Selected Readings on the Human Side of Information Technology

Edward J. Szewczak
Canisius College, USA

 **INFORMATION SCIENCE REFERENCE**

Hershey · New York

Director of Editorial Content: Kristin Klinger
Senior Managing Editor: Jennifer Neidig
Managing Editor: Jamie Snavely
Assistant Managing Editor: Carole Coulson
Typesetter: Amanda Appicello
Cover Design: Lisa Tosheff
Printed at: Yurchak Printing Inc.

Published in the United States of America by
        Information Science Reference (an imprint of IGI Global)
        701 E. Chocolate Avenue, Suite 200
        Hershey PA 17033
        Tel: 717-533-8845
        Fax: 717-533-8661
        E-mail: cust@igi-global.com
        Web site: http://www.igi-global.com

and in the United Kingdom by
        Information Science Reference (an imprint of IGI Global)
        3 Henrietta Street
        Covent Garden
        London WC2E 8LU
        Tel: 44 20 7240 0856
        Fax: 44 20 7379 0609
        Web site: http://www.eurospanbookstore.com

Library of Congress Cataloging-in-Publication Data

Selected readings on the human side of information technology / Edward J. Szewczak, editor.

      p. cm.

 Summary: "This book presents quality articles focused on key issues concerning the behavioral and social aspects of information technology"--Provided by publisher.

 Includes bibliographical references and index.

 ISBN 978-1-60566-088-2 (hbk.) -- ISBN 978-1-60566-089-9 (ebook)

 1. Information technology--Social aspects. 2. Information resources management. 3. Information technology--Management. I. Szewczak, Edward.

 T58.5.S436 2009

 303.48'33--dc22

                        2008019461

British Cataloguing in Publication Data
A Cataloguing in Publication record for this book is available from the British Library.

All work contributed to this book set is original material. The views expressed in this book are those of the authors, but not necessarily of the publisher.

Table of Contents

Section IV
Utilization and Application

Section V
Critical Issues

Detailed Table of Contents

Section I
Fundamental Concepts and Theories

Chapter I

Mario Morcellini, University "La Sapienza", Rome, Italy

This chapter asserts that digital media, more than any other medium, has become an expression of new social and cultural conditions. By first exploring the three dimensions of communication-related change and then defining the self in the era of new media, this chapter seeks to understand varying definitions of communication and interaction in modern society.

Chapter II

John Weckert, Centre for Applied Philosophy and Public Ethics, Charles Sturt University, Australia

This chapter examines the concept of offence and argues that such an examination can shed some light on global ethical issues. It examines the nature of offence, what, if anything, is wrong in giving offence, the obligations on the offended, whether or not offence is objective, and offence in a global setting. It argues for the view that choice and context provide some way of distinguishing between offence, which is a serious moral issue and that which is not. It is morally worse to offend those who have no choice in the area of the offence, for example race, than in areas where there is choice. Context is important in that offending the vulnerable is morally worse than offending those in more powerful, or privileged groups.

Chapter III

Philip Brey, University of Twente, The Netherlands

This chapter examines whether information ethics is culture relative. If it is, different approaches to information ethics are required in different cultures and societies. This would have major implications for the current, predominantly Western approach to information ethics. If it is not, there must be concepts and principles of information ethics that have universal validity. The descriptive evidence is for the cultural relativity of information ethics is studied by examining cultural differences between ethical attitudes towards privacy, freedom of information, and intellectual property rights in Western and non-Western cultures.

Chapter IV

Yingxu Wang, University of Calgary, Canada

Cognitive Informatics (CI) is a transdisciplinary enquiry of the internal information processing mechanisms and processes of the brain and natural intelligence shared by almost all science and engineering disciplines. This chapter presents an intensive review of the new field of CI. The structure of the theoretical framework of CI is described encompassing the Layered Reference Model of the Brain (LRMB), the OAR model of information representation, Natural Intelligence (NI) vs. Artificial Intelligence (AI), Autonomic Computing (AC) vs. imperative computing, CI laws of software, the mechanism of human perception processes, the cognitive processes of formal inferences, and the formal knowledge system. Three types of new structures of mathematics, Concept Algebra (CA), Real-Time Process Algebra (RTPA), and System Algebra (SA), are created to enable rigorous treatment of cognitive processes of the brain as well as knowledge representation and manipulation in a formal and coherent framework. A wide range of applications of CI in cognitive psychology, computing, knowledge engineering, and software engineering has been identified and discussed.

Section II
Development and Design Methodologies

Chapter V

Hannakaisa Isomäki, University of Lapland, Finland

This chapter describes a study clarifying information systems (IS) designers' conceptions of human users of IS by drawing on in-depth interviews with 20 designers. The designers' experiences in their work create a continuum of levels of thought that range from more limited conceptions to more comprehensive ones reflecting variations of the designers' situated knowledge related to human-centred design. The resulting forms of thought indicate three different but associated levels in conceptualising users. The separatist form of thought provides designers predominantly with technical perspectives and a capability for objectifying things. The functional form of thought focuses on external task information and task productivity, nevertheless, with the help of positive emotions. The holistic form of thought provides designers with competence of human-centred information systems development (ISD). Furthermore, the author hopes that understanding the IS designers' tendencies to conceptualise human users facilitates the mutual communication between users and designers.

This chapter introduces a qualitative study of user's information-seeking tasks on Web-based media, by investigating user's cognitive behaviors when they are searching for particular information on various kinds of Web sites. The experiment particularly studies cognitive factors including user goals and modes of searching. The main objective is to identify the corresponding impact of these factors on their needs and behaviors in relation to Web site design. By taking a user-based qualitative approach, the author hopes that this study will open the door to a careful consideration of actual user needs and behaviors in relation to information-seeking tasks on Web-based media.

Chapter VII

This chapter describes the user-centered design approach the authors adopted in the development and evaluation of an adaptive Web site. The development of usable Web sites, offering easy and efficient services to heterogeneous users, is a hot topic and a challenging issue for adaptive hypermedia and human-computer interaction. User-centered design promises to facilitate this task by guiding system designers in making decisions, which take the user's needs in serious account.

An interactive motivation-attitude theory is developed based on the Layered Reference Model of the Brain (LRMB) and the object-attribute-relation (OAR) model. This chapter presents a rigorous model of human perceptual processes such as emotions, motivations, and attitudes. This work is a part of the formalization of LRMB, which provides a comprehensive model for explaining the fundamental cognitive processes of the brain and their interactions. The current research demonstrates that the complicated human emotional and perceptual phenomena can be rigorously modeled and formally treated based on cognitive informatics theories and denotational mathematics.

This chapter presents a conceptual framework for an emerging type of user interface for mobile ubiquitous computing systems, and focuses in particular on the interaction through motion of people and objects in physical space. The authors introduce the notion of Kinetic User Interface as a unifying framework and a middleware for the design of pervasive interfaces, in which motion is considered as the primary input modality.

Section III
Tools and Technologies

Chapter X

Lorenzo Cantoni, University of Lugano, Switzerland
Stefano Tardini, University of Lugano, Switzerland

This chapter provides a conceptual framework for the newest digital communication tools and for the practices they encourage, stressing the communication opportunities they offer and the limitations they impose. In this chapter, Internet-based communication technologies are regarded as the most recent step in the development of communication technologies. This approach helps have a broad perspective on the changes information and communication technologies (ICT) are bringing along in the social practices of so called knowledge society. In the second part of the chapter, the authors present two examples of relevant social practices that are challenged by the most recent ICT, namely journalism (news market) and Internet search engines.

Chapter XI

Masataka Yoshikawa, Hakuhodo Inc., Japan

This chapter aims to explore the future trajectory of digital music entertainment among consumers by comparing the characteristics of the usage patterns of digital music appliances in the U.S. to those in Japan. The author conducted two empirical surveys in the U.S. and Japan, and found some basic differences in the usage patterns of a variety of digital music appliances. Ethnographical research among Japanese women also found that sharing music via mobile phone ring tones is a new trend, though hard disk music players like iPod have become the standard of digital music appliances in the world.

Chapter XII

Jeffrey Hsu, Fairleigh Dickinson University, USA

A number of new communications technologies have emerged in recent years that have been largely regarded and intended for personal and recreational use. However, these "conversational technologies" and "constructivist learning tools," coupled with the power and reach of the Internet, are viable choices for both educational learning and knowledge-oriented applications. The technologies given attention in this article include instant messaging (IM), Weblogs (blogs), wikis, and podcasts. A discussion of the technologies and uses, underlying educational and cognitive psychology theories, and also applications for education and the management of knowledge, are examined in detail.

Chapter XIII

    David Peebles, University of Huddersfield, UK
    Anna L. Cox, University College London, UK

This chapter discusses a number of recent studies that demonstrate the use of rational analysis (Anderson, 1990) and cognitive modelling methods to understand complex interactive behaviour involved in three tasks: (1) icon search, (2) graph reading, and (3) information retrieval on the World Wide Web (WWW). The authors describe the underlying theoretical assumptions of rational analysis and the adaptive control of thought-rational (ACT-R) cognitive architecture (Anderson & Lebiere, 1998), a theory of cognition that incorporates rational analysis in its mechanisms for learning and decision making. In presenting these studies, the authors aim to show how such methods can be combined with eye movement data to provide detailed, highly constrained accounts of user performance that are grounded in psychological theory.

Section IV
Utilization and Application

Chapter XIV

    Mary R. Lind, North Carolina A&T State University, USA

In this chapter, wireless technology use is addressed with a focus on the factors that underlie wireless interaction. A de-construction of the information processing theories of user/technology interaction is presented. While commercial and useful applications of wireless devices are numerous, wireless interaction is emerging as a means of social interaction—an extension of the user's personal image—and as an object of amusement and play. The technology/user interaction theories that have driven the discussions of computer assisted communication media are information richness, communicative action, and social influence modeling. This chapter will extend this theoretical view of wireless devices by using flow theory to address elements of fun, control, and focus.

Chapter XV

    Hugo Liu, The Media Laboratory, USA
    Pattie Maes, The Media Laboratory, USA
    Glorianna Davenport, The Media Laboratory, USA

Popular online social networks such as Friendster and MySpace do more than simply reveal the superficial structure of social connectedness — the rich meanings bottled within social network profiles themselves imply deeper patterns of culture and taste. If these latent semantic fabrics of taste could be harvested formally, the resultant resource would afford completely novel ways for representing and reasoning about Web users and people in general. This chapter narrates the theory and technique of such a feat — the natural language text of 100,000 social network profiles were captured, mapped into a diverse ontology of music, books, films, foods, etc., and machine learning was applied to infer a semantic fabric of taste. Taste fabrics bring us closer to improvisational manipulations of meaning, and afford us at least three semantic functions—the creation of semantically flexible user representations, cross-domain taste-based recommendation, and the computation of taste-similarity between people — whose use cases are demonstrated within the context of three applications — the InterestMap, Ambient Semantics, and IdentityMirror.

Recently, the ubiquitous use of mobile phones by people from different cultures has grown enormously. In this chapter, the authors attempt to understand if cultural differences influence the way people use their mobile phones in public places. The material considered draws on the existing literature of mobile phones, and quantitative and qualitative work carried out in the UK (as a mature mobile phone market) and the Sudan (that is part of Africa and the Middle East culture with its emerging mobile phone market).

This chapter examines the use of the Internet for gathering health information by boomers and seniors. This study attempts to determine whether online health seekers have changed their behaviors from the information they found online. This research analyzes the Kaiser Family Foundation e-Health and the Elderly public opinion dataset of access by boomers and seniors to online health information. The major results indicate that boomers marginally use online health information more than seniors for the management of their health. The most significant results indicated that boomers and seniors who are more aware and have positive feelings toward online health information would use it more to manage their health.

This chapter explores the use of evolutionary game theory (EGT) (Nowak & May, 1993; Taylor & Jonker, 1978; Weibull, 1995) to model the dynamics of adaptive opponent strategies for a large population of players. In particular, the authors explore effects of information propagation through social networks in evolutionary games. The key underlying phenomenon that the information diffusion aims to capture is that reasoning about the experiences of acquaintances can dramatically impact the dynamics of a society.

Section V
Critical Issues

Chapter XIX

This chapter explores cultural aspects of information-communications systems embedded into new media environments and a new age of social responsibility has emerged for information technology professionals. This chapter also discusses digital e-culture and the new media's role in cultural heritage. As current information-communications systems converge with media, we are confronted with a new form of primarily-digital media that reshapes not only industry but also the cultural fabric of the world on a regional and global basis.

Chapter XX

Previous research has shown that the open source movement shares a common ideology. Employees belonging to the open source movement often advocate the use of open source software within their organization. Hence, their belief in the underlying open source software ideology may influence the decision making on the adoption of open source software. This may result in an ideological—rather than pragmatic—decision. A recent study has shown that American organizations are quite pragmatic in their adoption decision. This chapter argues that there may be circumstances in which there is more opportunity for ideological behavior. Organizational adoption decision was investigated in Belgian organizations and results indicate that while most organizations are pragmatic in their decision making, the influence of ideology should not be completely disregarded in small organizations.

Chapter XXI

Most computer applications feature visual user interfaces that assume that all users have equivalent propensities to perceive, interpret, and understand the multidimensional spatial properties and relationships of the objects presented. However, the hunter-gatherer theory (Silverman & Eals, 1992) suggests that there are modern-day differences between the genders in spatial and cognitive abilities that stem from differentiated prehistoric sex roles. If true, there may be discrepancies in how males and females differentially utilize particular spatial visual cues and interface features. This chapter reports three experiments in which participants engage in visual spatial tasks using 2D and 3D virtual worlds: (1) matching object shapes; (2) positioning objects; and (3) resizing objects. Female subjects under-perform male subjects in the matching and positioning experiments, but they outperform male subjects in the resizing experiment. Moreover, male subjects make more use of motion cues. Implications for the design of gender effective user interfaces and virtual environments are considered.

Chapter XXII

Social and healthcare industries offer demanding occupations, as these jobs are human-contact intensive and, moreover, customers are usually met in critical situations. This chapter focuses on how information systems affect the stress levels of health and social-care workers. An empirical study shows a strong correlation between the use of computers and stress levels in the healthcare professions: The more computer use, the more stress. The authors conclude that when users understand the total collaborative work setting, computer work obtains meaning, and stress levels reduce.

Section VI
Emerging Trends

Chapter XXIII

This chapter is to re-addresses the vision of human-computer symbiosis as originally expressed by J.C.R. Licklider nearly a half-century ago and to argue for the relevance of this vision to the field of cognitive informatics. A central concept of this vision is that humans need to be incorporated into computer architectures. The state of this technology is assessed within the context of contemporary theory and practice, and the authors describe what they regard as this emerging field of neo-symbiosis. Examples of neo-symbiosis are provided, but these are nascent examples and the potential of neo-symbiosis is yet to be realized.

Chapter XXIV

This chapter describes how social politeness is relevant to computer system design. As the Internet becomes more social, computers now mediate social interactions, act as social agents, and serve as information assistants. To succeed in these roles, computers must learn a new skill—politeness. Yet selfish software is currently a widespread problem and politeness remains a software design "blind spot." Using an informational definition of politeness, as the giving of social choice, suggests four aspects: 1. respect, 2. openness, 3. helpfulness, and 4. remembering. Examples are given to suggest how polite computing could make human-computer interactions more pleasant and increase software usage. In contrast, if software rudeness makes the Internet an unpleasant place to be, usage may minimize. For the Internet to recognize its social potential, software must be not only useful and usable, but also polite.

Cross-cultural literature, often discusses differences among people and how their respective culture and history may affect their adoption and preference usage patterns of ITC. Considering language is one of the major defining attributes of culture, this chapter takes a sociolinguistic approach to argue that there is also a cross-cultural aspect to ITC adoption within the same culture. This article examines the socio-linguistic perspective that men and women communicate differently in the context of online courses. A key finding is that although cultural and gender differences can be eliminated if participants wish to do so through ITC, gender-based cultural patterns still emerge.

This chapter illustrates the role of the mobile phone in the rise of new cultural models of parenting. According to a phenomenological theoretical approach to culture and everyday life, the author argues that the relationship between technologies, culture, and society should be conceived as a mutual construction. Analysing new social phenomena such as "hyperparenting" and the "dialogic use" of mobile phones, the author argues upon the role of mobile communication technologies in articulating the paradoxical nature of the contemporary cultural model of family education.

Chapter XXVII

This chapter introduces the concept and activities of the digitally-enabled tourist and the impact such as tourist has on the travel and tourism industry. It summarizes the existing and emerging technical environments that encourage the use of hand held digital recording devices and personal Internet communications. Additionally, it looks at ways tourists publish and exhibit digital visual and written artifacts of their travel experience. The chapter introduces general types of digital communication infrastructure to be considered by the industry to create an experience to support this type of tourism.

Today's media are vast in both form and influence; however, few cultural studies scholars address the video gaming industry's role in domestic maintenance and global imposition of U.S. hegemonic ideologies. In this chapter, video games are analyzed by cover art, content, and origin of production. Whether it is earning more "powers" in games such as Star Wars, or earning points to purchase more powerful artillery in Grand Theft Auto, capitalist ideology is reinforced in a subtle, entertaining fashion. This study shows that oppressive hegemonic representations of gender and race are not only present, but permeate the majority of top-selling video games. Finally, the study traces the origins of best-selling games, to reveal a virtual U.S. monopoly in the content of this formative medium.

Prologue

I'm always trying to stave off technology. I can't help it. I have this deep-seated feeling that technology somehow is anti-human, anti-biological, anti-relationship. When am I going to realize that it doesn't matter? I can't stop it... Now maybe we staver-offers just have to quit wanting so much control. Couldn't we just allow new ideas and things into our lives? And let the folks who enjoy them – even ourselves – embrace them? Even the word sounds more graceful: embrace.
—Mary Scalzi, My View, The Buffalo News (February 12, 2008)

Mary Scalzi's perspective on technology intrigues me. Humans have a love-hate relationship with machines. Machines are useful. They can do some things better than humans can. But there is something about machines that humans do not entirely trust. Charlie Chaplin's antics in *Modern Times* were played out against a background of dead seriousness. When Frederick Winslow Taylor fathered scientific management – an attempt to apply the scientific method to the management of workers, thereby rendering the worker more machine-like – workers protested that Taylorism was dehumanizing. Of course, *Modern Times* and Taylorism took place in the world of low technology. Are the same things true about humans and machines in the world of high technology? The quote above suggests that perhaps it is, at least for some humans.

In late 1993 I was on the phone with Mehdi Khosrow-Pour, who was the founder and head of the Information Resources Management Association (IRMA), who during the course of the conversation asked me to suggest a new track for the Association's annual conference that was meeting for only the fifth time in San Antonio, Texas the following spring. Not wanting to appear daft, I blurted "the human side of IT." The phrase stuck and is still being used today at IRMA conferences.

When IGI Global asked me to contribute this prologue, I was somewhat hesitant at first to commit to the project. My hesitancy was based on what I believe is a natural uneasiness about revisiting in memory events that happened some fifteen years ago. After all, memory is fallible and, like recalling history, subject to invention. Yet at the same time the prospect of recalling why I coined the phrase in the first place, on the fly as it were, intrigued me. What influences were at work in the recesses of my mind at the time? After some reflection, I believe there were three – why information systems fail, the Minnesota experiments, and human factors.

As a student of MIS in the 1980s, certain research efforts impressed upon me the importance of focusing on the role of people in systems. Henry Lucas' study of why information systems fail (Lucas, 1975) is a case in point. In particular, his finding that human behavior is at least as important as technical excellence to the success of an information system left a lasting impression on me. It is easy to be dazzled by the stream of technological innovations in hardware and software. However systems are built for people. It is how people react to technology that is of fundamental importance to systems' success. Today the concept of the "operational feasibility" of a systems idea is included in all textbooks on systems analysis and design. To be assured that a systems idea has a fighting chance of succeeding, the people for whom the system is being developed must ultimately accept the system and use it in the manner it was developed to be used.

The "Minnesota Experiments" (Dickson, Senn & Chervany, 1977) were another influence on my thinking about people and systems. These experiments were conducted to study the significance of IS characteristics on decision activity. Decision effectiveness was seen as dependent on the decision maker, the decision environment, and the characteristics of the IS. One aspect of these experiments appealed to me greatly at the time – the consideration of individual differences, especially the concepts of psychological type and cognitive style. That individuals may gather information differently and then use that information in different ways opened up possibilities for studying people and systems that seemed limitless. My earlier college course work in psychology and sociology suddenly seemed truly meaningful and useful. I even thought briefly about incorporating psychological types into my dissertation work – until I realized that my dissertation committee would not be amused. In any event, individual differences and decision making continue to interest me to this day.

"Human factors" as a field of study began to address the need to understand how people are affected by and respond to IT. A good definition of human factors is provided by Beard & Peterson (1988, pp. 12-13): "Human factors is the scientific study of the interaction between people, machines, and their work environment. The knowledge gained from this study is used to create systems and work environments which help to make people more productive and more satisfied with their work life." To more clearly define major research themes on human factors, Beard and Peterson (1988) divided the existing research into five categories: human-machine interaction (how people and computers communicate); interface specification tools (formal techniques for the design of the focus of interaction between people and computers); information presentation (the way data are displayed to the user (including graphic, numeric, alphanumeric, tabular, text, audible, tactile); system user documentation (producing documentation in a form and style suitable to the expert or novice system user); and end-user involvement (methods used to involve users directly in the various stages of system development).

Within these five fundamental categories are included many different topics and issues relevant to the human side of IT. These topics and issues are often featured as tracks at professional conferences or form the focus of special issues of scholarly journals. Prior to my telephone conversation with Mehdi Khosrowpour, I had noted that all of the tracks in the earlier IRMA conferences had a technological focus and that a new track that emphasized the human aspects of systems was sorely needed. I can't recall if I was asked to suggest a list of topics that would be appropriate for the track, but if I did I'm sure the list was short, general in nature, and woefully inadequate to the task. In any event, the Human Side of IT track was created for the 5th Information Resources Management Association International Conference. If the number of paper contributors is any indication of success, the new track focused on people and IT was a big hit. It was evident that many researchers had an interest in the human side of IT and wanted an outlet for their work. I'm still not sure what the boundaries of the human side of IT may be. I do know that they are not technological.

The new-found popularity of the Human Side of IT track gave way to the publication of three books of readings: Szewczak, E. & Khosrowpour, M. (Eds.), *The Human Side of Information Technology Management*; Szewczak, E. & Snodgrass, C. (Eds.), *Managing the Human Side of Information Technology: Challenges and Solutions*; and Szewczak, E. & Snodgrass, C. (Eds.), *Human Factors in Information Systems*. Contributors to these books of readings canvassed a wide range of topics, including but not limited to human-centered methods in IS, user satisfaction in IS, IT assimilation, computer anxiety, the impact of office automation on user health and stress, multimedia computing in support of knowledge work and group collaboration, attitude and use of computer mediated communication, student personality traits and expert systems, cultural diversity and group DSS, IT and privacy, IT and leadership, the cultural characteristics of IT professionals, motivation for using IT, individual differences and computer attitudes, and ethics and IT. This wide range of topics is indicative of the many avenues of research afforded to scholars interested in the human side of IT. It should be noted that the continual introduction of new technologies will provide ample opportunities for researchers to further explore the human side of IT and to add to the list of relevant topics.

Professional conferences are an ideal outlet for researchers to present their work on a wide range of different, often only distantly related, topics. But more focused efforts in the field of human factors in particular have yielded results of both theoretical as well as practical importance. The work of Ben Schneiderman at the University of Maryland is a notable case in point. He has compiled an impressive collection of results of many different researchers (including himself) focusing on the dimensions of the issue of *human-computer interaction* that is relevant to researchers and practitioners in many fields of endeavor, including computer science, psychology, library and information science, business and information systems, education technology, communication arts and media studies, and technical writing and graphic design. According to Shneiderman (1998, p. 10), "[e]ffective systems generate positive feelings of success, competence, mastery, and clarity in the user community. The users are not encumbered by the computer and can predict what will happen in response to each of their actions. When an interactive system is well designed, the interface almost disappears, enabling users to concentrate on their work, exploration, or pleasure. Creating an environment in which tasks are carried out almost effortlessly and users are 'in the flow' requires a great deal of hard work from the designer."

What is involved in the "great deal of hard work from the designer?" To begin with, the designer must recognize the human diversity involved in the environment wherein the system is to be used. Are the users novices or first-time users, knowledgeable intermittent users, or expert frequent users? What tasks will the users be expected to perform? For example, in a medical clinic, will users be expected to perform queries by patient, update data, perform queries across patients, add relations, and/or evaluate the system? The designer must then consider the various interaction styles available. Is direct manipulation using a mouse appropriate or do users feel better entering commands directly using a keyboard? Will menu selection be acceptable, or will form fillin be more desirable? However these questions are answered, the designer should adhere to the eight golden rules of interface design (Adapted from Shneiderman, 1998, p. 74-75):

Rule #1: Strive for consistency. Consistent sequences of actions should be required in similar situations; identical terminology should be used in prompts, menus, and help screens; and consistent color, layout, capitalization, fonts, and so on should be employed throughout. Exceptions, such as no echoing of passwords or confirmation of the delete command, should be comprehensible and limited in number.

Rule #2: Enable frequent users to use shortcuts. As the frequency of use increases, so do the user's desire to reduce the number of interactions and to increase the pace of interaction. Abbreviations, special keys, hidden commands, and macro facilities are appreciated by frequent knowledgeable users. Short response times and fast display rates are other attractions for frequent users.

Rule #3: Offer informative feedback. For every user action, there should be system feedback. For frequent and minor actions, the response can be modest, whereas for infrequent and major actions, the response should be more substantial. Visual presentation of the objects of interest provides a convenient environment for showing changes explicitly, for example, using a direct manipulation interface.

Rule #4: Design dialogs to yield closure. Sequences of actions should be organized into groups with a beginning, middle, and end. The informative feedback at the completion of a group of actions gives users the satisfaction of accomplishment, a sense of relief, the signal to drop contingency plans and options from their minds, and an indication that the way is clear to prepare for the next group of actions.

Rule #5: Offer error prevention and simple error handling. Design the system such that users cannot make a serious error; for example, prefer menu selection to form fillin and do not allow alphabetic characters in numeric entry fields. If users make an error, the system should detect the error and offer simple, constructive, and specific instructions for recovery. Erroneous actions should leave the system state unchanged, or the system should give instructions about restoring the state.

Rule #6: Permit easy reversal of actions. Actions should be reversible. This feature relieves anxiety, since the user knows that errors can be undone, thus encouraging exploration of unfamiliar options.

Rule #7: Support internal locus of control. Experienced users strongly desire the sense that they are in charge of the system and that the system responds to their actions. Surprising system actions, tedious sequences of data entries, inability or difficulty in obtaining necessary information, and inability to produce the action desired all build anxiety and dissatisfaction.

Rule #8: Reduce short-term memory load. The limitation of human information processing in short-term memory requires that displays be kept simple, multiple page displays be consolidated, window-motion frequency be reduced, and sufficient training time be allotted for codes, mnemonics, and sequences of actions. Where appropriate, online access to command-syntax forms, abbreviations, codes, and other information should be provided.

As straightforward and "obvious" as these guidelines may seem today, they are the result of years of careful study and research in the area of human factors. They have also been implemented in modern interface technologies, especially graphical user interface (GUI) technologies. As impressive as these research results are, as an educator I find that the idea that people are at least as important as technology in systems is a hard sell to IS students. After all, IS programs at colleges and universities are fundamentally focused on various aspects of technology – hardware, software, database management systems, telecommunications, Web site development, Internet security, etc. IS graduates need to be technologically proficient in order to compete successfully in the job market. Even in the area of systems analysis and design there are many tools and techniques that are fundamentally technical that IS students need to master. Still, when I teach systems analysis and design, I cannot resist relating an experience which speaks to the role of people in systems. As a Ph.D. student, one of my jobs was to work with the MBA Program Director ("PD") in the redesign of the MBA admissions program. The program used a database management system called System 1022 through a COBOL interface. "PD" wanted me to rewrite the COBOL interface in the language of System 1022. For me this was an enjoyable technical exercise which involved taking 30 plus pages of COBOL and reducing the program to just 7 pages of System 1022 code with system enhancements that were transparent to the system user. "PD" was delighted with the results. But delight soon turned to misery when "PD" tried to convince people in the MBA office to change the way they did things. "PD" learned firsthand the power of "resistance to change" over the course of the 12 months it took to convince people that the new system was actually a good thing for all concerned and that the old COBOL interface was really a bad thing. (Thankfully, I was not involved with the people issue.) Also, "PD" probably learned a few things on the job about the importance of "user involvement" during systems development.

Yet most students readily respond to topics related to the human side of IT. For example, the topic of personal information privacy and IT has great interest for me. It has been my observation that most students are very much aware of the information privacy issue and that most do care about keeping their personal information private. Take, for instance, the topic of "cookies." I explain that cookies are small text files that are surreptitiously stored on the students' computer hard disks when they visit various websites on the Internet and that contain information about what websites they have visited. I further explain why the cookies are created and stored; namely, so businesses can use the information in the cookies to develop "profiles" of the students for use in, among other possible things, creating marketing pitches in the form of things like pop-up ads. When I'm finished, most students want to know how to get rid of the cookies, so I explain to the best of my ability the many approaches to managing cookies that are available today, including the use of anti-spyware programs and even Microsoft's Internet Options under Windows Tools.

But here is my concern – do students actually act on my suggestions? If not, why not? Now I know that my concerns about safeguarding my personal information privacy when using the Internet (as well as in the low tech world) affect the way I approach using IT in a negative way. I do not give away my personal to *any* website, even if it means some kind of reward (say, free shipping) will be withheld from me. I'm afraid of being a victim of identity theft. I worry about nameless, faceless people in cyberspace who are ready and waiting to do me harm, the nature of which I can only conceive in a dark moment of reflection. I do not join social networks in cyberspace for fear that my personal information will somehow in some way be compromised. I will not use Google's Gmail because I'm aware of the possibility that anything I send may be saved in Google's server farms for a very long time to come. This is *my* response to Internet technology. But what about my students? I know that they do not always follow my prescriptions for doing well in my courses. So why would they listen to my concerns about sharing personal information with websites?

I think that one key avenue for further research in the human side of IT is studying how Internet users respond to IT in the face of threats to their personal information privacy. We know, for example, that when Facebook.com added a feature that makes it easier for users to keep abreast of their friends by tracking users' activities on the website and then communicating these activities to all the people in the friends' social network, hundreds of thousands of Facebook.com users expressed outrage at what was perceived as an unwarranted use of their personal information. How will the human-computer interface be affected by personal and social issues such as concerns about personal information privacy? Does the human need to belong to social networks overcome concerns about safeguarding personal information? Or does concern about protecting personal information mitigate against joining social networks? These are just a few of the interesting questions that further research into the human side of IT can help to answer. As technology evolves, so will people's response to it. And along with the response will come the need to understand it.

In any event, I wonder what Mary Scalzi would think about all this.

Edward J. Szewczak, Professor of IS, Canisius College

Edward J. Szewczak is Professor of Information Systems at Canisius College. He has co-edited a number of scholarly readings texts for Idea Group Publishing, including Human Factors in Information Systems (with Coral Snodgrass), Managing the Human Side of Information Technology: Challenges and Solutions (with Coral Snodgrass), Measuring Information Technology Investment Payoff (with Mo Mahmood), The Human Side of Information Technology Management (with Mehdi Khosrowpour), and Management Impacts of Information Technology: Perspectives on Organizational Change and Growth (with Coral Snodgrass and Mehdi Khosrowpour). He is currently serving as an Associate Editor of The Information Resources Management Journal.

REFERENCES

Beard, J.W., & Peterson, T.O. (1988). A taxonomy for the study of human factors in management information systems (MIS). In Carey, J.M. (Ed.), *Human factors in management information systems*. Norwood, NJ: Ablex Publishing. 7-25.

Dickson, G.W., Senn, J.A., & Chervany, N.L. (1977). Research in management information systems: The Minnesota experiments. *Management Science*, 23(9), 913-923.

Lucas, Henry C. (1975). *Why information systems fail*. New York, NY: Columbia University Press.

Shneiderman, B. (1998). *Designing the human interface: Strategies for effective human-computer interaction*, 3rd Ed. Reading, MA: Addison-Wesley.

Szewczak, E. & Khosrowpour, M. (Eds.). (1996). *The human side of information technology management*. Hershey, PA: Idea Group Publishing.

Szewczak, E. & Snodgrass, C. (Eds.). (2002). *Managing the human side of information technology: Challenges and solutions*. Hershey, PA: Idea Group Publishing.

Szewczak, E., & Snodgrass, C. (Eds.). (2002). *Human factors in information systems*. Hershey, PA: IRM Press.

Taylor, F.W. (1911). *The principles of scientific management*. New York, NY: Harper & Row.

Section I
Fundamental Concepts and Theories

Chapter I
Digital Media and Socialization

Mario Morcellini
University "La Sapienza", Rome, Italy

ABSTRACT

The chapter reflects about the idea of crisis making evident that, in the case of communication, it doesn't mean a reduction of importance, but on the contrary increasing and growth. The actual communication fortune is in fact built on what seems a lack in our societies that is the vaporization and loss of social capital. In front of the modern individualism, the social system moves people to search other functions able to balance it: communication is certainly one of the functions. It doesn't help only individuals to get through the crisis, but it also promotes the increase of relations in the social system. The communication covers up the decline of traditional institutions (school, family, and religion) configuring a chance. Digital media, more than any other medium, becomes an expression of new social and cultural conditions.

INTRODUCTION

In order to understand the action of communication on individuals and on society, both as an industrial force and as a narrative and poetic force, it is important to look beyond the syntax of communication and to start from a reflection on the sociocultural framework of the passage to "late-modernity," which is often identified as a "crisis" from which to interpret the new meaning of communication with regard to the process of the construction of the self.

In the modern condition, the passage to modernity hinges on three elements of modification: the social actors, the institutions, and the liquid substitute of the media.

With regard to the first, the change solicited by communication relates to three dimensions:

1. **To the sphere of the self** and to the construction and redefinition, therefore, of the subjective identity of the social actors by means of the stimulation of an *interior revolution*: self-reflection. It is as though communication helps the individual to prepare for new visions of the world and for different styles of life which, in the long term, reflect on social relations and on the narration of the scenarios of life.

2. **To relationships,** whereby with a double key of interpretation communication is both

a *symbolic gesture* to measure and improve oneself with regard to others, and also *passion*, in that modern man, overwhelmed by contextual crises, looks for a sense to life and for orientation in dealings with others.

3. **To action,** since communication helps both to multiply the exchanges between individuals and to react to states of crisis.

As far as the institutions are concerned, we intend to emphasize the semantic and sociocultural transformations undergone by the school, the family, and at work in the passage to the modern; that is to say, everything which in the past was defined as a source of stability, equilibrium, and social and personal certainty.

Many sociologists use the term *crisis* to describe this transformation, a term which is today a part of the history of any society (starting from the premodern world). However, the present state of sociocultural transition presents different characteristics in that rather than a crisis of sector or of a social subsystem, it regards all those institutions which, in past societies, organised time in society (religion, school, the family, work). In this scenario the crisis regards socialization in particular; that is, those processes which allow for the reproduction of values, of collective orientation and, therefore, of that cultural orientation which is the basis of subjective action.

A world in search of itself could be a suitable metaphor to describe the image of a time which is characterized by the triumph of uncertainties, the great accumulation of sources of insecurity, of fear, and of lack of trust, counterpoised to the idea of a society founded principally on certainty, on trust, and on the possibility of recognition (Bauman, 2000; Beck, 2000; Giddens, 1991).

It is as though there had been a change in the relationship between rights and obligations compared with the past, and the unravelling of the sense of obligation corresponded to an exponential increase in the expectations of the individual (the rights) with regard to social organization.

This liquid dimension (Bauman, 1998) of modern society gives substance to the subject and to the individualistic matrix of communication, removing sense from social prescriptions. In this respect, communication, and digital communication in particular, becomes the liquid substitute of the late-modern crisis.

From here we arrive at the third key concept: the media. The fortunes of communication are constructed literally on the vaporization and the loss of the weight of society on the individual. The scant involvement and sense of orientation of the social system often causes the subject to look for other repairing functions. One of these is certainly communication, which is viewed as a low cost resource with which to react to the crisis of the emptying of social relationships (the liquid substitute of the media). Communication reacts powerfully to change, reacting to the weakening of the system, to the devaluation of the values, to the growth of disvalues, that is, those individual values which are not recognized by others.

Communication, in fact, does not only help to get through the crisis, to fill the "black holes" in our interactions (Morcellini, 1997, 2004), but it also fills these gaps with relationships with the social system. That is to say, it literally carries out a function of substitution for socialization. This means that communication, in fact, covers the decline in all the institutions which in the past organized and prescribed individual behaviour (the school, the family, and religion).

Starting from this viewpoint, the "crisis" takes on another meaning: in connection with the sense of change in communication, it is no longer seen as "diminishing in importance," but rather as "multiplication and growth." *The theatre of communication* is useful not only to stimulate exchanges and interrelations between individuals, but also to stimulate the individuals themselves to change. Communication does not simply gratify the need for relationships, it multiplies them.

Specifically, the media stimulate the three dimensions of the social actors: that of the self, filtered and explored in the dream dimension of the media and of the interaction mediated by technology, which induces the individual to prepare a new vision of the world and new styles of life; that of behaviour and of action, that is to say, that transformation which it is possible to meet in the symbolic scenarios of representation, identification and information in social interaction. There has been enough research to maintain that the good fortune of communication lies in its capacity to educate people to interiorize knowledge in a mitridatic way, that is, with a daily homeopathic dose of communication. In this way the organism prepares to react to the virus of change, which we perceive as a risk, or a threat, as a result of the effort associated with the idea itself of change; that which exalts the group as a privileged situation of change: people change in groups.

THE SELF IN THE ERA OF THE NEW MEDIA

Evolution or metamorphosis are terms which conjure up a process which is too linear to relate the complex and reticular nature of modern change. To emphasize the upheaval and the transformation of the social contest, in which unpredictable or uncontrollable forms emerge in the area of cultural and value models, in attitudes and behaviour, in customs and lifestyle, as well as in the transformation of the social order, it is therefore far more appropriate to use the term *revolution* (Morcellini, 2004, 2005).

The progressive weakening of memory and of inherited values, the consequent loss of points which anchor us to tradition, the exaltation of dynamism, of flexibility, of the capacity of subjective adaptation to the multiplicity of situations of the present, have favoured this "passage" to the late-modern.

The impact and the development of communication have contributed to the acceleration of these processes of social change, in some cases determining the phenomenon of *transitionality* (Grasso,1989), often used by sociologists to narrate the youth culture and the sense of discomfort which has developed from the revolutionary unpredictability of the modern condition.

On the basis of this first reflection, the media is far more than simply an environment for the transmission of knowledge. The media appears as places for exchanging and sharing values, ideas, and symbols which condition the processes of individual and collective identification (Morcellini, 1997) creating what is almost a semantic environment of socialization in which the young satisfy their need for individualization, on the one hand, and on the other reconstruct symbolic and linguistic membership within a sociocultural framework which is now empty of points of reference and of anchors of values (Bessotti, 2006). From this angle, communication takes on a new significance: it no longer carries out a *function of substitution* (Morcellini, 1997, 2004) to the modern crisis, but it produces a multiplication of opportunities for dialogue and for interaction, thanks above all to the continual updating offered by technology. The universe of the media and in particular of the new media has become for the individual a space of *capitalistic accumulation* (almost flexible) of symbols, of signs which increase the chances of identification, of recognition, of discovery and exploration of the self, and of the surrounding sociocultural dimension.

The process of modernization and of technological and scientific development, which have also taken place in the field of communications, have certainly favoured the exercising of citizenship and of democratic practices. Possession of the media, in fact, legitimizes the processes of participation of the individual in the dynamics of our times, above all with regard to access strategies to territories of knowledge and the symbolic sphere. This first interpretation is an integral part of a widely accepted point of view, of a lifestyle and expectations about communications which are referable to a vision of a *society of knowledge* founded on the search for and the promise of a social well-being, in which education (Ranieri, 2006) and communications are the emerging infrastructures.

"Only those who know more than they can do will avoid being swept away by change" (Ranieri, 2006, p. 52) because they can move more freely in society and can face the flexibility and socio-cultural heterogeneity. Today knowledge has, in fact, become the means of constructing a sense of identity and belonging; that is to say, the way in which individuals continually redefine themselves in relation to their surrounding reality. Investment in permanent further education, in knowledge, and in culture represent, therefore, one of the actions which will guarantee more competitiveness in the job market and will help cope with social and cultural complexity and lack of homogeneity (Ranieri, 2006; Rullani, 2004).

In this context, communication represents, to an even greater extent than in the past, the most immediate and all-involving of forms with which to know the social world. By nature it is not impositional, or it does not at least present itself as such, and it is handy, available, immediately consumable, friendly, and low-cost. All of this means that the type of socialization which derives from it is not authoritarian, where the competencies of the adult meet the supposed incompetence of the pupil, but in tendency egalitarian. This key-aspect is still waiting to be explored, but if we consider with greater attention the sphere of those needs which are satisfied by communication and the modality by means of which this particular type of relationship unfolds (for example, through media education), it will certainly be possible to improve the structure of the media narration and the mechanisms of production and distribution of information which conquer the imagination and meet the imaginary and the need of the modern individual to dream.

This new investiture of communication is easily seen in the relationship of young people to cultural consumption; young people prove to be capable of independence and self-orientation when placed in front of a multimedial keyboard, and they form a relationship which is almost symbiotic with the media, with a natural organization and control of the language and of the codes (Meyrowitz, 1985).

Yet if on the one hand innovation and the technological "race" promote a cultural democratization, on the other they signal new differences because of the increase in the opportunities of access to communicative "competencies." The chance to participate in democratic life, in fact, does not resolve the problem of the new forms of inequality which communication consigns to the *society of change*, marking further the loss of social reference points and the radical sense of loss of traditional cultural mediations (Morcellini, 2004). Thus, from the more traditional gap relating to the different technological availability of the media, which does not consent the construction of personal experiences to all, we pass to the intergenerational gap, determined by the embarrassment and discomfort of adults in comparison with the experience and media competence shown by the young.

A further gap regards the capital of the individual with regard to culture and knowledge, or, rather, the disparity of competence in the field of communication, which is useful to handle and interpret the sociocultural changes of the media and to develop a mature and independent orientation regarding both decision and action. In synthesis, behind the appearance of an isomorphic distribution of communication and of its instruments, are hidden forms of different properties, different title, and different capital.

As far as this gap is concerned, there is a close connection with the issue of the "crisis of cultural mediation." The Italian education system has always been behind when it comes to progress in communication. It is sufficient to remember that Italy was the only European country in which the spread of the media, and in particular of television, came before mass literacy.

In this process, which was all but linear, television fulfilled a wide-scale educational function which the school itself was not able to develop, contributing therewith to the spread not only of a common language, but also of a shared culture (Farnè, 2003; Morcellini, 2005).

FAMILY, SCHOOL, WORK: AN ALBUM OF SEMANTIC CHANGES

Modern times have certainly contributed towards the erosion of the mediation function of the school and of the family, in order to celebrate the value of direct experience, of subjective self-searching, and of the active exploration of the individual (Maffesoli, 1988).

The first critical problem regards *the family*: young people today are faced with a dimension which in the past was always a guarantee of stability but which today has been fragmented.

The weakening of this social institution dates back to the years of youth protest, when the bourgeois model with its functionalist nature, was condemned. According to this scheme, the task of the family was to contribute to the emancipation of the individual so as to guarantee an efficient social integration, the function of which was the maintenance of structural and cultural equilibrium. This model was thrown into crisis in the 1970s at the same time as the affirmation of educational and cultural polycentrism and following a series of social transformations. It has lost the typical connotations of the institution, transforming itself into a social group, or indeed into a space wherein to construct projects of personal life, relationships, and affective and educative relations (Besozzi, 2006). We come, thus, to delineate a framework which it is difficult to circumscribe in a standard model. This is because the quality of the interaction between parents and children comes under scrutiny, which determines its educative efficacy in the process of construction of the self.

In spite of the heterogeneity and the complexity of the picture which has just been outlined, today the sense of the family still seems to be present in the universe of values of the individual. According to the findings of a recent national survey by ISTAT (2005), confirmed by more localised and restricted research, the family is to be found in first place among the values recognized by the young in the hierarchy of the "most important things," in spite of the fact that relations within the domestic walls are in fact often conflictual, contradictory, and, therefore, difficult to reconcile with quality relationships. Besozzi (2006) describes this trend through a game of expectations and desires for the future, typical of the young, and closely connected to the sense of precariousness and of social uncertainty; in other words, for young people the family represents the symbol of security, of stability, and of protection compared with a reality which is fragmented and fragile. The value of this agency of socialization increases above all in the dimension of the imaginary, representing for young people the desire for stability as opposed to the state which is eternally transitory. However, if the family represents a *value-refuge*, it does not constitute a future projection around which to construct a project for living, probably because of the sense of individual responsibility and of subjective effort that the construction of a family nucleus involves (Besozzi, 2006).

The second critical problem regards the *work crisis*. In the past this represented an economic resource which led to a stable positioning in society, but it was above all a dimension which resulted in identity and socialization. The job determined a significant form of individual emancipation, functioning as an instrument of access and legitimization within social categories and classes, as well as a motor of mobility and of meritocratic reward. The choice of flexibility, apparently comprehensible within the prospective of an enlarging of the job market, has resulted in a fundamental error: that of considering the question as merely economic, overlooking its function of socialization, of preparation for roles, and of the attaining of objectives, but above all of the construction of identity (Bauman, 1998). The modern society no longer provides a safety net for individual behaviour and the weakening of prescriptions regarding action and socialization, and the weakening of values and of behavioural norms has put the burden on the individual, who has become the protagonist not only of his or her choices, but also of defeats. Placing this weight and focusing attention on the individual, however, involves an assumption of responsibility for the sociocultural orientation towards action, causing the subject an increase in discomfort and difficulty in front of the many choices society presents.

An indicator of excessive individualism is given by the concentration of attention on the corporal, which is ever more the territory of recapitulation of the need for happiness and of subjective realization, and it is not chance that in these modern times, compared with the past, human beings have more consumer goods, through which they seek to satisfy the sense of satisfaction of the individual identity (Codeluppi, 2003). But the desired expectations, however, do not seem commensurate to the possibility of restitution: the increase in wealth and material goods corresponds paradoxically to a sharpening of the sense of discomfort. Society today seems to be less and less a dispenser of well-being and of participation, and has become a territory in which individual expectations take precedence by force, overriding the mediations upheld by society.

The third critical problem regards the *educational improbability of the school system*. This more than other areas has suffered from the weakening of society's capacity to transfer culture and knowledge which are not negotiable to the new generations. In the past, values and knowledge were transmitted to young people, but what they assimilated was in reality the architecture of the adult age and the relative learning of that role. Today it is the school itself which is feeling the effects of the weakening of society and is

in a state of crisis because it is still founded on traditional pedagogical prescriptions which are ill adapted to the requirements and the characteristics of modern society. It is in the scenario of *educational improbability* that we see that the idea of school as a "parking lot" has become to an ever greater extent incorporated into the institution. It is here that we see the sense of an absence of values and a lack of communication particularly between the generations, except in those cases where the teacher, with significant effort, manages to regain the role of mediation. Evidence of this is the increasing lack of interest of the young in the education, which is visible in the evident arrogance and vulgarity present to an ever greater extent in their attitudes and, on the other hand, in a decrease in the willingness of teachers to involve themselves more in the educational process. One of the triggering factors of this crisis, therefore, is the loss of confidence and of "faith" of the teachers; the school runs the risk of becoming *a void-producing mechanism*, because it produces architecture and schemes, but not culture.

To this we must add the rapid penetration of communication technologies in the social and cultural experience of the individual, which has intensified this perception of an emptying of sense. The media, in fact, by its technological nature, often gives priority to direct experiences of the use of the medium and stimulate processes of symbolic construction of individual and subjective realities, which therefore lack cultural filters. For this reason, those intellectual spaces through which the learning processes of the individual were often *mediated* in the past (such as, for example, the school and the family), are today in decline in comparison with the development of communication.

In the face of this transformation, the school has always had to confront the dilemma of its social function: should it uphold the conservation of a cultural heritage by the transmission of what has been legitimated by tradition as "knowledge," or should it risk adapting to innovation and to the changes which surround it, taking on the responsibility for filtering cultural forms and knowledge that are too new?

Since the 1960s a number of researchers have observed that over the course of time the school seems to have been over-concerned to affirm traditional values, giving priority to an abstract dimension, which was often coldly ultracognitive, to the detriment of those more concrete aspects which are connected to the development of the individual's personality emotions (Alfassio Grimaldi & Bertoni, 1964, p. 63). This attitude was without a doubt consistent with the social characteristics and the dominant cultural model of those years, but it is a resistance which we have not yet left behind us. The scholastic institution still today, in fact, maintains forms of influence on the sociocultural condition which are present in the language and in the instruments of the media. Inevitably this conditions the position of teachers with regard to communication and risks compromising their passion for education, increasing the difficulty of adapting the content of the programmes to the expressive forms and dynamics of the media. The same condition reflects, moreover, on the students and removes value from the educational context, which is perceived and experienced as a place of socialization but not of learning and education.

Through communication, this institution can find again its cultural impetus and represent itself as the intellectual terrain in which and through which to interpret modern change. Technological progress is not enough to guarantee cultural sense and quality to the contents of the media; the channel and its signifier, which are present in the codes of the means of communication, are not enough to convey meaningful messages. As Luciano Galliani affirmed in the title of a thought-provoking book in 1979, *The Process is the Message*, certainly not the technology.

Intellectual space and critical comparison are also the basis of the cultural *humus* of media prod-

ucts. Investment in a communicative policy and ethic would, on the one hand, serve to rejuvenate, or rather reinvigorate, the expressive language and the contents of the media, balancing the processes of the handling of the communicative apparatus. On the other hand it would serve to re-establish, particularly in the action of consumption, situations of dialogue and symbolic comparison from which to stimulate a process of semantic construction of the experiences.

Through communication, the school could carry out its task of accompanying the young in this modern sociocultural evolution, observing and investigating in what way the changes affect and condition the need for identification, and modifying the dynamics of socialization in a project of intervention and qualification of the requests for participation, relationships, and comprehension of the modern world. In fact, if it is true that the young develop a harmonious relationship with the media from early infancy (Buckingham, 2004), it is also true that this *naturalism* is not always a guarantee of an equally natural acquisition of awareness of the mechanisms of the process, which are hidden in the construction of a message. For this reason, a progressive education in communication and in its languages (media education) could contribute to the development of an awareness of the sociocultural function and of the power to condition the media with regard to everyone's symbolic universe. Only on this condition can the school become the preferred environment of the culture of change, taking back that role of mediation which will enable it, and also serve mass culture, to reclaim its function as guarantor of equal opportunities.

THE DIGITAL MEDIA AS EXPRESSION OF THE LATE-MODERN

The digital media, more than any other, can be considered emblematic of the new late-modern sociocultural condition in that they inaugurate forms of interaction and of action, both individual and collective, which reflect the relations of the subject to a complex and "multimedial" reality.

The first common factor regards the reticular articulation of the digital world and its extension free from space-time limits which grants the subject an open explorative navigation, directed only by individual interests and motivations and guided by the sense of responsibility and by the level of independence and subjective critical sense which condition the choices. The process of individualization of the modern condition (Beck, 2000), in the digital media translates, thus, into the capacity of orientation, of independence of choice and of subjective action in front of the many cultural proposals of the virtual Web, and in the construction of a personalized path of consumption, starting from those needs and desires which need constantly to be satisfied and from the capacity to construct new media diets according to the social circumstances in which each of us acts.

Individualism can be found, therefore, in the capacity of choice and of selection of virtual and real information on the Web, in the ability to combine and hybridize it in a creative and selective way, without letting it enter into contradiction. In this way there is the development of the so-called *subjective activism* (Morcellini & Cortoni, 2007) or *consumeristic attitude* (Codeluppi, 2003), according to which the critical character of a cultural and medial behaviour derive from the capacity of the individual to release, during the moment of decodification, the dominant ideological interpretations, connected to the productive act, in order to reconstruct subjective interpretative pathways, which are often hybridized with personal life experiences. This renewed behaviour has been defined *networked individualism* (Marinelli, 2004), in that it allows for the satisfying of new forms of subjective identification, for the appeasement of the need for protagonism, and for explorativity,

leading to new processes of interpretation of the self, of the others, and of reality. The young are the principle protagonists of these technologies, often activating processes of auto-socialization in that they succeed in declining with flexibility the characteristics of the different technologies to different uses, contexts, and opportunities to such an extent that they can be defined the *networked generation* (Tirocchi, Andò, & Antenore, 2002). In this space all are transformed at the same time into producers and consumers, transmitters, and receivers. In other words, the spectator becomes actor, expressing his or her willingness to enter the text and actualize it, taking as a starting point the personal prospective of interpretation.

If this form of virtual individualism can appear as an expression of liberty and of subjective emancipation, it risks, however, transforming itself into a condition of excess, and of scant cultural mediation, resulting in fragmentation and a loss of direction. The capacity for self-orientation, in fact, depends on the level of independence, responsibility, and personality which each individual matures, starting from daily experience and educational experience; that is, depending on the individual background of culture and experience. Also in this case, the cultural, affective, and informative patrimony of the family and of the school have a strong effect on socialization in the age of digital media, on the level of self-respect and assuredness, and, as a result, on the sociocultural attitudes of the individual which are expressed when surfing the Internet. In other words, a solid cultural mediation from the family and from the school in the process of socialization helps to guarantee all the basic instruments the individual needs to orientate him or herself in the digital world in an independent and creative manner, and when this is lacking the subject has difficulty in the media network.

Moreover, a strong instability and fluidity of knowledge and of values often corresponds to the immateriality of place in the late-modern era, so much so that the same process of socialization takes on a symbolic value. Thus, if the identity fragments and becomes fragile due to a lack of solid and concrete points of reference, the processes of identification become multiple and parallel, in that the subject seeks elsewhere for that which the traditional agencies of socialization are not able to guarantee. This allows for the appeasing of heterogeneous needs and the satisfying of aspects of the personality which are equally divergent through their immersion in virtual worlds.

The objective is always the same: the realization of the self and the attainment of an internal well-being by constantly involving oneself in the experiences of daily life, although the contexts and the times of the socialization change.

Through digital technology, therefore, new forms of interaction and immediate communication, without filters, are realized. They are independent of spatial distances and make it possible to satisfy the need to relate in a way which is coherent with the characteristics of a late-modern condition and of a digitalized society (Maffesoli, 2004).

According to some researchers, in fact, one of the peculiarities of the post condition in today's society regards the rediscovery of the social, of the sharing and collective participation which lead to a new form of interaction and intersubjective comparison. This is a form of reaction to the excesses of modern individualism, a "cure" for its side effects of subjective sense of loss, which has developed due to the lack of solid reference points to which the individual can anchor him or herself in the process of definition of identity. This leads the subject to seek new forms of participation, giving origin to the so-called phenomenon of de-individualization (Bauman, 2000; Maffesoli, 2004).

This reclaiming of the relational dimension in the digital world can be interpreted starting from two aspects of interpretation: that which is carried out within the virtual space and that which is closely connected to real experience.

In the first case, we are speaking of those relationships of virtual interaction which are played out in the semantic sharing of ideas, myths, rites, and interpretations of reality in the new spatial dimensions which are generated by technological convergence. Far from being impersonal, these new environments make it possible to appease the need for identification and the search for the self through comparison and exchange with those who choose to share the same semantic community, exploring different worlds according to the presuppositions of the classic sociology of Alfred Schutz. It thus becomes possible to satisfy the need for a "common understanding" through contact with the other and the re-appropriation of the relational dimension, developing a sense of belonging and sharing, often semantic or symbolic, which affects the process of the search for and the construction of the self, social network (Marinelli, 2004).

On the other hand, the increase in relationships in the virtual environment does not necessarily mean the weakening of concrete experience and interaction. Paradoxically in the late-modern era we are seeing the rediscovery of certain dimensions of the real connected to traditional experience, such as, for example, aesthetics, physical space as space-symbol of the bond, of celebration, and of rituality and, therefore, as *alchemy of the social*, of contact and comparison with the alter (Maffesoli, 2004, p. 81).

In support of this new dimension of late-modern relationships there have been a number of studies by ISTAT in recent years into the cultural behaviour of young Italians which announce a new tendency: the discovery of and search for collective, shared experiences in which the dimension of relationships is reclaimed, for direct participation , and for plurisensorial involvement through the experience (Morcellini, 2005, 2004a). In the last few years, in fact, there have been cultural modifications in all those areas which in the past were labelled elite or niche markets. So we find in a 10-year period (from 1996 to 2005) that the theatre, classical music, and visits to archaeological sites have increased their appeal, not only among the young, in spite of the explosion that has taken place regarding the means of communication.

In spite, therefore, of the structural instability of the social context, particularly of the economic sector, there has been an increase in cultural activity founded on contact and on social and emotional involvement. There has been an increase in the number of cinema goers of 16.1%, for the theatre of 10.6%, and so on for other activities: museums and exhibitions (+17.3%); classical music concerts (+3.1%); other music (+0.6%); sports events (+4.5%).

It is 2005 specifically in which all the forms of live entertainment reach their maximum historical level in terms of users over a 10-year period. The only form of entertainment which is in decline is the discotheque (-2.53% from 1996 to 2005). This data helps to radicalize the differences between the new generation and that of the 1980s (see Table 1).

If we wish to narrow the research to the year 2005 and focus attention on different cultural behaviour, taking into consideration the different age groups among the young, it is possible to see that the cinema occupies the first place in the classification of entertainment. It is therefore the most popular medium among all age groups,

Table 1. New encyclopedia of culture and communication. Spectators between 6 and 19 years of age at different entertainment events between 1996 and 2005.

YEAR	The-atre	Cin-ema	Museums and exhi-bitions	Classi-cal music concerts	Concerts of other music	Sports events	Disco-theques and dancing
1996	19.1	-64	26.1	5.8	23.1	39.3	31.1
1997	13.9	69	39.2	8.3	24.6	43	31
1998	20.6	71.3	38.2	6.3	-22	40.4	28.9
1999	23.2	69.3	38.6	7.5	22.6	40.8	30.2
2000	22.7	66.9	41.3	7.3	23.5	41.7	30.4
2001	25.6	75.8	40.6	7.5	23.6	42.8	30.3
2002	25.1	78.6	42.3	7.6	24.4	42.5	28.6
2003	23.4	74	41.2	7.1	24.8	44.2	28.8
2005*	29,7	80,1	43,4	8,9	23,7	43,8	28,6
Escursione 2000/2005	+7	+13.2	+2.1	+1.6	+0.2	+2.1	-1.8
Escursione 1996/2005	+10.6	+16.1	+17.3	+3.1	+0.6	+4.5	-2.5

Source: elaboration based on ISTAT data

* data not at present available for 2004

although with different percentages. Discotheques and dance halls, on the other hand, are frequented by the over-15s and their popularity increases with age, reaching second place in the classification of outdoor activities in 2005. As far as the younger members of the group are concerned (from 6 to 10 and from 11 to 14), museums and exhibitions are the most popular activities, in third place after the cinema and sports events. The theatre also shows a significant number of spectators, particularly among children between 6 and 10 (28.4%), followed by pop music and classical music concerts.

A new way of relating to the context of reality and of forming relationships has been established. This is certainly fluctuating and dynamic, consistent with the social flexibility and cultural fragmentation/fragility of the real which is still to be explored. In general the young pass from one space to another to satisfy their need to belong in different contexts, which reinforces the semantic or symbolic sharing of gestures, and expressive and ideological forms. In other words, the post-modern ethos is acted out in shared spaces, in participation and in collective and material events.

If we wish to synthesize the cultural behaviour of young Italians with reference to the stimuli of modern society, it is worth highlighting certain key points:

1. **Multimediality** and **explorativity** as styles of consumption and individual attitudes in front of the range of cultural and media stimuli of modern society; according to ISTAT data, from 2000 to 2005 there was an enormous increase in the cultural activities of the young who have at their disposal different media contemporarily in a productive and creative way to satisfy multiple needs, or rather desires. There is no longer competition between the media, but a synergy of stimuli, instruments, and languages.

2. **Subjective activism and protagonism** as symbols of the centrality of the individual in the choice and personalization of the different media stimuli. The received wisdom in that the subject has been transformed from consumer into producer of symbols, knowledge, and meanings conveyed by the media and recontextualized in everyday experience.

3. **Relationships and participations** which define the cultural behaviour of the young and the processes of socialization in the late-modern context. ISTAT data, for example, shows that between 1998 and 2005 there is a growth in young people's need to spend time with their contemporaries, a characteristic which increases with age in correspondence with the process of socialization. Naturally, there is a progressive abandoning of the domestic environment in favour of the informal world of their peers. Along with friends, we must not underestimate the practice of sport in free time. This increased between 2000 and 2005, particularly among girls and it gains in popularity with age. In conclusion, participation in cultural events represents a form of reaction to modern hyper-technology and is a symbol of the re-appropriation of a traditional dimension, that of face-to-face interaction.

PC AND THE INTERNET: TERRAIN OF DESIRES AND RISKS

"After twenty years of hypnosis by the television, the new generations are beginning to rub their eyes and the audience is changing from passive to active." In an interview Paolo Ferri, lecturer in Didactic Technology and Theory and Techniques of the New Media at the Bicocca University of Milan used these words to synthesize the metamorphosis in act in the relationship of the young with the new technologies. "The PC beats the TV, Here is the Generation" is the title of an article in a section of *Repubblica*, following the publication of data by Nielson on the new technologies (2005), which recounts the increase of these media in the diet of the young. The PC, in its different forms, is experiencing the same history of penetration that the TV experienced with regard to the cultural habits of the Italians 50 years ago. The risk seems to be the same: the speed of this process is such that it does not allow the social institutions, in particular the family and the school, to keep pace with the times, so that they risk yet again appearing inadequate with regard to the communicative, interactive, and creative characteristics which the new media offer. The question, therefore, is no longer whether or not to use the medium, but how to use it correctly within the different social and educational contexts so as to emphasize the potentials and reduce the possible risks of an undesirable use. The ISTAT data of 2005 confirm that the use of the PC and Internet has literally doubled within the family compared with the year 2000, to the extent that 83.3% of children between 3 and 17 use it. The use of the PC increases with age and is prevalently a male activity, particularly when we consider daily use. Females seem to have a less familiar and less frequent relationship with this technology; indeed, as age increases its use decreases even more until by adulthood it has all but disappeared (see Table 3). Statistics naturally only make it possible to provide a photograph of the extension and the radicalization of a social and cultural phenomenon such as that which regards the new technologies. However it is not possible to provide adequate information to enable us to motivate a certain use or to restrict the use to specific social and cultural contexts. Every analysis, therefore, is only partial when it comes to reconstructing an overview of a generation also with regard to the use of new technologies.

If almost every family possesses this technological artefact, the same situation is not present in the scholastic context where, according to ISTAT data and in spite of the policy of technological investment undertaken by the state, there is still a reduced use of the medium in the classroom compared with the rapidity of the processes of technological advancement and scientific investment abroad. A more consistent investment and attention on the part of the schools and of the ministry to the use of the new media, therefore, could help to reduce the number of children who do not use the PC simply because they do not have one at home. Possession, however, relieves us from the need to ask further questions regarding the new technologies: knowing how to use this media with "awareness of cause," in a way which is focused and not casual is a problem which *in primis* regards adults rather than the young.

According to the ISTAT data of 2005 on the frequency of use of the PC by age and sex, it is possible to affirm that males in particular, and specifically young males, have a better, more natural, and more continuous relationship with the new technologies, and specifically with the PC. This latter group are in fact the most assiduous and frequent users (they use it every day in greater numbers than females), while girls and women seem to congregate at the antipodes of the classification regarding styles of use; that is to say, they use the PC less than males and in a more sporadic manner.

If we analyze the picture presented by ISTAT 2005 (Table 2) vertically and focus our attention on females, we can see that in spite of their scarce familiarity with the new technologies, girls are more open and well disposed towards the digital media compared with women: until the age of 24 they use this medium once or more a week in greater numbers than males, even if this habit weakens as age increases (see Table 2).

The scenario which is gradually emerging has led many researchers, among paedagogists, psychologists, sociologists, and mass-mediologists, to question the cognitive, perceptive, behavioural, and relational metamorphoses that this new symbiotic relationship risks determining.

Table 2. Towards the Technoeval Age. Use of the Internet by sex and age group (2005).

Age group	Every day		Once or more a week		A few times a month		A few times a year		Does not use the PC	
	M	F	M	F	M	F	M	F	M	F
3-5	4.4	1.4	8.6	5.4	5.7	5.5	0.9	1.9	74.9	81.6
6-10	9.1	6.2	33.3	37.1	8.0	9.0	1.5	2.2	46.0	43.9
11-14	27.4	14.9	41.6	44.2	4.8	9.0	1.2	3.9	23.5	27.4
15-19	36.5	21.7	35.5	47.9	4.6	6.5	2.2	1.6	20.1	20.6
20-24	38.3	30.6	24.1	30.2	5.1	5.8	1.4	2.6	27.6	27.4
25-34	38.4	32.7	17.7	14.8	3.2	4.0	1.6	2.8	37.3	42.8
35-44	39.6	26.4	13.1	12.5	3.4	4.8	1.6	2.4	40.3	52.4
45-54	32.6	19.2	11.5	9.2	2.8	3.1	1.2	2.0	50.3	64.3
55-59	19.4	9.3	10.0	4.2	2.6	1.2	1.7	1.5	63.4	81.2
60-64	9.6	3.0	7.5	2.1	2.0	1.1	0.8	1.8	77.5	89.8
65-74	4.5	0.6	3.6	0.9	1.1	0.2	0.6	0.4	87.8	94.3
75 +	1.5	0.1	1.0	0.2	0.3	0.3	-	-	94.1	96.5
Totale	25.6	16.0	15.3	13.4	3.2	3.5	1.2	1.8	52.3	62.8

Source: elaboration of ISTAT data 2005
Key: for each age group the higher percentage value of use between the sexes has been highlighted.

It is not a question of assuming apocalyptic and integrated positions towards this new reality, but rather of reflecting and analyzing in a strategic, synergic, and transversal manner the social effects, the psychological consequences, and the strategies with which to use these instruments to the best in everyday life. The objective could be to predispose conditions so that the new media can become a support for the "do-it-yourself" process in children, transforming them from surfers to planners.

It is worth adding a few reflections to the above on the process of familiarization with the new technologies (Silverstone, 1999) or indeed on the new forms of socialization which derive from their modality of use and from social practices constructed around the act of consumption. According to researchers in the field of digital technologies, the virtual and the real dimension are progressively demolishing the confines which previously delimitated them and are constructing forms of parasocial communication in which the virtual dimension is transformed into a cultural humus and stimulus for sharing and participation in a relationship between equals, nourishing, fortifying, and enriching the exchange of emotions and meanings in face to face interaction. It is as though reciprocal forms of influence and conditioning were activated between the real world and the virtual world.

Table 3. Towards the Technoeval Age. Use of the Internet by sex and age group (2005).

Classi di età	Tutti i giorni		Una o più volte a set-timana		Qualche volta al mese		Qualche vol-ta all'anno		Non usano Internet	
	M	F	M	F	M	F	M	F	M	F
3-5	-	-	-	-	-	-	-	-	-	-
6-10	1.3	0.9	5.4	6.5	4.0	4.1	2.0	1.9	84.0	84.8
11-14	7.1	4.2	22.8	21.1	10.9	11.3	6.2	4.6	52.7	57.9
15-19	18.0	9.4	34.7	38.5	9.4	11.5	3.5	3.6	32.5	32.6
20-24	25.2	15.4	27.8	40.8	8.1	10.0	2.5	4.4	32.9	33.9
25-34	24.6	18.2	21.1	19.5	5.1	7.1	3.0	2.7	43.1	49.4
35-44	22.6	12.6	19.6	14.6	5.0	6.2	2.3	3.5	48.2	61.4
45-54	16.6	8.7	15.9	9.4	5.2	4.5	2.2	2.6	58.1	71.9
55-59	9.8	4.1	11.3	4.6	4.2	2.0	2.0	0.8	69.3	84.4
60-64	5.3	1.4	7.6	2.0	1.7	1.0	1.3	1.6	80.9	91.0
65-74	2.4	0.3	2.9	0.5	1.3	0.3	0.6	0.1	90.0	94.6
75 +	0.6	0.0	1.1	0.0	0.2	0.2	0.2	-	93.8	96.4
Totale	14.5	7.9	15.7	12.1	4.7	4.7	2.2	2.2	60.2	70.2

Source: elaboration of data ISTAT 2005
Key: for each age group the higher percentage value of use between the sexes has been highlighted.

Among the new technologies, the Internet warrants a separate chapter. According to data collated by ISTAT in 2005, the use of the Web is established among minors, and it increases with age. Also in this case the tendency towards "regular" virtual surfing (every day or almost), is prevalently male. If girls do not use the PC, they will not as a rule use Internet. In fact, from the ISTAT data of 2005 on the frequency of use of Internet by age group and sex it again emerges that the highest percentage of those who do not use Internet are predominantly female, regardless of age (see Table 3). Starting from the picture which

has just been delineated, if we wish to focus our attention on females and identify a profile of a "Web surfer" among those few who relate to the new technologies, this would be of a girl between 6 and 24 years old who surfs a few times a month more than males, even if the girls lose this habit progressively, again with age.

It is certain that the pragmatism implicit in the use of the new technologies, the protagonism in the processes of construction of knowledge, the perceptive, cognitive, and emotional immersion in virtual reality, and the simulation of experiences separated from the physicality of the acts, represent determining characteristics which help to intensify the interaction of the young with these technologies. This union which was already presumed in the 1990s, when the technological explosion was merely an intuition and a wager for the future, has today been transformed into a condition sine qua non which characterizes the experience of the young, "the best teachers of communicative technologies" (Tirocchi et al., 2002). Restricting the analysis of the new media to the PC and Internet, as some national institutes of research such as ISTAT still do today, is however reductive because it does not allow for the question of technological convergence, of the hybridization of languages and meanings which satisfy the desire for eclecticism, explorativity, and protagonism of the subject. The terminological choice of "digital media" itself with which to describe the new *new-medial* world lets us understand a reality which is more complex and articulated than the Internet, which also embraces the new frontiers of TV, the mobile phone, the radio, or indeed of those generalist media which, to respond to the activity of exploration and manipulation of the technological contents of the subjects according to the logic of constructivism, develop new forms of interaction and of action.

The dimension of the community, the new prospective of dialogue among equals, the different opportunities for socialization, the perception of an expressive freedom behind the mask of an identity which could be fictitious, as well as the possibility of being open to change without necessarily destabilizing oneself, all the above represent keys of interpretation, perhaps over-optimistic, which help to edify a relationship of reciprocal trust between the young and the new communicative technologies

The experience of reaffirmation of the self and of the construction or search for an identity are at the basis of every educational process, whether real or virtual, for the young and for many behavioural orientations with regard to the technological possibilities of today. In the case of the Internet,

the awareness of the virtuality of the real and the perception of a dimension which is parallel to the tangible one, stimulate the individual to expose him or herself to risk, in the awareness that experiences lived through the screen do not constitute real life.

CONCLUSION

We could compare the technologies to a "no-man's-land" where identities and roles are played out, certainties, equilibriums, and knowledge are both constructed and destabilized, a sense of belonging is established and acquaintances developed, but risks and dangers are also met. It is a place of risk, where everything is mobile and dynamic and the possibility of cognitive growth is proportional to the possibility of encountering environments which are insalubrious and often dangerous for the young, above all on the Internet. Also in this case the responsibility for the journey falls on the explorer, on the safety of the route, on the compass and the map, but also on the destination and the previous experience of *surfing*. In other words, the framework of reality conditions the approach and the experience of the young with respect to the prospects of socialization offered by the new technologies. A cultural and socio-educational humus which is constantly present in the choices and experiences of consumption can facilitate the maturing of a critical sense which is sufficient to conduct the relationship with these technologies harmoniously and independently. In this way the risk of transforming the actors of the virtual into "victims" can be avoided.

When we speak of digital technologies, we are not referring exclusively to the Internet; digital TV, the potential of the mobile phone for digitalization, and the recent arrival of the radio on the Web are symbols of the integration of two realities, the virtual and the real, which influence each other, exchanging symbols, signifiers, and signs, and exerting a strong influence on the development of socialization in the young. Virtual experiences thus echo real ones, particularly in those aspects which do not manage to emerge through concrete everyday experience, while real life provides a key of interpretation to relate to and exploit adequately the experiences and activities connected to the new technologies.

The virtual reality of the Web and that which is perceived, put into practice, constructed, or imagined in the continuous relationship with the digital technologies mirrors the real world, particularly when, through immersion and integration with the languages and characteristics of the new media, it attempts to gratify needs and desires which the individual is not always able to satisfy in everyday life. The hybridization of languages and multimedial convergence, therefore, increase the possibility of contact, of communicative and semantic exchange between individuals, removing the barriers not only of space and time but also of sex, creed, ideology, and so forth, producing a sensation of communication between equals. However, it is also true that they can conceal unexpected situations of violation of privacy, of violence, and particularly psychological violence, which invade personal space. This too, however, is a reflection of what happens in the tangible world, but at an experiential acceleration which is directly proportionate to the prospective of interaction and contact offered by the digital media.

In second place, this interpretation of the relationship of the young with technology in the adult world seems yet again to present a point of view which does not always correspond to the view they put forward of themselves. The young are born and brought up in a technological environment and they learn to handle independently the different media and the multitude of stimuli which come from a reality which is in itself complex. They get used to progressively facing, observing, listening to, and selecting or reorganizing in their experience of life the wide range of inputs offered. The propensity towards the digital media produces

with time a modification in the way of observing, thinking, and interpreting the surrounding reality, which becomes eclectic and reticular, in accordance with a precise order which is closely connected to subjective experience. The young, who have grown up immersed in these continual cultural and technological stimuli, develop a *forma mentis* which is able to handle and control these same stimuli and they present themselves to the adult world with this awareness and cultural and experiential maturity.

The story of the numbers recounts a process of cultural appropriation by Italian society which, while certainly not linear, is seductive and interesting. However, the reaching of certain percentages does not solve the problem of the cultural competence of the Italians in the use of the languages and instruments of the media. The numbers recount neither the position of this communication in people's lives, the intensity of the media experiences in everyday life, nor indeed the level of influence they have on life style. They limit themselves to supplying a photograph of the situation from which to investigate in depth into the cultural, symbolic, expressive, and behavioural relationship between the media and the young.

The numbers indicate an encouraging trend. An observation of the data, in fact, indicates that the change is determined principally by the young. It is therefore possible to introduce the concept of *communicative activation* with which to intend not only the activism of the public but also a different attitude of independence in the new generation with regard to the communicative and technological stimulation of which they are protagonists. This communicative analysis should be carried out as part of their education to show that it is enough to have access to the media to find forms of communication and thereby avoid anxiety-provoking incomprehension between the generations. As these processes are taking place with such rapidity, the least we can do is help them along.

REFERENCES

Alfassio Grimaldi, U., & Bretoni, I. (1964). *I giovani degli anni '60*. Bari: Laterza.

Bauman, Z. (1998). *Work, consumerism, new poor*. London: Open University Press.

Bauman, Z. (2000). *Liquid modernity*. Cambridge, UK: Polity Press.

Beck, U. (2000). *Risk society: Towards a new modernità*. New Deli, India: Sage.

Besozzi, E. (2006). *Società, cultura, educazione*. Roma: Carocci.

Buckingham, D. (2006). *Media education. Literacy, learning and contemporary culture*. Cambridge, UK: Polity Press.

Codeluppi, V. (2003). *Il Potere del consumo*. Torino: Bollati Boringhieri.

Farné, R. (2003). *Buona maestra tv. La rai e l'educazione da Non è mai troppo tardi a Quark*. Roma: Carocci.

Giddens, A. (1991). *Modernity and self-identity: Self and society in the late modern age*. Stanford, CA: Stanford University Press.

Grasso, P. (1974). *Personalità e innovazione: Ricerca psicologico-sociale sulla condizione giovanile di transizionalità culturale*. Roma: Coines.

Grasso, P. (1989). *Parabola giovanile dagli anni '50 agli anni '80*. Roma: Euroma.

Griswold, W. (1994). *Cultures and societies in a changing world*. Thousand Oaks, CA: Pine Forge.

Maffesoli, M. (1988). *Le temps des tribus*. Paris: Le Livre de Poche.

Maffesoli, M. (2004). *Le rythme de vie. Variation sur l'imaginaire post-moderne*. Paris: Editions Table Ronde.

Marinelli, A. (2004). *Connessioni*. Milano: Guerini e associati.

Meyrowitz, J. (1985). *No sense of place*. New York: Oxford University Press.

Morcellini, M. (1997). *Passaggio al futuro. Formazione e socializzazione tra vecchi e nuovi media*. Milano: FrancoAngeli.

Morcellini, M. (1999). *La TV fa bene ai bambini*. Roma: Meltemi.

Morcellini, M. (2004). *La scuola della modernità. Per un manifesto della media education*. Milano: FrancoAngeli.

Morcellini, M. (2005). *Il Mediaevo. TV e industria culturale nell'Italia del XX secolo*. Roma: Carocci.

Morcellini, M., & Cortoni, I. (2007). *Provaci ancora, scuola. Idee e proposte contro la svalutazione della scuola nel Tecnoevo*. Trento: Erickson.

Ranieri, A. (2006). *I luoghi del sapere*. Roma: Il sole 24ore.

Rullani, E. (2004). *Economia della conoscenza*. Roma: Carocci.

Sciolla, L. (2002). *Sociologia dei processi culturali*. Bologna: Il Mulino.

Silverstone, R. (1999). *Why study the media?* London: Sage.

Tirocchi, S., Andò, R., & Antenore, M. (2002). *Giovani a parole. Dalla generazione media alla networked generation*. Roma: Guerini e Associati.

This work was previously published in Digital Literacy: Tools and Methodologies for Information Society, edited by P. Rivoltella, pp. 45-66, copyright 2008 by IGI Publishing, formerly known as Idea Group Publishing (an imprint of IGI Global).

Chapter II
Giving and Taking Offence in a Global Context[1]

John Weckert

Centre for Applied Philosophy and Public Ethics, Charles Sturt University, Australia

ABSTRACT

This article examines the concept of offence, both its giving and taking, and argues that such an examination can shed some light on global ethical issues. It examines the nature of offence, what, if anything, is wrong in giving offence, the obligations on the offended, whether or not offence is objective, and offence in a global setting. It argues for the view that choice and context provide some way of distinguishing between offence which is a serious moral issue and that which is not. It is morally worse to offend those who have no choice in the area of the offence, for example race, than in areas where there is choice. Intermediate cases such as religious belief, choice depends largely on education and exposure to alternatives. Context is important in that offending the vulnerable is morally worse than offending those in more powerful, or privileged groups.

INTRODUCTION: WHY BOTHER WITH OFFENCE?

A study of the concept of offence can shed some light on global ethical issues. While offence is frequently not taken very seriously, the contention here is that it should be. A better understanding of why offence is taken and why some instances of giving offence are reprehensible and others are not can assist our understanding of what is necessary in a global ethics. The argument here focuses on the morality of giving offence rather than on what kinds of offence, if any, should be subject to legal restrictions. The recent case of the Danish cartoons illustrates the importance of the notion of offence. Unless offence is taken seriously, that case has no interesting moral dimension. It is simply an instance of someone exercising their legitimate right to freedom of expression and others unjustifiably objecting. The Danish publisher was right to do what he did and the offended Muslims were wrong to object. If, however, offence is taken seriously, then the question of who was right and who was wrong becomes more problematic, and the issue can be seen as a real clash of values. In liberal democratic states, freedom of expression is highly valued, but this is not universal. Perhaps it should be, but when considering ethics in a global context, we are not starting with a clean slate. The realities of the world are where we start. In some parts of the world the general the notion of freedom of expression is not even entertained. It simply is not an issue to be taken into account. Social cohesion and religious beliefs are all important. The society rather than the individual comes first. Once that is realised, the offence that was taken is more comprehensible. From the perspective of the offended, there is a good reason for taking offence; there has been a violation of an important religious value for no apparent reason other than denigration of the Muslim faith. While the situation was undoubtedly more complicated and some took advantage of the cartoons for their own ends, the fact is that it was relatively easy for them to do this, partly because of a lack of understanding of the importance of freedom of speech in most Western countries and the feeling that their religion was not being respected.

It is impossible to limit offence to national or cultural borders given the current state of the electronic media, particularly the Internet. Some action, acceptable in one country or culture, can be extremely offensive in another. As noted above, cartoons have played a prominent role in recent times in causing offence in countries other than those in which they were published, particularly those published in Denmark. Those cartoons depicted the prophet Mohammad in ways that much of the Muslim world considered blasphemous. Earlier a cartoon in Australia depicted a scene in which certain Israeli actions were compared with Nazi actions at Auswitch. This cartoon was severely criticised because of its offensiveness to Jews and was withdrawn. More recently an Indonesian newspaper published a cartoon showing the Australian Prime Minister and Minister for Foreign Affairs as copulating dogs. This was in response to Australia granting temporary visas to a group of illegal immigrants from the Indonesian province of Papua. In retaliation, an Australian newspaper published a cartoon of the Indonesian President and a Papuan as dogs copulating, with the President in the dominant position. Each of these cartoons was condemned in the other country as being offensive. These cases highlight various cultural differences, for example, different views on freedom of speech and expression, and on blasphemy. Where there are incompatible positions on fundamental issues, some way must be sought to solve or avoid conflict. In the Danish case mentioned, the offence caused by the cartoons led to a tragic loss of life as well as to tension between various countries. The offensiveness of the cartoons of the copulating dogs too led to an increase in tensions, in this case between Indonesia and Australia. Given the importance of the concept of offence in the global arena, it warrants examination in that context.

WHAT IS OFFENCE?

Offence is some sort of hurt or pain, displeasure, disgust, mental distress or mental suffering of some variety (see Feinberg, 1985, p. 1). Something is offensive if some people do not like it in a certain way; it hurts their feelings, it disgusts them, or something of that ilk. Strictly speaking, things do not give offence; people do through their actions. An outcrop of rock shaped like some part of the human anatomy is not offensive although a sculpture of the same shape might be. While it is common to talk of pictures, cartoons, and language as offensive, what is really offensive is that someone has acted in some way, by photographing, painting, drawing, talking, writing, or some similar activity. Giving offence involves intention. It need not be the case that the action is intended to offend (although it might be) but the action must be intentional (to emphasis the point, I am ignoring the fact that actions are often defined as intentional). An intentional action can give offence in a way that an unintentional one will not. Public nudity is often considered offensive but if on some occasion, it is a result of someone escaping a burning house, it is not likely to be seen as such. Many things done intentionally cause offence unintentionally. Often we do not know that something that we do will be offensive to some. Much offence too is a result of carelessness. Some people may not bother perhaps too much about the feelings of others. It is not that they want to cause offence, it is rather that they do not care enough to avoid causing offence or perhaps are just not perceptive enough.

Many things are described as offensive, ranging from public nudity and copulating to racist and religious actions and blasphemy, from snubs from acquaintances to insults about one's appearance. These offences are what Tasioulas (2006) calls *norm-governed*. In these cases certain norms have been violated, or at least the offended party believes so. Tasioulas distinguishes these offences from what he calls *primitive* offences. Offensive smells, for example, dihydrogen sulfide (rotten egg gas), are an example. Norm-governed offences are the ones of interest here.

Discussions of giving offence are commonly conducted in the context of freedom of speech and possible restrictions that might be justified by offensive material, or in the context of criminalisation of certain actions (Feinberg, 1973; Tasioulas, 2006). Much everyday offence is of course more personal. I am offended when I alone am not invited to the party, or when someone implies that I am incompetent or poorly dressed. Most of this kind of offensive behaviour is not seen as the proper concern of the law, except perhaps in the workplace where it can be related to harassment or bullying. The most important instances of offence however, at least in the public arena,

concern things like racist language, blasphemy, and indecency (although personal offence to a prominent figure can cause widespread public offence).

Taking offence might be said to involve three elements: the hurt, the judgement that the action was wrong, and some action, for example, demanding an apology or recompense. The argument here will be that, contra Barrow (2005), action is not properly part of taking offence but that, contra Tasioulas, some judgement is.

First, Barrow suggests that offence involves a demand of an apology or compensation and on this he builds his case for there being a duty not to take offence, an argument to which we will return later. The position taken here, however, is that any demand for an apology or compensation is a consequence of taking offence but not part of taking offence itself. If I am offended I might or might not demand that anything be done about it. It depends on the severity of the offence, my timidity, and other factors.

Taking offensive, however, does involve a judgement that the offending action is wrong, something that should not be done. Tasioulas (2006, p. 152-153), argues that this, while perhaps commonly the case, is not necessary. His counter-example is of a middle-aged man who has overcome his strict upbringing but still takes offence at a same-sex couple holding hands in public, even though he does not believe it wrong. He simply cannot overcome his feelings. It seems to me that a better way of describing this situation is that he does not take offence at all but merely feels uncomfortable. Having been raised a fundamentalist Lutheran, I feel uncomfortable, sometimes extremely, with certain blasphemous language even though I no longer believe it to be wrong in itself (even though I almost expect a bolt of lightening to strike the blasphemer), but to describe my feelings as offence would be inaccurate. I might judge it wrong, however, in certain contexts because it offends others.

WRONGNESS AND OFFENSIVENESS

Taking offence is clearly associated with our beliefs, in that taking offence at any particular action can only occur in certain contexts where certain beliefs are held. If I say or do something potentially offensive but nobody takes offence, it is not at all obvious that I have given offence. Perhaps it will be objected that what is important is not *giving* offence but *offence*, pure and simple. However, unless there is an *objective* norm-governed offence, something that will be contested, it is not clear that there is anything interesting in offence apart from its giving and taking. When offence is discussed as a reason for criminalising or banning certain behaviour, it is because it is offensive, that is, it gives offence and some people take offence. The behaviour might still be wrong in the absence of giving or taking offence but that is another matter that has nothing to do with offence. Feinberg divides offensive actions into two categories, those that are offensive because they are wrong and those that are wrong because they are offensive. Racist language is offensive because such language is wrong while not being invited to a party is wrong, if wrong at all, simply because it is offensive. I prefer to say that racist language is both wrong *and* offensive. It is wrong because, at least, it is disrespectful to a race and it is offensive when members of that race are subjected to it and take offence. When those racial members are subjected to it, it is doubly wrong; wrong because of the lack of respect and because it gives offensive. If there is nobody around to take offence, it is still wrong but hardly offensive.

The focus of this article is on behaviour that is, in Feinberg's terminology, wrong because it is offensive, that is, *offensive nuisances*. This of course includes, for the purposes here, behaviour that is both wrong in itself and wrong because it is offensive if offence is taken, but the focus here is on the latter.

Is giving offence really wrong? We are talking here, it must be emphasized, of things that are wrong (if they are wrong as all) *because* they are offensive, not things that are wrong in themselves and are offensive on that account alone. Nor are we talking about everything that the offended parties judge to be wrong on the grounds that they are offended. Essentially what we are talking about are those cases of offence where the offended justifiably judge that they have been wronged. One may be inclined to say that there are no such cases; that is, that there is nothing really wrong with giving offence where the only wrong is the offence itself. After all, if people are so sensitive that they become offended at something heard or seen, so much the worse for them. While this contains an element of truth, it is not the whole story. It is probably true that any offence taken at not being invited to a dinner might not matter much, but the mocking of a physical disability or a tragedy, for example, might be extremely hurtful and offensive even for those not overly sensitive. However, most offence discussed in the contest of freedom of expression or criminalization is not of these kinds. Rather it involves blasphemy, sexually explicit language, racial vilification, ridicule of culture, public nudity, or sexual activity, and a host of other things.

In order to understand more about what is wrong with giving offence, if anything is, we will consider why people take offence. Obviously, offence is taken for different reasons by different people and over a wide range of areas. Three areas will be considered. The first of these concerns things which are not necessarily directed at any person or group, such as sexually explicit language and public nudity. Some people are offended by certain language and pictures. Part of the explanation for the offence taken clearly has to do with upbringing and socialization. This, however, is not a complete explanation. Taking offence is more than merely not liking. There are many things that I do not like that do not offend me, for example, certain types of music and art.

If I find something offensive, I take it personally in some way. I am *hurt*. A reasonable explanation of why I am hurt is that I identify closely with beliefs that this sort of behavior or material is wrong, and in a way I feel violated. If you expose me to these things that you know I do not like, then you are not showing me the respect that I deserve as a person. Even if it was not directed at me in particular, I may feel that people like me, those who hold the beliefs that I hold, are not respected enough. In both cases, that is, where it is directed at us in particular and where it is not, we may feel devalued as persons

The second, and related, area is the ridiculing, mocking or even just criticizing of beliefs, commitments, and customs, particularly those based on religion and culture. We tend to identify with a set of beliefs or with a group in a way that makes those beliefs or that group part of our self-image. So when ridicule is directed at those beliefs or that group, we feel that we are being mocked or ridiculed, and again can feel that we are not being respected as persons. Those who are mocking or criticizing portray themselves as being superior to us.

The third and final area is the offence taken at language or conduct which is racist or sexist. What these share is that there is no choice involved in being a member of either of these groups. There is a real sense here in which our identity and self-image is inextricably linked with groups of these types of which we find ourselves members. Here there seems to be a particularly close link between offence and self-respect.

These three examples all show that there is a close connection between the taking of offence and respect, both respect for others and self-respect or esteem. When someone makes a remark or exhibits conduct that we find offensive, we may feel that we are not being respected as persons in the way that we ought to be. Our self-respect may be lessened to some extent. Too much of this conduct may cause us to see ourselves as people of little worth. If something which is an integral part

of me is mocked – say, my height, race, gender, or intelligence – this is evidence that others do not value me as a person to the extent that they ought. They are not showing me the respect that I deserve as a person. If I identify very closely with a political party or with a religion and if that party or religion is mocked, I may feel the same (although it will be argued later that there are relevant differences in these cases). So perhaps we can say that what is wrong with giving offence in general is that it is showing a lack of respect for others and that it may cause them to lose some of their self-respect.

It is not being argued here that showing disrespect to someone will always lead to a loss of self-respect by that person, nor does it imply that all that is wrong with showing a lack of respect is this link with self-respect. However, it is claimed that there is an important link. Not everyone has enough self-confidence to disregard all instances of perceived disrespect.

This account that links offence with respect fits our intuitions in at least two ways. First, it explains why offence connected with race, gender, and physical disability, for example, seems to be much more serious than offence related to football or political allegiances, musical taste or sensitivity to pictures of naked humans or to not being invited to the party. If we make a commitment to something, or admit that we do not like something, we should be prepared, to some extent anyway, to accept the consequences of making that commitment or admission. At any rate, there is an important difference between areas in which we have some choice, like football team allegiance, and those in which we do not, for example, race.

There are, of course, some cases which are anything but clear-cut, for example, religious belief. We will return to that in a later section.

The second way that this account of offence fits in with common feelings is that it also helps to explain why it seems more objectionable to mock or ridicule the disadvantaged than the advantaged. If someone takes offence at some mockery of an advantaged group, that person must first identify him or herself with that group; that is, they must see themselves as privileged in some way. If they can only take offence to the extent that they identify with some favored section of society, their self-respect is unlikely to suffer much. Barrow (2005, pp. 272-273) discusses this kind of case and comes to a conclusion not so different from that espoused here. He argues that he, as an Englishman and clearly in a privileged position in English society, can be offended by certain anti-English remarks, but that he has no grounds for taking any action; he has not been morally wronged.

THE DUTY NOT TO TAKE OFFENCE

Barrow argues that there is a duty not to take offence. He cannot, and does not, mean that there is a duty not to have the hurt feeling. We have little choice about that, at least in the short term. We may over time no longer feel the hurt over certain comments or actions that we once did, but it is not something that we can just turn on and off like a tap. His view is more plausible if taking offence involves judging to be wrong. We might not be able to stop the hurt but we might have some control over whether or not we judge something to be wrong. But again, while over time we change our minds regarding what we judge to be wrong in some cases, it is not something that can be done just on cue. What he really means is that there is an obligation not to demand an apology or compensation or something of that ilk when one takes offence, and this is certainly plausible. In essence, this is a plea for tolerance. I might be offended by some action; that is, I feel the hurt and I judge the action to be wrong, but it does not follow that I have a right to demand anything in return. This is of particular importance in the global context created by the electronic media. Given the

variety in cultures, customs, and religions that now come into regular contact at many different levels of society, there is bound to be much that is said and done that many find offensive. If there is to be any hope of living together more or less peacefully, not only must there be an effort not to give offence but also, and equally important, tolerance of the views and actions of others even when we find them, perhaps, extremely offensive. It has been argued here that the actions to which Barrow objects are not part of taking offence itself, so it is more accurate to say that there is a duty not to demand compensation or retribution when offended. While there is no duty not to take offence, there is a duty not to demand action as a result of the offence taken.

ARE SOME OFFENCES OBJECTIVE?

Tasioulas argues so (2006, pp. 157ff). We are talking here just of norm-governed offences, those that violate some norm. Objective offences are, or are supposed to be, actions that are offensive in themselves regardless of whether anyone takes offence at them. They violate some moral norm and moral norms can be objective and therefore so can offence. Objective offences have properties that constitute a reason for being offended. Tasioulas gives two examples of such offences: racist language and public copulation. The former has more plausibility than the latter. Racist language reveals lack of respect and lack of respect is always wrong. If I am shown lack of respect, then I have a reason for being offended. Public copulation is more problematic. While it *in fact* violates norms in, for example, Australia, it is not at all clear that it necessarily does. A society could presumably function perfectly well if public copulation were the norm. In such a society it would not be showing any lack of respect and nobody would be harmed in any way, and it would be difficult to make a case that it was objectively morally wrong. If public copulation were the norm and was not showing any lack of respect for those who might witness the event, it is difficult to see how it could have properties that would constitute a reason for taking offence. In countries where it does violate a norm, as in Australia, it can still be considered wrong on the grounds that it is offensive (and not merely because it is against the law), but that implies nothing about it being objectively wrong in any sense.

Is racist language objectively offensive? Suppose that in some homogenous society, racist language is common. No one takes offence because there is nobody of the despised race around and none of the locals care. A good case can be made that the behaviour is wrong regardless of whether anyone takes offence because, if for no other reason, it reinforces the view that one race is inferior to another. But that seems quite different from saying that it is offensive. Things are offensive in a context. Jokes ridiculing particular Australian traits are not offensive if told by an Australian in a room full of Australians, but might be in another context. In any case, not everything that is wrong is offensive, except in a trivial sense in which our moral sensibilities are offended by all wrong actions, but then the offence taken at those actions is not worth discussing. We can get what we want just by considering the wrongness of the actions. It might be argued that the fact that it is happening at all is offensive to people of that race simply because they know that it is occurring even though none is exposed to it. We will return to this issue later.

It could still be argued of course that the mere fact that nobody is in fact offended by racist language does not show that it is not inherently offensive. Consider offensive smells. Certain smells just are offensive to humans. That is just a fact of the way that we are, and presumably is a result of our evolution. There was survival advantage in avoiding things with particular smells. So in this sense some smells are objectively offensive. Why then resist the view that some actions are

also objectively offensive? Offensive smells, as we know, frequently become less offensive once we have been continually exposed to them for some time. By analogy certain actions are offensive in themselves, and the fact that some people do not see them as such is no argument that they are not. Some people and some cultures simply have become desensitised or have not yet developed the sensitivities to recognise them as such. It is well-known that we can develop our sense of smell (and other senses) by practice. We can learn to notice smells that we had not before and learn to make distinctions that previously we had missed. The point of this is not that offensive smells are subtle and require learning to be noticed. Rather it is that the fact that some smell is not noticed or recognised does not show that it is not there in an objective sense. Similarly, actions might be offensive but not recognised as such simply as a result of undeveloped sensitivities.

It is odd though to say that some smell that we no longer find offensive is really offensive. If the smell, in the sense of a physical event, does not cause an offensive olfactory sensation, then surely it is not an offensive smell, and in the same way, if racist language does not cause offence it is not offensive, even if wrong. Something about the smell is objective, its physical properties, but its offensiveness is not objective. The utterance of the racist language is objective, but the offensiveness is not.

It might be objected that the analogy is not a good one because the offensiveness of smells does not rely on beliefs in the way that norm-governed offences do. But the situation is not so simple. The information that we receive through our senses is mediated to some extent by our beliefs and concepts; it is to some extent "theory-laden", so the difference between primitive and norm-governed offences is one of degree rather than one of kind, at least with respect to beliefs. What is different is that in the second case, but not the first, we make a judgement about the moral wrongness of an action, but that is irrelevant here where we are only concerned with the supposed objectivity of some offensiveness.

OFFENCE IN A GLOBAL CONTEXT

We will now focus on offence in a global setting. The previous sections have discussed or raised various aspects of offence that will be used to highlight its importance in discussions of global ethics. In particular we will consider the subjectivity of offences, the role of choice, that is, the difference between offences related to what we choose and those related to what we are, the context in which the offensive actions were performed, and finally indirect offence, that is, offensive actions that those offended only hear about or otherwise know about but do not directly experience.

Subjectivity

It is plausible to argue that some things are just wrong regardless of any cultural beliefs or practices. For example, murder, human sacrifice, female genital mutilation, and slavery are surely wrong even if they are an accepted part of some culture. Bernard Gert (1999) argues that there are morals that all impartial, rational persons would support and lists 10:

- Do not kill
- Do not cause pain
- Do not disable
- Do not deprive of freedom
- Do not deprive of pleasure
- Do not deceive
- Keep your promises
- Do not cheat
- Obey the law
- Do your duty

While these are not absolute and can be overridden, they are objective in the sense that they would be agreed to by impartial, rational persons. If this is correct, then there is an obvious starting point for a global ethics. If it were the case that some offences were wrong in themselves, that is, objectively, then another rule could be added to Gert's 10, something like "Do not perform any actions that are objectively offensive". If some actions were offensive in an objective sense, then those actions, even if only wrong because offensive, would be wrong irrespective of culture. Suppose, for example, that blasphemy is objectively offensive. Publishing the Danish cartoons then was wrong regardless of the attitudes toward them in Denmark and other Western countries. We have argued however that offence is not objective, so if it is to play any role in a global ethics, that role must lie elsewhere. The offensiveness rule could of course be modified to "Do not perform any actions that are offensive" but this is much too broad and could prohibit almost anything. What is required is some way of distinguishing between different offences that does not rely on some being objective. It will be argued that choice and context give some indication of how to delineate those instances of giving offence that are serious and those that are not.

Choice

The question of choice was raised in an earlier section where it was noted that there is, or seems to be, a difference between mocking one for wearing outlandish clothes and mocking one's race. It could be argued, as it has been by Barrow, that saying something that could be taken as offensive, for example, ridiculing religious beliefs, could be a sign of respect. That person is considered an autonomous human being who is mature enough and secure enough in his or her beliefs not to take offence when those beliefs are criticised or held up to ridicule. There is something in this. Treating people as mature adults is showing more respect than treating them as people who must have their feelings protected. This argument, if it holds at all, only holds in those areas where there is genuine choice. I have no control over my race, so ridiculing that can hardly be a sign of respecting my maturity regarding my beliefs. Ridiculing my outlandish clothes, at the other extreme, does not seem so important. I choose to wear them and could wear others, in a way that I cannot become a member of another race. Culture and religion, often closely interwoven, present an intermediate and more difficult case. Religion and culture are a bit like race in that they help define who we are. I identify with them as I do with my race. On the other hand, I do have some choice in a way that I do not with my race. I can choose to be a Christian but cannot choose to be Caucasian. The situation clearly is not so straightforward. While I can chose to become a Christian or choose to leave the faith if I were one, it is not quite like choosing a new brand of breakfast cereal. The choice will usually be a culmination of belief changes over time. But choose to join or leave religions we do. There is however a difference between those with a moderately good education and those without. An educated person who knows about other religions, about scientific explanations of the world and so on, can make an informed choice in a way that someone lacking those advantages cannot. They have a greater ability to weigh up evidence and to then make their choices based on that process. An illiterate peasant farmer has probably never entertained the possibility that his religious beliefs might be, or even could be, false. Given upbringing and culture, there is little choice but to believe.

What does this have to do with giving offence? We are talking here of actions that are wrong because they are offensive. The suggestion is that there is a relationship between the degree of wrongness and the amount of choice that someone has. Mocking of race is worse than mocking of the wearing of outlandish clothes because (at least partly) one has no choice in the former while one does in the latter. Mocking the religious beliefs of an uneducated peasant, who has no real choice,

is worse than mocking the religious beliefs of a well-educated person who has the ability to weight up the evidence and make a informed choice. In the latter case, the mocking could be a sign of recognising that person's autonomy and affording him or her the opportunity to defend his or her beliefs. In the former case, this is not so. It can only be interpreted as showing disrespect.

This issue of choice clearly has relevance for offence in the global arena, even apart from offence related to race. A large proportion of the world's population is poor and relatively uneducated and without easy access to sources of information, including the Internet, that would increase their range of options regarding lifestyle and belief. If the argument of this article is correct, it is more important to try to avoid actions that would be offensive to these people than to those who are more privileged. Mocking those without choice is not respecting them as they deserve to be respected as persons.

Context

The context in which offensive actions are performed is important in assessing their wrongness. What are essentially the same actions can be very different with regard to their offensiveness. It is instructive to consider Barrow's examples (2005, pp. 267, 272-273). He suggests, though does not say explicitly, that saying offensive things about the English, Pakistanis, and Nazis is more-or-less the same; one is no worse than the others. However, being English or Pakistani is racial, in the sense that the terms are being used here. In this sense, those called Pakistanis, even if born in England, are not considered English, because of their race. On the other hand, being a Nazi is a result of choice. On the argument of the preceding section, offending Pakistanis because that is what they are is worse than offending Nazis. One is born a Pakistani but one is not born a Nazi.

The main point of this section however is highlighted by comparing offending the English and offending the Pakistanis, in England. The kind of offensive actions in mind are ones such as mocking of race, culture, or religion. Is it worse to offend Pakistanis in England than it is to offend the English in England? Barrow, as we saw, suggests not, but there are reasons for thinking otherwise. Consider again the case of the cartoons published in Denmark that seriously offended many Muslims around the world, sparking riots and a considerable number of deaths. The context in which these cartoons were published is clearly relevant to assessing the morality of the action. Many Muslims, if the press is to be believed, feel under threat. The powerful Western nations are perceived as having exploited Muslim nations for decades, and this perception has been given impetus by recent invasions and talk of invasions. Regardless of the rightness or wrongness of the wars in Afghanistan and Iraq, they are clear signs of who has the military and economy power and who has not. In this situation, it is not surprising that the cartoons caused offence. It could be easily seen as just another sign of Western lack of respect for the Muslim religion. In a different context the action might not have been wrong. Suppose that a Muslim newspaper published cartoons ridiculing Christ. In countries where Christians were dominated by Muslims, it may well cause extreme offence if the Christians felt under threat, but in the Christian world at large, it probably would not, at least in the affluent West. The difference in the situations reflects how many Christian and Muslim groups see themselves relative to the other in the current world.

We will return for a moment to the copulating dogs cartoons published in both Indonesia and Australia. If the press is to be believed, there seems to have been more offence in Indonesia over the Australian cartoon that in Australia over the Indonesian one. If this is so, context provides one reason. In recent times, the relationship between Australia and Indonesia has been uneasy at best, particularly from the time that Australia took an active part in East Timor's fight for independence from Indonesia. The granting of visas, albeit temporary ones, to a group of illegal immigrants from the Indonesian province of Papua, where there is also an independence movement, was seen by the Indonesians as a sign that Australia was supporting that movement. It was also seen as evidence that Australia believed the Papuans claims that they were being persecuted by the Indonesian authorities. Additionally, the Australian government had been taking a very hard line against illegal immigrants and the approach to the Papuans appeared to be much more lenient. In this context, the retaliatory cartoon published in Australia could be seen as just another sign of contempt and lack of respect for the Indonesians. In Australia, while some politicians claimed that the Indonesian cartoon was offensive, the reaction has been more muted. In Australia there are no independence movements and nothing that could be interpreted as an attack on its sovereignty by Indonesia. The context is quite different.

Indirect Offence

According to Tasioulas, at least regarding criminalization, the only offences that should be taken into account are direct offences, that is, those that are directly experienced. Seeing a copulating couple in a public park is offensive in a way that merely knowing that it is happening is not. Feinberg's position regarding pornography is similar:

When printed words hide decorously behind covers of books sitting passively on bookstore shelves, their offensiveness is easily avoided. ... There is nothing like the evil smell of rancid garbage oozing right out through the covers of a book. When an "obscene" book sits on the shelf, who is there to be offended? Those who want to read it for the sake of erotic stimulation presumably will not be offended (or else they wouldn't read it), and those who choose not to read it will have no experience by which to be offended. (1973, p. 45)

The example given by Feinberg makes his argument look plausible, and it is commonly used in relation to television programmes containing explicit sex and violence. It you do not like it, do not watch it. However, those who find something offensive commonly do not need to directly experience it to be offended. That it is happening at all is offensive. Wolgast makes this point in relation to pornography:

The felt insult and indignity that women protest is not like a noise or bad odor, for these are group-neutral and may offend anyone, while pornography is felt to single women out as objects of insulting attention. ... With pornography there is a felt hostile discrimination. (1987, p. 112)

A similar point can be made with regard to the Danish cartoon case. Most of those who took offence would not have seen the cartoons, certainly those in regions where the Internet is not widespread. But this lack of direct experience was largely irrelevant. The *fact* that they were published was offensive.

If offence is related to respect for others and to self-respect, as was argued earlier, the issue of reasonable avoidability does not arise. If women or some race or any particular group is singled out for treatment which shows lack of respect and which is of the type to lower self-respect, it is not an issue whether or not someone can easily avoid some instance of that type of offensive action. Some members of the racial group might avoid hearing some racially offensive language, some religious members might avoid seeing offensive cartoons, and some woman might avoid seeing pornography, but these individuals are still being shown less respect than they deserve, simply because they are members of these targeted groups.

It must be noted of course that neither Tasioulas nor Feinberg are claiming that actions or material are only offensive when directly experienced. Their argument is rather that in those cases where it is not, it is not a serious contender for criminalisation. The suggestion here is that even

in at least some of those cases, indirect offence needs to be taken seriously. This is particularly so in the global case. Most of those offended by some action will be aware that it has occurred but will not have directly experienced it, but that is largely irrelevant. *That* it occurred is what is important.

CONCLUSION

The purpose of the article was to examine the concept of offence and on the basis of that examination to show its importance in considerations of a global ethic. The argument has been that offence, even actions that are thought wrong merely because they are offensive but not wrong in themselves, should not be overlooked. Careful thought should be given to actions that could be deemed offensive to certain groups, even if we think that those actions are protected by freedom of speech or expression, or by some other right or principle. It was argued that actions that offend because of attributes over which people have no choice are of more concern than those which offend because of attributes over which there is choice, and context is important. Giving offence in some contexts, for example, where the offended already feel vulnerable, is worse than giving offence in contexts where they do not. In murky areas such as religious belief, the amount of choice is related to the options available, and this in turn is related to the level of education and the information readily accessible. This suggests that one way of alleviating some problems of offence is to make a greater effort to make more information readily available to a greater number of people. On the other hand there is a duty not to take action against those who have offended. Tolerance of the views of others is always important and is especially so in a global community where there is no common legal framework and disputes are frequently settled by violence.

ACKNOWLEDGMENT

I would like to thank the participants of a seminar at the Centre for Applied Philosophy and Public Ethics (Charles Sturt University and Australian National University) for many useful comments on a draft of this article. I also wish to acknowledge the informative discussions that I have had over recent years with my colleague Yeslam Al-Saggaf.

REFERENCES

Barrow, R. (2005). On the duty of not taking offence. *Journal of Moral education, 34*(3), 265-275.

Feinberg, J. (1973). *Social philosophy.* Englewood Cliffs, NJ: Prentice Hall.

Feinberg. J. (1985). *The moral limits of the criminal law. Vol. 2: Offense to others.* Oxford: Oxford University Press.

Gert, B. (1999). Common morality and computing. *Ethics and Information Technology, 1,* 57-64.

Tasioulas, J. (2006). Crimes of offence. In A. Simester & A. von Hirsh (Eds.), *Incivilities: Regulating offensive behaviour.* Oxford: Hart.

Wolgast, E. H. (19 8 7). *The grammar of justice.* Ithaca, NY: Cornell University Press.

ENDNOTE

[1]   Parts of this article are based on earlier work published in Weckert, J. (2003). Giving offense on the Internet. In S. Rogerson & T. W. Bynum (Eds.), *Computer ethics and professional responsibility* (pp. 327-339). Basil Blackwell Publishers, and in G. Collste (Ed.), *Ethics and information technology* (pp. 104-118). New Academic Publishers.

Chapter III
Is Information Ethics
Culture–Relative?

Philip Brey
University of Twente, The Netherlands

ABSTRACT

In this article, I examine whether information ethics is culture relative. If it is, different approaches to information ethics are required in different cultures and societies. This would have major implications for the current, predominantly Western approach to information ethics. If it is not, there must be concepts and principles of information ethics that have universal validity. What would they be? The descriptive evidence is for the cultural relativity of information ethics will be studied by examining cultural differences between ethical attitudes towards privacy, freedom of information, and intellectual property rights in Western and non-Western cultures. I then analyze what the implications of these findings are for the metaethical question of whether moral claims must be justified differently in different cultures. Finally, I evaluate what the implications are for the practice of information ethics in a cross-cultural context.

INTRODUCTION

Information ethics[1] has so far mainly been a topic of research and debate in Western countries, and has mainly been studied by Western scholars. There is, however, increasing interest in information ethics in non-Western countries like Japan, China, and India, and there have been recent attempts to raise cross-cultural issues in information ethics (e.g., Ess, 2002; Gorniak-Kocikowska, 1996; Mizutani, Dorsey & Moor, 2004). Interactions between scholars of Western and non-Western countries have brought significant differences to light between the way in which they approach issues in information ethics. This raises the question whether different cultures require a different information ethics and whether concepts and approaches in Western information ethics can be validly applied to the moral dilemmas of non-Western cultures. In other words, is information ethics culturally relative or are there concepts and principles of information ethics that have universal validity? The aim of this essay is to arrive at preliminary answers to this question.

MORAL RELATIVISM AND INFORMATION ETHICS

In discussions of moral relativism, a distinction is commonly made between descriptive and metaethical moral relativism. *Descriptive moral relativism* is the position that as a matter of empirical fact, there is extensive diversity between the values and moral principles of societies, groups, cultures, historical periods, or individuals. Existing differences in moral values, it is claimed, are not superficial but profound, and extend to core moral values and principles. Descriptive moral relativism is an empirical thesis that can in principle be supported or refuted through psychological, sociological, and anthropological investigations. The opposite of descriptive moral relativism is *descriptive moral absolutism*, the thesis that there are no profound moral disagreements exist between societies, groups, cultures, or individuals. At issue in this essay will be a specific version of descriptive moral relativism, *descriptive cultural relativism*, according to which there are major differences between the moral principles of different cultures.

Much more controversial than the thesis of descriptive moral relativism is the thesis of metaethical moral relativism, according to which the truth or justification of moral judgments is not absolute or objective, but relative to societies, groups, cultures, historical periods, or individuals.[2] Whereas a descriptive relativist could make the empirical observation that one society, polygamy, is considered moral whereas in another it is considered immoral, a metaethical relativist could make the more far-reaching claim that the statement "polygamy is morally wrong" is true or justified in some societies while false or unjustified in others. Descriptive relativism therefore makes claims about the values that different people or societies actually have, whereas metaethical relativism makes claims about the values that they are justified in having. Metaethi-

cal moral relativism is antithetical to *metaethical moral absolutism*, the thesis that regardless of any existing differences between moral values in different cultures, societies, or individuals, there are moral principles that are absolute or objective, and that are universally true across cultures, societies, or individuals. Metaethical moral absolutism would therefore hold that the statement "polygamy is morally wrong" is either universally true or universally false; it cannot be true for some cultures or societies but false for others. If the statement is true, then societies that hold that polygamy is moral are in error, and if it is false, then the mistake lies with societies that condemn it.

The question being investigated in this essay is whether information ethics is culturally relative. In answering this question, it has to be kept in mind that the principal aims of information ethics are not descriptive, but normative and evaluative. That is, its principal aim is not to describe existing morality regarding information but rather to morally evaluate information practices and to prescribe and justify moral standards and principles for practices involving the production, consumption, or processing of information. A claim that information ethics is culturally relative therefore a claim that metaethical moral relativism is true for information ethics. It is to claim that the ethical values, principles, and judgments of information ethics are valid only relative to a particular culture, presumably the culture in which they have been developed. Since information ethics is largely a product of the West, an affirmation of the cultural relativity of information ethics means that its values and principles do not straightforwardly apply to non-Western cultures.

But if the cultural relativity of information ethics depends on the truth of metaethical relativism, does any consideration need to be given to descriptive relativism for information ethics? This question should be answered affirmatively. Defenses of metaethical relativism usually depend on previous observations that descriptive relativism is true. If descriptive relativism is false, it follows that people across the world share a moral framework of basic values and principles. But if this is the case, then it seems pointless to argue for metaethical moral relativism: why claim that the truth of moral judgments is different for different groups if these groups already agree on basic moral values? On the other hand, if descriptive relativism is true, then attempts to declare particular moral principles of judgments to be universally valid come under scrutiny. Extensive justification would be required for any attempt to adopt a particular moral framework (say, Western information ethics) as one that is universally valid. In the next section, I will therefore focus on the question whether there are good reasons to believe that there are deep and widespread moral disagreements about central values and principles in information ethics across cultures, and whether therefore descriptive cultural relativism is true for information ethics.

THE DESCRIPTIVE CULTURAL RELATIVITY OF INFORMATION-RELATED VALUES

In this section, I will investigate the descriptive cultural relativity of three values that are the topic of many studies in information ethics: privacy, intellectual property, and freedom of information. Arguments have been made that these values are distinctly Western, and are not universally accepted across different cultures. In what follows I will investigate whether these claims seem warranted by empirical evidence. I will also relate the outcome of my investigations to discussions of more general differences between Western and non-Western systems of morality.

How can it be determined that cultures have fundamentally different value systems regarding notions like privacy and intellectual property?

I propose that three kinds of evidence are relevant:

1. **Conceptual:** the extent to which there are moral concepts across cultures with similar meanings. For example, does Chinese culture have a concept of privacy that is similar to the American concept of privacy?
2. **Institutional:** the extent to which there is similarity between codified rules that express moral principles and codified statements that express moral judgments about particular (types of) situations. For example, are the moral principles exhibited in the laws and written rules employed in Latin cultures on the topic of privacy sufficiently similar to American laws and rules that it can be claimed that they embody similar moral principles?
3. **Behavioral:** the similarity between customs and behaviors that appear to be guided by moral principles. This would include tendencies to avoid behaviors that are immoral regarding a moral principle, tendencies to show disapproval to those who engage in such behaviors, and to show disapproval to those who do not, and tendencies to show remorse or guilt when engaging in such behaviors. For instance, if a culture has a shared privacy principle that states that peeking inside someone's purse is wrong, then it can be expected that most people try not to do this, disapprove of those who do, and feel ashamed or remorseful when they are caught doing it.

It is conceivable that in a particular culture a value or moral principle is widely upheld at the behavioral level, but has not (yet) been codified at the institutional and conceptual level. But this is perhaps unlikely in cultures with institutions that include extensive systems of codified rules, which would include any culture with a modern legal system. It is also conceivable that a moral value or principle is embodied in both behavioral customs and codified rules, but no good match can be found at the conceptual level. In that case, it seems reasonable to assume that the value or principle at issue is embodied in the culture, but different concepts are used to express it, making it difficult to find direct translations.

A full consideration of the evidence for descriptive moral relativism along these three lines is beyond the scope of this article. I only intend to consider enough evidence to arrive at a preliminary assessment of the cultural relativity of values in contemporary information ethics.

Privacy

It has been claimed that in Asian cultures like China and Japan, no genuine concept or value of privacy exists. These cultures have been held to value the collective over the individual. Privacy is an individual right, and such a right may not be recognized in a culture where collective interest tend to take priority over individual interests. Using the three criteria outline above, and drawing from studies of privacy in Japan, China and Thailand, I will now consider whether this conclusion is warranted.

At the conceptual level, there are words in Japanese, Chinese, and Thai that refer to a private sphere, but these words seem to have substantially different meanings than the English word for privacy. Mizutani et al. (2004) have argued that there is no word for "privacy" in traditional Japanese. Modern Japanese, they claim, sometimes adopt a Japanese translation for the Western word for privacy, which sounds like "puraibashii", and written in katakana. Katakana is the Japanese phonetic syllabary that is mostly used for words of foreign origin. According to Nakada and Tamura (2005), Japanese does include a word for "private", "Watakusi", which means "partial, secret and selfish". It is opposed to "Ohyake", which means "public". Things that are Watakusi are considered less worthy than things that are Ohyake. Mizutani et al. (2004) point out, in addition, that there are certainly behavioral customs in Japan that amount to a respect for privacy. There are conventions that restrict access to information, places, or objects. For example, one is not supposed to look under clothes on public streets.

In China, the word closest to the English "privacy" is "Yinsi", which means "shameful secret" and is usually associated with negative, shameful things. Lü (2005) claims that only recently that "Yinsi" has also come to take broader meanings to include personal information, shameful or not, that people do not want others to know (see also Jingchun, 2005; McDougall & Hansson, 2002). This shift in meaning has occurred under Western influences. As for institutional encoding of privacy principles, Lü maintains that there currently are no laws in China that protect an individual right to privacy, and the legal protection of privacy has been weak and is still limited, though there have been improvements in privacy protection since the 1980s.

Kitiyadisai (2005), finally, holds that the concept of privacy does not exist in Thailand. She claims that the Western word privacy was adopted in the late nineteenth or early twentieth century in Thailand, being transliterated as "privade," but this word gained a distinctly Thai meaning, being understood as a collectivist rather than an individual notion. It referred to a private sphere in which casual dress could be worn, as opposed to a public sphere in which respectable dress had to be worn. In the Thai legal system, Kitiyadisai claims there has not been any right to privacy since the introduction of privacy legislation in 1997 and a Thai constitution, also in 1997, that for the first time guarantees basic human rights. Kitiyadisai argues, however, that Thai privacy laws are hardly enacted in practice, and many Thais remain unaware of the notion of privacy.

It can be tentatively concluded that the introduction of a concept of privacy similar to the Western notion has only taken place recently in Japan, China, and Thailand, and that privacy legislation has only taken place recently. In traditional Japanese, Chinese, and Thai culture, which still has a strong presence today, distinctions are made that resemble the Western distinction between public and private, and customs exist that may be interpreted as respective of privacy, but there is no recognized individual right to privacy.

Intellectual Property Rights

In discussing the cultural relativity of intellectual property rights (IPR), I will limit myself to one example: China. China is known for not having a developed notion of private or individual property. Under communist rule, the dominant notion of property was collective. All means of production, such as farms and factories, were to be collectively owned and operated. Moreover, the state exercised strict control over the means of production and over both the public and private sphere. A modern notion of private property was only introduced since the late 1980s. Milestones were a 1988 constitutional revision that allowed for private ownership of means of production and a 2004 constitutional amendment that protects citizens from encroachment of private property.

The notion of intellectual property has only recently been introduced in China, in the wake of China's recent economic reforms and increased economic interaction with the West. China is currently passing IPR laws and cracking down on violations of IPR in order to harmonize the Chinese economic system with the rest of the world. But as journalist Ben Worthen observes, "the average citizen in China has no need and little regard for intellectual property. IPR is not something that people grew up with … and the percent of citizens who learn about it by engaging in international commerce is tiny." Worthen also points out that Chinese companies "have no incentive to respect IPR unless they are doing work for Western companies that demand it"

and that "since most of the intellectual property royalties are headed out of China there isn't a lot of incentive for the government to crack down on companies that choose to ignore IPR."[3] All in all, it can be concluded that China's value system traditionally has not included a recognition of intellectual property rights, and it is currently struggling with this concept.

Freedom of Information

Freedom of information is often held to comprise two principles: freedom of speech (the freedom to express one's opinions or ideas, in speech or in writing) and freedom of access to information. Sometimes, freedom of the press (the freedom to express oneself through publication and dissemination) is distinguished as a third principle. In Western countries, freedom of information is often defined as a constitutional and inalienable right. Laws protective of freedom of information are often especially designed to ensure that individuals can exercise this freedom without governmental interference or constraint. Government censorship or interference is only permitted in extreme situations, pertaining to such things as hate speech, libel, copyright violations, and information that could undermine national security.

In many non-Western countries, freedom of information is not a guiding principle. There are few institutionalized protections of freedom of information; there are many practices that interfere with freedom of information, and a concept of freedom of information is not part of the established discourse in society. In such societies, the national interest takes precedence, and an independent right to freedom information either is not recognized or is made so subordinate to national interests that it hardly resembles the Western right to freedom of information. These are countries in which practices of state censorship are widespread; mass media are largely or wholly government-controlled, the Internet, databases, and libraries are censored, and messages that do not conform to the party line are cracked down upon.

Let us, as an example, consider the extent to which freedom of information can be said to be a value in Chinese society. Until the 1980s, the idea of individual rights or civil rights was not a well-known concept in China. Government was thought to exist to ensure a stable society and a prosperous economy. It was not believed to have a function to protect individual rights against collective and state interests. As a consequence of this general orientation, the idea of an individual right to freedom of information was virtually unknown. Only recently has China introduced comprehensive civil rights legislation. In its 1982 constitution, China introduced constitutional principles of freedom of speech and of the press. And in 1997, it signed the International Convention on Economic, Social, and Cultural Rights, and in 1998 the International Convention on Civil and Political Rights (the latter of which it has not yet ratified).

Even though the Chinese government has recently come to recognize a right to freedom of information, as well as individual human rights in general, and has introduced legislation to this effect, state censorship is still rampant, and the principle of upholding state interest still tends to dominate the principle of protecting individual human rights. Internet censorship presents a good example of this. Internet traffic in China is controlled through what the Chinese call the Golden Shield, and what is known outside mainland China as the Great Firewall of China. This is a system of control in which Internet content is blocked by routers, as well as at the backbone and ISP level, through the "filtering" of undesirable URLs and keywords. A long list of such "forbidden" URLs and keywords has been composed by the Chinese State Council Information Office, in collaboration with the Communist Party's Propaganda Department. This system is especially geared towards censorship of content coming from outside mainland China (Human Rights Watch, 2006).

Rights-Centered and Virtue-Centered Morality

A recurring theme in the above three discussions has been the absence of a strong tradition of individual rights in the cultures that were discussed – those of China, Japan, and Thailand --—and the priority that is given to collective and state interests. Only very recently have China, Japan, and Thailand introduced comprehensive human rights legislation, which has occurred mainly through Western influence, and there is still considerable tension in these societies, especially in China and Thailand, between values that prioritize the collective and the state and values that prioritize the individual.

Various authors have attempted to explain the worldview that underlies the value system of these countries. In Japan and Thailand, and to a lesser extent China, Buddhism is key to an understanding of attitudes towards individual rights. Buddhism holds a conception of the self that is antithetical to the Western conception of an autonomous self which aspires to self-realization. Buddhism holds that the self does not exist and that human desires are delusional. The highest state that humans can reach is Nirvana, a state of peace and contentment in which all suffering has ended. To reach Nirvana, humans have to become detached from their desires, and realize that the notion of an integrated and permanent self is an illusion. In Buddhism, the self is defined as fluid, situation-dependent, and ever-changing. As Mizutani et al. and Kitiyadisai have noted, such a notion of the self is at odds with a Western notion of privacy and of human rights in general, notions which presuppose a situation-independent, autonomous self which pursues its own self-interests and which has inalienable rights that have to be defended against external threats.

In part through Buddhism, but also through the influence of other systems of belief such as Confucianism, Taoism, and Maoism, societies like those of China and Thailand have developed a value system in which the rights or interests of the individual are subordinate to those of the collective and the state. To do good is to further the interests of the collective. Such furtherances of collective interests will generally also benefit the individual. The task of government, then, is to ensure that society as a whole functions well, in a harmonious and orderly way, and that social ills are cured, rather than the ills of single individuals. In other words, government works for the common good, and not for the individual good.

Only recently have countries like China and Thailand come to recognize individual human rights and individual interests next to collective interests. But according to Lü (2005), the collectivist ethic still prevails:

Adapting to the demands of social diversity, the predominant ethics now express a new viewpoint that argues against the simple denial of individual interests and emphasizes instead the dialectical unification of collective interests and individual interests: in doing so, however, this ethics points out that this kind of unification must take collective interests as the foundation. That is to say, in the light of the collectivism principle of the prevailing ethics, collective interests and individual interests are both important, but comparatively speaking, the collective interests are more important than individual interests. (Lü, 2005, p. 12)

If this observation is correct, then the introduction of human rights legislation and property rights in countries like China is perhaps not motivated by a genuine recognition of inalienable individual human rights, but rather a recognition that in the current international climate, it is better to introduce human rights and property rights, because such principles will lead to greater economic prosperity, which is ultimately to the benefit of the collective.

The dominant value systems prevalent in China, Thailand, and Japan are examples of what philosopher David Wong (1984) has called virtue-centered moralities. According to Wong, at least two different approaches to morality can be found in the world: a *virtue-centered morality* that emphasizes the good of the community, and a *rights-centered morality* that stresses the value of individual freedom. Rights-centered morality is the province of the modern West, although it is also establishing footholds in other parts of the world. Virtue-centered morality can be found in traditional cultures such as can be found in southern and eastern Asia and in Africa. Wong's distinction corresponds with the frequently made distinction between individualist and collectivist culture, that is found, amongst others, in Geert Hofstede's (1991) well-known five-dimensional model of cultural difference. However, this latter distinction focuses on social systems and cultural practices, whereas Wong makes a distinction based in differences in moral systems.

In Wong's conception of virtue-centered moralities, individuals have duties and responsibilities that stem from the central value of a common good. The common good is conceived of in terms of an ideal conception of community life, which is based on a well-balanced social order in which every member of the community has different duties and different virtues to promote the common good. Some duties and virtues may be shared by all members. The idea that human beings have individual rights is difficult to maintain in this kind of value system, because recognition of such rights would have to find its basis in the higher ideal of the common good. But it seems clear that attributing rights to individuals is not always to the benefit of the common good. The recognition of individual property rights, for example, could result in individual property owners not sharing valuable resources that would benefit the whole community. In virtue-centered moralities, the ideal is for individuals to be virtuous, and virtuous individuals are those individuals whose individual good coincides with their contribution to the common good. Individual goods may be recognized in such communities, but they are always subordinate to the common good. Individuals deserve respect only because of their perceived contribution to the common good, not because they possess inalienable individual rights.

Conclusion

The discussion of privacy, intellectual property rights, and freedom of information has shown that a good case can be made for the descriptive cultural relativity of these values. These values are central in information ethics, as it has been developed in the West. Moreover, it was argued that the uncovered cultural differences in the appraisal of these values can be placed in the context of a dichotomy between two fundamentally different kinds of value systems that exist in different societies: rights-centered and virtue-centered systems of value. Information ethics, as it has developed in the West, has a strong emphasis on rights, and little attention is paid to the kinds of moral concerns that may exist in virtue-centered systems of morality. In sum, it seems that the values that are of central concern in Western information ethics are not the values that are central in many non-Western systems of morality. The conclusion therefore seems warranted that descriptive moral relativism is true for information ethics.

METAETHICAL MORAL RELATIVISM AND INFORMATION ETHICS

In the first section, it was argued that descriptive moral relativism is a necessary condition for metaethical moral relativism, but is not sufficient to prove this doctrine. However, several moral arguments exist that use the truth of descriptive relativism, together with additional premises, to argue for metaethical relativism. I will start with a consideration of two standard arguments of this form, which are found wanting, after which I will consider a more sophisticated argument.

Two Standard Arguments for Metaethical Relativism

There are two traditional arguments for metaethical moral relativism that rely on the truth of descriptive moral relativism (Wong, 1993). The one most frequently alluded to is the *argument from diversity*. This argument starts with the observation that different cultures employ widely different moral standards. Without introducing additional premises, the argument goes on to conclude that therefore, there are no universal moral standards. This argument rests on what is known in philosophy as a naturalistic fallacy, an attempt to derive a norm from a fact, or an "ought" from an "is". The premise of the argument is descriptive: there are different moral standards. The conclusion is normative: no moral standard has universal validity. No evidence has been presented that the truth of the premise has any bearing on the truth of the conclusion.

A second, stronger argument for moral relativism is the *argument from functional necessity*, according to which certain ethical beliefs in a society may be so central to its functioning that they cannot be given up without destroying the society. Consequently, the argument runs, these ethical beliefs are true for that society, but not necessarily in another. However, this argument is also problematic because it grounds the truth of ethical statements in their practical value for maintaining social order in a particular society. Such a standard of justification for ethical statements is clearly too narrow, as it could be used to justify the moral beliefs of societies whose beliefs and practices are clearly unethical, for instance, fascist societies. If a society operates in a fundamentally unethical way, then the transformation of some of its social structures and cultural forms would seem acceptable if more ethical practices are the result.

Wong's and Harman's Argument for Metaethical Relativism

More convincing arguments for moral relativism have been presented by David Wong (1984, 2006) and Gilbert Harman (1996, 2000). Their argument runs, in broad outline, as follows. There are deep-seated differences in moral belief between different cultures. Careful consideration of the reasons for these moral beliefs they have shows that they are *elements of different strategies to realize related but different conceptions of the Good.* No good arguments can be given why one of these conceptions of the Good is significantly better than all the others. Therefore, these moral beliefs are best explained as different but (roughly) equally valid strategies for attaining the Good.

This is a much better argument than the previous two, since it puts the ball in the metaethical absolutist's court: he will have to come up with proof that it is possible to provide good arguments for the superiority of one particular conception of the Good over all other conceptions. Metaethical absolutists can respond to this challenge in two ways. First, they may choose to bite the bullet and claim that a rational comparison of different conceptions of the Good is indeed possible. Different conceptions of the Good, they may argue, rely on factual or logical presuppositions that may be shown to be false. Alternatively, they may argue that there are universally shared moral intuitions about what is good, and these intuitions can be appealed to in defending or discrediting particular conceptions of the Good. For instance an individual who believes that physical pleasure is the highest good could conceivably be persuaded to abandon this belief through exposure to arguments that purport to demonstrate that there are other goods overlooked by this individual that are at least as valuable. Such an argument could conceivably rely on someone's moral intuitions about the Good that could be shown to deviate from someone's explicit concept of the Good.

Second, a mixed position could be proposed, according to which it is conceded that individuals or cultures may hold different conceptions of the Good that cannot be rationally criticized (*pace* metaethical relativism) but that rational criticism of individual moral beliefs is nevertheless possible (*pace* metaethical absolutism) because these beliefs can be evaluated for their effectiveness in realizing the Good in which service they stand. After all, if moral beliefs are strategies to realize a particular conception of the Good, as Wong and Harman have argued, then they can be suboptimal in doing so. A belief that Internet censorship is justified because it contributes to a more stable and orderly society can be wrong because it may not in fact contribute to a more stable and orderly society. Empirical arguments may be made that Internet censorship is not necessary for the maintenance of social order, or even that Internet censorship may ultimately work to undermine social order, for example, because it creates discontentment and resistance.

In the existing dialogue between proponents of rights-centered and virtue-centered systems of morality, it appears that both these approaches are already being taken. Western scholars have criticized the organicist conception of society that underlies conceptions of the Good in many Asian cultures, while Western definitions of the Good in terms of individual well-being have been criticized for their atomistic conception of individuals. Rights-based systems of morality have been criticized for undervaluing the common good, whereas virtue-based systems have been criticized for overlooking the importance of the individual good. In addition, both rights-centered and virtue-centered systems of morality have been criticized for not being successful by their own standards. Western individualism has been claimed to promote selfishness and strife, which results in many unhappy individuals plagued by avarice, proverty, depression, and loneliness. Western societies have therefore been claimed to be unsuccessful in attaining their own notion of the Good, defined in terms of individual well-being. Virtue-centered cultures have been claimed to be have difficulty in developing strong economies that serve the common good, because good economies have been argued to require private enterprise and a more individualist culture. In addition, strong state control, which is a feature of many virtue-centered cultures, has been argued to lead to corruption and totalitarianism, which also do not serve the common good.

In light of the preceding observations, it seems warranted to conclude, *pace* metaethical absolutism, that rational criticism between different moral systems is possible. It does not follow, however, that conclusive arguments for universal moral truths or the superiority of one particular moral system over others are going to be possible. Critics of a particular moral system may succeed in convincing its adherents that the system has its flaws and needs to be modified, but it could well be that no amount of criticism ever succeeds in convincing its adherents to abandon core moral beliefs within that system, however rational and open-minded these adherents are in listening to such criticism.

Conclusion

I have argued, *pace* metaethical relativism, that it is difficult if not impossible to provide compelling arguments for the superiority of different notions of the Good that are central in different moral systems, and by implication, that it is difficult to present conclusive arguments for the universal truth of particular moral principles and beliefs. I have also argued, *pace* metaethical absolutism, that is nevertheless possible to develop rational arguments for and against particular moral values and overarching conceptions of the Good across moral systems, even if such arguments do not result in proofs of the superiority of one particular moral system or moral principle over another.

From these two metaethical claims, a normative position can be derived concerning the way in which cross-cultural ethics ought to take place. It follows, first of all, that it is only justified for proponents of a particular moral value or principle to claim that it ought to be accepted in another culture if they make this claim on the basis of a thorough understanding of the moral system operative in this other culture. The proponent would have to understand how this moral system functions and what notion of the Good it services, and would have to have strong arguments that either the exogenous value would be a good addition to the moral system in helping to bring about the Good serviced in that moral system, or that the notion of the Good serviced in that culture is flawed and requires revisions. In the next section, I will consider implications of this position for the practice of information ethics in cross-cultural settings.

INFORMATION ETHICS IN A CROSS-CULTURAL CONTEXT

It is an outcome of the preceding sections that significant differences exist between moral systems of different cultures, that these differences have important implications for moral attitudes towards uses of information and information technology, and that there are good reasons to take such differences seriously in normative studies in information ethics. In this section, I will argue, following Rafael Capurro, that we need an intercultural information ethics that studies and evaluates cultural differences in moral attitudes towards information and information technology. I will also critically evaluate the claim that the Internet will enable a new global ethic that provides a unified moral framework for all cultures.

Intercultural Information Ethics

The notion of an *intercultural information ethics* (IIE) was first introduced by Rafael Capurro (2005, in press), who defined it as a field of research in which moral questions regarding information technology and the use of information are reflected on in a comparative manner on the basis of different cultural traditions. I will adopt Capurro's definition, but differ with him on what the central tasks of an IIE should be. Capurro defines the tasks of IIE very broadly. For him, they not only the comparative study of value systems in different cultures in relation to their use of information and information technology, but also studies of the effect of information technology on customs, languages, and everyday problems, the changes produced by the Internet on traditional media, and the economic impact of the Internet to the extent that it can become an instrument of cultural oppression and colonialism.

I hold, in contrast, that studies of the effects of information technology in non-Western cultures are more appropriately delegated to the social sciences (including communication studies, cultural studies, anthropology and science, and technology studies). An intercultural information ethics should primarily focus on the comparative study of moral systems. Its overall aim would be to interpret, compare, and critically evaluate moral systems in different cultures regarding their moral attitudes towards and behavior towards information and information technology.

This task for IIE can be broken down into four subtasks, the first two of which are exercises in descriptive ethics and the latter two of which belong to normative ethics. First, IIE should engage in *interpretive studies* of moral systems in particular cultures, including the systems of value contained in the religious and political ideologies that are dominant in these cultures. The primary focus in such interpretive studies within the context of IIE should be on resulting moral attitudes towards the use and implications of information technology and on the moral problems generated by uses of information technology within the context of the prevailing moral system. Second, IIE should engage in *comparative studies* of moral systems from different cultures, and arrive at analyses of both similarities and differences in the way that these moral systems are organized and operate, with a specific focus on the way in which they have different moral attitudes towards implications of information technology and on differences in moral problems generated by the use of information technology.

Third, IIE should engage in *critical studies* in which the moral systems of particular cultures are criticized based on the insights gained through the interpretive and comparative studies alluded to above, particularly in their dealings with information technology. Critical studies may be directed towards critizing moral values and beliefs in cultures other than one's own, and proposing modifications in the culture's moral system and ways in which it should solve moral problems, but may also involve self-criticism, in which one's own moral values and the moral system of one's own culture is criticized based on insights gained from the study of alternative moral systems. Fourth, IIE should engage in *interrelational studies* that focus on the construction of normative models for interaction between cultures in their dealings with information and information technology that respect their different moral systems. Interrelational studies hence investigate what moral compromises cultures can make and ought to make in their interactions and what shared moral principles can be constructed to govern their interactions.

Global Ethics and the Information Revolution

Some authors have argued that globalization and the emergence of the Internet have created a global community, and that this community requires its own moral system that transcends and unifies the moral systems of all cultures and nations that participate in this global community. The ethics needed for the construction of such a moral system has been called *global ethics*. The idea of a global ethics or ethic was first introduced by German theologian Hans Küng in 1990 and later elaborated by him in a book (Küng, 2001). His aim was to work towards a shared moral framework for humanity that would contain a minimal consensus concerning binding values and moral principles that could be invoked by members of a global community in order to overcome differences and avoid conflict.

Krystyna Górniak-Kocikowska (1996) has argued that the computer revolution that has taken place has made it clear that a future global ethic will have to be a computer ethic or information ethic. As she explains, actions in cyberspace are not local, and therefore the ethical rules governing such actions cannot be rooted in a particular local culture. Therefore, unifying ethical rules have to be constructed in cyberspace that can serve as a new global ethic. Similar arguments have been presented by Bao and Xiang (2006) and De George (2006).

No one would deny that a global ethic, as proposed by Küng, would be desirable. The construction of an explicit, shared moral framework that would bind all nations and cultures would evidently be immensely valuable. It should be obvious, however, that such a framework could only develop as an addition to existing local moral systems, not as a replacement of them. It would be a framework designed to help solve global problems, and would exist next to the local moral systems that people use to solve their local problems. In addition, it remains to be seen if cross-cultural interactions over the Internet yield more than a mere set of rules for conduct online, a global netiquette, and will result in a global ethic that can serve as a common moral framework for intercultural dialogue and joint action. Hongladarom (2001) has concluded, based on empirical studies, that the Internet does not create a worldwide monolithic culture but rather reduplicates existing cultural boundaries. It does create an umbrella cosmopolitan culture to some extent, but only for those Internet users who engage in cross-cultural dialogue, which is a minority, and this umbrella culture is rather superficial. Claims that the Internet will enable a new global ethic may therefore be somewhat premature. In any case, such intercultural dialogue online will have to be supplemented with serious academic work in intercultural information ethics, as well as intercultural ethics at large.

CONCLUSION

It was found in this essay that very different moral attitudes exist in Western and non-Western countries regarding three key issues in information ethics: privacy, intellectual property, and freedom of information. In non-Western countries like China, Japan, and Thailand, there is no strong recognition of individual rights in relation to these three issues. These differences were analyzed in the context of a difference, proposed by philosopher David Wong, between rights-centered moralities that dominate in the West and virtue-centered moralities that prevail in traditional cultures, including those in South and East Asia. It was then argued that cross-cultural normative ethics cannot be practiced without a thorough understanding of the prevailing moral system in the culture that is being addressed. When such an understanding has been attained, scholars can proceed to engage in moral criticism of practices in the culture and propose standards and solutions to moral problems. It was argued, following Rafael Capurro, that we need an intercultural information ethics that engages in interpretive, comparative, and normative studies of moral problems and issues in information ethics in different cultures. It is to be hoped that researchers in both Western and non-Western countries will take up this challenge and engage in collaborative studies and dialogue on an issue that may be of key importance to future international relations.

REFERENCES

Bao, X., & Xiang, Y. (2006). Digitalization and global ethics. *Ethics and Information Technology, 8*, 41-47.

Capurro, R. (2005). Privacy: An intercultural perspective. Ethics and Information Technology, 7(1), 37-47.

Capurro, R. (in press). Intercultural information ethics. In R. Capurro, J. Frühbaure, & T. Hausmanningers (Eds.), *Localizing the Internet. Ethical issues in intercultural perspective.* Munich: Fink Verlag. Retrieved January 25, 2007, from http://www.capurro.de/iie.html

De George, R. (2006). Information technology, globalization and ethics. *Ethics and Information Technology, 8*, 29–40.

Ess, C. (2002). Computer-mediated colonization, the renaissance, and educational imperatives for an intercultural global village. *Ethics and Information Technology, 4*(1), 11-22.

Gorniak-Kocikowska, K. (1996). The computer revolution and the problem of global ethics. *Science and Engineering Ethics, 2*, 177–190.

Harman, G. (1996). Moral relativism. In G. Harman & J. J. Thompson (Eds.), *Moral relativism and moral objectivity (pp. 3-64).* Cambridge, MA: Blackwell Publishers.

Harman, G. (2000). Is there a single true morality? In G. Harman (Ed.), *Explaining value: And other essays in moral philosophy* (pp. 77-99). Oxford: Clarendon Press.

Hofstede, G. (2001). *Culture's consequences.* Thousand Oaks, CA: Sage.

Hongladarom, S. (2001). Global culture, local cultures and the Internet: The Thai example. In C. Ess (Ed.), *Culture, technology, communication: Towards an intercultural global village* (pp. 307-324). Albany, NY: State University of New York Press.

Human Rights Watch. (2006). Race to the bottom. Corporate complicity in Chinese Internet censorship. *Human Rights Watch Report, 18*(8C). Retrieved January 25, 2007, from http://www.hrw.org

Johnson, D. (2000). *Computer ethics* (3rd ed.). Upper Saddle River, NJ: Prentice Hall.

Jingchun, C. (2005). Protecting the right to privacy in China. *Victoria University of Wellington Law Review, 38*(3). Retrieved January 25, 2007, from http://www.austlii.edu.au/nz/journals/VUWL-Rev/2005/25.html

Kitiyadisai, K. (2005). Privacy rights and protection: Foreign values in modern Thai context. *Ethics and Information Technology, 7*, 17-26.

Küng, H. (2001). *A global ethic for global politics and economics.* Hong Kong: Logos and Pneuma Press.

Lü, Y.-H. (2005). Privacy and data privacy issues in contemporary China. *Ethics and Information Technology, 7*, 7-15.

McDougall, B., & Hansson, A. (Eds.). (2002). *Chinese concepts of privacy.* Brill Academic Publishers.

Mizutani, M., Dorsey, J., & Moor, J. (2004). The Internet and Japanese conception of privacy. *Ethics and Information Technology, 6*(2), 121-128.

Nakada, M., & Tamura, T. (2005). Japanese conceptions of privacy: An intercultural perspective. *Ethics and Information Technology, 7*, 27-36.

Wong, D. (1984). *Moral relativity.* Berkeley, CA: University of California Press.

Wong, D. (1993). Relativism. In P. Singer (Ed.), *A companion to ethics* (pp. 442-450). Blackwell.

Wong, D. (2006). *Natural moralities: A defense of pluralistic relativism.* Oxford: Oxford University Press.

ENDNOTES

[1] By information ethics I mean the study of ethical issues in the use of information and information technology. Contemporary information ethics is a result of the digital revolution (or information revolution) and focuses mainly on ethical issues in the production, use, and dissemination of digital information and information technologies. It encloses the field of computer ethics (Johnson, 2000) as well as concerns that belong to classical information ethics (which was a branch of library and information science), media ethics, and journalism ethics.

[2] This doctrine is called metaethical rather than normative because it does not make any normative claims, but rather makes claims about the nature of moral judgments. *Normative moral relativism* would be the thesis that it is morally wrong to judge or interfere with the moral practices of societies, groups, cultures, or individuals who have moral values different from one's own. This is a normative thesis because it makes prescriptions for behavior.

[3] Worthen, B. (2006). Intellectual property: China's three realities. *CIO Blogs.* Online at http://blogs.cio.com/intellectual_property_chinas_three_realities. Accessed October 2006.

This work was previously published in the International Journal of Technology and Human Interaction, edited by B. C. Stahl, Volume 3, Issue 3, pp. 12-24, copyright 2007 by IGI Publishing, formerly known as Idea Group Publishing (an imprint of IGI Global).

Chapter IV
The Theoretical Framework of Cognitive Informatics

Yingxu Wang
University of Calgary, Canada

ABSTRACT

Cognitive Informatics (CI) is a transdisciplinary enquiry of the internal information processing mechanisms and processes of the brain and natural intelligence shared by almost all science and engineering disciplines. This article presents an intensive review of the new field of CI. The structure of the theoretical framework of CI is described encompassing the Layered Reference Model of the Brain (LRMB), the OAR model of information representation, Natural Intelligence (NI) vs. Artificial Intelligence (AI), Autonomic Computing (AC) vs. imperative computing, CI laws of software, the mechanism of human perception processes, the cognitive processes of formal inferences, and the formal knowledge system. Three types of new structures of mathematics, Concept Algebra (CA), Real-Time Process Algebra (RTPA), and System Algebra (SA), are created to enable rigorous treatment of cognitive processes of the brain as well as knowledge representation and manipulation in a formal and coherent framework. A wide range of applications of CI in cognitive psychology, computing, knowledge engineering, and software engineering has been identified and discussed.

INTRODUCTION

The development of classical and contemporary informatics, the cross fertilization between computer science, systems science, cybernetics, computer/software engineering, cognitive science, knowledge engineering, and neuropsychology, has led to an entire range of an extremely interesting and new research field known as Cognitive Informatics (Wang, 2002a, 2003a, b, 2006b; Wang, Johnston & Smith 2002; Wang & Kinsner, 2006). *Informatics* is the science of information that studies the nature of information; it's processing, and ways of transformation between information, matter, and energy.

Definition 1. *Cognitive Informatics* (CI) is a transdisciplinary enquiry of cognitive and information sciences that investigates the internal information processing mechanisms and processes of the brain and natural intelligence, and their engineering applications via an interdisciplinary approach.

In many disciplines of human knowledge, almost all of the hard problems yet to be solved share a common root in the understanding of the mechanisms of natural intelligence and the cognitive processes of the brain. Therefore, CI is a discipline that forges links between a number of natural science and life science disciplines with informatics and computing science.

The structure of the theoretical framework of CI is described in Figure 1, which covers the Information-Matter-Energy (IME) model (Wang, 2003b), the Layered Reference Model of the Brain (LRMB) (Wang, Wang, Patel & Patel, 2006), the Object-Attribute-Relation (OAR) model of information representation in the brain (Wang, 2006h; Wang & Wang, 2006), the cognitive informatics model of the brain (Wang, Liu, & Wang, 2003; Wang & Wang, 2006), Natural Intelligence (NI) (Wang, 2003b), Autonomic Computing (AC) (Wang, 2004), Neural Informatics (NeI) (Wang, 2002a, 2003b, 2006b), CI laws of software (Wang,

Figure 1. The theoretical framework of CI

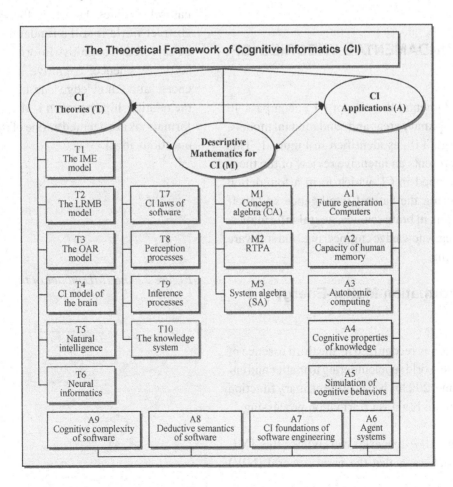

2006f), the mechanisms of human perception processes (Wang, 2005a), the cognitive processes of formal inferences (Wang, 2005c), and the formal knowledge system (Wang, 2006g).

In this article, the theoretical framework of CI is explained in the fundamental theories of CI section. Three structures of new descriptive mathematics such as Concept Algebra (CA), Real-Time Process Algebra (RTPA), and System Algebra (SA) are introduced in the denotational mathematics for CI in order to rigorously deal with knowledge and cognitive information representation and manipulation in a formal and coherent framework. Applications of CI are discussed, which covers cognitive computing, knowledge engineering, and software engineering. Then, it draws conclusions on the theories of CI, the contemporary mathematics for CI, and their applications.

THE FUNDAMENTAL THEORIES OF CI

The fundamental theories of CI encompass 10 transdisciplinary areas and fundamental models, T1 through T10, as identified in Figure 1. This section presents an intensive review of the theories developed in CI, which form a foundation for exploring the natural intelligence and their applications in brain science, neural informatics, computing, knowledge engineering, and software engineering.

The Information-Matter-Energy Model

Information is recognized as the third essence of the natural world supplementing to matter and energy (Wang, 2003b), because the primary function of the human brain is information processing.

Theorem 1. A generic worldview, the IME model states that the natural world (NW)

that forms the context of human beings is a dual world: one aspect of it is the physical or the concrete world (PW), and the other is the abstract or the perceptive world (AW), where matter (M) and energy (E) are used to model the former, and information (I) to the latter, that is:

$$
\begin{aligned}
NW &\triangleq PW \parallel AW \\
&= \wp\,(M, E) \parallel \alpha\,(I) \qquad (1) \\
&= \mathfrak{n}\,(I, M, E)
\end{aligned}
$$

where $\parallel$ denotes a parallel relation, and $\wp$, α, and $\mathfrak{n}$ are functions that determine a certain *PW*, *AW*, or *NW*, respectively, as illustrated in Figure 2.

According to the IME model, information plays a vital role in connecting the physical world with the abstract world. Models of the natural world have been well studied in physics and other natural sciences. However, the modeling of the abstract world is still a fundamental issue yet to be explored in cognitive informatics, computing, software science, cognitive science, brain sciences, and knowledge engineering. Especially the relationships between I-M-E and their transformations are deemed as one of the fundamental questions in CI.

Figure 2. The IME model of the worldview

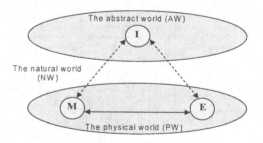

Corollary 1. The natural world $NW(I, M, E)$, particularly part of the abstract world, $AW(I)$, is cognized and perceived differently by individuals because of the uniqueness of perceptions and mental contexts among people.

Corollary 1 indicates that although the physical world $PW(M, E)$ is the same to everybody, the natural world $NW(I, M, E)$ is unique to different individuals because the abstract world $AW(I)$, as a part of it, is subjective depending on the information an individual obtains and perceives.

Corollary 2. The *principle of transformability between IME* states that, according to the IME model, the three essences of the world are predicated to be transformable between each other as described by the following generic functions f_1 to f_6:

$$I = f_1(M) \tag{2.1}$$
$$M = f_2(I) \stackrel{?}{=} f_1^{-1}(I) \tag{2.2}$$
$$I = f_3(E) \tag{2.3}$$
$$E = f_4(I) \stackrel{?}{=} f_3^{-1}(I) \tag{2.4}$$
$$E = f_5(M) \tag{2.5}$$
$$M = f_6(E) \stackrel{?}{=} f_5^{-1}(E) \tag{2.6}$$

where a question mark on the equal sign denotes an uncertainty if there exists such a reverse function (Wang, 2003b).

Albert Einstein revealed Functions f_5 and f_6, the relationship between matter (m) and energy (E), in the form $E = mC^2$, where C is the speed of light. It is a great curiosity to explore what the remaining relationships and forms of transformation between I-M-E will be. To a certain extent, cognitive informatics is the science to seek possible solutions for f_1 to f_4. A clue to explore the relations and transformability is believed in the understanding of the natural intelligence and its information processing mechanisms in CI.

Definition 2. *Information* in CI is defined as a generic abstract model of properties or attributes of the natural world that can be distinctly elicited, generally abstracted, quantitatively represented, and mentally processed.

Definition 3. The *measurement of information*, I_k, is defined by the cost of code to abstractly represent a given size of internal message X in the brain in a digital system based on k, that is:

$$I_k = f : X \rightarrow S_k$$
$$= \lceil \log_k X \rceil \tag{3}$$

where I_k is the content of information in a k-based digital system, and S_k is the measurement scale based on k. The unit of I_k is the number of k-based digits (Wang, 2003b).

Equation 3 is a generic measure of information sizes. When a binary digital representation system is adopted, that is $k = b = 2$, it becomes the most practical one as follows.

Definition 4. The metalevel representation of information, I_b, is that when $k = b = 2$, that is:

$$I_b = f : X \rightarrow S_b$$
$$= \lceil \log_b X \rceil \tag{4}$$

where the unit of information, I_b, is a *bit*.

Note that the *bit* here is a concrete and deterministic unit, and it is no longer probability-based as in conventional information theories (Bell, 1953; Shannon, 1948). To a certain extent, computer science and engineering is a branch of modern informatics that studies machine representation and processing of external information; while CI is a branch of contemporary informatics that studies internal information representation and processing in the brain.

Theorem 2. The most fundamental form of information that can be represented and processed is binary digit where *k = b = 2.*

Theorem 2 indicates that any form of information in the physical (natural) and abstract (mental) worlds can be unified on the basis of binary data. This is the CI foundation of modern digital computers and NI.

The Layered Reference Model of the Brain

The LRMB (Wang et al., 2006) is developed to explain the fundamental cognitive mechanisms and processes of natural intelligence. Because a variety of life functions and cognitive processes have been identified in CI, psychology, cognitive science, brain science, and neurophilosophy, there is a need to organize all the recurrent cognitive processes in an integrated and coherent framework. The LRMB model explains the functional mechanisms and cognitive processes of natural intelligence that encompasses 37 cognitive processes at six layers known as the *sensation, memory, perception, action, metacognitive,* and *higher cognitive layers* from the bottom-up as shown in Figure 3. LRMB elicits the core and highly repetitive recurrent cognitive processes from a huge variety of life functions, which may shed light on the study of the fundamental mechanisms and interactions of complicated mental processes, particularly the relationships and interactions between the inherited and the acquired life functions as well as those of the subconscious and conscious cognitive processes.

Figure 3. LRMB model

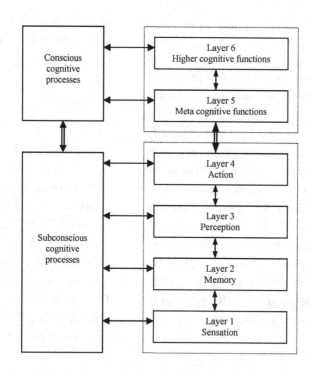

The OAR Model of Information Representation in the Brain

Investigation into the cognitive models of information and knowledge representation in the brain is perceived to be one of the fundamental research areas that help to unveil the mechanisms of the brain. The *Object-Attribute-Relation* (OAR) model (Wang, 2006h; Wang et al., 2003) describes human memory, particularly the long-term memory, by using the *relational metaphor*, rather than the traditional *container metaphor* that used to be adopted in psychology, computing, and information science. The OAR model shows that human memory and knowledge are represented by relations, that is, connections of synapses between neurons, rather than by the neurons themselves as the traditional container metaphor described. The OAR model can be used to explain a wide range of human information processing mechanisms and cognitive processes.

The Cognitive Informatics Model of the Brain

The human brain and its information processing mechanisms are centred in CI. A cognitive informatics model of the brain is proposed in Wang and Wang (2006), which explains the natural intelligence via interactions between the inherent (subconscious) and acquired (conscious) life functions. The model demonstrates that memory is the foundation for any natural intelligence. Formalism in forms of mathematics, logic, and rigorous treatment is introduced into the study of cognitive and neural psychology and natural informatics. Fundamental cognitive mechanisms of the brain, such as the architecture of the thinking engine, internal knowledge representation, long-term memory establishment, and roles of sleep in long-term memory development have been investigated (Wang & Wang, 2006).

Natural Intelligence (NI)

Natural Intelligence (NI) is the domain of CI. Software and computer systems are recognized as a subset of intelligent behaviors of human beings described by programmed instructive information (Wang, 2003b; Wang & Kinsner, 2006). The relationship between Artificial Intelligence (AI) and NI can be described by the following theorem.

Theorem 3. The law of *compatible intelligent capability* states that *artificial intelligence (AI)* is always a subset of the *natural intelligence* (NI), that is:

$$AI \subseteq NI \tag{5}$$

Theorem 3 indicates that AI is dominated by NI. Therefore, one should not expect a computer or a software system to solve a problem where humans cannot. In other words, no AI or computing system may be designed and/or implemented for a given problem where there is no solution being known by human beings.

Neural Informatics (NeI)

Definition 5. *Neural Informatics* (NeI) is a new interdisciplinary enquiry of the biological and physiological representation of information and knowledge in the brain at the neuron level and their abstract mathematical models (Wang, 2004; Wang & Wang, 2006).

NeI is a branch of CI, where memory is recognized as the foundation and platform of any natural or artificial intelligence (Wang & Wang, 2006).

Definition 6. The *Cognitive Models of Memory* (CMM) states that the architecture of human memory is parallel configured by the Sensory Buffer Memory (SBM), Short-

Term Memory (STM), Long-Term Memory (LTM), and Action-Buffer Memory (ABM), that is:

$$CMM \triangleq SBM$$
$$\| STM$$
$$\| LTM$$
$$\| ABM \qquad (6)$$

where the ABM is newly identified in Wang and Wang (2006).

The major organ that accommodates memories in the brain is the cerebrum or the cerebral cortex. In particular, the association and premotor cortex in the frontal lobe, the temporal lobe, sensory cortex in the frontal lobe, visual cortex in the occipital lobe, primary motor cortex in the frontal lobe, supplementary motor area in the frontal lobe, and procedural memory in cerebellum (Wang & Wang, 2006).

The CMM model and the mapping of the four types of human memory onto the physiological organs in the brain reveal a set of fundamental mechanisms of NeI. The OAR model of information/knowledge representation described in the OAR model of information representation in the brain section provides a generic description of information/knowledge representation in the brain (Wang, 2006h; Wang et al., 2003).

The theories of CI and NeI explain a number of important questions in the study of NI. Enlightening conclusions derived in CI and NeI are such as: (a) LTM establishment is a subconscious process; (b) The long-term memory is established during sleeping; (c) The major mechanism for LTM establishment is by sleeping; (d) The general acquisition cycle of LTM is equal to or longer than 24 hours; (e) The mechanism of LTM establishment is to update the entire memory of information represented as an OAR model in the brain; and (f) Eye movement and dreams play an important role in LTM creation. The latest development in CI and NeI has led to the determination of the magnificent and expected capacity of human memory as described in the Estimation of the Capacity of Human Memory section.

Cognitive Informatics Laws of Software

It is commonly conceived that software as an artifact of human creativity is not constrained by the laws and principles discovered in the physical world. However, it is unknown what constrains software. The new informatics metaphor proposed by the author in CI perceives software is a type of instructive and behavioral information. Based on this, it is asserted that software obeys the laws of informatics. A comprehensive set of 19 CI laws for software have been established in Wang (2006f), such as:

1. Abstraction
2. Generality
3. Cumulativeness
4. Dependency on cognition
5. Three-dimensional behavior space known as the object (O), space (S), and time (T)
6. Sharability
7. Dimensionless
8. Weightless
9. Transformability between I-M-E
10. Multiple representation forms
11. Multiple carrying media
12. Multiple transmission forms
13. Dependency on media
14. Dependency on energy
15. Wearless and time dependency
16. Conservation of entropy
17. Quality attributes of informatics
18. Susceptible to distortion
19. Scarcity

The informatics laws of software extend the knowledge on the fundamental laws and properties of software where the conventional product metaphor could not explain. Therefore, CI forms one of the foundations of software engineering and computing science.

Mechanisms of Human Perception Processes

Definition 7. *Perception* is a set of interpretive cognitive processes of the brain at the subconscious cognitive function layers that detects, relates, interprets, and searches internal cognitive information in the mind.

Perception may be considered as the *sixth sense* of human beings, which almost all cognitive life functions rely on. Perception is also an important cognitive function at the subconscious layers that determines personality. In other words, personality is a faculty of all subconscious life functions and experience cumulated via conscious life functions.

According to LRMB, the main cognitive processes at the perception layer are emotion, motivation, and attitude (Wang, 2005a). The relationship between the internal emotion, motivation, attitude, and the embodied external behaviors can be formally and quantitatively described by the *motivation/attitude-driven behavioral* (MADB) *model* (Wang & Wang, 2006), which demonstrates that complicated psychological and cognitive mental processes may be formally modeled and rigorously described by mathematical means (Wang, 2002b, 2003d, 2005c).

The Cognitive Processes of Formal Inferences

Theoretical research is predominately an inductive process, while *applied research* is mainly a deductive one. Both inference processes are based on the cognitive process and means of abstraction. *Abstraction* is a powerful means of philosophy and mathematics. It is also a preeminent trait of the human brain identified in CI studies (Wang,

2005c). All formal logical inferences and reasonings can only be carried out on the basis of abstract properties shared by a given set of objects under study.

Definition 8. *Abstraction* is a process to elicit a subset of objects that shares a common property from a given set of objects and to use the property to identify and distinguish the subset from the whole in order to facilitate reasoning.

Abstraction is a gifted capability of human beings. Abstraction is a basic cognitive process of the brain at the metacognitive layer according to LRMB (Wang et al., 2006). Only by abstraction can important theorems and laws about the objects under study be elicited and discovered from a great variety of phenomena and empirical observations in an area of inquiry.

Definition 9. *Inferences* are a formal cognitive process that reasons a possible causality from given premises based on known causal relations between a pair of cause and effect proven true by empirical arguments, theoretical inferences, or statistical regulations.

Formal inferences may be classified into the deductive, inductive, abductive, and analogical categories (Wang, 2005c). *Deduction* is a cognitive process by which a specific conclusion necessarily follows from a set of general premises. *Induction* is a cognitive process by which a general conclusion is drawn from a set of specific premises based on three designated samples in reasoning or experimental evidences. *Abduction* is a cognitive process by which an inference to the best explanation or most likely reason of an observation or event. *Analogy* is a cognitive process by which an inference about the similarity of the same relations holds between different domains or systems, and/or examines that if two

Table 1. Definitions of formal inferences

.	Inference technique	Formal description		Usage
		Primitive form	**Composite form**	
1	Abstraction	$\forall S, p \Rightarrow \exists e \in E \subseteq S, p(e)$	-	To elicit a subset of elements with a given generic property.
2	Deduction	$\forall x \in X, p(x) \Rightarrow \exists a \in X, p(a)$	$(\forall x \in X, p(x) \Rightarrow q(x))$ $\forall x \in X, p(x) \Rightarrow \exists a \in X, p(a)$ $(\exists a \in X, p(a) \Rightarrow q(a))$	To derive a conclusion based on a known and generic premises.
3	Induction	$((\exists a \in X, P(a)) \wedge (\exists k, k+1 \in X, (P(k) \Rightarrow P(k+1))) \Rightarrow \forall x \in X, P(x)$	$((\exists a \in X, p(a) \Rightarrow q(a)) \wedge (\exists k, k+1 \in X, ((p(k) \Rightarrow q(k)) \Rightarrow (p(k+1) \Rightarrow q(k+1)))) \Rightarrow \forall x \in X, p(x) \Rightarrow q(x)$	To determine the generic behavior of the given list or sequence of recurring patterns by three samples.
4	Abduction	$(\forall x \in X, p(x) \Rightarrow q(x)) \Rightarrow (\exists a \in X, q(a) \Rightarrow p(a))$	$(\forall x \in X, p(x) \Rightarrow q(x) \wedge r(x) \Rightarrow q(x)) \Rightarrow (\exists a \in X, q(a) \Rightarrow (p(a) \vee r(a)))$	To seek the most likely cause(s) and reason(s) of an observed phenomenon.
5	Analogy	$\exists a \in X, p(a) \Rightarrow \exists b \in X, p(b)$	$(\exists a \in X, p(a) \Rightarrow q(a)) \Rightarrow (\exists b \in X, p(b) \Rightarrow q(b))$	To predict a similar phenomenon or consequence based on a known observation.

things agree in certain respects, then they probably agree in others. A summary of the formal definitions of the five inference techniques is shown in Table 1.

For seeking generality and universal truth, either the objects or the relations can only be abstractly described and rigorously inferred by abstract models rather than real-world details.

The Formal Knowledge System

Mathematical thoughts (Jordan & Smith, 1997) provide a successful paradigm to organize and validate human knowledge, where once a truth or a theorem is established, it is true until the axioms or conditions that it stands for are changed or extended. A proven truth or theorem in mathematics does not need to be argued each time one uses it. This is the advantage and efficiency of formal knowledge in science and engineering. In other words, if any theory or conclusion may be argued from time-to-time based on a wiser idea or a trade-off, it is an empirical result rather than a formal one.

The Framework of Formal Knowledge (FFK) of mankind (Wang, 2006g) can be described as shown in Figure 5. An FFK is centered by a set of theories. A *theory* is a statement of how and why certain objects, facts, or truths are related. All objects in nature and their relations are constrained by invariable laws, no matter if one observed them or not at any given time. An *empirical truth* is a

Figure 4. The framework of formal knowledge (FFK)

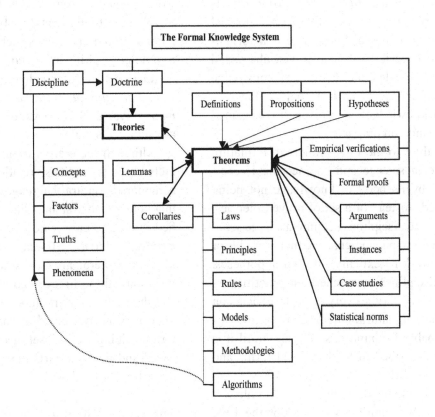

Figure 5. The structural model of an abstract concept

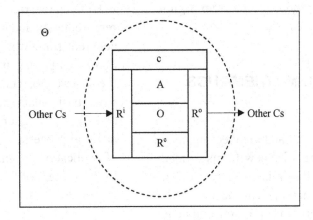

truth based on or verifiable by observation, experiment, or experience. A *theoretical proposition* is an assertion based on formal theories or logical reasoning. Theoretical knowledge is a formalization of generic truth and proven abstracted empirical knowledge. Theoretical knowledge may be easier to acquire when it exists. However, empirical knowledge is very difficult to be gained without hands-on practice.

According to the FFK model, an immature discipline of science and engineering is characterized by its body of knowledge not being formalized. Instead of a set of proven theories, the immature disciplines document a large set of observed facts, phenomena, and their possible or partially working explanations and hypotheses. In such disciplines, researchers and practitioners might be able to argue every informal conclusion documented in natural languages from time-to-time probably for hundreds of years, until it is formally described in mathematical forms and proved rigorously.

The disciplines of mathematics and physics are successful paradigms that adopt the FFK formal knowledge system. The key advantages of the formal knowledge system are its stability and efficiency. The former is a property of the formal knowledge that once it is established and formally proved, users who refers to it will no longer need to reexamine or reprove it. The latter is a property of formal knowledge that is exclusively true or false that saves everybody's time from arguing a proven theory.

DENOTATIONAL MATHEMATICS FOR CI

The history of sciences and engineering shows that new problems require new forms of mathematics. CI is a new discipline, and the problems in it require new mathematical means that are descriptive and precise in expressing and denoting human and system actions and behaviors. Conventional *analytic mathematics* are unable to solve the fundamental problems inherited in CI and related disciplines such as neuroscience, psychology, philosophy, computing, software engineering, and knowledge engineering. Therefore, *denotational mathematical structures and means* (Wang, 2006c) beyond mathematical logic are yet to be sought.

Although there are various ways to express facts, objects, notions, relations, actions, and behaviors in natural languages, it is found in CI that human and system behaviors may be classified into three basic categories known as to *be*, to *have*, and to *do*. All mathematical means and forms, in general, are an abstract and formal description of these three categories of expressibility and their rules. Taking this view, mathematical logic may be perceived as the abstract means for describing "to be," set theory describing "to have," and algebras, particularly process algebra, describing "to do."

Theorem 4. The utility of mathematics is the means and rules to express thought rigorously and generically at a higher level of abstraction.

Three types of new mathematics, Concept Algebra (CA), Real-Time Process Algebra (RTPA), and System Algebra (SA), are created in CI to enable rigorous treatment of knowledge representation and manipulation in a formal and coherent framework. The three new structures of contemporary mathematics have extended the abstract objects under study in mathematics from basic mathematical entities of numbers and sets to a higher level, that is, concepts, behavioral processes, and systems. A wide range of applications of the denotational mathematics in the context of CI has been identified (Wang, 2002b, 2006d, e).

Concept Algebra

A *concept* is a cognitive unit (Ganter & Wille, 1999; Quillian, 1968; Wang, 2006e) by which the meanings and semantics of a real-world or an abstract entity may be represented and embodied based on the OAR model.

Definition 10. An *abstract concept c* is a 5-tuple, that is:

$$c \triangleq (O, A, R^c, R^i, R^o) \qquad (7)$$

where

- O is a nonempty set of object of the concept, $O = \{o_1, o_2, ..., o_m\} = \mathbb{P}U$, where $\mathbb{P}U$ denotes a power set of U.
- A is a nonempty set of attributes, $A = \{a_1, a_2, ..., a_n\} = \mathbb{P}M$.
- $R^c \subseteq O \times A$ is a set of internal relations.
- $R^i \subseteq C' \times C$ is a set of input relations, where C' is a set of external concepts.
- $R^o \subseteq C \times C'$ is a set of output relations.

A structural concept model of $c = (O, A, R^c, R^i, R^o)$ can be illustrated in Figure 6, where c, A, O, and R, $R = \{R^c, R^i, R^o\}$, denote the concept, its attributes, objects, and internal/external relations, respectively.

Definition 11. *Concept algebra* is a new mathematical structure for the formal treatment of abstract concepts and their algebraic relations, operations, and associative rules for composing complex concepts and knowledge (Wang, 2006e).

Concept algebra deals with the algebraic relations and associational rules of abstract concepts. The associations of concepts form a foundation to denote complicated relations between concepts in knowledge representation. The associations among concepts can be classified into nine categories, such as inheritance, extension, tailoring, substitute, composition, decomposition, aggregation, specification, and instantiation as shown in Figure 6 and Table 2 (Wang, 2006e). In Figure 6, $R = \{R^c, R^i, R^o\}$, and all nine associations de-

Figure 6. The nine concept association operations as knowledge composing rules

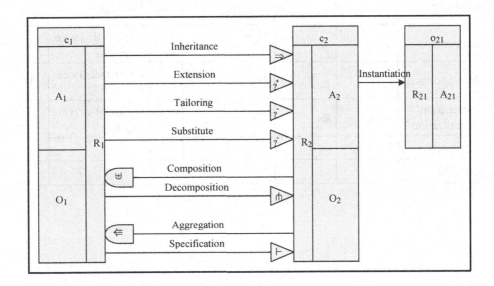

Table 2. Taxonomy of contemporary mathematics for knowledge representation and manipulation

Operations	Concept Algebra	System Algebra	Real-Time Process Algebra			
			Meta Processes		Relational Operations	
Super/sub relation	≻ / ≺	⊒ / ⊑	Assignment	:=	Sequence	→
Related/ independent	↔ / ↮	↔ / ↮	Evaluation	◆	Jump	⌢
Equivalent	=	=	Addressing	⇒	Branch	|
Consistent	≅		Memory allocation	⇐	Switch	| ... | ...
Overlapped		Π	Memory release	⇍	While-loop	R^*
Conjunction	+	⊔	Read	>	Repeat-loop	R^+
Elicitation	*		Write	<	For-loop	R^i
Comparison	~		Input	|>	Recursion	↻
Definition	≜		Output	|<	Procedure call	↦
Difference		⊟	Timing	@	Parallel	||
Inheritance	⇒	⇒	Duration	≙	Concurrence	∯
Extension			Increase	↑	Interleave	|||
Tailoring			Decrease	↓	Pipeline	»
Substitute			Exception detection	!	Interrupt	↯
Composition	⊎ +⇒	⊎⇒	Skip	⊘	Time-driven dispatch	↳$_t$
Decomposition	⋔⇒	⊕	Stop	⊠	Event-driven dispatch	↳$_e$
Aggregation/ generalization	⇐⇒	≢	System	§	Interrupt-driven dispatch	↳$_i$
Specification	⊢	⊢				
Instantiation	↦	↦				

scribe composing rules among concepts, except instantiation that is a relation between a concept and a specific object.

Definition 12. A *generic knowledge K* is an *n*-nary relation R_k among a set of *n* multiple concepts in *C*, that is

$$K = R_k : (\overset{n}{\underset{i-1}{X}} C_i) \to C \tag{8}$$

where $\overset{n}{\underset{i=1}{\bigcup}} C_i = C$, and

$R_k \in \Re = \{\Rightarrow, \overset{+}{\Rightarrow}, \overset{}{\Rightarrow}, \overset{\sim}{\Rightarrow}, \uplus, \Cap, \Leftleftarrows, \vdash, \mapsto\}$.

In Definition 12, the relation R_k is one of the concept operations in CA as defined in Table 2 (Wang, 2006e) that serves as the knowledge composing rules.

Definition 13. A *concept network CN* is a hierarchical network of concepts interlinked by the set of nine associations $\Re$ defined in CA, that is:

$$CN = R_e : \overset{n}{\underset{i-1}{X}} C_i \to \overset{n}{\underset{i-j}{X}} C_j \tag{9}$$

where $R_k \in \Re$.

Because the relations between concepts are transitive, the generic topology of knowledge is a hierarchical concept network. The advantages of the hierarchical knowledge architecture *K* in the form of concept networks are as follows: (a) *Dynamic*: The knowledge networks may be updated dynamically along with information acquisition and learning without destructing the existing concept nodes and relational links. (b) *Evolvable*: The knowledge networks may grow adaptively without changing the overall and existing structure of the hierarchical network.

A summary of the algebraic relations and operations of concepts defined in CA are provided in Table 2.

Real-Time Process Algebra (RTPA)

A key metaphor in system modeling, specification, and description is that a software system can be perceived and described as the *composition* of a set of interacting *processes*. Hoare (1985), Milner (1989), and others developed various algebraic approaches to represent communicating and concurrent systems, known as process algebra. A *process algebra* is a set of formal notations and rules for describing algebraic relations of software processes. *Real-Time Process Algebra* (Wang, 2002b, 2005b) extends process algebra to time/event, architecture, and system dispatching manipulations in order to formally describe and specify architectures and behaviors of software systems. A process in RTPA is a computational operation that transforms a system from a state to another by changing its inputs, outputs, and/ or internal variables. A process can be a single metaprocess or a complex process formed by using the process combination rules of RTPA known as process relations.

Definition 14. *Real-Time Process Algebra* is a set of formal notations and rules for describing algebraic and real-time relations of software processes.

RTPA models 17 metaprocesses and 17 process relations. A metaprocess is an elementary and primary process that serves as a common and basic building block for a software system. Complex processes can be derived from metaprocesses by a set of process relations that serves as process combinatory rules. Detailed semantics of RTPA may be referred to in Wang (2002b).

Program modeling is on coordination of computational behaviors with given data objects. Behavioral or instructive knowledge can be modeled by RTPA. A generic program model can be described by a formal treatment of statements, processes, and complex processes from the bottom-up in the program hierarchy.

Definition 15. A *process P* is a composed listing and a logical combination of *n* metastatements p_i and p_j, $1 \leq i < n$, $1 < j \leq m = n+1$, according to certain composing relations r_{ij}, that is:

$$P = \mathop{R}_{i=1}^{n-1}(p_i \ r_{ij} \ p_j), j = i+1$$
$$= (...(((p_1) \ r_{12} \ p_2) \ r_{23} \ p_3) \ ... \ r_{n-1,n} \ p_n) \qquad (10)$$

where the big-R notation (Wang, 2002b, 2006i) is adopted to describes the nature of processes as the building blocks of programs.

Definition 16. A *program* $\mathfrak{P}$ is a composition of a finite set of *m* processes according to the time-, event-, and interrupt-based process dispatching rules, that is:

$$\mathfrak{P} = \mathop{R}_{k=1}^{m}(@ e_k \hookrightarrow P_k) \qquad (11)$$

Equations 9.1 and 10.1 indicate that a program is an *embedded relational algebraic* entity. A statement *p* in a program is an instantiation of a metainstruction of a programming language that executes a basic unit of coherent function and leads to a predictable behavior.

Theorem 5. The *embedded relational model (ERM)* states that a software system or a program $\mathfrak{P}$ is a set of complex embedded relational processes, in which all previous processes of a given process form the context of the current process, that is:

$$\mathfrak{P} = \mathop{R}_{k=1}^{m}(@ e_k \hookrightarrow P_k)$$
$$= \mathop{R}_{k=1}^{m}[@ e_k \hookrightarrow \mathop{R}_{i=1}^{n-1}(p_i(k) \ r_{ij}(k) \ p_j(k))], j = i+1$$

$$(12)$$

ERM presented in Theorem 5 provides a *unified mathematical model of programs* (Wang, 2006a) for the first time, which reveals that a program is a finite and nonempty set of embedded binary relations between a current statement and *all previous ones* that formed the *semantic context* or environment of computing.

Definition 17. A *metaprocess* is the most basic and elementary processes in computing that cannot be broken up further. The set of *metaprocesses P* encompasses 17 fundamental primitive operations in computing as follows:

$$P = \{:=, \blacklozenge, \Rightarrow, \Leftarrow, \underset{\sim}{\Leftarrow}, >, <, |>, |<, \underline{@}, \triangleq, \uparrow, \downarrow, !,$$
$$\oslash, \boxtimes, \S\} \qquad (13)$$

Definition 18. A *process relation* is a composing rule for constructing complex processes by using the metaprocesses. The *process relations R* of RTPA are a set of 17 composing operations and rules to built larger architectural components and complex system behaviors using the metaprocesses, that is:

$$R = \{\rightarrow, \curvearrowright, |, |...|, R^*, R^+, R^i, \circlearrowleft, \rightarrowtail, \|,$$
$$\oiint, \|\|, \gg, \not\leqslant, \hookrightarrow_t, \hookrightarrow_e, \hookrightarrow_i\} \qquad (14)$$

The definitions, syntaxes, and formal semantics of each of the metaprocesses and process relations may be referred to RTPA (Wang, 2002b, 2006f). A complex process and a program can be derived from the metaprocesses by the set of algebraic process relations. Therefore, a program is a set of embedded relational processes as described in Theorem 5.

A summary of the metaprocesses and their algebraic operations in RTPA are provided in Table 2.

System Algebra (SA)

Systems are the most complicated entities and phenomena in the physical, information, and social worlds across all science and engineering disciplines (Klir, 1992; von Bertalanffy, 1952; Wang, 2006d). Systems are needed because the physical and/or cognitive power of an individual component or person is not enough to carry out a work or solving a problem. An *abstract system* is a collection of coherent and interactive entities that has stable functions and clear boundary with external environment. An abstract system forms the generic model of various real world systems and represents the most common characteristics and properties of them.

Definition 19. *System algebra* is a new abstract mathematical structure that provides an algebraic treatment of abstract systems as well as their relations and operational rules for forming complex systems (Wang, 2006d).

Abstract systems can be classified into two categories known as the closed and open systems. Most practical and useful systems in nature are open systems in which there are interactions between the system and its environment. However, for understanding easily, the closed system is introduced first.

Definition 20. A *closed system* $\widehat{S}$ is a 4-tuple, that is :

$$\widehat{S} = (C, R, B, \Omega) \tag{15}$$

where

- C is a nonempty set of components of the system, $C = \{c_1, c_2, ..., c_n\}$.
- R is a nonempty set of relations between pairs of the components in the system, $R = \{r_1, r_2, ..., r_m\}$, $R \subseteq C \times C$.
- B is a set of behaviors (or functions), $B = \{b_1, b_2, ..., b_p\}$.
- Ω is a set of constraints on the memberships of components, the conditions of relations, and the scopes of behaviors, $\Omega = \{\omega_1, \omega_2, ..., \omega_q\}$.

Most practical systems in the real world are not closed. That is, they need to interact with external world known as the *environment* Θ in order to exchange energy, matter, and/or information. Such systems are called open systems. Typical interactions between an open system and the environment are inputs and outputs.

Definition 21. An *open system* S is a 7-tuple, that is:

$$S = (C, R, B, \Omega, \Theta)$$
$$= (C, R^c, R^i, R^o, B, \Omega, \Theta) \tag{16}$$

where the extensions of entities beyond the closed system are as follows:

- Θ is the environment of S with a nonempty set of components C_Θ outside C.
- $R^c \subseteq C \times C$ is a set of internal relations.
- $R^i \subseteq C_\Theta \times C$ is a set of external input relations.
- $R^o \subseteq C \times C_\Theta$ is a set of external output relations.

An open system $S = (C, R^c, R^i, R^o, B, \Omega, \Theta)$ can be illustrated in Figure 7 (Wang, 2006d).

Figure 7. The abstract model of an open system

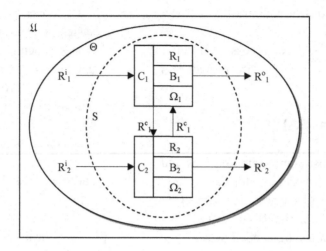

Theorem 6. The equivalence between open and closed systems states that an open system S is equivalent to a closed system $\hat{S}$, or vice versa, when its environment Θ_S or $\Theta_{\hat{S}}$ is conjoined, respectively, that is:

$$\begin{cases} \hat{S} = S \sqcup \Theta_S \\ S = \hat{S} \sqcup \Theta_{\hat{S}} \end{cases} \tag{17}$$

According to Theorem 6, any subsystem $\widehat{S_k}$ of a closed system $\hat{S}$ is an open system S. That is, any supersystem S of a given set of n open systems S_k, plus their environments Θ_k, $1 \le k \le n$, is a closed system. The algebraic relations and operations of systems in SA are summarized in Table 2.

Theorem 7. The Wang's *first law* of system science, *system fusion*, states that system conjunction or composition between two systems S_1 and S_2 creates *new relations* ΔR_{12} and/or *new behaviors* (functions) ΔB_{12} that are solely a property of the new supersystem S determined by the sizes of the two intersected component sets $\#(C_1)$ and $\#(C_2)$, that is:

$$\begin{aligned} \Delta R_{12} &= \#(R) - (\#(R_1) + \#(R_2)) \\ &= (\#(C_1 + C_2))^2 - ((\#(C_1))^2 + (\#(C_2))^2) \\ &= 2 \, (\#(C_1) \bullet \#(C_2)) \end{aligned} \tag{18}$$

The discovery in Theorem 7 reveals that the mathematical explanation of system utilities is the newly gained relations ΔR_{12} and/or behaviors (functions) ΔB_{12} during the conjunction of two systems or subsystems. The empirical awareness of this key system property has been intuitively or qualitatively observed for centuries. However, Theorem 7 is the first rigorous explanation of the mechanism of system gains during system conjunctions and compositions. According to Theorem 7, the maximum *incremental* or *system gain* equals to the number of by-directly interconnection between all components in both S_1 and S_2, that is, $2(\#(C_1) \bullet \#(C_2))$.

Theorem 8. The Wang's *2nd law* of system science, the *maximum system gain*, states that work done by a system is always larger than any of its components, but is less than or is equal to the sum of those of its components, that is:

$$\begin{cases} W(S) \le \sum_{i=1}^{n} W(e_i), & \eta \le 1 \\ W(S) > \max(W(e_i)), & e_i \in E_S \end{cases} \qquad (19)$$

There was a myth on an ideal system in conventional systems theory that supposes the work down by the ideal system $W(S)$ may be greater than the sum of all its components $W(e_i)$, that is:

$$W(S) \ge \sum_{i=1}^{n} W(e_i).$$

According to Theorems 7 and 8, the ideal system utility is impossible to achieve.

A summary of the algebraic operations and their notations in CA, RTPA, and SA is provided in Table 2. Details may be referred to in Wang (2006d, g).

APPLICATIONS OF CI

The last two sections have reviewed the latest development of fundamental researches in CI, particularly its theoretical framework and descriptive mathematics. A wide range of applications of CI has been identified in multidisciplinary and transdisciplinary areas, such as: (1) The architecture of future generation computers; (2) Estimation the capacity of human memory; (3) Autonomic computing; (4) Cognitive properties of information, data, knowledge, and skills in knowledge engineering; (5) Simulation of human cognitive behaviors using descriptive mathematics; (6) Agent systems; (7) CI foundations of software engineering; (8) Deductive semantics of software; and (9) Cognitive complexity of software.

The Architecture of Future Generation Computers

Conventional machines are invented to extend human physical capability, while modern information processing machines, such as computers, communication networks, and robots, are developed for extending human intelligence, memory, and the capacity for information processing (Wang, 2004). Recent advances in CI provide formal description of an entire set of cognitive processes of the brain (Wang et al., 2006). The fundamental research in CI also creates an enriched set of contemporary *denotational mathematics* (Wang, 2006c), for dealing with the extremely complicated objects and problems in natural intelligence, neural informatics, and knowledge manipulation.

The theory and philosophy behind the next generation computers and computing methodologies are CI (Wang, 2003b, 2004). It is commonly believed that the future-generation computers, known as the cognitive computers, will adopt non-von Neumann (von Neumann, 1946) architectures. The key requirements for implementing a conventional *stored-program controlled* computer are the generalization of common computing architectures and the computer is able to interpret the data loaded in memory as computing instructions. These are the essences of stored-program controlled computers known as the von Neumann (1946) architecture. Von Neumann elicited five fundamental and essential components to implement general-purpose programmable digital computers in order to embody the concept of stored-program-controlled computers.

Definition 22. A *von Neumann Architecture* (VNA) of computers is a 5-tuple that consists of the components: (a) the *arithmetic-logic unit* (ALU), (b) the *control unit* (CU) with a *program counter* (PC), (c) a *memory* (M), (d) a set of *input/output* (*I/O*) *devices*, and (e) a *bus* (B) that provides the data path between these components, that is:

$$VNA \triangleq (ALU, CU, M, I/O, B) \qquad (20)$$

Definition 23. *Conventional computers* with VNA are aimed at stored-program-controlled *data* processing based on mathematical logic and Boolean algebra.

A VNA computer is centric by the bus and characterized by the all purpose memory for both data and instructions. A VNA machine is an extended Turing machine (TM), where the power and functionality of all components of TM including the control unit (with wired instructions), the tape (memory), and the head of I/O, are greatly enhanced and extended with more powerful instructions and I/O capacity.

Definition 24. A *Wang Architecture* (WA) of computers, known as the *Cognitive Machine*

as shown in Figure 8, is a parallel structure encompassing an Inference Engine (IE) and a Perception Engine (PE) (Wang, 2006b, g), that is:

$$
\begin{aligned}
WA \triangleq (IE \parallel PE) \\
= (\ & KMU// \text{ The knowledge manipulation unit} \\
& \parallel BMU// \text{The behavior manipulation unit} \\
& \parallel EMU // \text{ The experience manipulation unit} \\
& \parallel SMU// \text{ The skill manipulation unit} \\
) \\
\parallel (\ & BPU \ // \text{ The behavior perception unit} \\
& \parallel EPU // \text{ The experience perception unit} \\
) & \qquad (21)
\end{aligned}
$$

As shown in Figure 8 and Equation 21, WA computers are not centered by a CPU for data manipulation as the VNA computers do. The WA computers are centered by the concurrent IE and PE for cognitive learning and autonomic perception based on abstract concept inferences and empirical stimuli perception. The IE is designed

Figure 8. The architecture of a cognitive machine

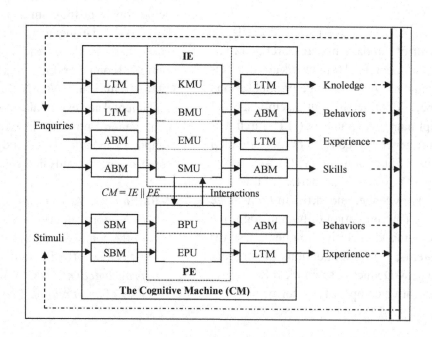

for concept/knowledge manipulation according to concept algebra (Wang, 2006e), particularly the nine concept operations for knowledge acquisition, creation, and manipulation. The PE is designed for feeling and perception processing according to RTPA (Wang, 2002b) and the formally described cognitive process models of the perception layers as defined in the LRMB model (Wang et al., 2006).

Definition 25. *Cognitive computers* with WA are aimed at cognitive and perceptive *concept/ knowledge* processing based on contemporary *denotational mathematics*, that is, CA, RTPA, and SA.

As that of mathematical logic and Boolean algebra are the mathematical foundations of VNA computers. The mathematical foundations of WA computers are based on denotational mathematics (Wang, 2006b, c). As described in the LRMB reference model (Wang et al., 2006), since all the 37 fundamental cognitive processes of human brains can be formally described in CA and RTPA (Wang, 2002b, 2006e). In other words, they are simulatable and executable by the WA-based cognitive computers.

Estimation of the Capacity of Human Memory

Despite the fact that the number of neurons in the brain has been identified in cognitive and neural sciences, the magnitude of human memory capacity is still unknown. According to the OAR model, a recent discovery in CI is that the upper bound of memory capacity of the human brain is in the order of $10^{8,432}$ bits (Wang et al., 2003). The determination of the magnitude of human memory capacity is not only theoretically significant in CI, but also practically useful to unveil the human potential, as well as the gaps between the natural and machine intelligence. This result indicates that the next generation computer memory systems may be built according to the OAR model rather than the traditional container metaphor, because the former is more powerful, flexible, and efficient to generate a tremendous memory capacity by using limited number of neurons in the brain or hardware cells in the next generation computers.

Autonomic Computing

The approaches to implement intelligent systems can be classified into those of biological organisms, silicon automata, and computing systems. Based on CI studies, *autonomic computing* (Wang, 2004) is proposed as a new and advanced computing technique built upon the routine, algorithmic, and adaptive systems as shown in Table 3.

The approaches to computing can be classified into two categories known as imperative and autonomic computing. Corresponding to these, computing systems may be implemented as imperative or autonomic computing systems.

Table 3. Classification of computing systems

		Behavior (O)	
		Constant	**Variable**
Event	**Constant**	Routine	Adaptive
(I)	**Variable**	Algorithmic	Autonomic
Type of behavior		*Deterministic*	*Nondeterministic*

Definition 26. An *imperative computing system* is a passive system that implements deterministic, context-free, and stored-program controlled behaviors.

Definition 27. An *autonomic computing system* is an intelligent system that autonomously carries out robotic and interactive actions based on goal- and event-driven mechanisms.

The imperative computing system is a traditional passive system that implements deterministic, context-free, and stored-program controlled behaviors, where a behavior is defined as a set of observable actions of a given computing system. The autonomic computing system is an active system that implements nondeterministic, context-dependent, and adaptive behaviors, which do not rely on instructive and procedural information, but are dependent on internal status and willingness that formed by long-term historical events and current rational or emotional goals.

The first three categories of computing techniques as shown in Table 3 are imperative. In contrast, the autonomic computing systems are an active system that implements nondeterministic, context-sensitive, and adaptive behaviors. Autonomic computing does not rely on imperative and procedural instructions, but are dependent on perceptions and inferences based on internal goals as revealed in CI.

Cognitive Properties of Knowledge

Almost all modern disciplines of science and engineering deal with information and knowledge. According to CI theories, cognitive information may be classified into four categories known as *knowledge, behaviors, experience,* and *skills* as shown in Table 4.

Definition 28. The taxonomy of *cognitive information* is determined by its types of inputs and outputs to and from the brain during learning and information processing, where both inputs and outputs can be either abstract information (concept) or empirical information (actions).

It is noteworthy that the approaches to acquire knowledge/behaviors and experience/skills are fundamentally different. The former may be obtained either directly based on hands-on activities or indirectly by reading, while the latter can never be acquired indirectly.

According to Table 4, the following important conclusions on information manipulation and learning for both human and machine systems can be derived.

Theorem 9. The *principle of information acquisition* states that there are four sufficient categories of learning known as those of

Table 4. Types of cognitive information

		Type of Output		Ways of Acquisition
		Abstract Concept	Empirical Action	
Type of Input	Abstract Concept	Knowledge	Behavior	*Direct or indirect*
	Empirical Action	Experience	Skill	*Direct only*

knowledge, behaviors, experience, and skills.

Theorem 9 indicates that learning theories and their implementation in autonomic and intelligent systems should study all four categories of cognitive information acquisitions, particularly behaviors, experience, and skills rather than only focusing on knowledge.

Corollary 3. All the four categories of information can be acquired directly by an individual.

Corollary 4. Knowledge and behaviors can be learnt indirectly by inputting abstract information, while experience and skills must be learned directly by hands-on or empirical actions.

The above theory of CI lays an important foundation for learning theories and pedagogy (Wang, 2004, 2006e). Based on the fundamental work, the IE and PE of cognitive computers working as a virtual brain can be implemented on WA-based cognitive computers and be simulated on VNA-based conventional computers.

Simulation of Human Cognitive Behaviors using the Contemporary Mathematics

The contemporary denotational mathematics as described in The Denotational Mathematics for CI section, particularly CA and RTPA, may be used to simulate the cognitive processes of the brain as modeled in LRMB (Wang et al., 2006). Most of the 37 cognitive processes identified in LRMB, such as the learning (Wang, 2006e), reasoning (Wang, 2006b), decision making (Wang et al., 2004), and comprehension (Wang & Gafurov, 2003) processes, have been rigorously modeled and described in RTPA and CA. Based on the fundamental work, the inference engineering and perception engine of a virtual brain can be imple-

mented on cognitive computers or be simulated on conventional computers. In the former case, a working prototype of a fully autonomic computer will be realized on the basis of CI theories.

Agent Systems

Definition 29. A *software agent* is an intelligent software system that autonomously carries out robotic and interactive applications based on goal-driven mechanisms (Wang, 2003c).

Because a software agent may be perceived as an application-specific virtual brain (see Theorem 3), behaviors of an agent are mirrored human behaviors. The fundamental characteristics of agent-based systems are autonomic computing, goal-driven action-generation, knowledge-based machine learning. In recent CI research, *perceptivity* is recognized as *the sixth sense* that serves the brain as the thinking engine and the kernel of the natural intelligence. Perceptivity implements self-consciousness inside the abstract memories of the brain. Almost all cognitive life functions rely on perceptivity such as consciousness, memory searching, motivation, willingness, goal setting, emotion, sense of spatiality, and sense of motion. The brain may be stimulated by external and internal information, which can be classified as willingness-driven (internal events such as goals, motivation, and emotions), event-driven (external events), and time-driven (mainly external events triggered by an external clock). Unlike a computer, the brain works in two approaches: the internal willingness-driven processes, and the external event- and time-driven processes. The external information and events are the major sources that drive the brain, particularly for conscious life functions.

Recent research in CI reveals that the foundations of agent technologies and autonomic computing are CI, particularly goal-driven action generation techniques (Wang, 2003c). The

LRMB model (Wang et al., 2006) described in the Layered Reference Model of the Brain section may be used as a reference model for agent-based technologies. This is a fundamental view toward the formal description and modeling of architectures and behaviors of agent systems, which are created to do something repeatable in context, to extend human capability, reachability, and/or memory capacity. It is found that both human and software behaviors can be described by a 3-dimensional representative model comprising *action*, *time*, and *space*. For agent system behaviors, the three dimensions are known as *mathematical operations*, *event/process timing*, and *memory manipulation* (Wang, 2006g). The 3-D behavioral space of agents can be formally described by RTPA that serves as an expressive mathematical means for describing thoughts and notions of dynamic system behaviors as a series of actions and cognitive processes.

CI Foundations of Software Engineering

Software is an intellectual artifact and a kind of instructive information that provides a solution for a repeatable computer application, which enables existing tasks to be done easier, faster, and smarter, or which provides innovative applications for the industries and daily life. Large-scale software systems are highly complicated systems that have never been handled or experienced precedent by mankind.

The fundamental cognitive characteristics of software engineering have been identified as follows (Wang, 2006g):

- The inherent complexity and diversity
- The difficulty of establishing and stabilizing requirements
- The changeability or malleability of system behavior
- The abstraction and intangibility of software products

- The requirement of varying problem domain knowledge
- The non-deterministic and polysolvability in design
- The polyglotics and polymorphism in implementation
- The dependability of interactions among software, hardware, and human beings

The above list forms a set of fundamental constraints for software engineering, identified as the cognitive constraints of intangibility, complexity, indeterminacy, diversity, polymorphism, inexpressiveness, inexplicit embodiment, and unquantifiable quality measures (Wang, 2006g).

A set of psychological requirements for software engineers has been identified, such as: (a) Abstract-level thinking; (b) Imagination of dynamic behaviors with static descriptions; (c) Organization capability; (d) Cooperative attitude in team work; (e) Long-period focus of attentions; (f) Preciseness; (g) Reliability; and (h) Expressive capability in communication.

Deductive Semantics of Software

Deduction is a reasoning process that discovers new knowledge or derives a specific conclusion based on generic premises such as abstract rules or principles. In order to provide an algebraic treatment of the semantics of program and human cognitive processes, a new type of formal semantics known as deductive semantics is developed (Wang, 2006f, g).

Definition 30. *Deductive semantics* is a formal semantics that deduces the semantics of a program from a generic abstract semantic function to the concrete semantics, which are embodied onto the changes of status of a finite set of variables constituting the semantic environment of computing (Wang, 2006g).

Theorem 10. The *semantics of a statement p*, *θ(p)*, on a given semantic environment Θ in deductive semantics is a double partial differential of the semantic function, $f_\theta(p)$ $= f_p : T \times S \to V = v_p(t,s), t \in T \wedge s \in S \wedge v_p \in V$, on the sets of variables S and executing steps T, that is:

$$\theta(p) = \frac{\partial^2}{\partial t\, \partial s} f_\theta(p) = \frac{\partial^2}{\partial t\, \partial s} v_p(t,s)$$

$$= \mathop{R}_{i=0}^{\#T(p)} \mathop{R}_{j=1}^{\#S(p)} v_p(t_i, s_j)$$

$$= \mathop{R}_{i=0}^{1} \mathop{R}_{j=1}^{\#\{s_1, s_2, \ldots, s_m\}} v_p(t_i, s_j)$$

$$= \begin{pmatrix} & s_1 & s_2 & \cdots & s_m \\ t_0 & v_{01} & v_{02} & \cdots & v_{0m} \\ (t_0, t_1] & v_{11} & v_{12} & \cdots & v_{1m} \end{pmatrix} \quad (22)$$

where t denotes the discrete time immediately before and after the execution of p during $(t_0, t_1]$, and # is the *cardinal calculus* that counts the number of elements in a given set, that is $n = \#T(p)$ and $m = \#S(p)$.

The first partial differential in Equation 22 selects all related variable $S(p)$ of the statement p from Θ. The second partial differential selects a set of discrete steps of p's execution $T(p)$ from Θ. According to Theorem 10, the semantics of a statement can be reduced onto a semantic function that results in a 2-D matrix with the changes of values for all variables over time along program execution.

Deductive semantics perceives that the carriers of software semantics are a finite set of variables declared in a given program. Therefore, software semantics can be reduced onto the changes of values of these variables. The deductive mathematical models of semantics and the semantic environment at various composing levels of systems are formally described. Properties of software semantics and relationships between the software behavioral space and the semantic environment are discussed. Deductive semantics is applied in the formal definitions and explanations of the semantic rules of a comprehensive set of software static and dynamic behaviors as modeled in RTPA. Deductive semantics can be used to define abstract and concrete semantics of software and cognitive systems, and facilitate software comprehension and recognition by semantic analyses.

Cognitive Complexity of Software

The estimation and measurement of functional complexity of software are an age-long problem in software engineering. The cognitive complexity of software (Wang, 2006j) is a new measurement for cross-platform analysis of complexities, sizes, and comprehension effort of software specifications and implementations in the phases of design, implementation, and maintenance in software engineering. This work reveals that the cognitive complexity of software is a product of its architectural and operational complexities on the basis of deductive semantics and the abstract system theory. Ten fundamental basic control structures (BCSs) are elicited from software architectural/behavioral specifications and descriptions. The cognitive weights of those BCSs are derived and calibrated via a series of psychological experiments. Based on this work, the cognitive complexity of software systems can be rigorously and accurately measured and analyzed. Comparative case studies demonstrate that the cognitive complexity is highly distinguishable in software functional complexity and size measurement in software engineering.

On the basis of the ERM model described in Theorem 5 and the deductive semantics of software presented in The deductive semantics of software section, the finding on the cognitive complexity of software is obtained as follows.

Theorem 11. The sum of the cognitive weights of all r_{ij}, $w(r_{ij})$, in the ERM model determines the operational complexity of a software system C_{op}, that is:

$$C_{op} = \sum_{i=1}^{n-1} w(r_{ij}), j = i + 1 \qquad (23)$$

A set of psychological experiments has been carried out in undergraduate and graduate classes in software engineering. Based on 126 experiment results, the equivalent cognitive weights of the 10 fundamental BCSs are statistically calibrated as summarized in Table 5 (Wang, 2006j), where the relative cognitive weight of the sequential structures is assumed one, that is, $w_1 = 1$.

According to deductive semantics, the complexity of a software system, or its semantic space, is determined not only by the number of operations, but also by the number of data objects.

Theorem 12. The *cognitive complexity* $C_c(S)$ of a software system S is a product of the operational complexity $C_{op}(S)$ and the architectural complexity $C_a(S)$, that is:

$$C_c(S) = C_{op}(S) \bullet C_a(S)$$
$$= \{\sum_{k=1}^{n_C} \sum_{i=1}^{\#(C_s(C_k))} w(k, i)\} \bullet$$
$$\{\sum_{k=1}^{n_{CLM}} \mathrm{OBJ}(CLM_k) + \sum_{k=1}^{n_C} \mathrm{OBJ}(C_k)\} \quad [\mathrm{FO}] \qquad (24)$$

Based on Theorem 12, the following corollary can be derived.

Corollary 5. The cognitive complexity of a software system is proportional to both its operational and structural complexities. That is, the more the architectural data objects and the higher the operational complicity onto these objects, the larger the cognitive complexity of the system.

Based on Theorem 11, the cognitive complexities of four typical software components (Wang, 2006j) have been comparatively analyzes as summarized in Table 6. For enabling comparative analyses, data based on existing complexity

Table 5. Calibrated cognitive weights of BCSs

BCS	RTPA Notation	Description	Calibrated cognitive weight
1	$\rightarrow$	Sequence	1
2	|	Branch	3
3	|... |...	Switch	4
4	R^i	For-loop	7
5	R^*	Repeat-loop	7
6	R^*	While-loop	8
7	$\rightarrowtail$	Function call	7
8	$\circlearrowleft$	Recursion	11
9	|| or □	Parallel	15
10	↯	Interrupt	22

Table 6. Measurement of software system complexities

System	Time complexity $(C_t [OP])$	Cyclomatic complexity $(C_m [-])$	Symbolic complexity $(C_s [LOC])$	Cognitive complexity		
				Operational complexity $(C_{op} [F])$	Architectural complexity $(C_a [O])$	Cognitive complexity $(C_c [FO])$
IBS (a)	ε	1	7	13	5	65
IBS (b)	O(n)	2	8	34	5	170
MaxFinder	O(n)	2	5	115	7	805
SIS_Sort	O(m+n)	5	8	163	11	1,793

measures, such as *time, cyclomatic,* and *symbolic* (LOC) complexities, are also contrasted in Table 6.

Observing Table 6 it can be seen that the first three traditional measurements cannot actually reflect the real complexity of software systems in software design, representation, cognition, comprehension, and maintenance. It is found that (a) Although four example systems are with similar symbolic complexities, their operational and functional complexities are greatly different. This indicates that the symbolic complexity cannot be used to represent the operational or functional complexity of software systems. (b) The symbolic complexity (LOC) does not represent the throughput or the input size of problems. (c) The time complexity does not work well for a system where there are no loops and dominate operations, because in theory that all statements in linear structures are treated as zero in this measure no matter how long they are. In addition, time complexity cannot distinguish the real complexities of systems with the same asymptotic function, such as in Case 2 (IBS (b)) and Case 3 (Maxfinder). (d) The cognitive complexity is an ideal measure of software functional complexities and sizes, because it represents the real semantic complexity by integrating both the operational and architectural complexities in a coherent measure. For example, the difference between IBS(a) and IBS(b) can be successfully captured by the cognitive complexity. However, the symbolic and cyclomatic complexities cannot identify the functional differences very well.

CONCLUSIONS

This article has presented an intensive survey of the recent advances and ground breaking studies in *Cognitive informatics*, particularly its theoretical framework, denotational mathematics, and main application areas. CI has been described as a new discipline that studies the natural intelligence and internal information processing mechanisms of the brain, as well as processes involved in perception and cognition. CI is a new frontier across disciplines of computing, software engineering, cognitive sciences, neuropsychology, brain sciences, and philosophy in recent years. It has been recognized that many fundamental issues in knowledge and software engineering are based on the deeper understanding of the mechanisms of human information processing and cognitive processes.

A coherent set of theories for CI has been described in this article, such as the Information-Matter-Energy model, Layered Reference

Model of the Brain, the OAR model of information representation, Natural Intelligence vs. Artificial Intelligence, Autonomic Computing vs. imperative computing, CI laws of software, mechanisms of human perception processes, the cognitive processes of formal inferences, and the formal knowledge system. Three contemporary mathematical means have been created in CI known as the *denotational mathematics*. Within the new forms of denotational mathematical means for CI, *Concept Algebra* has been designed to deal with the new abstract mathematical structure of concepts and their representation and manipulation in learning and knowledge engineering. *Real-Time Process Algebra* has been developed as an expressive, easy-to-comprehend, and language-independent notation system, and a specification and refinement method for software system behaviors description and specification. *System Algebra* has been created to the rigorous treatment of abstract systems and their algebraic relations and operations.

A wide range of applications of CI has been identified in multidisciplinary and transdisciplinary areas, such as the architecture of future generation computers, estimation the capacity of human memory, autonomic computing, cognitive properties of information, data, knowledge, and skills in knowledge engineering, simulation of human cognitive behaviors using descriptive mathematics, agent systems, CI foundations of software engineering, deductive semantics of software, and cognitive complexity of software systems.

ACKNOWLEDGMENT

The author would like to acknowledge the Natural Science and Engineering Council of Canada (NSERC) for its support to this work. The author would like to thank the anonymous reviewers for their valuable comments and suggestions.

REFERENCES

Bell, D. A. (1953). *Information theory*. London: Pitman.

Ganter, B., & Wille, R. (1999). *Formal concept analysis* (pp. 1-5). Springer.

Hoare, C. A. R. (1985). *Communicating sequential processes*. Prentice Hall.

Jordan, D. W., & Smith, P. (1997). *Mathematical techniques: An introduction for the engineering, physical, and mathematical sciences* (2nd ed.). Oxford, UK: Oxford University Press.

Klir, G. J. (1992). *Facets of systems science*. New York: Plenum.

Milner, R. (1989). *Communication and concurrency*. Englewood Cliffs, NJ: Prentice Hall.

Quillian, M. R. (1968). Semantic memory. In M. Minsky (Ed.), *Semantic information processing*. Cambridge, MA: MIT Press.

Shannon, C. E. (1948). A mathematical theory of communication. *Bell System Technical Journal, 27*, 379-423, 623-656.

von Bertalanffy, L. (1952). *Problems of life: An evolution of modern biological and scientific thought*. London: C. A. Watts.

von Neumann, J. (1946). The principles of large-scale computing machines. Reprinted in *Annals of History of Comp., 3*(3), 263-273.

Wang, Y. (2002, August). On cognitive informatics (Keynote Speech). In *Proceedings of the 1st IEEE International Conference on Cognitive Informatics (ICCI'02)* (pp. 34-42), Calgary, Canada. IEEE CS Press.

Wang, Y. (2002). The real-time process algebra (RTPA). *The International Journal of Annals of Software Engineering, 14*, 235-274.

Wang, Y. (2003). Cognitive informatics: A new transdisciplinary research field. *Brain and Mind: A Transdisciplinary Journal of Neuroscience and Neurophilosophy, 4*(2), 115-127.

Wang, Y. (2003). On cognitive informatics. *Brain and Mind: A Transdisciplinary Journal of Neuroscience and Neurophilosophy, 4*(2), 151-167.

Wang, Y. (2003, August). Cognitive informatics models of software agent systems and autonomic computing (Keynote Speech). In *Proceedings of the International Conference on Agent-Based Technologies and Systems* (ATS'03) (p. 25), Calgary Canada. University of Calgary Press.

Wang, Y. (2003). Using process algebra to describe human and software system behaviors. *Brain and Mind: A Transdisciplinary Journal of Neuroscience and Neurophilosophy, 4*(2), 199–213.

Wang, Y. (2004, August). On autonomic computing and cognitive processes (Keynote Speech). In *Proceedings of the 3rd IEEE International Conference on Cognitive Informatics (ICCI'04)* (pp. 3-4), Victoria, Canada. IEEE CS Press.

Wang, Y. (2005, August). On the cognitive processes of human perceptions. In *Proceedings of the 4th IEEE International Conference on Cognitive Informatics (ICCI'05)* (pp. 203-211), Irvin, California. IEEE CS Press.

Wang, Y. (2005, May 1-4). On the mathematical laws of software. In *Proceedings of the 18th Canadian Conference on Electrical and Computer Engineering (CCECE'05)* (pp. 1086-1089), Saskatoon, Saskatchewan, Canada.

Wang, Y. (2005, August). The cognitive processes of abstraction and formal inferences. In *Proceedings of the 4th IEEE International Conference on Cognitive Informatics (ICCI'05)*, (pp. 18-26), Irvin, California. IEEE CS Press.

Wang, Y. (2006, May 8-10). A unified mathematical model of programs. In *Proceedings of the 19th Canadian Conference on Electrical and Computer Engineering (CCECE'06)* (pp. 2346-2349), Ottawa, Ontario, Canada.

Wang, Y. (2006, July). Cognitive informatics towards the future generation computers that think and feel. In *Proceedings of the 5th IEEE International Conference on Cognitive Informatics (ICCI'06)* (pp. 3-7), Beijing, China. IEEE CS Press.

Wang, Y. (2006, July). Cognitive informatics and contemporary mathematics for knowledge representation and manipulation (invited plenary talk). In *Proceedings of the 1st International Conference on Rough Set and Knowledge Technology (RSKT'06)* (pp. 69-78), Chongqing, China. Lecture Notes in AI (LNAI) 4062. Springer.

Wang, Y. (2006, July). On abstract systems and system algebra. In *Proceedings of the 5th IEEE International Conference on Cognitive Informatics (ICCI'06)*, (pp. 332-343), Beijing, China. IEEE CS Press.

Wang, Y. (2006, July). On concept algebra and knowledge representation. In *Proceedings of the 5th IEEE International Conference on Cognitive Informatics* (ICCI'06) (pp. 320-331), Beijing, China. IEEE CS Press.

Wang, Y. (2006). On the informatics laws and deductive semantics of software. *IEEE Transactions on Systems, Man, and Cybernetics (Part C), 36*(2), 161-171.

Wang, Y. (2006). *Software engineering foundations: A transdisciplinary and rigorous perspective* (CRC Book Series in Software Engineering 2). Boca Raton, FL: CRC Press.

Wang, Y. (2006, May). The OAR model for knowledge representation. In *Proc. of the 19th IEEE Canadian Conference on Electrical and Computer Engineering* (CCECE'06) (pp. 1696-1699), Ottawa, Canada.

Wang, Y. (2006, July). On the Big-R notation for describing iterative and recursive behaviors. In

Proceedings of the 5th IEEE International Conference on Cognitive Informatics (ICCI'06) (pp. 132-140), Beijing, China. IEEE CS Press.

Wang, Y. (2006, July). Cognitive complexity of software and its measurement. In *Proceedings of the 5th IEEE International Conference on Cognitive Informatics (ICCI'06)* (pp. 226-235), Beijing, China. IEEE CS Press.

Wang, Y., Dong, L., & Ruhe, G. (2004, July). Formal description of the cognitive process of decision making. In *Proceedings of the 3rd IEEE International Conference on Cognitive Informatics (ICCI'04)* (pp. 124-130), Victoria, Canada. IEEE CS Press.

Wang, Y., & Gafurov, D. (2003, August). The cognitive process of comprehension. In *Proceedings of the 2nd IEEE International Conference on Cognitive Informatics (ICCI'03)* (pp. 93-97). London: IEEE CS Press.

Wang, Y., Johnston, R., & Smith, M. (2002). Cognitive informatics. In *Proc. of the 1st IEEE International Conference (ICCI02)*, Calgary, Alberta, Canada. IEEE CS Press.

Wang, Y., & Kinsner, W. (2006, March). Recent advances in cognitive informatics. *IEEE Transactions on Systems, Man, and Cybernetics (Part C), 36*(2), 121-123.

Wang, Y., Liu, D., & Wang, Y. (2003). Discovering the capacity of human memory. *Brain and Mind: A Transdisciplinary Journal of Neuroscience and Neurophilosophy, 4*(2), 189-198.

Wang, Y., & Wang, Y. (2006, March). On cognitive informatics models of the brain. *IEEE Transactions on Systems, Man, and Cybernetics, 36*(2), 203-207.

Wang, Y., Wang, Y., Patel, S., & Patel, D. (2006, March). A layered reference model of the brain (LRMB). *IEEE Transactions on Systems, Man, and Cybernetics (Part C), 36*(2), 124-133.

This work was previously published in the International Journal of Cognitive Informatics and Natural Intelligence, edited by Y. Wang, Volume 1, Issue 1, pp. 1-27, copyright 2007 by IGI Publishing, formerly known as Idea Group Publishing (an imprint of IGI Global).

Section II
Development and Design Methodologies

Chapter V
Different Levels of Information Systems Designers' Forms of Thought and Potential for Human–Centered Design

Hannakaisa Isomäki
University of Lapland, Finland

ABSTRACT

This article describes a study clarifying information systems (IS) designers' conceptions of human users of IS by drawing on in-depth interviews with 20 designers. The designers' lived experiences in their work build up a continuum of levels of thought from more limited conceptions to more comprehensive ones reflecting variations of the designers' situated knowledge related to human-centred design. The resulting forms of thought indicate three different but associated levels in conceptualising users. The separatist form of thought provides designers predominantly with technical perspectives and a capability for objectifying things. The functional form of thought focuses on external task information and task productivity, nevertheless, with the help of positive emotions. The holistic form of thought provides designers with competence of human-centred information systems development (ISD). Furthermore, the author hopes that understanding the IS designers' tendencies to conceptualise human users facilitates the mutual communication between users and designers.

INTRODUCTION

As information systems (IS) increasingly pervade all aspects of everyday life, of utmost importance is how applications of IS are adjusted to human action. In particular, in current information systems development (ISD) it is essential to take into account human characteristics and behaviour; that is, to humanise IS (Sterling, 1974). In the same vein, Checkland (1981) argues that ISD should be seen as a form of enquiry within which IS designers' understandings regulate an operationalisation of their intellectual framework into a set of guidelines for investigation that require particular methods and techniques for building the system. Regarding the humanisation of IS, a notion concerning the nature of the human being is a crucial element of the intellectual framework. As a consequence, within this kind of enquiry, the way humans are taken into account in ISD is dependent on the operationalisation of the IS designers' conceptualisations of users. With respect to human-centeredness, attention should be paid to the fundamental qualities of people without any explicit or implicit domination of the other elements of IS, such as data, formal models and technical appliances, or managerial belief systems that treat humans instrumentally. This is necessary in order to conceptualise humans in their own right, and thus avoid the reduction of humans to something that exists only in relation to particular instrumental needs and purposes (cf. Buber, 1993).

Of essential importance is the nature of IS designers' insights into human characteristics and behaviour that are essential with respect to the IS-user relationship. The most crucial insight regarding human-centred design is to be able to conceptualise users as active subjects comprised of physical, cognitive, emotional, social and cultural qualities, an insight which is the prerequisite for design that promotes subsequent user acceptance and satisfaction. Yet conspicuously absent from contemporary IS literature are empirical studies investigating IS designers' conceptions of the human users, which have been studied more intensively two decades ago when the systems designers' inadequate view of the user has been stated to be one reason for the behavioural problems often experienced while implementing IS (Bostrom & Heinen, 1977; Dagwell & Weber, 1983). Also, the lack of knowledge of human needs and motivation on the part of the systems designers has been claimed to cause IS implementation failures (Hawgood, Land & Mumford, 1978). Further, Hedberg and Mumford (1975) have

defined the nature of the view of human being held by systems designers as an essential factor in the IS design process. The systems designers' view of the user is also included in some studies as one of the targets of value choices during the ISD process (Kumar & Bjørn-Andersen, 1990; Kumar & Welke, 1984) and is therefore defined as a value rather than an insight in these studies. Dagwell and Weber (1983), in their replication study, rely on Hedberg-Mumford's definition of the concept but also refer to Kling (1980). "we know very little about the perceptions that computer specialists have of the users they serve and the ways in which they translate these perceptions into concrete designs (p. 47)." Bostrom & Heinen (1977), in turn, define systems designers' assumptions of people as one of the system designers' implicit theories or frames of reference. These previous works do not take an explicit stance toward the definition of the concept "conception," and do not align the nature of conceptions in detail. For instance, from where do conceptions derive their origins, and what is the nature of those conceptions? In a more recent study, Orlikowski and Gash (1994) discuss their definition of the IS designers' views. They elaborate the concept *"frame of reference"* by comparing it to the concept *"schema"* (Neisser, 1976, pp. 9-11), *"shared cognitive structures"* or *"cognitive maps"* (Eden, 1992, pp. 261-262), *"frames"* (Goffman, 1974, pp. 10-11), *"interpretative frames"* (Bartunek & Moch, 1987, p. 484), *"thought worlds"* (Dougherty, 1992, p. 179), *"interpretative schemes"* (Giddens, 1984, pp. 29-30), *"scripts"* (Gioia, 1986, p. 50), *"paradigms"* (Kuhn, 1970, p. 43), and *"mental models"* (Argyris & Schön, 1978). They end up by defining their own meaning for the concept frames as a general concept of shared cognitive structures, not especially regarding humans.

This article describes a study which aims to clarify IS designers' conceptions of users of IS by drawing on in-depth interviews with 20 IS designers. The analytical choices carried out in this study regard IS designers' conceptions of users as experiences inherent in their lifeworlds, particularly during the different phases of ISD. The lived experiences build up conceptions that form a structure of meaning, which incorporates a continuum of levels from more limited understandings to more comprehensive notions; that is, different levels of thought reflecting variations of the designers' situated, practical knowledge. In this way the development of IS is understood as knowledge work. It is an intellectual and personal process which takes its form according to the conceptions of the performers of the process. IS designers are then applying the ISD methodologies according to their own observations and thinking (Avison & Fitzgerald, 1994; Hirschheim et al, 1995; Mathiassen, 1998). Then the most important tool for ISD, and a key resource in contemporary IT companies, is the IS designers' thought and insight (Nonaka & Takeuchi, 1995; Quinn, 1992). Particularly with respect to the humanisation of IS, designers' conceptualisations of the human users are seen as knowledge that reflects the designers' competence in humanising IS. In this way, IS designers' conceptions may be seen as intellectual capital that mirrors the know-how, practices, and accumulated expertise of practitioners within a particular profession (Kogut & Zander, 1992).

In what follows, first, the assumptions informing this study are presented by introducing the interpretative approach referred to as phenomenography. Second, the resulted forms of thought are presented and discussed. The IS designers' conceptualisations presenting their mental schemes of the human user result in three forms of thought, revealing both context-centred and human-centred understandings of what humans are. These three levels of understanding indicate that IS designers tend to conceptualise uses in terms of technology, business and work, and that seldom are users taken into account according to their human qualities. Finally, the different levels of conceptualisation are discussed in relation to human-centred ISD.

DIFFERENT LEVELS OF UNDERSTANDING

This study merges with the principles of phenomenography, which is a qualitatively oriented method of empirical research for investigating the different ways in which people experience aspects of reality (Marton, 1981; Marton & Booth, 1997). Essentially, phenomenography is about individual meaning construction, which results in a conception. The primary focus is on the structure of the meaning of conceptions, which are seen in the light of the phenomenological notion according to which person and world are inextricably related through a person's lived experience of the world (e.g., Husserl, 1995; Merleau-Ponty, 1962). Our intentionality is seen as qualitatively varying foci on the horizon of our life worlds. While experiencing the world, individuals form conceptions, including qualitative dissimilarities, which are inherent in the intertwined referential and structural aspects of an experience. Different levels are due to the way the structural aspect and the referential aspect merge with each other. Then an experience is specified by the analytical distinctions of a structural aspect and a referential aspect (Figure 1). The structural aspect denotes how a particular phenomenon is both discerned from its environment and how the phenomenon's parts relate to each other as well as to the whole phenomenon. That which surrounds the phenomenon experienced, including its contours, is its external horizon. The parts and their relationships, together with the contours of the phenomenon, are its internal horizon. The referential aspect signifies the meaning of the conception. These two aspects are dialectically intertwined and occur simultaneously within an experience. Thus, people create conceptions with respect to the structural aspect's external and internal horizons of a phenomenon

Figure 1. The analytical distinctions of an experience (Marton & Booth, 1997)

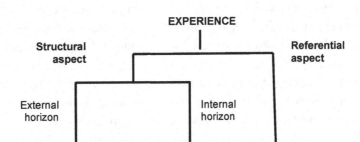

that are dialectically merged with the referential aspect of that particular phenomenon.

On the one hand, conceptions differ in terms of content, and on the other hand, they differ in terms of the extent of the form that a certain phenomenon is experienced, as a part of that phenomenon, or more as a whole. When detached parts of a phenomenon are the focus of thought instead of relating the parts meaningfully to the whole phenomenon, the meaning of the phenomenon is understood in a way that refers to a more narrow view. Respectively, when the focus of thought is more comprehensive regarding the whole meaning of a phenomenon instead of on separate parts of it or even the surroundings of the phenomenon, the more explanatory conceptions are. Further, the more explanatory power conceptions have, the better they support competent action with respect to the phenomenon in question (Sandberg, 2000). Based on these differences, conceptions form a structure of meaning, which incorporates a continuum of levels from more limited understandings to more comprehensive notions. The qualitative variation in the ways that IS designers conceptualise users reflects their different conceptions of users, and simultaneously forms different levels in the designers' understandings, reflecting variations of their situated, practical

knowledge as forms of thought. These forms of thought, in turn, suggest different levels of competence in humanising IS, because the subjective conceptualisations of IS designers refer to their intention of action (Säljö, 1994).

The interview method is accomplished with respect to phenomenographic principles. To promote multiple interpretations within individual designers, first, opening questions with varying perspectives into the different phases of ISD, such as planning, design, implementation, use and maintenance, was incorporated in the interview framework. Second, to sustain the connection between the designers' reflection and the actual work within ISD phases while the in-depth interviews aimed at achieving mutual and authentic understanding that proceeded from the interviewees' expressions. The interviews were taped at the designers' workplaces to maintain the work practice orientation and to facilitate the expression of the connection between the respondents' immediate experiences and the subsequent conception. Second, the respondents represent a variety of geographical location, age, gender, educational background and work experience. They came from various different application areas of IS practice, such as e-commerce, tele and media communications, groupware, health care systems, office automation and insurance systems.

The analysis of the interview data was carried out against the phenomenographical theory. Since phenomenography does not offer grounds for defining the content of conceptions within data, a coding paradigm was developed from the data in order to facilitate the identification and categorisation of meanings in the data (Glaser & Strauss, 1967; Tesch, 1990; Strauss & Corbin, 1990). The development of the coding paradigm was based on the phenomenographical principle regarding the intentionality of conceptions. Conceptions are context-dependent and every experience is described in content-loaded terminology (Säljö, 1994,). That is, the descriptions are carried out in terms of the nature of the situational experiences in question. Consequently, the meanings are to be found in accordance with the underlying assumptions concerning the intentional nature of ISD. In addition, since it is assumed in phenomenography that the meanings of the respondents' mental acts exist in the data and are constitutive of the data (Walsh, 1994), the way meanings are understood in this study should also be in accordance with the types of intentionality existing in the data. Thus, the coding paradigm was finalised by bracketing away any preconceived ideas of what the IS designers' views might be like (Francis, 1993), and letting the analysis be informed by the underlying assumptions of intentionality in ISD.

First, the data includes utterances that describe various actions and objectives concerning ISD. These expressions indicate intentionality as defined by Hirschheim et al. (1995, p. 16). They state that "IS development is intentional, to the extent it reflects a planned change. It is based on developers' intentions to change object systems towards desirable ends", and go on to say that (1995, p. 17) "intentions in systems development are expressed by objectives. These are related to general value-orientations and represent what 'one ought to do' or 'what is good'." From this it can be concluded, in the first place, that intentionality in

ISD is expressed by intentional action. That is to say, IS designers' descriptions of the actions and means they are involved with when developing an IS reveal the meanings they give to the phenomena they deal with concerning ISD. This notion is in accordance with the principle of contextuality in phenomenography, which denotes that people's conceptualisations are not detachable, either from their context or the content of the task at hand. This stance also reinforces the interpretative nature of phenomenographical analysis in that the researcher must see the designers' action as inherently meaningful (cf. Schwandt, 2000). In the second place, as Hirschheim et al. (1995) point out, intentions are expressed by objectives of ISD. Consequently, it is an appropriate way to define that the way the IS designers understand the human user of an IS is revealed through descriptions in which the respondents' focus of reflection is on the objectives of ISD. That is to say, in addition to the actions and means the designers refer to, the IS designers' intentions to change object systems toward desirable ends reveal the meanings they give to the phenomena they deal with concerning ISD. These desirable ends or objectives represent the things that are regarded most important in ISD. In this way, the IS designers' descriptions of action, means and objectives also implicitly indicate value orientations included in the process of ISD. Therefore, the described actions and objectives represent the things that are regarded important, and thus reveal the referential aspect in terms of intentionality as an implied value orientation. This means that the initial referential aspects of conceptions may be found in utterances in which the designers refer to their way and means of building systems and the objectives of their actions.

Second, the data includes descriptions in which the respondents' thoughts are attached to human objects. These descriptions of people indicated human features and also value orientations toward people. Often these descriptions also included expressions which indicated emotionally toned reactions. These kinds of expressions within the data indicate intentionality that is in accordance with Uljens (1991), who states that the process of qualitative individuation of a mental act has been done when an object and a psychological mode, referred to as an attitude, is shown. In other words, how a particular object of thought is experienced denotes the respondents' attitudes toward the phenomenon that is being reflected on. In brief, the inherent meaning of an utterance may be seen as the correlation between the what- and how-aspects in that they are not detachable from each other, but are interrelated in a particular logical way, indicating what a particular phenomenon is, in what it is revealed, and what kind of values and attitudes are related to it. As described above, the search for the meanings in the data, data analysis, was initiated by establishing a coding paradigm, which suggests that the meanings in the data are found in utterances in which the designers refer to their actions, means, and objectives concerning ISD, as well as to human characteristics.

The subsequent analysis procedures followed the idea, firstly, of iterating between the meaning (referential aspect) of single statements, their surrounding statements, and the data as a whole, and second, iterating between the features that reveal different levels in these meanings (structural aspect). The analysis appreciates the phenomenological notion of "Lebenswelt" in that the continuum of levels from more limited forms of thought to more comprehensive understandings reflects associative connections within the designers' conceptions rather than direct, law-like logical relations between them (cf. Husserl, 1995). The analysis revealed the designers' conceptions as different levels of understanding, which appear as the separatist, functional, and holistic forms of thought. These forms of thought reveal three different levels of understandings incorporating both context-centred and human-centred notions. In the descriptions associated with the context-centred conceptions, the designers' focus of reflection is on

technology, work, and business. The human-centred conceptions deal with knowledge, emotions, and the designers' selves. The following description delineates the specific contents of the conceptions as parts of the three forms of thought by highlighting some exemplary conceptions.

THE SEPARATIST FORM OF THOUGHT

The most partial way in which the IS designers conceptualise humans is through the separatist form of thought. It demonstrates how IS designers see humans within the affordances and constraints of contemporary IS and their development as separated from fluid and coherent interactions. Within this form of thought, the user is positioned outside the IS designers' awareness through objectivist conceptualisations. An objectivist pattern is evident in the context-centred separatist conceptions, which reflect understandings according to which reality exists independent of humans and can thus be understood independent of humans (cf. Lakoff, 1987; Orlikowski & Baroudi, 1991). In this case, when discussing human-centred issues of ISD, the designers' focus of reflection is directed to technology, job titles, and market mechanisms. For example, within the conception of *"the human being displaced by technology"* IS designers refer to humans in terms of technology:

R: What are these requirements and wishes like? Could you tell me more about them?
D16: Well, because it is a question of – let's say — a feedback channel that our company offers as a product to its clients, it means that if the client purchases, for instance, a datanet-based customer network, they have datanet and router accesses through which they operate between their networks and use the whole telecommunication network. Then there are a lot of this kind of usability issues, response times and load percentages, or in a way, how it (telecommunication network) sort

of behaves, what happens there.

In the above interview extract, the designer considers the customers' needs as a piece of software — "a feedback channel" — and the main point that emerges is how this item of software works with the functions of a telecommunications network. The designer's train of thought becomes focussed on technology instead of human-centred issues and needs, such as how the software is built in regard to the humans that will be using it. In the same vein, within the conception of *"the human being as a market"* the designers make use of expressions which show their intention is to build products that are profitable and, therefore easy to sell. Yet they do not base their intentions upon human features, such as spontaneous and mood-related online behaviour that could be a prerequisite for selling their products (e.g., Hoffman & Novak, 1996; Bellman et al, 1999):

D5: It is more reasonable to develop a mass product which has a lot of users. The point here is that then it can be copied and sold.

In contrast to notions that emphasise understanding human consumption behaviour, the IS designers adhere to the idea that humans are simply a featureless mass of consumers who form a market for IT products. Because the above conception does not incorporate any human characteristics, but refers to a mass market, it is thereby making a clear distinction between the market and the features of the people assumed to form that market. For this reason, the conception appears as objectivist. This conception also implies a predisposition according to which the current development of IS as an industry is that of a rational institution which produces mass culture by reducing humans to members of a mass (cf. Slater, 1997). Furthermore, humans become separated attitudinally from IS and their development due to a presumed lack of technological knowledge,

and thus are forced to encounter disparaging attitudes. The separatist human-centred conception of *"the technology-illiterate human bein'"* produces accounts according to which the most distinct characteristic of humans is that they are ignorant of technology, specifically computers, software and ISD methodologies. In particular, this illiteracy is seen as a contrast to the literacy of the IS designers:

R: Have you ever wondered why people behave in that way — that they cannot say what they want from the system?
D17: I think that it's because they don't know how these [IS] are defined. If one doesn't know these methods, one can't do it. That is the biggest reason, not that they aren't willing to say what they want but they don't have the know-how.

Beath and Orlikowski (1994) report similar findings in their analysis of a relatively new representative of the ISD methodologies' rationalist tradition, information engineering (IE). According to the analysis, the IE text creates and sustains both implicitly and explicitly a dichotomy between users and IS designers by characterising the users as technologically ignorant in regard to the use of technology. When operationalised, these characterisations are likely to generate nonviable and unsatisfactory interactions between users and IS designers. It seems also that the designers do not consider the weaknesses in users' knowledge and thought as an issue that deserves to be taken into account in design. However, when humans are included in the design considerations, the weaknesses in people's thinking should be understood as natural flaws in human cognitive behaviour that can be appropriately guided, or even prevented by adequate design (Kirs, Pflughoeft, & Kroeck, 2001; Norman, 1989; Robillard, 1999). The idea then is that designers should have awareness of and be able to recognise these erroneous tendencies in users in order to carry out IS planning and design with the express aim of preventing people from committing faulty actions during computer use, rather than conceptualising users as technologically ignorant.

Moreover, negative emotions and physical stress symptoms have the effect of separating humans from IS. The conception of *"the computer anguished human being"* reveals views acknowledging that IS cause negative emotional arousal in users. These reactions are manifested as negative attitudes, resistance, fear and discomfort in situations where people are confronted by plans for the future use of computers or in situations in which individuals are using computers:

R: How in your mind do people learn to use software?
D6: ... I have also met users who have so much fear of the user interface that they don't dare to explore or try anything, they just do what is familiar and safe.

These conceptualisations are consistent with statements concerning the widespread existence of technophobia (Brosnan, 1998a). Besides being an obviously unpleasant and undesired experience, negative emotions, such as anxiety and fear, make people's behaviour withdrawn and elusive by narrowing their action (Fredrickson & Branigan, 2001), as well as decreasing the quality of their performance (Brosnan, 1998b).

In brief, within the separatist form of thought, the human being becomes separated from viable interactions with both the IS designers themselves and IS. This is due to a tendency to an objectivist conceptualisation, which blurs the designers' thought to such an extent that people are no longer recognised as humans. The overall narrative style of this form of thought is reminiscent of the style of a nomothetic science reflecting technical, strategic views aiming at controlling the IS-related social system with the technical system (cf. Deetz, 1996). Further, people become separated from the

development of IS due to disparaging attitudes inherent in designers' assumptions that users are technologically ignorant. Moreover, this form of thought brings to the fore human characteristics, such as negative emotions, which are seen as an obstacle to a viable IS-user relationship.

THE FUNCTIONAL FORM OF THOUGHT

The functional form of thought consists of conceptualisations in which humans are seen to act in an insubstantial manner, adapting to the external functions of technology, work tasks and the way the IS designers themselves use computers. Within this adaptive response, positive emotions are required in order to create and sustain viable interactions with IS. In this way, the IS-user relationship is seen as functional: the action of people is seen as determined by their external environment, and the role of human emotion is to facilitate this process. The different conceptions that build up this form of thought reveal a behaviourist understanding of the human being.

For instance, the conception of *"the invisible human being"* denotes humans as using IS in an insubstantial manner. Typical of this conception is the belief that there is a user who uses an IS. Yet the user is not characterised further but is assumed just to use the system:

R: If you think of a situation where you are creating an application, who do you think you're making it to?
D16: Hm.....
R: Do you think of certain types of people or how does it show that you are making it for people?
D16: I don't think of particular types of people but I think that the human being is in some sense always a part of the system. If it is a system that has a user interface so there must be somebody who uses it. Even if it is a system that runs by

timer initiation, there must be a user interface, too, for setting the timer parameters in the system, so there must be somebody to use it, too. To my mind there is always someone using the systems, they (systems) are not fully automated.

A functioning relation between people and IS is thus acknowledged, but this does not include any features originating from the mental, social or cultural human modes of being. In other words, humans and their behaviour are understood as purely physical-organic responses to technology, as established in the tenets of Skinnerian behaviourism (Skinner, 1938, 1991). Similarly, the IS designers' conception of *"the human being behind the process of work"* denotes humans in conformity with behaviourist thinking. Within this conception individuals are seen in terms of their work tasks or organisational work processes. Characteristic of these conceptualisations is that the people performing the tasks are not portrayed further, but are assumed merely to use IS according to the external task flows:

R: How would you define users' needs?
D8: They consist of the utilising organisation's needs at all levels, beginning with what the people need in order to continually do their work tasks, and ending with the things that the organisation expects from the system, what can be abstracted from the process and be used to develop and control action.

Here, human action is seen as a series of direct responses to external work tasks issued to people. Zuboff's (1988) well-known distinction between "automating work" and "informating work" highlights the difference between implied behaviourist and nonbehaviourist assumptions concerning human action in computerised work (pp. 9-10). Automating work refers to deploying technology in ways that increase the self-acting and self-regulating capacities of technical systems, which are expected to minimise human intervention. Because human intervention is minimised and machines perform the work tasks, interactions between individuals and computers become determined by the structure and sequence of computerised workflows to which, in turn, humans are supposed to respond. Zuboff's term of automating work, thus, implies a behaviourist assumption of humans and their behaviour.

Quite the opposite is suggested by the term informating work, which adds to the automating view of work in that information technology can be used to automate, but at the same time, it has the ability to translate the automated activities into a form that renders work processes, objects, events and behaviours visible, knowable and sharable for people (Zuboff, 1988). That is to say, within the interaction of humans and computers, people actively observe, interpret and share the information which is mediated to them by IS. They do not just respond like marionettes to the information offered by IS, but actively construct their own conceptions of the computer-mediated tasks they are given and act according to their own interpretations of the particular situation. Thus, in order to accomplish fluid and coherent interaction designs between humans and computers in regard to particular tasks, the users' mental models, especially those concerning the tasks submitted to them, should also be designed (Norman, 1989; Preece, 1994).

Also typical of the functionalist form of thought is that the role of human emotion is to facilitate people's adaptation to technology. Within the conception of *"The techno-enthusiast human being"* the designers depict positive emotions, such as enthusiasm, as essential features in humans:

R: Do you think there are common features in those people for whom you have built systems?
D17: Well, at least during very recent years, it has been enthusiasm.

In particular, positive emotional reactions

in people are seen to be induced by technology. Positive feelings are especially seen as a prerequisite for the successful use of IS. These conceptualisations reveal a functional understanding of positive emotions. Whereas negative emotions are associated with specific tendencies, such as an urge to escape or to avoid disquieting things, positive emotions seem to spark changes in cognitive activity in addition to producing behavioural tendencies (Fredrickson & Branigan, 2001). Therefore, the IS designers' accounts of positive emotions as a prerequisite for the use of computers imply an understanding of the role of human emotional features in promoting successful functioning.

To sum up, within the functional form of thought humans and their behaviour are understood from a behaviourist stance, which renders human substance only as physical and organic by nature, denoting that the movements of people can be explained by the laws of mechanics (Wilenius, 1978). However, this form of thought adds to the previous separatist way of thinking in so far as humans are actually depicted as performing tasks with computers, whereas in the separatist form of thought the conceptualisations either totally omit human features or humans are seen as unable to use computers. In addition, the human emotional feature that is recognised in this form of thought appears as positive — even though functional — in nature. This way of thinking acknowledges humans as users, and therefore is more developed than the previous separatist form of thought.

THE HOLISTIC FORM OF THOUGHT

The most developed form of thought by which the IS designers conceptualise humans as users of IS is the one characterised as holistic. Its holistic quality is revealed in several ways. First, unlike the preceding forms of thought, the designers recognise a number of human characteristics. Second, these observed human features are often seen to coexist or intertwine with each other. Third, these conceptualisations suggest that the relationship between users and designers, as well as the IS-user relation, is a reciprocal process, including characteristics typical of human behaviour.

To begin with, the conception of *"the human being reflected in technology"* reveals the specific goal of constructing computer interfaces with human-like features: the interaction between people and computers is then envisaged as enriched with dialogues conveying both the rational and emotional meanings of the information in question (e.g., Nakazawa, Mukai, Watanuki & Miyoshi, 2001). Respectively, the depictions of various human features in technology reveal understandings suggesting human features built into technology render the interaction between users and IS as resembling the interplay of cognitive, emotional and social aspects that occur between humans:

R: What kind of user interface do you think that people would want to use?
D4: I strongly believe that 3D interfaces are coming. They could offer kind of human-like facial features as agents, which would bring a human sense to the systems. The third dimension could also be utilised so that interfaces become tangible and accessible.

Further, the context-centred conception of *"the human being as an organisational learner,"* which highlights people as organisations which learn about their own work processes, refers indirectly to learning, which stresses both cognitive and social human features. Collective cognitive features are referred to as an organisation's ability to form new insights into its work processes and to guide the deployment of IS effectively (Robey, Boudreau & Rose, 2000). A social dimension is also implied when it is assumed that people learn as an organisation:

D8: Needs are prone to change rapidly, especially after the implementation of the system, because they teach an organisation a lot about itself, and an organisation's self-knowledge increases and usually needs change in a more clever direction. Then there very quickly happens a sort of 'learning leap', which is often experienced as if the system is not valid at all although it is a question of the organisation's increased knowledge of its own activity.

Within the conception of *"the knowledge sharing human being"* the designers open up their view of learning by specifying mutual understanding between users and designers as essential. *"It is important to be able to explain things so that we understand each other."* The capability of taking another's perspectives into account form the core of this conception, which highlights knowledge sharing as a particularly important instance within the processes of organisational learning. Knowledge sharing is the link between individual and group learning, and signifies the expansion of individuals' cognitive maps into shared understandings (Crossan, Lane & White, 1999). In particular, the ability to take the perspective of others into account is an indispensable prerequisite for knowledge sharing (Boland & Tenkasi, 1995). Buber (1993) ascertains that, in order to be able to take others' perspectives into account fully, one has to treat others as equal human beings and respect the current circumstances of others. In these kinds of relationships positive emothional features, such as care and joy, need to be acknowledged and combined with cognitive and social abilities (Fredrickson & Branigan, 2001)

Moreover, the conception of *"the emotionally coping human being"* refers to an ability to regulate in a successful way both negative and positive subjective feelings in computerised situations. In this way, the designers see emotional coping in the light of positive outcomes (cf. Folkman & Moskowitz, 2000, pp.648-649):

D8: ... a skilful user always has such peace of

mind and attitude. She or he kind of has a better tolerance for stress, and an ability to cope with contradictions in a better way than others. For some reason this kind of attitude leads to a particular resourcefulness and an ability to utilise the system in a more natural way, compared to a person who has some negative emotional features, fear or hostility towards the system, and who then ends up having difficulties with the system due to her/his heavy attitude.

A cognitive aspect is seen as inherent in emotional coping in that it requires that individuals' recognise their different emotional experiences. However, in addition to these internal cognitive-affective features, emotion regulation refers to the external social and cultural factors that redirect, control, and shape emotional arousal in such a way that an individual is able to act adaptively in emotionally activating situations (Pulkkinen, 1996). While ISD is often seen as a stressful process which requires an ability to endure changing emotional experiences, such as interest and frustration (Newman & Noble, 1990) in recurrent situations of failure and subsequent success (Robey & Newman, 1996), it is understandable that the designers regard people who are able to regulate their emotions successfully as skilful.

Briefly, the holistic form of thought is comprised of conceptualisations that regard humans as cognitive, emotional, social and cultural creatures. The conceptions belonging to this form of thought embody similar basic human modes of being, as shown above. However, the aforementioned basic modes of being emerge in these conceptions as different behavioural affordances. The cognitive mode of being is seen as intellect, reasoning, learning, reflection, understanding and awareness of something. Similarly, the emotional mode of being is conceptualised as empathy, stress, tranquillity, commitment, contentment and a feeling of mastery. Further, the social mode of being is referred to as a need for communication, group learning, interpersonal power and connection, as well as knowledge sharing. These behavioural affordances are seen as incorporated in technology, appearing between humans, or within the interaction of humans and IS.

THE FORMS OF THOUGHT IN ISD

The IS designers' forms of thought revealed in the results of this study are regarded as important tools for ISD, and are seen to have implications for the ways that humans are taken into account as users within the different situations of ISD. These different situations refer to the phases of ISD such as planning, design, implementation, use and maintenance. The phases are cyclical and intertwining (e.g., Beynon-Davies, Carne, Mackay, & Tudhope, 1999). Planning refers to initiation and requirements analysis actions, including client contacts and definition of user requirements. During this phase the greatest degree of interaction occurs between users and designers (Newman & Noble, 1990). In order to accomplish requirements analysis, the designers should understand many human issues in addition to technical ones (Holtzblatt & Beyer, 1995). Design denotes procedures where requirements are refined and turned into specifications and finally software. Then technical reliability and maintainability of the system, user interface's applicability for the intended purpose of the system, as well as the aesthetical appearance of the system, are designed (Smith, 1997). Winograd (1995) emphasises that, in addition to technical requirements, the properties of a user interface should meet with the social, cognitive and aesthetic needs of people. Especially within new ubiquitous technological environments, the design of IS-user relationship should focus, in addition to social and cultural features, on individuals' perceptual, cognitive and emotional space (Stephanidis, 2001).

How would the designers then perform according to their forms of thought? The strength of the designers utilising a separatist form of thought

would be technical knowledge, especially the ability to fluently conceptualise issues of design in accordance with objective definitions, a skill that is needed in creating formal specifications. However, the validity of objectifying design issues is dependent on the focus of such definitions. From a human-centred perspective, valid definitions would require being theoretically sensitive to human activity and deriving second-order conceptions from that activity (see Walsham, 1995), rather than creating objectivist conceptualisations, which overlook humans and their behaviour. An obvious disutility would be a tendency to treat users as technologically ignorant, which implies incompetence in social relationships with users.

The designers embracing the functional form of thought possess technical knowledge, and value such knowledge in users. They tend to focus on formal job descriptions, external work tasks and individuals' task productivity. A deficit from a human-centred perspective would be the tendency to overlook human issues and to focus instead on the functional purposes of IS; that is, external task information regarding an organizations' process improvements. Often such conceptualisations are regarded to yield Tayloristic designs, which underestimate the social context. However, they possess competence in functional and technical systems design. Their strength would be increased social competence to fulfil the demand for mutual understanding, which is regarded of utmost importance in ISD (cf. Heng, Traut, & Fischer, 1999).

The designers building upon the holistic form of thought emphasise clients' satisfaction, which ensures sustainable customer relationships and regard mutual understanding during ISD as essential between users and designers. Their strength would be increased social competence fulfil the demand for mutual understanding, which is regarded of utmost importance in ISD (e.g., Klein & Hirschheim, 1993; Lyytinen & Ngwenyama, 1992). It seems also likely that they have competence in IS planning which aims at the improvement of organisational processes and are identified as functional, such as sales and purchasing processes, and emphasise mutual understanding. Also, they understand how to maintain customership instead of just visioning economic gains or focusing on people's task productivity. Besides possessing technical competence, these holistic designers would be able to consolidate definitions of formal and external work tasks into human issues. A particularly significant capability would be to understand the process of organisational learning, which is essential in order to adjust the evolving requirements during the process of ISD. Moreover, they value balanced emotional behaviour, and thus intuitively grasp the possible dangers of relying on superfluous emotional behaviour.

With respect to the humanisation of IS, a holistic conception is required in ISD. It is then assumed that the human being is actualised in intertwined physical, cognitive, emotional, social and cultural qualities, and that these qualities are fundamentally different. Without the simultaneous existence of all of the qualities, it is not possible to consider a creature as a human. Yet the qualities cannot be reduced from one quality to another, but rather need to be understood as a whole (Rauhala, 1983). Considering the human being as an actor, as a user of an IS, the whole of a human being is understood as an active subject adjoining to IS. Then the IS-user relationship consists of human action involving explicit and tacit affordances that emerge dynamically in the interaction between humans and IS. In other words, the static characteristics of humans and technology take on a new form within their intertwining activity, which is shaped according to the affordances that, on the one hand, the human substance embodies, and which, on the other hand, the properties of IS support or ignore. Consequently, understanding humans and their behaviour as users of IS requires insight into these emerging human experiences appearing within the affordances and constraints of contemporary IS and their development. Especially at present when the IS are no longer merely tools for personal and professional instrumental productivity, but also (re)constituting and mediating different social structures and practices (e.g., Orlikowski, 1992; Orlikowski, 2000), IS acts as social spaces that are important growing social and cultural reference points for users and, thus also for IS designers. Design that takes into account the consequences of the form and functions of IS to usersl social qualities, such as self-identity, is indeed and necessity if contemporary IS development aims at high-quality and usable systems (Greenhill & Isomäki, 2005).

In summary, the resulting forms of thought indicate three different but associated levels of intellectual competence in conceptualising humans as users of IS. The separatist form of thought provides designers predominantly with technical perspectives and a capability for objectifying things. However, it is worth noticing that the validity of objectifying design issues is dependent on the focus of such definitions. From a human-centred perspective, valid definitions would require being theoretically sensitive to human activity and deriving abstracted conceptions from that activity rather than creating objectivist conceptualisations, which overlook humans and their behaviour. The functional form of thought focuses on external task information and task productivity, nevertheless, with the help of positive emotions. The holistic form of thought provides designers with competence of human-centred ISD, even though all the aspects of the richness of the human condition are not revealed. It seems the designers are intellectually more oriented toward designing IS for objectified, streamlined organisational processes consisting of external work tasks, and that this orientation challenges the human-centred orientations.

REFERENCES

Avison, D.E., & Fitzgerald, G. (1994). Information systems development. In W. Currie & R. Galliers (Eds.), *Rethinking management information systems: An interdisciplinary perspective* (pp. 250-278). Oxford: Oxford University Press.

Beath, C.M., & Orlikowski, W. (1994). The contradictory structure of systems development methodologies: Deconstructing the IS-user relationship in information engineering. *Information Systems Research, 5*(4), 350-377.

Bellman, S., Lohse, G.L., & Jordan, E.J. (1999). Predictors of online buying behavior. *Communications of the ACM, 42*(12), 32-38.

Beynon-Davies, P., Carne, C., Mackay, H., & Tudhope, D. (1999). Rapid application development (RAD): An empirical review. *European Journal of Information Systems, 8*, 211-223.

Boland, R.J., & Tenkasi, R.V. (1995). Perspective making and perspective taking in communities of knowing. *Organization Science, 6*(4), 350-372.

Bostrom, R.P., & Heinen, J.S. (1977). MIS problems and failures: A socio-technical perspective. Part I: The causes. *MIS Quarterly, 1*(3), 17-32.

Brosnan, M. (1998a). *Technophobia. The psychological impact of information technology.* London: Routledge.

Brosnan, M. (1998b). The impact of computer anxiety and self-efficacy upon performance. *Journal of Computer Assisted Learning, 14*, 223-234.

Buber, M. (1993). *Sinä ja minä* [I and Thou]. Juva: WSOY.

Checkland, P. (1981). *Systems thinking, systems practice.* Chichester: Wiley.

Cotterman, W.W., & Kumar, K. (1989). User cube: A taxonomy of end users. *Communications of the ACM, 32*(11), 1313-1320.

Crossan, M.M., Lane, H.W., & White, R.E. (1999). An organizational learning framework: From intuition to institution. *Academy of Management Review, 24*(3), 522-537.

Dagwell, R., & Weber, R. (1983). System designers' user models: A comparative study and methodological critique. *Communications of the ACM, 26*(11), 987-997.

Deetz, S. (1996). Describing differences in approaches to organization science: Rethinking Burrell and Morgan and their legacy. *Organization Science, 7*(2), 191-207.

Folkman, S., & Moskowitz, J.T. (2000). Positive affect and the other side of coping. *American Psychologist, 55*(6), 647-654.

Francis, H. (1993). Advancing phenomenography: Questions of method. *Nordisk Pedagogik, 13*, 68-75.

Fredrickson, B.L., & Branigan, C. (2001). Positive emotions. In T. Mayne & G. Bonanno (Eds.), *Emotions: Current issues and future directions* (pp. 123-151). New York: Guilford Press.

Glaser, B.G., & Strauss, A.L. (1967). *The discovery of grounded theory. Strategies for qualitative research.* London: Weidenfeld and Nicolson.

Greenhill, A., & Isomäki, H. (2005). Incorporating self into Web information system design. In A. Pirhonen, H. Isomäki, C. Roast, & P. Saariluoma (Eds.), *Future interaction design* (pp. 52-66). London: Springer-Verlag.

Hawgood, L., Land, F., & Mumford, E. (1978). A participative approach to forward planning and systems change. In G. Bracchi, & P.C. Lockermann (Eds.), *Information systems methodology. Proceedings of the 2ⁿᵈ Conference of the European Cooperation in Informatics* (pp. 39-61), Venice, Italy. Springer-Verlag.

Hedberg, B., & Mumford, E. (1975). The design of computer systems: Man's vision of man as an integral part of the system design process. In E. Mumford, & H. Sackman (Eds.), *Human choice and computers* (pp. 31-59). Amsterdam: North Holland.

Heng, M.S.H., Traut, E.M., & Fischer, S.J. (1999). Organisational champions of IT innovation. *Accounting, Management and Information Technology, 9*(3), 193-222.

Hirschheim, R., & Klein, H.K. (1989). Four paradigms of information systems development. *Communications of the ACM, 32*(10), 1199-1216.

Hirschheim, R., Klein, H.K., & Lyytinen, K. (1995). *Information systems development and data modeling. Conceptual and philosophical foundations.* Cambridge University Press.

Hoffman, D.L., & Novak, T.P. (1996). Marketing in hypermedia computer-mediated environments: conceptual foundations. *Journal of Marketing, 60*(3), 50-68.

Holtzblatt, K., & Beyer, H.R. (1995). Requirements gathering: The human factor. Communications of the ACM 38(5), 31-32.

Husserl, E. (1995). Fenomenologian idea. Viisi luentoa [The phenomenological idea. Five lectures] (Himanka, Hämäläinen & Sivenius, Trans.). Helsinki: Loki-kirjat.

Kirs, P.J., Pflughoeft, K., & Kroeck, G. (2001). A process model cognitive biasing effects in information systems development and usage. *Information & Management, 38*, 153-165.

Klein, H.K., & Hirschheim, R.A. (1993). The application of neo-humanist principles in information systems development. In D.E. Avison, T.E. Kendall, & J.J. DeGross (Eds.), *Human, organizational, and social dimensions of information systems development* (pp. 263-280). Amsterdam: Elsevier.

Kling, R. (1977). The Organizational Context of User-Centered Software Designs. MIS Quarterly 1(4), 41-52.

Kogut, B., & Zander, U. (1992). Knowledge of the firm, combinative capabilities and the replication of technology. *Organization Science, 3*(5), 383-397.

Kumar, K., & Bjørn-Andersen, N. (1990). A cross-cultural comparison of IS designer values. *Communications of the ACM, 33*(5), 528-538.

Kumar, K., & Welke, J. (1984). Implementation failure and system developer values: Assumptions, truisms and empirical evidence. In *Proceedings of the 5th International Conference on Information Systems* (pp. 1-12), Tucson, AZ.

Lakoff, G. (1987). *Women, fire and dangerous things.* University of Chicago Press.

Marton, F. (1981). Phenomenography: Describing conceptions of the world around us. *Instructional Science, 10*, 177-200.

Marton, F., & Booth, S. (1997). *Learning and awareness.* Mahwah, NJ: Lawrence Erlbaum.

Mathiassen, L. 1998. Reflective systems development. *Scandinavian Journal of Information Systems, 10*(1/2), 67-118.

Merleau-Ponty, M. (1962). *Phenomenology of perception.* London: Routledge.

Nakazawa, M., Mukai, T., Watanuki, K., & Miyoshi, H. (2001). Anthropomorphic agent and multimodal interface for nonverbal communication. In N. Avouris, & N. Fakotakis (Eds.), *Advances in human-computer interaction I. Proceedings of the PC HCI 2001* (pp. 360-365), Athens, Greece.

Newman, M., & Noble, F. (1990). User involvement as an interaction process: A case study. *Information Systems Research, 1*(1), 89-110.

Nonaka, I., & Takeuchi, H. (1995). *The knowledge-creating company: How Japanese companies create the dynamics of innovation.* Oxford University Press.

Norman, D.A. (1989). *Miten avata mahdottomia ovia? Tuotesuunnittelun salakarit* [The psychology of everyday things]. Jyväskylä: Gummerus.

Orlikowski, W.J. (1992). The duality of technology: Rethinking the concept of technology in organizations. *Organization Science, 3*(3), 398-427.

Orlikowski W.J. (2000). Using technology and constituting structures: A practice lens for studying technology in organizations. *Organization Science, 11*(4), 404-428.

Orlikowski, W.J., & Baroudi, J.J. (1991). Studying information technology in organizations: Research approaches and assumptions. *Information Systems Research, 2*(1), 1-28.

Orlikowski, W.J., & Gash, D.C. (1994). Technological frames: Making sense of information technology in organizations. *ACM Transactions on Information Systems, 12*(2), 174-207.

Preece, J. (1994). *Human-computer interaction.* Harlow, UK: Addison-Wesley.

Pulkkinen, L. (1996). Female and male personality styles: A typological and developmental analysis. *Journal of Personality and Social Psychology, 70*(6), 1288-1306.

Quinn, J.B. (1992). The intelligent enterprise: A new paradigm. *Academy of Management Executive, 6*(4), 48-63.

Rauhala, L. (1983). *Ihmiskäsitys ihmistyössä* [The conception of the human being in human work]. Helsinki: Gaudeamus.

Robey, D., Boudreau, M.C., & Rose, G.M. (2000). Information technology and organizational learning: A review and assessment of research. *Accounting, Management & Information Technology, 10*(1), 125-155.

Robey, D., & Newman, M. (1996). Sequential patterns in information systems development: An application of a social process model. *ACM Transactions of information systems, 14*(1), 30-63.

Robillard, P.N. (1999). The role of knowledge in software development. *Communications of the ACM, 42*(1), 87-92.

Säljö, R. (1994). Minding action. Conceiving the world vs. participating in cultural practices. *Nordisk Pedagogik, 14*, 71-80.

Sandberg, J., (2000). Understanding human competence at work: An interprettive approach, *Academy of Management Journal* 43(1), 9-25.

Schwandt, T., (2000). Three epistemological stances for qualitative inquiry. Interpretivism, hermeneutics, and social constructionism. In Denzin, N.K. &Y.S. Lincoln (Eds.) The handbook of qualitative research (2nd ed.). Thousand Oaks, CA: Sage, 189-213.

Skinner, B.F. (1991). The behavior of organisms: An experimental analysis. Acton, MA: Copley. Originally published in 1938.

Slater, D. (1997). *Consumer culture and modernity.* Malden, MA: Blackwell.

Smith, A. (1997). *Human computer factors: A study of users and information systems.* London: McGraw-Hill.

Stephanidis, C. (2001). Human-computer interaction in the age of the disappearing computer. In N. Avouris, & N. Fakotakis (Eds.), *Advances in human-computer interaction I. Proceedings of the PC HCI 2001* (pp. 15-22), Athens, Greece.

Sterling, T.D. (1974). Guidelines for humanizing computerized information systems: A report from Stanley House. *Communications of the ACM, 17*(11), 609-613.

Strauss, A., & Corbin, J. (1990). *Basics of qualitative research: Grounded theory procedures and techniques.* Newbury Park, CA: Sage Publications.

Tesch, R. (1990). *Qualitative research: Analysis types and software tools.* New York: Falmer Press.

Uljens, M. (1991). Phenomenography: A qualitative approach in educational research. In L. Syrjälä, & J. Merenheimo (Eds.), *Kasvatustutkimuksen laadullisia lähestymistapoja.* Oulun yliopiston kasvatustieteiden tiedekunnan opetusmonisteita ja selosteita 39 (pp. 80–107).

Walsh, E. (1994). Phenomenographic analysis of interview transcripts. In J.A. Bowden, & E. Walsh (Eds.), *Phenomenographic research: Variations in method* (pp. 17-30). The Warburton

Symposium. Melbourne: The Royal Melbourne Institute of Technology.

Walsham, G. (1995). Interpretive case studies in IS research: Nature and method. *European Journal of Information Systems, 4*(2), 74-81.

Wilenius, R. (1978). *Ihminen, luonto ja tekniikka* [The human being, nature and technology]. Jyväskylä: Gummerus.

Winograd, T. (1995). From programming environments to environments for designing. *Communications of ACM, 38*(6), 65-74.

Zuboff, S. (1988). *In the age of the smart machine: The future of work and power.* New York: Basic Books.

This work was previously published in the International Journal of Technology and Human Interaction, edited by B. C. Stahl, Volume 3, Issue 1, pp. 30-48, copyright 2007 by IGI Publishing, formerly known as Idea Group Publishing (an imprint of IGI Global).

Chapter VI
A Qualitative Study in User's Information–Seeking Behaviors on Web Sites:
A User–Centered Approach to Web Site Development

Napawan Sawasdichai
King Mongkut's Institute of Technology, Ladkrabang, Thailand

ABSTRACT

This chapter introduces a qualitative study of user's information-seeking tasks on Web-based media, by investigating user's cognitive behaviors when they are searching for particular information on various kinds of Web sites. The experiment, which is a major part of the recently completed doctoral research at the Institute of Design-IIT, particularly studies cognitive factors including user goals and modes of searching in order to investigate if these factors significantly affect users' information-seeking behaviors. The main objective is to identify the corresponding impact of these factors on their needs and behaviors in relation to Web site design. By taking a user-based qualitative approach, the author hopes that this study will open the door to a careful consideration of actual user needs and behaviors in relation to information-seeking tasks on Web-based media. The results may compliment the uses of existing quantitative studies by supplying a deeper user understanding and a new qualitative approach to analyze and improve the design of information on Web sites.

INTRODUCTION

When visiting a Web site, each user has a specific goal that relates to a pattern of needs, expectations, and search behaviors. They also approach with different modes of searching based on varied knowledge, experience, and search sophistication.

This leads to differences in information-seeking strategies and searching behaviors. Since information on Web sites is traditionally structured and presented based on Web sites' goals and contents, it may or may not match with user goals or search behaviors.

Because of these problems, information structuring is the essence of Web design since these problems cannot be solved by the development of technically sophisticated systems alone. User search behaviors need to be studied and deeply understood in order to design systems that allow them to perform their information-seeking tasks easily, without struggle and frustration. The contents need to be authored, organized, structured, and presented to fit their needs, expectations, and search behaviors, while being able to carry out the goal of the Web site simultaneously. Both the provider and user must benefit at the same time to ensure the Web site success. As a result, user-centered design process is important in Web development to help people succeed within an information context that seeks to achieve business goals (Brinck, Gergle, & Wood, 2002).

In attempts to move toward user-centered design, many studies have been developed to establish design principles that better serve Web-based media. Among these attempts, Web usability, grounded in human-computer interaction (HCI), has currently assumed a significant role underpinning the design of many Web sites in order to maximize efficient use. Web usability studies and practices are primarily concerned with people performing a task accurately, completely, and easily. These may involve making information accessible, retrievable, legible, and readable, ensuring that all Web pages are reachable and practically navigated, or dealing with technical aspects of media interface and Web system by ensuring that all system functionality can be operated correctly and easily.

User Research in Web Development

User research in relation to Web site development is mostly conducted by using quantitative methods or automated programs, such as data mining and Logs File Analysis (analyze usage data), GOMS analysis (predict execution and learning time), and Information Scent modeling (mimic Web site navigation) serve different purposes. These automated methods are particularly essential to usability testing (evaluation), especially in cases where numerous users are involved since they can reveal a substantial amount of information with regard to usage patterns by representing the actual usage characteristics. Some also provide in-depth statistical analysis of usage. For example, *logs file analysis* can show overall hits, conversion rates, entrance pages, search terms, peak times, demographics, and system down-time (see Figure 1 and 2). These develop an understanding of how the Web site is being used by the actual users, which helps identify potential problems of the Web site, and may assist in suggesting a change or directing the future design (Brinck et al., 2002).

However, the limitations of these automated methods are that they cannot be employed without an existing Web site; the Web site needs to be prototyped or implemented at some level before these methods can be applied since they are intended as an analytical means rather than a generative one. More importantly, these automated methods cannot capture important qualitative and subjective information such as user preferences and misconceptions (Ivory & Hearst, 2001). They tend to yield a higher level of user data — what they do or what they do not do — but they usually fail to capture and analyze user cognitive behaviors such as their satisfaction, decision-making pattern, or reasons that underpin their needs and behaviors.

Figure 1. An example page from logs file analysis: Visits

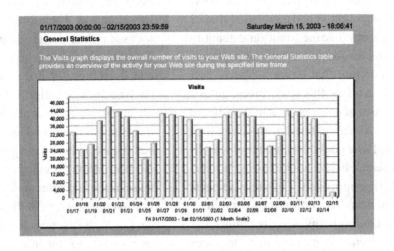

Figure 2. An example page from logs file analysis example: Top entry pages

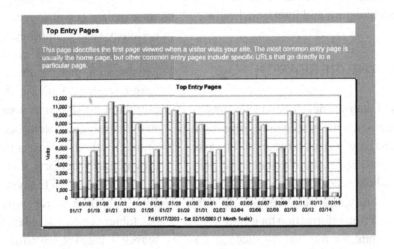

Therefore, qualitative study using nonautomated methods such as user observation, focus groups, user interviews and surveys still play an important role in Web development. These nonautomated methods can be used in the design process to capture, analyze, and conceptualize Web structure before usability evaluation takes place. They can be employed in the evaluation process as complements to the automated methods as well, in order to help capture and analyze qualitative and subjective user information that is missing from the automated methods alone. Applying both quantitative and qualitative studies can significantly improve the quality and quantity of user input and feedback that may help suggest a change or direction that better supports user satisfaction. As a result, this study investigates a relatively new area of user research in Web-based media, offering a user-centered perspective with consideration of user goals, user modes of searching and their search behaviors by taking a user-based qualitative approach. The study expects to expand understanding within the area of user studies, and accordingly investigates how these user cognitive factors contribute to differences in user information needs and their information-seeking behaviors on Web-based media, particularly in view of user search strategies and user search methods. Understanding within this area will contribute to the further development of information architecture and interface design.

SCOPE OF THE RESEARCH

The practices of Web site development are fundamentally concerned with two equally important and interrelated parts: (1) Web functionality and (2) Web information. In the user-centered perspective, usability, accessibility, sustainability, suitability, credibility, and usefulness of both Web functionality and Web information for its intended users are important for the Web to succeed. In most current practices, the user-centered approach is usually taken into design consideration in a general sense; for example, by conducting user studies to establish who are the intended users of the Web site (user profiles), and what do they want to achieve (user goals)? Others may perform user testing with regard to usability evaluation in terms of what is working, and what is not (usability of Web functionality). These current user-centered approaches are concerned with Web functionality rather than Web information. Furthermore, they

pay considerably more attention to usability aspects while the Web information content receives less attention. Therefore, this research primarily focuses on the design of Web information, particularly in view of the importance, suitability, and usefulness of information design provided on Web sites (see Figure 3).

The study is particularly concerned with user information needs and user information-seeking behaviors; it also investigates whether the design of information provided on the Web site supports these needs and behaviors. Secondly, the research is also concerned with the suitability and usefulness of Web functionality necessary for users to gain access to the information they need. The research also looks into different types of search methods or search tools provided on Web sites to investigate whether these search methods or tools are useful and suitable to user search strategies.

When searching, each user has a different search plan: For instance, they lightly explore or seriously search and they select search methods and tools in order to easily achieve their goal. This search plan is primarily based on their search strategy, which is the scheme that generally distinguishes user search patterns. Besides search strategies, each user may use a particular search method, which is the procedure for how they actually perform their search. User search method is based on the types of search tools they choose for their search, which may include menu bar, table of contents, index, or search engine. User search strategies can range from general or less-focused search to more specific or purposeful search. Furthermore, it may change from time to time based on the current context or situation that unfolds while they are searching as well as the search results that they find or retrieve. Based on user search strategies and its results, user search methods are changed accordingly. As a result, this research is aimed to uncover the primary factors governing or influencing these user search strategies and methods.

Figure 3. Primary focuses of the research: The design of Web information-based on user-centered approach, particularly with regard to usefulness and suitability

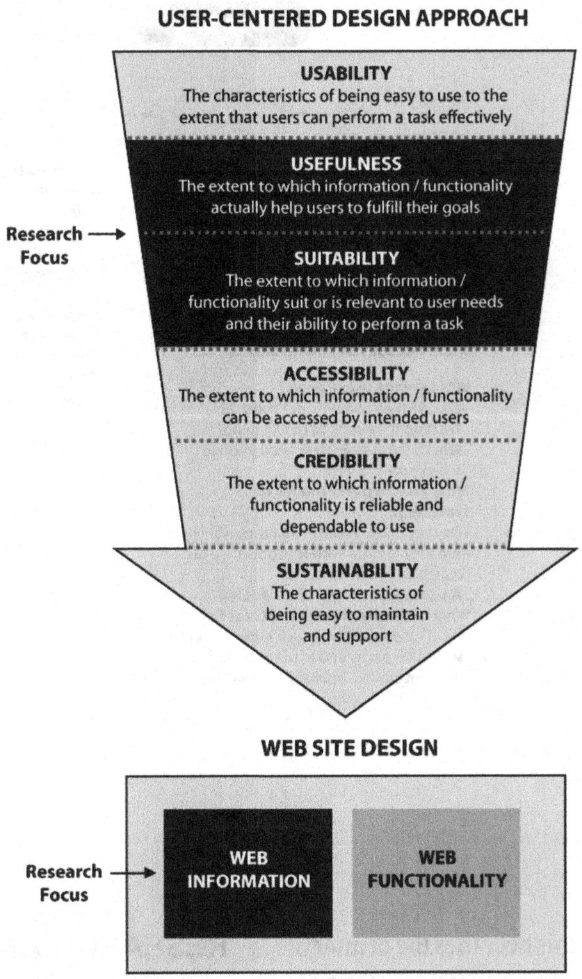

USER-CENTERED DESIGN APPROACH

USABILITY
The characteristics of being easy to use to the extent that users can perform a task effectively

USEFULNESS
The extent to which information / functionality actually help users to fulfill their goals

Research → Focus

SUITABILITY
The extent to which information / functionality suit or is relevant to user needs and their ability to perform a task

ACCESSIBILITY
The extent to which information / functionality can be accessed by intended users

CREDIBILITY
The extent to which information / functionality is reliable and dependable to use

SUSTAINABILITY
The characteristics of being easy to maintain and support

WEB SITE DESIGN

Research → Focus

WEB INFORMATION

WEB FUNCTIONALITY

More importantly, in order to understand and eventually determine what types, characteristics, formats, and presentation methods for information is suitable and useful for users, the research needs to investigate the relatively new areas of user-centered approaches to Web site design: user goals and user modes of searching (see Figure 4).

Information scientists have studied user modes of searching for decades, and these ideas are well categorized by Rosenfeld and Morville (1998) in their book *Information Architecture for the World Wide Web*. However, since the notion of user modes of searching has never been elaborated in terms of what to expect from their differences, it needs

Figure 4. Primary focus of the research: User goals and user modes of searching

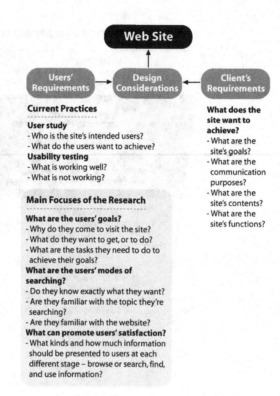

further investigation—this becomes the primary focus of this research to uncover its substantial impact on user needs, expectations, search strategies, or information-seeking behaviors in this medium. In addition, typical user profiles are also categorized in order to determine whether these profiles exert any substantial impact on user needs, expectations, or search patterns. These profiles particularly focus on user demographic and techno-graphic data, including prior knowledge in the content they are searching, prior experience in the particular or similar Web site interface, and sophistication in general Internet use.

RESEARCH ANALYTIC FRAME

The research begins with defining and categorizing the important elements or factors of the study, including user goals, user modes of searching, as well as Web site goals and contents. Accordingly, the research analytic frame is established to help identify potential cases for the study. User goals and modes of searching were investigated within the context of specific Web site goals to reveal common user search patterns, search strategies, and search methods associated with each case and to identify the primary problems that occur in each pattern.

User Goals

Each user has a specific goal when visiting a Web site. Different goals suggest different kinds of needs, expectations, and search behaviors, which are factors in Web usage and success. Further, users may access the same Web site with different goals at different times; moreover, they often link several goals and explore them sequentially. User goals may be categorized as follows:

- **To seek specific information:** In this category, users may engage a Web site to search for specific information that helps them to stay updated, make decisions, fulfill a specific inquiry, perform tasks, learn, or conduct research.
- **To fulfill personal interests:** Some users may engage a Web site as a resource for pleasure to fulfill a personal interest (e.g., watching a video clip or listening to music on an entertainment Web site).
- **To communicate and/or perform tasks:** Others may use Web sites as a channel for communicating or as a means for performing tasks (e.g., connecting to a community Web site or paying bills on a company Web site).

Among these three categories of user goals, the information-seeking goal is prevalent and poses the greatest problem for users. Consequently this is the primary investigative focus in this research.

User Modes of Searching

Besides user goals, users also approach a Web site with varied levels of specification of their needs and different levels of search specification and determination, this leads to differences in information-seeking behaviors including search strategies, search methods, and selection of search tools. Some users may know exactly what they

are looking for and where to find it, while others are without a clue. Since these search behaviors and user expectations vary widely, it is important to recognize and distinguish among them noting their differences.

A current study (Rosenfeld & Morville, 1998) has delineated users' different modes of searching as known-item searching, existence searching, exploratory searching, and comprehensive searching (research). Based on Rosenfeld and Morville's model, user modes of searching are modified and extended in this research to include topical searching which falls between existence and known-item searching. User modes of searching may be categorized as follows:

- **Exploratory searching (browsing):** Users have a vague idea of their information needs. They do not know exactly what they are hoping to find, but some may know how to phrase their question. They want to explore and learn more.
- **Existence searching:** Users have an abstract idea or concept of what they are hoping to find, but do not know how to describe it clearly or whether the answer exists at all. They want to search for what matches their idea or mental image.
- **Topical searching:** Users know what they want in general. Some may want to search for an answer to their specific question. They know what they are hoping to find, but do not know where/which categories they should look for.
- **Known-item searching:** Users know exactly what they want, and usually know where/which categories they should look for. Users' information needs are clearly defined and have a single, correct answer.
- **Comprehensive searching (research):** Users want to search for specific information, and they want everything available regarding this information. Users' information needs

are clearly defined, but might have various or many answers.

Users Search Behaviors

When users are searching for information and trying to accomplish their goals, they move between two cognitive states (thoughts/decisions — with regard to their goal and interest) and physical states (interactions — concern with functions, navigation, and computer performance) with regard to information provided on each Web page.

For instance, some users may want to keep searching because they need detailed information,

Table 1. Users' cognitive and physical search behaviors

Users' Cognitive Behaviors (thoughts/decisions)	Users' Physical Behaviors (interactions)
— Some information is found, and they want to learn more, or want to know the details of the retrieval documents. — The intended information is found. Users' primary information needs are fulfilled, but users are interested in finding other relevant or related information. — The intended information is found. Users' primary information needs are fulfilled. Users are ready to use information they found to take further action(s). — The intended information is not found, or not enough to take further action(s). Users' primary needs are not fulfilled. Users need to keep searching. — Users make a positive decision (decide to proceed) about something according to information they found. — Users make a negative decision (decide not to proceed) about something according to information they found. — Users are satisfied. All users' needs are fulfilled. Users are able to accomplish their goals based on the information they found. — Users are not satisfied. Users' needs are not fulfilled. Users are unable to accomplish their goal(s).	— Users keep searching in the current retrieval results. — Users keep searching by changing search strategy. — Users record the information they found. — Users go back to the selected (bookmarked) page or results. — Users give up.

while others may be satisfied with only a short descriptive text presented on the first page. Some may prefer textual information, but others may feel more satisfied with visual information. These search behaviors may be identified as shown in Table 1. These cognitive and physical behaviors with regard to user search, previously observed from initial user observation, will be further used to establish a coding scheme used in an analytical process of the research.

Web Site Goals and Contents

While this research focuses on the relatively new areas of user studies: user goals and user modes of searching, other factors such as site contents,

Figure 5. The research analytic frame: Generating 10 different study cases for the research

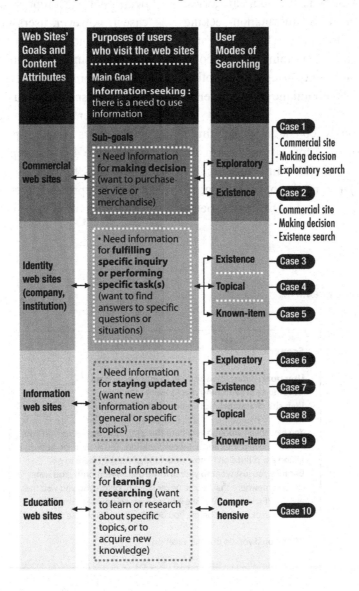

site goals, and site functions nevertheless play a significant role in determining the design of a Web site. Each Web site contains unique contents and goals depending on the nature of the company, institution, or individual that owns that Web site. Based on the book *Web Navigation: Designing the User Experience* (Fleming, 1998), these Web sites can be distinguished and generalized by the similarities of their goals and contents into six categories: (1) commercial Web site, (2) identity Web site (Web site for company or institution), (3) information Web site, (4) education Web site, (5) entertainment Web site, and (6) community Web site. However, only the first four categories, in which the problems of information-seeking tasks are primarily found, will be investigated in this study. Moreover, entertainment and community Web sites are quite different from other Web sites because of their unique goals, contents, and functions.

By simultaneously considering the three important factors of information design on Web sites: (1) Web site goals and contents, (2) user goals, and (3) user modes of searching, an analytic frame is constructed. Different aspects of each factor are systematically combined with one another to establish prominent cases or scenarios for the study; each of which presents a unique combination of the three factors: (1) Web site goals and contents, (2) user goals, and (3) user modes of searching.

Nevertheless, these cases are not mutually exclusive; they might overlap or combine since one Web site may consist of two or more combinations (see Figure 5). As shown in Figure 6, case 1 represents the scenario in which users with exploratory searching mode visit a commercial Web site in order to find information to make a decision. Case 2 represents a similar scenario to case 1; however, users in case 2 arrive with an existence mode of searching. Cases 3, 4, and 5 represent similar scenarios in which users visit identity (company) Web sites to find information to fulfill a specific inquiry.

However, each case has a distinctive search mode. Users in case 3 approach with an existence mode; case 4 with a topical mode; while case 5 approaches with a known-item mode. Cases 6, 7, 8, and 9 represent the scenarios in which users visit information Web sites to find information to

Figure 6. An example scenario

Scenario 1

User goal : Information-seeking to make a decision
User mode of searching : Exploratory searching
Web site characteristic : Commercial website

You have been working very hard this year. Your boss surprised you with a $5,000 bonus and a 2-week vacation. You're thinking about taking a trip, but don't know what kind of trip, or where to go because you just went to your favorite place last month. You want to go somewhere that you've never been to before. So you visit the website "Expedia.com" to see if there is anything interesting. You want to explore more before you decide what you should do.

What would you do on your vacation ?

stay updated. Though, they are assigned different modes of searching, which include exploratory, existence, topical, and known-item modes respectively. Case 10 represents a scenario in which users with a comprehensive mode of searching approach an educational Web site to find information for learning or researching a specific content. Each of these 10 cases will be investigated and analyzed to uncover similarities and differences in patterns of user information-seeking behaviors, as well as to identify user information needs, user search strategies, and user search methods associated with different user goals, modes of searching, and Web site characteristics.

RESEARCH QUESTIONS

The study is specifically conducted within these selected 10 cases generated from the research analytic frame shown in Figure 5 in order to find the answers to these research questions:

- What are the common patterns of user information-seeking behavior presented in each study case?
- What are the user search strategies, search methods, or selected search tools commonly found or employed in each study case?
- What kinds of information do users need in each study case in terms of the types, characteristics, formats, presentation methods, quantity and quality of information?
- What are the key factors in each study case that help or obstruct users to accomplish the information-seeking task?

The research findings that answer these questions will be analyzed to identify the relationships existing among user goals and user modes of searching with their information needs, search strategies, and search methods. These results will help establish the classification of cognitive

factors, as well as provide an analysis framework for information design on Web sites.

RESEARCH METHODOLOGY

Research Methods

A qualitative research method is used in this study to explore the similarities and differences of user search patterns. Users' information-seeking behaviors are observed through controlled observation, through video observation combined with protocol analysis. User profiles are also collected through a series of questionnaires. Ten scenarios are designed to create the 10 study cases originating from the research analytic frame to help the participants enter the situation and the tasks they needed to accomplish. Each scenario is embedded with a particular mode of searching, and a different search goal resulting in the performance of a task, ranging from open-ended to very specific purpose and search.

- *Scenario 1* **explores a commercial Web site:** Expedia.com. User goal is to make a decision; user search mode is exploratory searching.
- *Scenario 2* **explores a commercial Web site:** Toyrus.com. User goal is to make a decision; user search mode is existence searching.
- *Scenario 3* **explores an identity Web site:** Paris-ile-de-France.com. User goal is to fulfill a specific inquiry; user search mode is existence searching.
- *Scenario 4* **explores an identity Web site:** Apple.com. User goal is to fulfill a specific inquiry; user search mode is topical searching.
- *Scenario 5* **explores an identity Web site:** FoodTV.com. User goal is to fulfill a specific inquiry; user mode is known-item searching.

- *Scenario 6* **explores an information Web site:** TVGuide.com. User goal is to stay updated on some interesting topics; user search mode is exploratory searching.
- *Scenario 7* **explores an information Web site:** ABCNews.com. User goal is to stay updated on a specific topic; user search mode is existence searching.
- *Scenario 8* **explores an information Web site:** DiscoveryHealth.com. User goal is to stay updated on a specific topic; user search mode is topical searching.
- *Scenario 9* **explores an information Web site:** CNN.com. User goal is to stay updated on a specific topic; user mode is known-item searching.
- *Scenario 10* **explores an information/education Web site:** WebMD.com. User goal is to research and learn about a specific topic; user search mode is comprehensive searching.

Fifty participants from different cultures, all of whom were literate in English, are observed regarding how they search for information and try to accomplish the tasks defined by the scenario they received. The participants approached the selected Web site with unspecified and various modes of searching and searched for information with goals appropriate to the selected scenario. Ten participants are randomly selected to participate in each scenario, with each participant doing two cases or two different scenarios.

As a result, the research collects in total 100 observation cases, which consist of 10 cases for each of 10 scenarios. The participants' interactions (physical behaviors) on Web sites are simply captured through a video recorder. Furthermore, by using protocol analysis, the participants express verbally what they think while performing tasks in order to reveal their thoughts (cognitive behaviors) and comments, which are extremely important for the analytical process.

Analysis Methods

Since the research data collected from participants is qualitative in nature, several methods of qualitative analysis are used in this research to carefully analyze various aspects of the data, in order to obtain integrated research findings that answer the related but different research questions on which this research focuses. Each analysis method used in the study delivers distinctive analytical results answering a specific research question. The analytical results obtained from these different analysis methods are also cross-examined in order to accumulate further findings. This collective analysis process helps to uncover the pattern of relationship that exists among various user cognitive factors, as well as to identify their substantial impact on user search behaviors and information needs.

Thematic analysis (Boyatzis, 1998), the process used for encoding qualitative information, is performed in this study to analyze the overall user search behaviors including user task list and process. In order to uncover the differences and similarities in user search behaviors, a thematic analysis framework with a coding scheme is designed based on an initial observation on user search behaviors. Participants' search behaviors are captured through video and sound recording, then analyzed and encoded by using the coding scheme (see Table 2).

User search behaviors are analyzed at each Web page the user visited as cognitive behaviors (thoughts/decisions) and physical behaviors (interactions). Each behavior is encoded using the preset coding scheme. The result is the sequence of user tasks performed by each user when searching for specific information on the particular Web site as described in the scenario they received (see Table 3).

The results, displayed as the encoded information of user search behaviors, are then further analyzed and generalized to determine the com-

Table 2. The coding scheme used in thematic analysis

Thematic Analysis: Coding Scheme	
User's Search Behaviors: **Cognitive Behaviors (Thoughts, Decisions)**	**Physical Behaviors (Interactions)**
(SR) Some information is found and they want to learn more, or want to know about the details of the retrieval documents.	(SR) Users keep searching in the current retrieval results.
[C] The intended information is found. Users' primary information needs are fulfilled, but users are interested in finding other relevant or related information.	[C] Users record the information they found.
[C] The intended information is found. Users' primary information needs are fulfilled. Users are ready to use information they found to take further action(s).	[?] Users keep searching by changing search strategy or search methods.
[?] The intended information is not found, or not enough to take further action(s). Users' primary needs are not fulfilled. Users need to keep searching.	[D] Users go back to the selected (bookmarked) page or result.
[D] Users make a positive decision (to proceed) about something according to information they found.	
[D] Users make a negative decision (not to proceed) about something according to information they found.	
[S] Users are satisfied. All users' needs are fulfilled. Users are able to accomplish their goals based on the information they found.	**Integrated Behaviors**
[S] Users are somewhat satisfied, but not completely satisfied. Users' primary needs are fulfilled, and users are able to accomplish their goals based on the information they found. However, users still need more information to fulfill all their needs completely.	Initial searching (SR) (SR) Information-collecting [C] [C] [C] Struggling [?] [?] Decision-making [D] [D] [D] Satisfactory / Unsatisfactory [S] [S] [U]
[U] Users are not satisfied. Users' needs are not fulfilled. Users are unable to accomplish their goal(s).	

mon patterns of information-seeking tasks that are associated with each study case (scenario) by using a *time-ordered matrix* (Robson, 1993). The time-ordered matrix is used to systematically

display the encoded information of user search behaviors in *time-ordered sequences* by presenting various types of user search behaviors, both physical and cognitive behaviors, observed in

Table 3. An example analysis of thematic analysis by using the pre-designed coding scheme

Information display on Web page	User's key actions	User's key speech/thoughts	User's cognitive and physical behaviors
page 1 **Homepage** • Menu bar • Table of contents • Search field • Recommend features	scrolling up-down select table of content	• "Well ... I want to look around first." • "There're lots of categories to choose from here, but I think I should start searching by 'Ages.'"	(SR) Some information is found, and they want to learn more, or want to know about the details of the retrieval documents. (SR) Users keep searching in the current retrieval results.
page 2 **Result Page** • Table of contents • Recommend products (small image + short description)	scrolling up-down read table of content look at image select table of content	• "Let's see if anything interesting is here." • "Visual stimulation ... um ... it sounds interesting." • "Well ... let's see what's in it."	(SR) Some information is found, and they want to learn more, or want to know about the details of the retrieval documents. (SR) Users keep searching in the current retrieval results.
page 3 **Result Page** • Small images + short descriptions	scrolling up-down look at image read short text select related categories	• "Well ... nothing interesting here." • "Maybe I should try another category to see if it has more interesting items."	(?) The intended information is not found, or not enough to take further action(s). Users' primary needs are not fulfilled. Users need to keep searching. (?) Users keep searching by changing search strategy.

each Web page from the start to completion of the task (see Figure 7).

Color coding is also added to help identify and group the same or similar tasks together. This enables one to see the overall task list and its sequence visually and practically in order to compare the differences and similarities that occur within and across different scenarios.

In addition, the results gained from thematic analysis are eventually summarized as *procedural analysis*, which presents the common process or pattern of user search behaviors in each study case (scenario) including search methods and task descriptions (see Figure 8).

The encoded information of user search behaviors is also further transformed into Chernoff

Figure 7. *An example use of time-ordered matrix used for further analyzing and generalizing the encoded information gained from the earlier thematic analysis by presenting user search behaviors in the time-ordered sequences*

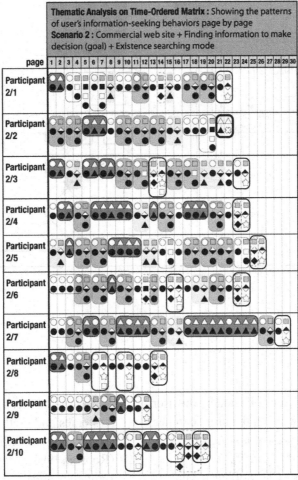

Participant N/n means scenario 'N' / participant 'n'.

Faces (Chernoff, 1973; Wainer & Thissen, 1981) in order to further identify and compare the common patterns of search behaviors that are associated with each user goal and mode of searching. Chernoff Faces are another coding scheme that is, in this case, used to help identify user's search behaviors holistically with regard to how frequent each behavior occurs, or which behavior occurs more often than the others.

Chernoff Faces also help visualize the frequency of tasks performed within and across different scenarios. For example, in this coding scheme, the face is used to represent the user's information-collecting state. The bigger the face, the

Figure 8. An example of procedural analysis used for presenting the process of user search patterns

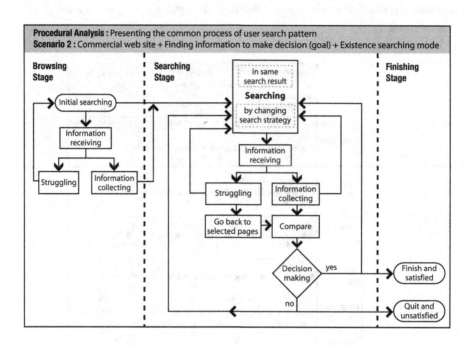

more information has been collected by the user. The eyes represent how much the user searches, while the eyebrows represent a struggling state (see Tables 4.1, 4.2, and Figure 9).

As shown in Figure 9, Chernoff Face Analysis reveals the patterns of user's prominent tasks performed in each different scenario. For example, users in scenario 2, as shown in the top row, need to perform an extensive decision-making task indicated by the gray and black hair they are all wearing; in contrast to users in scenarios 4 and 9 who all appear with no hair signifying that they do not perform any decision-making task at all. The analysis also visually addresses user search struggle or satisfaction clearly. As seen clearly in Figure 9, all users in scenario 9 appear with complete satisfaction while most users in scenario 4 are unsatisfied with their search.

In order to identify the patterns of user search strategies and methods commonly used in each scenario, a checklist with a sequence record (Robson, 1993) is designed to record participants' frequency and sequence of use of various search tools available on each Web site. The recorded data is then further analyzed to identify the common patterns of user search strategies and search methods primarily used in each scenario, as well as to compare the differences and similarities of user search patterns within and across different scenarios (see Table 5).

Similarly, in order to identify the patterns of user information needs commonly found in each study case, another Checklist Record (Robson, 1993) is designed to record the frequency of use of different kinds of information available on each Web site. Different types, characteristics,

Table 4.1. The coding scheme used in Chernoff Face Analysis

Chernoff Faces Analysis: Coding Scheme	
Users' cognitive states and physical states	**Chernoff Faces coding system**
Initial searching states Some information is found, and they want to learn more, or want to know about the details of the retrieval documents. Users keep searching in the current retrieval results.	**EYES** less often ··· 5 ⓘⓘ 10 ⊙⊙ 15 more often ᵇᵒᵈ 20
Information-collecting states The intended information is found. Users' primary information needs are fulfill, but users are interested in finding other relevant or related information. The intended information is found. Users' primary information needs are fulfill. Users are ready use information they found to take further action(s). Users record the information they found.	**HEAD** ◯ 5 less often ◯ 10 more often ◯ 15 ◯ 20
Struggling states The intended information is found. Users' primary information needs are fulfill. Users are ready use information they found to take further action(s). Users keep searching by changing search strategy.	**EYEBROWS** less often ⌒⌒ 0 – – 5 ‿ 10 ╲ ╱ 15 more often W 20

Table 4.2. The coding scheme used in Chernoff Face Analysis

Chernoff Faces Analysis: Coding Scheme	
Users' cognitive states and physical states	**Chernoff Faces coding system**
Decision-making states ◇ D Users make a **positive** decision (to proceed) about something according to information they found.	**CHEEK** less often ↕ more often 1 / More than 1
◆ D Users go back to the previously selected or recorded (bookmarked) pages or results, and/or compare the selected pages or results side by side in case there are more than one page or result selected.	**NOSE** less often ↕ more often 1 / More than 1
◈ D Users make a **negative** decision (not to proceed) about something according to information they found.	**HAIR** less often ↑ more often 5 / 10 / 15
Satisfactory states ☆ S Users are satisfied. All users' needs are fulfilled. Users are able to accomplish their goals based on the information they found.	**MOUTH** ⌣
⬟ S Users are somewhat satisfied, but not completely satisfied. Users' primary needs are fulfilled, and users are able to accomplish their goals based on the information they found. However, users still need more information to fulfill all their needs completely.	**MOUTH** ⊢
✕ U Users are not satisfied. Users' needs are not fulfilled. Users are unable to accomplish their goal(s).	**MOUTH** ⌢

Figure 9. Examples of Chernoff Face Analysis used to visually identify various types of user search behaviors regarding the frequency of each behavior

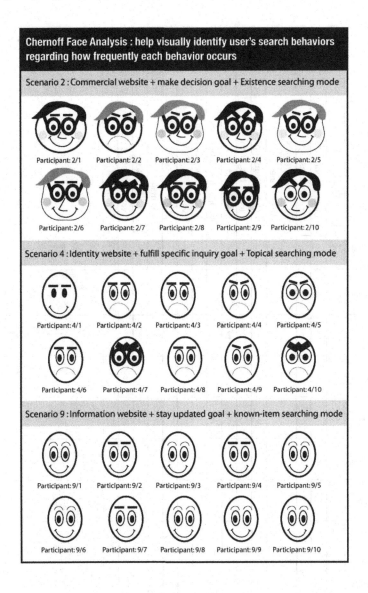

formats, and presentation methods of information display that are viewed by users while performing information-seeking tasks are captured by using the Checklist Record. This process is used to analyze and identify the main types, characteristics, formats, and presentation methods of information needed by users to accomplish the given task within and across different scenarios (see Table 6).

The analysis of user profiles is collected and built upon user data acquired through a series of questionnaires provided to the research par-

Table 5. An example analysis of user search strategies and user search methods by using the Checklist and Sequence Record

	Exploring/Browsing							Purposeful searching						Auxiliary			Sequence
Checklist and Sequence Record: Showing the frequency and sequence of use of different search tools — **Scenario 2: commercial** Web site + **making decision** goal + **existence searching** mode																	
	Menus	Table of content	Feature items/topics	list of items/topics	Advertising	Related items/topics	Table or diagram w/ link text	Search field	Simple search function	Advanced search function	Index	Shortcut	Site map	"Back" button	"Next" button	"See more" button	
Participant 2/1*	2**	5						1						7		7	browsing categories ⇄ browsing results ↔ purposeful searching
Participant 2/2		2						6						6		9	purposeful searching ⇄ retrieval results ↔ exploring, browsing
Participant 2/3		3	2			4		2						5		7	browsing categories ⇄ browsing results ↔ purposeful searching retrieval results
Participant 2/4		4				2		1		1				4	6	5	browsing categories ⇄ browsing results ↔ purposeful searching retrieval results
Participant 2/5						2		2		3				8		10	purposeful searching ⇄ retrieval results ↔ exploring, browsing
Participant 2/6		6												14		11	browsing categories ⇄ browsing results
Participant 2/7		13						1						15	1	7	browsing categories ⇄ browsing results ↔ purposeful searching
Participant 2/8		3						1						6		7	browsing categories ⇄ browsing results ↔ purposeful searching
Participant 2/9		4												5		6	browsing categories ⇄ browsing results
Participant 2/10		8						1						10	2	7	browsing categories ⇄ browsing results ↔ purposeful searching
Central tendency: mean	0.2	4.8	0.2	0	0	0.8	0	1.4	0	0.4	0	0	0	8	0.9	7.6	browsing categories ⇄ browsing results ↔ purposeful searching
Central tendency	**6.0**							**1.8**						**16.5**			purposeful searching ⇄ retrieval results ↔ exploring, browsing; browsing categories ⇄ browsing results ↔ purposeful searching retrieval results

Table 6. An example analysis of user information needs by using the Checklist Record

Scenario 2
Commercial Web site, making decision goal, existence searching mode

	Characteristics of Information								Formats of Information display					Presentation Methods of Information display				Types of Information			Remarks: Users thoughts, comments on their information needs
	Quick references, Bullet points	FAQs, questions and answers	Step-by-step instructions	Comparison information	Recommendations, feature articles	Glossary explanations	Stories, sequence information	Complete descriptions	Topics, keywords, headlines	Abstracts, summaries	Short or brief text/information	Full or long text/information	Biography references	Textual descriptions	Diagrams, maps	Matrix, tables	Images, icons, illustrations	Opinions, reviews recommendations	News, reports	Facts, scientific information	
Partici-pant 2/1	8				2			7	15	9	23	7		24			21	YES		YES	Many users would like to see more and bigger pictures, or some interactive displays showing the usage of product. Some users expect to see the same or similar information to what they would see on the package of the product when they buy in a store. Most users want to see comparison information or want a comparison tool.
Partici-pant 2/2	25				2			3	14	8	22	3		22			23	YES		YES	
Partici-pant 2/3	22				4			7	11	11	22	7		22			24	YES	YES	YES	
Partici-pant 2/4	22				4			3	15	7	23	3		23			24	YES		YES	
Partici-pant 2/5	24				1			4	11	15	26	4		26			27	YES		YES	
Partici-pant 2/6	25				6			2	19	11	30	2		30			30	YES	YES	YES	
Partici-pant 2/7	29				10				30	6	36			35			36	YES		YES	
Partici-pant 2/8	36				4			2	9	7	16	2		16			18	YES	YES	YES	
Partici-pant 2/9	16				4				8	4	12			12			15			YES	
Partici-pant 2/10	27				8				21	6	27			26			30	YES		YES	
Central tendency (mean)	23.8				4.5			2.8	15.4	8.4	23.7	2.8		23.6			24.8				

Figure 10. An example of analysis of user profiles

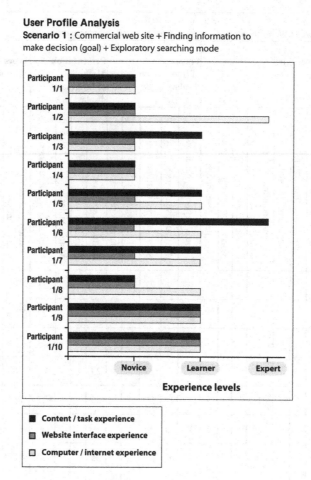

User Profile Analysis
Scenario 1 : Commercial web site + Finding information to make decision (goal) + Exploratory searching mode

ticipants when the observation took place (see Figure 10). The questionnaire was designed to acquire user demographic and techno-graphic data focusing on different aspects of user experience, including users' prior knowledge and experience in the specific content they are searching, users' prior experience in the particular or similar Web site interface, and users' general experience in Internet use for information-seeking purposes.

Furthermore, qualitative comparison is conducted by constructing truth tables (Ragin, 1987, 1994) to help further identify additional insights and various factors that may reveal additional information about user search struggle or success, and help confirm the results from other analytical methods (see Table 7). This particular analysis is important for the research since it looks across all 100 cases simultaneously, in contrast to other analyses that examine 10 observation cases of each scenario collectively.

Table 7. The construction of truth table 1

Causal conditions				Total instances among 100 cases	Output code: presence/ absence of instance (P)	Output code: achieving goal-search success (S)
A	**B**	**C**	**D**			
Have prior knowledge and/or experience in content?	Have visited the Web site before (return user)?	Utilize different kinds of search tools?	Read text or detailed information thoroughly?			Achieve original goal-search success?
1*	1	1	1	3	1*	1*
1	1	1	0	3	1	1
1	1	0	1	6	1	1
1	0	1	1	8	1	1
0	1	1	1	0	0	n/a**
1	1	0	0	9	1	0
1	0	0	1	12	1	1
0	0	1	1	3	1	1
1	0	1	0	15	1	1
0	1	0	1	3	1	1
0	1	1	0	0	0	n/a**
1	0	0	0	22	1	1
0	0	0	1	6	1	1
0	1	0	0	0	0	n/a**
0	0	1	0	3	1	1
0	0	0	0	7	1	0
				= 100 cases		

*Number '1' indicates the presence of a causal condition or an output, and '0' indicates its absence. **Code 'n/a' indicates that the output code for the particular row is not applicable or it cannot be identified because the instance of the causal combination on that row is absent.

Validation of Coding System

Reliability and validity of coding schemes specifically designed to use for analysis in this research is fundamentally important and needs to be examined before the study proceeds further. In qualitative research, the observer's consistency and bias in interpreting user behaviors and using coding schemes to code events are a primary concern. As a result, to measure reliability and validity of the coding scheme and analysis methods, a second observer is invited to independently interpret and code the same video data. The scripts encoded by both observers are then compared to identify the degree to which both observers agree in their interpretation and coding. This validation process is called *double coding,* which is perhaps the most used technique to attain sufficient reliability to proceed with analysis and interpretation (Boyatzis, 1998; Miles & Huberman, 1984).

After the double coding process is completed, the *confusion matrix* is constructed to show where the two observers are different in their judgment when coding the events. Agreement takes place when both observers use the same code for the same event. On the contrary, disagreement occurs when observers use different codes to code the same event. To read the confusion matrix, the scores on the diagonal from top left to bottom right indicate agreement between the two observers, while the scores off this diagonal indicate their disagreement (Robson, 1993) (see Figure 11).

As shown in Figure 11, the scores on the diagonal from top left to bottom right appearing in coding 'A', 'B', 'C', 'D', and 'L' indicate agreement between the two observers. However, for the coding 'E', there is also a score appearing off this diagonal which indicates an event of their disagreement. Note that in this particular case, both observers do not assign coding 'F', 'G', 'H', 'I', 'J', 'K', and 'M' to any events. Therefore, there is no score for unused coding in the matrix; this will be different from one case to another.

Then, based on the scores on the confusion matrix, the proportion of agreement, the proportion expected by chance, and the Cohen's Kappa are respectively calculated to measure inter-observer agreement (see Figure 12). "The inter-observer agreement is the extent to which two or more observers obtain the same results

Figure 11. An example construction of the confusion matrix showing the scores of agreement and disagreement between two observers in their judgment when coding the events

Confusion Matrix

Observer 1	Observer 2													Total
	A ○	B ●	C △	D ▲	E □	F ▣	G ■	H ◇	I ◈	J ◆	K ☆	L ✣	M X	
A ○	6				1									7
B ●		8												8
C △			4											4
D ▲				4										4
E □					2									2
F ▣														
G ■														
H ◇														
I ◈														
J ◆														
K ☆														
L ✣												1		1
M X														
Total	6	8	4	4	3							1		26

when measuring the same behaviors (e.g. when independently coding the same tape)." (Robson, 1993, p. 221).

In order to assess the significance of Kappa scores, Fliess (1981) has suggested the following rules of thumb: the Kappa scores of 0.40 to 0.60 is considered "fair"; the Kappa scores of 0.60 to 0.75 is considered "good"; and the Kappa scores above 0.75 is considered "excellent." The results obtained from this validation process show that validity of the coding schemes used in this study, in

the view of inter-observer agreement, is positively strong. The Kappa scores of seven observation cases acquire "excellent" points (0.75-0.95), and the other three cases also show "good" scores (0.64-0.71).

However, the extent of agreement between two observers who use the coding scheme to code the same events independently is also affected by some other factors. One primary factor may be the observer's learning curve with regard to the coding scheme; one observer is more familiar with

Figure 12. An example calculation of the proportion of agreement, the proportion expected by chance, and the Cohen's Kappa Score to measure the extent of inter-observer agreement

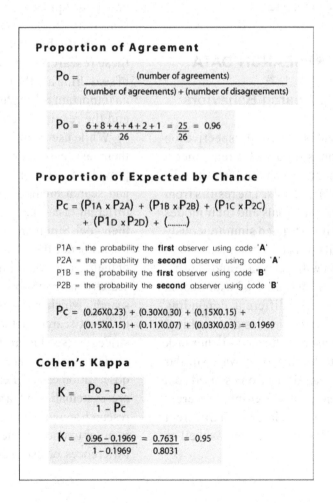

the coding scheme while the other observer is new and still learning to use the codes and/or interpret the events. Another important factor may be the observer's lack of experience or direct contact with the actual participants in the prior observation when the events were recorded. This occurs when one observer attended the observation in person when the events were recorded while the other observer was absent. The observer who had experience or direct contact with the actual participants when the events were recorded will be able to capture the participants' emotions or thoughts that are hard to detect through watching video data alone. As a result, the two observers may interpret the same user behavior differently since the first observer also makes judgments based on experience with the actual participant. These are factors that may play an important role in the inter-observer agreement.

ANALYSIS OF RESEARCH DATA

Patterns of User Search Behaviors

The research provides a new perspective on design considerations for a Web site by incorporating requirements from both Web site (client) intentions and user goals. The results from this study in which user goals and their modes of searching were investigated simultaneously with Web site goals to reveal common search patterns associated with each case and significantly show that the patterns of user search behaviors are uniquely different depending on their goals and current modes of searching. Even though each user performed his/her task in isolation and in his/her own way, similar search patterns appeared based on a shared goal and/or the same mode of searching. Different search patterns were associated with different user goals and modes of searching, as well as Web site intentions.

In this research, user search behaviors are primarily analyzed by using the thematic analysis (Boyatzis, 1998) with time-ordered matrix (Robson, 1993) (see Table 3 and Figure 7), along with procedural analysis (see Figure 8), and Chernoff Faces (Chernoff, 1973, Wainer and Thissen, 1981) (see Figure 9), to uncover the patterns of user tasks in each scenario, while Checklist and Sequence Record (Robson, 1993) (see Table 5) is used to identify the types of user search strategies and methods. The analyses (see an example in Figure 7) show that users who begin with the same goal will perform their search similarly in terms of what tasks are necessary to reach the goal. However, if they use different modes of searching, which depend mainly on how precisely they know what they want, they will have different search strategies and consequently choose different kinds of search methods even though they begin their search with the same goal. Therefore, based on these research findings, user goals and modes of searching are the main mechanisms that play an important role in determining user behaviors and the resulting search patterns.

While user goal is the main factor regulating their task description, user mode of searching provides the major impact on search strategies and search methods. User goals determine the different tasks they need to perform to achieve their goal. Simultaneously, user modes of searching influence their search strategies, or the plans of their search, determining how hard or easy the search can be and how much time is spent on their search, which accordingly results in selecting different search methods based on their search strategies (see Figure 13).

The analyses are collectively done on 10 observation cases of each of 10 scenarios which are systematically fabricated according to the research analytic frame previously demonstrated, in order to uncover the patterns of similarities or differences of user search behaviors. Based on

Figure 13. User goals and user modes of searching, the main factors regulating user search behaviors and the resulting search patterns

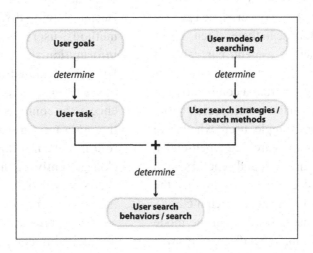

research findings, the participants in scenarios 1 and 2 share the same search goal. As a result, even though they have different modes of searching and perform their tasks on different Web sites, the patterns of their task descriptions are very alike. Likewise the participants in scenarios 3, 4, and 5, or the participants in scenarios 6, 7, 8, and 9 have different modes of searching on different Web sites but have very similar tasks. Each group of these participants who share the same search goal, perform their tasks similarly although they do not share the same search modes and they visit different Web sites.

Patterns of User Search Strategies and Methods

When performing their search, individuals need a search plan — how to perform their search and which kinds of search tools to use in order to easily achieve their original goal. This plan is different from person-to-person based on user search strategy. However as stated earlier, one's

search strategy is influenced by one's mode of searching (see Figure 13).

As a result, when visiting a Web site, individuals who arrive with different modes of searching will form different intentions as well as plan different search strategies, and accordingly perform their search in different ways to reach the same goal. Search strategies range from a general or less objective search (browse) to a more specific or purposeful search. These are directly proportional to user modes of searching which range from open-ended to specific search. They may also plan a fast or slow search based on time available and the urgency of their need. Users who plan a slow search usually want to record their search results by using the bookmark function or simply print out the results of retrieval pages for later use. Search strategy may change from time to time in accordance with modes of searching, which are based on the current context or situation that unfolds while they are searching as well as in response to the search results they find or retrieve.

While search strategy is the scheme that generally characterizes user search patterns, search method is the procedure for how they actually perform their search. This concerns the types of search tools chosen for use in their search. These search tools may include a menu bar, table of contents, index, site map, shortcut, search engine, and so forth. Users select from a combination of these search tools to perform their search based on their strategy. For example, users who are in the mode of exploratory searching (open-ended search), will likely plan a slow and general search (search strategy) and explore by browsing the menu bar and table of contents (search method). On the other hand, users who are in the mode of known-item searching (specific search), will usually plan a fast and purposeful search (search strategy) and comfortably use the index or shortcut (search method) to pursue their search.

The analyses (see an example in Table 5) show that users who begin with the same mode of searching have similar search strategies and choose similar methods. Based on research findings, the participants in scenarios 1 and 6 begin their search with the same mode of searching. As a result, even though they have different search goals and perform their tasks on different Web sites, they choose similar search strategies and methods. Each group of participants who share the same mode of searching chooses similar search strategies and methods although they do not share the same search goals and they visit different Web sites. However, note that even though the participants in scenarios 2, 3, and 7 have different modes of searching from the participants in scenarios 4 and 8, they also share similar search strategies and methods.

Patterns of User Information Needs

In this research, user information needs are primarily analyzed by using the Checklist and Sequence Record (Robson, 1993) (see Table 6) to identify the types, characteristics, formats, as well as quality and quantity of information preferred or needed by users to fulfill their original goals. Besides having different search strategies and methods, users also have different needs for information that can fulfill their goals. The findings demonstrate that user goals, modes of searching, and prior knowledge and experience in the contents they search are collectively the main mechanisms that play an important role in determining their information needs. Consequently, each user who comes to visit a Web site with a different goal, mode of searching, and prior knowledge and experience will need different kinds of information in order to fulfill his/her goal. Information provided on a Web site may be categorized based on various aspects of information including the characteristics of the information; formats and presentation methods of information display; types of information; as well as quality and quantity of given information.

Information characteristics differ widely including quick reference information such as short or brief information organized and presented using bullet points; frequently asked question (FAQ); glossary or explanation; procedural guideline or step-by-step instruction; comparison information; recommendation; sequential story or report; and complete description. Based on the research findings, user need for different characteristics of information is influenced by their different goals.

Types of information can be categorized into three different groups. The first group includes information that comes from personal or expert opinion, critique, review, or recommendation such as an editor's choice or customer's review. The second group may include the information that is collected from news or reports such as today's news or weekly reports, and the last group includes the information that presents the facts or scientific information for any given topic or item. Similar to user need for different information characteristics, the research findings demonstrate that user information needs for different types of information are influenced by different user goals.

Formats of information display range from an abstract level, including keyword; topic or headline; abstract; summary, to the detailed level including brief/short text or information, full/long text or information, reference, and bibliography. Based on the research findings, user needs for different formats of information display are influenced by different modes of searching. Presentation methods for information display range from textual to visual presentation, including textual or descriptive information (text), diagram, matrix, table, icon, image, illustration, or combinations of these methods. The research findings show that information needs for different presentation methods of information display are influenced by the type and character of the site contents.

Quality and quantity of information range from shallow information, which is usually not enough to help individuals to take further actions, to a variety of deep and detailed information. Based on the research findings, user information needs for different levels of quality and quantity of given information are influenced by various factors related to both the user and the Web site simultaneously. These factors include user goal; modes of searching; prior knowledge and experience in the contents they search; as well as the characteristics of Web contents — simple, everyday topics, or complicated, hard topics.

Discussion on Relevant Factors for User Search Success

Even though the accuracy of a search engine is one of the most recognized factors determining user search success or failure, qualitative comparison conducted by constructing truth tables and applying *Boolean algebra method* (Ragin, 1987, 1994) demonstrates that there are other relevant factors that play an important role to influence user search success or struggle. These influencing factors derive from both user profiles and behaviors as well as Web site attributes.

The qualitative comparison method is used in this study to examine among cases the combinations of causal conditions that help produce the positive outcome (users achieve the goal). These causal conditions include user prior experience in the content and Web site interface, their behaviors while searching, and several Web site attributes. Two truth tables (truth table 1 [see Table 7], and truth table 2 [see Table 10]) are constructed from observation data, which is recorded into nominal-scale and represented in binary form, to display different combinations of values on the conditions and outputs.

A presence-absence dichotomy is used in the tables to specify what outcomes and causal conditions are either present or absent in each observation case. Code number 1 indicates the presence of a condition or an output; code number 0 indicates the absence (see Tables 7 and 10). Truth table 1, as demonstrated in Table 7, is constructed to examine the causal conditions of user prior experience and search behavior and identify the combinations that significantly contribute to user search success.

With uppercase letters indicating presence and lowercase letters indicating absence of a particular causal condition shown in the combination, the data on user search success (S) from truth table 1 can be represented in the Boolean equation as follows:

$$S = ABCD + ABCd + ABcD + AbCD + AbcD + abCD + AbCd + aBcD + Abcd + abcD + abCd$$

This equation for S (search success) shows 11 primitive combinations of causal conditions that help users to achieve their goal. In order to simplify these primitive expressions, the concept of Boolean minimization is used. The most fundamental of Boolean minimization rules is (Ragin, 1987):

If two Boolean expressions differ in only one causal condition yet produce the same outcome, then the causal condition that distinguishes the two expressions can be considered irrelevant and can be removed to create a simpler, combined expression (p. 93).

The *Boolean minimization process* is conducted in a bottom-up fashion until no further stepwise reduction of Boolean expression is possible. This process is applied to the primitive expressions derived from truth table 1 as demonstrated in Table 8. With the Boolean minimization process applied, the reduced expressions (prime implicants) on user search success (S) from truth table 1 can be represented in the simpler equation as follows:

$$S = AC + AD + Ab + bC + bD + cD + ABD + Abd + Acd$$

Then, the final step of Boolean minimization is conducted by using the prime implicant chart (see Table 9) to map the links between nine prime

implicants (see the second equation previously shown) and 11 primitive expressions (see the first equation). This process helps to eliminate redundant prime implicants in order to produce a logically minimal number of prime implicants which cover as many of the primitive Boolean expressions as possible.

Eventually, with the final process of Boolean minimization applied, the final equation (S) from truth table 1 demonstrates six combinations of causal conditions that produce the positive outcome (user search success) as follows:

$$S = AC + AD + Ab + bC + bD + cD$$

This final equation significantly demonstrates the result showing that causal condition 'A' (users have prior knowledge and/or experience in the content), condition 'C' (users utilize different kinds of search tools), and condition 'D' (users read text or detailed information thoroughly) are the important variables that help users to achieve their goals.

Table 8. Boolean minimization process applied to the primitive expressions from truth table 1

Minimization : Step 1	Minimization : Step 2
ABCD *combines with* ABCd *to produce* ABC	ABC *combines with* AbC *to produce* AC
ABCD *combines with* ABcD *to produce* ABD	ACD *combines with* ACd *to produce* AC
ABCD *combines with* AbCD *to produce* ACD	ACD *combines with* AcD *to produce* AD
ABCd *combines with* AbCd *to produce* ACd	AbC *combines with* Abc *to produce* Ab
ABcD *combines with* aBcD *to produce* BcD	AbC *combines with* abC *to produce* bC
ABcD *combines with* AbcD *to produce* AcD	AcD *combines with* acD *to produce* cD
AbCD *combines with* AbCd *to produce* AbC	BcD *combines with* bcD *to produce* cD
AbCD *combines with* abCD *to produce* bCD	bCD *combines with* bcD *to produce* bD
AbcD *combines with* abcD *to produce* bcD	bCD *combines with* bCd *to produce* bC
AbcD *combines with* Abcd *to produce* Abc	
abCD *combines with* abCd *to produce* abC	
AbCd *combines with* Abcd *to produce* Abd	
AbCd *combines with* abCd *to produce* bCd	
aBcD *combines with* abcD *to produce* acD	

Table 9. Prime implicant chart showing coverage of original terms by prime implicants

Primitive Expressions

Prime Implicants

	ABCD	ABCd	ABcD	AbCD	AbcD	abCD	AbCd	aBcD	Abcd	abcD	abCd
AC	X	X		X			X				
AD	X		X	X	X						
Ab				X	X		X		X		
bC				X		X	X				X
bD				X	X	X				X	
cD			X		X			X		X	
ABD	X		X								
Abd							X		X		
Acd		X					X				

Contrary to the traditional view on user experience with Web site interface (first-time versus return users), the result shows that causal condition 'B' (users have visited the Web site before) is not the primary factor contributing to users' accomplishment in their search.

In addition, the second truth table (truth table 2) is constructed to examine the impact of various causal conditions including user prior knowledge in the contents they search (condition 'A') and prior experience in Web interface (condition 'B'), combined with different causal conditions from various Web site attributes (see Table 10). These variables include condition 'E' (Web site provides different approaches to content classification), condition 'F' (Web site has well-organized search retrieval results), and condition 'G' (Web site provides search tips or examples).

With all processes of Boolean minimization applied, the final Boolean equation (S) from truth table 2 demonstrates six combinations of causal conditions that produce the positive outcome (user search success) as follows:

$$S = AeF + AEFg + AEfG + BeFg + bEFg + Abefg$$

Significantly, this final equation derived from truth table 2 also confirms that causal condition 'A' (users have prior knowledge and/or experience in the content) is the important variable that helps users to achieve their goals. Besides the condition 'A,' the Web site variables that have significant impact on user search success include condition 'E' (Web sites that provide different approaches to content classification) and condition 'F' (Web

Table 10. The construction of truth table 2

Causal conditions					Total instances among 100 cases	Output code: presence/ absence of instance (P)	Output code: achieving goal– search success (S)
A	**B**	**E**	**F**	**G**			
Have prior knowledge and/or experience in content?	Have visited the Web site before (return user)?	Provide different approaches to content classifi-cation?	Have well organized search (retrieval) results?	Provide search tips or examples?			Achieve original goal– search success?
1*	1	1	1	1	0	0	n/a**
1	1	1	1	0	5	1*	1*
1	1	1	0	1	1	1	1
1	1	0	1	1	1	1	1
1	0	1	1	1	0	0	n/a
0	1	1	1	1	0	0	n/a
1	1	1	0	0	0	0	n/a
1	1	0	0	1	0	0	n/a
1	0	0	1	1	9	1	1
0	0	1	1	1	0	0	n/a
0	1	1	1	0	0	0	n/a
1	1	0	1	0	7	1	1
1	0	1	0	1	9	1	1
0	1	0	1	1	0	0	n/a
1	0	1	1	0	9	1	1
0	1	1	0	1	0	0	n/a
1	1	0	0	0	7	1	0
1	0	0	0	1	0	0	n/a
0	0	0	1	1	0	0	n/a
1	0	0	1	0	5	1	1
0	0	1	0	1	0	0	n/a
0	1	0	0	1	0	0	n/a
1	0	1	0	0	0	0	n/a
0	0	1	1	0	6	1	1
0	1	1	0	0	0	0	n/a
0	1	0	1	0	3	1	1
1	0	0	0	0	25	1	1
0	1	0	0	0	0	0	n/a
0	0	1	0	0	0	0	n/a
0	0	0	1	0	5	1	0
0	0	0	0	1	0	0	n/a
0	0	0	0	0	8	1	0
					= 100 cases		

*Number '1' indicates the presence of a causal condition or an output, and '0' indicates its absence. **Code 'n/a' indicates that the output code for the particular row is not applicable or it cannot be identified because the instance of the causal combination on that row is absent.*

sites that have well-organized search retrieval results). The result also shows that condition 'B' (users have visited the Web site before), and 'G' (Web sites provide search tips or examples) have less impact on user search success compared with other variables. These analytical results as well as others are further summarized and synthesized, in order to develop explanatory frameworks of user search behaviors and needs, as well as to establish classifications of substantial user factors and analytical frameworks to evaluate information design on Web sites.

CONCLUSION

This investigation demonstrates that a user-centered approach can improve information design on Web-based media through study of various factors, especially user cognitive factors including user goals and modes of searching, to identify the corresponding impact of these factors on information and functional needs in terms of user behaviors. As an attempt to solve the problems of information-seeking tasks in Web-based media, the research is successful in providing a new perspective on Web site design considerations by strongly taking a user-centered approach to incorporate a careful consideration of actual user needs and behaviors together with requirements from a Web site.

By conducting extensive qualitative research on user study in relation to search needs and behaviors on Web sites as well as employing various analytical methods to uncover different aspects of the research data, the study answers the research questions. The common patterns of user information-seeking behavior, user search strategies and methods, as well as user information needs presented in different cases are revealed. These valuable findings will be further synthesized to develop frameworks and classifications.

Deeper understanding of these various factors, especially user cognitive factors, may complement the use of existing analytical or design methods such as task analysis and scenario-based design, by helping Web developers to recognize the important factors that may be subtle or previously unidentified yet substantially affect user task performances. By recognizing these elements, Web developers can identify the useful and appropriate functions and/or information to include in each particular case, in order to support user needs and task performances and eventually promote their satisfaction.

REFERENCES

Boyatzis, R. E. (1998). *Transforming qualitative information: Thematic analysis and code development*. Thousand Oaks, CA: Sage.

Brinck, T., Gergle, D., & Wood, S. D. (2002). *Usability for the Web: Designing Web sites that work*. San Francisco: Morgan Kaufmann.

Chernoff, H. (1973). The use of faces to represent points in k-dimensional space graphically. *Journal of the American Statistical Association, 68,* 361-368.

Fleming, J. (1998). *Web navigation: Designing the user experience*. Sebastopol, CA: O'Reilly & Associates.

Fliess, J. L. (1981). Statistical methods for rates and proportions. New York: Wiley.

Ivory, M. Y., & Hearst, M. A. (2001). The state of the art in automating usability evaluation of user interface. *ACM Computing Surveys, 33*(4), 470-516.

Miles, M. B., & Huberman, A. M. (1984). *Qualitative data analysis: A sourcebook of new methods*. Newbury Park, CA: Sage.

Ragin, C. C. (1987). *The comparative method: Moving beyond qualitative and quantitative strategies.* Berkeley; Los Angeles: University of California Press.

Ragin, C. C. (1994). *Constructing social research: The unity and diversity of method.* Thousand Oaks, CA: Pine Forge Press.

Robson, C. (1993). *Real world research: A resource for social scientists and practitioner-researchers.* Malden, MA: Blackwell.

Rosenfeld, L., & Morville, P. (1998). *Information architecture for the World Wide Web.* Sebastopol, CA: O'Reilly & Associates.

Wainer, H., & Thissen, D. (1981). Graphical data analysis. *Annual Review of Psychology, 32,* 191-241.

This work was previously published in Human Computer Interaction Research in Web Design and Evaluation, edited by P. Zaphiris, pp. 42-77, copyright 2007 by Information Science Publishing (an imprint of IGI Global).

Chapter VII
A User–Centered Approach to the Retrieval of Information in an Adaptive Web Site

Cristina Gena
Università di Torino, Italy

Liliana Ardissono
Università di Torino, Italy

ABSTRACT

This chapter describes the user-centered design approach we adopted in the development and evaluation of an adaptive Web site. The development of usable Web sites, offering easy and efficient services to heterogeneous users, is a hot topic and a challenging issue for adaptive hypermedia and human-computer interaction. User-centered design promises to facilitate this task by guiding system designers in making decisions, which take the user's needs in serious account. Within a recent project funded by the Italian Public Administration, we developed a prototype information system supporting the online search of data about water resources. As the system was targeted to different types of users, including generic citizens and specialized technicians, we adopted a user-centered approach to identify their information needs and interaction requirements. Moreover, we applied query analysis techniques to identify further information needs and speed up the data retrieval activity. In this chapter, we describe the requirements analysis, the system design, and its evaluation.

INTRODUCTION

The development of a *Web-based information system* targeted to different types of users challenges the Web designer because heterogeneous requirements, information needs, and operation modes have to be considered. As pointed out by Nielsen (1999) and Norman and Draper (1986), the user's mental model and expectations have to be seriously taken into account to prevent her/him from being frustrated and rejecting the services offered by a Web site. Indeed, this issue is particularly relevant to Web sites offering task-oriented services, because most target users utilize them out of their leisure time, if not at work. Being under pressure, these users demand ease of use as well as efficient support to the execution of activities.

The positive aspect of a technical Web site is, however, the fact that the users can be precisely identified and modeled; moreover, their information needs, representing strong requirements, can be elicited by means of a suitable domain analysis. Therefore, utilities, such as data search and retrieval, can be developed to comply with different goals and backgrounds. Of course, users' involvement and testing have to be carried out also in this case because they support the development of effective and usable services (see Dumas & Redish, 1999; Keppel, 1991).

In our recent work, we faced these issues in the development of ACQUA, a prototype Web-based information system for the Italian Public Administration presenting information about water resources (a demo is available at http://acqua.di.unito.it). During the system design phase, we put in practice traditional *usability* principles and *adaptive hypermedia* best practices and we derived general guidelines for the development of *usable Web-based systems* for technical users (see Brusilovsky, 1996, 2001; Fink, Kobsa, & Nill, 1999; Maybury & Brusilovsky, 2002). The system described in the rest of this chapter is targeted to two main classes of users:

- Generic users, such as the citizen, who want to be informed about the general health state of rivers, lakes, and underground waters.
- Technical users, such as the public administration employees, who retrieve specific pieces of information for analysis purposes.

In this chapter we describe the requirements analysis, the design, and the evaluation of ACQUA,

focusing on the *user-centered approach* adopted in the prototype design and development phases. We involved domain experts and end users since the beginning of our work in order to assess the usefulness and suitability of the functionality offered by the system, as well as of its user interface. For further information about the system, see Gena and Ardissono (2004).

The rest of this chapter is organized as follows: Section "Background" provides an overview of the relevant user-centered design research. Section "The ACQUA Project" presents our work. Specifically, Section "Application Requirements" describes the interaction and user interface requirements that emerged during the design phase; Section "Adaptive Features" presents the adaptive features we developed for our system; Section "Association Rules" describes the techniques supporting the personalized information search; Section "Evaluation of ACQUA" presents the results of an evaluation we carried out to test the system functionality with real users; and Section "Comparison with Other Solutions" compares our proposal with some related work. Finally, section "Future Trends" discusses some open technical issues and suggests how to address them, and Section "Conclusion" concludes the chapter.

BACKGROUND

Several researchers suggested to address usability issues by developing *adaptive systems*. For instance, Benyon (1993) proposed adaptivity as a solution, because a single interface cannot be designed to meet the usability requirements of all the groups of users of a system. However, it is possible to prove that adaptivity enhances the usability of a system only if it can be shown that, without the adaptive capability, the system performs less effectively. Benyon identifies five interdependent activities to be considered when designing an adaptive system:

1. *Functional analysis*, aimed at defining the main functions of the system.
2. *Data analysis*, concerned with understanding and representing the meaning and structure of data in the application domain.
3. *Task knowledge analysis*, focused on the cognitive characteristics required by the system users, such as the user's mental model, cognitive load, and the required search strategy.
4. *User analysis*, aimed at determining the scope of the user population to which the system is targeted. This analysis concerns the identification of the user attributes that are relevant for the application, such as required intellectual capability, cognitive processing ability, and similar. The target population is analyzed and classified according to the aspects of the application derived from the above-mentioned points.
5. *Environment analysis* is aimed at identifying the characteristics of the environment in which the system is going to operate.

Notice that these phases are similar to the steps followed during the requirements analysis phase of a generic software system (Preece, Rogers, Sharp, & Benyon, 1994). Benyon underlined the fact that adaptive systems should benefit more than other systems from a requirements analysis before starting any kind of evaluation, because the development of these systems has to take a high number of features into account. The recognition that an adaptive capability may be desirable leads to an improved system analysis and design. As a demonstration, he reported an example of an adaptive system development, wherein he prototyped and evaluated the system with a number of users. Several user characteristics were examined to determine their effects on the interaction. Then, further task knowledge and functional analysis were carried out.

Also Oppermann (1994) proposed a user-centered perspective and suggested a *design-evaluation-redesign* approach. He noticed that the adaptive features can be considered as the main part of a system and thus have to be evaluated during every development phase. The problem is circular:

*   A problem solvable by means of the adaptivity has to be identified.
*   The user characteristics related to the problem have to be selected.
*   Ways of inferring user characteristics from interaction behavior have to be found.
*   Adaptation techniques offering the right adaptive behavior have to be designed.

This process requires a bootstrapping method: first some initial adaptive behavior is implemented, then tested with users, revised, and tested again. The reason is that it is hard to decide which particular adaptations should be associated to specific user actions. Furthermore, the adaptations must be potentially useful to the user. The necessity of an iterative process is due to the fact that the real behavior of users in a given situation is hard to foresee; therefore, some evidence can be shown only by monitoring the users' activity. From the iterative evaluation point of view, the design phases and their evaluation have to be repeated until good results are reached.

Oppermann's iterative process is very similar to the *user-centered system design* approach originally phrased by Gould and Lewis (1983) and extended by Norman and Draper (1986).

Dix, Finlay, Abowd, and Beale (1998) pointed out that the iterative design is also a way to overcome the inherent problems of incomplete requirements specification, as only a subset of the requirements for an interactive system can be determined from the start of the project. The iterative evaluation process requires empirical knowledge about the users' behavior from the first development phases. In the case of an adaptive system, prior knowledge about the real users, the context of use, and domain experts facilitates the selection of the relevant data for the user model, such as personal features, goals, plans, domain knowledge, and context. Deep knowledge about users also offers a broad view of the application goals and prevents the system designer from serious mistakes, especially when dealing with innovative applications.

Petrelli, De Angeli, and Convertino (1999) proposed the user-centered approach to user modeling as a way to move from designer questions to guidelines by making the best use of empirical data; they advocated incremental system design as a way to satisfy large sets of users. They reported that at the early stage of development of a mobile device presenting contextual information to museum visitors, they decided to revise some of their initial assumptions about the user model. Indeed, they made this decision after having analyzed the results of a questionnaire distributed to 250 visitors. For instance, they discarded the former user modeling techniques based on stereotypes (because the sociodemographic and personal data taken in consideration did not characterize the users' behavior in a satisfactory way) in favor of a socially oriented and context-aware perspective. For instance, they noticed that people do not like to visit museums on their own and prefer looking at paintings to interacting with a device.

As discussed by Höök (2000), intelligent user interfaces may violate many usability principles developed for direct manipulation systems. The main problem is that these systems may violate many good principles, such as enabling the user to control the system, making the system predictable (given a certain input, the system always generates the same response), and making the system transparent so that the user understands at least partially how it works. In addition, most adaptive interface developers are more concerned with defining inference strategies than with interface design. For Höök, intelligent user interfaces sometimes require a new way of addressing usability, different from the principles outlined for direct-manipulation systems. Instead of measur-

ing factors such as task completion time, number of errors, or number of revisited nodes, other aspects have to be considered. For instance, "if the system should do information filtering, then we must check whether subjects find the most relevant information with the adaptive system and not necessarily whether they find it fast. This is not to say that the traditional measurements are always wrong—this of course depends upon the task that user and (adaptive) system should solve together" (Höök, 2002, p. 12).

Finally, Palmquist and Kim (2000) investigated the effects of (field independent and field dependent) *cognitive style* and online database search experience on WWW search performance. They concluded that cognitive style significantly influences the performance of novice searchers. In contrast, experienced searchers display a common behavior: they usually do not get lost in Web pages including many links, but they are able to choose useful navigation strategies. Therefore, Palmquist and Kim suggested that novice users should benefit from Web pages that have a simple design and few links providing information necessary to perform analytic search.

THE ACQUA PROJECT

Application Requirements

In 2003, the Water Resources Division (*Direzione Risorse Idriche*) of the Piedmont Region and the University of Torino started a project for the development of ACQUA, a Web-based information system presenting data about water resources derived from the monitoring activities on the territory. The goal was to make information available on a Web site that describes the Division and supports a search for data in real time, in order to limit the distribution of information on a one-to-one basis via e-mail messages and paper publications. The technicians of the Division guided us in the system development by specifying application requirements and by sharing with us a repository of e-mail messages they exchanged with users asking for information throughout the years. The repository provided us with evidence about the users' interested in water resources data, the inspected information, and the regularities in the search for data. Most questions were posed by the following:

- Employees of other Public Administrations, such as technicians and researchers, who are often interested in environmental impact studies, construction feasibility studies, and historical data.
- Technicians, such as companies working at the construction of bridges and houses.
- Attorneys, who are typically interested in the examination of data concerning specific regions, for example, as a consequence of an environmental disaster.
- Farmers, who wish to monitor the biochemical state of their fields.
- Students attending secondary school, university, and also doctoral programs. These users collect information for the preparation of reports concerning, for example, historical changes in biological and chemical composition of waters, or the evolution of the capacity and hydrometric levels of rivers, and similar.

Following a user-centered approach, we developed the system by involving domain experts and end users since the first design phases. After a requirements analysis phase, we developed a number of mock-ups, which we discussed and redesigned after several focus group sessions with the experts and the users involved in the project. We decided to adopt a cooperative design approach (Greenbaum & Kyng, 1991) in order to utilize the experience of domain experts and technicians in the design of an effective user interface. We based the development of our first prototype on the collected feedback. As the ACQUA system

is devoted to the Public Administration, we had to satisfy usability and predictability requirements that imposed the design of a simple user interface. Specifically, our interlocutors suggested the following:

- The interface should be usable and intuitive in order to satisfy user needs and expectations. This first requirement should be followed in every interface design project; however, Public Administrations have the mandatory goal of satisfying all the citizens, thus usability is also intended as a service for the collectivity.
- The system behavior should be highly predictable (Dix et al., 1998) to support first-time visitors in their search task, but also to avoid frustrating professional users who would regularly use it at work. Notice that the predictability requirement has some subtle aspects: for instance, not only the user should foresee what is going to happen next, but also what should *not* be expected from the service. This is very important to prevent the user from starting the exploration of paths that will not provide her/him with the information, or the functionality (s)he is looking for.
- The system should provide the user with data that can be analyzed without preprocessing. Therefore, search results should be presented in machine-processable formats, in addition to the pictorial ones suitable for a general-purpose presentation in Web pages.
- For the sake of accessibility, the pages of the user interface should be optimized for standard browsers, without the need of special equipments or software environments.

In order to maximize the usefulness of the information that can be retrieved from the Web site, we decided to make the system generate the search results in formats, such as MS Excel® tables and textual (TXT) files, directly supporting the data analysis and interpretation at the user side. We also tried to address efficiency in the retrieval of information by reconsidering the design of the general Web site to be presented. We wanted to offer the right information the user is looking for; thus, we decided to show the main search functions in the home page of the Web site, and to move textual information, such as the pages describing the Public Administration divisions, in secondary pages, which can be reached by following hypertextual links.

Moreover, having analyzed the data about the users interested in water resources, we identified two main targets to which the system should adapt. For shortness, we denote these categories as novices and experts.

- *Novice users*, such as students and generic citizens, visit the Web site on an occasional basis and are not familiar with the content presented by the information system.
- *Expert users*, such as technicians, farmers, and the personnel of other Public Admin-

istrations, frequently visit the site and are familiar with the domain-specific information provided by the system.

In order to take the interaction requirements of these users into account, we defined two search functions:

(i) The *simple search* is a geographical search modality and guides the user step by step in the retrieval of information;

(ii) The *advanced search* offers forms where the expert user may compose the queries in single step. Figure 1 shows the user interface of the ACQUA prototype supporting the advanced search; the menus enable the user to specify the river ("Scegli il corso d'acqua"), observation point ("Scegli il punto di monitoraggio"), start date ("Data Inizio"), and end date ("Data Fine"). Moreover, the user interface enables the user to select the hydrometric and chemical-physical parameters to be inspected.

Figure 1. Searching quantitative data (continuous hydrometric and chemical-physical parameters) about Po River in the Torino-Murazzi observation point

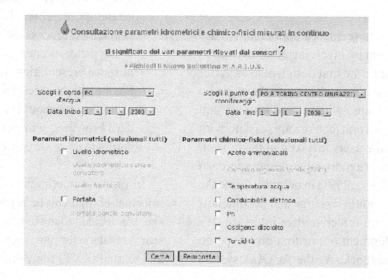

Thus, novice users may search for information in a friendly modality and the eligible choices are restricted and presented along the path, while expert users benefit from a faster search function.

As a matter of fact, the information about water resources exploited by the system is unavoidably incomplete. For instance, some data are collected by automatic stations, which have been set up at different times over the years and sometimes are out of order. Moreover, unfortunately, data collected in manual observation points have been stored in unstructured formats and the historical series has been reconstructed only for the very recent past.

For the sake of predictability, the simple and advanced search functions prevent the user from composing any queries that are incorrect, or are aimed at searching for unavailable data. The idea is that, in both cases, the system should only present the choices leading to available results. For instance, as shown in Figure 1, the labels of

the parameters, which are not available for the Po River, are shaded and cannot be selected by the user to define a query.

Adaptive Features

The information about water resources concerns rivers, lakes, and underground waters and includes the following:

- Descriptive data about resources and observation points: for example, maps of the points, charts representing environmental changes, pictures, documents, publications, and descriptions of the monitoring stations. For instance, Figure 2 ("Caratteristiche della stazione di monitoraggio TORINO" ["Features of the Torino monitoring station"]) shows the coordinates and other information about the observation point on Po River located in Torino, Parco Michelotti.

Figure 2. Portion of the page describing the Torino observation point on Po River

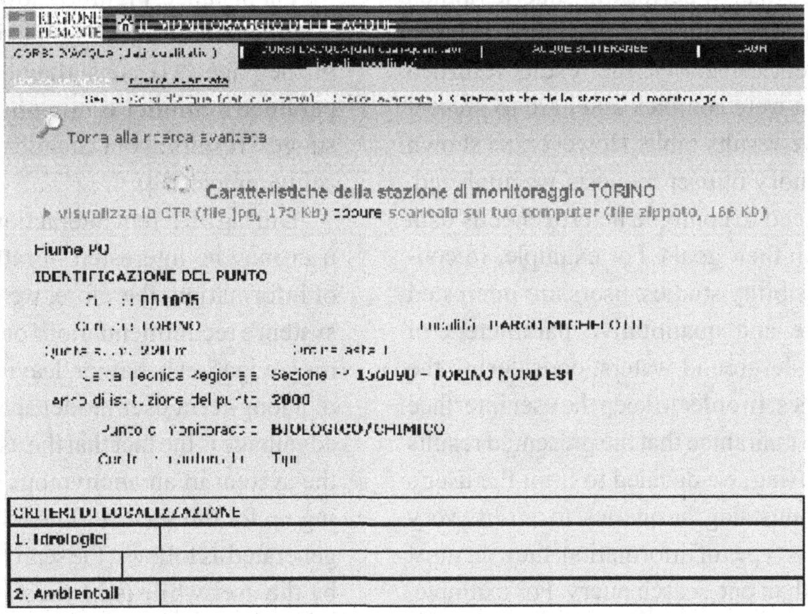

- Measurement parameters concerning physical dimensions and other features, which characterize the environmental state of the resources. These parameters are grouped in two main classes:

  - *Qualitative parameters*, which are periodically measured: technicians visit the observation points, collect data, and take samples for laboratory tests.

  - *Quantitative parameters*, which are monitored by automatic stations.

These stations carry out the measurements on a daily basis.

The ACQUA Web site is organized in four main sections, respectively devoted to the presentation of qualitative and quantitative information about rivers, information about lakes, and information about underground waters. The system enables the user to retrieve data about water resources by performing a simple or advanced search in all the sections of the site. Therefore, a large amount of heterogeneous data is accessible, ranging from biological and chemical data to capacity measurement and hydrometric levels (for details, see Gena & Ardissono, 2004).

We noticed that, by performing queries aimed at selecting a large number of data items, belonging to different categories, the results returned by the system were complex and hard to present in an intuitive results table. However, as shown by the repository of user requests we analyzed, users often need to combine heterogeneous data to accomplish their goals. For example, in construction feasibility studies, users are interested in qualitative and quantitative parameters of rivers and underground waters, considering the historical series. In order to keep the user interface simple and to guarantee that the presented results are not confusing, we decided to limit the user's freedom in composing the queries: to retrieve very heterogeneous types of information, the user must define more than one search query. For example,

as shown in Figure 1, the ACQUA query interface enables the user to choose from different rivers, observation points, years, and data types. Other categories, such as qualitative and quantitative data about rivers, lakes, and underground waters are treated as separate sections of the Web site and have their own query functions.

Unfortunately, although this approach enforces the clarity of the results, it makes the search for multiple types of information a lengthy task. Therefore, a compromise between clarity and efficiency must be found. In order to address this issue, we extended the system with an *intelligent search component*, which complements the user's explicit queries with *follow-up queries* (Moore & Mittal, 1996) frequently occurring together in navigation paths. When possible, the system anticipates the user's queries and makes the extended search results available as personalized suggestions that can be downloaded on demand. If the user is interested in the recommended information, (s)he can retrieve it by clicking on the adaptive suggestion links, without performing any further queries. At the same time, the system retrieves the extended results only after the user clicks on a suggestion link in order to avoid precaching possibly useless data.

For instance, Figure 3 shows the recommendations generated by the system in the lower portion of the page ("Ti consigliamo anche i valori dei parametri chimici e microbiologici" ["We also suggest results about chemical and microbiological parameters"]).

During different interaction sections, the same user may be interested in rather different types of information; therefore, we decided to base the system's recommendations on the analysis of her/his navigation behavior, leaving the management of a long-term user model apart. One immediate advantage is the fact that the user can interact with the system in an anonymous way, without signing up for the service. The follow-up queries are generated as follows: the search queries performed by the user while (s)he browses the Web site are

Figure 3. Annotated link for the suggested information and descriptions of the monitoring stations

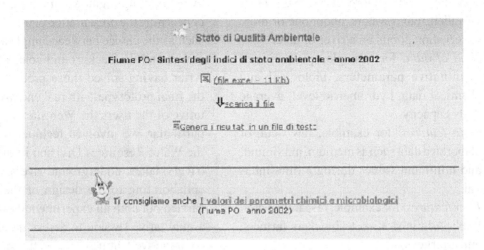

monitored and association rules which suggest other, strictly related queries are applied.

Each association rule has a condition part specifying constraints on the previous navigation behavior, and an action part defining a relevant follow-up query to be performed in order to retrieve complementary information. The rules we defined in our current prototype are mutually exclusive and they are selected and fired by applying a very tiny and efficient inference engine. This engine would not be suitable to manage a large set of conflicting rules: a general-purpose rule-based engine should be employed to that purpose. However, we prefer to maintain a simple set of adaptation rules, and to avoid embedding complex rule-based engines in order to keep the adaptive features as lightweight as possible. In fact, the management of the interaction is subject to a relevant overload due to the generation of results in multiple formats, which is a main requirement for the information system. In this situation, minimalist but efficient adaptation to the user is strongly preferred to flexible but complex one.

Association Rules

In order to define the *association rules* to be applied for anticipating the user's information needs, we analyzed a repository of requests, which real users posed to the Water Resources Division over the years; the requests consisted of e-mail messages and fax documents. As we noticed that different kinds of information frequently occurred together in these requests, we decided to analyze the frequency of co-occurrence in order to identify the regularities. Specifically, we analyzed 97 requests and we selected a set of features describing the requests in a systematic way. These features concerned rather different aspects of the requests; thus, for clarity purposes, we grouped them in subcategories. In the following, we report the subcategories we defined and for each one we list some sample features:

- *Kind of request:* for example, environmental impact study, construction feasibility studies, and lawyers' studies.

- *Request features:* for example, information about one or more rivers, about lakes or underground waters, about one or more observation points on a river or lake.
- *Kind of data:* for example, qualitative or quantitative parameters, biological and chemical data, hydrometric level, average daily capacity.
- *Data features:* for example, raw data, or elaborated data such as medium, maximum, and minimum values during a time interval.
- *User features:* for example, research center, Public Administration, technicians, farmers, and attorneys.

We computed the frequency with which the features co-occurred in the requests: if the frequency exceeded a given threshold, the set of involved features became a possible candidate for an association rule. Then we compared the extracted associations with their original requests in order to validate our findings with factual knowledge, and finally we asked the technicians of the Water Resources Division if our conclusions were correct. After this last check, we selected the correct associations and we encoded the rules in the system.

For instance, a rule suggests to retrieve qualitative parameters about a water resource if the user has asked for quantitative historical data for more than one observation point on that resource, supposing that (s)he is looking for information for a construction feasibility study. Another rule suggests retrieving the environmental state indexes of a resource if the user has requested biological and chemical data, under the hypothesis that (s)he is involved in an environmental impact study.

Evaluation of ACQUA

We first evaluated the ACQUA prototype in a usability test by involving external users who were not cooperating at the project (see Dumas

& Redish, 1999, for methodological details). The evaluation highlighted some usability problems concerning the presentation of basic information, such as the choice between simple and advanced search and the background color of the menus. After having solved those problems, we tested the final prototype with real end users representative of the users the Web site is devoted to. In particular, we involved technicians working at the Water Resources Division in different fields (rivers, lakes, underground rivers, etc.) and not collaborating to the design of the project. We carried out both an experimental evaluation and a qualitative session to assess the suitability of the adaptive features offered the system.

Subjects. We evaluated 10 potential users of the ACQUA system, four females and six males, aged 30–50. All the users worked in the water resource area and none of them was involved in the project.

Procedure. The subjects were split up in two groups (five subjects each) and randomly assigned to one of the two groups. The experimental group had to solve some tasks using the adaptive Web site, which applies the association rules described in Section "Adaptive Features" to compute the results of follow-up queries related to the users' explicit queries. Instead, the control group had to solve the tasks without adaptation.

Experimental tasks. Every subject had to solve seven tasks, each one representing a real task the user can perform in the Web site. As suggested by our correlation study, the tasks were strictly correlated and could be grouped in three search activities the user often performs together. The first activity conveyed the whole information useful to an environmental impact study. The second one supported construction feasibility studies. The third activity supported lawyers' studies and activities.

- In the control group, the users had to submit a new query for every task, in order to obtain the requested results. The new queries were submitted by filling in the query specification forms (see, e.g., Figure 1).

- In the experimental group, the users could obtain the extra information related to the next task to be performed by clicking on an adaptive suggestion link that supports the immediate retrieval of the suggested information (see, e.g., Figure 3).

Experimental design. Single-factor (the adaptivity) between-subjects design.

Measures. The subjects' navigation behavior was recorded by using Camtasia Studio®. We measured the task completion time and then the subjects' satisfaction, by means of a post-task walk-through.

Hypothesis. We hypothesized that the users working in the experimental group could obtain better performance results than those of the control group.

Results. The ANOVA (analysis of variance) showed that the subjects of the experimental group achieved the best performance results. In addition, we calculated the effect size (treatment magnitude) and the power (sensitivity) as suggested in Chin (2001). The effect size (ω^2) measures the strength, or the magnitude, of the treatment effects in an experiment. In behavioral sciences, small, medium, and large effects of ω^2 are 0.01, 0.06, and >0.15, respectively. The power of an experiment (n') is the ability to recognize treatment effects and the power can be used for estimating the sample size. In social science, the accepted value of the power is equal to 0.80, which means that the 80% of repeated experiments will give the same results. In the following, we show a summary of the results:

Task 2.
    ANOVA: $F(1.8) = 12.45$ $p<0.01$;
    $\omega^2=0.53$; $n'=3.49$

Task 3.
    ANOVA: $F(1.8) = 12.12$ $p<0.01$;
    $\omega^2=0.53$; $n'=3.60$

Task 5.
    ANOVA: $F(1.8) = 14.16$ $p<0.01$;
    $\omega^2=0.57$; $n'=3.04$

Task 7.
    ANOVA: $F(1.8) = 9.23$ $p<0.05$;
    $\omega^2=0.45$; $n'=4.86$

It should be noticed that all the results are significant and have a large estimate of the magnitude of the treatment effect. In addition, by exploiting a power of 0.80 and the corresponding ω^2 for each task we could determine the requested sampled size, which fits our sample size ($n=5$) (for details about statistics, see Keppel, 1991).

Post-task walk-through. During any *post-task walk-through*, test subjects are asked to think about the event and comment on their actions. Thus, after each test we talked to the subjects to collect their impression and to discuss their performance and the problems encountered during the test. In this session, we also aimed at retrieving useful feedback for a qualitative evaluation of the site. In fact, although our experimental evaluation reported significant results supporting our hypothesis, the actual user behavior could be different. As recently pointed out by Nielsen (2004), statistical analyses are often false, misleading, and narrow; in contrast, insights and qualitative studies are not affected by these problems because they strictly rely to the users' observed behavior and reactions.

In most cases, the interviewed users were satisfied with the site. Most of them encountered some problems in the execution of the starting query of task 2, thus we modified the interface form.

- All the users of the experimental group followed the adaptive suggestion link provided by the system but they did not realize that it represented a personalization feature. When we explained the adaptations, they noticed the particularity of the suggestion ("We also recommend you ..."). Anyway, they were attracted from the suggestions and they appreciated the possibility of skipping the execution of a new query. The adaptive suggestions were considered visible and not intrusive.

- The users of the control group reported similar considerations when we described the adaptive features offered by the Web site. Even if they did not receive any suggestions during the execution of tasks, they explored the result pages in order to find a shortcut to proceed in the task execution. After having followed some links, they went back to the previous query page or to the home page by clicking on the "Back" button of the browser.

Both groups displayed a common behavior pattern: the users explored a results page before starting a new search. Nevertheless, their behavior could be influenced by the test condition, because tested users tend to pay a lot of attention to their own actions and to the page design.

We conclude by admitting that although the test subjects were satisfied with the adaptation features, only the real system usage can demonstrate our hypothesis. However, both quantitative and qualitative test results are encouraging and we think that the adaptations are correctly placed. After this test, we presented the adaptive version of the Web site to the technicians of the Water Resources Division collaborating on the project. They confirmed the correctness of association rules we defined and they decided to replace the non-adaptive version of the prototype system with the adaptive one.

Comparison with Other Solutions

The ACQUA system has a plain user interface, designed to meet simplicity, usability, and predictability requirements, but it offers advanced interactive features enabling the user to create a personal view of the information space. Two search features, targeted to novice and expert users, are available, and the search results are presented in both pictorial and machine-readable formats in order to support direct data manipulation at the user side. Moreover, the system analyzes the user's queries to identify her/his information needs, and it employs association rules to propose follow-up queries complementing the search results with strictly related information. The follow-up queries are applied on demand; thus, the user can ignore them if (s)he is not interested in the additional data, and the system does not need to retrieve any uninteresting information.

The advanced search features we presented differ from the related work in various aspects. On the one hand, the inferences performed by our system are simpler than the probabilistic ones applied in other automated assistants, such as Lumière (Horvitz, Breese, Heckerman, Hovel, & Rommelse, 1998) and ACE (Bunt & Conati, 2003), which exploit Bayesian networks to capture the dependencies among the user actions. The point is that the user interacting with the ACQUA system does not carry out a complex task requiring a problem-solving activity. Therefore, lightweight rules associating contextually related search queries are sufficient to predict the implicit information needs and to complement the search for information accordingly. Our approach also differs from the follow-up question answering techniques proposed by Moore and Mittal (1996): in order to efficiently manage the query selection process, our follow-up queries are precompiled in a set of association rules, instead of being generated by a planner.

On the other hand, we apply query analysis techniques to identify regularities in search patterns. This differs from the typical inferences carried out in recommender systems, which reason about the features of the selected items to identify the user's priorities (see, e.g., Billsus & Pazzani, 1999), or about the regularities in the selection of individual items (see, e.g., the work by Cotter & Smyth, 2000; GroupLens, 2002).

Liu, Yu, and Meng (2002) propose other query analysis strategies for personalized Web search. However, instead of personalizing the proposed results, their system supplies a small set of categories as a context for each query. The system combines the user's search history with a general user profile automatically extracted from a category hierarchy to offer a personalized context for disambiguating the proposed query results. In ACQUA, we do not manage long-term user preferences because we noticed that, in different interaction sections, the same users are interested in rather different types of information. We thus decided to base the recommendations only on the analysis of the user's search behavior.

FUTURE TRENDS

It is worth mentioning that the manual definition of the first set of association rules supporting the user's search task was a lengthy work and might not be easily replicated to revise the rules along time. However, if the Water Resources Division employs the ACQUA system as its official Web site, the log files generated by the system will provide structured evidence about user behavior (in addition to e-mails and faxes). Thus, data-mining techniques could be exploited to automatically recognize usage patterns and revise the association rules accordingly.

Indeed, we believe that these techniques can support the analysis of user behavior in an effec-

tive way, but they still have to be coupled with human analysis, in order to validate and interpret results: in several cases, these techniques have generated some very interesting results, but also other irrelevant or hardly understandable findings, which have been discarded.

At any rate, Web usage mining techniques, derived from machine learning methods such as knowledge discovery in data (KDD or data mining) can contribute to automate the adaptation of Web-based systems to the users. According to the scheme proposed by Pierrakos, Paliouras, Papatheodorou, and Spyropoulos (2003), ACQUA can be classified as a Web personalization system offering *task performance support*: this functionality involves the execution of a particular action on behalf of the user. In our case, the system generates queries and makes the results available as links to some files storing them. This functionality is considered as the most advanced personalization function and it is seldom offered by Web-based personalized services.

The most suitable data-mining technique, given the adaptive goals of the ACQUA system, is the *sequential pattern discovery*, which is aimed at identifying navigational patterns (event sequences) in the analyzed data (in our case, Web usage data). This methodology supports the discovery of event sequences that can be summarized as follows: "If event A, B, and C occur in that order, then events D, E, and F always follow." Two types of methods are generally applied to discover sequential patterns: *deterministic techniques*, which record the navigational behavior of the users and extract knowledge from the analyzed data, and *stochastic methods*, which use the sequence of already-visited Web pages to predict the behavior occurring in the next visits. Once sequential patterns have been discovered, the extracted knowledge can be automatically integrated in the personalization process, and the system behavior adapted accordingly.

CONCLUSION

We presented our experience in the design and development of ACQUA, an interactive prototype Web site for the Public Administration. The system presents information about water resources and supports the user in the search for generic information, as well as technical information about the rivers, lakes, and underground waters.

The usability and functional requirements that emerged during the design of the ACQUA system were very interesting and challenging, as they imposed the development of functions supporting the efficient retrieval of data by means of a simple user interface. We found out that the introduction of basic adaptivity features, aimed at understanding the user's information needs in detail, was very helpful to meet these requirements.

We were asked to develop a system having a simple user interface, designed to meet usability and predictability requirements. This fact limited our freedom to add advanced interaction features, desirable in a Web site visited by heterogeneous users; however, it challenged us to find a compromise between functionality and simplicity. In order to address this issue, we developed two interactive features enabling the user to create a personal view on the information space:

- The system offers a simple and an advanced search functions targeted to novice and expert users, respectively.
- Moreover, the system carries out a query analysis aimed at identifying the user's information needs, and applies association rules to extend the user's queries and complete the search results with data that is usually retrieved together by end users.

Qualitative and quantitative evaluation results showed that the adaptive user interface was more successful than the nonadaptive one. The reason was probably the concrete help offered by the adaptive suggestions, which speed up the execution of time-consuming search tasks. Moreover, the adaptive features were not perceived as intrusive and the user was allowed to skip useless suggestions. Furthermore, the system did not impose a previous annoying and discouraging registration phase.

As discussed in Section "Future trends," the adaptive features offered by the ACQUA system could be improved by the integration of Web-usage mining techniques aimed at discovering real usage patterns. In that way, the association rules employed to identify the user's implicit information needs could be automatically updated along time. However, we believe that the rules we manually defined provide a knowledge base that cannot be replaced with automatically extracted rules. In principle, both kinds of rules could be integrated in order to enhance the effectiveness of the system adaptations.

ACKNOWLEDGMENTS

This work was funded by Regione Piemonte, Direzione Risorse Idriche. We thank Giovanni Negro, Giuseppe Amadore, Silvia Grisello, Alessia Giannetta, Maria Governa, Ezio Quinto, Matteo Demeo, and Vincenzo Pellegrino, who assisted us during the system development and provided the domain-specific knowledge.

REFERENCES

Benyon, D. (1993). Adaptive systems: A solution to usability problems. *International Journal of User Modeling and User-Adapted Interaction, 3*, 65–87.

Billsus, D., & Pazzani, M. (1999). A personal news agent that talks, learns and explains. *In Proceedings of 3rd International Conference on Autonomous Agents* (pp. 268–275).

Brusilovsky, P. (1996). Methods and techniques of adaptive hypermedia. *International Journal of User Modeling and User-Adapted Interaction, 6*(2–3), 87–129.

Brusilovsky, P. (2001). Adaptive hypermedia. *International Journal of User Modeling and User-Adapted Interaction, 11*(1–2), 87–110.

Bunt, A., & Conati, C. (2003). Probabilistic student modelling to improve exploratory behaviour. *International Journal of User Modeling and User-Adapted Interaction, 13*(3), 269–309.

Chin, D. N., (2001). Empirical evaluation of user models and user-adapted systems. *International Journal of User Modeling and User-Adapted Interaction, 11*(1–2), 181–194.

Cotter, P., & Smyth, B. (2000). WAPing the Web: Content personalization for WAP-enabled devices. *Proceedings of International Conference on Adaptive Hypermedia and Adaptive Web-Based Systems* (pp. 98–108).

Dix, A., Finlay, J., Abowd, G., & Beale, R. (1998). *Human computer interaction* (2nd ed.). Prentice Hall.

Dumas, J. S., & Redish, J. C. (1999). *A practical guide to usability testing*. Norwood, NJ: Ablex.

Fink, J., Kobsa, A., & Nill, A. (1999). Adaptable and adaptive information for all users, including disabled and elderly people. *New Review of Hypermedia and Multimedia, 4*, 163–188.

Gena, C., & Ardissono, L. (2004). Intelligent support to the retrieval of information about hydric resources. *Proceedings of 3rd International Conference on Adaptive Hypermedia and Adaptive Web-Based Systems* (pp. 126–135).

Gould, J. D., & Lewis, C. (1983). Designing for usability: Key principles and what designers think. *Proceedings of CHI '83* (pp. 50–53).

Greenbaum, J., & Kyng, M. (1991). *Design at work: Cooperative design of computer systems*. Hillsdale, NJ: Lawrence Erlbaum.

GroupLens. (2005). GroupLens Research. Retrieved November 2, 2005, from www.GroupLens.org

Höök, K. (2000). Steps to take before IUIs become real. *Journal of Interacting With Computers, 12*(4), 409–426.

Horvitz, E., Breese J., Heckerman D., Hovel D., & Rommelse, K. (1998). *The* Lumière project: Bayesian user modeling for inferring the goals and needs of software users. *Proceedings of 14th Conference on Uncertainty in Artificial Intelligence,* San Francisco.

Keppel, G. (1991). *Design and analysis: A researcher's handbook*. Englewood Cliffs, NJ: Prentice-Hall.

Liu, F., Yu, C., & Meng, W. (2002). Personalized Web search by mapping user query to categories. *Proceedings of the 2002 ACM Conference on Information and Knowledge Management,* McLean, VA.

Maybury, M., & Brusilovsky, P. (Eds.). (2002). The adaptive Web. *Communications of the ACM, 45.*

Moore, J. D., & Mittal, V. O. (1996). Dynamically generated follow-up questions. *IEEE Computer, 29*(7), 75–86.

Nielsen, J. (1999). *Web usability*. Indianapolis, IN: New Riders Publishing.

Nielsen, J. (2004). *Risks of quantitative studies*. Retrieved March 9, 2004, from www.useit.com/alertbox/20040301.html

Norman, D. A., & Draper, S. W. (1986). *User centered system design: New perspective on HCI*. Hillsdale, NJ: Lawrence Erlbaum.

Oppermann, R. (1994). Adaptively supported adaptivity. *International Journal of Human-Computer Studies, 40,* 455–472.

Palmquist, R. A., & Kim, K. S. (2000). Cognitive style and on-line database search experience as predictors of Web search performance. *Journal of the American Society for Information Science, 51*(6), 558–566.

Petrelli, D., De Angeli, A., & Convertino, G. (1999). A user centered approach to user modeling.

Proceedings of the 7th International Conference on User Modeling (pp. 255–264).

Pierrakos, D., Paliouras, G., Papatheodorou, C., & Spyropoulos, C. D. (2003). Web usage mining as a tool for personalization: A survey. *International Journal of User Modeling and User-Adapted Interaction, 13*(4), 311–372.

Preece, J., Rogers, Y., Sharp, H., & Benyon, D. (1994). *Human-computer interaction.* Addison Wesley.

Chapter VIII
On the Cognitive Processes of Human Perception with Emotions, Motivations, and Attitudes

Yingxu Wang
University of Calgary, Canada

ABSTRACT

An interactive motivation-attitude theory is developed based on the Layered Reference Model of the Brain (LRMB) and the object-attribute-relation (OAR) model. This paper presents a rigorous model of human perceptual processes such as emotions, motivations, and attitudes. A set of mathematical models and formal cognitive processes of perception is developed. Interactions and relationships between motivation and attitude are formally described in real-time process algebra (RTPA). Applications of the mathematical models of motivations and attitudes in software engineering are demonstrated. This work is a part of the formalization of LRMB, which provides a comprehensive model for explaining the fundamental cognitive processes of the brain and their interactions. This work demonstrates that the complicated human emotional and perceptual phenomena can be rigorously modeled and formally treated based on cognitive informatics theories and denotational mathematics.

INTRODUCTION

A variety of life functions and cognitive processes has been identified in cognitive informatics (Wang, 2002a, 2003a, 2003b, 2007b) and cognitive psychology (Payne & Wenger, 1998; Pinel, 1997; Smith, 1993; Westen, 1999; Wilson & Keil, 1999). In order to formally and rigorously describe a comprehensive and coherent set of mental processes and their relationships, an LRMB has been developed (Wang & Wang, 2006; Wang, Wang, Patel, & Patel, 2006) that explains the functional mechanisms and cognitive processes of the brain and the natural intelligence. LRMB encompasses 39 cognitive processes at six layers known as the *sensation, memory, perception, action, meta* and *higher cognitive layers* from the bottom up.

Definition 1: Perception is a set of internal sensational cognitive processes of the brain at the subconscious cognitive function layer that detects, relates, interprets, and searches internal cognitive information in the mind.

Perception may be considered as the sixth sense of human beings since almost all cognitive life functions rely on it. Perception is also an important cognitive function at the subconscious layers that determines personality. In other words, personality is a faculty of all subconscious life functions and experience cumulated via conscious life functions. It is recognized that a crucial component of the future generation computers known as the *cognitive computers* is the *perceptual engine* that mimic the natural intelligence (Wang, 2006a, 2007c).

The main cognitive processes at the perception layer of LRMB are *emotion, motivation,* and *attitude* (Wang et al., 2006). This article presents a formal treatment of the three perceptual processes, their interrelationships, and interactions. It demonstrates that complicated psychological and cognitive mental processes may be formally modeled and rigorously described. Mathematical models of the psychological and cognitive processes of emotions, motivations, and attitudes are developed in the following three sections. Then, interactions and relationships between emotions, motivations, and attitudes are analyzed. Based on the integrated models of the three perception processes, the formal description of the cognitive processes of motivations and attitudes will be presented using RTPA (Wang, 2002b, 2003c, 2006b, 2007a). Applications of the formal models of emotions, motivations, and attitudes will be demonstrated in a case study on maximizing strengths of individual motivations in software engineering.

THE HIERARCHICAL MODEL OF EMOTIONS

Emotions are a set of states or results of perception that interprets the feelings of human beings on external stimuli or events in the binary categories of pleasant or unpleasant.

Definition 2: An emotion is a personal feeling derived from one's current internal status, mood, circumstances, historical context, and external stimuli.

Emotions are closely related to desires and willingness. A *desire* is a personal feeling or willingness to possess an object, to conduct an interaction with the external world, or to prepare for an event to happen. A *willingness* is the faculty of conscious, deliberate, and voluntary choice of actions.

According to the study by Fischer, Shaver, and Carnochan (1990) and Wilson and Keil (1999), the taxonomy of emotions can be described at three levels known as the sub-category, basic, and super levels as shown in Table 1.

It is interesting that human emotions at the perceptual layer may be classified into only two opposite categories: *pleasant* and *unpleasant*. Various emotions in the two categories can be classified at five levels according to its strengths of subjective feelings as shown in Table 2 (Wang, 2005), where each level encompasses a pair of positive/negative or pleasant/unpleasant emotions.

Definition 3: The strength of emotion $|E_m|$ is a normalized measure of how strong a person's emotion on a five-level scale identified from 0 through 4, that is:

$$0 \leq |E_m| \leq 4 \qquad (1)$$

where $|E_m|$ represents the absolute strength of an emotion regardless whether it is positive (pleasant)

Table 1. Taxonomy of emotions

Level	Description				
Super level	Positive (pleasant)		Negative (unpleasant)		
Basic level	Joy	Love	Anger	Sadness	Fear
Sub-category level	Bliss, pride, contentment	Fondness, infatuation	Annoyance, hostility, contempt, jealousy	Agony, grief, guilt, loneliness	Horror, worry

Table 2. The hierarchy of emotions

Level (Positive/Negative)		Description
0	No emotion	-
1	Weak emotion	Comfort	Safeness, contentment, fulfillment, trust
		Fear	Worry, horror, jealousy, frightening, threatening
2	Moderate emotion	Joy	Delight, fun, interest, pride
		Sadness	Anxiety, loneliness, regret, guilt, grief, sorrow, agony
3	Strong emotion	Pleasure	Happiness, bliss, excitement, ecstasy
		Anger	Annoyance, hostility, contempt, infuriated, enraged
4	Strongest emotion	Love	Intimacy, passion, amorousness, fondness, infatuation
		Hate	Disgust, detestation, abhorrence, bitterness

or negative (unpleasant), and the scope of $|E_m|$ is corresponding to the definitions of Table 2.

It is observed that an organ known as *hypothalamus* in the brain is supposed to interpret the properties or types of emotions in terms of pleasant or unpleasant (Payne & Wenger, 1998; Pinel, 1997; Smith, 1993; Wang et al., 2006; Westen, 1999).

Definition 4: Let T_e be a type of emotion, ES the external stimulus, IS the internal perceptual status, and BL the Boolean values true or false. The perceptual mechanism of the hypothalamus can be described as a function, that is:

$$T_e : ES \times IS \to BL \tag{2}$$

It is interesting that the same event or stimulus *ES* may be explained in different types, in terms of pleasant or unpleasant, due to the difference of the real-time context of the perceptual status *IS* of the brain. For instance, walking from home to the office may be interpreted as a pleasant activity for one who likes physical exercise, but the same walk due to car breakdown will be interpreted as unpleasant. This observation and the taxonomy provided in Tables 1 and 2 leads to the following Theorem.

Theorem 1: The human emotional system is a binary system that interprets or perceives an external stimulus and/or internal status as pleasant or unpleasant.

Although there are various emotional categories in different levels, the binary emotional system of the brain provides a set of pairwise universal solutions to express human feelings. For example, angry may be explained as a default solution or generic reaction for an emotional event when there is no better solution available; otherwise, delight will be the default emotional reaction.

THE MATHEMATICAL MODEL OF MOTIVATIONS

Motivation is an innate potential power of human beings that energizes behavior. It is motivation that triggers the transformation from thought (information) into action (energy). In other words, human behaviors are the embodiment of motivations. Therefore, any cognitive behavior is driven by an individual motivation.

Definition 5: A motivation is a willingness or desire triggered by an emotion or external stimulus to pursue a goal or a reason for triggering an action.

As described in LRMB (Wang et al., 2006), motivation is a cognitive process of the brain at the perception layer that explains the initiation, persistence, and intensity of personal emotions and desires, which are the faculty of conscious, deliberate, and voluntary choices of actions.

Motivation is a psychological and social modulating and coordinating influence on the direction, vigor, and composition of behavior. This influence arises from a wide variety of internal, environmental, and social sources, and is manifested at many levels of behavioral and neural organizations.

The taxonomy of motives can be classified into two categories known as learned and unlearned (Wittig, 2001). The latter is the primary motives such as the *survival motives* (hunger, thirst, breath, shelter, sleep, and eliminating pain). The former are the secondary motives such as the need for achievement, friendship, affiliation, dominance of power, and relief anxiety, which are acquired and extended based on the primary motives.

Definition 6: The strength of motivation M is a normalized measure of how strong a person's motivation on a scale of 0 through 100, that is:

$$0 \leq M \leq 100 \tag{3}$$

where $M = 100$ is the strongest motivation and $M = 0$ is the weakest motivation.

It is observed that the strength of a motivation is determined by multiple factors (Westen, 1999; Wilson & Keil, 1999) such as:

a. The *absolute motivation* $|E_m|$: The strength of the emotion.
b. The *relative motivation E - S*: A relative difference or inequity between the expectancy of a person *E* for an object or an action towards a certain goal and the current status *S* of the person.

c. The *cost* to fulfill the motivation *C*: A subjective assessment of the effort needed to accomplish the expected goal.

Therefore, the strength of a motivation can be quantitatively analyzed and estimated by the subjective and objective motivations and their cost as described in the following theorem.

Theorem 2: The strength of a motivation M is proportional to both the strength of emotion $|E_m|$ and the difference between the expectancy of desire E and the current status S, of a person, and is inversely proportional to the cost to accomplish the expected motivation C, that is:

$$M = \frac{2.5 \bullet |E_m| \bullet (E\text{-}S)}{C} \qquad (4)$$

where $0 \leq |E_m| \leq 4$, $0 \leq (E,S) \leq 10$, $1 \leq C \leq 10$, and the coefficient 2.5 makes the value of M normalized in the scope of [0 .. 100].

In Theorem 2, the strength of a motivation is measured in the scope $0 \leq M \leq 100$. When $M > 1$, the motivation is considered being a desired motivation, because it indicates both an existing emotion and a positive expectancy. The higher the value of M, the stronger the motivation.

According to Theorem 2, in a software engineering context, the rational action of a manager of a group is to encourage individual emotional desire, and the expectancy of each software engineer and to decrease the required effort for the employees by providing additional resources or adopting certain tools.

Corollary 1: There are super strong motivations toward a resolute goal by a determined expectancy of a person at any cost.

It is noteworthy that a motivation is only a potential mental power of human beings, and a strong motivation will not necessarily result in a behavior or action. The condition for transform-

ing a motivation into a real behavior or action is dependent on multiple factors, such as values, social norms, expected difficulties, availability of resources, and the existence of alternative goals.

The motivation of a person is constrained by the attitude and decision-making strategies of the person. The former is the internal (subjective) judgment of the feasibility of the motivation, and the latter is the external (social) judgment of the feasibility of the motivation. Attitude and decision-making mechanisms will be analyzed in the following subsections.

THE MATHEMATICAL MODEL OF ATTITUDES

As described in the previous section, motivation is the potential power that may trigger an observable behavior or action. Before the behavior is performed, it is judged by an internal regulation system known as the attitude.

Psychologists perceive attitude in various ways. Fazio (1986) describes an *attitude* as an association between an act or object and an evaluation. Eagly and Chaiken (1992) define that an attitude is a tendency of a human to evaluate a person, concept, or group positively or negatively in a given context. More recently, Wittig (2001) describes attitude as a learned evaluative reaction to people, objects, events, and other stimuli. Attitudes may be formally defined as follows.

Definition 7: An attitude is a subjective tendency towards a motivation, an object, a goal, or an action based on an intuitive evaluation of its feasibility.

The modes of attitudes can be positive or negative, which can be quantitatively analyzed using the following model.

Definition 8. The mode of an attitude A is determined by both an objective judgment of its conformance to the social norm N and a subjective judgment of its empirical feasibility F, that is:

$$A = \begin{cases} 1, & N = \mathbf{T} \wedge F = \mathbf{T} \\ 0, & N = \mathbf{F} \vee F = \mathbf{F} \end{cases} \tag{5}$$

where $A = 1$ indicates a positive attitude; otherwise, it indicates a negative attitude.

INTERACTIONS BETWEEN MOTIVATION AND ATTITUDE

This section discusses the relationship between the set of interlinked perceptual psychological processes such as emotions, motivations, attitudes, decisions, and behaviors as formally modeled in the preceeding sections. A motivation/attitude-driven behavioral model will be developed for formally describing the cognitive processes of motivations and attitudes.

It is observed that motivation and attitude have considerable impact on behavior and influence the

ways a person thinks and feels (Westen, 1999). A reasoned action model is proposed by Fishbein and Ajzen (1975) that suggests human behavior is directly generated by behavioral intensions, which are controlled by the attitude and social norms. An initial motivation before the judgment by an attitude is only a temporal idea; with the judgment of the attitude, it becomes a *rational* motivation (Wang et al., 2006), also known as the *behavioral intention.*

The relationship between an emotion, motivation, attitude, and behavior can be formally and quantitatively described by the Motivation/Attitude-Driven Behavior (MADB) model as illustrated in Figure 1. In the MADB model, motivation and attitude have been defined in Equations 4 and 5. The rational motivation, decision, and behavior can be quantitatively analyzed according to the following definitions. It is noteworthy that, as shown in Figure 1, a motivation is triggered by an emotion or desire.

Definition 9: A rational motivation M_r is a motivation regulated by an attitude A with a positive or negative judgment, that is:

Figure 1. The motivation/attitude-driven behavior (MADB) model

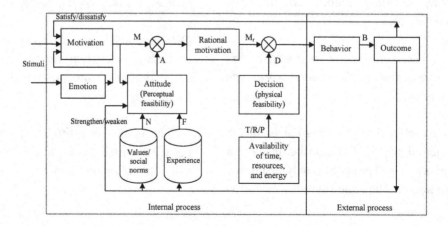

$$M_r = M \cdot A$$

$$= \frac{2.5 \bullet |E_m| \bullet (E\text{-}S)}{C} \bullet A \qquad (6)$$

Definition 10: A decision D for confirming an attitude for executing a motivated behavior is a binary choice on the basis of the availability of time T, resources R, and energy P, that is:

$$D = \begin{cases} 1, & T \wedge R \wedge P = \mathbf{T} \\ 0, & T \vee R \vee P = \mathbf{F} \end{cases} \qquad (7)$$

Definition 11. A behavior B driven by a motivation M_r and an attitude is a realized action initiated by a motivation M and supported by a positive attitude A and a positive decision D toward the action, that is:

$$B = \begin{cases} \mathbf{T}, & M_r \cdot D = \dfrac{2.5 \bullet |E_m| \bullet (E\text{-}S)}{C} \bullet A \cdot D > 1 \\ \mathbf{F}, & otherwise \end{cases} \qquad (8)$$

FORMAL DESCRIPTION OF COGNITIVE PROCESSES OF MOTIVATION AND ATTITUDE

The formal models of emotion, motivation, and attitude have been developed in previous sections. This section extends the models and their relationship into detailed cognitive processes based on the OAR model (Wang, 2007d) and using RTPA (Wang, 2002b, 2003c, 2006b, 2007a), which enable more rigorous treatment and computer simulations of the MADB model.

The Cognitive Process of Motivations

The mathematical model of rational motivation is described in Equation 6. Based on Equation 6, the cognitive process of motivation is presented in Figure 2. The motivation process is divided into four major sub-processes known as: (1) to form motivation goal; (2) to estimate strength of motivation; (3) to form rational motivation; and (4) to stimulate behavior for the motivation.

The MADB model provides a formal explanation of the mechanism and relationship between motivation, attitude, and behavior. The model can be used to describe how the motivation process drives human behaviors and actions, and how the attitude as well as the decision-making process help to regulate the motivation and determines whether the motivation should be implemented.

The Cognitive Process of Attitudes

The mathematical model of attitude has been described in Equation 5. Based on Equation 5, the cognitive process of attitude is presented in Figure 3. The attitude process is divided into three major sub-processes known as: (1) to check the mode of attitude; (2) to determine physical availability; and (3) to stimulate behavior for the motivation.

The Integrated Process of Motivation and Attitudes

According to the MADB model and the formal description of the motivation and attitude processes as shown in Figures 1 through 3, the cognitive processes of motivation and attitude are interleaved. An integrated process that combines both motivation and attitude is given in Figure 4 via the following sub-processes: (1) to form motivation goals; (2) to estimate strength of motivation; (3) to check the mode of attitude; (4) to form rational motivation; (5) to determine physical availability; and (6) to stimulate behavior for the rational motivation.

Figure 2. The cognitive process of motivation

The Motivation Process

Motivation (I:: o$\mathbf{S}$; O:: OAR $\mathbf{ST}$) $\triangleq$
{ I. Form motivation goal(s)
  $\rightarrow$ ObjectIdentification (o, A , R)

II. Estimate strength of motivation M(o)$\mathbf{N}$
  $\rightarrowtail$ Quantify (E$_m$(o)$\mathbf{N}$)   // The strength of emotion
  $\rightarrowtail$ Quantify (S(o)$\mathbf{N}$)   // The current status
  $\rightarrowtail$ Quantify (E(o)$\mathbf{N}$)   // The expectancy of desire
  $\rightarrowtail$ Quantify (C(o)$\mathbf{N}$)   // The cost to accomplish

$$\rightarrow M(o)\mathbf{N} = \frac{2.5\ E_m(o)\mathbf{N} \circ (E(o)\mathbf{N}\mathbf{N}S(o)\ )}{C(o)\mathbf{N}}$$

  $\rightarrow$ ($\blacklozenge$ M(o)$\mathbf{N}$ > 1
      $\rightarrow$ ⓈM(o)$\mathbf{BL}$ = $\mathbf{T}$ // Positive motivation
   | $\blacklozenge$ ~
      $\rightarrow$ ⓈM(o)$\mathbf{BL}$ = $\mathbf{F}$ // Negative motivation
)

III. Check the mode of attitude A(o)$\mathbf{N}$
  // Refer to the Attitude process

IV. Form rational motivation M$_r$(o)
  $\rightarrow$ M$_r$(o)$\mathbf{N}$:= M(o)$\mathbf{N}$ $\bullet$ A(o)$\mathbf{N}$
  $\rightarrow$ ($\blacklozenge$ M$_r$(o)$\mathbf{N}$ > 1
      $\rightarrow$ ⓈM$_r$(o)$\mathbf{BL}$ = $\mathbf{T}$ // Rational motivation
   | $\blacklozenge$ ~
      $\rightarrow$ ⓈM$_r$(o)$\mathbf{BL}$ = $\mathbf{F}$ // Irrational motivation
)

V. Determine physical availability D(o)$\mathbf{N}$
  // Refer to the Attitude process

VI. Stimulate behavior for M$_r$(o)
  $\rightarrow$ ($\blacklozenge$ D(o)$\mathbf{N}$ = 1   // Implement motivation o
      $\rightarrowtail$ GenerateAction (M$_r$(o))
      $\rightarrowtail$ ExecuteAction (M$_r$(o))
      $\rightarrow$ R := R $\cup$ <o, M$_r$(o)>
   | $\blacklozenge$ ~   // Give up motivation o
      $\rightarrow$ D(o)$\mathbf{N}$:= 0
      $\rightarrow$ o :=
      $\rightarrow$ R :=
)
  $\rightarrow$ OAR $\mathbf{ST}$ = <O $\cup$ o, A $\cup$ A , R $\cup$ R > // Form new OAR model
  $\rightarrowtail$ Memorization (OAR $\mathbf{ST}$)
}

Figure 3. The cognitive process of attitude

The Attitude Process

Attitude (I:: o**S**; O:: OAR **ST**) ≜
{   I. Form motivation goal(s)
  → ObjectIdentification (o, A , R)

  II. Estimate strength of motivation M(o)**N**
    // Refer to the Motivation process

  III. Check the mode of attitude A(o)**N**
    // Perceptual feasibility
  ↦ Qualify (N(o)**BL**)   // The social norm
  ↦ Qualify (F(o)**BL**)   // The subjective feasibility
  → (◆ N(o)**BL** ∧ F(o)**BL** = **T**
      → A(o)**N** := 1
   | ◆ ~
      → A(o)**N** := 0
)

  IV. Form rational motivation M_r(o)
    // Refer to the Motivation process

  V. Determine physical availability D(o)**N**
  ↦ Qualify (T(o)**BL**)   // The time availability
  ↦ Qualify (R(o)**BL**)   // The resource availability
  ↦ Qualify (P(o)**BL**)   // The energy availability
  → (◆ T(o)**BL** ∧ R(o)**BL** ∧ P(o)**BL** = **T**
      → D(o)**N** := 1   // Confirmed motivation
   | ◆ ~
      → D(o)**N** := 0   // Infeasible motivation
)

  VI. Stimulate behavior for M_r(o)
  → (◆ D(o)**N** = 1   // Implement motivation o
      ↦ GenerateAction (M_r(o))
      ↦ ExecuteAction (M_r(o))
      → R := R ∪ <o, M_r(o)>
   | ◆ ~   // Give up motivation o
      → D(o)**N** := 0
      → o :=
      → R :=
)
  → OAR **ST** = <O ∪ o, A ∪ A , R ∪ R > // Form new OAR model
  ↦ Memorization (OAR **ST**)
}

Table 3. Motivation factors of a project

Role	E_m	C	E	S
The manager	4	3	8	5
Programmers	3.6	8	8	6

Figure 4. The integrated process of motivation and attitude

The Motivation and Attitude Process

Motivation-Attitude (I:: o**S**; O:: OAR'**ST**) ≙

{ I. Form motivation goal(s)
→ ObjectIdentification (o, A', R')

II. Estimate strength of motivation M(o)**N**
↦ Quantify (E$_m$(o)**N**)　　　　　// The strength of emotion
↦ Quantify (S(o)**N**)　　　　　　// The current status
↦ Quantify (E(o)**N**)　　　　　　// The expectancy of desire
↦ Quantify (C(o)**N**)　　　　　　// The cost to accomplish
→ M(o)**N** = $\frac{2.5\ E_m(o)\mathbf{N} \circ (E(o)\mathbf{N} - S(o)\mathbf{N})}{C(o)\mathbf{N}}$
→ (◆ M(o)**N** > 1
　　→ Ⓢ M(o)**BL** = **T**　　　// Positive motivation
　| ◆ ~
　　→ Ⓢ M(o)**BL** = **F**　　　// Negative motivation
　)

III. Check the mode of attitude A(o)**N**
// Perceptual feasibility
↦ Qualify (N(o)**BL**)　　　　　// The social norm
↦ Qualify (F(o)**BL**)　　　　　// The subjective feasibility
→ (◆ N(o)**BL** ∧ F(o)**BL** = **T**
　　→ A(o)**N** := 1
　| ◆ ~
　　→ A(o)**N** := 0
　)

IV. Form rational motivation M$_r$(o)
→ M$_r$(o)**N** := M(o)**N** • A(o)**N**
→ (◆ M$_r$(o)**N** > 1
　　→ Ⓢ M$_r$(o)**BL** = **T**　　// Rational motivation
　| ◆ ~
　　→ Ⓢ M$_r$(o)**BL** = **F**　　// Irrational motivation
　)

V. Determine physical availability D(o)**N**
↦ Qualify (T(o)**BL**)　　　　　// The time availability
↦ Qualify (R(o)**BL**)　　　　　// The resource availability
↦ Qualify (P(o)**BL**)　　　　　// The energy availability
→ (◆ T(o)**BL** ∧ R(o)**BL** ∧ P(o)**BL** = **T**
　　→ D(o)**N** := 1　　　　　// Confirmed motivation
　| ◆ ~
　　→ D(o)**N** := 0　　　　　// Infeasible motivation
　)

VI. Stimulate behavior for M$_r$(o)
→ (◆ D(o)**N** = 1　　　　　// Implement motivation o
　↦ GenerateAction (M$_r$(o))
　↦ ExecuteAction (M$_r$(o))
　→ R' := R' ∪ <o, M$_r$(o)>
　| ◆ ~　　　　　　　　// Give up motivation o
　　→ D(o)**N** := 0
　　→ o := ∅
　　→ R' := ∅
　)
→ OAR'**ST** = <O ∪ o, A ∪ A', R ∪ R'> // Form new OAR model
↦ Memorization (OAR'**ST**)
}

MAXIMIZING STRENGTHS OF INDIVIDUAL MOTIVATIONS

Studies in sociopsychology provide a rich theoretical basis for perceiving new insights into the organization of software engineering. It is noteworthy that in a software organization, according to Theorem 2, the strength of a motivation of individuals *M* is proportional to both the strength of emotion and the difference between the expectancy and the current status of a person. At the same time, it is inversely proportional to the cost to accomplish the expected motivation *C*. The job of management at different levels of an organization tree is to encourage and improve E_m and *E*, and to help employees to reduce *C*.

Example 1: In software engineering project organization, the manager and programmers may be motivated to the improvement of software quality to a different extent. Assume the following factors as shown in Table 3 are collected from a project on the strengths of motivations to improve the quality of a software system, analyze how the factors influence the strengths of motivations of the manager and the programmers.

According to Theorem 2, the strengths of motivations of the manager M_1 and the programmers M_2 can be estimated using Equation 4, respectively:

$$M_1(manager) = \frac{2.5 \bullet |\ E_m\ | \bullet (E\text{-}S)}{C}$$
$$= \frac{2.5 \bullet 4 \bullet (8\text{ - }5)}{3}$$
$$= 10.0$$

and

$$M_2(programer) = \frac{2.5 \bullet 3.6 \bullet (8\text{ - }6)}{8}$$
$$= 2.3$$

Figure 5. The chain of motivation in a software organization

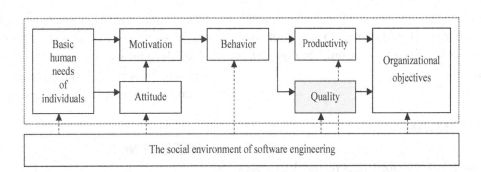

The results show that the manager has much stronger motivation to improve the quality of the software system than that of the programmers in the given project. Therefore, the rational action for the manager is to encourage the expectancy of the programmers or to decrease the required effort for the programmers by providing additional resources or adopting certain tools.

According to sociopsychology (Wiggins, Eiggins, & Zanden, 1994), social environment, such as culture, ethical norms, and attitude greatly influences people's motivation, behavior, productivity, and quality towards collaborative work. The chain of individual motivation in a software organization can be illustrated as shown in Figure 5.

Cultures and values of a software development organization helps to establish a set of ethical principles or standards shared by individuals of the organization for judging and normalizing social behaviors. The identification of a larger set of values and organizational policy towards social relations may be helpful to normalize individual and collective behaviors in a software development organization that produces information products for a global market.

Another condition for supporting creative work of individuals in a software development organization is to encourage diversity in both ways of thinking and work allocation. It is observed in social ecology that a great diversity of species and a complex and intricate pattern of interactions among the populations of a community may confer greater stability on an ecosystem.

Definition 12: Diversity refers to the social and technical differences of people in working organizations.

Diversity includes a wide range of differences between people such as those of race, ethnicity, age, gender, disability, skills, educations, experience, values, native language, and culture.

Theorem 3: The diversity principle states that the more diversity of the workforce in an organization, the higher the opportunity to form new relations and connections that leads to the gain of the system fusion effect.

Theorem 3 is particularly useful for software development organizations where creative work products are engineered. System theory indicates that if the number of components of a system reaches a certain level—the critical mass—then the functionality of the system may be dramatically increased (Wang, 2007a). That is, the increase of diversity in a system is the condition to realize the system fusion effect, which results in a more powerful system with newly created relations and behaviors that only belong to the system as a whole.

CONCLUSION

This article has described the perceptual processes of emotions, motivations, and attitudes based on which complicated psychological and mental processes may be formally modeled and rigorously explained. Relationships and interactions between motivation and attitude have been formally described in RTPA. It has been recognized that the human emotional system is a binary system that interprets or perceives an external stimulus and/or internal status as in the categories of pleasant or unpleasant. It has revealed that the strength of a motivation is proportional to both the strength of the emotion and the difference between the expectancy of desire and the current status of a person and is inversely proportional to the cost to accomplish the expected motivation. Case studies on applications of the interactive motivation-attitude theory and cognitive processes of motivations and attitudes in software engineering have been presented.

This work has demonstrated that the complicated human emotional and perceptual phenomena, as well as their natural drives and constraints, can be rigorously modeled in denotational mathematics and be formally treated and described. This work has been based on two fundamental cognitive informatics models: the LRMB and the OAR model. The former has provided a blueprint to exploring the natural intelligence and its mechanisms. The latter has established a contextual foundation to reveal the logical representation of information, knowledge, and skills in the perceptual space of the brain.

ACKNOWLEDGMENT

The author would like to acknowledge the Natural Science and Engineering Council of Canada (NSERC) for its support to this work. We would like to thank the anonymous reviewers for their valuable comments and suggestions.

REFERENCES

Eagly, A. H., & Chaiken, S. (1992). *The psychology of attitudes*. San Diego, CA: Harcourt Brace.

Fazio, R. H. (1986). How do attitudes guide behavior? In R. M. Sorrentino & E. T. Higgins (Eds.), *The handbook of motivation and cognition: Foundations of social behavior*. New York: Guilford Press.

Fischer, K. W., Shaver, P. R., & Carnochan, P. (1990). How emotions develop and how they organize development. *Cognition and Emotion, 4*, 81-127.

Fishbein, M., & Ajzen, I. (1975). *Belief, attitude, intention, and behavior: An introduction to theory and research*. Reading, MA: Addison-Wesley.

Payne, D. G., & Wenger, M. J. (1998). *Cognitive psychology*. New York: Houghton Mifflin.

Pinel, J. P. J. (1997). *Biopsychology* (3rd ed.). Needham Heights, MA: Allyn and Bacon.

Smith, R. E. (1993). *Psychology*. St. Paul, MN: West Publishing Co.

Wang, Y. (2002a). On cognitive informatics (Keynote Lecture). In *Proceedings of the 1st IEEE International Conference on Cognitive Informatics (ICCI'02)* (pp. 34-42). IEEE CS Press.

Wang, Y. (2002b). The real-time process algebra (RTPA). *The International Journal of Annals of Software Engineering, 14*, 235-274.

Wang, Y. (2003a). Cognitive informatics: A new transdisciplinary research field. *Brain and Mind: A Transdisciplinary Journal of Neuroscience and Neurophilosophy, 4*(2), 115-127.

Wang, Y. (2003b). On cognitive informatics. *Brain and Mind: A Transdisciplinary Journal of Neuroscience and Neurophilosophy, 4*(2), 151-167.

Wang, Y. (2003c). Using process algebra to describe human and software behaviors. *Brain and Mind: A Transdisciplinary Journal of Neuroscience and Neurophilosophy, 4*(2), 199-213.

Wang, Y. (2005). On the cognitive processes of human perceptions. In *Proceedings of the 4th IEEE International Conference on Cognitive Informatics (ICCI'05)* (pp. 203-211). IEEE CS Press.

Wang, Y. (2006a). Cognitive informatics—Towards the future generation computers that think and feel (Keynote speech). In *Proceedings of the 5th IEEE International Conference on Cognitive Informatics (ICCI'06)* (pp. 3-7). IEEE CS Press.

Wang, Y. (2006b). On the informatics laws and deductive semantics of software. *IEEE Transactions on Systems, Man, and Cybernetics, 36*(2), 161-171.

Wang, Y. (2006c). On abstract systems and system algebra. In *Proceedings of the 5th IEEE International Conference on Cognitive Informatics (ICCI'06)* (pp. 332-343). IEEE CS Press.

Wang, Y. (2007a). Software engineering foundations: A software science perspective. *CRC Software Engineering Series, 2*(1), 580.

Wang, Y. (2007b). The theoretical framework of cognitive informatics. *The International Journal of Cognitive Informatics and Natural Intelligence, 1*(1), 1-27.

Wang, Y. (2007c). Towards theoretical foundations of autonomic computing. *The International Journal of Cognitive Informatics and Natural Intelligence, 1*(3), 1-15.

Wang, Y. (2007d). The OAR model of neural informatics for internal knowledge pepresentation in the brain. *The International Journal of Cognitive Informatics and Natural Intelligence, 1*(3), 64-75.

Wang, Y., & Wang, Y. (2006). Cognitive informatics models of the brain. *IEEE Transactions on Systems, Man, and Cybernetics, 36*(2), 203-207.

Wang, Y., Wang, Y., Patel, S., & Patel, D. (2006). A layered reference model of the brain (LRMB). *IEEE Transactions on Systems, Man, and Cybernetics, 36*(2), 124-133.

Westen, D. (1999). *Psychology: Mind, brain, and culture* (2nd ed.). New York: John Wiley & Sons.

Wiggins, J. A., Eiggins, B. B., & Zanden, J. V. (1994). *Social psychology* (5th ed.). New York: McGraw-Hill.

Wilson, R. A., & Keil, F. C. (Eds.). (1999). *The MIT encyclopedia of the cognitive sciences.* Cambridge, MA: The MIT Press.

Wittig, A. F. (2001). *Schaum's outlines of theory and problems of introduction to psychology* (2nd ed.). New York: McGraw-Hill.

Chapter IX
Kinetic User Interfaces:
Physical Embodied Interaction with Mobile Ubiquitous Computing Systems

Vincenzo Pallotta
University of Fribourg, Switzerland

Pascal Bruegger
University of Fribourg, Switzerland

Béat Hirsbrunner
University of Fribourg, Switzerland

ABSTRACT

This chapter presents a conceptual framework for an emerging type of user interfaces for mobile ubiquitous computing systems, and focuses in particular on the interaction through motion of people and objects in physical space. We introduce the notion of Kinetic User Interface as a unifying framework and a middleware for the design of pervasive interfaces, in which motion is considered as the primary input modality.

INTRODUCTION

Internet and mobile computing technology is changing the way users access information and interact with computers and media. *Personal Computing* in its original form is fading and shifting towards the ubiquitous (or pervasive) computing paradigm (Want et al., 2002). Ubiquitous Computing systems are made up of several interconnected heterogeneous computational devices with different degrees of mobility and computing power. All of these devices and appliances are embedded in everyday objects, scattered in space, capable of sensing the environment and of communicating with each other, and carried or exchanged by people. Therefore, we are facing a new ecology of computing systems that poses new issues in their integration and usability. Human-computer interfaces that were designed for desktop personal computers must be re-conceived for this new scenario. Due to the different capabilities of mobile and embedded devices, the pervasive computing infrastructure, and the nature of their expected usage, it is apparent that new types of user interfaces are needed in order to unleash the usability of new generation distributed computing applications (see (Rukzio, 2006) for a classification of mobile devices interfaces). Additionally, the concept of user interface itself seems to be no longer adequate to cope with ubiquitous computing systems. Rather, it is the concept of interaction and user experience that will take over (Beaudouin-Lafon, 2004).

Ubiquitous Computing

Ubiquitous Computing (henceforth Ubicomp) is an emerging research sub-area of Distributed Systems whose main focus is studying how heterogeneous, networked computing devices can be embedded in objects of daily use in order to enable new applicative scenarios and user experiences. Mark Weiser (1991; 1993; 1994) introduced the term Ubiquitous Computing in the '90s as a new way to understand computer technology and to lay the foundations of an expected and necessary computing paradigm revolution. Weiser's vision has been adopted and interpreted by a great number of researchers, among whom we consider relevant for our goals the works of (Abowd & Mynatt, 2000; Abowd et al., 2002; Banavar & Bernstein, 2004; Bellotti et al., 2002; Greenfield, 2006; Norman, 1999; Want et al., 2002). We summarize the Ubicomp vision in four fundamental points that motivate our effort of providing a new conceptual framework for Ubicomp user interfaces:

1. Today's computer (e.g., the personal computer) will disappear, and the computing power will fade inside the network infrastructure, as it is already the case to some extent with existing web-services.

2. Computing will be extremely distributed and heterogeneous. This will result from the interconnection of several computing devices, each specialized in specific tasks and scattered in the physical environment (ranging from embedded devices to high-performance servers).

3. Computer interfaces will no longer capture the full attention of users. Rather, computer applications will run in "background" most of the time, accomplishing "routinized" operations, and they will try to gain user's attention only when strictly required.

4. Computer interfaces will be unobtrusive and based on new emerging interaction models obtained by direct interaction with physical objects and with the whole environment.

Ubiquitous Computing is often equated to (or better, confused with) nomadic computing (Kleinrock, 1997). Nomadic computing is a form of computing environment that offers its users access to data or information from any device and network while they are in state of motion. In nomadic computing, the use of portable devices (such as laptops and handheld computers) in conjunction with mobile communications technologies enables users to access the Internet and data on their home or work computers from anywhere in the world. Mobile connectivity certainly does play an important role in Ubicomp, but it is not the only one. We consider of central importance the *user's mobility* intended as the user's *ability of moving objects and themselves in the physical space*. In fact, in using Ubicomp systems, users are no longer forced to sit in front of a desktop computer and to operate it with mice, keyboards and local input/output devices.

Users will interact through actions performed on everyday objects that surround them. As pointed again by Weiser[1]:

[ubiquitous computing] *is different from PDAs, dynabooks, or information at your fingertips. It is invisible, everywhere computing that does not live on a personal device of any sort, but is in the woodwork everywhere.*

User Interfaces for Ubicomp Systems

Human-computer interaction (HCI) is a very large domain of research, which includes all related aspects of interaction with digital appliances. Although HCI has been mostly focused on graphical user interfaces (GUIs), we consider here those aspects that pertain to how users will interact with computers in the 21st century (Winograd, 2000), that is, by direct manipulation of objects in their physical environment. Paul Dourish (2001) defined this paradigm as *embodied interaction.* According to his definition, meaningful embodied interaction with a digital system can be obtained only if an alignment is maintained between the physical and the digital world. In other terms, "bits" and "atoms" must live together in peace (Negroponte, 1995). As recently pointed out in (Sparacino, 2005, p. 2):

[…] *computation and sensing are moving from computers and devices into the environment itself. The space around us is instrumented with sensors and displays, and this tends to reflect a widespread need to blend together the information space with our physical space.*

Embodied interaction is thus aimed at exploring new *interaction patterns* where people are exploring how to move the interface "off the screen" and into the real world (Shafer et al., 2001).

For instance, in Tangible User Interfaces (TUIs) (Ulmer and Iishi, 2000; Holmquist et al., 2004), tangible interaction is intended to replace desktop GUI's interaction and elements with operations on physical objects. The motion of objects in the physical space determines the execution of actions, such as item selection (by means of what in TUI are called "phicons" i.e., *physical icons*), service requests, database updates, and so forth. Rekimoto (1997) proposed the Pick&Drop pattern, an extension of the Drag&Drop pattern, to move items across computers. In his work on graspable user interfaces, Fitzmaurice (2000) proposed to extend the interaction with classical GUI by means of physical objects (such as LEGO bricks) over an augmented desktop surface. Tangible and graspable user interfaces are undoubtedly a great achievement in HCI. However, they are strongly biased by GUIs interfaces; nearly no new types of interaction induced by the nature of the physical space and objects have been proposed other than replications of those available on ordinary desktop GUIs.

The development of the ideas introduced by TUIs, combined with the ubiquity of information over the Internet, has led to a new concept of what counts as an Ubicomp system. Moving from the assumption that only information appliances could constitute a ubiquitous system, the whole material world of things and people now can be made computational and connected. The movement of the "Internet of Things" (ITU, 2005; Bleeker, 2006) is aimed at promoting the idea that any object can have a *virtual identity* in the Internet realm, as long as the object can embed a unique identifier, which corresponds to an IP address. This is now possible because of the larger 128 bits IP address space offered by the new IPv6 protocol (i.e., 3.4×10^{38} addresses). According to (Greenfield, 2006), the type of infrastructure that enables Ubiquitous Computing is already technically feasible and it will soon scale up to a level that will make it possible to safely connect a huge number of small heterogeneous devices, possibly embedded in everyday objects.

Augmented Reality (AR) (Mackay, 1998) and Wearable Interfaces (Barfield & Caudell, 2001) are emerging technologies that support embodied interaction for Ubicomp systems. We believe that Augmented Reality focuses more on how feedback is provided, whereas Wearable Interfaces focuses on the types of devices that can support embodied interaction.

Unobtrusive Interfaces

When HCI intersects Ubicomp, many assumptions that were made when designing interaction for ordinary computing devices are no longer valid. In Ubicomp, computers exist in different forms and only in a minimal portion as ordinary desktop computers (i.e., where interaction is performed through screens, keyboards, mice). As pointed out by Weiser and other promoters of Ubicomp, interacting with a ubiquitous system should be realized through an *unobtrusive interface*, more precisely, an interface that does not capture the full attention of the user, who can still use the system to perform the foreground tasks (Nardi, 1996). In contrast, an obtrusive interface is one that requires an unjustified cognitive effort to be operated, thus interfering with the normal usage of the system. Weiser & Seely Brown (1996) call this setting "Calm Technology" in order to stress the importance of adapting the computers and their interfaces to human pace, rather that the other way around. In this vision, computers should follow users in their daily activity and be ready to provide information or assistance on demand. Moreover, they should not require much attention from the user by asking information that can be autonomously obtained from the actual usage context. They must be "aware" of the context and be able to adapt their behaviour and interfaces to differ-

ent usage situations. In other words, ubiquitous computers must be *smart* and *adaptive*.

Kinetic-Awareness

Context-awareness is considered as the most important issue in Ubicomp (Baldauf et al., 2006; Dourish, 2004; Hong et al., 2005). Specifically, location-awareness is considered a key component of context in designing user interfaces for mobile systems. Location-awareness has been always treated as a sub-case of context-awareness, and motion as a form of context change. Location change is taken as a context change for adapting the application's behaviour, rather than as an explicit intentional act within the application's interface.

We believe that location changes occurring over time can represent more than just context-change. It can be considered as input modality. This does not mean that location or motion context has to be neglected. Motion input and location context can be used together in the same way as in handheld GUIs, where interaction with the mobile devices can be contextualized through location or motion. For instance, it does make sense to consider a different interpretation for an object's motion that occurs in a different location, or to interpret the GUI input differently when the mobile device is moving with different kinetic properties. To clarify this aspect let us consider two examples.

The first example is about two possible situations where a paraglide is flying i) over a lake, or ii) over the ground. Motion input is treated accordingly to the actual situation; when flying over the lake some manoeuvres are considered risky, while they are considered safe if flying over the ground (landing is possible everywhere).

The second example is a situation where implicit interaction with GUI is enabled if the handheld device is detected moving with a certain speed. For instance, suppose that a dialogue box asking for a confirmation pops up on the handheld's GUI. If the user is moving, at a speed of more than 5 Km/h, then after a timeout, the interface assumes that the default choice has been (implicitly) selected. If the user is moving at lower speed or is still, the interface will wait for input without the timeout.

According to Dix et al. (2000), *space* and *location* define a new design space for interactive mobile systems. Mobile devices have increasing capacity in providing location and motion information as part of their usage context. They also acknowledged that accounting for motion as an input modality for location-aware mobile Ubicomp systems opens potential research opportunities. In fact, they propose and instantiate a taxonomy of the degrees of mobility with available technologies and applications. They categorize degrees of mobility along three dimensions *level of mobility* (i.e., the physical bound of the device to the environment), *level of independence* (i.e., the relation of the used location-aware device with other devices or to the environment), *level of cooperativeness* (i.e., the extent to which the device is bound to a particular individual or group). Some existing mobile devices and applications are then categorized according to this three-dimensional taxonomy. Some difficult or even impossible cases, such as a *fixed-pervasive-personal*, that might be instantiated by a fully isolated active cell (e.g., a prison cell with motion sensors). The combination that is relevant for us is that of *pervasive-mobile-personal/group* devices. Such devices might be location/motion-aware objects that can be used to interact with Ubicomp systems.

Systems combining location and motion awareness, henceforth, will be referred to as *kinetic-aware systems*. Our analysis of how kinetic information is taken into account in existing Ubicomp systems revealed that there are two main views on the role of kinetic information in user interfaces:

1. In the first view, location and motion are used as a component of the usage context that is exploited by applications running on the mobile information computing devices for adapting their behaviour. In this view, there is no physical interaction with the place (and its contained artefacts) where the users are using their own devices. The environment is not "sensing" the presence and the physical action of the user. Moreover, neither the system nor the environment is supposed to handle spatio-temporally located events.

2. In the second view, location change and motion are considered as *primary input modalities* reflecting the user's goals and intentions while using Ubicomp applications. That is, users can intentionally perform explicit and implicit actions through physical motion. These actions are recognized and contextualized in the place where they occur, by possibly affecting the state of co-located devices and remote systems. Interaction through motion with physical space becomes the main focus, rather than simply contextualizing applications based on ordinary user interfaces running on mobile devices.

While the majority of research on location-aware Ubicomp systems focuses on the first view on kinetic awareness, we focus instead on the second view, which can be achieved by recognizing users' goals and intentions from various properties of motion of objects in the physical space through what we call the *Kinetic User Interface* (KUI).

Kinetic awareness can be seen as part of a more general paradigm, defined in (Dix et al., 2004) as *context-aware computing*. This emerging paradigm poses several challenges. One of the biggest recognized difficulties for this type of system is *interpreting human activity*. We do not propose algorithms for automatic recognition of human activities (which is a machine learning task). Instead, we propose a framework in which activities can be decomposed into smaller and easier-to-detect patterns. These patterns are instantiated by acquiring input from sensors that are linked to software components representing physical objects. We believe that providing a level of abstraction for activities will make easier the design and the implementation of Kinetic User Interfaces for Ubicomp systems.

Related Works and Technologies

Location-aware services are nowadays available to mobile Internet users. With the advent of Web2.0[2], a great deal of applied research and development recently has been devoted to embedding Internet technology into everyday life mobile devices, ranging from pure entertainment to critical applications such as healthcare, national security, military (Cáceres et al., 2006). The rationale behind these efforts is to provide the mobile Internet users with great flexibility in authoring, publishing, and retrieving information, as well as in accessing services that are relevant in a given situation and place. A remarkable example of Web2.0 mobile application for multimedia information retrieval is SocialLight[3], which allows the tagging of geographical location with multimedia tags (e.g., shadow-tags). The roaming users can "geo-tag" a place either by using a mobile phone when they are physically present there, or by attaching the tag on the SocialLight Web page with a GoogleMap mash-up. Information can further be retrieved from the Web site through the mashed-up map or by querying the system by using a mobile, GPS-enabled Internet device. Geo-tagging is also the focus of the Mobile Multimedia Metadata project of the Garage Cinema Lab (Davis et al., 2004), whose main purpose is to cooperatively annotate geo-located pictures. (Ashbrook et al., 2006) push this concept further and propose a roadmap for future research with a new type of scenario based on location-awareness and motion tracking, in which users can capture media while moving, and share their experience by making the captured media stream available to Internet users in real-time.

Location-awareness in Ubicomp has been the main focus of several projects since 1990. Among the projects that heavily rely on location context are the Aware Home (Kidd et al., 1999) at GeorgiaTech, the GUIDE project at Lancaster University (Chervest et al., 2000), the AURA project at Carnegie Mellon University (Sousa & Garlan, 2002), the GAIA's Active Space project at University of Illinois Urbana Champaign (Román et al., 2002), the Interactive Maps at ETHZ (Norrie, 2005), and the Global Smart Places project (Meyer et al., 2006). It might seem that this is a widely explored research area, but a closer analysis reveals that all of these projects deal with a very basic form of motion-awareness. Location change is taken as a user's context change, which is used for dynamically adapting the application's behaviour. They all consider a user's location as an additional parameter of an explicit service request. Then, the service's output is delivered on the handheld device carried by the user or on a nearby display.

The Cyberguide project (Abowd et al., 1996) is one among the first attempts in taking a user's motion into account (see also (Schilit, 1995)). A tourist equipped with indoor (IR beacons) and outdoor (GPS) localization devices can automatically receive contextual relevant information on a PDA while moving, and feed a trip journal.

In the EasyLiving project at Microsoft (Brumitt et al., 2000), a geometric model of the physical space is used in order to enable physical embodied interaction by representing the physical relationships between entities in the world. Unfortunately, this model has a limited scope since it is adapted to room scale, and it only considers current spatial relationships between objects, while ignoring their motion within the tracked space.

The Intelligent Workspace project at MIT (Koile et al., 2003) is a system that records the user's location history and learns the so-called *activity zones*. Activity zones are portions of the physical space where the user is doing specific activities and which are repeatedly observed by the system. Once an activity zone is learned, the settlement of user in it will automatically trigger a number of pre-defined services that support the observed activity. In other words, the system reacts to context change and, in particular, to the user's location change.

However, none of the above-mentioned systems explicitly recognize motion as the primary input modality and as a mean of performing a purposeful (explicit or implicit) action within the application's interaction space. The following systems make a further step towards a more explicit notion of kinetic-awareness.

In the Sentient Computing project at AT&T Cambridge Research labs (Addlesee et al., 2001), motion tracking is an essential feature for interacting with the system. The system is built around the ActiveBat infrastructure for tracking location and motion using ultrawide-band sensors (now commercialized by Ubisense[4]). A few applications for the ActiveBat have been proposed, such as "FollowMe" that allows users to move their input-output environments over several devices scattered in the environment (e.g., phone call forwarding, virtual desktop displacement), or the "Virtual Mouse" that allows users carrying the ActiveBat device to use it as a mouse over a wall display. A relevant aspect of this project for us is the adopted context modelling techniques. The application-level and the user-level (mental) model of the environment are kept aligned by the system (Harter et al., 2002). In other words, when users perform actions, they update their mental representation of the resulting state of the environment by directly observing it. This representation might not be consistent with the information that applications have gathered through sensors. The system must take care of checking and possibly restabilising the lost alignment.

The Sonic City project (Gaye et al., 2003) exploits motion in the urban landscape as a way for interactively creating a musical experience. The user motion is tracked, as well as the current position over the city map. Motion and location contexts are combined with other contexts obtained through wearable sensors in order to influence the composition of music content in real-time. Users of the Sonic City interface can hear the result of musical composition during their walking activity.

Other applications of the motion context are pervasive games and races. Games that involve location tracking (like trails in (Spence et al., 2005)) are suited for exploiting the motion context. For instance, in CatchBob (Nova et al., 2006), a multi-player game developed at EPFL, the players' motion is tracked and their paths are made visible to other team members on a digital map. The goal of the game is to cooperatively perform a task by looking at the motion of the other team members on a handheld display and by communicating direction suggestions in real-time.

Overview of the Chapter

In this chapter, we propose a unifying framework for the design and implementation of Kinetic User Interfaces for Ubicomp systems by (i) defining a set of fundamental concepts and (ii) by presenting a middleware that enables the use of motion in physical spaces as the primary interaction modality.

The remainder of this chapter is structured as follows. In Section 2, we provide some backgrounds and intuitions about the distinguishing features of KUIs compared to other types of user interfaces. We also present a few motivating applicative KUI-based scenarios. In Section 3, we detail the main concepts of KUI and we present the structure of its middleware architecture. Conclusions are finally discussed in Section 4.

KINETIC USER INTERFACES

The term "Kinetic" is derived from the Greek *kinetikos*, which means "moving of, relating to or resulting from motion (the action or process of moving)." In physics, kinetic theory explains the physical properties of matter in terms of the movement of its constituent parts; kinetic energy refers to energy, which a body possesses by virtue of being in motion. Kinetic abilities of humans are of no question. People move and change their current spatial location all the time and in a mostly unconscious way. Humans are also capable of "modulating" motion in several ways, by keeping or varying their speed, by following different trajectories or patterns (e.g., dancing), or by executing various types of motion in parallel (e.g., gesturing while walking).

At different scales and contexts, motion (or absence of motion) can be recognized as a purposeful action. For instance, if a tourist stops long enough in front of a statue, it might be reasonable to assume that he or she is observing the monument. What if the statue (or the environment) would be smart enough to provide the tourist with relevant information about its author or style, or, even smarter, to figure out that the tourist has already stopped at the statue, to avoid repeating the old information unless the tourist explicitly requests it?

A familiar everyday situation occurs when items are passed through a bar code reader in a grocery store counter. Their motion (the passage in a given place) is recognized as a purchase transaction. Another typical KUI situation takes place when somebody, possibly unconsciously, performs dangerous actions such as moving into dangerous areas. In these cases, a monitoring system could alert the user by signalling the potential danger.

KUI vs. GUI

Motion in the physical space is such a common and pervasive phenomenon that we hardly recognize its status of an interaction modality with a computer. While it is apparent that motion plays an essential role in WIMP[5] Graphical User Interfaces (GUI), the virtual and limited nature of GUI's space, the "desktop," seems not to afford the full bodily motion interaction (Beaudoin-Lafon, 2000). For instance, it does make little or no sense to talk about speed or acceleration of the pointer. Sometimes, however, these properties are taken into account by specific types of PC applications like games or flight simulators.

We introduce the concept of *Kinetic User Interface* (KUI) as a way of endorsing Weiser's Ubiquitous Computing vision (Weiser, 1993) and the Dourish's Embodied Interaction vision (Dourish, 2001) discussed in the previous section. Accordingly, KUIs are intended to enable a new interaction model for pervasive computing systems in which the motion of objects and users in the physical space are recognized as events and processes to which the system reacts. To make a parallel with ordinary, pointer-controlled Graphical User Interfaces (GUIs), moving the pointer on the display and clicking on a graphical item is recognized by the system as an intentional act, which usually triggers a system's reaction on the software representation of the domain object associated to the selected graphical item and, possibly, the execution of an action on the domain object specified in the application currently running on the computer. Similar to "hovering" the pointer over a desktop in GUIs, in KUIs users can trigger input events for the computing environment by moving themselves and by displacing tracked objects. Users can exploit the physical space by executing actions/operations on physical objects, such as moving, grabbing, touching, juxtaposing, whose effects are reflected in the application objects. For instance, following a path or executing a pre-defined motion pattern can be viewed as similar to "mouse gestures" in ordinary desktop GUIs and can consequently trigger reactions by the gesture-enabled application.

KUIs are not limited to single-user interfaces and do not impose a unique locus of interaction. Hence, it enables richer interactions than GUIs and it is better suited to ubiquitous and mobile computing environments. Motion as an input modality can be used alone or in combination with other input modalities available to the user for interaction with the system, which are directly afforded by other mobile devices carried by the users and by fixed input devices located in the interaction space (e.g., ordinary point and click, or speech recognition).

Feedback Management

As in GUIs, an important issue in KUIs is *feedback management*. Due to the different nature of physical space with respect to GUI's synthetic space, feedback cannot be provided in the same way as for GUIs. Since one of the goals of KUI is to help build unobtrusive interfaces, we give back to users only the minimal amount of information required to inform them that their interaction with the physical space has been successfully recognized. In turn, the system should avoid interfering with the user's current activity if the effects of the recognized action have only a peripheral importance to the current foreground task (i.e., if the effects impact only objects that are not in the current focus of attention of the user). Moreover, since the physical space already allows for the direct manipulation of real objects, feedback should only inform users about those effects produced in the computing space to (virtual) domain objects.

Although users might not always be aware of what effects are caused by their motion and the motion of tracked objects, they will be unobtrusively notified when their motion has been detected and interpreted by the system. Different than GUIs or even in Augmented Reality systems, there will be no need to display a synthetic image of the moving object. The only graphical components of the interface will be those corresponding to additional modalities. For example, we can imagine a scenario where a dialog box is prompted on a mobile device or on an embedded display when the user is detected[6] to walk by or stop at a specific point of interest.

A feedback mechanism of control is also necessary for other reasons, such as privacy; to grant a certain level of protection, users must be somehow aware when their presence and motion is being currently tracked. Consequently, they must always be given the possibility to stop the tracking of the mobile device and to be allowed to use an alternative interaction modality.

KUI Interaction Patterns

Although KUI interaction patterns can be radically different from GUI patterns, some of the most effective GUI patterns, such as Drag&Drop, can be transferred and adapted to KUI interaction with physical space. For instance, in a KUI-enabled SmartHome, the user can "drag" the media being currently played in the living room and "drop" it to the bedroom just by moving a representative localizable object such as the remote controller. It is worth noting that the "Drag&Drop" pattern is provided as an interaction pattern by the KUI middleware and can be activated (and recognized) for specific applications such as the SmartHome control system[7].

Another useful pattern we include in KUI is *continuous tracking*. Continuous physical motion is comparable to mouse-gestures in GUIs. KUI-enabled applications are supposed to recognize certain *kinetic patterns* that might be naturally performed by users during other activities or specific situations.

As an example of the continuous tracking pattern, consider the scenario where the user is driving a car and some of the car's motion parameters are obtained by embedded sensors such as a GPS tracking system and an accelerometer. The sensors reveal that the car is decelerating in the proximity of a gas station (i.e., a geo-located point of interest already known by the application). This kinetic pattern (deceleration) is detected by the KUI and interpreted by the application as the user's intention of refuelling at the gas station. This hypothesis might be corroborated by other contextual information from the current car's sensors (e.g., the fuel level being almost zero). As a result of this behaviour, the system will pro-actively prompt the driver with the current gas prices at the approaching gas station. The application might also perform further contextual inferences and inform the user that keeping the current speed and considering the current fuel level he/she can reach the next gas station that has better gas prices. However, if the system detects that the fuel level is high or the fuel tank is even full, it will not react because it can infer that the driver stops for other (unknown) reasons (e.g., to take a pause).

This is a clear example of how KUI interaction differs from ordinary location-aware user interfaces. In this scenario, the driver passing by a gas station does not need to explicitly inquire about the gas prices. Current location information is only used to contextualize the query that is triggered as a result of the speed change occurring in the proximity of a given point of interest.

With regard to enabling technologies, continuous motion tracking is already available with current GPS-based car navigation systems, and easily can be integrated with personal mobile devices (e.g., SmartPhones, PDAs) connected to mobile Internet infrastructures (such as UMTS, GPRS, WiMax). With ordinary GPS navigation systems, the user can always check the current location on a graphical map and the proximity to point of interests. With KUI, we extend the possibilities of these systems with an additional level of interactivity and integration with networked services (Pallotta et al., 2006).

KUI-Enabled Scenarios

KUI-enabled applications have a different purpose compared to ordinary location-aware ones. Since motion is used as an input modality, KUI-based applications are expected to provide a higher level of fluidity in interaction and user experience. In those situations in which the interface should not interfere with the foreground user's activity (which in turn might or might not be a computer-based one), KUI will allow unobtrusive interaction with a computer. We consider here three case studies that have been developed so far and that exemplify the benefits of KUI interaction patterns.

Safety in Air Sports

Jane is flying with her paraglide over the Alps and is trying to reach the other side of a lake she is currently over. Can she do it without any risks? The UbiGlide flight navigator detects the motion of the paraglide. By interpreting her current activity UbiGlide infers Jane's intention to cross the lake. UbiGlide then senses the environment, namely, the wind's force and direction, the lake altitude, the distance between the paraglide and the opposite shore, and finally concludes that the crossing is not possible. Jane is informed immediately about the risk of danger. Later, she is so focused on the flight that she finds herself approaching a no-fly zone (e.g., an airplane landing strip). UbiGlide detects this possibility and alerts her about the danger.

In this scenario the current paraglide motion is not only tracked but also interpreted. An activity report is obtained by composing a number of basic flight movements in order to recognize more complex behaviour patterns. For instance, *spiral ascension* is made of several *turns* and *altitude changes*. Moreover, activities are filtered by other contextual information such as wind speed and direction, air humidity, and so forth.

SmartHome and SmartCity

Julia, Steve, and their daughter Monica live in Geneva. Julia is a busy businesswoman and Steve is a researcher at the university. Monica is in her last year of college. They live in a flat equipped with latest IT technology. They own a networked SmartFridge, which detects when food items go in and out, and automatically generates a list of missing items. The UbiShop system looks at the list generated by the SmartFridge and sends requests to buy the missing items to any family members who pass by a grocery store. Monica is on her way back home after school and passes by a grocery store. A reminder to buy milk is sent on her mobile phone by the UbiShop system. She decides to ignore the reminder since she knows that another grocery store is on her way home. Meanwhile, Steve is also on his way home and near a grocery store. He also receives the reminder and decides to buy the milk. This purchase causes the deletion of the milk from the shopping list, so that Monica will no longer be bothered. When back home, Steve does not put the milk in the fridge. After a while, the SmartFridge "wonders" why the milk has not yet been put inside, so a request about this item is sent to Steve who had simply forgot the milk in the car.

This illustrates how KUI can contribute to context-aware collaboration[8] in a mixed urban/home environment. Family members' activities are coordinated according to actual members' mobility. The system decides to adapt a workflow by interpreting team members' behaviors in context. Here, the role of the KUI interface is twofold. First, it allows triggering the task

assignment when the user is moving into a zone where the task could be accomplished. Second, it detects from the user's speed whether he/she is likely to be willing to perform the assigned task. For instance, if the user is running, the application could interpret this motion pattern as "being in a hurry" and might decide not to bother the user. Another interesting aspect where KUI plays a role is when the user is expected to perform an action and this action does not occur. This is the case when, in our scenario, Steve forgot to put the milk in the fridge. The application subscribed to a motion event that does not occur within a time interval.

Safe-Critical Work Environments

Bill is a specialized worker in a chemical plant. He typically operates an industrial chemical reactor. He wears a head-mounted display and he is connected to the main control desk through wireless radio communication gears. While normally operating the reactor, suddenly Bill starts running (accelerates) toward the emergency exit. He is not able to alert the control desk about what is happening. The KUI interface detects this motion pattern as abnormal and figures out that the operator is trying to escape from a dangerous situation. The system then opens the doors on the pathway toward the exit of the reactor building and then immediately closes them after the operator is sensed to have passed through them.

In certain industrial settings such as chemical plants, it is important that the operator keeps his hands free in order to be able to do his usual manual work, while at the same time he/she accesses the automated commands and looks at the supervision information needed to complete the task. The role of KUI is apparent because it provides an additional implicit input modality that might serve to detect sudden instinctive reactions to dangerous situations.

THE KUI MODEL

In this section, we present the main concepts of Kinetic User Interfaces that are implemented as software components in the KUI middleware architecture.

The KUI Conceptual Taxonomy

In KUI, motion is a main (or primary) interaction modality afforded by the physical space to users through the motion of *tracked entities*. Tracked entities are any objects or autonomous (possibly living) things for which we can provide location and motion information. Tracked entities are represented by KUI components called *Kuidgets*. Interaction with Kuidgets happens when users affect their motion properties or change spatio-temporal relationships among them (e.g., an object is entering into an area). For instance, when the user is driving a car, the motion properties of its corresponding Kuidget will be continuously updated with its current position, speed, acceleration, and direction.

The term "Kuidget" has been chosen to make the parallel with a GUI's widgets, that is, software components that provide public interfaces for a hardware sensor and whose interaction is implemented in terms of messages and call-backs (Winograd, 2001). Kuidgets are the software counterpart of some real world entities that can be used for interaction in KUIs. A KUI-enabled system is thus able to recognize the current location of Kuidgets, and makes sense of their motion parameters such as path, speed, acceleration, and direction. Location and motion sensors (e.g., GPS or other tracking devices, accelerometers, compasses, altimeters) typically provide three-dimensional location and motion information to Kuidgets. Kuidgets are classified according to four main dimensions: *geometry*; *kinetic properties*; *degree of autonomy*; and *type of motion*.

From the geometric point of view, Kuidgets can be arbitrary three-dimensional objects. However,

it makes sense to distinguish between those objects whose size is not relevant and those for which it matters. Entities of the first type are considered as points while others are considered as geometric shapes. This distinction is application-dependent, because one entity can be considered a point in one application and a shape in others. For instance, a vehicle (a car, a train, a ship, a plane) is a point when considered as a moving object in the space, and it is a space when considered as a container of objects and people. In the KUI model, the same entity plays two roles at the same time and is linked to two distinct Kuidgets.

Kuidgets can be *fixed* or *mobile*. Fixed Kuidgets are typically places or landmarks in the physical space, while mobile Kuidgets are physical entities whose location and motion can be observed by tracking the entity or can be provided by their embedded location and motion sensors.

In modelling KUI's dynamics we adopt the *status-event semantics*, which means that KUI-based applications should be able to effectively deal both with the *status* of objects and with the *events* they generate. Thus, as an underlying model for dealing with Status-Event semantics in KUI, we adopt the Environment and Artefacts theory for multi-agent systems as proposed by (Ricci et al., 2006). Accordingly, we further classify Kuidgets along their degree of autonomy as *artefact Kuidgets* and *agent Kuidgets*. Artefact Kuidgets correspond to mobile physical objects that cannot move autonomously (e.g., a mobile phone, a car). The motion properties of an artefact Kuidget can be directly determined and communicated by the artefact itself (e.g., a GPS sensor + a mobile network connection) or observed by another entity (e.g., the infrastructure of the containing object, a nearby artefact, or an agent). The events of moving, grabbing, dragging, and dropping artefact Kuidgets are triggered by the detection of their current kinetic properties in the physical space and by the actions performed through their interfaces for direct manipulation (e.g., pressing a button on the object while moving it). Agent Kuidgets correspond to autonomous moving entities (people, animals, robots). Agent Kuidgets have a higher degree of autonomy, and they can induce motion to other artefact Kuidgets.

At the physical level, there is not much difference between artefacts and agent Kuidgets; they are essentially KUI's components, and as long as their corresponding physical objects are providing their location and motion information, they are treated equally in KUIs. At a conceptual level, however, they differ because agents can control and operate artefacts and have a higher degree of autonomy. This distinction is particularly useful when KUI-enabled applications need to determine the location and motion of Kuidgets in the absence of up-to-dated information. Motion of artefact Kuidgets typically has to be somehow causally linked to agent Kuidgets; sometimes artefacts cause the motion of agents, and sometimes it is the other way around.

Artefact Kuidget typically keeps its last observed (communicated) location if they are not linked to any moving entity (i.e., the law of inertia). Even in cases where no information can be obtained for an artefact Kuidget, its current location can be inferred by default just by knowing that it is unlinked from a moving Kuidget. Different from artefact Kuidgets, agent Kuidgets have more freedom. When unlinked from any moving artefact Kuidgets, their current location and motion status cannot be safely inferred; they can move without being tracked. Of course, there also might be the case that an artefact is no longer tracked, but this case is considered as an error condition rather than a choice selected by the user. In other words, in KUI agent Kuidgets can decide when they can be tracked, while artefacts cannot.

Two Kuidgets can be logically linked and they can provide location and motion information to each other. For instance, a car equipped with a GPS sensor (an artefact Kuidget) can provide location and motion information to its driver (an agent Kuidget). Conversely, a user carrying a GPS sensor can provide location and motion information to the car Kuidget by setting a logical link between the car and the user who is driving the car. It is important to notice that when the user leaves the car, even if the link is destroyed, the car Kuidget keeps its last location.

It is also our goal to make KUI as general as possible in order to uniformly cope with different geographical scales (e.g., tabletop, room, building, cities) and with different types of location-aware devices (e.g., GPS, RFID, Wireless cell triangulation, ultrasonic, ultra-wideband, infrared). For this purpose, we also distinguish between different *types* of physical space. Following (Dix et al., 2000), we consider *topological* and *symbolic* spaces[9]. In topological spaces, objects are localized by their exact position by means of an absolute coordinate system and through a notion of distance. In symbolic spaces, locations are considered as symbolic elements (e.g., rooms, buildings, cities), and object are localized through spatial relations with other objects (e.g., in the bedroom, near the red table). For topological spaces, the two basic types of references are *points* and *zones*, while for symbolic spaces, entities are explicitly connected through symbolic spatial relations such as containment, accessibility, and so forth. Different from (Dix et al., 2000), we do not make any distinction between real and virtual spaces. In our approach, virtual spaces are managed by applications and they do not need to be represented at the KUI level. However, KUI allows the geo-localization of virtual objects; these are entities of the computing space mapped to the geographical space (e.g., a geo-tag or a zone).

The detection of particular spatio-temporal relations between Kuidgets can trigger application-specific KUI events. There are several spatio-temporal relations that can be modelled. We propose here that a basic KUI should provide at least two types of spatio-temporal relations: *proximity* and *containment*. For these relations it is important to consider their temporal dimension, namely the start and end time, and the duration of the relation. For instance, if two mobile Kuidgets (e.g., two agents) are observed while moving together along the same path or into the same location, the application will be notified with a "joint motion" event by the KUI manager. Then, the application might make inferences, and as a result, establish an application-dependent relation between the two Kuidgets. For instance, when the two agent Kuidgets are moving together, the application can infer (with the help of other contextual information) that they might be friends. Similarly, when two Kuidgets that are supposed to jointly move cease to do so, an event could be triggered that in certain circumstances could denote an unusual situation. For instance, a car moving somewhere while its owner moves elsewhere else might denote that the car has been stolen.

The last dimension for our classification is the type of motion of mobile Kuidgets. In order to cope with most possible situations, we consider both *endogenous* and *exogenous* motion. Endogenous motion occurs when objects move without any change of location. For instance, a rotating object that remains in the same place counts as endogenous motion; another example is the sudden motion sensors embedded in Apple Macintosh[10] laptops that can be exploited as an input modality in games. Exogenous motion represents the familiar case in which objects are displaced in the space. However, even if an entity is affected by exogenous motion, this does not necessarily mean that the exact change of location is tracked. For instance, if motion is detected by an accelerometer, the interface can use this information to trigger an event. This is the case of a Nintendo Wii™ controller WiiMote that is used to interact with games without detecting the exact change of location of players. More precisely, endogenous motion pertains to the fact that the spatial coordinate system is centred on the moving object, while exogenous motion is referenced to an external coordinate system.

The KUI Middleware

The software architecture we propose for KUI is supposed to be integrated within a larger context-aware middleware for Ubicomp. As in GUI, KUI should be independent from the underlying OS, and should enable rich interaction for context-aware Ubicomp systems. For this reason, we do not commit ourselves to a specific middleware. Rather, we focus on a general "pluggable" software component, which would allow us to make KUI available in an arbitrary *context-aware middleware* (see (Baldauf et al., 2006) for a review). However, KUI can be used as a standalone system if the interface between the KUI manager and motion-aware mobile devices is made through ad-hoc drivers.

The KUI middleware is made of three layers of abstraction (as shown in Figure 1). Below, we provide details about each layer:

- The *Observation Layer* is the lower level. Its role is to collect kinetic contexts from location and motion aware devices and from other hardware sensors.

- The *KUI-Space Layer* is an object-oriented environment that contains and manages Kuidgets state and their semantic relationships. Information flow coming from the observation layer is used to update the state of Kuidgets. Location information pertaining to Kuidgets is stored in a suitable data structure, the GeoDB (e.g. a GIS[11]), that is also used to store and manage physical space references of fixed and mobile Kuidgets for both topological and symbolic spaces.

- The *Activity Layer* manages the context history, and aggregates KUI events into higher-level semantic events (i.e., for the detection of specific interaction patterns) that are sent to the applications. In this layer, representations of *situations* will be constructed by aggregating kinetic informa-

Figure 1. KUI Middleware

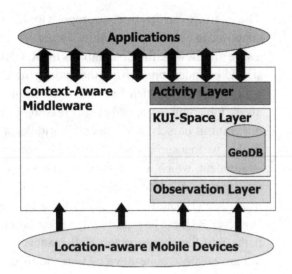

tion from Kuidgets and other contextual information. Moreover, models of activities will be matched with the spotted situations in order to determine the occurrence of anomalous behaviours.

More specifically, in the KUI software components location and motion information are linked to either fixed Kuidgets or mobile Kuidgets that are localizable by means of tracking hardware.

The KUI Components

The KUI Middleware can be seen as a user interface server that connects client applications to motion-aware input devices. In that sense, our

Figure 2. Sketch of the KUI Toolkit

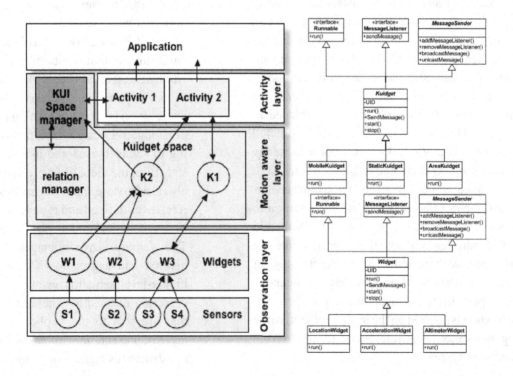

model is similar to the X-Windows toolkit model. KUI provides an API to applications for subscribing aggregated events from the Activity Layer and encapsulates motion-aware devices through the Observation Layer. The main components of the KUI middleware are detailed in Figure 2.

A number of location and motion-aware devices can be connected to any Kuidget for which they cooperate in providing its kinetic information. Kuidgets are identified by universally unique identifiers (UUID), and are linked to entries in the GeoDB that provides both direct localization and indirect localization through explicit relationships with other Kuidgets not linked to directly localizable elements. When the Observation Layer produces fresh kinetic information for a given Kuidget, a callback is sent to KUI-Space manager component, which updates the corresponding geographical information in the GeoDB and manages the relations between active Kuidgets.

The KUI-Space Manager is responsible for the aggregation and filtering of low-level events produced by the Observation Layer. Observations also can be obtained from the hosting context-aware middleware through *context widgets* (Dey et al., 2001). Context widgets are abstractions for different types of context sensors. They hide the complexity of the sensor communication protocols and offer a hot-plugging mechanism for dynamically adding and removing sensors to the system. As for GUIs, the application does not have to be modified when the pointing system changes, for instance, from mouse to pen. In our case, Kuidgets connected to location and motion Widgets do not know what kind of sensor is actually in use when they get kinetic information.

The Relation Manager receives location updates from the KUI-space and processes them according to the (programmable) relation rules. Relations between Kuidgets are created, deleted or updated and dispatched to the KUI-space manager, which then sends them to the upper Activity Layer through a notification mechanism. When some pre-defined geographical relationship change occurs (e.g., an object enters an active zone), the Relation Manager is responsible of notifying these events to the Activity Layer or directly to the subscribing Kuidgets. These events can be programmed as triggers that check conditions matched against the GeoDB, while aggregate events can be subscribed by objects in the upper Activity Layer. Relations between Kuidgets can be created either by the Kuidget's internal logic in response to Kuidget events triggered when retrieving information from the GeoDB, or explicitly by applications. The latter case is useful when we logically link agent and artefact Kuidgets together, allowing one of them to inherit motion properties from the other one.

The Activity Layer is responsible of aggregating motion information from one or several Kuidget, as well as dynamic information generated by the Relation Manager. Relations and Kuidgets status are used as the building blocks for the recognition of the previously described kinetic interaction patterns.

Enabling Technology

The KUI middleware can be implemented on top of a context-aware middleware such as the *Context Toolkit* (Dey et al., 2001) and it can be integrated within any enterprise architecture like J2EE or .NET. Kinetic-aware devices typically will be connected through wireless Internet so that client-server software architecture is apparently justified. Applications exploit localization infrastructures for indoor and outdoor tracking. Indoor localization technologies include RFID antennas, ultrasonic, ultrawide-band, and IR sensors. For outdoor localization and motion tracking, GPS offers the most available tracking solution, which, combined with wireless Internet communication (e.g., GPRS, EDGE or UMTS) is nowadays available on commercial mobile phone and handheld devices. Additionally, we expect to detect others (more local) motion parameters (such as acceleration and direction) by using wearable sensors like accelerometers and digital compasses. For this point, it is crucial for the Observation Layer to be capable of dealing with several location and motion tracking technologies at the same time and of easily associating them with Kuidgets. The accuracy of different localization devices and motion sensors is not considered to be an issue in this discussion that pertains to the conceptual framework for the development of user interfaces based on kinetic input. We expect, in any case, that motion tracking and wearable sensor technology will rapidly improve, as already has been the case for other enabling technology like, for instance, the diffusion of broadband Internet connection for the Web.

CONCLUSION

In this chapter, we explored the notion of *kinetic-awareness* in Ubicomp user interfaces by means of the seamless and transparent integration of objects motion detection in the physical space as a primary input modality. Kinetic User Interfaces enable the users of Ubicomp systems to establish an interaction through continuous tracking of kinetic-aware mobile devices at different spatial scales and by the acquisition of kinetic input through motion-aware embedded sensors. KUI interfaces allow the seamless integration of contextual (implicit) and intentional (explicit) interaction through motion. We presented a conceptual framework for KUI interfaces and a middleware as the basis for implementing the KUI component in standard Ubicomp architectures.

Kinetic-awareness in Ubicomp seems to take over simple location-awareness. Motion-based interaction is a complementary notion to context-awareness. It is not just a matter of acting while moving, but *acting by moving*. Motion is a great source of information that leverages new dimensions of user experience in Ubicomp systems. As noted in (Beaudouin-Lafon, 2004), in post-WIMP user interfaces, it will be necessary to shift towards a more holistic view of user interaction. Users are expected to interact through *activities* rather than single actions. Moreover, they will try to achieve higher-level goals through activities, rather than to accomplish tasks through planned actions. KUI provides a framework for designing Ubicomp applications with embodied interaction with a special focus on unobtrusiveness and fluidity.

REFERENCES

Abowd, G.D., Mynatt, E.D., & Rodden. T. (2002, January-March). The Human Experience. *Pervasive Computing 1*(1), 48-57.

Abowd, G.D., & Mynatt, E.D. (2000). Charting Past, Present, and Future Research in Ubiquitous Computing. *ACM Transactions on Computer-Human Interaction, 7*(1), 29–58.

Addlesee, M., Curwen, R., Hodges, S., Newman, J., Steggles, P., Ward, A.., & Hopper, A. (2001). Implementing a Sentient Computing System. *IEEE Computer, 34*(8), 50-56.

Ashbrook, D., Lyons, K., & Clawson, J. (2006). Capturing Experiences Anytime, Anywhere. *IEEE Pervasive Computing 5*(2), 8-11.

Baldauf, M., Dustdar, S., & Rosenberg, F. (2007). A Survey on Context Aware Systems. *International Journal of Ad Hoc and Ubiquitous Computing*, Inderscience Publishers. forthcoming. Pre-print from: http://www.vitalab.tuwien.ac.at/~florian/papers/ijahuc2007.pdf

Banavar, G., & Bernstein, A. (2004). Challenges in Design and Software Infrastructure for Ubiquitous Computing Applications. *Communications of the ACM, 45*(12), 92-96.

Barfield, W., & Caudell, T. (Eds.). (2001) *Fundamentals of Wearable Computers and Augmented Reality*. LEA Books.

Beaudouin-Lafon, M. (2000). Instrumental Interaction: An Interaction Model for Designing Post-WIMP User Interfaces. In *Proceedings of ACM Human Factors in Computing Systems, CHI 2000, La Haye (Pays-Bas), Avril 2000, CHI Letters 2(1)*:446-453, ACM Press.

Beaudouin-Lafon, M. (2004). Designing Interaction, not Interfaces. In Costabile, M.F. (Ed.), In *Proceedings of the working conference on Advanced visual interfaces AVI 2004*, (pp. 15-22). Minneapolis: ACM Press.

Bellotti, V., Back, M., Edwards, K., Grinter, R, Lopes, C., & Henderson, A. (2002). Making Sense of Sensing Systems: Five Questions for Researchers and Designers. In *Proceedings of CHI 2002* (pp. 415-422), Minneapolis: ACM Press.

Bleecker, J. (2006). *Why Things Matter: A Manifesto for Networked Objects — Cohabiting with Pigeons, Arphids and Aibos in the Internet of Things*. Retrieved from http://research.techkwondo.com/files/WhyThingsMatter.pdf

Brumitt, B., Meyers, B. Krumm, J., Kern, A.,. & Shafer, S. (2000). EasyLiving: Technologies for Intelligent Environments. In *Proceedings of Second International Symposium on Handheld and Ubiquitous Computing HUC2K*, (pp. 12-29). Bristol, UK, Springer Verlag.

Chen, G., & Kotz, D. (2000). *A Survey of Contex-Aware Mobile Computing Research*. (Tech. Rep. No. TR2000-381), Darthmouth Science Department.

Cheverst, K., Davies, N., Mitchell, K., Friday, A., & Efstratiou, C. (2000). Developing a Context-aware Electronic Tourist Guide: Some Issues and Experiences. In *Proceedings of CHI 2000* (pp. 17-24). The Netherlands.

Davis, M. King, S., Good, N., & Sarvas, R. (2004). From Context to Content: Leveraging Context to Infer Media Metadata. In *Proceedings of 12th Annual ACM International Conference on Multimedia MM2004* (pp. 188-195). New York, ACM Press.

Dey, A.K., & Abowd, G.D. (2000). CyberMinder: A Context-Aware System for Supporting Reminders. In *Proceedings of the 2nd International Symposium on Handheld and Ubiquitous Computing HUC2K* (pp. 25-27), Bristol, UK, Springer Verlag.

Dey, A.K., Salber, D., & Abowd, G.D. (2001). A Conceptual Framework and a Toolkit for Supporting the Rapid Prototyping of Context-Aware Applications (anchor article of the special issue on Context-Aware Computing). *Human-Computer Interaction Journal, 16*(2-4), 97-166.

Dix, A., Rodden, T., Davies, N., Trevor, J., Friday, A., & Palfreyman, K. (2000). Exploiting space and location as a design framework for interactive mobile systems. *ACM Transactions on Computer-Human Interaction, 7*(3), 285-321.

Dix, A. (2002a). Managing the Ecology of Interaction. In Pribeanu, C., & Vanderdonckt, J. (Eds.), *Proceedings of Tamodia 2002 - First International Workshop on Task Models and User Interface Design* (pp. 1-9). Bucharest, Romania: INFOREC Publishing House, Bucharest.

Dix, A. (2002b). Beyond intention - pushing boundaries with incidental interaction. In *Proceedings of Building Bridges: Interdisciplinary Context-Sensitive Computing*, Glasgow University, Sept. 9th 2002.

Dix, A., Finlay, J., Abowd, G., & Beale, R. (2004). *Human-Computer Interaction* (Third Edition). Prentice Hall. 2004.

Dourish, P. (2001). *Where the Action Is: The Foundations of Embodied Interaction*. Cambridge, MIT Press.

Fitzmaurice, G.W. (1996). *Graspable User Interfaces*. Unpublished doctoral dissertation, Department of Computer Science, University of Toronto.

Gaye, L., Mazé, R., & Holmquist, L.E. (2003). Sonic City: The Urban Environment as a Musical Interface. In *Proceedings of the Conference on New Interfaces for Musical Expression* NIME-03 (pp. 109-115), Montreal, Canada.

Greenfield, A. (2006). *Everyware: the dawning age of ubiquitous computing.* New Riders publishers, Berkeley. 2006.

Harter, A., Hopper, A., Steggles, P. Ward, A., & Webster, P. (2002). The anatomy of a Context-Aware Application. *Wireless Networks,* 8, 187-197.

Hightower, J., & Borriello, G. (2001). Location systems for ubiquitous computing. *IEEE Computer 34*(8), 57-66.

Holmquist, L., Schmidt, A., & Ullmer, B. (2004). Tangible interfaces in perspective: Guest editors' introduction. *Personal and Ubiquitous Computing 8*(5), 291-293.

Hong, D., Chiu, D.K.W., & Shen, V.Y. (2005). Requirements elicitation for the design of context-aware applications in a ubiquitous environment. In *Proceedings of ICEC'05* (pp. 590-596).

International Telecommunication Union (2005). *The Internet of Things: Executive Report.* Retrieved from http://www.itu.int/pub/S-POL-IR.IT-2005/e. Geneva, 2005

Kleinrock, L. (1997). Nomadic computing. *Telecommunication Systems 7*(1-3): 5-15.

Kidd, C.K., Orr, R.J., Abowd, G.D. Atkeson, C.G., Essa, I.A., MacIntyre, B., Mynatt, E., Starner, T.E., & Newstetter, W. (1999, October 1-2)). The Aware Home: A Living Laboratory for Ubiquitous Computing Research. Paper presented at *the Second International Workshop on Cooperative Buildings* CoBuild99, Pittsburgh, PA (LNCS 1670).

Koile, K., Tollmar, K., Demirdjian, D., Shrobe, H., & Darrell, T. (2003). Activity Zones for Context-Aware Computing. In *Proceedings of Ubicomp 2003,* (pp. 90-106).

Mackay, W.E. (1998). Augmented reality: linking real and virtual worlds. A new paradigm for interacting with computer. In *Proceedings of International Conference on Advanced Visual Interfaces* AVI'98, (pp. 13-21).

Meier, R., Harrington, A. Termin, T., & Cahill, V. (2006). A Spatial Programming Model for Real Global Smart Space Applications. In Eliassen, F. & Montresor, Al. (Eds.) *Proceedings of the 6th IFIP International Conference on Distributed Applications and Interoperable Systems* DAIS 06 (pp. 16-31). Bologna, Italy, 2006. Lecture Notes in Computer Science, Springer-Verlag.

Nardi, B.A. (Ed.) (1996). *Context and consciousness: activity theory and human-computer interaction.* Cambridge, MA: MIT Press.

Negroponte, N. (1995). *Being Digital.* Vintage Editions. 1996.

Norman, D.A. (1999). *The Invisible Computer.* Cambridge, MA. MIT Press.

Norrie, M.C., & Signer, B. (2005, January). *Overlaying Paper Maps with Digital Information Services for Tourists,* In proceedings of *The 12th International Conference on Information Technology and Travel and Tourism* ENTER 2005, Innsbruck, Austria.

Nova, N., Girardin, F., & Dillenbourg, P. (2006, May 9-12)). The Underwhelming Effects of Automatic Location-Awareness on Collaboration in a Pervasive Game. In proceedings of *The International Conference on the Design of Cooperative Systems* COOP06 (pp. 224-238). Carry-le-Rouet, Provence, France.

Pallotta, V., Brocco, A., Guinard, D., Bruegger, P., & De Almeida, P. (2006, June 27). RoamBlog: Outdoor and Indoor Geoblogging Enhanced with Contextual Service Provisioning for Mobile Internet Users. In *Proceedings of the 1st International Workshop on Distributed Agent-Based Retrieval Tools* (pp. 103-121). Cagliari, Italy.

Rekimoto, J. (1997). Pick-and-Drop: A Direct Manipulation Technique for Multiple Computer Environments. In *Proceedings of International Conference on 10th annual symposium on User Interface Software and Technology* UIST'97 (pp. 31-39).

Ricci, A., Viroli, M., & Omicini, A. (2006, April 18-21). Construenda est CArtAgO: Toward an Infrastructure for Artifacts in MAS. In *Proceedings of the European Meeting on Cybernetics and Systems Research* EMCSR'06 (vol. 2 pp. 569–574). University of Wien, Vienna, Austria.

Román, M., Hess, C.K., Cerqueira, R., Ranganathan, A., Campbell, R.H., & Nahrstedt, K. (2002). GAIA: A Middleware Infrastructure to Enable Active Spaces. *IEEE Pervasive Computing, 1*(4), 74-83.

Rukzio, E. (2006). *Physical Mobile Interactions: Mobile Devices as Pervasive Mediators for Interactions with the Real World.* Unpublished doctoral dissertation, University of Munich.

Salkham, A., Cunningham, R., Senart, A., & Cahill, V. (2006). *A Taxonomy of Collaborative Context-Aware Systems* (Tech. Rep. No. TCD-CS-2006-30). Dept. of Computer Science, University of Dublin, Trinity College.

Shafer, S.A.N., Brumitt, B., & Cadiz, J. (2001). Interaction issues in context-aware intelligent environments. *Human-Computer Interaction, 16*(2), 363-378.

Schilit, B.N. (1995). *System architecture for context-aware mobile computing.* Unpublished doctoral dissertation, Columbia University, 1995. Retrieved from http://citeseer.ist.psu.edu/schilit-95system.html

Sousa, J.P., & Garlan, D. (2002). *AURA: an Architectural Framework for User Mobility in Ubiquitous Computing Environments.* In *Proceedings of the IEEE Conference on Software Architecture* (pp. 29-43), Montreal.

Sparacino, F. (2005). Intelligent Architecture: Embedding Spaces with a Mind for Augmented Interaction. In Costabile, M.F. & Paternò, F. (Eds.): *Proceedings of the* INTERACT 2005 *- Human-Computer Interaction* IFIP TC13 *International Conference* (pp. 2-3). LNCS 3585 Springer Verlag.

Spence, M., Driver, C., & Clarke, S. (2005). Sharing Context History in Mobile. Context-Aware Trails-Based Applications. Paper presented at the *1st international workshop on exploiting context histories in smart environments* ECHISE 2005, Part of PERVASIVE 2005, Munich, Germany, 2005.

Ullmer, B., & Ishii, H. (2000). Emerging Frameworks for Tangible User Interfaces. *IBM Systems Journal* 9(3-4), 915-931.

Want, R., Pering, T., Borriello, G., & Farkas, K.I. (2002). Disappearing Hardware. *IEEE Pervasive Computing 1*(1), 26-35.

Weiser, M. (1991). The Computer for the 21st Century. *Scientific American, 265*(3), 94-104.

Weiser, M. (1993). Hot topic: Ubiquitous computing. *IEEE Computer*, October 1993, 71-72.

Weiser, M. (1994). The world is not a desktop. *ACM Interactions, 1*(1), 7-8.

Weiser, M. & Seely Brown, J. (1996). *The Coming Age of Calm Technology* (Tech. Rep.) Xerox PARC.

Winograd, T. (2000). Towards a Human-Centered Interaction Architecture. In Carroll, J. (Ed). *Human-Computer Interaction in the New Millennium.* Addison-Wesley, Reading, MA.

Winograd, T. (2001). Architectures for context. *Human-Computer Interaction*, 16(2,3,4).

ENDNOTES

1. http://www.ubiq.com/hypertext/weiser/UbiHome.html
2. http://en.wikipedia.org/wiki/Web_2.0
3. http://www.socialight.com
4. http://www.ubisense.com
5. WIMP stands for "Windows, Icons, Menus, Popups".
6. The motion detection can be obtained either by the mobile device itself (e.g. a GPS-enabled handheld) or by external device or infrastructure (e.g. a badge tracked by a sensing space).
7. This interaction pattern is similar to the Teleport application (Addlesee et al., 2001), which allows users wearing ActiveBadges to move their desktop environments from a PC to another.
8. See (Salkham et al., 2006) for an overview.
9. We changed the names attributed to these types of space by (Dix et al., 2000). Our "topological" corresponds to their "cartesian" and our "symbolic" corresponds to their "topological".
10. http://www.apple.com/
11. Geographical Information Systems

This work was previously published in Advances in Ubiquitous Computing: Future Paradigms and Directions, edited by S. Mostefaoui, Z. Maamar, and G. Giaglis, pp. 201-228, copyright 2008 by IGI Publishing, formerly known as Idea Group Publishing (an imprint of IGI Global).

Section III
Tools and Technologies

Chapter X
Communicating in the Information Society:
New Tools for New Practices

Lorenzo Cantoni
University of Lugano, Switzerland

Stefano Tardini
University of Lugano, Switzerland

ABSTRACT

The present chapter provides a conceptual framework for the newest digital communication tools and for the practices they encourage, stressing the communication opportunities they offer and the limitations they impose. In this chapter, Internet-based communication technologies are regarded as the most recent step in the development of communication technologies. This approach helps have a broad perspective on the changes information and communication technologies (ICT) are bringing along in the social practices of so called knowledge society. As a matter of fact, these changes need to be considered within an "ecological" approach, that is, an approach that provides a very wide overview on the whole context (both in synchronic terms and in diachronic ones) where ICT are spreading. In the second part of the chapter, the authors present two examples of relevant social practices that are challenged by the most recent ICT, namely journalism (news market) and Internet search engines.

INTRODUCTION

New digital communication tools (information and communication technologies, or ICT) rapidly spreading worldwide have a deep impact on the way we interact and communicate, both in everyday life and in our professional activities; they are changing our social life and our social practices. For instance, the way we can access, edit and share documents (movies, songs, pictures, images, texts or any other kind of documents) has changed, as well as the way we relate to government, access health, banking, and other public services, the way we work, play, learn, buy and sell, search information, meet (un)known people, and so on (Cantoni & Tardini, 2006).

The rapid growth of these new technologies has raised the issue of *digital literacy*, creating a divide between those who can (are able/have access to) manage them and those who cannot (are not able/do not have access to), as well as between those who are *digital natives* and those who have "migrated" into digital technologies (*digital immigrants*). The term *digital divide* refers to "the inequalities that exist in Internet access based on income, age, education, race/ethnicity, and ... between rural and metropolitan areas, through such factors as pricing and infrastructure" (Hill, 2004, p. 27).

However, a first important clarification is needed here: it is not the first time new communication technologies have arisen and caused changes in a society, nor will it be the last. Suffice it to think of the enormous changes brought along by the invention of writing and the alphabet, which made it possible also for people who are both spatially and temporally separated to communicate (Danesi, 2006); again, the invention and the diffusion of letterpress print gave rise to the first assembly line, embedding "the word itself deeply in the manufacturing process and [making] it into a kind of commodity" (Ong, 2002, p. 118).

Generally speaking, every "technology of the word" has always brought along larger or smaller, positive or negative changes in the contexts where it was adopted (McLuhan, 2001), always raising the issues of literacy and access to information.

In a sense, every new communication technology spreading in a given society has always configured social class of "scribes," that is, of those people who are able to use that given technology within that society. After being managed only by social elite of the scribes, some technologies are then "socialized," that is, they get to be mastered by most of the society. It is the case, for instance, of reading and writing, which remained a long while after it was invented only

a matter for scribes: those who needed a written text had necessarily to turn to them. For instance, Charlemagne (747-814) could be the emperor of the Holy Roman Empire even though he was hardly able to write (hence the legend that he could not write at all) and learned to read only in his adulthood; nowadays illiterate people are in fact almost excluded from social life. Not all communication technologies reach the stage of socialized literacy: for example, the use of the telegraph has always remained in the hands of some operators who had the knowledge of how to send and receive telegrams. Furthermore, some technologies get to be socialized only with regard to the fruition of the message, while its production remains a matter for experts. In the Western society, for instance, TV and radio are nowadays completely socialized in the sense that everybody is able to use TV sets and radios in order to receive the programs they broadcast; but when it comes to the production of TV and radio messages, only skilled operators can do that (although this state of affairs is being challenged by digital audio and video editing).

Something similar is happening to digital information and communication technologies (ICT), which are becoming more and more a necessary tool in order to be fully introduced into the information society ("a society in which low-cost information and ICT are in general use") or "knowledge society"—where "knowledge" stresses "the fact that the most valuable asset is investment in intangible, human, and social capital and that the key factors are knowledge and creativity" (europa.eu.int/comm/employment_social/knowledge_society/index_en.htm). In other terms, digital literacy is more and more a requirement in the knowledge society, at least in terms of digital fruition: being able to access digital information is something that cannot be anymore referred to "digital scribes," but is becoming more and more a personal requirement.

The comparison with the model of linguistic change can help explain how a technology is accepted or rejected by a given community/society. The introduction of a new element into a language system follows three steps: the new element is created/invented by someone who first coins it and uses it (or a new sense is given to an existing element: *innovation*), the new element is then adopted and used by the hearer (*adoption*), and finally, the new element spreads in the system: a new word becomes part of the lexicon of a language, is inserted in the language dictionaries, and so on (*change*). "Linguistic change is the diffusion or the generalization of an innovation, that is, necessarily, a series of subsequent adoptions" (Coseriu, 1981, p. 56). Similarly, a technological innovation needs different steps and—often—a long-term process (Rogers, 1995) in order to be accepted and to spread in a society, where it must partly overlap with other existing technologies, partly overcome old ones (Cantoni & Tardini, 2006, pp. 7-18).

As a matter of fact, the media market is like an ecological system where the introduction of a new element (e.g., a new animal species) affects the whole system, entering in competition with the other existing elements and causing a re-organization of the whole system. With respect to this process, Roger Fidler coined the term of *mediamorphosis*, stressing the fact that new communication media do not arise from nothing, as through spontaneous generation, but emerge step by step from the metamorphoses of earlier media, in a context where other communication technologies pre-existed, which had their own role in supporting specific social practices. Furthermore, pre-existing media are usually not completely displaced, but they go on evolving and adapting themselves to the new context, usually by carving out a niche for themselves (Fidler, 1997).

Thus, it is crucial to understand the context where new ICT are spreading. Generally speaking, the emerging of digital technologies is driving the media market towards globalization thanks to the opportunities offered by digitization.

The present chapter aims at providing a conceptual framework for understanding the newest digital communication tools and the practices they encourage, stressing the communication opportunities these technologies offer and the limitations they impose. The first paragraph will outline the framework, presenting the main tools and devices that allow digital communication and the characteristics of the settings they rely on, and providing a four-layer taxonomy for the understanding of new digital communication tools. The second paragraph will present two examples of relevant social practices where ICT play a seminal role, namely journalism (news market) and Internet search engines. It will then explore how they are changing as a consequence of the diffusion of new ICT.

BACKGROUND

Before presenting some new practices that new communication technologies support, and in order to better understand them, it is important to have an overview of the devices and the tools that make these practices possible.

Devices and Tools

The most common device that supports communication in the knowledge society is no doubt the *computer*: it is no accident that the kind of communication that takes place by means of new ICT has been often referred to as *computer mediated communication* (CMC), usually intended as the interpersonal communication through a computer. However, this term, referring to this particular device, does not take into account the interactions that ICT allow by means of other devices, such as mobile phones, PDAs, iPods, and other mp3 players, TV sets, videogames consoles, and others. As a matter of fact, nowadays the same kind of interaction that is made possible by a computer is made possible also (at least partially, in some cases) by these devices. The basic technology that underlies communication mediated by new ICT is the *Internet*, the "global network connecting millions of computers" (http://www.Webopedia.com/TERM/I/Internet.html). Through the Internet almost every kind of communication is allowed: it is possible to have spoken conversations as well as written interactions; one-to-one communications as well as one-to-many or even many-to-many ones; it is possible to publish written texts with images and audio and video as well; it is possible to communicate in real time or to send messages that will be read later; it is possible to send and share documents of all kinds; and so on. The features of the communications taking place over the Internet are strongly dependent on the tools employed: different tools impose different constraints and offer different options to interlocutors. (Cantoni & Tardini, 2006, p. 43)

The Internet offers indeed a variety of communication tools. The most common and most diffused one is *e-mail*. Through e-mail it is possible to send a text message to one or more addressees simultaneously. E-mail is a low-bandwidth, text-based technology, but since it is possible to attach all kinds of files to an e-mail message, it allows also the exchange of multimedia documents between interlocutors. E-mail is mostly used as an asynchronous tool, somehow like normal mail. Two other tools, based on the technology of e-mail, are to be mentioned here: *mailing lists* and *newsgroups*, which allow for an easy delivery of a text message to a group of addressees.

Over the Internet it is possible to have also interpersonal synchronous communications, either spoken or written. *Chat* or *messenger systems*, for instance, allow for a synchronous exchange of written text messages, while *desktop (audio/video) conference systems* and *VoIP systems* allow for spoken interactions over the Internet, where interlocutors can either hear each other (as in VoIP systems and in audioconferences) or even

(partially) see each other, as in videoconferences. A more complex interaction environment is that of *3D multi-user virtual environments*, where subscribed participants are represented in a 3D virtual world (also called *metaverse*) by an *avatar*, that is, a virtual character users can move in the virtual space in order to get closer to other participants, chat with them, perform actions allowed by the virtual world, and so on. One of the most known and diffused of such environments is *Second Life* (http://secondlife.com), a 3D online digital world imagined, created, and owned by its residents. In June 2007 Second Life had more than 7,500,000 residents; its virtual environment has been exploited by companies, businesses, universities, and other institutions to expand and support their commercial, educational, and institutional activities (see, for instance, Kemp & Livingstone, 2006).

Of course, the Internet-based communication tool that, together with e-mail, is the most known and used is the *World Wide Web* (WWW), a system of Internet servers that support specially formatted documents. The documents are formatted in a markup language called HTML (*HyperText Markup Language*) that supports links to other documents, as well as graphics, audio, and video files. This means you can jump from one document to another simply by clicking on hot spots. (http://www.Webopedia.com/TERM/W/World_Wide_Web.html)

The most important "space" of the WWW are the well-known *Web sites*; however, we will focus here on the main tools and services of so-called *Web 2.0*, that is, the second generation of the World Wide Web that is focused on the ability for people to collaborate and share information online. Web 2.0 basically refers to the transition from static HTML Web pages to a more dynamic Web. (http://www.Webopedia.com/TERM/W/Web_2_point_0.html)

In other terms, rather than aiming at providing users with information, Web 2.0 tools "enable user participation on the Web and manage to recruit a large number of users as authors of new content," thus obliterating "the clear distinction between information providers and consumers" (Kolbitsch & Maurer, 2006, p. 187). Thus, we can claim that Web 2.0 tools have the potential of moving further the process of socialization of Internet-based communication technologies, by socializing also the activity of publishing on the Web.

The main tools we are referring to here are blogs and wikis. *Blogs* (short for *Web logs*) are Web pages that serve as a publicly accessible personal journal for an individual or a group, a sort of Web-based electronic diaries that reflect the personalities of their authors. Blogs are very useful tools for micropublishing, since they "enable the process of quickly and easily committing thoughts to the Web, offer limited discussion/talkbacks, and syndicate new items to make it easier to keep up without constant checking back" (Hall, 2002). Blogs "are not open to the public for authoring, and there is no well-defined publishing process as in newspapers" (Kolbitsch & Maurer, 2006, p. 190). The rapid spread of blogs has given rise to the creation of a real network of more or less loosely interconnected Weblogs (so-called *blogosphere*), where the author of one blog can easily comment on the articles of other blogs.

Strictly connected to blogs is RSS (Rich Site Summary or RDF Site Syndication), an XML format developed to syndicate Web content, thus helping people receive new information items as soon as they are published. Users can subscribe to RSS content, and automatically receive new info, such as news feeds, updates, blog's items, and the like. Similar in nature is *podcasting*, the possibility of automatic download of audio files onto an iPod (or other mp3 players) from Web services one has subscribed to.

Wikis (from the Hawaiian word "wiki wiki," which means "quick") are collaborative Web sites comprised of the perpetual collective work of many authors. Similar to a blog in structure and logic, a wiki allows anyone to edit, delete or modify content that has been placed on the Web site using a browser interface, including the work of previous authors. (http://www.Webopedia. com/TERM/w/wiki.html)

In a sense, wikis seem to have materialized the dreams of the pioneers of hypertext, such as Vannevar Bush, Ted Nelson, and Douglas Engelbart, and of the early hypertext theorists, that of having a shared environment where anybody could produce, edit, and store any kind of information, thus blurring the distinction between authors and readers. The most famous wiki-based Web site is no doubt the Wikipedia, the "free encyclopedia that anyone can edit" (http://en.wikipedia.org/ wiki/Main_Page). As observed by Kolbitsch and Maurer (2006), "the success of Wikipedia builds on the tight involvement of the users, the sense of the community, and a dedication to developing a knowledge repository of unprecedented breadth and depth" (p. 195). Started in 2001, in December 2007 the English version of Wikipedia had more than 2,100,000 articles, the German and French Wikipedias more than 500,000, and also the Polish, Dutch, Japanese, Spanish, Italian, Portuguese, Russian, Swedish, and Chinese versions had more than 150,000 articles; in December 2007, 250 different Wikipedias were online (the complete list can be found at: http://meta.wikimedia. org/wiki/List_of_Wikipedias).

Finally, the diffusion of *community-based networking services* has to be mentioned. These are Web-based services that rely on the community of their users in order to let them store, organize, and share different kind of documents, such as photos (e.g., Flickr—www.flickr.com) and bookmarked Webpages (e.g., del.icio.us—http:// del.icio.us). Users of such services can add their documents to their online space in the service, tag them, comment on them, and share them with other users; the key element of the system is the tagging activity, since the tags added by a user to his/her documents are used for describing and categorizing the documents, thus making them available for other users' searches. Such services can be seen as a Web-based evolution of file sharing systems (such as Napster and Kazaa), which allow users to share (sometimes illegally) their files by means of a peer-to-peer architecture.

Conceptually similar to community-based networking systems are some features of Web services like eBay, Amazon, and similar ones; in these services the behaviors and the opinions of users (in the form of a rating given to a seller, of a comment on a book, and so on) are used to create "social" (in a broad sense) networks, such as clusters of users with similar interests, which are in some way connected with each other, but cannot communicate. Community-based networking services are often used as an alternative to "traditional" search engines; however, as we will see in the next section, also Internet search engines are undergoing a pragmatic/social turn, in the sense that they are trying to take more and more into account the actual behaviors of their users (Cantoni, Faré, & Tardini, 2006).

Features of Electronic Communication

All these tools allow for different kinds of communications, since they provide different communication settings. Generally speaking, Internet-based communication has peculiar features that differentiate it from both oral and written communication; at the same time, it shares many features with both oral and written communication. Some authors coined the word Netspeak (Crystal, 2001, p. 17), which emphasizes the double face of CMC: "The heart of the matter seems to be its relationship to spoken and written language" (Crystal, 2001, p. 24). We will not focus here on the different settings allowed by the different tools; we will just outline the main features of electronic texts, which depend both on their support and on the communication setting in which they are produced (Cantoni & Tardini, 2006, pp. 54-57).

Electronic texts are *directly inaccessible to human senses.* Whereas books can be directly accessed by human senses (sight in particular), texts coded in computer files need the mediation of other tools (hardware and software) in order to be seen and read. Electronic documents share this feature with other supports for information, such as, for instance, vinyl records, or audio and video cassettes. Furthermore, electronic texts are inaccessible as a whole, since it is possible to access only a part of an electronic text at a time, namely the part that appears on the monitor.

Electronic texts are *immaterial*, since they are physically just a sequence of bits. The immateriality of digital documents makes them very easy to transport, reproduce, and access.

Electronic texts are perfectly *reproducible*. Of course, technical reproduction is not a novelty of electronic texts (Benjamin, 1973). However, digitization brought this process to an end. In electronic texts, not only it is impossible to distinguish the master from the copies, as, for instance, in printed books and in cinematographic films, but often it is not even possible to locate them in the space, due to their immateriality.

Electronic texts may be made—thanks to computer networking—*always accessible* without any limit of space. A document published on the Internet is always "close" and available to its readers, wherever they are, provided that they have an Internet access.

An electronic text *can be modified* as much as one wants. In digital documents, parts of a text can be added, deleted, or edited at a user's will. Unlike printed texts, which cannot be modified anymore once they have been concluded and printed, electronic texts remain always at the author's (and reader's) disposal and can be altered whenever required; in this sense, electronic texts may be said to be "never over," as wikis clearly show. With regard to this feature, digital writing is similar to hand writing, which allows as many text modifications as one wants; however, in hand written texts, modifications leave tracks and remain visible always, while electronic ones can be altered without leaving any trace.

Electronic texts are potentially *multimedia* documents. As a matter of fact, thanks to their digital nature, in electronic documents elements belonging to different semiotic codes can be integrated, such as pictures, images, audios, videos, and animations.

Electronic texts are *persistent*: persistency is a basic feature of CMC, because of the very nature of the medium used. Digital documents leave a persistent trace in the electronic world, which can be recorded and read many times.

Electronic texts are often the result of *interactive communications*: as a matter of fact, computer mediated communication is always interactive, since it makes it easy and fast for senders and receivers to interact. In this way, Internet communication is really (potentially) dialogic and interactive, thus differentiating itself from the mass-media model where the message is unilaterally broadcast. Furthermore, Internet communication allows a higher degree of *customization* than mass-media communication: electronic messages may be designed in order to meet more closely the needs of single users or of specific groups.

A Four-Layer Taxonomy

The different technologies of the word mankind has invented can be organized according to different perspectives, taking into account their peculiarities as well as their common features. We thus propose the following taxonomy, organized along four relevant layers to be considered in relation to the Internet, and underline what is the place of the Internet (Cantoni & Tardini, 2006, pp. 23-25).

The first layer considers *which aspects of communication a technology is able to fix* outside the evanescent live act of communication. In fact, every technology can represent only some aspects of the world communicative acts refer to, such as their verbal content, still images (black and white or colored), moving images, sounds, and so forth, while omitting many others: intonation, physical setting, flavors, smells, and so on. From this point of view electronic media allow for a great convergence of previous media. Written digital texts can be combined with digital images, sounds, movies, graphics, and so forth.

The second layer considers *the activities and processes required for fixing and objectifying* parts of reality into a communicative act, the resources and costs needed. What are the processes required to produce, modify, replicate, and preserve a communication object belonging to a given technology of the word? If we think of handwriting, we know that it requires a big effort to reproduce a book but we know also that manuscripts can last many centuries without being corrupted or damaged. With the printing press, reproducing a text has become much more efficient (both from the point of view of time and resources and from the point of view of accuracy). In handwriting, cancellations and modifications are easy to carry out, while in print they are not at all easy, and require the set-up of a new "original" document. Electronic texts, on the other hand, partake of both modes, since they can be modified and reproduced very easily. Yet, the electronic world seems very fragile in terms of preservation, and we do not know whether an electronic document will be preserved for centuries. What we do know is that physical supports are not strong, and hardware and software standards change at a very fast pace, requiring a continuous upgrading of every digital collection.

Connected with the physical supports of communication is also *the possibility of moving them in space*, which constitutes the third layer of taxonomy. While in the period of orality, knowledge moved along with the knowing persons, distribution of written and printed documents made this movement much easier. If books are physical objects to be moved in space, the telegraph and the telephone required only a physical connection (the wire) and allowed for almost immediate transmissions. Wireless telegraph, radio, television, and mobile phones are all technologies which dispensed with the need for any physical link (besides the obvious hardware for sending and receiving signals). The Internet, from this point of view, allows for almost instant bidirectional and multidirectional communications, at a global level, being able to convey elements belonging to all sorts of semiotic codes.

Communication artifacts need also to *be accessed and interpreted*. Every technology of the word imposes a number of conditions for its fruition: speaking requires the air (the simplest condition to be met); writing requires light, whether natural or artificial; the telegraph, radio, and TV require electricity and suitable apparatuses. Electronic documents require hardware and software to be accessed. This raises the very delicate issue of *obsolescence*. Today we can read cuneiform documents because they require just eyes and light to be accessed, but we are unable to access a CD-ROM or a file on a hard-disk or the Internet without having suitable hardware and an appropriate piece of software. Obsolescence here is so fast that some supports used only a few years ago are no longer available (think, for example, of many data cassettes' or floppy-disks' formats), and files codified in "old" operating systems and software cannot communicate anything anymore. In the electronic world changes are the only stable rule.

TWO EXAMPLES: THE PRACTICES OF PROVIDING AND SEARCHING INFORMATION IN THE KNOWLEDGE SOCIETY

In this section two examples of practices that in the last years have been seriously challenged by the spread of new technologies will be presented: journalism (and the news market) and Internet

search engines. As it is clear, these practices are strictly related to one another, since both of them have to do with information. The news market deals with providing specific kinds of information, while Internet search engines deal with making any kind of information easily available to Internet users.

The News Market

Since the 1980s, the news market has been challenged by the diffusion of digital technologies: the computer first, the Internet and the latest tools, such as blogs. The changes these technologies are bringing in the sector are thorough:

The development of communications technologies in the news sector is transforming workplace relations and encouraging labour mobility. ... It is also enabling new media organizations to emerge with new types of work and new workplace activities. ... Opportunities to develop new types of content, use new forms of delivery and to develop new workplace practices are consequently challenging traditional practices within established news media organizations. (Harrison, 2006, p. 72)

Generally speaking, the situation digital technologies are configuring in the news market is a convergence of new technologies with existing ones: on the one side,

The Internet is being incorporated into other mass-media, in particular acting as a new and very important information source for them; on the other side, the Internet tends to include the existing media as an extra channel for the information they broadcast. (Cantoni & Tardini, 2006, p. 152)

As concerns the Internet as an information source for journalists, several studies show that the number of journalists using online sources is increasing more and more over time: for instance, the Eleventh Annual Survey of the Media, conducted by Euro RSCG Magnet together with the Columbia University, which in 2005 for the first time involved not only U.S. journalists, but also international ones, claims that:

Online news sites grew dramatically in importance, with 64% of journalists reporting that they often or sometimes use Web news in their day-to-day reporting, up from 34% in 2003 ... Reporters are increasingly taking advantage of the wealth of up-to-the-minute information at their fingertips ... This increasing reliance on online sources suggests that journalists, pressured by deadlines and other factors, may be forced by the challenges of their profession to sacrifice accuracy in their stories for immediacy of information. (Euro RSCG Magnet, 2005, pp. 16-17)

Among the online sources which journalists rely upon, blogs are gaining more and more consideration. Blogs are growing on the whole. According to a research conducted by comScore Networks, in the first quarter of 2005 50 million U.S. Internet users (i.e., about 30% of all U.S. Internet users) visited a blog, up from 34 million in the first quarter of 2004 (comScore Networks, 2005). In the particular case of journalists, according to Euro RSCG Magnet, 51% of them use Weblogs, a percentage that is significantly higher than that of blog visitors as a whole. Of those journalists who use blogs, 70% do so for work-related purposes, and in particular for finding story ideas, 53% for research and reference, 42%, and 36% for finding sources for their stories (Euro RSCG Magnet, 2005, p. 2). However, the reverse of the medal must be considered as well: the widespread use of blogs—and of online sources in general—by journalists has raised some critical issues. We dwell here upon two of them: the issue of trust and that of the role of journalists itself.

The issue of the credibility of Web information sources is one of the main concerns when dealing with the relationship between the Internet and other mass media. In a sense, the Internet has reproposed a situation similar to that which occurred when radio emerged (see Gackenbach & Ellerman, 1998, pp. 9-15):

Since the same receiving set and the same procedure allowed access to the programs of broadcasting stations that were very different with regard to the quality of their contents and to the target public they addressed, how, then, was it possible to distinguish high-quality stations from low-quality ones? The hierarchy of sources the press had established suddenly appeared to be disrupted, in an undifferentiated jumble of words, sounds and programs. Analogously, in the Internet everything can be accessed by means of the same software (the browser), in a seemingly flat and indistinct network. (Cantoni & Tardini, 2006, p. 133)

Of course, this point becomes even more relevant in journalism. The same survey by Euro RSCG Magnet, points out also that journalists admit that they do not trust blogs: they see blogs as just another advertising outlet for corporations. Only 1% of them consider blogs as very credible sources, and only 22% foresee that blogs will become valuable journalistic tools (Euro RSCG Magnet, 2005). The big challenge brought along by online sources in terms of trust is proved also by the fact that in 2005, 93% of journalists agreed "that they are excruciatingly careful about fact-checking their stories" (Euro RSCG Magnet, 2005, p. 21), while in 2003 only 59% of them agreed with this statement.

The widespread diffusion of blogs has challenged journalists' perception of their role and their work (and bloggers' perception as well). On one side, often journalists have a blog of their own, where they can express their opinions more freely than in traditional mass-media. On the other side, bloggers are "struggling to define their role as it relates to the media" (Euro RSCG Magnet, 2005,

p. 27). What is their role within the mainstream media? Are they to be considered as journalists? Do they want to be considered as journalists? As a matter of fact, many bloggers do consider themselves as journalists, while others prefer to stress their outsider status, thus eschewing the name of journalist and making of blogging a real profession (*professional blogger*). Furthermore, blogs are strongly fostering the diffusion of so-called *citizen journalism* (or *grassroots journalism*), that is, a kind of journalism where citizens have an active role in gathering, analyzing, and spreading news and information; the power of this kind of journalism consists in the quickness and easiness with which a citizen can tell the world what s/he has seen and experienced. For instance, in the case of a sudden and disastrous event, citizen journalists and bloggers are quicker than any other journalist, because they happen to be on the scene. This occurred, among other events, with the tsunami—when the lists of the survivors in the hospitals that were published on the blogs were more updated than those published by governments and institutions—and with the terrorist attack in London, when blogs could publish almost in real time news, comments, photos, and so on (Faré, 2006). In this context, of course, the issue of trust and credibility is—once again—pivotal, as some recent scandals concerning unfounded and unverified information published and spread by bloggers confirm. Blogs, however, have proved also to be useful in unmasking unfair journalistic practices, thus playing a role of control towards the media system, as well as the political and economical ones.

When it comes to the Internet as a channel for broadcasting news, the situation seems to be—at least in the U.S.—that of a deeper and deeper integration of online capabilities into "traditional" practices.

Still, Ross and Middleberg (1999, p. 3) noticed that broadcast stations have been slow to establish Web sites, and to showcase news over promotional material. Of the Web sites affiliated with local broadcast television stations, only a small fraction take full advantage of the capabilities of the Internet by offering "real news."

Only 3 years later the situation looked very different, and the integration of online and offline information was accelerating: Middleberg and Ross (2002) found that "Web readership now often rivals or surpasses print readership. The Web is not an incremental add-on to readership, viewership or profitability. Increasingly, it is the soul of a publication" (p. 4). Moreover, original content on Web sites increased as well, in particular for newspapers, thus showing that more journalism jobs were becoming online-only. With the advent of Web 2.0, new challenges have arisen for newspapers: a survey conducted in 2006 with the most 100 circulated newspapers in the U.S. showed that "newspapers are taking advantages of online capabilities, and have expanded upon their traditional strategies to launch aggressive online programs that include many sophisticated elements" (The Bivings Group, 2006, p. 2). According to this survey, 76 of these newspapers offer RSS feeds on their Web sites, 31 offer podcasts, 80 offer at least one reporter blog, 33 offer a sort of "most popular" function, only 7 a bookmarking function. It is interesting to note that only 23 Web sites of these newspapers require registration to view articles online (significantly, 7 of the 10 most circulated, and only 2 of the bottom 10), and in most of them registration is free of charge. From this research it might be concluded that "newspaper publishers are responding to decreasing print circulation and audiences by developing more aggressive and extensive Web strategies" (The Bivings Group, 2006, p. 22).

However, the situation in other countries is not the same as in the U.S. An analogous research conducted in Italy on the 50 most diffused newspapers, for instance, shows a different situation, where the adoption of the most recent Web capabilities is still very low, as if the Internet were still considered as a competitor to newspapers rather than a complementary opportunity: 19 of the 50 most diffused Italian newspapers require registration, very often with a charge, to access the newspaper's archive; 13 of these newspapers offer RSS feeds, 8 offer a blog, only 8 offer videos and only 3 offer podcasts; furthermore, a large gap emerges between the 10 top newspapers and the 10 bottom ones (Conti, 2006).

To sum up the issue, we can single out five areas where online information presents a clear added value: (1) *multimedia*, online information sources can offer information coded through different media: texts, audio, pictures, photos, animations, movies; (2) *interaction*, information Web sites can offer a higher level of interactivity than any other mass medium, allowing users to interact both with the Web site's system and with other people through the Web site; as we have seen, the interaction possibilities offered by Web 2.0 tools are currently the major challenge for the online presence of newspapers; (3) *persistence,* online information can be easily archived, re-used, and left continuously at readers' disposal; (4) *in-depth studies,* the easiness of online publishing makes it possible also to provide in-depth analyses and studies of given information, and to make them always available to readers; (5) *immediateness,* nowadays online information can be published almost just-in-time, updated very easily, and used just-in-time, as the case of blog clearly shows (Cantoni & Tardini, 2006, pp. 155-157).

Internet Search Engines

As it has been already mentioned before, one of the advantages of ICT, information availability at levels never possible or even thinkable before, is at the same time one of its most relevant issues and challenges, the so called *information overload.* Users can access so many resources and so many documents on the Internet that they are flooded with information and are not able to understand which ones are really relevant and useful to them and to select them among the others (Cantoni et al., 2006).

Over the Internet, search engines are the tools specifically developed to address this issue, helping users finding relevant sources, which can answer their informative needs.

In this section, a brief presentation of search engines is done, stressing how they have integrated and are integrating users themselves to better their own answering strategies.

First of all, search engines can be divided into two different families: that of directories and that of proper (full text) search engines.

The first ones (e.g., Yahoo! Directories, About, and Dmoz) have a tree-shaped structure, list Web sites as a whole, and are managed by human editors. In fact, a human editor has to decide whether a Web site is of enough quality to be included in the directory, and—in case the answer is yes—on which branch.

Proper search engines (e.g., Google, Yahoo! Search, MSN, AOL, Ask, etc.) are, on the contrary, pieces of software, which crawl the Internet (an activity usually referred to as "spidering"), copy single Web pages in their databases and index them following given rules, according to which pages are assigned to given keywords in a given order/rank. While strategies to analyze Web pages in order to identify their relevant keywords have been bettered over the last years, due to great improvements in natural language processing (computational linguistics), search engines had to incorporate in their ranking algorithms also "extrinsic" elements, that is, elements that are not deducible from the code and the address (URL) of the Web page itself.

In fact, in order to provide relevant answers, search engines started to consider (of course, we are using the verb as a metaphor, being applied to a piece of software) not only the single pages, but also the Web as an ecological system, and the way users behave when accessing it.

The most used extrinsic element is the so called "link popularity," which plays a relevant role, for instance, in Google. According to it, pages are given a page rank depending on the number of back-links they have (the links referring to the page from other Web sites), and on the page rank of the Web sites from which the back-links come. In other words, link popularity reinterprets a link as being a citation. The more a document is cited, the more it is considered important, or, like votes, the more a page is voted, the higher it goes. Links are furthermore also an indirect measure of accesses: the more back-links a Web site has, the more it is likely that visitors will access it (in ancient times, there was the motto: *all roads bring to Rome...*, that is, the capital of the empire).

If link popularity takes into consideration *directly* the actual citations/votes by Web publishers, and *inferentially,* the actual paths of Web surfers, click popularity measures them directly. It takes into consideration the actual clicks of users on the search engine's result page, reorganizing the presented elements depending on how users react to them, clicking or not.

Another extrinsic element being integrated into search engines' ranking algorithms is money: Web publishers can buy given keywords, getting then a better positioning for them. Of course, it is a quite extra-content element, but it can be useful to measure the commitment of the publisher, which "puts its money where its mouth is," to quote a popular saying, and goes perfectly in line with the search engine business (unfortunately this sometimes makes them accept political censorship in order to be allowed in given countries, as it happens, for instance, in China; see Deibert & Villeneuve, 2005).

Other extrinsic elements take into consideration how much frequently the Web site is updated, on the publisher's side, or the position of the users, on their side (for instance, if one is looking for a laundry, no point in answering the "better laundry" in itself as it is much better to provide a list of laundries in close proximity).

A few words are to be spent to present the Alexa service, which is quite similar to that of a search engine. It relies onto the actual navigations of its users, who have to install a dedicated plug-in in their browser: once its users visit a Web site, Alexa tells them which other Web sites are shared by those who visited that same Web site, offering a service similar to that of Amazon, which tells "Customers who bought this item also bought..."

For a certain period, search engines used in their indexing activities dedicated meta-tags, namely the keywords meta-tag, a tag listing the keywords relevant for a Web page, added by its own editor in the source code itself. After a while, however, due to a massive search engine spamming (i.e., an unfair use of that meta-tag, for instance listing, for the Website of a little B&B in Tuscany keywords like: "tourism in Italy," "Florence," etc.) its use in ranking algorithm has dramatically declined. To provide the same kind of information, in the Web 2.0, folksonomies were born (see, for instance, del.icio.us at http://del.icio.us). A folksonomy, or social tagging, is a list of tags collaboratively attached to a resource by its users (and publishers). While a single publisher can lie declaring a document's meta tags, many independent readers will not, at least if numbers are high enough, this is the folksonomy's claim, a claim similar to the one supporting the Wikipedia.

In this section, a brief presentation of search engines has shown how they have to take into consideration not only the content of Web sites, as it can be understood through its Web pages' source code, but also their context, be it the ecological system of the Web itself, or the actual navigation practices of Web surfers.

CONCLUSION AND FUTURE TRENDS

In this chapter, Internet-based communication technologies (and Web 2.0 tools, in particular) have been regarded as the last step in the development of communication technologies. This approach is particularly useful in order to have a broad perspective on the changes ICT are bringing along in the social practices of so called knowledge society. As a matter of fact, new ICT emerged in a media market already covered by other technologies, where they had to "negotiate" their space. The new configuration of the media market has brought along new communication practices, and these, in turn, made new social practices emerge, since communication permeates any other social practice.

Two specific practices have been presented in the chapter, both dealing directly with information management, namely journalism and Internet search engines.

Journalism and the news market have been seriously challenged by the spread of Internet-based technologies and of Web 2.0 in particular. As has been shown, the information sources of journalists are changing, thus reraising the issue of their trust and credibility; the process of delivering news is changing, since the Internet is gaining more and more space in comparison to newspapers; the role itself of journalists is challenged, since bloggers are entering the market; and so on.

Analogously, even a very recent and ICT-based practice, such as that of searching information over the Internet, is undergoing some radical changes, due mainly to the diffusion of Web 2.0 tools. Internet search engines, "are trying more and more to rely upon pragmatic features of Web sites, that is, they are taking into account the behaviors of people who publish a Web site and people who visit it. This turn can be traced back to the growing awareness that Web sites—and, broadly speaking, electronic communication—

are used by real communities of persons in order to fulfill real communicative needs." (Cantoni et al., 2006, p. 61)

Both examples show the importance of digital literacy in the knowledge society: in the specific fields of journalism and Internet search engines, being able to publish online information and/or to retrieve it guarantees inclusion in the society, while those who are not able to deal with online information will be more and more excluded from social life. As has been shown, Web 2.0 tools and services are increasing the possibility for Internet users to publish information on the Web, thus lowering the digital divide not only in terms of access to digital information or services, but also in terms of the publication of digital content.

These changes concern not only the field of information management, but also many other social practices, as is shown by the changes in the way we teach and learn (e-learning), work, buy, and sell (e-business and e-commerce), relate to government and other public services (e-government), access health (e-health), use banking services (e-banking), and so on.

REFERENCES

Benjamin, W. (1973). The work of art in the age of mechanical reproduction. In H. Arendt (Ed.), *Illuminations* (pp. 211-44). London: Fontana Press.

Bivings Group. (2006, August 1). *The use of the Internet by America's newspapers*. Retrieved October 3, 2007, from http://www.bivingsreport. com/campaign/newspapers06_tz-fgb.pdf

Cantoni, L., Faré, M., & Tardini, S. (2006). A communicative approach to Web communication: The pragmatic behavior of Internet search engines. *QWERTY. Rivista italiana di tecnologia cultura e formazione*, 1(1), 49-62.

Cantoni, L., & Tardini, S. (2006). *Internet (Routledge introductions to media and communications)*. London, New York, NY: Routledge.

comScore Networks. (2005, August). *Behaviors of the blogosphere: Understanding the scale, composition and activities of Weblog audiences.* Retrieved October 3, 2007, from http://www.comscore.com

Conti, L. (2006, August 7). *I quotidiani italiani e internet.* Retrieved October 3, 2007, from http://www.pandemia.info/studio%20giornali%20online.pdf

Coseriu, E. (1981). *Sincronia, diacronia e storia. Il problema del cambio linguistico.* Torino: Boringhieri.

Crystal, D. (2001). *Language and the Internet.* Cambridge: Cambridge University Press.

Danesi, M. (2006). Alphabets and the principle of least effort. *Studies in Communication Sciences*, 6(1), 47-62.

Deibert, R.J., & Villeneuve, N. (2005). Firewalls and power: An overview of global state censorship of the Internet. In M. Klang & A. Murray (Eds.), *Human rights in the digital age* (pp. 111-24). London, Sydney, Portland: GlassHouse Press.

Euro RSCG Magnet. (2005). *Rebuilding trust: Rebuilding credibility in the newsroom and the boardroom. Eleventh annual survey of the media with Columbia University Graduate School of Journalism.* New York, NY: Euro RSCG Magnet.

Faré, M. (2006). *Blog e giornalismo, l'era della complementarietà.* Lugano, Switzerland: University of Lugano, European Journalism Observatory. Retrieved October 3, 2007, from http://www.ejo.ch/analysis/newmedia/blog.pdf

Fidler, R. (1997). *Mediamorphosis. Understanding new media.* Thousand Oaks, CA: Pine Forge Press.

Gackenbach, J., & Ellerman, E. (1998). Introduction to psychological aspects of Internet use. In J. Gackenbach (Ed.), *Psychology and the Internet: Intrapersonal, interpersonal, and transpersonal implications* (pp. 1-26). London, San Diego, CA: Academic Press.

Hall, M. (2002, December 16). Give your users the power of the press with Weblogs and wikis. *Intranet Journal.* Retrieved October 3, 2007, from http://www.intranetjournal.com/articles/200212/ij_12_16_02a.html

Harrison, J. (2006). *News (Routledge introductions to media and communications)*. London, New York, NY: Routledge.

Hill, E. (2004). Some thoughts on e-democracy as an evolving concept. *Journal of E-Government*, 1(1), 23-39.

Kemp, J., & Livingstone, D. (2006, August 26). Putting a Second Life metaverse skin on learning management systems. In D. Livingstone & J. Kemp (Eds.), *Proceedings of the Second Life Education Workshop at the Second Life Community Convention* (pp.13-18), San Francisco, Paisley, UK: The University of Paisley. Retrieved October 3, 2007, from http://www.sloodle.com/whitepaper.pdf

Kolbitsch, J., & Maurer, H. (2006). The transformation of the Web: How emerging communities shape the information we consume. *Journal of Universal Computer Science*, 12(2), 187-213.

McLuhan, M. (2001). *Understanding media. The extensions of man.* London, New York, NY: Routledge.

Middleberg, D., & Ross, S.S. (2002). *The Middleberg/Ross media survey. Change and its impact on communications, 8th annual national survey.* Middleberg and Associates.

Ong, W.J. (2002). *Orality and literacy. The technologizing of the word.* London, New York, NY: Routledge.

Rogers, E.M. (1995). *Diffusion of innovations.* New York, NY: The Free Press.

Ross, S.S., & Middleberg, D. (1999, October). *The first annual Middleberg/Ross broadcast media in cyberspace study.* Middleberg and Associates.

Chapter XI
Foreseeing the Future Lifestyle with Digital Music:
A Comparative Study Between Mobile Phone Ring Tones and Hard–Disk Music Players Like iPod

Masataka Yoshikawa
Hakuhodo Inc., Japan

ABSTRACT

This chapter aims to explore the future trajectory of enjoying digital music entertainment among consumers comparing the characteristics of the usage patterns of digital music appliances in the U.S. and those in Japan. As the first step of this research, the author conducted two empirical surveys in the U.S. and Japan, and found some basic differences in the usage patterns of a variety of digital music appliances. Next, a series of ethnographical research based on focus-group interviews with Japanese young women was done and some interesting reasons of the differences were discovered. In Japan, sharing the experiences of listening to the latest hit songs with friends by playing them with mobile phones that have the high quality, ring tone functions can be a new way of enjoying music contents, while hard-disk music players like iPod have become a de facto standard of the digital music appliances in the world.

INTRODUCTION: CENTRAL QUESTIONS

The November 2001 debut of iPod and the subsequent opening of iTunes Music Store have brought a rapid expansion of the digital music market around the world. Some estimate that the market will be worth $1.7 billion dollars by 2009 (Jupiter Research). Now, iTunes Music Store service is available in 30 countries around the world, with the total number of downloaded songs surpassing the 500 million mark in July 2005.

The store only opened in Japan in August 2005 and sold over 1 million songs in the first 4 days. This is an astonishing achievement, considering that Japan's largest online music store Mora has monthly sales of around 450,000 songs. In March and April 2005, SONY, which has long led the portable music player market, released a new digital music player under the Walkman brand, offering both the hard disk type and USB flash memory type to launch a marketing drive against iPod. The developments have finally begun to provide Japanese music lovers with an environment whereby digital music contents are broadly enjoyed in terms of both services and hardware devices.

One of the major characteristics of Japan's digital music market has been the presence of digital music contents for use on mobile phones. The use of digital music contents on mobile phones, which started as regular ring tones, has gradually evolved into Chaku-uta® (true-tone ring tones) by December 2002, and to Chaku-uta Full™ (mobile-phone-based music distribution service launched in December 2004 by the mobile carrier "au"). Chaku-uta® and Chaku-uta Full™ have sold over 100 million songs and 10 million songs respectively, making the digital music service the largest segment in mobile-phone content services.

The environment for enjoying digital music content is set to expand even further into the future. How would such a development affect the way Japanese music fans listen to music in general? This paper examines future ways of enjoying digital music content in Japan, and the competition between music players like iPod for use with personal computers and mobile phones that have adopted the usage as music players.

JAPAN'S DIGITAL MUSIC CONTENT MARKET AND THE PROLIFERATION OF MOBILE PHONES BEFORE 2005

Firstly, let us examine past developments of the digital music content market in Japan. Japan's first digital music distribution service started in April 1997. A company called MUSIC.CO.JP began offering songs mainly from independent labels. Coinciding with the launch of numerous music download services in the U.S., a number of online music Web sites opened one after another, orchestrated by individual artists and record labels. In December 1999, SONY Music Entertainment became the first major record company to start an online music store bitmusic. Toshiba EMI, Avex Records, and other major companies followed suit. Yet, since early 2005, the system for online distribution of digital music contents has been underdeveloped, as can be seen in the fact that Mora's supposed largest online music catalog in Japan contained just 100,000 songs, as opposed to iTunes Music Store's lineup of 1 million songs upon its launch in August in Japan.

There is no denying that mobile-phone-related music services have been the driving force of the nation's digital music market. The launch of the i-mode service by NTT DoCoMo in February 1999 marked the start of digital content downloading services via mobile phones. The connection speed of 9600bps in those days made it, initially, difficult to distribute songs in high audio quality. Faced with the adversity, businesses began offering Chaku-melo music ring tones, instead of distributing actual music contents, achieving dramatic growth. The Chaku-melo market has rapidly expanded to 80-90 billion yen in 2002. What makes this development unique was the fact that this service was initiated not by record companies rather by major online Karaoke service providers like GIGA and XING, computer game companies like SEGA, and other companies operating in the peripheral areas of the music industry itself. The market size of 80-90 billion yen as of 2002 is among the highest of all mobile-related digital content services, proving the market-led proliferation of digital content services for mobile phones.

Amidst the flourishing success of the Chaku-melo market, supported by peripheral music businesses, record companies that lead the music industry initiated a move to provide the Chaku-uta® service, offering true-tone music as ring tones, instead of Chaku-melo MIDI-based ring tone melodies. The service was initially started solely by Japan's second largest mobile carrier au in December 2002. While the Chaku-melo service was employed by all mobile carriers rapidly, the Chaku-uta® service was not adopted by the industry leader NTT DoCoMo until February 2004 and by the number three mobile carrier Vodafone until March 2004. However, the service picked up substantial support from younger generations. As the preceding proliferation of the Chaku-melo service had already familiarized mobile phone users with the concept of *obtaining music over mobile phone*, Chaku-uta® sales reached 100 million songs by July 2004, and surpassed 200 million songs by April 2005 to establish a market of substantial scale. Record companies joined forces to establish Label Mobile, which currently provides around 300,000 songs, approximately three times the catalog size of computer-based online music stores.

After Chaku-uta® came the Chaku-uta Full™ service, which provides whole songs as ring tones to become a de facto digital music store over mobile phones. It reached its fifth million download in April, just 6 months after its launch in October 2004. The cumulative total of downloaded songs reached 10 million in June, causing a dramatic expansion in market size. Although the number of songs available remains smaller than Chaku-uta® at 37,000, the catalog is expected to keep on expanding.

As described thus far, the digital-music-content industry has rapidly mushroomed as one of mobile phone services, but it has been less than 1 year since a full-scale music distribution service (Chaku-uta Full™) was launched. Music has been merely distributed as an additional function to mobile phones, that is, the ring tone. Consumption has been initiated by mobile phone use, instead of music itself. In other words, an explosive proliferation of a new communications device called mobile phones, has triggered the consumption of digital music content as a natural course of evolution. Amidst this situation, a series of dedicated digital music players called iPod has emerged with major success, triggering the launch of the iTunes Music Store offering downloads of digital music content. With the development of a fully fledged environment for computer-based consumption of digital music contents, what has been the course of competition between different types of devices in today's digital music content market? Let us examine the overview based on the results of a quantitative survey.

TODAY'S DIGITAL MUSIC CONTENT MARKETS: JAPAN AND U.S. MARKETS

In order to grasp the state of today's digital music content market in Japan, we have simultaneously conducted a survey consisting of identical questions for use in both Japan and the U.S. Results from the two countries were compared against each other in order to identify characteristics of the Japanese market. The survey was titled *Survey on Digital Contents*, and the survey period it ran online was between February and March 2005.[1] The following samples were included: Japan, N=677 aged 15-59 and in the U.S., N=700 aged 18-59.

First, let us take a look at the rate of music-terminal use in the two countries: 6.9% of Japanese respondents used hard-disk music players like iPod, whereas the ratio was almost double at 11.5% in the U.S. The ratio of people using USB flash-memory music players was 7.2% in Japan and 16.1% in the U.S., more than double the Japanese figure. However, the ratio of those using mobile phones as music players was 19.8% in Japan, nearly three times the U.S. result of 6.1%. These figures demonstrated a clear tendency of U.S. users opting for hard-disk or flash-memory devices with music transferred via computers, and Japanese users choosing mobile phones to listen to music.

Next, the survey examined how samples typically downloaded digital music contents: 28.9% of U.S. respondents have downloaded music via computer, over 10 percentage points higher than the Japanese ratio of 17.4%. On the other hand, 42.2% have downloaded music (music ring tones) over mobile phones in Japan, around three times the equivalent U.S. figure of 14.2%. The ratio of people who have downloaded true-tone ring tones was 20.4% in Japan, an astonishing lead of around seven fold compared to the U.S. result of 3.0%. The clear tendency of computer orientation in the U.S. and mobile phone orientation in Japan, observed in the choice of music-playing terminals, was also evident in terms of the practice of music downloading.

As explained in the previous section, these findings are a natural outcome reflecting how the digital-music-content market emerged and established itself around mobile phones from the early days in Japan in contrast to market development that evolved around computers and the Internet in the U.S. However, there is some interesting data—the survey asked those who do not own a portable digital music player which type of device they would like to possess. The results indicated almost identical tendencies between Japanese and U.S. respondents, unlike the stark differences they demonstrated in previous questions. Those who intend to purchase a hard-disk music player accounted for 26.7% in Japan and 26.1% in the U.S. The figures for flash-memory players were also very similar at 21.4% in Japan and 21.7% in the U.S. Finally, the ratio of those using a mobile phone as a music player is 5.3% in Japan and 3.0% in the U.S. Even though the Japanese figure is slightly higher than the U.S. figure, they can be viewed as almost at the same level, in comparison to the ratio gaps observed in other questions.

This data demonstrates a strong contrast to previous data, which showed a noticeable computer orientation for the U.S., and mobile phone orientation for Japan. In both countries, purchase intention appears higher for computer-based music players based on either hard disk or USB flash memory, and relatively low for mobile phones doubling as music players.

Until now, Japan's digital-music-content market has been characterized, in terms of hardware, with proliferated use of mobile phones, as opposed to the U.S. market where more users download music via computer. However, as the results of the aforementioned survey suggest, computer-based music players will be used increasingly for the consumption of digital music content, in addition to mobile phones, in the future Japanese market. Then, what changes will emerge in consumer's music playing styles when such hardware competition (spread of computer-based music players) evolves?

FUTURE STYLE OF DIGITAL MUSIC LISTENING IN JAPAN: OVERALL TREND

We have projected future changes in the style of digital music listening in Japan, dividing the samples of the aforementioned survey into the following three groups and comparing the profiles, music listening styles, and mentalities of the current and future users.

1. Current digital music content users—Those who own hard-disk/USB flash-memory music players N=42.
2. Digital music content potential users—Those who intend to purchase hard-disk/USB flash-memory music players N=307.
3. Nonusers of digital music contents—Those excluding the above two groups N=319.

We made a particular comparison between current digital music content users who have constituted the computer-oriented digital music market, and digital-music-content potential users who intend to join the market from now, so as to identify how the listening style of this market is likely to change, and what impact such changes will have on the market, which has evolved through downloading by means of mobile phones thus far. First, we compared samples' demographic profiles and basic indicators in music consumption.

Gender Comparison

Current digital-music-content users mainly consist of men, accounting for 66.7%, as opposed to women at 33.3%. Digital-music-content potential users have a more even gender distribution, consisting of men and women at respectively 54.4% and 45.6%. Nonusers of digital music contents have a greater proportion of women at 58.4%, compared to men at 43.6%.

Comparison by Gender and Generation

The generation factor was then incorporated to characterize the three groups more clearly. Among current digital-music-content users, men in their 20s claimed the largest proportion at 29.6%, followed by women in their 20s at 23.8%, and men in their 30s at 16.7%. These three groups alone represent over 70% (70.1%), indicating that digital music content is primarily enjoyed among younger people—both men and women. In comparison, among digital-music-content potential users, men in various age groups accounted for around 10% each, that is, men in their 20s at 11.1%, men in their 30s at 10.7%, men in their 40s at 15.3%, and men in their 50s at 11.7%. Women in their 20s and 30s also represented, around the same proportion, at 11.4% and 8.5% respectively. Compared to current digital-music-content users, there is a more

even distribution of age and gender groups. As for nonusers of digital music contents, women in the middle to high age groups made up over 40%, including women in their 30s at 14.7%, women in their 40s at 12.3%, and women in their 50s at 16.3%. The data analysis incorporating generation factors highlighted distinctive characteristics among the three user categories.

Comparison of the Number of CDs Owned

When asked how many CDs they own, 18.7% of current digital-music-content users said 50 to 99, followed by 23.8% owning 100-199 CDs and 11.9% owning over 200 CDs. These three groups represent over 50% (54.4%). Among digital-music-content potential users, 18.2% own 0-9 CDs, whereas those owning 10-19 CDs, 20-29 CDs, and 30-49 CDs accounted for 14.0%, 13.7%, and 16.3% respectively. Combined, over 60% (62.2%) owned less than 50 CDs. Almost 70% (69.8%) of nonusers of digital music contents also own less than 50 CDs, broken down into those with 0-9 CDs, 10-19 CDs, 20-29 CDs, and 30-49 CDs at respectively 31.7%, 14.7%, 12.2%, and 11.6%. As the figures show, current users have a large proportion of people with a substantial CD collection, whereas nonusers have a large proportion of people with limited CD ownership.

Comparison of Monthly Music Spending

Similarly to the former, the ratio of those spending over 3,000 yen (equivalent to the cost of one CD album) per month was 61.8% among current digital-music-content users but less than 40% (39.1%) among digital-music-content potential users. Over 70% (75.9%) of potential users spent at least 1,000 yen (equivalent to the cost of one CD single) per month. Nonusers of digital music contents demonstrated a similar tendency to potential users, with 28.8% spending over 3,000 yen, and 66.1% spending over 1,000 yen. As the figures indicate, current users have a large proportion of people who spend more on CDs, whereas nonusers have a large proportion of people who spend less on them.

Summarizing the results thus far, current digital-music-content users are mainly young men and women in their 20s, with substantial CD ownership and high music-related spending per month. They can be described as *music fans* with substantial music-related consumption. Potential users of digital music content, who are expected to enter this market, are distributed across both genders and broad generations, from youth to those in middle age. They are characterized as middle-level users in music consumption. Nonusers of digital music content are mainly women in higher age groups, with relative inactiveness in terms of music consumption. The results illustrate clear differences in demographic characteristics and music consumption behavior. There are major differences between consumers who have bolstered the computer-based, digital-music-content market until now, and those who will support the market from now on. These facts alone point to the possibility that the current market is set to undergo substantial changes in its nature. In order to examine details of anticipated changes, we have compared the three groups in their attitude and mentality in listening to music.

Formats of Music Ownership

Of current digital-music-content users 61.9% acknowledge the desire to store all of their CD collection on the computer, a significantly higher ratio than digital-music-content potential users at 26.7% and nonusers of digital music contents at 17.2%. Current users appear to have a strong desire to manage their music by computer and use computers as the main device for handling music content. In comparison, such desire is not as strong among the other two groups.

Intention Regarding Songs Available for Downloading

Next, in order to examine the number of songs that are available for downloading, we looked at whether people want a greater selection from download services via computer or those via mobile phone. When asked whether the number of songs downloadable via computer on the Internet should be increased, 45.2% of current digital-music-content users said "yes," much greater than 30.0% among digital-music-content potential users and 15.0% among nonusers of digital music content. As for whether they want to see the number of songs available via mobile phone increased, just 7.1% of current users agreed, whereas the ratio was more than double at 15.0% among potential users, and 9.7% among nonusers. Although with not as stark a difference as the last paragraph, these groups clearly demonstrated different preferences in catalog enhancement between downloading services via computers or those via mobile phones. In short, current users want to see enhancement of the computer-downloadable catalogs, while potential users want enhancement of mobile-phone-based catalogs just as much as of computer-based catalogs. The results, once again, indicate a strong preference among current users on computer-based services. In comparison, potential users are requesting catalog enhancement to both computer-based and mobile-phone-based services. In other words, potential users and nonusers wish to use both computers and mobile phones to listen to music rather than mere computers.

Style of Using Songs

We also asked several questions on how people wish to use songs they own. Of current digital-music-content users 35.7% said they want to store all CDs they own on a computer and edit them, for example, compiling a collection of favorite songs. The ratio was 22.5% among digital-music-content potential users and 11.0% among nonusers of digital music contents. These figures again confirmed the computer-oriented style of current users and highlighted another of their characteristics, that is, actively using downloaded songs for their personal enjoyment. This characteristic became even more evident in the next question.

People were asked whether they like to compile a collection of songs from CDs they own according to specific themes and use the original CD as a gift for friends on a suitable occasion of some sort. Of current users 11.9% said "yes," whereas the ratio was 15.3% among potential users and 6.0% among nonusers. A greater proportion of potential users expressed preference to this style than current users.

The third question was on whether they wanted to burn their favorite songs on CD-R or DVD more casually to give away to friends and acquaintances. The results showed a similar tendency to the results for the second question. Of current users 7.1% agreed, while the ratio among potential users was greater at 12.7%. Even nonusers had a greater proportion at 9.1%. Looking at the results to these three questions, current users have a self-contained approach in enjoying music with a preference to downloading via computers, whereas potential users are more inclined towards exchanging and distributing music with others.

Finally, we asked whether they wanted to give away or exchange songs, downloaded via mobile phone, to friends over the mobile phone. Again, only 7.1% of current users, who have the preference to computer-based song purchase, agreed to the concept, whereas the ratio was greater among potential users (9.1%), with even nonusers reaching the same level as potential users (8.8%). All the numbers point to the computer-oriented and self-contained nature of current users, and the potential users' tendency of combined computer and mobile phone use and a strong inclination towards distributing and exchanging songs.

When these analysis results are combined with the demographic characteristics and basic indicators in music consumption, current digital-music-content users can be defined as those with a strong computer preference, wishing to use digital music content for their personal enjoyment in a self-contained approach. In contrast, digital music content, potential users who are entering the market from now, are combining computers and mobile phones for this purpose and are inclined towards enjoying music with others in addition to appreciating it by themselves. This group has a particular tendency of using music as one of the tools for communicating with other people around them.

Let us take a closer look as the results to enable us to explore the direction of how Japan's digital music market may change, while reflecting upon the trends of both hardware and people's music listening styles.

The digital-music-content market in Japan originally evolved from the distribution of mobile phone ring tones. Then, music content was merely one of the functions or menus available in using mobile phones. They did not go beyond the ring tone boundary. Amidst this situation, the market embraced the emergence of a new type of music device that contains a hard disk or USB flash memory, designed to be used with a computer. Contemporary music fans were among the first to adhere to such devices, consisting of men and women in their 20s that are most active consumers of music. They stored and managed all music content they already had in a computer, thereby converting them into digital content, and began carrying songs in portable music players and in so doing they were enjoying music for themselves in a rather self-contained fashion.

Today, digital music content that takes the form of mobile phone ring tones exists alongside digital music content that can be carried on hard-disk or USB flash-memory music players. We have investigated the future course of the market in view of the profile and music mentality of potential users of digital music content, who are making a full-scale entry into this market in the future. Future users will be combining computers and mobile phones, and, unlike contemporary users, enjoying music as both a communication tool with others and for personal entertainment purposes. Digitizing music contents gives music a new function as a communication promotion factor, in addition to the current functions as ring tones and personal enjoyment.

In order to further clarify this new style of enjoying digital music content, we conducted an oral qualitative survey on two groups, that is, current iPod users who represent those enjoying digital music content via computers, and Chaku-uta® and Chaku-uta Full™ users who represent those enjoying digital music content via mobile phones. The survey clarified their styles in listening to digital music content, so as to obtain an insight into the future direction of music-listening styles.

FUTURE OF THE DIGITAL MUSIC CONTENT MARKET IN JAPAN: CHANGES IN MUSIC CONTENT CONSUMPTION

The *Survey on the usage of iPod and Chaku-uta®* was conducted in the period between December 2004 and February 2005. In-depth interviews were held with three male and female iPod users in their 20s and 30s, and with three male and female Chaku-uta® Mobile users in their 10s and 20s.[2]

Comments From iPod Users

What follows are typical comments made by iPod users on their style of enjoying music:

I find the Random Play function to be very refreshing. I can 'rediscover' songs on CDs that I did not pay much attention previously. [...] I

can store a lot of songs without having to worry about how much space is left. Now, I am storing whatever songs I have, even ones that I would skip if I am playing it on CD. [A 37-year-old man who has used iPod for 1.5 years, SOHO, 6,000 songs are held]*

I now realize how much I have restricted myself with frameworks of genres and artists when listening to music. The Shuffle function highlights the raw power of individual songs. [...] Occasions like that have broadened the range of music genres I listen to, making me feel like trying out CDs I would never have dreamed of listening to before. [26-year-old woman who has used iPod for 1 year, office worker, 1,500 songs are held]

I never used to carry music around, but now I do not go anywhere without my iPod. This has widened the variety of occasions I listen to music, for example, while on a train or on the way home after a drink. [...] There are times when a song I frequently listened to on CD sounds very different on a portable player, because of various situations you are in at the time. That gives me fun. [39-year-old man who has used iPod for 6 months, office worker, 700 songs are held]

As suggested in the results of the quantitative survey, they typically—to some extent—have a self-contained approach in music entertainment. Their remarks illustrate new ways of enjoying music (consumption styles) they have attained through hard-disk music players like iPod. For them, a hard-disk music player is a device that allows them to randomly enjoy music out of a greater selection of songs than previously possible in conventional devices (cassette player, MD player), loaded from their CD collection. A hard-disk music player is a true portable music player strictly for personal use. In order for the device to be self-contained, it must be able to carry a massive number of songs, which in turn, facilitates random playing. This random playing then releases listeners from the boundaries of existing music context (by genre, by artist, etc.) and invites the creation of new contexts, thereby enhancing the self-contained nature even further. They are enjoying music in this cycle.

For them, consumption of music content is not about listening to each individual song, but about enjoying a stream of music. It must always be a fresh string or stream of music different from what they have already experienced previously. Their consumption of digital music content is characterized as *self-contained context consumption*. This is an emergence of a new style of music consumption, only possible for hard-disk music players like iPod. The style is facilitated with the concept of *play list* in iPod and other devices. The ability to compile a new string or stream of music, has diluted the concept of *album*, presented conventionally from package providers and artists as producers, and encouraged individual users to compile their own music streams. Consequently, music is increasingly evaluated on the merit of each song. One example is the way iTunes Music Store presented its proliferation scale in the unit of individual songs downloaded, rather than albums. This kind of presentation appears to depict a transition of mentality, with listeners focusing more on individual songs, rather than embracing the supplier-defined unit of *album*.

The following comments are derived from Chaku-uta® Mobile users on their style of enjoying music:

During a break time at work, I just leave my mobile phone to play songs to provide some background music. [...] They are all songs that everyone knows, and will not trigger any music talk. However, it is better than having no music, and stimulates conversation. [...] I don't mind if each song may be just 30 seconds long. It is actually better to have short tunes to enjoy them with my colleagues and build up a lively atmosphere. [25-year-old man who has used Chaku-uta® Mobile for 6 months, office worker, 10 songs are held]

I like upbeat Techno music. I use these types of songs as Chaku-uta, and play them during break time when my friends are around, so that I can show them how to dance to the tunes. [...] The other day, I had my mobile hanging around my neck, and playing Chaku-uta, as I danced across a Shinjuku intersection with my friend. [21-year-old woman who has used Chaku-uta® Mobile for 6 months, university student, three songs are held]

I might listen to and check out music with my friends, but I am more likely to use it as the Sleep Timer when I go to bed. [...] I can operate it by hand, and put it on charge at the same time. It is very convenient. [...] I don't care about (each song being the ring tone length of 30 seconds and) not having the complete song. I fall asleep as I listen to the same songs repeatedly. [19-year-old woman who has used Chaku-uta® Mobile for 1 year, vocational school student, five songs are held]

The analysis of the quantitative survey results also indicated that persons entering the digital-music-content market from now use *both computer-based music players and mobile phones*, and *use music to enhance their relationship or communication with their friends and acquaintances* instead of merely enjoying music by themselves. Comments from Chaku-uta® Mobile users substantiate the tendency, that is, using music as a tool for sharing various occasions with friends.

As part of the quantitative survey described earlier, people were asked how they use ring tones and Chaku-uta® on mobile phones. The top three answers were as "ring tones (87.3%)," "alarm clock (60.4%)," and "other alarm sounds (46.3%)," The fourth highest ranked answer, however, was to "enjoy them alone as music" (44.0%), and 41.7% said they "enjoy them together with friends or use them to entertain others"—as such indicating that people are beginning to enjoy mobile-downloaded tunes as stand alone songs with friends.

What can be noted in these comments is that songs are enjoyed in the ring tone length of 30 seconds, rather than in their entirety, which is quite different to that of hard-disk music player users, who consume a massive amount of randomly replayed music in various contexts. Their consumption style is summarized as "sharing the occasion of playing popular songs, rather than personal favorites with others to magnify enjoyment." What counts is how good each NETA (=song as conversation topic) is, rather than how many songs you have in store. Their consumption of digital music content is characterized as "NETA consumption to be shared among friends." For them, Chaku-uta® Mobile is perceived as a "music player that plays 30-seconds of everyone's favorite songs for a shared experience." The emergence of a new service called Chaku-uta® has brought about this new style in music consumption, while now, the style seems to transform formats of music content.

CONCLUSION

As we have examined, Japan's digital-music-content market—which started off with the distribution of ring tones as one mobile phone service—has embraced the arrival of fully fledged digital music players and online stores, both designed to be used via computers, such as iPod and iTunes Music Store. From the viewpoint of hardware competition, the market has now entered a stage of combined development of mobile-phone-based devices and computer-based devices. It has brought about two contrasting consumption styles with distinctive characteristics (computer-based and mobile-phone-based consumption of digital music content), and diversified people's styles in enjoying music at the same time.

People who use a computer-based means to enjoy digital music content, have a self-contained style of consuming music in a specific context, loading a hard-disk music player with a greater amount of music from their personal CD collection

than previously possible and enjoying songs in random order. In contrast, people who use mobile-phone-based devices, employ a mobile phone as a communal music player for playing 30-second tunes of high popularity and consume music as topics (information) for sharing various occasions with friends or enhancing the atmosphere.

At present, these styles are separate tendencies and can be observed among users of hard-disk music players and users of mobile phones as music players as two extremes. However, a steady proliferation of hard-disk or USB flash-memory music players may cause these styles to merge on the side of individual users. Competition between two types of devices has created two distinctive styles of listening to music. Now, each user may start using both of these devices at the same time, hence adopting both styles alongside each other. Such a user may eventually begin to seek both of the styles in one of the two types of devices, which may amount to hardware integration, brought about by the symbiosis of the two different music-listening styles. Closely paying attention to consumer behavior and practices in the future will then give way to rich empirical data to be used to develop and elaborate the stream of thought outlined in this study further.

FURTHER READING

Institute for Information and Communications Policy. (Eds.). (2005). *Henbou suru contents business. (Contents business.)* Tokyo: Toyo keizai shinpo sha.

Masuda, S. (2005). *Sono ongaku no sakusha toha dare ka.* Tokyo: Misuzu shobo.

Masuda, S., & Taniguchi, F. (2005). *Ongaku mirai kei.* Tokyo: Yosen sha.

Ministry of Internal Affairs and Communications. (Eds.). (2005). *Information and communications in Japan 2005.* Tokyo: Gyousei.

Tsuda, D. (2004). *Dare ga ongaku wo korosu no ka.* Tokyo: Shoei sha.

Yoshimi, S. (2004). *Media bunka ron. (Invitation to media cultural studies.)* Tokyo: Yuhikaku.

ENDNOTES

[1]   The survey was conducted by Macromill Inc. in Japan and Zoomerang, Inc. in the U.S. And, it was organized by Hakuhodo Institute of Life and Living and Hakuhodo DY Media Partners' Media Environment Laboratory.

[2]   The survey was conducted by Oval Communication and was organized by Hakuhodo Institute of Life and Living and Hakuhodo DY Media partners' Media Environment Laboratory.

Chapter XII
Innovative Technologies for Education and Learning:
Education and Knowledge–Oriented Applications of Blogs, Wikis, Podcasts, and More

Jeffrey Hsu
Fairleigh Dickinson University, USA

ABSTRACT

A number of new communications technologies have emerged in recent years that have been largely regarded and intended for personal and recreational use. However, these "conversational technologies" and "constructivist learning tools," coupled with the power and reach of the Internet, have made them viable choices for both educational learning and knowledge-oriented applications. The technologies given attention in this article include instant messaging (IM), Weblogs (blogs), wikis, and podcasts. A discussion of the technologies and uses, underlying educational and cognitive psychology theories, and also applications for education and the management of knowledge, are examined in detail. The implications for education, as well as areas for future research are also explored.

INTRODUCTION

For many years, the mediums employed for education have remained fairly constant and traditional: tried and true methods such as the blackboard and chalk, whiteboards, flipcharts, and overhead projectors. The employment of computing technologies has resulted in the use of PowerPoint, e-mail, and Web-based course portals/enhancements such as Blackboard and WebCT.

There have been numerous studies done, and papers written, about the use of technology in the classroom, together with work on the related areas of e-learning, Web-based learning, and online learning. The usage of computing technologies in education has been examined in numerous studies, and there is a sizable body of work on Web and online learning, including the studies by Ahn, Han, and Han (2005), Liu and Chen (2005), Beck, Kung, Park, and Yang (2004), and numerous others.

In particular, some of these technologies have been recognized as useful in the classroom, and have been engaged in innovative ways. The technologies of particular interest are those that are referred to as "conversational technologies," which allow for the creation and sharing of information (KPMG, 2003; Wagner, 2004). Another term often used to describe these technologies is the concept of "constructivist learning tools," which encourage, and are focused on, users creating, or constructing, their own content (Seitzinger, 2006).

The interest in employing these kinds of technologies stems not only from the unique pedagogical benefits gained, but also from the basic need to stay in tune with the focus and strengths of today's students. Prensky (2001) suggests that the students being taught today are "no longer the people our educational system was designed to teach" and that while the students of today can be termed "digital natives," many educators could be better termed "digital immigrants." Yet another way to look at this is to view earlier educational approaches as "print-based," while those of the current environment can be called "digitally-based, secondly-oral" (Ferris & Wilder, 2006).

The purpose of this article is to examine these technologies and explore both the evolution of their use from personal applications to that of educational tools, and also to examine the key educational applications for which these are being used. Relevant research and applications are examined and analyzed. The future of these technologies for educational and professional use, together with viable research areas, is examined as well.

CONVERSATIONAL TECHNOLOGIES AND CONSTRUCTIVIST LEARNING TOOLS

The notion of conversational technologies is not a new one, as it encompasses many types of systems that have been widely used for some time, including e-mail, video conferencing, and discussion forums.

The term "conversational technology" is derived from the work of Locke et al. (2000) relating to conversational exchanges and his Cluetrain Manifesto. One of the key concepts here is that "markets are conversations" and that knowledge is created and shared using question and answer dialog. Specific theses that relate to this form of "conversational knowledge management" suggest that aggregation and abstraction of information helps to create information. Other characteristics of conversational knowledge management include the fact that it is fast, stored in different locations, and does not require sophisticated technologies in order to be accomplished (Wagner, 2004).

Conversational technologies encompass a wide range of systems and software, many of which are familiar, including e-mail, instant messaging, Web pages, discussion forums, video and audio content/streaming, wikis, and Weblogs. While there are specific aspects that are of interest in terms of the more mature technologies, the ones that will be given attention in this article are the issues, impacts, and applications relating to IM, blogs, wikis, and podcasts. These are technologies that are newer, have a growing base of users, and are starting to become recognized as viable tools for education.

The term "constructivist learning tool" has also become associated with these, particularly blogs and wikis, in that they have a key characteristic of allowing users to develop and maintain their own content. Some of the characteristics of constructivist learning include engagement, active learning, collaboration, real world based, and the usage of reflection as a part of the learning process (Seitzinger, 2006).

It should be noted that these technologies and tools are best suited to course structures where class collaboration and communication are encouraged, rather than those with an emphasis on lectures and a presentation of factual information. In addition, in courses where there is substantial group work, or projects where a collaborative document is created, the use of these would be especially helpful and useful. Both hybrid and full distance learning courses would be situations where these could also be used effectively.

TEACHING AND LEARNING: NEW TRENDS

Conversational and constructivist technologies are certainly here to stay, as evidenced by their extensive role in our society. It would therefore be useful to examine their applicability in the educational realm. While usage based on popularity or student preference seems to be one factor, there are also theoretical and conceptual bases for employing these kinds of technologies in the classroom.

Earlier paradigms of teaching emphasized print-based materials for instruction, which included printed textbooks, paper-based instructional materials, and written tutorials, all of which are grounded in the notion that the teacher, lecture, and instructional materials form not only the basis, but also the authority in the educational process. The transmission of material from the teacher (lecture) and/or textbook to the student (called the "print model") is still the central basis

of most teaching, even if they are supplemented with other methods including discussion and other forms of student interaction/participation (Ferris & Wilder, 2006).

However, the advent of digital and conversational technologies has brought forth the new concept of secondary orality (Ong, 1982). This concept emphasizes that teaching and learning should go beyond printed materials toward a greater emphasis on group work, fostering student communities, and encouraging student participation. The concept encourages a greater sense of interaction with and "ownership" of knowledge, emphasizing self-awareness and expression, and effectively using electronic tools (Gronbeck, Farrell, & Soukup, 1991).

The use of conversational technologies can have a positive impact, because they attempt to not only improve upon the print approach, but also use secondary-oral techniques. In other words, while a student can still be presented with material (in different formats) using the print model, the introduction of secondary-oral methods can be used to improve the overall learning experience. Using the latter, there is the opportunity to work and learn collaboratively, explore, analyze, engage in discussion, and otherwise "learn" in new and innovative ways (Ferris & Wilder, 2006; Wallace, 2005).

INSTANT MESSAGING (IM)

It is unlikely that there would be many college students who are unfamiliar with the use of IM. Allowing for interactive and real-time synchronous communications with instant response, instant messenger is truly conversational in that it allows for "chat" and communications between both individuals and groups. The major instant messaging systems in use include AOL (AIM), MSN Messenger, Yahoo! Messenger, and ICQ.

IM is a means for users to "chat" and communicate in real-time. While originally the domain of personal users, over time the unique benefits and effectiveness of this medium were realized, and IM started to become accepted as a form of communication in businesses (particularly high-tech firms), and now has been studied and tested as an educational tool (Kinzie, Whitaker, & Hofer, 2005).

The important features of IM include both its synchronous nature and its ability to support both chat and phone-like interaction. While real-time interaction allows for rapid communications to occur, there is also no need to enter an interaction "space" as with chat rooms. Instead, the main usage of IM is in one-on-one communications, which can be more formally termed as a dyadic "call" model, which more closely resembles phone call interaction. It should be noted that even though much of the communication is done between two individuals, there are some systems that support multiparty instant messaging.

Some of the salient features of IM include the ability for users to see user details as to current status (online, idle, away, out to lunch), and also on a user's changes in status (active, logged out, etc.). Lists of users can be displayed on the screen, so that contact can be made when desired. If a "chat" is initiated, a special window comes up, and the interaction can commence, provided that both parties are online and willing to proceed.

The real-time nature of IM has resulted in the technology being used for reasons aside from personal "chat." In business, IM has become in some industries an accepted form of communication. A number of studies have concluded that instant messaging is ideal for informal interaction. In particular, the use of IM has been shown to be helpful in cases where collaborative coordination and problem solving is involved. Social bonding and interaction, which is a component contributing to the success of more complex collaboration situations, is also enhanced by using instant messenger technology (Nardi & Bradner, 2000).

An important difference between IM and e-mail is the tendency for instant messenger interaction to be more casual and informal than e-mails, which helps to bring about a more "friendly" communication atmosphere. This may in part be due to a reduction in the formalities that are typically involved when using e-mail or the phone. In particular, IM has been considered more suitable for such tasks as scheduling meetings, asking or answering quick questions, and for other kinds of tasks that are brief, require a prompt response, or are less formal. It is perceived to be far simpler to IM someone to ask a quick question, for example, or to confirm a meeting or lunch, rather than to e-mail or call (Nardi & Bradner, 2000).

It is also of interest that IM communications tend to be more flexible in terms of their uses (everything from task-related questions to a new joke), and can allow for greater expressiveness in terms of emotion, humor, and personality (Nardi & Bradner, 2000). Another interesting aspect is what Nardi and Bradner (2000) refer to as "outeraction," which focuses on the processes associated with IM. These include conversational availability, communications zones, intermittent conversations, awareness, and conversational progress/media switching. IM is useful in certain communications situations, since it tends to be less disruptive and interrupting, while at the same time a user's availability is more clearly known (scanning buddy list status, for example). It is also a convenient means for setting up more formal interactions, such as arranging a conference call (media switching). Intermittent, dispersed communications can be conducted over a longer period of time, which includes interruptions. Another benefit includes the knowledge that others are "there" and available, even if not currently in chat mode; however there is always the opportunity to make contact, whether through IM or a different form of communications.

While some educators may scoff at and even express criticism at the thought of instant messaging as a viable educational tool, others believe there is potential in the medium.

In terms of educational uses for IM, they are being explored and tested. Clearly, IM not only allows students to collaborate more effectively on homework assignments and projects, but also helps to maintain a closer social network between students, which could have a positive impact on learning. In addition, if IM is carefully targeted and focused toward the material or lecture topic in hand, the use of IM may actually help and stimulate deeper and more active learning.

On the other hand, it has been hypothesized that the distraction of working on various other tasks in parallel with IM, known as "distracted attention," may have a negative impact on learning (Hembrooke & Gay, 2003).

Table 1.

INSTANT MESSAGING	
Description	Real-time communications that allow for informal communications to be conducted easily and quickly
Advantages	Availability and acceptance by students Social presence (know the status of other users online) Real-time (synchronous) communications Encourages collaboration Reduces formality in communications
Disadvantages	Distracted attention, especially in a classroom setting "Time waster" that is not directed toward course content, but on personal discussions Expectations of 24-7 instructor access Can be time consuming for instructors Benefits are uncertain in classroom settings
Educational applications	Virtual office hours (instructor-student) Collaboration on group projects Real-time class discussions Mentoring
Course/ subject suitability	Courses with group projects and assignments Distance learning support
Theoretical foundations	Active learning Dual (verbal and visual) processing

Active learning (Grabinger, 1996) and dual (verbal and visual) processing (Clark & Paivio, 1991) are at work here. It could be said that using IM to encourage greater discussion and reflection on the course contents would be likened to the use of discussion boards; however, since IM is a real-time technology, the interaction is conducted during the lecture or class, not afterward. Some studies have reported positive effects and student satisfaction from IM being used to discuss course subjects in real-time (Guernsey, 2003).

A study by Kinzie et al. (2005) examined the use of IM during classroom lectures and found that while the general idea of using IM online discussions was positively received, the actual process and experience of using IM to conduct discussions during class lecture sessions was not found to be less than a positive experience by both teachers and students. It was suggested that the difficulties of multitasking and dividing one's attention between the lecture and instructor, doing the IM discussion, contributed to the lack of satisfaction with the process.

Burke (2004) used instant messaging as a medium for creating course diaries in three different mathematics courses. IM was chosen since it was thought to be popular, widely used by students, and considered more "fun," so there was some hope that this popularity would transfer over to greater and more enthusiastic usage by students. In fact, the choice was made to use IM over a seemingly more suitable choice, blogs. A bot was created that would retrieve IM diary entries from students and store them in a PostgreSQL database, and there was also a program set up to display diary entries from each student, viewable by both the student and the instructor. The main finding of the study was that the IM media was not ideally suited for all kinds of courses, especially those that involved creating longer portions of text, or involved diagramming. Error detection and recovery was also not that well developed, and also there was a need for better editing tools.

In summary, while instant messenger can be appropriate for various applications, in particular for information communications in a business setting, the results from educational studies appear to be mixed, with both positive and negative effects noted. While there seem to be advantages to real-time communications between students, between students and instructors, and also between groups working on a project, it appears that there are problems and limitations if the technology is used in a classroom setting. The challenges of focusing on a class lecture, together with maintaining a conversation online, seem to be a problem that has not yet been resolved. In addition, while instructors can often establish closer relationships with students using IM, there is also the problem of unreasonable student expectations of continuous teacher access, which may not be present if IM was not available as an option. In connection with this, using IM for student help can result in a greater time commitment, since sessions can become lengthy with many questions and responses being sent back and forth.

BLOGS (WEBLOGS)

Blogs started as a means for expressive individuals to post online diaries of themselves. Complete with text and photos, these logs were essentially an individual's online narrative or diary, with events, stories, and opinions. While its original use was for personal expression, recently its effectiveness as a tool for education has been discovered, including its use as an extension of "learning logs," which are created online (Barger, 1997). One of the earliest blogs, as we know and use them today, was Dave Winer's Scripting News, which was put online in 1997. While the use of Weblogs can be considered generally new, the concepts of keeping a "log" or "learning log" is not.

The concept of "learning logs" has been in use since before the advent of the Weblog. The concept of this is to enable someone to document his or her learning, and also to do some critical reflection (Fulwiler, 1987) and self-analysis. The use of a learning log or journal is related to action research learning strategies (Cherry, 1998) and attempts to link previous knowledge and new information learned. Blogs are a natural extension of learning logs/journals in that they are electronic and can be made available ("published") more easily (Armstrong, Berry, & Lamshed, 2004).

The use of electronic Weblogs as educational tools offers the benefits of increased information sharing, simplified publication of information, and improved instructor monitoring and review (Flatley, 2005; Wagner, 2003). The use of blogs has been expanding, as Perseus Development reported that there were some 10 million blogs in 2004, and the number is ever increasing (Nussbaum, 2004). The growth in this area is expected to increase in the years to come.

Blogs can be defined more formally as being "frequently updated Web sites consisting of dated entries arranged in reverse chronological order" (Walker, 2005) and can take several forms, including the personal diary/journal, knowledge-based logs, and filter blogs. The first, an electronic, online diary of one's life events and opinions, is probably the most common. The online diary/journal blog is one that, being on the Internet, is public, as opposed to the traditional (typically paper) diaries, which are generally kept private. It should come as no surprise that there are many different online diary/journal blogs that are currently online, where one can find out details, often much more than one might want to know, about someone's life and thoughts. Personal blogs form the majority of the blogs that are currently online and available, which make up roughly 70% of all the blogs in existence (Herring et al., 2003).

The second type (knowledge-based) captures knowledge and places it online in various formats. The third type (filter) attempts to select, rate, or comment on information contained in other sites (Herring et al., 2004).

There are software packages that are designed to help users create blogs, including Blogger, Xanga, Blurty, and MovableType. While the basic features of most blog software emphasize the creation of blog pages, some of the more sophisticated ones offer the capability to track readership, see who followed what links, add photos, and set up more advanced structures. When online, blogs can range from being totally public (listed in the blog service directory), to being "unlisted" but still open to being highly restricted (password-protected).

Blogs are also interesting and unique in that they are not merely online versions of paper diaries and journals. Rather, as a communications medium under the control of the main writer (author), it is reflective of the fact that an audience is "watching and listening." What is put on a blog is not merely a one-sided set of thoughts and reporting of events; there can also be responses to feedback and reactions from the "viewing audience." Therefore, blogging is considered a highly social activity, rather than a personal one. In fact, recent work has indicated that the momentum for creating, and also updating a blog, came about as a result of encouragement from friends and the viewing audience (Nardi et al., 2004). In addition, blogging can have negative repercussions when posted information is perceived to be confidential, proprietary, or improper. In some cases, employees posting what was considered by their employers as "confidential" information can cause problems.

Blogs do not, in general, exhibit a free-flow of information between the blogger and the outside audience. While feedback is often requested, received, and desired by the blogger, the level and quantity of feedback from readers is generally limited compared with the output from the blog writer. In addition, while blogs may have sections where hyperlinks are mentioned, the number of hyperlinks in blog pages is frequently not very large (Schiano, Nardi, Gumbrecht, & Swartz, 2004).

More formally, Weblogs can be considered to be objects motivating human behavior, which is related to activity theory. Activity theory states that there are objects that have motives that respond to a human need or desire, and that they manifest a person's desire to accomplish that motive (Leontiev, 1978; Vygotsky, 1986). The objects that connect bloggers to their own social networks include letting people know what is happening in their lives, voicing opinions, asking for feedback, and "letting off steam" about certain challenges or difficulties currently being experienced, to name a few (Nardi et al., 2004).

Blogs have been categorized by Krisnamurthy (2002) as being categorized into four different types, along the dimensions of individual versus community, and personal versus topical. A blog can therefore range from being very individual and personal, all the way to being open to the community, however very focused on a particular topic.

The acceptance of blogs for educational purposes is gaining interest, with one university, the University of Maryland, attempting to implement blogging software campus-wide (Higgins, Reeves, & Byrd, 2004).

In addition, the educational uses of blogs take advantage of their ability to encourage expression and the development of online relationships. Blogs allow for learning and interaction to be more knowledge-centered, especially if the assignments are structured in the format of encouraging feedback and input from the instructor and outside experts. Blogs also allow students to gain a better understanding of a subject's knowledge domain (Glogoff, 2005). As an example of this type of blog-enhanced class structure, students might be provided with a Weblog from which to complete certain course assignments. After researching the indicated subject, the student would present the new information by "publishing" it to the Weblog. The Weblog would constitute the student's assignment, which would then be subject to review and critique by not only the instructor, but also by other students in the class. Supplementing this could be discussion boards, where threads would be devoted to discussions on the Weblogs created by the students. This kind of assignment and interaction would be especially useful for both hybrid and fully online distance learning courses (Glogoff, 2005).

There are other benefits of Weblogs. These could be expressed using the learning theories and concepts of guided discovery, directive learning, receptive learning, and social/community-centered instruction.

Guided discovery allows for the exploration and study of a certain topic, which is then followed by assignments that emphasize the synthesis of information. In effect, a student can be asked to research an area and "construct knowledge" using the Weblog as a medium. Part of the assignment goes beyond merely explaining or presenting the material, and asks for the application of the concept using a real-world situation. The ability for students to post and make comments about other students' blogs provides an atmosphere of interactivity and collaboration. One of the advantages of using blogs together with guided discovery is that it encourages the use of cognitive scaffolding, where students would approach learning (together with the use of blogs and interaction) by repeatedly seeking information, reflecting and thinking about what has been learned, and then going back and obtaining more information, so as to build upon and dig deeper into the subject area. This can result in a more active and productive form of learning (Betts & Glogoff, 2004; Glogoff, 2005).

Directive learning, where responses from students are followed by prompt feedback from instructors, can also be supported using blogs. In this case, students would not only use a blog to submit assignments, but also to review instructor feedback. In additional to feedback, there would be opportunities for the instructor to ask additional questions, in effect, to encourage further exploration and "drilling down" into the subject (Betts & Glogoff, 2004; Glogoff, 2005).

Receptive learning is where instructional modules are presented that focus on certain broader areas, from which certain sub-areas within these are highlighted for a student to research and report on. Generally, the areas are contained within a designated theoretical context (Betts & Glogoff, 2004; Glogoff, 2005).

Social/community-centered instruction is a logical component of educational work using blogs, and in particular the use of peer and social interaction as a part of the learning process. The use of blogs functions as an easily accessible medium for students to present their findings (and to be read by others) and also to integrate not only the information presented, but also related links and references to other resources. This form of interaction helps to encourage further exploration by students. A blog-based discussion can then be

Table 2.

WEBLOGS (BLOGS)	
Description	A technology that allows a sequence of entries (online diary, journal) to be posted and published online
Advantages	Reflection and critical thinking are encouraged Authenticity through publication Social presence Development of a learning community Active learning encouraged Ability to receive and respond to feedback
Disadvantages	Controlled primarily by blog author Editing/modifications not open as in a wiki
Educational applications	Online learning journal Problem solving/manipulation space Online gallery space (writings, portfolio, other work) Peer review exercises
Course/ subject suitability	Writing courses Foreign language courses Research seminars
Theoretical foundations	Activity theory Guided discovery Cognitive scaffolding Receptive learning Social cognition Community practice Communities of inquiry

continued by conducting peer reviews of other students' blogs, which may include commentary, critique, the posing of questions, and opening up the way for further inquiry. The ability to share and benefit from the findings of other students (and to explore further) is another important outcome. The theories of community practice (Snyder, 2002), social cognition (Vygotsky, 1978), and communities of inquiry (Lipman, 1991) provide support for the blog-related techniques mentioned previously.

Ducate and Lomicka (2005) discuss their experiences in using Weblogs to support foreign language classes. Weblogs help the foreign language student to learn during the process of reading, and then creating blog entries. Students can learn by reading blogs that are written in the new, target language, including learning new vocabulary, checking out links and further information on words, and learning associated cultural information. The reading and absorption of blogs on the culture associated with the target language, including literature and lifestyles, all would contribute to the learning process.

Another approach would be to have students maintain blogs written in their new, target language, and then the goal would be to seek commentary and critique on these blogs by others in the class. Yet another innovative method might be to share blogs with other classes studying the same language, and for students to read and comment on each other's postings. In the case where students travel to a country where the target language is spoken, the compilation of travel blogs would be a useful learning tool as well (Ducate & Lomicka, 2005).

Wang and Fang (2005) looked at whether the use of blogs encouraged or enhanced cooperative learning in an English rhetoric/writing class taught in Taiwan. The main premise was that blogs can encourage students to spend more time working within a class "community" and can benefit from a greater sharing of contributions and inputs. In general, cooperative learning benefits can be di-

vided into three different types: formal, informal, and base groups. Formal cooperative learning is where the instructor explicitly provides course materials and assignments to a group and then observes the students' learning processes. When the instructor provides information more generally (such as detailing how to use a blog for course assignments) and then lets the group work out their own methods for handling an assignment, that is known as informal cooperative learning. When a learning-oriented group is maintained for an extended period of time, such as throughout a semester, then this form of cooperative learning is known as a cooperative base group (Johnson & Johnson, 1998; Johnson, Johnson, & Holubec, 1991). The study, run over the course of a semester, found that the use of blogs contributed not only to cooperative learning in general, but also to autonomous learning. Autonomous learning is focused on how much students take responsibility for their own learning, and also develop self-confidence in the task or skill (Wenden, 1991). The use of blog technologies was also found to help improve information processing, learning self-evaluation, and effective time management (Wang & Fang, 2005).

Martindale and Wiley (2005) also used blogs in their courses and looked at two cases of the impact of this technology on teaching and learning. Martindale taught a doctoral-level course on instructional design and technology. In it, students were introduced to blogs and used them throughout the course, which overall tended to promote higher levels of quality in their course work. Blogs were used to post ideas and abstracts of their projects, and also to place links for relevant research papers and Web-based resources. The end result was a course "knowledge base" that represented the cumulative output of the students in the course. The blogs were also used for article critiques, which were an integral part of each weekly class. Students were given access to the blogs of other students and were able to offer feedback.

Wiley taught two different courses, one on online learning research, and the other on online interaction culture. Both included the use of blogs as a supporting technology, the first employing a general course blog where information about the course, student assignments, and class updates and student/instructor interaction exchanges were posted on an ongoing basis. In the second, blogs were used to discuss experiences using different online communications technologies, causing students to become highly engaged, resulting in passionate discussions and detailed commentaries posted to the blogs, far exceeding the level and depth of feedback that was expected (Martindale & Wiley, 2005).

In summary, blogs can be useful for educational purposes, particularly where there is the need to encourage and stimulate critical thinking and reflection on a work, concept, or idea. The submission or publication of a document or text as a blog can then lead others in a class to review and comment, setting the stage for greater analysis and study. In particular, blogs are suited to writing courses, where a text can be analyzed and critiqued, or for a situation where a peer review is desired. The use of blogs is also ideal for the situation where someone keeps an online journal of one's learning, or wants to display her or her work to an audience. The blog approach is also considered useful for group study of a certain focused problem or case, such as those used in graduate courses and seminars.

WIKIS

Yet another technology, known as the wiki, has emerged, which allows for improved collaboration compared with Weblogs. While the major emphasis of Weblogs is the creation of a set of pages and documents primarily by a single individual, the strength of a wiki is the ability for numerous interested readers and users to express ideas on-line, edit someone else's work, send and receive ideas, and post links to related resources and sites. As a result, wikis go a step further and allow for greater collaboration and interactivity (Chawner & Gorman, 2002). Wikis have been found to have value for educational purposes, and their use has begun to be integrated into a number of university courses, in particular (Kinzie, 2005).

The term "wiki" comes from the Hawaiian word "wikiwiki," which means "fast." The technology is computer-based and can be generally described as a knowledge sharing and creation system that has as its basis a set of Web pages, which can be created and updated on an iterative and collaborative basis, and is in many ways a form of groupware. A wiki is designed to run on the Internet and World Wide Web, uses the HTTP protocol, and resembles traditional Web sites in terms of its underlying structure. Some of the benefits of wikis include the ability to easily create pages (using a simplified form of HTML or basic HTML) and the ability for a document to be authored collaboratively and collectively. In particular, simplicity is the key to wikis, and wiki pages have been designed to be easy to create, (simpler than the process of creating standard Web pages). One of the better-known examples of a wiki is www.wikipedia.org, which is an online encyclopedia with entries authored and edited by different persons worldwide, and in several different languages as well. In essence, it is an online information resource that is authored by interested and knowledgeable persons from around the world.

Wagner (2004) developed a set of design principles that relate to wikis. These are the principles of open, incremental, organic, mundane, universal, overt, unified, precise, tolerant, observable, and convergent wikis. *Open* means that anyone can edit a wiki, creating an "open source" environment for the sharing of knowledge. *Incremental* means that new pages can be added, even if they do not yet exist. *Organic* means that the information can be continuously evolving, as changes and edits are made. Wikis are *mundane* because they involve the use of a simplified set of essential commands. The design of wikis is also *universal*, meaning that writing and editing is a "combined" activity, formatting is related to input (*overt*), page names are not context specific (*unified*), and pages are generally named with some precision *(precise)*. Wikis should be *tolerant* of error; activity should be *observable* by all, and duplications are undesirable and should be deleted (*convergent*).

There are a number of software programs that enable the effective creation of wiki pages, including TikiWiki, TWiki, and Pmwiki. These allow for the effective creation, modification/editing, and management of wikis, including creating pages, creating links, formatting, and feature modules (discussion forums, photo pages, download areas, etc.) (Chawner & Lewis, 2006)

Wikis are set up to allow for easy collaboration, and more specifically, editing. Rather than passively reading a passage of text or related information (which may include graphics, multimedia, hyperlinks, etc.), a reader of a wiki can also take on the role of a writer, making changes to the text (re-organizing, editing, re-writing, and marking up) at will. In essence, the document is open to changes by a "collaborative community," which allows for the secondary-oral model in education to be applied.

One reservation on the part of educators to embrace wikis is the fact that wikis are designed to allow for open and free access and editing by all members of a "community." As a result, if improperly managed, a wiki's content can become an unreliable, inaccurate, or biased source of information due to its largely unmonitored format. There is also the issue of having little or no "quality control," resulting in a wiki not being trusted by its readers and users. An example of this was the controversy over the accuracy and reliability of Wikipedia, in the case of John Seigen-thaler, in which the subject alleged that false and incorrect statements were posted in his biography (Seigenthaler, 2005). However, other studies have attempted to prove that Wikipedia was overall an accurate information source. One article reported that after analyzing a set of Wikipedia's science articles, they were judged to be, by the British journal Nature, as reliable as the Encyclopedia Britannica (BBC News, 2005).

Wikis are useful for education in that they help to promote student participation and also a sense of group community and purpose in learning. Indeed, an important element of this is the relaxed sense of control over the content, allowing students to have a greater role in managing its focus and direction.

Wikis are not all the same, and there is significant diversity between various forms and implementations of wiki systems. In fact, it could be debated what features truly characterize a "true" wiki. The features inherent in most include the ability for users to both read and edit information, without the need for security or access restrictions. The emphasis is on simplicity, and the informal, "never finished" nature of wikis, which may constitute the contributions of multiple authors, is another key characteristic. While the emphasis of many wikis is on simplicity and a lack of access restrictions, that does not mean that all wikis work this way. In reality, there can be a continuum of features from simple to complex. At the complex end of the scale can be capabilities for security/access restrictions, complex organizational structures, and for integrated with content management systems (Lamb, 2004).

Now that the strengths and weaknesses of wikis have been established, it would be useful to examine the educational applications of wikis. In general, the most suitable applications are those that take advantage of the wiki's free, open structure. As such, the use of wikis as discussion/bulletin boards, brainstorming tools, and online sketchpads is appropriate. Meeting planning is another viable application area, in that the organizer can start with a preliminary agenda, from which the other participants can then add their own additions or make modifications or comments.

An important application area for wikis has been identified in knowledge management (KM). The use of wikis for knowledge management may allow for an improvement over existing systems and technologies. Currently, with existing KM systems, there does exist a number of bottlenecks relating to knowledge acquisition, namely acquisition latency, narrow bandwidths, knowledge inaccuracy, and "maintenance traps." Basically, these knowledge acquisition bottlenecks result from a time lag between when the knowledge is created, and then distributed. In addition, there are the problems of limited channels of knowledge

input, possibilities of erroneous information being received, and also the difficulties of maintaining the knowledge base as it grows larger (Land, 2002; Wagner, 2006; Waterman, 1986).

The use of wikis to elicit a "bazaar" approach to knowledge management, rather than a "cathedral" approach, is proposed as a better alternative. These terms are derived from software development, whether the "bazaar" allows for more continuous and open access to code (or information), as opposed to the "cathedral" approach where access is only provided on certain (release) dates to certain persons. The difference between the "cathedral" (closed), sources of knowledge acquisition management and "bazaar" (open) could be illustrated by the difference between encyclopedias that are created by a single firm, such as Encarta or the Encyclopedia Brittanica, and those that obtain

Table 3.

WIKI	
Description	A technology that allows for material to be easily published online, and also allows open editing and inputs by a group
Advantages	Contributions and editing by a group Open access to all users Collaborative
Disadvantages	Lack of organization and structure may result in an unmanageable wiki Tracking of contributions and modifications can be difficult Quality control
Educational applications	Collaborative writing/authoring Group project management Brainstorming activities Knowledge base creation (knowledge management)
Course/subject suitability	Knowledge management Writing Group work in courses
Theoretical foundations	Conversational technology Constructivist learning tool

information from readers and users, such as the well-known Wikipedia.

The emphasis therefore is on teamwork, continuous review and testing, and the development of conversational sharing (Wagner, 2006). Inherent in the workings of wikis is support for an open, collaborative environment, where many people can contribute to the development of knowledge instead of being limited to a set of "experts." It appears that conversational knowledge acquisition and management are appropriate for wikis (Cheung, Lee, Ip, & Wagner, 2005). As for educational applications and KM, a study by Raman, Ryan, and Olfman (2005) examined the use of a wiki to help encourage and support collaborative activities in a knowledge management course. More specifically, using wikis in the course helped to encourage openness and better sharing and updating of knowledge bases. Many-to-many communication is supported, and the persistence of the created pages formed the basis of a knowledge repository. In short, the impact of easy page creation and improved updating and editing, together with effective maintenance of knowledge histories, were seen as positives (Raman et al., 2005; Bergin, 2002).

Activities in the KM course activities included group article review assignments, answering questions about sharing knowledge and uses of the wiki technology, and also creating a wiki-based knowledge management system. Students were asked to create, update, refine, and then maintain a class knowledge management system. In terms of these experiences, while the use of the wiki technology was generally viewed positively, feedback received indicated that, since the goals of using the wiki were not made clear, using one was perceived to be counter-productive. More specific guidance on goals and objectives, a clearer system structure, and advanced training were suggested as ways to make the wiki a more effective educational tool. The availability of too many features made the task of doing the course activities more difficult, since much time was spent learning the various features rather than focusing on the task at hand. A simpler, less feature-rich version was therefore preferred (Raman et al., 2005).

Another popular application of wikis in the classroom is in supporting writing courses. The use of this technology can help to foster the impression that writing is "fun," and that there can be a shared and collaborative side to writing, revising, and commenting on written work. In other words, the technology can benefit not only the writing and editing process, but also in bringing about an awareness that writing is being done for a specific audience.

An example of the use of wikis in English is the Romantic Audience Program at Bowdoin College, where students used a wiki to discuss and examine Romantic literature, focusing on poetry, poets, and related topics. The technology was used to elicit discussion and analyses by the group, encourage elaboration on areas where further study or insight was sought, and to seek out linkages to additional sources and commentary. Another project is Auburn University's Wikifish, which was created by one school within the university, where questions are posed, and opinions and comments by all are encouraged.

Difficulties encountered in using wikis for education include the difficulty of tracking the new pages and contributions made by students, since modification can be made to another student's text without specifically identifying the author or editor. As a result, it can be difficult to monitor, and properly attribute, what contributions were made by whom, on a particular page. A proposed solution to this was an instructor's use of categories and topics, requiring that students link to and add, rather than simply modify, the contributions of other students. Another issue was how much of a balance in terms of the tradeoff between total freedom, and total control, was ideal. Since a clear benefit of a wiki is the emphasis on free expression and on spontaneous inputs, reducing this may have a negative effect on open interaction and student contributions (Lamb, 2004).

An interesting application of the use of wikis in the classroom was the work by Bruns and Humphreys (2005), where wikis were used in a New Media Technologies course to collaboratively develop entries for an online wiki encyclopedia called the M/*Cyclopedia of New Media*, an actual live wiki resource made available online. The effort to develop entries involved over 150 students spanning six classes in the program. Feedback indicated that while students had little difficulty with using the wiki system, obstacles came about more with the writing and format of the encyclopedia entries.

Another study examined the use of wiki technology in German-speaking communities in Switzerland (Honegger, 2005), while Desilets, Paquet, and Vinson (2005) looked at how usable wikis are and found that the main problems encountered related to the management of hyperlinks. Wikis were also examined from the perspective of structure: how did the use of certain templates affect the appearance and layout of wiki pages? The results suggested that they are useful in certain circumstances and could be helpful overall to end users (Haake, Lukosch, & Schummer, 2005).

In summary, wikis are best suited to course and activities where there is a document, text, or other project to be worked on jointly by a class or group. In a sense, it is a tool for collaboration, and a form of groupware. The compilation of a class or group report or project, the creation of a knowledge base, or brainstorming sessions appear to be viable applications. The free and open structure, however, can fall prey to disorganization and degradation in quality, and so it is important to have safeguards and procedures in place to ensure an effective result.

PODCASTS

While the terms "pod" and "podcast" at first mention might evoke visions of "Invasion of the Body Snatchers," for most tech people in the know, the reference to Pod is almost certainly a reference to Apple's popular and ubiquitous iPod.

However, podcasts are in actuality not what their name might imply them to be. A "podcast," a combination of "iPod" and "broadcast," neither refers to a technology specifically requiring an iPod, nor broadcasts information to users. Instead, podcasts are multimedia files (typically audio or video) that are downloaded to users on a subscription basis. Because of the potential confusion due to the use of the word "pod," some have called for the letters to mean "personal option digital" or "personal on demand, " rather than iPod.

Podcasts can be played back on any device or system that can play digital audio (typically MP3) or video files, and are not broadcast to a large audience, in the way that television, radio, or spam e-mails are sent. Instead, they are sent to users who have specifically subscribed to a podcast service, and as such, files are automatically downloaded to the user's computer when they are ready and available. In addition, podcast files are generally not streamed (as video is streamed), but rather are downloaded for later playback (Lim, 2005; Lum, 2006). Podcasts are delivered to subscribers through the use of RSS or RFD XML format media feeds, rather than more traditional forms of downloading (Descy, 2005).

Podcasts are considered to be a viable educational tool for several reasons. First, because of the popularity and wide use of devices such as the iPod and similar units, it would seem like a good medium from which to distribute educational materials. Secondly, the ease with which information can be retrieved and accessed makes this a good choice for students, who are using these devices on a regular basis for music and should have few technical difficulties or learning curves (Lum, 2006).

There are multiple facets to podcasts. First, there is the consumption perspective, where someone downloads the podcast and then listens or views it. This involves subscribing to a service (or enrolling in a course), finding the relevant file, and then downloading and playing it. Alternately, someone can actually create podcasts; an instructor can produce lessons for students, or students can produce an assignment in the form of a podcast file (Lum, 2006).

Education is one area where the power of the podcast has been used in various ways. At Duke University, orientation material was distributed as podcasts, loaded onto iPod units, and given to students in its 2004 incoming freshman class. The units were provided not only for orientation purposes, but also for use in playing podcast lectures when the students take certain courses at the university. At Mansfield University, students were sent podcasts about various student life issues, and at Arizona State University, President Michael Crow used podcasts to deliver messages to the university community (Lum, 2006).

While there appear to be sound reasons for using podcasts, there is also a theoretical basis behind the use of podcasting. This is based on cultural-historical activity theory (Engestrom, 2002) and is based on the fact that podcasting can be considered a tool that can be used to help learners to better interact with or understand a task and its environment. Vygotsky (1978) argues that the effectiveness of podcasts rests in its linkage

Table 4.

PODCASTS	
Description	The ability to create audio (and other media) based files to be distributed on a regular/subscription basis to users; these can be easily retrieved and played back on handheld devices, computers, and through other means
Advantages	Allows for information to be retrieved and played back on widely available, ubiquitous devices More suitable to auditory and visual learners
Disadvantages	In consumption (playback) mode, does not directly support collaboration Is not inherently interactive in nature
Educational applications	Recorded class lectures Case-based instruction Guest lectures in the form of podcasts Supplemental course materials Support for distance learning courses
Course/subject suitability	Subject matter lends itself to auditory format
Theoretical Foundations	Cultural-historical activity theory

between social/cultural influences present in the environment and the cognitive development of the learner. Expressed another way, the concept is that since so many student have access to iPods and MP3 players, it would make sense to explore the viability of using such a device for learning and educational purposes.

Lim (2005) discussed experiences in using podcasts for teaching geography. Because of the nature of the subject, it was found that video would have a greater impact and result than audio. Students were asked to submit assignments to be created and submitted as podcasts. Overall, this helped to bring about satisfaction and interest in terms of the subject. Ractham and Zhang (2006) looked at the potential for podcasts in a classroom setting. While there are the obvious benefits in terms of being able to distributing class materials, there also are benefits in terms of contributing to social networking in the class and continuing a flow of academic knowledge. Class discussions, announcements of research activities and conferences, and also campus activities could be distributed as podcasts. Review materials could be distributed effectively on an automatic basis to interested students. In addition, the ability for students to create podcasts to be distributed to others would also be a new means of submitting assignments or expressing creativity.

Podcasts, unlike IM, blogs, and wikis, offer a greater emphasis on providing engaging auditory and visual course materials to students, rather than on collaboration and group work. While not generally a substitute for traditional lectures and knowledge presentation, they offer the benefits of easily accessible and "digestible" course material. Whether it is excerpts from class lectures, highlights from a guest speaker, or an oral test review, the use of podcasts provides a means by which students can obtain and easily receive course-related information. In addition, it also provides a means by which students can express and present their work, which can then be "published" and distributed in podcast format.

DISCUSSION AND CONCLUSION

The face of education, whether online, hybrid, or classroom, is constantly changing, and it is important for educators to stay abreast of the many opportunities and possibilities that are available.

In this article, several technologies, generally termed as conversational technologies due to their interactive and collaborative nature, were discussed in detail, together with their capabilities, benefits, and educational applications. Relevant research and case studies as they relate to classroom and educational applications were discussed.

In general, the tools discussed here fall into the class known as "conversational technologies" or "constructivist learning tools." As such, they emphasize student interaction, group learning, and collaboration, rather than the more traditional classroom mode. In light of this, they are more suited to educational courses or environments where the emphasis is on student communication, where students have access to technology, and where creative output and thinking is encouraged.

In the situation where a course is primarily lecture-based, or is mainly concerned with the delivery of factual or conceptual information, these tools may have limited applicability. The one application that may be helpful in this case may be for interaction to be extended outside of the classroom, through the use of instant messenger, or for supplemental materials to be distributed as podcasts.

Since each of the tools has its own characteristics and suitable applications, it would be up to the educator to select those that are most appropriate to one's course and activity.

Instant messenger, which is commonly used by students for personal use, has found its way not only into the business community, but also into the classroom, because of its strengths in terms of informal communications that are conducted real-time. There are some mixed results regarding the use of IM for use for education; benefits are claimed by some, but there are limitations as well. The use of IM would best be employed in situations where group work, student communication, and real-time discussion would be helpful. However, it should be used cautiously, since it can be distracting, and students may end up carrying on personal, rather than course-related discussions.

Both blogs and wikis have been hailed as useful tools for education, and the specific advantages and disadvantages of each are noted and discussed. Blogs tend to be more one-sided, with an author presenting his of her information, with generally limited input from the readers and public. However, the use of the technology has been used effectively to promote information sharing and to support writing courses. The use of blogs to support online learning journals, class article/peer reviews, creating online portfolios and galleries, and for solving a specific problem or case would be advantageous. It would also appear to be a good medium for graduate research seminars, where papers and studies are analyzed and critiqued.

Wikis, which allow freedom in creation and in editing and enhancement by others, are especially useful in collaborative situations where the input of an entire group is desired instead of a single person's contribution. In the classroom, wiki support for collaborative writing and group activities, where students contribute to the creation of a common result, would be useful. In general, any kind of learning activity that involves the collection and maintenance of knowledge or information may benefit from the use of wiki technology.

The use of podcasts, which may include audio or video, is growing in popularity and is being used for delivery of information to subscribers on an automatic basis. Educational podcasts, both for the delivery of audio and video-based knowledge to students, and also as a new medium for the creation and presentation of assignments, appear to have potential. While podcasts are useful as a means for publishing and distributing files of multimedia-based class materials, there also exists the potential to create new podcast content, both for educators and as a course activity.

Clearly, the use of these new conversational technologies is allowing for the enhancement and continued evolution of new and innovative forms of support for teaching and learning.

FUTURE RESEARCH AREAS

Certainly, there are many benefits to the use of conversational technologies and constructivist tools for educational use. However, more research needs to be done, not only in terms of identifying additional types of applications and uses, but also in terms of how to more effectively identify and apply new approaches to learning with the aid of these kinds of technologies.

Some of the broader research issues that can be examined include measuring both learning, and the perceived quality of education, depending on the specific technology or tool employed. Are there measurable benefits to using a certain technology in terms of the material learned, better class performance, or more subjective factors? It would also be useful to determine, particularly when using blogs and wikis, the neutrality or bias in the entries, and how much these contribute to (or detract from) the material submitted for a course assignment.

Other research areas are more technology specific. It was mentioned earlier that wikis can be a useful tool in knowledge management. The application of wikis to effective knowledge management deserves further attention, both in terms of developing or adapting the wiki structure and features to knowledge management uses, and also for identifying various kinds of user interfaces and functionality that would improve usability.

The establishment of wiki-supported communities of practice is one area where the tool could possibly be useful.

Podcasting also has many areas that are ripe for further investigation. There are issues that can be explored in the areas of knowledge management, collaboration, and the adoption of podcasts. Some of the specific topics of interest include the management and sharing of knowledge using podcasts, examining whether their use actually improves learning, studying their effects on collaboration and networking, and what the factors (or features) are that would help to promote its use.

There also has been work on the psychological aspects of distance learning and online courses (Dickey, 2004), and a study of learners' reactions to using IM, blogs, and wikis, for example, would yield insights into its appropriateness for its further use in education. Does the use of these technologies contribute to the satisfaction of students, or is more classroom face-to-face still better?

The realm of these new technologies is certainly ripe with a host of opportunities for both interesting and meaningful research studies.

REFERENCES

Ahn, J., Han, K., & Han, B. (2005). Web-based education: Characteristics, problems, and some solutions. *International Journal of Innovation and Learning 2005, 2*(3), 274-282.

Armstrong, L., Berry, M., & Lamshed, R. (2004). Blogs as electronic learning journals. *E-Journal of Instructional Science and Technology, 7*(1). Retrieved from http://www.usq.edu.au/electpub/e-jist/docs/Vol7_No1/CurrentPractice/Blogs.htm

Barger, J. (1997). Weblog resources FAQ, Robot Wisdom Werblog. Retrieved from http://www.robotwisdom.com/weblogs

BBC News. (2005). Wikipedia survives research test. BBC News, December 15, 2005.

Beck, P., Kung, M., Park, Y., & Yang, S. (2004). E-learning architecture: Challenges and mapping of individuals in an Internet-based pedagogical interface. *International Journal of Innovation and Learning 2004, 1*(3) 279-292.

Bergin, J. (2002). Teaching on the Wiki Web. *ACM SIGCSE Bulletin*, 1.

Betts, J. D., & Glogoff, S. (2004). Instruction models for using Weblogs in e-learning. In *Proceedings of Syllabus 2004*. San Francisco.

Blood, R. (2004). How blogging software reshapes the online community. *Communications of the ACM, 47*(12), 53-133.

Bruns, A., & Humphreys, S. (2005). Wikis in teaching and assessment: The M/Cyclopedia Project. In *Proceedings WikiSim'05*. San Diego, CA.

Burke, M. (2004). Instant messaging and course diaries. *CCSC Northeastern Conference Proceedings, 19*(5), 207-274.

Chawner, B., & Gorman, G. E. (2002), Wikis are wicked. *New Library World, 103*(1182/1183), 483.

Chawner, B., & Lewis, P. (2006). Wiki wiki webs: New ways to communicate in a Web environment. *Information Technology and Libraries, 25*(1), 33-43.

Cherry, N. (1998). *Action research: A pathway to action, knowledge, and learning.* RMIT Publishing.

Cheung, K., Lee, F., Ip, R., & Wagner, C. (2005). The development of successful online communities. *International Journal of the Computer, the Internet, and Management, 13*(1).

Clark, J. M., & Paivio, A. (1991). Dual coding theory and education. *Educational Psychology Review, 3*, 149-210.

Cold, S. (2005). Using RSS to enhance student research. *ACM SIGITE Newsletter, 3*(1).

Dearstyne, B. (2005). Blogs: The new information revolution. *Information Management Journal,* (September/October), 38-44.

Descy, D. (2005). Podcasting: Online media delivery...with a twist. *TechTrends, 49*(5), 4-6.

Desilets, A., Paquet, S., & Vinson, N. (2005). Are wikis usable? In *Proceedings WikiSim'05.* San Diego, CA

Dickey, M. (2004). The impact of Weblogs on student perceptions of isolation and alienation in a Web-based distance learning environment. *Open Learning, 19*(3), 279-291.

Ducate, L., & Lomicka, L. (2005). Exploring the blogosphere: Use of Weblogs in the foreign language classroom. *Foreign Language Annals, 38*(3), 410-421.

Efimova, L., & Fiedler, S. (2004). Learning webs: Learning in Weblog networks. In Kommers, Isaias, & Nunes (Eds.), *Proceedings of the IADIS Intl. Conference on Web Based Communities 2004.* Lisbon: IADIS Press.

Engestrom, Y. (2002). Cultural historical activity theory. Retrieved from http://www.helsinki.fi/~jengestr/activity/6a.htm

Engstrom, M. E., & Jewitt, D. (2005). Collaborative learning the wiki way. *TechTrends, 49*(6), 12-15.

Ferris, S. P., & Wilder, H. (2006). Uses and potentials of wikis in the classroom. *Innovate, 1*(5).

Fisher, M., & Baird, D. (2005). Online learning design that fosters support, self-regulation, and retention. *Campus-Wide Information Systems, 22*(2), 88-107.

Flatley, M. (2005). Blogging for enhanced teaching and learning. *Business Communication Quarterly, 68*(2005).

Fuchs-Kittowski, F., & Kohler, A. (2002). Knowledge creating communities in the context of work processes. *SIGGROUP Bulletin, 23*(3).

Fuchs-Kittowski, F., & Kohler, A. (2005). Wiki communities in the context of work processes. In *Proceedings WikiSim'05.* San Diego, CA.

Fulwiler, T. (1987). *The journal book.* Portsmouth, NH: Boynton/Cook.

Glogoff, S. (2005). Instructional blogging: Promoting interactivity, student-centered learning, and peer input. *Innovate, 1*(5).

Grabinger, R. S. (1996). Rich environments for active learning. In D. H. Jonassen (Ed.), *Handbook of research for educational communications and technology* (pp. 665-692). New York: Macmillan.

Gronbeck, B., Farrell, T., & Soukup, P. (1991). *Media consciousness and culture.* Newbury Mark, CA: Sage.

Guernsey, L. (2003, July 24). In the lecture hall, a geek chorus. *The New York Times.*

Haake, A., Lukosch, S., & Schummer, T. (2005). Wiki templates. In *Proceedings WikiSym'05* (pp. 41-51). San Diego, CA.

Hargis, J., & Wilson, B. (2005). Fishing for learning with a podcast net. Instruction and Research Technology, Univ. of North Florida.

Hembrooke, H., & Gay, G. (2003). The laptop and the lecture. *Journal of Computing in Higher Education, 15*(1).

Herring, S., Scheidt, L., Bonus, S., & Wright, E. (2004). Bridging the gap: A genre analysis of Weblogs. In *Proceedings of HICSS 2004.* Big Island, HI.

Higgins, C., Reeves, L., & Byrd, E. (2004). Interactive online journaling. In *Proceedings SIGUCCS'04.* Baltimore, MD.

Honegger, B. (2005). Wikis—A rapidly growing phenomenon in the German-speaking school community. In *Proceedings WikiSim'05*. San Diego CA.

Hsu, K., & Tanner, J. (2006). An assessment of classroom technology usage in business. *International Journal of Innovation and Learning, 3*(5), 488-498.

Johnson, D. W., & Johnson, R. T. (1998). *Cooperation and competition*. Edina, MN: Interaction.

Johnson, D. W., Johnson, R. T., & Holubec, E. (1991). *Cooperation in the classroom* (3rd ed.). Edina, MN: Interaction.

Kinzie, S. (2005, February 12). Colleges land lines nearing an end. *The Washington Post*.

Kinzie, M., Whitaker, S., & Hofer, M. (2005). Instructional uses of instant messaging during classroom lectures. *Educational Technology and Society, 8*(2), 150-160.

KPMG. (2003). Insights from KPMG's European Knowledge Management Survey 2002/2003. KPMG Knowledge Advisory Services, Amsterdam.

Krisnamurthy, S. (2002). *The multidimensionality of blog conversations. Internet research 3.0*. Maastricht, The Netherlands.

Lamb, B. (2004). Wide open spaces Wikis ready or not. *Educause, September/October*, 36-48.

Leontiev, A. (1978). *Activity, consciousness, and personality*. Englewood Cliffs, NJ: Prentice Hall.

Leuf, B., & Cunningham, W. (1999). *The WIKI way: Quick collaboration on the Web*. Reading, MA: Addison Wesley.

Lim, K. (2005). *Now hear this—Exploring podcasting as a tool in geography education*. Nanyang Technological University.

Lipman, M. (1991). *Thinking in education*. New York: Cambridge University Press.

Liu, C., & Chen, S. (2005). Determinants of knowledge sharing of e-learners. *International Journal of Innovation and Learning 2005, 2*(4), 434-445.

Locke, C. et al. (2000). *The Cluetrain Mainfesto: The end of business as usual*. Cambridge, MA: Perseus.

Louridas, P. (2006). Using wikis in software development. *IEEE Software, March/April*, 88-91.

Lum, L. (2006). The power of podcasting. *Diverse Issues in Higher Education, 23*(2), 32.

Martindale, T., & Wiley, D. (2005). Using Weblogs in scholarship and teaching. *TechTrends, 49*(2).

Mock, K. (2002). The use of Internet tools to supplement communication in the classroom. *CCSC Northeastern Conference Proceedings, 17*(2), 4-21.

Nardi, B., & Bradner, E. (2000). Interaction and outeraction. In *Proceedings of CSCW'00*. Philadelphia, PA.

Nardi, B., Schiano, D. J., & Gumbrecht, M. (2004). Blogging as social activity. In *Proceedings of CSCW 2004* (pp. 222-231). Chicago.

Nardi, B., Schiano, D. J., Gumbrecht, M., & Swartz, L. (2004). Why we blog. *Communications of the ACM, 47*(12), 41-46.

Nussbaum, E. (2004, January 11). My so-called blog. *The New York Times*.

O'Neill, M. (2005). Automated use of a wiki for collaborative lecture notes. In *Proceedings SIGCSE'05* (pp. 267-271).

Ong, W. (1982). *Orality and literacy*. New York: Routledge.

Prensky, M. (2001). Digital natives, digital immigrants. *On the Horizon, 9*(5).

Ractham, P., & Zhang, X. (2006). Podcasting in Academia. In *Proceedings SIGMIS-CPR'06*.

Raman, M., Ryan, T., & Olfman, L. (2005). Designing knowledge management systems for teaching and learning with wiki technology. *Journal of Information Systems Education, 16*(3), 311-320.

Schiano, D., Nardi, B., Gumbrecht, M., & Swartz, L. (2004). Blogging by the rest of us. In *Proceedings CHI 2004* (pp. 1143-1146).

Seigenthaler, J. (2005, November 29). A false Wikipedia biography. *USA Today.*

Seitzinger, J. (2006). Be constructive: Blogs, podcasts, and wikis as constructivist learning tools. *Learning Solutions, July.*

Seng, J., & Lin, S. (2004). A mobility and knowledge-centric e-learning application design method. *International Journal of Innovation and Learning 2004, 1*(3), 293-311.

Vygotsky, L. (1986). *Thought and cognition.* Cambridge, MA: MIT Press.

Wagner, C. (2004). Wiki: A technology for conversational knowledge management and group collaboration. *Communications of the AIS, 13*(2004), 265-289.

Wagner, C. (2006). Breaking the knowledge acquisition bottleneck through conversational knowledge management. *Information Management Resources Journal, 19*(1), 70-83.

Walker, J. (2005). Weblog. Definition from the Routledge Encyclopedia of Narrative Theory.

Wallace, M. (2005). *Notes towards a literacy for the digital age.* Retrieved from http://uclaccc.ucla.edu/articles/article-digitalage.htm

Wang, J., & Fang, Y. (2005). Benefits of cooperative learning in Weblog networks. In *Proceedings APAMALL2005 and ROCMELIA2005, Kun Shan University.*

Wenden, A. (1991). *Learning strategies for learner autonomy.* New York: Prentice-Hall.

Wickramasinghe, N., & Lichtenstein, S. (2006). Supporting knowledge creation with e-mail. *International Journal of Innovation and Learning 2006, 3*(4), 416-426.

Wikipedia. (2006). Mobile computing, definition. Retrieved August 25, 2006, from http://en.wikipedia.org/wiki/Mobile_computing

This work was previously published in the International Journal of Information and Communication Technology Education, edited by L. A. Tomei, Volume 3, Issue 3, pp. 70-89, copyright 2007 by IGI Publishing, formerly known as Idea Group Publishing (an imprint of IGI Global).

Chapter XIII
Modelling Interactive Behaviour with a Rational Cognitive Architecture

David Peebles
University of Huddersfield, UK

Anna L. Cox
University College London, UK

ABSTRACT

In this chapter we discuss a number of recent studies that demonstrate the use of rational analysis (Anderson, 1990) and cognitive modelling methods to understand complex interactive behaviour involved in three tasks: (1) icon search, (2) graph reading, and (3) information retrieval on the World Wide Web (WWW). We describe the underlying theoretical assumptions of rational analysis and the adaptive control of thought-rational (ACT-R) cognitive architecture (Anderson & Lebiere, 1998), a theory of cognition that incorporates rational analysis in its mechanisms for learning and decision making. In presenting these studies we aim to show how such methods can be combined with eye movement data to provide detailed, highly constrained accounts of user performance that are grounded in psychological theory. We argue that the theoretical and technological developments that underpin these methods are now at a stage that the approach can be more broadly applied to other areas of Web use.

INTRODUCTION

With the rapid increase in Internet use over the past decade there is a growing need for those engaged in the design of Web technology to understand the human factors involved in Web-based interaction. Incorporating insights from cognitive science about the mechanisms, strengths, and limits of human perception and cognition can provide a number of benefits for Web practitioners. Knowledge about the various constraints on cognition, (e.g., limitations on working memory), patterns of strategy selection, or the effect of design decisions (e.g., icon style) on visual search, can inform the design and evaluation process and allow practitioners to develop technologies that are better suited to human abilities.

The application of cognitive psychology to human-computer interaction (HCI) issues has a long history going back to Card, Moran, and Newell's (1983) introduction of the goals, operators, methods, and selection rules (GOMS) task analysis technique and model human processor (MHP) account of human information processing in the early 1980s. Since then, their cognitive engineering approach has developed into a family of methods (John & Kieras, 1994; Olson & Olson, 1990) which are widely used to produce quantitative models of user performance in interactive tasks.

Another, more recent approach to modelling human performance in interactive tasks has emerged in the last decade from theoretical and technological advances in research into cognitive architectures. Cognitive architectures are theories of the fundamental structures and processes that underlie all human cognition, of which there are several currently in existence including EPIC (executive process / interactive control; Kieras & Meyer, 1997), Soar (Laird, Newell, & Rosenbloom, 1987; Newell, 1990), and ACT-R (Anderson & Lebiere, 1998; Anderson et al., 2004). An important feature of these architectures is that they are all implemented as computer programming systems so that cognitive models may be specified, executed, and their outputs (e.g., error rates and response latencies) compared to human performance data.

Originally ACT-R and Soar were theories of central cognition only and did not explicitly specify mechanisms for perception or motor control. EPIC however, was unique in that from its inception it incorporated processors for cognition, perception, and motor control. Recent adaptations to ACT-R (Byrne & Anderson, 1998) and Soar (Chong & Laird, 1997) have now ensured that both architectures incorporate perceptual motor

components that allow models to include visual attention processes and manual interactions with a keyboard and mouse. This is an important development for the study of HCI as cognitive models can now be *embodied* (Kieras & Meyer, 1997) in the sense that the architectures are now able to simulate perceptual-motor contact with computer interfaces and devices and so capture the complex interactions between the task environment, cognition, and perceptual-motor behaviour.

Modelling interactive behaviour with an embodied cognitive architecture has a number of advantages over the traditional cognitive engineering approach exemplified by GOMS and its relatives. Perhaps the most important of these is that computational models can actually execute the task, allowing a direct test of the sufficiency of the hypothesised processes. Second, although most cognitive architectures contain built-in timing parameters taken from the psychological literature, unlike cognitive engineering models, they do not require prior estimated times for all subcomponents of a task. In addition, some architectures — such as ACT-R and Soar — contain learning mechanisms which allow them to model various effects of practice on performance. This allows cognitive architectures to be used to model novel tasks, novice users, or tasks involving components without prior time estimates.

One of the promises of embodied cognitive architectures is that, once they are equipped with sufficient knowledge, they will begin to provide a priori predictions of user performance and eventually evolve into artificial users that can be employed to evaluate novel tasks and environments (Ritter, Baxter, Jones, & Young, 2000; Young, Green, & Simon, 1989). In this chapter we will describe one of these architectures, ACT-R, and show how it has been used to provide detailed and sophisticated process models of human performance in interactive tasks with complex interfaces. ACT-R is an appropriate choice for this discussion because, in contrast to other cognitive architectures, ACT-R also embodies the rational theory of cognition (Anderson, 1990) which analyses cognitive phenomena in terms of how they are adapted to the statistical structure of the environment. Rational analysis and ACT-R's mechanisms have been used recently to provide novel insights into Web-based interactions. The chapter proceeds as follows: First we describe the basic assumptions and mechanisms of rational analysis and the ACT-R cognitive architecture. We then show how these have been used to develop a model of information foraging on the Web and discuss the model in relation to a rational analysis model of the task and the data from eye-tracking studies of interactive search. In the final sections of this chapter we briefly outline ACT-R models of two interactive tasks; graph reading (Peebles & Cheng, 2003) and icon search (Fleetwood & Byrne, in press). Although neither of these studies involves a specifically Web-based task, they both describe user interaction with items commonly found on Web pages. They are also illustrative of a methodology that combines task analysis, eye tracking, and formal modelling to provide a detailed account of the cognitive, perceptual, and motor processes involved in the performance of the task. These studies are also useful because in both cases the model is validated by comparing the simulated eye movements with those recorded from human subjects. Both studies, therefore, are clear demonstrations of a novel approach to understanding interactive behaviour that can be applied to Web-based tasks.

RATIONAL ANALYSIS

Rational analysis (Anderson, 1990) is a method for understanding the task an agent attempts to complete. It assumes that humans have evolved cognitive mechanisms that are useful for completing tasks that we encounter in our environment, and that these mechanisms work in an efficient way to complete these tasks. Therefore, rather than concerning ourselves with firstly trying to

define the cognitive mechanisms required by the agent to solve the task, rational analysis suggests that we should consider the structure of the task itself, the environment in which it is encountered, together with some minimal assumptions about the computational limitations of the system. From these initial statements the analysis proceeds by the specification of an optimal solution to the problem and the comparison of human behavioural data to see how close an approximation it is to the optimal solution.

By identifying the best way to complete the task (the optimal strategy) we can often infer what the cognitive mechanisms of a rational agent must be as although humans do not always complete tasks in the most optimal way their behaviour is usually similar to the optimal strategy. That is, humans usually behave in such a way that they appear to be trying to complete their tasks in the most efficient manner, that is, they try to maximise their returns while minimising the cost of achieving their goals.

Rational analysis has been applied to several aspects of human cognition (see e.g., Oaksford & Chater, 1998), from the original analyses of memory, categorisation, causal inference, and decision making conducted by Anderson (1990), to more recent analyses of exploratory choice (Cox & Young 2004; Young, 1998) and the updating of memory during tasks in dynamic environments (Neth, Sims, Veksler, & Gray, 2004).

THE ACT-R COGNITIVE ARCHITECTURE

ACT-R is a theory of human cognition developed over a period of 30 years by John Anderson and his colleagues (Anderson & Lebiere, 1998; Anderson et al., 2004) that incorporates the theory of rational analysis. It is a principal effort in the attempt to develop a unified theory of cognition (Newell, 1990). As a cognitive architecture, ACT-R attempts to specify the basic cognitive structures and processes that underlie all human cognition.

Figure 1 illustrates the components of the architecture relevant to our discussion. ACT-R consists of a set of independent modules that acquire information from the environment, process information, and execute motor actions in the furtherance of particular goals. There are four modules that comprise the central cognitive components of ACT-R. Two of these are memory stores for two types of knowledge: a declarative memory module that stores factual knowledge about the domain, and a procedural memory module that stores the system's knowledge about how tasks are performed. The former consists of a network of knowledge chunks whereas the latter is a set of *productions*, rules of the form "IF <condition> THEN <action>": the condition specifying the state of the system that must exist for the rule to apply and the action specifying the actions to be taken should this occur. The other two cognitive modules represent information related to the execution of tasks. The first is a control state module that keeps track of the intentions of the system during problem solving, and the second is a problem state module that maintains the current state of the task.

In addition to these cognitive modules there are four perceptual-motor modules for speech, audition, visual, and motor processing (only the latter two are shown in Figure 1). The speech and audition modules are the least well-developed and, at present, simply provide ACT-R with the capacity to simulate basic audio perception and vocal output for the purpose of modelling typical psychology experiments. The visual and motor modules are more well-developed and provide ACT-R with the ability to simulate visual attention shifts to objects on a computer display and manual interactions with a computer keyboard and mouse.

Each of ACT-R's modules has an associated *buffer* that can hold only one chunk of information from its module at a time, and the contents of all of the buffers constitute the state of an ACT-R model at any one time. Cognition proceeds via

Figure 1. The modular structure of ACT-R 6.0

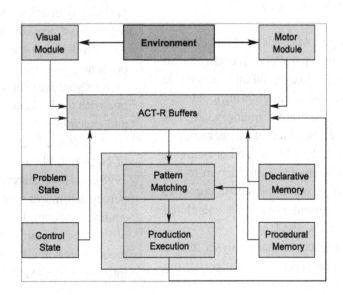

a pattern matching process that attempts to find productions with conditions that match the current contents of the buffers. There then follows a process to select the "best" production from those that match the conditions, after which the most appropriate production "fires" and the actions (visual or manual movements, requests for the retrieval of a knowledge chunk from declarative memory, or modifications to buffers) are performed. Then the matching process continues on the updated contents of the buffers so that tasks are performed through a succession of production rule firings. As an example, two production rules (written in English rather than in ACT-R code) that instantiate part of a search task may look something like this:

IF	the goal is to find the meaning of "eudaimonia" (control state)
AND	there is nothing in declarative memory about "eudaimonia" (declarative)
THEN	set the goal to search the WWW for "eudaimonia" (control state)
IF	the goal is to search the WWW for "eudaimonia" (control state)
AND	the Web browser is open (problem state)
THEN	look for the menu labelled "Bookmarks" (visual)
AND	update the problem state to "looking for Google" (problem state)

The processing in ACT-R's modules is serial but the modules run in parallel with each other so that the system can move visual attention while also moving the mouse and attempting to retrieve knowledge from declarative memory. ACT-R processes also have associated latency parameters taken from the psychology literature. For example, it typically takes 50 ms for a production to fire and the time taken to move the mouse cursor to an object on the computer screen is calculated using Fitts' Law (Fitts, 1954).

ACT-R implements rational analysis in two ways. The first is its mechanism for retrieving knowledge chunks from declarative memory which is based on the notion of activation. Each chunk in declarative memory has a level of activation which determines its probability and latency of retrieval, and the level of activation for a chunk reflects the recency and frequency of its use. This enables us to understand how rehearsal of items in a short-term memory task can boost the activation levels of these chunks and consequently increase the chances of recall/retrieval from declarative memory. The level of activation of a chunk falls gradually over time, and without retrieval or activation spreading from chunks in the current goal, it may fall below a threshold level which then results in retrieval failure. This enables ACT-R models to forget knowledge without having to explicitly delete chunks from the declarative memory store.

The second way that ACT-R implements rational analysis is in its mechanism for choosing between alternative production rules. According to rational analysis, people choose between a number of options to maximise their expected utility. Each option (i.e., production rule) has an expected probability of achieving the goal and an expected cost. It is assumed that when carrying out computer-based tasks people interact with the task environment and choose actions that will optimise their efficiency (i.e., maximise the probability of achieving the goal while minimising the cost, usually measured in units of time). At each decision step in the cycle, therefore, all possible production rules that match against the current goal are proposed in a choice set, and the one with the highest level of efficiency is chosen and executed.

ACT-R has been used to model a wide range of cognitive phenomena (Anderson & Lebiere, 1998), and in recent years, with the inclusion of the perceptual-motor modules, it has been applied to a number of complex interactive tasks in the area of HCI and human factors research, for example, menu selection (Byrne, 2001), cell phone menu interaction (St. Amant, Horton, & Ritter, 2004), and driving (Salvucci & Macuga, 2002). Although individually these models do not yet offer us a virtual "user" which can be sat in front of a Web browser and asked to complete any goal, together they provide us with insights into how and why users behave in particular ways, for example, when searching for information on the Web. In this chapter we will concentrate on three particular areas of work that are relevant to understanding Web behaviour: icon search, graph reading, and information foraging on the WWW.

MODELLING INTERACTIVE BEHAVIOUR

In the following section, we will summarise a number of recent studies which employ rational analysis, cognitive modelling, eye tracking, or a combination of all three, to understand human performance in Web-based or HCI tasks. We first discuss recent efforts to model information foraging and interactive search on the WWW. These studies show how ACT-R and rational analysis can be successfully applied to explain different aspects of people's behaviour when conducting interactive search tasks. This can include both high-level behaviours such as backtracking through Web-pages and low-level behaviours such as patterns of visual attention obtained from eye-tracking studies. We then describe two studies which combine experimental data collection, eye movement recording, and cognitive modelling methods using ACT-R to provide detailed accounts of the cognitive, perceptual, and motor processes involved in the tasks. These studies were chosen because both develop a detailed process model which not only captures the human response time data from the experiment, but also provides a close match to the patterns of visual attention revealed by the eye movement study. This level of detail in modelling is still relatively uncommon and the strong constraints added by seeking to match model and human eye movement scan paths

during the course of the task provide a further validation of the models.

Information Foraging on the World Wide Web

Information foraging theory (IFT; Pirolli & Card, 1999; Pirolli, 2005) describes an account of information gathering behaviour based on the ecological behaviours of animals when foraging for food. The account can be applied to situations in which people are searching for information in a number of different situations such as in a library or on the WWW. The theory rests on rational analysis in that it proposes that human behaviour is directed by the objective to maximise gain and minimise effort, and that this process is sensitive to changes in the environment. In contrast to animal studies, where the assumption is that animals seek to reduce the ratio of calorie intake to energy expenditure, the assumption in IFT is that people attempt to reduce the ratio of information gained to time spent.

The way in which the environment is structured determines the costs of search for information. For example, the structure of a Web site will determine how many pages the user has to navigate through in order to satisfy his/her goal. When searching for information on the WWW, many people make use of search engines. After entering some key words the user is presented with a list of search results which are usually ordered in terms of their relevance to the key words. Each of the results returned can be considered to be a "patch" of information. The user has to choose to either investigate one of the patches or to redefine their search criteria. Conducting another search using different key words will result in a change in the environment. This process is known as *enriching* the environment as it is hoped that the result is that the cost of obtaining the required information will be reduced compared to the perceived cost of obtaining it in the previous environment. Decisions about whether or not to pursue a particular information patch or to continue enriching the environment are based on a number of factors such as the perceived value of the information returned, the perceived costs of acquiring that information, interface constraints, and previous knowledge.

The decision to forage within a particular patch of information is based on an ongoing assessment of information *scent*. Information scent is the perception of the value of the distal information based on the proximal information available, that is, it is an estimate of the relevance of the information contained on a yet unseen page based on the cues from the icon or wording of the link on the page currently viewed. The theory predicts that as more time is allocated to within-patch foraging, the rate of information return increases but only up to an optimal point, after which the rate starts to decrease. Therefore, after a particular amount of within-patch foraging (searching within a Web site) it becomes more profitable to move to the next patch (select another Web site from the list of search results) even though there are still pages within the previous patch that have not yet been visited.

SNIF-ACT

Scent-based Navigation and Information Foraging in the ACT architecture (SNIF-ACT) (Pirolli & Fu, 2003) is a model of human behaviour in an interactive search task. The model makes use of ACT-R's spreading activation mechanism so that the information scent of the currently viewed Web page activates chunks in declarative memory as does the spreading activation from the goal. Where these two sources of activation coincide there are higher levels of activation and this indicates a high degree of relevance between the goal and the page being attended to. This activation is what ultimately drives the behaviour of the model. The model includes the use of search engines to provide a set of search results and the

processing of the page that is returned. The links on the page are attended to and eventually one of the links is selected.

The behaviour of the model is compared to user behaviour and successfully demonstrates that people tend to select the highest scent item in a list. SNIF-ACT does this by assessing the information scent of all the links on a page and then choosing the highest one. The model is also able to explain the point at which a user abandons a particular Web site and returns to the search results in order to select another item from the list or selects a link that takes them to another Web site. If the mean information scent of the currently viewed page is lower than the mean information scent of a page on another site the model selects that action that takes them to the other site.

Eye-Tracking Experiments in Interactive Search

When presented with a list of search results or items on a menu within a Web site (i.e., a patch of information), the user has to choose between selecting an item which will move him/her to another patch and doing some assessment on either the currently attended item or some other item in the list (i.e., consume the information presented within the current patch). As has been mentioned previously, IFT proposes that the user will make use of the information scent of the items to guide their behaviour. If the information scent of a particular item in the list is higher than the rest (i.e., that item appears to be relevant to the task and the user believes that clicking it will lead them to better information) then the item will be selected.

Eye-tracking experiments have been used to investigate what people attend to when conducting interactive search tasks (Brumby & Howes, 2004; Silva & Cox, 2005). Participants were given an information goal and a list of items and asked to select the label that they thought would lead to the information they required. Brumby and Howes demonstrated that people often examine only a subset of the list before selecting the target item, and that this behaviour is affected by the relevance of the other items in the list. When the other items in the list are more relevant to the goal (i.e., they have high levels of information scent), people tend to look at more items in the list and also tend to look at individual items on more occasions than when the items are irrelevant. When there are a number of items with high scent (i.e., two or more items look like they would lead to relevant information) people need to consider more items than when only one item looks sensible.

However, one limitation of this work is that the analysis of eye-tracking data is rarely sensitive enough to determine whether a lack of fixation of the eyes on an item really means that people have not assessed the relevance of the item. In order to address this, Silva and Cox (2005) additionally employed a recognition task in their study in order to assess the level of processing of each item in the list.

Figure 2 represents a simplified scan path of a participant completing one of these tasks. The items are represented on the y axis with time along the x axis. The highlighted item is the target item and was selected by the participant. The figure demonstrates how the user starts at the top of the list and scans down the list fixating items in the list. Some of the items (3 & 6) are skipped over. The results from Silva and Cox's (2005) recognition task suggest that in such cases the lack of fixations of particular items in the menu can be explained by parafoveal processing. However, parafoveal processing can only explain lack of fixations on up to two items below the last fixation (i.e., items 8 & 9) and cannot explain why the user does not attend to other items in the list (i.e., items 10 to 16).

SNIF-ACT would be able to produce a trace that would match the behaviour of users in these studies in terms of which items from the menus the user selected. However, the model does not account for the fact that some of the items in the menus were not assessed by the users as it assumes that users have knowledge about information scent of all the items in the list and then selects the item with the highest level of scent. Consequently, SNIF-ACT is unable to provide us with any explanation for why users should choose to select an item when they have not even read the entire list presented to them.

Cox and Young (2004) propose an alternative model to that of SNIF-ACT that is able to capture this fine-grained level of detail of user behaviour. Their model is a rational analysis of an interactive search task that provides a rational explanation of why the user would select an item without first assessing all the items in the list.

In interactive search, the agent has the goal of selecting the item that will lead to goal completion. However, as the menu presented is novel, the first thing that the model has to do is to gain

Figure 2. A simplified scan path of a participant performing an interactive search task

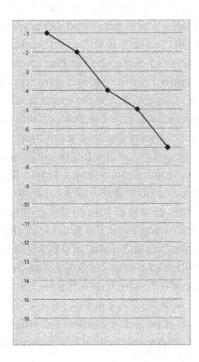

some information about the menu. The model therefore includes two types of exploratory acts (EAs) (these are the different types of things the model can do): assess information SCENT and ANTICIPATE the result of selecting this item. The SCENT EA should be thought of as being an amalgamation of perceiving the label, reading the label (at a lexical level), and considering the semantic similarity between the label and the current task. The ANTICIPATE EA should be thought of as some additional cognitive effort that considers whether the label is likely to lead to the goal. For example, given the goal of finding an armchair for your living room on a furniture shop Web site, imagine the model considering the first item in the menu "home." The SCENT EA would return a moderately high rating as the label has a moderately high level of information scent given the goal ("home" and "armchair"). The ANTICIPATE EA models the agent's consideration of whether the label *home* is likely to lead to the home page of the site, or to a list of home furnishings. Each of these EA types has a cost associated with it with the ANTICIPATE EA type being more expensive in mental effort than the first type. There is also a fixed cost of moving attention from one item in the menu to the next.

Before assessing any items, the model "knows" the number of items in the menu and considers each of these items to be equally (ir)relevant to completing the task. The scent ratings of the items in the menu are used as the basis for determining the new relevance (R) value of an item following an assessment. On each page, the set of relevancies R_i are mapped into a set of probabilities P_i by the transformation $P_i = odds(Ri)/\sum odds(R_j)$, where odds(R) is defined in the standard way as $odds(R) = R/(1-R)$. Note that $\sum P_i = 1$, reflecting the fact that exactly one option on the page leads to the goal.

When the model is run on a set of menus it demonstrates how different patterns of information scent result in different behaviours. As

Brumby and Howes (2004) demonstrated, the levels of information scent of both the goal item and the distractors affect behaviour. However, it is also interesting to note that the model predicts that just the change in position of the goal item relevant to the distractors results in different patterns of behaviour: Sometimes the model predicts that users will scan to the bottom of the menu before selecting the target item, and other times they will select the item immediately after assessing the item leaving other items in the menu unassessed. To explain how this occurs we will compare the behaviour of the model when the high scent item is in position two (as an example of occurring early in the menu) and in position 12 (as an example of occurring late in the menu) in more detail. In both examples, initially, all 16 menu items are rated equally and all have an R value of 0.06. The relevance values are translated into efficiencies (E) which are then used to determine which of the EAs is most likely to lead to the goal and therefore which EA is executed in each cycle. In the first cycle, the EA that proposes assessing the scent of the first item in the menu is rated as having the highest E value due to it having the lowest cost. Consequently, the model assesses the first item which gets rated as very low scent. As a result, the new R value of this item is set at 0. On the next cycle, the EA that proposes SCENT assessment on the second item in the list is the most efficient (due to the lower cost) so this item gets assessed. This behaviour continues until the model assesses the high scent item.

In menus where the high scent item occurs early on in the menu, the second item in the menu gets an R value of 0.5097 which raises the probability that this item will lead to the goal to 0.6220. On the following cycle the R value of the high scent item leads to an E value of 0.008 while the second best item (an item yet to be assessed) has an R value of 0.06 which results in an E value of 0.006. Although the E values of the two EAs are very similar, one is larger than the other, and this is what determines which EA is chosen.

In our example of a menu where the high scent item occurs later on in the menu, the relevance of each of the low scent items that have already been assessed falls to 0. When the model assesses the twelfth item its R value is 0.5097, which raises the probability that this item will lead to the goal to 0.6220. On the following cycle the R value of the high scent item only has an E value of 0.005 while the item with the best efficiency (an item yet to be assessed) has an R value of 0.05 which results in an E value of 0.006. The result is that the model continues to assess each item in the menu until it reaches the bottom because the efficiency of conducting a SCENT assessment of a new item is greater than the efficiency of conducting the ANTICIPATE assessment on the high scent item in position 12. This has the effect of slowly increasing the probability of the item in position 12 leading to the goal.

The detail of the model explains that the reason the behaviour is different for the two types of menus is because the detail of the mathematics of the rational analysis. Comparisons of the traces of the model with the empirical data suggest that the model provides a good explanation of the cognitive processes involved in this task. This suggests that participants make an assessment of the relevance of a label to the current goal and then, together with the estimated relevance of previous items, choose to either (1) select that item as the one that will lead to the goal, (2) conduct some further assessment of the current item, or (3) move on to another item and assess that. Which of these EAs is chosen is driven by the pattern of information scent that has been experienced so far.

The model provides us with an explanation of how and why the position of the goal and the quality of the distractor items affect the behaviour of the participants on the task. Regardless of the pattern of scent of the menu, the model predicts that the agent will tend to stop exploring the menu as soon as it comes across a menu item that has high information scent (self-terminates) if this is encountered early in the menu. On menus where

there is one high scent item among a set of low scent items and the high scent item occurs later in the menu, the agent continues to assess the other items in the menu before conducting further assessment of the high scent item and finally selecting it. The model enables us to explain why we see these different patterns of behaviour on menus which have such similar patterns of information scent. This is due to the effect of the interdependence of the probability that each of the items will lead to the goal. The actual point on the menu at which the model swaps from one behaviour to the other is sensitive to a number of factors such as the length of the menu and the costs of the EAs. It would appear therefore that it is in the nature of interactive search that there are close calls which suggest that people can rationally do either behaviour and that a number of factors have an effect on the behaviour of participants exploring real menus.

Together the two models described previously provide us with a good understanding of how people perform search tasks on the WWW. SNIF-ACT and the rational model explain different aspects of the interaction: SNIF-ACT demonstrates the higher level, page by page, link following behaviour seen in such tasks, whereas the rational model explains the lower level interactions with just one page. Given information about the information scent of the items on a new Web site both models are able to make predictions about user behaviour on the site.

Modelling Graph Reading

Peebles and Cheng (2003) conducted an experiment, eye movement study and cognitive modelling analysis to investigate the cognitive, perceptual, and motor processes involved in a common graph-reading task using two different types of Cartesian graph. The purpose of the study was to determine how graph users' ability to retrieve information can be affected by presenting the same information in slightly different types of the same class of diagram. The two types of graph, shown in Figure 3, represent amounts of UK oil and gas production over two decades. The only difference between the two graph types is in which variables are represented on the axes and which are plotted. In the *Function* graphs, the *argument* variable (AV: time in years) is represented on the x-axis and the *quantity* variables (QV: oil and gas) on the y-axis whereas in the *Parametric* graphs, the quantity variables are represented on the x and y axes and time is plotted on the curve.

In the experiment, participants were presented with the value of a "given" variable and required to use the graph to find the corresponding value of a "target" variable, for example, "when the value of oil is 2, what is the value of gas?" This type of

Figure 3. Function and parametric graphs used in Peebles and Cheng (2003) depicting values of oil and gas production for each year

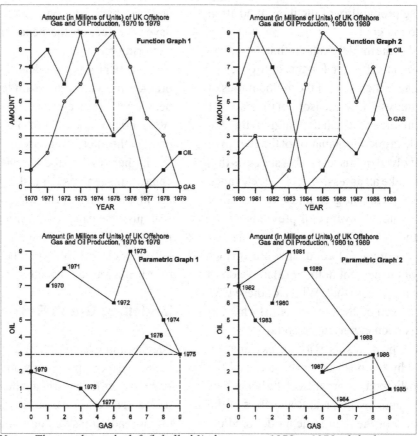

Notes: The graphs on the left (labelled 1) show years 1970 to 1979 while those on the right (labelled 2) show years 1980 to 1989. Dashed lines indicate the optimal scan path required to answer the question, "when the value of oil is 3, what is the value of gas?"

task has typically been analysed in terms of the minimum sequence of saccades and fixations required to reach the location of the given variable's value and then from there to the location of the corresponding value of the target variable (Lohse, 1993; Peebles & Cheng, 2001, 2002; Peebles, Cheng, & Shadbolt, 1999). Experiment participants (some of whom had their eye movements recorded) completed 120 trials, each participant using only one graph type. The 120 questions were coded into three classes (QV–QV, QV–AV, and AV–QV) according to which variable's value was given and which was required (QV denotes a *quantity* variable, oil or gas, and AV denotes the *argument* variable, time). On each trial, a question (e.g., "GAS = 6, OIL = ?") was presented above the graph and participants were required to read the question, find the answer using the graph on the screen and then enter their answer by clicking on a button labelled *Answer* in the top right corner of the window which revealed a circle of buttons containing the digits 0 to 9. RTs were recorded from the onset of a question to the mouse click on the Answer button.

The RT data from the experiment, displayed in Figure 4, showed that the graph used and the type of question asked both had a significant effect on the time it took for participants to retrieve the answer. This was all the more surprising because, for two of the three question types, participants were faster using the less familiar parametric graphs by nearly a second.

The results of the eye movement study were also surprising. It was found that in 63% of trials (irrespective of the graph used or question type being attempted), after having read the question at the start of a trial, participants redirected their visual attention to elements of the question at least once during the process of problem solving with the graph. This was not predicted by the simple minimal fixation sequence account outlined previously but two possible explanations may be provided: (1) participants initially encode the three question elements but are unable to retain all of them in working memory and retrieve them by the time they are required to do so, or (2) to reduce the probability of retrieval failure, participants break the problem into two sections,

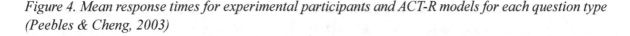

Figure 4. Mean response times for experimental participants and ACT-R models for each question type (Peebles & Cheng, 2003)

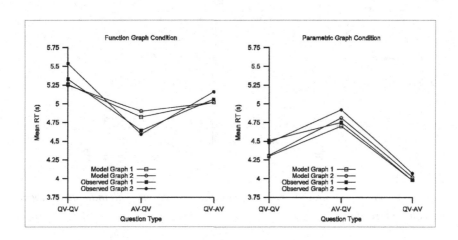

the first allowing them to reach the given location and the second to then proceed to the target location corresponding to the solution.

Peebles and Cheng (2003) constructed two ACT-R models of the experiment (one for each graph type) that were able to interact with an exact replica of the experiment software. The models consisted of a set of productions to carry out the six basic subgoals in the task; (1) read the question; (2) identify the *start location* determined by the given variable; (3) identify the *given location* on the graph representing the given value of given variable; (4) from the given location, identify the *target location* representing the required variable; (5) identify the *target value* at the target location; and (6) enter the answer. Many of the productions were shared by the two models, the main difference between them being the control structure that sequences the execution of the productions. Figure 4 shows that the mean RTs from the parametric

and function graph models are a good fit to the observed data (R^2 = .868, RMSE = 0.123, and R^2 = .664, RMSE = 0.199 respectively). Perhaps more importantly however, were the insights into the observed eye movement data that came from the modelling process itself. When ACT-R focuses attention on an object on the screen, representations of the object and its location are created in the system's visual buffers which can be accessed by productions. Eventually these representations go into declarative memory with initial activation values and, as long as these values are above a certain threshold, they can be retrieved by the cognitive system and replaced in a buffer. However, ACT-R includes a mechanism by which the activation of representations in declarative memory decreases over time which allows it to simulate processes involved in forgetting. These mechanisms played a crucial role in the ACT-R models' ability to capture the eye movement data

Figure 5. Screen shots showing an experimental participant's eye movement data (left) and the ACT-R model's visual attention scan path (right) for the QV–QV question "oil = 6, gas = ?" using the 1980's parametric graph

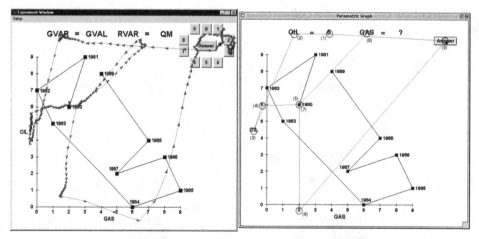

Note: In the model screen shot, numbered circles on the scan path indicate the location and sequence of fixations.

observed in the experiment. At the start of each trial, the models read the three question elements and during the problem solving these elements are placed in declarative memory. As a consequence, at least one question element must be retrieved from memory at each stage of the problem in order to continue. However, as soon as a question element is placed in declarative memory its activation starts to decay and, as a consequence, the probability that it cannot be retrieved increases. Typically, if a retrieval failure occurs, an ACT-R model will halt as it does not have the appropriate information to solve the problem. During the process of model development it was found that on a significant proportion of trials the model was not able to retrieve question elements at the later stages of the trial because their activation had fallen below the retrieval threshold. As a consequence new productions had to be added to allow the model to redirect attention to the question in order to re-encode the element and then return to solving the problem. This was precisely the behaviour observed in the eye movement study. This is illustrated in Figure 5 which compares screen shots of the model scan path and eye movements recorded from one participant for the same question using the 1980's parametric graph. The numbered circles on the model screen shot indicate the sequence of fixations produced by the model. The pattern of fixations in both screenshots is remarkably similar.

Modelling Icon Search

Fleetwood and Byrne's study of icon search (2002, in press) is a another demonstration of how an ACT-R cognitive model can provide a detailed account of the cognitive and perceptual processes involved in a common HCI task that closely matches people's response times (RTs) and patterns of eye movements. Fleetwood and Byrne's model differs from that of Peebles and Cheng (2003) in that it incorporates eye movements and movement of attention (EMMA) (Salvucci, 2001),

a computational model of the relationship between eye movements and visual attention. EMMA can be easily integrated into the ACT-R architecture, allowing models to make more detailed predictions of actual eye movements, rather than simple shifts of visual attention.

One of the main aims of Fleetwood and Byrne's research is to investigate the notion of icon "quality" (defined in terms of an icon's distinctiveness and visual complexity) and to examine the effect that differences in quality may have on identification performance. They created three classes of icon (examples of which are shown in Figure 6). "Good" quality icons were designed to be easily distinguishable from others based on the primitive features of colour and shape. All icons in this set were a combination of one colour (from six) and one shape (from two).

In contrast, "poor" quality icons were designed to be distinguishable only by a relatively careful inspection but to be relatively indistinguishable in a large distractor set. These poor quality icons were all of the same basic shape and colour (a combination of black, white, and shades of grey). An intermediate class of "fair" quality icons was also designed with shapes more distinctive than the poor quality icons but more complex than the good quality icons, and with the same range of greyscale colours as the poor quality icons. The

Figure 6. Examples of icons of good, fair, and poor quality used in the experiment of Fleetwood and Byrne (in press)

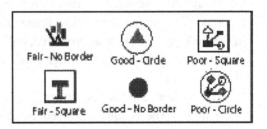

main effect of the manipulation was to produce a different similarity structure for each class of icons. Good quality icons could be identified as a single combination of features, for example, "yellow triangle." In contrast, fair quality icons were defined by more than one combination of features (typically three, for example: "grey rectangle; black square; black diagonal-right"), some of which were shared with other icons. In the poor quality group, icons were defined by an average of four feature combinations and many more of these were shared by several other icons in the group. From the visual search literature, it can be predicted that search time will increase as icon distinctiveness decreases. An additional factor in Fleetwood and Byrne's (2006) study also known to affect search time (at least for certain stimuli) is the number of distractors in the display, with search time increasing with the number of distractors in the search set. In their experiment, Fleetwood and Byrne had search sets of 6, 12, 18 and 24 icons.

In the experiment, participants were required to find, as rapidly as possible, different quality target icons in search sets of differing sizes. On each trial, a target icon and file name were presented followed 1500 ms later by a button labelled *Ready* for the participant to click when he/she felt ready to continue. When this button was clicked, the target icon was replaced by the search set and the participant had simply to look for the target icon and click on it as quickly as possible; when an icon was clicked upon, the next trial started. Participants completed a total of 144 trials, involving all levels of the search set and icon quality variables, and on each trial the participant's RT (the duration between clicks on the Ready button and an icon in the search set) was recorded. The results of the experiment (shown in Figure 7) revealed that, as predicted, both icon quality and search set size had a significant effect on search time.

To provide an explanation of their data, Fleetwood and Byrne (2006) produced an ACT-R

model of the task that was able to interact with the same experiment software as the participants. As described previously, each experiment trial is comprised of two stages, the first where the target icon and its file name are encoded and the second in which it is sought. The model has a set of seven productions to carry out the first stage: (1) locate the target icon and (2) encode an attribute pair (e.g., "grey rectangle"), (3) look below the icon and (4) encode the associated file name, and finally (5) locate and (6) click on the "Ready" button. In the second stage, the model locates and attends to an icon with the previously encoded target feature and then shifts visual attention to the file name below it. If the file name matches the target file name, visual attention is returned to the icon and the mouse clicks on it. If the file name is not the target, however, the model continues the search by locating another icon at random with the same target features. This sequence of events requires four productions and takes 285 ms to complete.

Figure 7 reveals a close correspondence between the mean RTs produced by the model and those of the experiment participants ($R^2 = .98$, RMSE = 126ms) and shows that an ACT-R model based on the similarity structure of the search set and the strategy of identifying a single combination of features and random search can provide a reasonable account of the data. However, Byrne, Anderson, Douglass, and Matessa (1999) had shown in an earlier study of visual search in a menu selection task that alternative strategies can produce similar aggregate RTs, necessitating the incorporation of eye movement data to add further constraints on the proposed theory. As a result, Fleetwood and Byrne (2006) carried out an eye movement study to test their model further and found two major discrepancies between the observed eye movements and the patterns of visual attention produced by their model. First, they found that, although the model successfully reproduced the patterns of visual attention across the icon quality and set size conditions, for all conditions the number of saccades per trial pro-

Figure 7. Response time by set size and icon quality for Fleetwood and Byrne's (in press) revised model and the experiment data

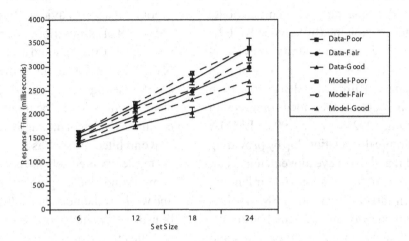

Figure 8. Mean number of shifts of visual attention per trial made by Fleetwood and Byrne's (in press) revised model relative to the mean number of gazes per trial made by participants

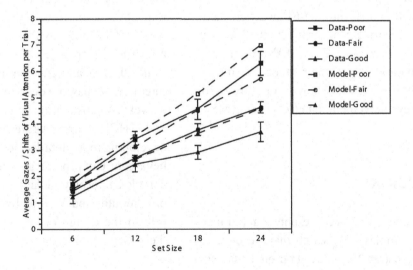

duced by the model was significantly greater than those recorded in the experiment. Second, when analysing the eye movement data, Fleetwood and Byrne found that patterns of icon search were not random as their model predicted, but were systematic, in the sense that participants sought to minimise the distance between successive fixations, typically looking at target icons closest to their current fixation point. This produced a search pattern that revealed a systematic scanning of areas of the display.

Both of the discrepancies between the model and human data are explained by Salvucci's (2001) EMMA model. It is been demonstrated previously that the relationship between eye movements and visual attention is not direct, and that people often do not move their eyes to their focus of attention (e.g., Henderson, 1992; Rayner, 1995). EMMA attempts to capture this relationship by providing an account of if and when eye movements occur, and if they do occur, the location of their landing relative to their targets. Integrating EMMA into ACT-R allows models to simulate actual eye movements rather than just visual attention shifts and provides a more realistic output to be compared with human eye movement data. In addition, EMMA predicts that efficient search strategies minimise average saccade distance, resulting in search patterns in which objects nearest to the current fixation point are examined soonest.

Fleetwood and Byrne (2006) modified their model's search strategy according to the EMMA account and incorporated EMMA's eye movement computations into their model, resulting in a greatly improved fit (shown in Figure 8) to the human eye movement data ($R^2 = .99$, RMSE $= 0.58$).

CONCLUSION

In this chapter we have presented a number of recent examples of research that we believe clearly demonstrate the value of rational analysis and cognitive modelling in the study of complex interactive behaviour. Such tasks typically involve the complex interaction of three elements: (1) the perceptual and cognitive abilities of the user; (2) the visual and statistical properties of the task environment; and (3) the specific requirements of the task being carried out. The use of rational analysis and an embodied cognitive architecture such as ACT-R allows all three of these elements to be brought together in an integrated theoretical account of user behaviour. Rational analysis provides a set of assumptions and methods that allow researchers to understand user behaviour in terms of the statistical structure of the task environment and the user's goal of optimising (i.e., reducing the cost/benefit ratio of) the interaction. Developing cognitive models of interactive behaviour in a cognitive architecture such as ACT-R allows researchers to specify precisely the cognitive factors (e.g., domain knowledge, problem-solving strategies, and working memory capacity) involved. In addition, the recent incorporation of perceptual-motor modules to cognitive architectures allows them to make predictions about users' eye movements during the entire performance of the task, which can be compared to observed eye movement data — a highly stringent test of the sufficiency and efficacy of a model. The use of these methods has increased rapidly over the last 5 years, as has the range of task interfaces being studied. Although we are still a long way from achieving the goal of an artificial user that can be applied "off the shelf" to novel tasks and environments, the models of interactive behaviour described here demonstrate a level of sophistication and rigour still relatively rare in HCI research. As these examples illustrate, developing more detailed accounts of interactive behaviour can provide genuine insights into the complex interplay of factors that affect the use of computer and Web technologies, which may inform the design of systems more adapted to their users.

NOTE

All correspondence to: David Peebles, Department of Behavioural Sciences, University of Huddersfield, Queensgate, Huddersfield, HD1 3DH, UK; D.Peebles@hud.ac.uk.

REFERENCES

Anderson, J. R. (1990). *The adaptive character of thought*. Hillsdale, NJ: Lawrence Erlbaum Associates.

Anderson, J. R., Bothell, D., Byrne, M. D., Douglass, S., Lebiere, C., & Qin, Y. (2004). An integrated theory of the mind. *Psychological Review, 111*(4), 1036-1060.

Anderson, J. R., & Lebiere, C. (1998). *The atomic components of thought*. Mahwah, NJ: Lawrence Erlbaum Associates.

Brumby, D. P., & Howes, A. (2004, July 30-August 1). Good enough but I'll just check: Web-page search as attentional refocusing. In *Proceedings of the 6th International Conference on Cognitive Modelling*, Pittsburgh, PA.

Byrne, M. D. (2001). ACT-R/PM and menu selection: Applying a cognitive architecture to HCI. *International Journal of Human-Computer Studies, 55*, 41-84.

Byrne, M. D., & Anderson, J. R. (1998). Perception and action. In J. R. Anderson & C. Lebiere (Eds.), *The atomic components of thought*, (pp. 167-200). Mahwah, NJ: Lawrence Erlbaum Associates.

Byrne, M. D., Anderson, J. R., Douglass, S., & Matessa, M. (1999). Eye tracking the visual search of click-down menus. In *Proceedings of the ACM CHI'99 Conference on Human Factors in Computing Systems* (pp. 402-409). New York: ACM.

Card, S. K., Moran, T. P., & Newell, A. (1983). *The psychology of human-computer interaction*. Hillsdale, NJ: Erlbaum.

Chong, R. S., & Laird, J. E. (1997). Identifying dual-task executive process knowledge using EPIC-Soar. In *Proceedings of the 19th Annual Conference of the Cognitive Science Society* (pp. 107-112). Mahwah, NJ: Lawrence Erlbaum Associates.

Cox, A. L., & Young, R. M. (2004). A rational model of the effect of information scent on the exploration of menus. In *Proceedings of 6th International Conference on Cognitive Modeling: Integrating Models*, (pp. 82-86). Mahwah, NJ: Lawrence Erlbaum Associates.

Fitts, P. M. (1954). The information capacity of the human motor systems in controlling the amplitude of movement. *Journal of Experimental Psychology, 47*, 381-391.

Fleetwood, M. D., & Byrne, M. D. (2002). Modeling icon search in ACT-R/PM. *Cognitive Systems Research, 3*, 25-33.

Fleetwood, M. D., & Byrne, M. D. (2006). Modeling the visual search of displays: A revised ACT-R/PM model of icon search based on eye tracking data. *Human Computer Interaction, 21*, 153-197.

Henderson, J. M. (1992). Visual attention and eye movement control during reading and picture viewing. In K. Rayner (Ed.), *Eye movements and visual cognition: Scene perception and reading*, (pp. 261-283). New York: Springer-Verlag.

John, B. E., & Kieras, D. E. (1994). *The GOMS family of analysis techniques: Tools for design and evaluation* (Tech. Rep. No. CMUHCII94106). Pittsburgh, PA: Carnegie Mellon University, Human-Computer Interaction Institute.

Kieras, D. E., & Meyer, D. E. (1997). An overview of the EPIC architecture for cognition and performance with application to human-computer interaction. *Human-Computer Interaction, 12*, 391-438.

Laird, J. E., Newell, A., & Rosenbloom, P. S. (1987). SOAR: An architecture for general intelligence. *Artificial Intelligence, 33*, 1-64.

Lohse, G. L. (1993). A cognitive model for understanding graphical perception. *Human-Computer Interaction, 8*, 353-388.

Neth, H., Sims, C. R., Veksler, V. D., & Gray, W. D. (2004). You can't play straight TRACS and win: Memory updates in a dynamic task environment. In K. D. Forbus, D. Gentner, & T. Regier (Eds.), *Proceedings of the 26th Annual Meeting of the Cognitive Science Society* (pp. 1017-1022). Hillsdale, NJ: Lawrence Erlbaum Associates.

Newell, A. (1990) *Unified theories of cognition*. Cambridge, MA: Harvard University Press.

Oaksford, M., & Chater, N. (Eds.). (1998). *Rational models of cognition*. UK: Oxford University Press.

Olson, J. S., & Olson, G. M. (1990). The growth of cognitive modeling in human-computer interaction since GOMS. *Human Computer Interaction, 5*, 221-265.

Peebles, D., & Cheng, P. C.-H. (2001). Graph-based reasoning: From task analysis to cognitive explanation. In *Proceedings of the 23rd Annual Conference of the Cognitive Science Society* (pp. 762-767). Mahwah, NJ: Lawrence Erlbaum Associates.

Peebles, D., & Cheng, P. C.-H. (2002). Extending task analytic models of graph-based reasoning: A cognitive model of problem solving with Cartesian graphs in ACT-R/PM. *Cognitive Systems Research, 3*, 77-86.

Peebles, D., & Cheng, P. C.-H. (2003). Modeling the effect of task and graphical representation on response latency in a graph reading task. *Human Factors, 45*, 28-46.

Peebles, D., Cheng, P. C.-H., & Shadbolt, N. (1999). Multiple processes in graph-based reasoning. In *Proceedings of the 21st Annual Conference of the Cognitive Science Society* (pp. 531-536). Mahwah, NJ: Lawrence Erlbaum Associates.

Pirolli, P. (2005) Rational analyses of information foraging on the Web. *Cognitive Science, 29*, 343-374.

Pirolli, P. L., & Card, S. K. (1999). Information foraging. *Psychological Review, 106*(4), 643-675.

Pirolli, P., & Fu, W.-T. (2003, June 22-26). *SNIF-ACT: A model of information foraging on the World Wide Web*. Paper presented at the Ninth International Conference on User Modeling, Johnstown, PA.

Rayner, K. (1995). Eye movements and cognitive processes in reading, visual search, and scene perception. In J. M. Findlay, R. Walker, & R. W. Kentridge (Eds.), *Eye movement research: Mechanisms, processes, and applications*, (pp. 3-22). New York: Elsevier.

Ritter, F. E., Baxter, G. D., Jones, G., & Young, R. M. (2000). Supporting cognitive models as users. *ACM Transactions on Computer-Human Interaction, 7*, 141-173.

Salvucci, D. D. (2001). An integrated model of eye movements and visual encoding. *Cognitive Systems Research, 1*(4), 201-220.

Salvucci, D. D., & Macuga, K. L. (2002). Predicting the effects of cellular-phone dialling on driver performance. *Cognitive Systems Research, 3*, 95-102.

Silva, M., & Cox, A. L. (2005, August 31-September 2) *Eye-movement behaviour in interactive menu search: Evidence for rational analysis*. Paper presented at the BPS Cognitive Section Conference 2005, University of Leeds.

St. Amant, R., Horton, T. E., & Ritter F. E. (2004). Model-based evaluation of cell phone menu interaction. In *Proceedings of the CHI'04 Conference on Human Factors in Computer Systems* (pp. 343-350). New York: ACM.

Young, R. M. (1998). Rational analysis of exploratory choice. In M. Oaksford & N. Chater (Eds.), *Rational models of cognition* (pp. 469-500). UK: Oxford University Press.

Young, R. M., Green, T. R. G., & Simon, T. (1989). Programmable user models for predictive evaluation of interface designs. In *Proceedings of CHI* '89: *Human Factors in Computing Systems* (pp. 15-19). AMC Press.

Section IV
Utilization and Application

Chapter XIV
A De–Construction of Wireless Device Usage

Mary R. Lind
North Carolina A&T State University, USA

ABSTRACT

In this article, wireless technology use is addressed with a focus on the factors that underlie wireless interaction. A de-construction of the information processing theories of user/technology interaction is presented. While commercial and useful applications of wireless devices are numerous, wireless interaction is emerging as a means of social interaction—an extension of the user's personal image—and as an object of amusement and play. The technology/user interaction theories that have driven the discussions of computer assisted communication media are information richness, communicative action, and social influence modeling. This article will extend this theoretical view of wireless devices by using flow theory to address elements of fun, control, and focus. Then, these technology/user interaction theories are used with respect to wireless devices to propose areas for future research.

INTRODUCTION

Within the United States, wireless devices have become ubiquitous communication devices. Yet, in Europe and the Far East, these devices are not only widely used as communication devices, but as vehicles of commerce and of entertainment. It is widely known that the GSM telecommunications standard is not fully implemented in the United States, inhibiting the development of wireless applications by firms to support their mobile customers. Yet, there seems to be more to this than telecommunication standards. This article will examine social behavioral issues that affect wireless usage and propose a model to better understand this usage.

Wireless devices, serving as transmitters of information at a reasonable cost from point to point without being tethered to a wired line, are profoundly impacting how we communicate and perform work (Rudy, 1996). Little research exists on how to design wireless technologies to better support wireless communications and applications (Te'eni et al., 2001). Research on information technology design finds that the technology should be fit to the user's task needs (Senn, 1998, Swanson, 1988). Since wireless devices provide a tool for convergence of voice, text, audio, photos, videos, and data (Yager, 2003), it is critical that the design of these wireless devices fits the multiple modes of data exchange and usage supported by the wireless devices.

Models to explain information technology design and adoption are rooted in the assumptions of the usefulness and usability afforded by the technology (Davis, 1989, Swanson, 1988), where the context for these technology design and adoption models is the workplace. As information technologies have become pervasive throughout the culture (Gaver, 2005), these technologies, while still an instrument to perform work more efficiently, have become a means of social networking, diversion, and entertainment for the homo luden (Huizinga, 1950). Yet along with this play aspect, the homo luden also gains control of his/her personal space. These aspects of mobile information technologies, usefulness, usability, play, and control will be explored in this article to determine how these dimensions of mobile information technology interaction can enable flow (Csikszentmihalyi, 1975) and enable homo ludens (Huizinga, 1950) to seamlessly process information for work and for play. Huizinga (1950) notes that play influences the culture of the players as well as Gaver (2005) observes that pervasive, "ambient" technologies also shape the culture in which the technologies are used. In this article, the discussion focuses on the use of these wireless technologies that have become artifacts representative of work, social, and play activities in our everyday cultural contexts, and how these same cultural contexts, in turn, are shaped by the wireless artifacts, and through this interaction, the enactment of additional uses for the wireless devices.

THEORETICAL FOUNDATION FOR WIRELESS MEDIA USAGE

Two theoretical approaches will be examined. First, the view of wireless devices as communication media based in information richness theory is presented, followed by the theoretical view of wireless devices using the social networking theory perspective. Secondly, wireless media will be addressed as objects of play and of control. Finally, a model is developed showing the bidirectional impact of wireless devices as artifacts that influence culture and the resulting culture that in turn impacts perceptions of the wireless artifacts.

Media Richness Theory

The rational choice model contends that users select the most effective medium for data exchange. Media richness theory (Daft & Lengel, 1984; Lind & Zmud, 1991) proposed that managers will use richer media in ambiguous contexts and the leaner media for more structured tasks. For example, face-to-face media that permit the transmission of nonverbal clues and immediate feedback will be used in contexts that are unclear and need to be sorted through in order to reduce the ambiguity of the context. In information richness theory (Daft & Macintosh, 1981; Daft & Weick, 1984; Daft & Lengel, 1984), it was proposed that communication channels vary in their ability to convey information and meaning. This theory suggests a continuum where the richest channels are those that provide for more face-to-face interaction and feedback, allowing for the communication of nuances, often unspoken, in adding meaning to communication. The leanest channels are those written or printed. Since research into information richness theory has met with conflicting results, especially in the area of e-mail studies, other theories and theory extensions have been explored. Neither voice mail nor e-mail allow for face-to-face interaction, but voice mail records the actual voice of the speaker while e-mail provides much quicker feedback than printed media. Thus, the underlying media richness theory is the assumption that individuals seek to be efficient communicators and make rational decisions, selecting a communication medium that fits the nature of the information being communicated.

Other theories have addressed the use of media as a social construct (El-Shinnawy & Markus, 1997). Using the social influence model of technology use, Fulk, Schmitz, and Steinfield (1990) proposed that perceptions of communication media, such as richness, are socially constructed. They found that individuals were more influenced in communication channel use and perceptions by their co-workers than by their supervisors. Also, they found that keyboard skill and computer experience were important predictors of perceptions of electronic mail richness. The communication medium became viewed as an artifact that reflects the social circumstances of the communicating partners that in turn impacts the social context for their social network, thus becoming an influence on the culture of that social group.

Ngwenyama and Lee (1997) proposed a critical social theory perspective for communication channel richness using the work of Weick (1969) and Habermas (1984), they posit that the richness of a communication channel is determined by how the person using that channel enacts the channel. Thus, critical social theory advocates the notion that the interpretation of the information conveyed through a channel is in the mind of the receiver. Some may filter complex, rich information and seek to simplify it to fit their simplistic view of the organization. While others may embrace complex, rich information and revel in trying to interpret the many dimensions of often ambiguous but rich information. It cannot be assumed that greater usage means a richer channel. It may just mean that the channel is more accessible or easier to use for short messages than the telephone or

face-to-face media. Thus, critical social theory shows that the enactment of the communication artifact is determined by that individual's context and the individual's perception of that context and as the use of the communication artifact becomes widespread then the culture will develop shared perceptions of its attributes, which can then have a broad impact on the culture.

Communicative Action Theory

The object of most communication is to convey information so that the communicating partners reach a mutual understanding, regarding the topic at hand. Habermas (1984), in his theory of communicative action, addresses the concept of communicative rationality, where a mutual understanding is reached through processes that signal commonalities in culture that promote understanding. Thus, the goal of communication is to reach a common understanding between the communicating parties. However, according to Habermas, different cultural groups may interpret different signals for enacting this mutual understanding. Hence, channel richness for one such group may differ from another group. Thus, communication action theory recognizes that the media are enacted differently in different cultural contexts, but the rational goal is to achieve a common understanding using the medium for communication.

Communication Channel Enactment

Addressing this issue of enacted meaning, Carlson and Zmud (1992) proposed communication channel extension theory and showed that one's past communication experiences, both in terms of the communication channels and the person with whom one is communicating via the channel, will in turn shape one's perception of a communication channel. Thus, different levels of experience with a computer mediated channel in an organizational context will shape one's perceptions, and use of such computer mediated channels, just as one's past experiences in engaging in face-to-face communication will influence face-to-face communication. This view of channel enactment then shows the circular impact of the channel on the communication content, within a cultural context where the perceptions of the communication partners influence future expectations of that channel.

Flow Theory

A different explanation has been proposed with little relationship to richness theory—flow theory (Trevino & Webster, 1992; Ghani & Deshpande, 1994). In flow theory, the channel is enacted as an article of amusement. Flow theory (Csikszentmihalyi, 1975; Miller, 1973) suggests that a flow state is a playful, exploratory experience where flow is a continuous variable from none to intense. Thus, some communication channels, particularly the computer mediated ones, may enact such playful behavior. Trevino and Webster (1992) proposed that, through flow, the individual has a sense of control of the interaction and thus finds it more interesting. This seems particularly true as the communication medium becomes a tool of commerce and work activity. Thus, control of the interaction engages the attention of the person using that medium. Csikszentmihalyi (1990, p. 4) developed the theory of optimal flow as, "the state in which people are so intensely involved in an activity that nothing else seems to matter; the experience itself is so enjoyable that people will do it even at great cost, for the sheer sake of doing it." Here, the context, rather than individual differences, is used to explain human motivation (Maehr, 1989; Weiner, 1990), and the focus is on the total concentration on an activity and the enjoyment resulting from that activity (Ghani, 1991; Malone & Lepper, 1987). Wireless devices serve as artifacts of communication and entertainment for many. When not talking on the

wireless device, people are observed looking at the screen for text messages, browsing the Web, playing games, and so forth. These artifacts of our culture have become a source of time absorption for many, as they wait for the next meeting or walk to their destinations.

Further, Csikszentmihalyi (1990, p. 25) characterized flow theory as, "A phenomenological model of consciousness based on information theory." Consciousness deals with the flow ordering of information regarding intended actions and goals (Parr and Montgomery, 1998). One of the dimensions of flow is the challenge of the experience (Ghani and Deshpande, 1994). Csikszentmihalyi (1990, p. 3) said, "The best moments usually occur when a person's body or mind is stretched to its limits in a voluntary effort to accomplish something difficult or worthwhile." Ghani and Deshpande (1994) state that a second dimension of flow is control by the users. Csikszentmihalyi (1994, p. 3) states, "We have all experienced times when, instead of being buffeted by anonymous forces, we do feel in control of our actions (on such occasions) we feel a sense of exhilaration, a deep sense of enjoyment." Turkle (1984) discussed how a computer user may work because of the fun of the interaction, not necessarily to achieve a specific goal. In flow, Csikszentmihalyi (1990) discussed how a person loses their sense of time. So flow enables a person to process information best when the effort expended by the individual is within that individual's control and when the challenge of the experience meets the skills of the person. The interaction with the wireless artifact must match the skill level of the user. The communication and Web browsing aspect of these wireless artifacts are compatible with already learned skills, using wireless artifacts for other activities, such as entertainment or games, requires skills interaction that match those the user will have to insure concentration on the activity. In any case, the control of the wireless artifact is in the hands of the user where this accessibility encourages increased usage.

Psychic-entropy is a counter force to flow in which there is disorder in consciousness. This occurs whenever, "Information…conflicts with extreme intentions or distracts us–from carrying them out." (Csikszentmihalyi, 1990, p. 36) Anxiety, fear, jealousy, or rage describes disordered experiences. Entropy drains our psychic energy, fragmenting attention. Attention is the process for collecting, storing, and retrieving information. Flow is an experience in which attention is freely invested in the accomplishment of goals allowing the self to develop, increasing complexity (Csikszentmihalyi, 1990). The control afforded by the wireless artifact helps to counter the force of psychic-entropy, giving the user more control over their environment (communication, schedules, messaging), where adjustments can be made in schedules easily, without the user being tethered to land based devices. Parr and Montgomery (1998, p. 27) state "Flow experiences have been characterized as the following, merging of action and awareness; centering of attention on a limited stimulus field; letting go of self-consciousness (transcendence of ego); a feeling of competence and control; having unambiguous goals and receiving immediate, specific feedback; and being intrinsically motivated." Thus, this aspect of flow looks for balance between one's goals and one's skills in achieving those goals. Flow is more closely associated with positive emotions, greater concentration, and a greater sense of control. A person must see that there is something worthwhile to do and that he/she has the ability to do it (Csikszentmihalyi, 1990). As one increases his/her skill level, she/he is motivated to seek out increasingly challenging activities (Mandigo & Thompson, 1998). Csikszentmihalyi (1990) indicates that the flow state is so enjoyable that the participant will want to continue with the activity for the sake of participation.

The communication, enabled by the wireless artifacts, creates a sense of flow for the wireless communities. These communities can achieve collaborative action (Crane, 1972) using the wirelessly connected communities. The wireless communities are not bounded by space and can connect easily to take action so that the communities are empowered by the collective strength and ability to influence actions in their space. So another aspect of flow enabled by the wireless artifacts is control over collective action.

Flow is about optimizing the happiness that occurs from the everyday immersion in life's activities, "It is by being fully involved with every detail of our lives whether good or bad, that we find happiness, not by trying to look for it directly." (Csikszentmihalyi, 1990, p. 2) A key component to the flow experience is participation or active involvement in something. It comes when an individual is participating in an activity that makes a difference in the person's life. "The concept of flow—the state in which people are so involved in an activity that nothing else seems to matter; the experience itself is so enjoyable that people will do it even at great cost, for the sheer sake of doing it." (Csikszentmihalyi, 1990, p. 4) This connectedness to communities can become an absorbing aspect of the wireless artifact. Yet paradoxically, the wireless artifact absorption can be with music, games, or Internet browsing afforded by the wireless artifact, which is largely a nonsocial activity. However, games are increasingly played via online networks, creating online gaming communities.

Much of the experience of finding flow is about order and goals. "When goals are clear, feedback relevant, and challenges and skills are in balance, attention becomes ordered and fully invested." (Csikszentmihalyi, 1990, p. 31) Here, a defining factor within a flow experience is the ability to recognize and accept clear boundaries in terms of the goals and acceptable behavior. This means that a flow activity must be ordered to some extent by conforming to cultural or social boundaries. "Athletes, mystics, and artists do very different things when they reach flow, yet their descriptions of the experience are remarkably similar." (Csikszentmihalyi, 1997b, p. 29) Although one person's experience with flow may be solitary and pertain simply to their specific circumstances, chances are that the flow is experienced as a member of a social network.

Therefore, within any given flow experience and particularly with usage of the wireless artifact, it is important to pinpoint the organizational frameworks or structural boundaries to which the participants adhere. It is within this willing submission to structural boundaries that highlights an important dimension for understanding the flow experience. What needs do these boundaries fulfill? And if the flow experience is a group activity, how is this mutual submission to ordered rules enhancing the flow experience and leading paradoxically to a freer, happier existence? Submission to overarching rules is found often within games, sports, social networks, and organizations. Membership in these groups brings meaning to its members, whereby meaning is imbued in the artifacts that provide the linkages for these groups. It is through these wireless artifacts, and the resulting linkages within the communities,

that trust in the social network develops. While the wireless devices enable multiple modes of communication between and within the communities, their interactions can be shared using common codes and symbols in text messaging and in gaming communities.

Csikszentmihalyi lays out three main qualities of a flow experience. These are: first, when there is a clear set of goals; second, when immediate feedback is provided; and third when all of a person's skills are being used to overcome challenges. (Csikszentmihalyi, 1997b, p. 29-30)

Because of the total demand on psychic energy, a person in flow is completely focused. There is no space in consciousness for distracting thoughts, irrelevant feelings. Self-consciousness disappears, yet one feels stronger than usual. The sense of time is distorted: hours seem to pass by in minutes. When a person's entire being is stretched in the full functioning of body and mind, whatever one does becomes worth doing for its own sake; living becomes its own justification. In the harmonious

Figure 1. Wireless artifact

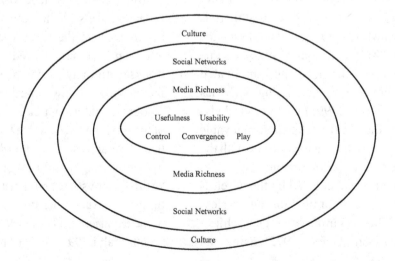

focusing of physical and psychic energy, life finally comes into its own. (Csikszentmihalyi , 1997b, p. 31-32)

It seems that, during the flow experience, the participant is able to forget about any larger problem and completely focus for the span of time while they are completing their activity. Absorption with games, online chats, blogging, and so forth, all provide clear rules and immediate feedback. In the context where the user's skills match the demands of the interface, the result can be total immersion.

From this discussion of the development of the theory for communications technology interaction and specifically wireless devices based in media richness theory and social network theory, the concept of flow was introduced, providing a multilayer perspective on wireless artifacts. So, in addition to the convergence achieved via the communication media, the media also engage the user by providing means for play and for control over, not only the play and communications activities enabled by the wireless device, but work activities as well. An assumption built into these wireless devices is that they are both useful and useable. The theoretical layers of wireless devices discussed in this section are shown in Figure 1.

Culture and Phratria—Wireless Artifact Interaction

Shiller (1979, p. 29) defines culture as a way of life in which our life's activities shape our culture. As technologies are adopted within society, these technologies shape our culture. For example, Tomlinson (1991) states, "The relationship implied in this is the constant mediation of one aspect of culture experienced by another: what we make of a television programme or a novel or a newspaper article is constantly influenced and shaped by whatever else is going on in our lives. But, equally, our lives are lived as representations to ourselves in terms of the representations present in our culture." Thus, the wireless technologies as artifacts enable communication, play, scheduling tasks, information search, and so forth, but the artifact itself shapes the culture and the expectations of those in the culture using these wireless devices. Huizinga (1950, p. 12) observed that play affects culture, "It would be rash to explain all the associations which the anthropologist calls "phratria"—for example, clans, brotherhoods, and so forth—simply as play-communities. Nevertheless, it has been shown again and again how difficult it is to draw the line between, on the one hand, permanent social groupings—particularly

Figure 2. Model of wireless usage

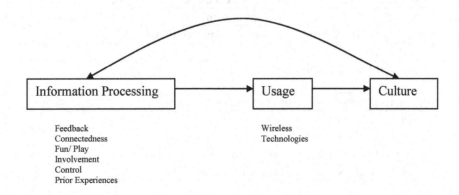

in archaic cultures with their extremely important, solemn, indeed sacred customs—and the sphere of play on the other." As discussed, these wireless artifacts enable social groupings. In some contexts, these phratria are for work purposes, but in many contexts, these groupings are social and for pleasure. Thus, the play is evidenced in the form of the type of phratia as well as the type of diversion, such as games or Internet browsing enabled by wireless devices.

Thus, flow applications are those that accomplish a repetitive activity, but do it in a way that makes doing the activity enjoyable, almost effortless with security. Flow applications blend

in with our daily lives, causing little disruption. As the widely accepted technology acceptance model (TAM) has shown (Davis, 1989), the user must perceive both usefulness and ease of use, while the flow model adds the dimensions of enjoyment and control. Table 1 shows the items for assessing usefulness and ease of use. Added to the TAM dimensions are the proposed flow dimensions of enjoyment and control.

Davis (1989) showed that task usefulness and ease of use of the technology are key components of technology acceptance. In flow theory, it is advocated that technology enables a carefree approach to doing a task that is effortless and

Table 1. Technology acceptance model and flow

Usefulness
Using technology x enabled me to accomplish tasks more quickly.
Using technology x improved my task performance.
Using technology x increased my task productivity.
Using technology x enhanced my effectiveness while performing the task.
Using technology x made it easier to do my task.
Technology x is useful in my task.
Ease of Use
Learning to use technology x is easy for me.
I find it easy to get technology x to do what I want to do.
My interaction with technology x is clear and understandable.
I find technology x flexible to interact with.
It is easy for me to become skillful at using technology x.
I find technology x easy to use.
Proposed Flow Dimenstion
Using technology x was a fun experience for me.
While using technology x I felt in control.
Using technology x gave me more control over my work activities.
Using technology x was a challenge that used my skills.
Using technology x was a pleasant adventure.

fun, while enabling greater control. Two other factors affecting use of a specific communication channel are accessibility of the channel (Zmud, Lind, & Young, 1991) and the degree to which the channel affords rapid feedback (Zmud, Lind, & Young, 1991). Few things are more accessible than a wireless device that can be carried in a person's pocket and these devices enable rapid feedback. So, the richness dimension of feedback, identified by Zmud et al. (1991), is an inherent factor discussed by Csikszentmihalyi (1997a) in flow theory.

FURTHER RESEARCH NEEDED

To move beyond using the devices as voice communication devices, applications that enable the dimension of flow are needed. These are applications for the user that enable them to carry out routine activities easily and with a great degree of control and applications that enable the connectedness with phatria. These applications will enable rich transaction exchanges within the phatria, whether the exchange is for social networking, collaborative action, gaming, or for mobile commerce. Applications enable the flow immersion, giving the user control over work activities and play activities. These applications should provide seamless intergration as the user moves from the work space to the play space to the social network space.

From a broad communication perspective, it has been shown that there are systematic differences in communication by gender. Women have a tendency to work harder at maintaining conversation in face to face situations (Fishman, 1983; Meyers et al., 1997). It has been shown that women value connection and cooperation more than men (Meyers et al., 1997), suggesting that this tendency to maintain the conversation level is evidence of insecurity. Both Allen and Griffeth (1977) and Gefen and Straub (1997) have examined the relationship between gender and

information processing. Allen and Griffeth (1997), counter to their hypothesis, found that women did not experience information under load as compared to their male coworkers in a study of 666 workers at a Midwestern telephone company. In the study, roughly 40% were female and about half the workers were hourly employees. Gefen and Straub (1997) found that women perceived electronic mail differently, but in practice, did not use it differently in a study of 392 respondents with three different airlines in three countries. The Gefen and Straub (1997) study showed that the women respondents perceived e-mail to be of higher social presence and more useful than men; however, these same women did not find e-mail easier to use than men and did not, in fact, make greater use of e-mail when measured through self report. Research is needed to determine if gender differences exist in wireless media use.

Certainly gender, culture, and age differences may influence acceptance of wireless media. Examination of these factors, in terms of the expanded TAM model, is needed. Is the greater acceptance of wireless media in Europe and Asia due to technological or cultural factors? Looking at the applications that drive usage of these wireless media, applications are needed that not only simplify work transactions, but are fun to use and not labor intensive in terms of data entry. A new paradigm for wireless applications may be instrumental in promoting flow. A paradigm that recognizes the need for work, play, and control by the user, which in turn, can change the culture of work and play, which through the interconnectedness of the phatria, leads to new uses in terms of work, play, and control for these wireless devices.

REFERENCES

Allen, D. W., & Griffeth, R. W. (1997). Vertical and lateral information processing: The effects of gender, employee classification level, and media richness on communication and work outcomes. *Human Relations, 50* (1), 1239-1260.

Carlson, J. R., & Zmud, R. W. ((1992). Channel expansion theory and the experiential nature of media richness perceptions. *Academy of Management Journal, 42*(2), 152-170.

Crane, D. (1972). *Invisible colleges: Diffusion of knowledge in scientific communities.* Chicago: The University of Chicago Press.

Csikszentmihalyi, M. (1975). *Beyond boredom and anxiety.* San Francisco: Jossey-Bass.

Csikszentmihalyi, M. (1997a). *Creativity: Flow and the psychology of discovery and invention.* New York: Harpers-Collins.

Csikszentmihalyi, M. (1997b). *Finding flow: The psychology of engagement with everyday life.* New York: Basic Books.

Csikszentmihalyi, M. (1990). *Flow: The psychology of optimal experience.* New York: Harper & Row.

Daft, R. L., & Lengel, R. H. (1984). Information richness: A new approach to managerial behavior and organization design. In L. L. Cummings and B. M. Staw (Ed.), *Research in organizational behavior.* Greenwich, CT: JAI, 6, 191-233.

Daft, R. L., & Macintosh, V. B. (1981). A tentative exploration into the amount and equivocality of information processing in organizational work units. *Administrative Science Quarterly, 26,* 207-224.

Daft, R. L., and Weick, K. E. (1984). Toward a model of organizations as interpretation systems. *Academy of Management Review, 9,* 284-295.

Davis, F.D. (1989). Perceived usefulness, perceived ease of use, and user acceptance of information technology. *MIS Quarterly,* September, 319-340.

El-Shinnawy, M., & Markus, M. L. (1997). The poverty of media richness theory: Explaining people's choice of electronic mail vs. voice mail. *International Journal of Human-Computer Studies, 46*(4), 443-467.

Fishman, P. (1983). Interaction: The work women do. In B. Thorne, C. Kramarae, & N. Henley (Eds.), *Language, gender and society* (pp. 89-101). Cambridge, MA: Newbury House.

Fulk, J., Schmitz, J. A., & Steinfield, C. W. (1990). A social influence model of technology use. In J. Fulk and C. Steinfield (Eds.), *Organizations and communication technology* (pp. 117-140). J. Newbury Park, CA: Sage.

Gaver, B. (2001, October). Designing for ludic aspects of everyday life. *ERCIM News,* 47. Retrieved from http://www.ercim.org/publication/ Ercim_News/enw47/gaver.html.

Gefen, D., and Straub, D. (1997). Gender differences in the perception and use of e-mail: An extension to the technology acceptance model. *MIS Quarterly, 21*(4), 389-401.

Ghani, J. A. (1991). Flow in human-computer interactions: Test of a model. In J. Carey (Ed.), *Human factors: Management information systems: An organizational perspective.* 229-237. Norwood, NJ: Ablex.

Ghani, J. A., and Deshpande, S. P. (1994). Task characteristics and the experience of optimal flow in human-computer interaction. *The Journal of Psychology, 128*(4), 381-391.

Habermas, J. (1984). *The theory of communicative action, Vol. 1, Reason and the rationalization of society.* Boston: The Beacon Press.

Huizinga, J. (1950). *Homo ludens.* Boston: The Beacon Press.

Lind, M. R., & Zmud, R. W. (1991). The influence of a convergence in understanding between technology providers and users on information technology innovativeness. *Organization Science, 2*(2), 195-217.

Maehr, M. L. (1989).Thoughts about motivation. In C. Ames & R. Ames (Eds.), *Research on motivation in education: Goals and cognition* (pp. 299-315). San Diego, CA: Academic Press.

Malone, T. W., & Lepper, M. R. (1987). Making learning fun: A taxonomy of intrinsic motivations for learning. In R. E. Snow & M. J. Farr (Eds.), *Aptitude, learning, and instruction* (pp. 223-253). Hillsdale, NJ: Erlbaum.

Mandigo, J. L., & Thompson, L. P. (1998). Go with their flow: How flow theory can help practitioners to intrinsically motivate children. *Physical Education, 55*(3), 145-160.

Meyers, R. A., Brashers, D. E., Winston, L., & Grob, L. (1997). Sex differences and group argument: A theoretical framework and empirical investigation. *Communication Studies, 48*, 19-41.

Miller, S. (1973). Ends, means, and galumphing: Some leitmotifs of play. *American Anthropologist, 75*, 87-98.

Ngwenyama, O. K., & Lee, A. S. (1997). Communication richness in electronic mail: Critical social theory and the contextuality of meaning. *MIS Quarterly, 21*(2), 145-168.

Parr, G. D., & Montgomery, M. (1998). Flow theory as a model for enhancing student resilience. *Professional School Counseling, 1*(5), 26-32.

Rudy, A. (1996). A critical review of research on electronic mail. *European Journal of Information Systems, 4*(4), 198-213.

Senn, J. A. (1998). *Information in business: Principles, practices and opportunities.* Englewood Cliffs, NJ: Prentice-Hall.

Shiller, H. I. (1979). Transnational media and national development. In K. Nordenstreng & H. I. Shiller (Eds.), *National sovereignty and international communication* (pp.21-29). Norwood, NJ: Ablex.

Swanson, E. B. (1988). *Information system implementation: Bridging the gap between design and utilization.*, Homewood, IL: Irwin.

Te'eni, D., Sagie, A., Schwartz, D. G., Zaidman, N. & Amichai-Hamburger, Y. (2001). The process of organizational communication: A model and field study. *IEEE Transactions on Professional Communication, 44*(1), 6-20.

Tomlinson, J. (1991). *Cultural imperialism.* Baltimore, MD: The Johns Hopkins University Press.

Trevino, L. K., & Webster, J. (1992). Flow in computer-mediated communication. *Communication Research, 19*(5), 539-574.

Turkle, S. (1984).*The second self: Computers and the human spirit.* New York: Simon and Schuster.

Yager, T. (2003). More than a cell phone. *Infoworld, 25*(5), 30.

Weick, K. E. (1969). *The social psychology of organizing.* Reading, MA: Addison-Wesley.

Weiner, B. (1990). History of motivational research in education. *Journal of Educational Psychology, 82*, 616-622.

Zmud, R., Lind, M., & Young, F. (1991). An attribute space for organizational communication channels. *Information Systems Research, 1*(4), 440-457.

This work was previously published in the International Journal of Technology and Human Interaction, edited by B. C. Stahl, Volume 3, Issue 2, pp. 34-44, copyright 2007 by IGI Publishing, formerly known as Idea Group Publishing (an imprint of IGI Global).

Chapter XV
Unraveling the Taste Fabric of Social Networks

Hugo Liu
The Media Laboratory, USA

Pattie Maes
The Media Laboratory, USA

Glorianna Davenport
The Media Laboratory, USA

ABSTRACT

Popular online social networks such as Friendster and MySpace do more than simply reveal the superficial structure of social connectedness — the rich meanings bottled within social network profiles themselves imply deeper patterns of culture and taste. If these latent semantic fabrics of taste could be harvested formally, the resultant resource would afford completely novel ways for representing and reasoning about web users and people in general. This paper narrates the theory and technique of such a feat — the natural language text of 100,000 social network profiles were captured, mapped into a diverse ontology of music, books, films, foods, etc., and machine learning was applied to infer a semantic fabric of taste. Taste fabrics bring us closer to improvisa-tional manipulations of meaning, and afford us at least three semantic functions — the creation of semantically flexible user representations, cross-domain taste-based recommendation, and the computation of taste-similarity between people — whose use cases are demonstrated within the context of three applications — the InterestMap, Ambient Semantics, and IdentityMirror. Finally, we evaluate the quality of the taste fabrics, and distill from this research reusable methodologies and techniques of consequence to the semantic mining and Semantic Web communities.

INTRODUCTION

Recently, an online social network phenomenon has swept over the Web — MySpace, Friendster,

Orkut, thefacebook, LinkedIn — and the signs say that social networks are here to stay; they constitute the *social Semantic Web*. Few could have imagined it — tens of millions of Web users joining these social network sites, listing openly their online friends and enlisting offline ones too, and more often than not, specifying in great detail and with apparent exhibitionism tidbits about who they are, what music they listen to, what films they fancy. Erstwhile, computer scientists were struggling to extract user profiles by scraping personal homepages, but now, the extraction task is greatly simplified. Not only do self-described personal social network profiles avail greater detail about a user's interests than a homepage, but on the three most popular sites, these interests are distributed across a greater spectrum of interests such as books, music, films, television shows, foods, sports, passions, profession, etc. Furthermore, the presentation of these user interests is greatly condensed. Whereas interests are sprinkled across hard-to-parse natural language text on personal homepages, the prevailing convention on social network profiles sees interests given as punctuation-delimited keywords and keyphrases (see examples of profiles in Figure 1), sorted by interest genres.

It could be argued that online social networks reflect — with a great degree of insight — the social and cultural order of offline society in general, though we readily concede that not all social segments are fairly represented. Notwithstanding, social network profiles are still a goldmine of information about people and socialization. Much computational research has aimed to understand and model the surface connectedness and social clustering of people within online social network through the application of graph theory to friend-relationships (Wasserman, 1994; Jensen & Neville, 2002; McCallum, Corrada-Emmanuel, & Wang, 2005); ethnographers are finding these networks new resources for studying social behavior in-the-wild. Online social networks have also implemented site features that allow persons to be searched or matched with others on the basis of shared interest keywords.

Liminal semantics. However, the full depth of the semantics contained within social network profiles has been under-explored. This paper narrates one such deep semantic exploration of social network profiles. Under the keyword mediation scheme, a person who likes "rock climbing" will miss the opportunity to be connected with a friend-of-a-friend (foaf) who likes "wakeboarding" because keyword-based search is vulnerable to the *semantic gap* problem. We envision that persons who like "rock climbing" and "wakeboarding" should be matched on the basis of them both enjoying common *ethoi* (characteristics) such as "sense of adventure," "outdoor sports," "and "thrill seeking." A critic might at this point suggest that this could all be achieved through the semantic mediation of an organizing ontology in which both "rock climbing" and "wakeboarding" are subordinate to the common governor, "outdoor sports." While we agree that *a priori* ontologies can mediate, and in fact they play a part in this paper's research, there are subtler examples where *a priori* ontologies would always fail. For example, consider that "rock climbing," "yoga," the food "sushi," the music of "Mozart," and the books of "Ralph Waldo Emerson" all have something in common. But we cannot expect *a priori* ontologies to anticipate such ephemeral affinities between these items. The common threads that weave these items have the qualities of being liminal (barely perceptible), affective (emotional), and exhibit shared identity, culture, and taste. In short, these items are held together by a liminal semantic force field, and united they constitute a *taste ethos*.

What is a taste ethos? A taste ethos is an ephemeral clustering of interests from the taste fabric. Later in this paper we will formally explain and justify inferring a taste fabric from social network profiles, but for now, it suffices to say that the taste fabric is an *n* by *n* correlation matrix, for all *n* interest items mentioned or implied on a social network (e.g., a book title, a book author, a musician, a type of food, etc.). Taste fabric specifies the pairwise affinity between *any* two interest items, using a standard machine learning numeric metric known as pointwise mutual information (PMI) (Church & Hanks, 1990). If a taste fabric is an oracle which gives us the affinity between interest items as $a(x_i, x_j)$, and a taste ethos is some set of interest items $x_1, x_2, \ldots x_k$, then we can evaluate quantitatively the strength, or *taste-cohesiveness*, of this taste ethos. While some sets of interest items will be weakly cohesive, other sets will demonstrate strong cohesion. Using *morphological opening* and *thresholding* (Serra, 1982; Haralick, Sternberg, & Zhuang, 1987), standard techniques for object recognition in the image processing field, we can discover increasingly larger sets of strong cohesiveness. The largest and most stable of these we term *taste neighborhoods* — they signify culturally stable cliques of taste. Visualizing these interconnected neighborhoods of taste, we see that it resembles a topological map of taste space!

Taste neighborhoods and taste ethoi, we suggest, are novel and deep mechanisms for taste-based intrapersonal and interpersonal semantic mediation. Rather than mapping two persons into interest keyword space, or into *a priori* ontological space, the approach advocated in this paper is to map the two persons first into taste-space, and then to use their shared *ethoi* and *neighborhoods* to remark about the taste-similarity of these persons.

Emergent and implicit semantics. While our work builds directly upon age-old language modeling techniques in Computational Linguistics, and graph-based associative reasoning in Artificial Intelligence (Collins & Loftus, 1975; Fellbaum, 1998; Liu & Singh, 2004), it is also sympathetic to trends in the Semantic Web literature — away from formal semantics, and toward an embrace of emergent and implicit semantics. In Volume 1 of this journal, Sheth, Ramakrishnan, and Thomas (2005) distinguish between formal, implicit, and powerful (soft) semantics for the Semantic Web movement. Whereas formal semantics must be manually specified, implicit semantics can be readily mined out of the unstructured Web using statistical approaches. Upon further refinement, implicit semantic resources can be transformed into powerful (soft) semantic resources that afford the ability to mediate informal and formal entities. Related to implicit semantics, emergent semantics is an evolutionary approach to knowledge management (Staab et al., 2002; Aberer et al., 2004) that advocates semantic organization to be shaped from the ground-up, *a posteriori,* and in accordance with the natural tendencies of the unstructured data — such a resource is often called a *folksonomy.* We suggest that online social network profiles give an implicit semantics for cultural taste-space, and that taste fabrics afford a semi-formal, soft semantics appropriate for semantic mediation between informal and formal entities. Finally, arising out of correlation analysis, topological features of the taste fabric — such as taste neighborhoods, identity hubs, and taste cliques — constitute an emergent semantics for taste-space.

Paper's organization. The rest of the paper has the following organization. Section Two lays out a theoretical foundation for representing and computing taste, framed within theories in the psychological and sociological literatures. In particular, it addresses a central premise of our taste-mining approach — "is the collocation of interest keywords within a single user's profile meaningful; how does that tell us anything about the fabric of taste?" The section titled "Weaving the Taste Fabric" narrates the computational architecture of the implementation of taste fabric, including techniques for ontology-driven natural language normalization, and taste neighborhood discovery. The section "What Is a Taste Fabric

Good For?" describes three semantic functions of a taste fabric — semantically flexible user modeling, taste-based recommendation, and interpersonal taste-similarity — within the context of three applications — InterestMap (Liu & Maes, 2005a), Ambient Semantics (Maes et al., 2005), and IdentityMirror. The following section evaluates the quality of the taste fabric by examining its efficacy in a recommendation task, and also entertains an advanced discussion apropos related work and reusable methodologies distilled from this research. The final section in the paper is the conclusion.

THEORETICAL BACKGROUND

This section lays a theoretical foundation for how taste, identity, and social network politics are approached in this work. For the purposes of the ensuing theoretical discussion, social network profiles of concern to this project can be conceptualized as a bag of interest items which a user has written herself in natural language. In essence, it is a self-descriptive free-text user representation, or harkening to Julie Andrews in *The Sound of Music*, "these are a few of my favorite things." A central theoretical premise of mining taste fabric from social network profiles by discovering latent semantic correlations between interest items is that "the collocation of a user's bag of interest items is meaningful, structured by his identity, closed within his aesthetics, and informs the total space of taste." Next, the paper argues that a user's bag of interests gives a true representation of his identity, and enjoys unified ethos, or, *aesthetic closure*. This is followed with a section which plays devil's advocate and betrays some limitations to our theoretical posture. The section theorizes a segregation of user's profile keywords into two species — identity-level items vs. interest-level items. This distinction has implications for the topological structure of the taste fabric.

Authentic Identity and Aesthetic Closure

In the wake of this consumer-driven contemporary world, the proverb "you are what you eat" is as true as it has ever been — we are what we *consume*. Whereas there was a time in the past when people could be ontologized according to social class, psychological types, and generations — the so-called demographic categories—today's world is filled with multiplicity, heterogeneity, and diversity. The idea that we now have a much more fine-grained vocabulary for expressing the self is what ethnographer Grant McCracken, echoing Plato, calls *plenitude* (McCracken, 1997). In a culture of plenitude, a person's identity can only be described as the sum total of what she likes and consumes. Romantic proto-sociologist Georg Simmel (1908/1971) characterized identity using the metaphor of our life's materials as a broken glass — in each shard, which could be our profession, our social status, our church membership, or the things we like, we see a partial reflection of our identity. These shards never fully capture our individuality, but taken together, they do begin to approach it. Simmel's fundamental explanation of identity is Romantic in its genre. He believed that the individual, while born into the world as an unidentified *content*, becomes over time reified into identified *forms*. Over the long run, if the individual has the opportunity to live a sufficiently diverse set of experiences (to ensure that he does not get spuriously trapped within some local maxima), the set of forms that he occupies — those shards of glass — will converge upon an authentic description of his underlying individuality. Simmel believes that the set of shards which we collect over a lifetime sum together to describe our true self because he believes in authenticity, as did Plato long before him, and Martin Heidegger after him, among others.

While Simmel postulated that earnest self-actualization would cause the collection of a person's shards to converge upon his true individuality, the post-Freudian psychoanalyst Jacques Lacan went so far as to deny that there could be any such true individual — he carried forth the idea that the ego (self) is always constructed in the Other (culture and world's materials). From Lacan's work, a mediated construction theory of identity was born — the idea that who we are is wholly fabricated out of cultural materials such as language, music, books, film plots, etc. Other popular renditions of the idea that language (e.g., ontologies of music, books, etc.) controls thought include the Sapir-Whorf hypothesis, and George Orwell's *newspeak* idea in his novel *1984*. Today, mediated construction theory is carried forth primary by the literature of feminist epistemology, but it is more or less an accepted idea.

At the end of the day, Simmel and Lacan have more in common than differences. Csikszentmihalyi and Rochberg-Halton (1981), succeed in the following reconciliation. Their theory is that the objects that people keep in their homes, plus the things that they like and consume, constitute a "symbolic environment" which both echoes (Simmel) and reinforces (Lacan) the owner's identity. In our work, we take a person's social network profile to be this symbolic environment which gives a true representation of self.

If we accept that a user profile can give a true representation of self, there remains still the question of closure. Besides all being liked by a person, do the interests in his bag of interests have coherence amongst themselves? If it is the case that people tend toward a tightly unified ethos, or *aesthetic closure*, then all the interests in a person's bag will be interconnected, interlocked, and share a common aesthetic rationale. If there is aesthetic closure, then it will be fair for our approach to regard every pair of interest co-occurrences on a profile to be significant. If we know there is not any closure, and that people are more or less arbitrary in what interests they choose, then our approach would be invalid.

Our common sense tells us that people are not completely arbitrary in what they like or consume, they hold at least partially coherent systems of opinions, personalities, ethics, and tastes, so there should be a pattern behind a person's consumerism. The precise degree of closure, however, is proportional to at least a person's ethicalness and perhaps his conscientiousness. In his *Ethics* (350 B.C.E.), Aristotle implied that a person's possession of ethicalness supports closure because ethics lends a person *enkrasia* or continence, and thus the ability to be consistent. Conscientiousness, a dimension of the Big Five personality theory (John, 1990), and perhaps combined with neuroticism, a second dimension in the same theory, would lead a person to seek out consistency of judgment across his interests. They need not all fall under one genre, but they should all be of a comparable quality and enjoy a similarly high echelon of taste. Grant McCracken (1991) coined the term Diderot Effect to describe consumers' general compulsions for consistency — for example, John buys a new lamp that he really loves more than anything else, but when he places it in his home, he finds that his other possessions are not nearly as dear to him, so he grows unhappy with them and constantly seeks to upgrade all his possessions such that he will no longer cherish one much more than the others. Harkening to the Romantic hermeneutics of Friedrich Schleiermacher (1809/1998), we might seek to explain this compulsion for uniformity as a tendency to express a unified emotion and intention across all aspects of personhood. Indeed, McCracken termed this uniformity of liking the various things we consume, Diderot Unity. Diderot Unity Theory adds further support to our premise that *for the most part*, a person's bag of interests will have aesthetic closure.

Upper Bounds on Theoretical Ideal

From the above discussion, we could conclude a theoretically ideal situation for our taste-mining approach – (1) a user's bag of interests is an authentic and candid representation of what the user really likes, and (2) none of the interests are out-of-place and there is strong aesthetic closure and share taste which binds together all of the interests in the bag. Here, we raise three practical problems which would degrade the theoretically ideal conditions, thus, constituting an upper bound; however, we suggest that these would degrade but not destroy our theoretical premise, resulting in noise to be introduced into the inference of the taste fabric.

A first corruptive factor is performance. Erving Goffman (1959) posed socialization as a theatrical performance. A social network is a social setting much like Goffman's favorite example of a cocktail party, and in this social setting, the true self is hidden behind a number of personae or masks, where the selection of the mask to wear is constrained by the other types of people present in that setting. Goffman says that we pick our mask with the knowledge of those surrounding us, and we give a rousing performance through this mask. In other words, the socialness of the social network setting would rouse us to commit to just one of our personae, and to give a dramatic performance in line with that persona. Performance might strength aesthetic closure, but it could also be so overly reductive that the bag of interests no longer represent all of the aspects of the person's true identity.

A second corruptive factor is publicity. In her ethnographic review of the Friendster social networking site, Danah Boyd (2004) raises concerns over the quality and truth of profiles in light of the fact that a personal profile is public, not only to strangers, but also to one's high school friends, college friends, professors, ex-girlfriends, and coworkers alike. Because social networking sites generally make a profile visible to all these different social circles at once, Boyd suggests that some users are cowed to the fear of potentially embarrassing exposure — for example, teacher exposing to his students, or teenager exposing to

his mother. As a result, users may be cowed into a lowest-common-denominator behavior, sanitizing the personal profile of all potentially embarrassing, incriminating, or offensive content.

Finally, a third corruptive factor also raised by Boyd, concerns the integrity and timeliness of social networks themselves. Boyd claims that Friendster profiles and friend connections are not frequently updated, leading to stale information which could distort the taste fabric if we were interested in looking at the temporal animation of the fabric. Boyd also writes about a phenomenon known as Fakesters — the creation of bogus user profiles such as for celebrities. However, the scope of Fakesters is arguably limited, and since Fakesters are chiefly imitations of actual people, aesthetic closure should still be observed and learning over Fakester profile examples should not greatly compromise the integrity of the meaning implied by the taste fabric.

Identity Keywords vs. Interest Keywords

While each social network has an idiosyncratic representation, the common denominator across all the major web-based social networks we have examined is the representation of a person's broad interests (e.g., hobbies, sports, music, books, television shows, movies, and cuisines) as a set of keywords and phrases. But in addition, more than just interests, higher-level features about a person such as cultural identities (e.g., "raver," "extreme sports," "goth," "dog lover," "fashionista") are also articulated via a category of special interests variously named, "interests," "hobbies & interests," or "passions."

As shown in the web page layout of the personal profile display (Figure 1), the *special interests* category appears above the more specific interest categories. We suggest that this placement encourages a different conceptualization for the special interests category — as a container for descriptions more central to one's own self-concept and self-

Figure 1. Examples of social network profile formats, on Orkut (left) and Friendster (right). Note the similarity of categories between the two.

identification. Of course, syntactic and semantic requirements are not enforced regarding what can and cannot be said within any of these profile entry interfaces, but based on our experiences, with the exception of those who are intentionally tongue-and-cheek, the special interests category is usually populated with descriptors more central to the self than other categories. For example, a person may list "Nietzsche" and "Neruda" under the "books" category, and "reading," "books," or "literature" under the special interests category. In the profile normalization process, identity descriptors are inferred from descriptors listed under the special interests category (e.g., "dogs" → "Dog Lover," "reading" → "Book Lover", "deconstruction" → "Intellectual").

Theoretically speaking, it is desirable to have two different granularities of description for a person. Identity descriptors are more general and constitute a far smaller ontology than interest descriptors, thus, the resulting effect is to create a taste fabric structured according to a hub-and-spoke topology. Identity descriptors serve as hubs and interest descriptors serve as spokes. The advantages to such an organization are revealed in a later section on applications, and

in the evaluation of the taste fabric in a recommendation task.

Having established a theoretical premise for mining taste fabric from social network profiles, and having argued for identity descriptors to be separate from interest descriptors, the following section dives into the architecture and techniques of the taste fabric implementation.

WEAVING THE TASTE FABRIC

The implementation of the taste fabric making system was completed in approximately 3,000 lines of Python code. As depicted in Figure 2, the architecture for mining and weaving the taste fabric from social network profiles can be broken down into five steps: (1) acquiring the profiles from social networking sites, (2) segmentation of the natural language profiles to produce a bag of descriptors, (3) mapping of natural language fragment descriptors into formal ontology, (4) learning the correlation matrix, and (5) discovering taste neighborhoods via morphological opening, and labeling the network topology. The following subsections examine each of these phases of pro-

Figure 2. Implemented architecture of the taste fabric maker

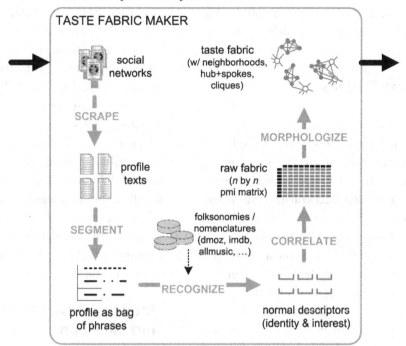

cessing more closely. A condensed description of the mining process, sans neighborhood discovery, can be found in Liu and Maes (2005a).

Acquiring Profiles from Social Networking Sites

The present implementation of the taste fabric sources from a one-time crawl of two Web-based social network sites, which took place over the course of six months in 2004. The shortcoming of this approach is that we were only able to mine 100,000 personal profiles from the sites, and only approximately 80% of these profiles contained substantive content because about 20% of users elected to not make their profile details publicly visible to our robotic crawler. Also, the one-time crawls prevents us from being able to engage in more interesting dynamic tracking of profiles which would potentially allow us to animate taste fabrics through time. At press time, we are in discussions with two social network Web sites to gain

research access to their user profiles, which should allow for the implementation that we discuss in this paper to be deployed on a larger scale.

At every step of mining, we are careful not to compromise the anonymity or personal information of social network users. In fact, in the end product, all traces of individual users, as well as their idiosyncratic speech, are purged from the taste fabric. From our 100,000 seed profiles, we used only the text of the categorical descriptors and none of the personal information including names and screen names. We chose two social networks rather than one, to attempt to compensate for the demographic and usability biases of each. One social network has its membership primarily in the United States, while the other has a fairly international membership. Both however, have nearly identical descriptor categories, and both sites elicit users to specify punctuation-delimited descriptors rather than sentence-based descriptors. One cost to mining multiple social networks is that there is bound to be some overlap in their memberships (by our estimates, this is about 15%), so these twice-profiled members may have disproportionately greater influence on the produced fabric.

Segmenting Profiles

Once profile texts are acquired, these texts need to be segmented. First, texts are easily segmented based on their interest categories. Recall in Figure 1 that texts are distributed across templated categories, e.g., passions/general interests, books, music, television shows, movies, sports, foods, "about me." Experience with the target social network websites tell us that most users type free-form natural language text into "about me," and natural language fragments for the specific interest categories. For the passions/general interest category, text is likely to be less structured than for specific interest categories, but still more structured than "about me." Perhaps this is due to the following psychology—for specific interests, it is clear what the instances would be, e.g., film names, director names, and film genres for the

films category, yet for the general interest category, the instance types are more ambiguous — so that field tends to elicit more idiosyncratic speech.

For each profile and category, its particular style of delimitation is heuristically recognized, and then applied. Common delimitation strategies were: comma-separated, semicolon-separated, stylized character sequence-separated (e.g. "item 1 \../ item 2 \../ ..."), new line –separated, commas with trailing 'and', and so on. Considering a successful delimitation as a category broken down into three or more segments, approximately 90% of specific categories were successfully delimited, versus about 75% of general categories. We did not attempt to segment "about me." Unsegmentable categories were discarded.

Ontology-Driven Natural Language Normalization

After segmentation, descriptors are normalized by mapping them into a formal ontology of identity and interest descriptors (Figure 3). Newly segmented profiles are represented as lists containing

Figure 3. Table of instance type ontology and data sources

TASTE FABRIC'S INSTANCE TYPES

category	types	ontology sources
identities	subculture, __ lover, taste echelon	wikipedia's "list of subcultures", dmoz
films	filmmaker, film title, film genre	imdb, dmoz
books	author, title, genre	amazon, wikipedia, dmoz
music	artist, album, song, genre/decade	allmusic, amazon, dmoz
foods	dish name, ethnicity, ingredient, course	allrecipes, foodsubs
sports	name, genre	dmoz, amazon
television	show name, genre	tvguide's "showguide", dmoz

casually-stated natural language fragments referring to a variety of things. They refer variously to authorships like a book author, a musical artist, or a filmmaker; to genres like "romance novels," "hip-hop," "comedies," "French cuisine"; to titles like a book's name, an album or song, a television show, the name of a sport, a type of food; or to any combination thereof, e.g., "Lynch's Twin Peaks," or "Romance novels of Danielle Steele." To further complicate matters, sometimes only part of an author's name or a title is given, e.g., "Bach," "James," "Miles," "LOTR," "The Matrix trilogy." Then of course, the items appearing under the general interest categories can be quite literally anything.

Figure 3 presents the ontology of descriptor instance types for the present taste fabric. At the top-level of the ontology are six specific interest categories plus one general interest category (i.e., "identities"). Also, as shown, there are roughly 25 second-level ontological types. There are a total of 21,000 recognizable interest descriptors, and 1,000 recognizable identity descriptors, sourcing from ontologies either scraped or XML-inputted from The Open Directory Project (dmoz)[1], the Internet Movie Database (imdb)[2], TV Tome[3], TV Guide[4], Wikipedia[5], All Music Guide[6], AllRecipes[7], and The Cook's Thesaurus[8]. Figure 3 only lists the primary sources, and lists them in order of descending saliency. The diversity and specificity of types ensures the maximal recognition capability over the free-form natural language in the profiles.

Ontologizing identity. The ontology of 1,000 identity descriptors required the most intensive effort to assemble together, as we wanted them to reflect the types of general interests talked about in our corpus of profiles; this ontology was hand-engineered out of a few nomenclatures and folksonomies — most prominently Wikipedia's extensive list of subcultures and The Open Directory Project's hierarchy of subcultures and hobbies. We also generated identity descriptors in the form "(blank) lovers" where blank was replaced with major genres in the rest of our ontology, e.g., "book lovers," "country music lovers," etc. Some profiles simply repeat a select subset of interest descriptors in the identity descriptors category, so having the "(blank) lovers" template would facilitate the system in recognizing these examples. The mapping from the general interest category into the identity descriptors ontology is far more indirect a task than recognizing specific interests because the general interest category does not insinuate a particular ontology in its phrasing. Thus, to facilitate indirect mapping, each identity descriptor is annotated with a bag of keywords which were also mined out from Wikipedia and The Open Directory Project — so for example, the "Book Lover" identity descriptor is associated with, inter alia, "books," "reading," "novels," and "literature." Because we employed two parallel mechanisms for identity descriptors, i.e., cultures versus "(blank) lovers," we cannot be completely assured that these do not overlap — in fact, they are known to overlap in a few cases, such as "Book Lovers" and "Intellectuals" or "Indie Rock Music Lovers" (genre of music) and "Indie" (subculture). Most cases of overlap, however, are much more justified because the cultural lexicon, just as natural language, cannot be flattened to a canon. Perhaps the most debatable choice we made was — for the sake of bolstering recognition rates — up-casting descriptors until they could be recognized in the identity ontology. For example, while "Rolling Stones" is not in the ontology of identity descriptors, we automatically generalize it until it is recognized, or all generalizations are exhausted — in the case of "Rolling Stones," it is up-cast into "Classic Rock Music Lovers."

Popularity-driven disambiguation. To assist in the normalization of interest descriptors, we gathered aliases for each interest descriptor and statistics on the popularity of certain items (most readily available in The Open Directory Project) that the system uses for disambiguation. For example, if the natural language fragment says simply "Bach," the system can prefer the more popular interpretation of "JS Bach" over "CPE Bach."

Situated semantic recognition. Once a profile has been normalized into the vocabulary of descriptors, they are relaxed semantically using a spreading activation (Collins & Loftus, 1975) strategy over the formal ontology, because more than simply being flat wordlists, the ontological instances are cross-annotated with each other to constitute a fabric of metadata. For example, a musical genre is associated with its list of artists, which in turn is associated with lists of albums, then of songs. A book implies its author, and a band implies its musical genre. Descriptors generated through metadata-association are included in the profile, but at a spreading discount of 0.5 (read: they only count half as much). This ensures that when an instance is recognized from free-form natural language, the recognition is situated in a larger semantic context, thus increasing the chances that the correlation learning algorithm will discover latent semantic connections.

In addition to popularity-driven disambiguation of, e.g., "Bach" into "JS Bach," we also leverage several other disambiguation strategies. Levenshtein (1965/1966) edit distance is used to handle close misspellings such as letter deletions, consecutive key inversions, and qwerty keyboard near-miss dislocations, e.g., "Bahc" into "Bach." Semantically empty words such as articles are allowed to be inserted or deleted for fuzzy matching, e.g. "Cardigans" into "The Cardigans" (band).

Using this crafted ontology of 21,000 interest descriptors and 1,000 identity descriptors, the heuristic normalization process successfully recognized 68% of all tokens across the 100,000 personal profiles, committing 8% false positives across a random checked sample of 1,000 mappings. Here, "tokens" refer to the natural language fragments outputted by the segmentation process; a recognition is judged successful if after stripping away semantically empty words, the token finds correspondence with an instance in the ontology, while remaining within the heuristically-specified tolerances for misspelling and popularity-driven disambiguation. We suggest that this is a good result considering the difficulties of working with free text input, and with an enormous space of potential interests and identities.

Correlation: Weaving the Raw Fabric

From the normalized profiles now each constituted by normalized identity and interest descriptors, correlation analysis using classic machine learning techniques reveals the latent semantic fabric of interests, which, operationally, means that the system should learn the overall numeric strength of the semantic relatedness of every pair of descriptors, across all profiles. In the recommender systems literature, our choice to focus on the similarities between descriptors rather than between user profiles reflects an item-based recommendation approach such as that taken by Sarwar et al. (2001).

Technique-wise, the idea of analyzing a corpus of profiles to discover a stable network topology for the interrelatedness of interests is similar to how *latent semantic analysis* (Landauer, Foltz, & Laham, 1998) is used to discover the interrelationships between words in the document classification problem. For our task domain though, we chose to apply an information-theoretic machine learning technique called *pointwise mutual information* (Church & Hanks, 1990), or PMI, over the corpus of normalized profiles. For any two descriptors f_1 and f_2, their PMI is given in equation (1). The probability of a descriptor, $\Pr(f)$, is defined here as the frequency of global occurrences of f_i divided by the summed frequency of global occurrences for all descriptors.

$$PMI(f_1, f_2) = \log_2\left(\frac{\Pr(f_1, f_2)}{\Pr(f_1)\Pr(f_2)}\right) \quad (1)$$

Looking at each normalized profile, the learning program judges each possible pair of descriptors in the profile as having a correlation, and updates that pair's PMI. What results is a 22,000×22,000 matrix of PMIs, because there are 21,000 interest descriptors and 1,000 identity descriptors in the ontology. After filtering out descriptors which have a completely zeroed column of PMIs, and applying thresholds for minimum connection strength, we arrive at a 12,000×12,000 matrix (of the 12,000 descriptors, 600 are identity descriptors), and this is the raw interest fabric. This is too dense to be visualized as a semantic network, but we have built less dense semantic networks by applying higher thresholds for minimum connection strength, and this is the reason why small clusters seem to appear in the InterestMap taste fabric visualization.

Criticism and limitations. A common critique heard about our approach is one that questions the efficacy of using the PMI metric for association. It has been suggested that we should look at collocations of greater rank than binary. Following our initial InterestMap publication, we extended the work by using morphological opening plus thresholding, as is done in image processing, to try to discover larger blocks of collocations which we call neighborhoods. This is to be discussed imminently. Additionally, another suggestion we are considering at press is negative collocation, that is, the collocation of a descriptor's absence with other descriptors. This would address an apparent flaw of pointwise mutual information, which is that it "overvalues frequent forms" (Deane, 2005), and would shed a new interpretation on the Semiotician Ferdinand de Saussure's structuralist enouncement that meaning must be 'negatively defined' (1915/1959).

Looking at Topological Features

The raw fabric has two extant topological features worthy of characterization — *identity hubs* and *taste cliques*. In addition, we describe what we believe to be a novel application of mathematical morphology (Serra, 1982; Haralick, Sternberg,

& Zhuang, 1987) in conjunction with spreading activation (Collins & Loftus, 1975) to discover the taste neighborhoods we hinted at in Section 1.

Identity hubs behave like seams in the fabric. Far from being uniform, the raw fabric is lumpy. One reason is that identity hubs "pinch" the network. Identity hubs are identity descriptor nodes which behave as "hubs" in the network, being more strongly related to more nodes than the typical interest descriptor node. They exist because the ontology of identity descriptors is smaller and less sparse than the ontology of interest descriptors; each identity descriptor occurs in the corpus on the average of 18 times more frequently than the typical interest descriptor. Because of this ratio, identity hubs serve an indexical function. They give organization to the forest of interests, allow interests to cluster around identities. The existence of identity hubs allows us to generalize the granular location of what we are in the fabric, to where in general we are and what identity hubs we are closest to. For example, it can be asked, what kinds of interests do "Dog Lovers" have? This type of information is represented explicitly by identity hubs.

Taste cliques as agents of cohesion. More than lumpy, the raw fabric is denser in some places than in others. This is due to the presence of taste cliques. Visible in Figure 5, for example, we can see that "Sonny Rollins," is straddling two cliques with strong internal cohesion. While the identity descriptors are easy to articulate and can be expected to be given in the special interests category of the profile, tastes are often a fuzzy matter of aesthetics and may be harder to articulate using words. For example, a person in a Western European taste-echelon may fancy the band "Stereolab" and the philosopher "Jacques Derrida," yet there may be no convenient keyword articulation to express this. However, when the taste fabric is woven, cliques of interests seemingly governed by nothing other than taste clearly emerge on the network. One clique for example, seems to demonstrate a Latin aesthetic: "Manu

Chao," "Jorge Luis Borges," "Tapas," "Soccer," "Bebel Gilberto," "Samba Music." Because the cohesion of a clique is strong, taste cliques tend to behave much like a singular identity hub, in its impact on network flow. In the following Section, we discuss how InterestMap may be used for recommendations, and examine the impact that identity hubs and taste cliques have on the recommendation process.

Carving Out Taste Neighborhoods with Mathematical Morphology

From the raw fabric, another step of processing is needed to reveal *taste neighborhoods* — patches of taste cohesion that are larger than taste cliques and more stable than ephemeral taste ethoi. Taste neighborhoods of course, overlap with one another, and the discovery and definition of taste neighborhoods seems even prone to the Ptolemaic dilemma — some nodes must be designated as "center of the universe," and the choice of these centric nodes can greatly affect the resultant neighborhood definition. Two taste neighborhoods with different Ptolemaic centers are shown in Figure 4.

Taste ethos from spreading activation. While the technical details for the discovery process are potentially lengthy, we sketch a conceptual overview of the implementation here. The raw n by n correlation matrix is reviewed as a classic spreading activation network (Collins & Loftus, 1975). That is to say, activation spreads outward from an origin node to all the connected nodes, then from all connected nodes to each of their connected nodes. The obvious observation here is that in our correlation situation, all nodes are connected to a large percentage of the graph, so our graph is super-connected. However, what makes the spreading activation meaningful is that the strength of the spread activation is proportional to the strength of the PMI along any edge in the graph. The energy of the spreading is also inhibited as the number of hops away from the origin grows, according to a per hop discount rate (e.g., 50%) So, spreading with a low tolerance (or, a high threshold for activation), and outward from "Jazz," "Yoga" (two-hops away) is reachable, but the energy attenuates before the "Football" (also, two-hops away) node can be activated.

Spreading activation outward from an origin node, the result can be likened to that node's

Figure 4. Two Ptolemaically-centered taste neighborhoods, computer generated with the follow parameters — a maximum of 50 nodes in each neighborhood, up to the first three instances of any category type are shown. Spatial layout is not implied by the neighborhood; nodes are manually arranged here.

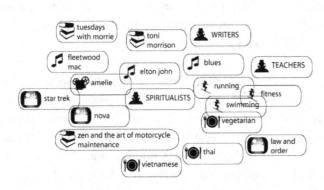

SPIRITUALISTS Taste Neighborhood

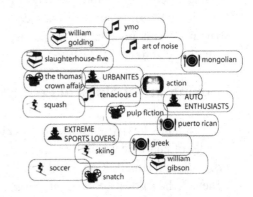

EXTREME SPORTS LOVERS Taste Neighborhood

defeasible (default, in the absence of other inputs or biases) taste ethos. This taste ethos is too small when spreading activation is configured with a modest tolerance. On the other hand, if the tolerance is increased too dramatically, the taste ethos will grow in size but its stability will be undermined due to this well-known problem in graph-based inference: beginning at two hops away, reached nodes lose their semantic relevance to the origin node very rapidly. Think of this as the *telephone game effect* — playing the childhood game of telephone, the first couple of hops are still recognizable, but recognition often rapidly tapers off after the first couple of hops. The effect is also observed by Google in their PageRank algorithm (Brin & Page, 1998) for scoring the salience of web pages by voting. They noted that high-rank pages tended to link to high-quality pages, and those to other high-quality pages, but after distance=2, reliability tapered off rapidly.

Mathematical morphology. To discover neighborhoods of taste which are larger than particular node-centric ethoi, but which are still nonetheless stable, we borrow two techniques from the field of mathematical morphology (Serra, 1982; Haralick, Sternberg & Zhuang, 1987) and that are widely used in the image processing literature which appropriates them for object segmentation — morphological opening and thresholding. Morphological opening is the mathematical composition of two operators erosion and dilation, in that order. The intuition is that erosion 'eats away' at the boundaries of an object, whereas dilation 'grows' the boundaries of the object. However, erosion and dilation are not inverses because both erosion and dilation are injective, that is, they are many-to-one and lossful transformations. The effect of morphological opening is also quite intuitive — it removes small objects 'disturbances' and opens up gaps when they are located near a boundary. There is morphological opening and there is also morphological closing which is dilation composed with erosion; closing fills in holes

and around boundaries more than opening. We employ opening because it is a bit crisper. Opening eliminates blemishes while closing magnifies blemishes. The other technique, thresholding, is frequently used to post-process an opened image. Applying a fixed threshold to an opened image simply turns every pixel above the threshold to 1, and below the threshold to 0.

Erosion and dilation over spread activations. We choose identity nodes as the centric origins for spreading because they are in general more stable places to start from. This follows the rationale that identities are stronger cultural fixtures than a book or a music album, generally speaking. From the identity nodes, we apply a relatively lenient discount, e.g., 0.8, and spread to define a fairly relevant neighborhood. This is repeated over all identity nodes, begetting an ethos for each identity node. Where ethoi overlap, the max of the node's energy is taken, rather than the sum of the node's energies. Now, erosion is applied, trimming back the weakest boundary nodes, followed by a dilation, growing the boundary by adding some energy to all nodes connected to the boundary, pushing some of them over the activation threshold and thus growing the mass. In the current implementation, two iterations of opening are performed, though the meaning of this varies widely with the choice of thresholds and other considerations.

In this manner, larger stable masses of nodes, termed taste neighborhoods, are discovered. Thresholding can help us trim a neighborhood to an arbitrary node-size. For visualizations such as InterestMap, neighborhoods comprised of up to thirty nodes seem visually appropriate. We believe that the application of morphological opening and thresholding to a spreading activation network in order to discover larger stable neighborhoods is a novel use, though we do not evaluate this claim within this paper's scope.

Summary. This section discussed an implementation of weaving the interest fabric out of social networks. Profiles mined from two social network websites were heuristically segmented and normalized according to a heterogeneous ontology assembled together from a variety of data sources. After normalization, correlation analysis learned the affinities between descriptors, and mathematical morphology over the "raw" fabric enabled taste neighborhoods to be discovered and overlaid onto the fabric. Next, we demonstrate the semantic uses of the taste fabric within application contexts.

WHAT IS A TASTE FABRIC GOOD FOR?

As a rich tapestry of interconnected interests and identities, the taste fabric brings us closer to improvisational manipulations of meaning, and affords us at least three semantic functions — the creation of semantically flexible user representations, cross-domain taste-based recommendation, and the computation of taste-similarity between people. This section explores these three basic semantic functions in the context of a survey of three applications we have developed. InterestMap is a taste-based recommendation system that leverages interactive visualization of neighborhoods to make the recommendation mechanism transparent, thereby enhancing users' trust perceptions of the recommender. Ambient semantics uses the taste fabric to facilitate social introductions between two strangers, based on their shared taste. IdentityMirror is a digital mirror for identity self-management. Whereas a real mirror shows you what you look like, IdentityMirror shows you who you are. It explores semantically flexible user representations by allowing time, orderliness, and current events in the world to nuance the representation of the viewer.

InterestMap

InterestMap (Liu & Maes, 2005a) visualizes the topology of the taste fabric, and in particular it depicts taste cliques, identity hubs, and taste neighborhoods as a navigatable map. As shown in Figure 5a, users can browse InterestMap's tapestry of neighborhoods, cliques and identity hubs, or, as depicted in Figure 5b, they can interactively build up their own taste ethoi, by searching for and attaching descriptors to a stationary "who am i?" node. The act of connecting a descriptor to the self is deeper than making a mere superficial keyword association since each descriptor is actually something more like a semantic cloud. Once a user has connected several descriptors to his self, those semantic clouds begin to intersect, overlap, and mingle. They begin to imply that other descriptors, which the user has not selected himself, *should* be within the user's taste. Hence, the notion of a visual recommendation.

Taste-based recommendation. InterestMap can, given a profile of the user's interests, recommend in a cross-domain way, books, songs, cuisines, films, television shows, and sports to that user based on taste. The user's interests are normalized according to aforementioned processes and mapped into the taste fabric. These nodes in the fabric constitute a particular activation configuration that is unique to the user, and the total situation described by this configuration is the fuzzy taste model of the user. To make recommendations, activation is spread outward from this configuration, into the surrounding nodes. Some nodes in the surrounding context will be activated with greater energy because they are more proximal to the taste signature of the starting configuration. The nodes activated with the highest energy constitute the user's recommendation. Figure 5b shows a visualization of the recommendation process. The user's self-described interests are the descriptors directly connected to the "who am i?" node. Each of these interests automatically entails other strongly connected descriptors. This is visually expressed well in the InterestMap visualization because a node getting pulled toward "who am i?" will tug a whole web of nodes behind it. Since the visualization starts with just the "who am i?" node

Figure 5. Two screenshots of the InterestMap interactive visualization. 5a (top) depicts a user browsing neighborhoods of taste visually. 5b (bottom) depicts a user visualizing his own taste ethos by dragging and connecting interesting nodes to the "who am i?" node.

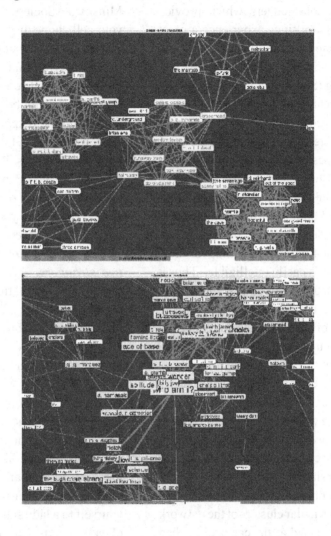

visible on the screen, specifying just a couple of interests can literally fill up the screen with its taste entailments. To visualize the spreading activation mechanism, the size and yellowness of nodes diminishes as activation spreads outward from the "who am i?" node.

Visual recommendation enhances transparency and trust. That a user trusts the recommen-

dations served to him by a recommender system is important if the recommender is to be useful and adopted. Among the different facilitators of trust, Wheeless and Grotz (1977) identify transparency as a prominent desirable property. When a human or system agent discloses its assumptions and reasoning process, the recipient of the recommendation is likely to feel less apprehensive toward the agent and recommendation. Also in the spirit of transparency, Herlocker, Konstan, and Riedl (2000) report experimental evidence to suggest that recommenders which provide explanations of its workings experience a great user acceptance rate than otherwise.

Unlike opaque statistical mechanisms like collaborative filtering (Shardanand & Maes, 1995), InterestMap's mechanism for recommendation can be communicated visually. The idiosyncratic topology of this taste fabric symbolizes the common taste tendencies of a large group of people. For example, in Figure 5a, it is plain to see that "Sonny Rollins" and "Brian Eno" are each straddling two different cliques of different musical genres. The rationale for each recommendation, visually represented as the spreading of flow across the network, is easily intelligible. Thus it may be easier for a user to visually contextualize the reasons for an erroneous recommendation, e.g., "I guess my off-handed taste for Metallica situated me in a group of metal heads who like all this other stuff I hate."

Although we have not yet implemented such a capability, the ability to interact with the Interest-Map network space would also afford the system an opportunity to *learn* more intelligently from user feedback about erroneous recommendations. Rather than a user simply stating that she did not like a particular recommendation, she could black out or deprecate particular clusters of the network which she has diagnosed as the cause of the bad recommendation, e.g., "I'll black out all these taste cliques of heavy metal and this identity hub of "Metal Heads" so the system will not make *that* mistake again."

Ambient Semantics

Ambient Semantics (Maes et al., 2005) is a wearable contextual information system that supports users in discovering objects and meeting people through pithy *just-in-time feedback* given in the crucial first moments of an encounter. Here is an example of a use case involving the discovery of a new book: Wearing the Ambient Semantics RFID reader wristband, you pick up a copy of Marvin Minsky's "Society of Mind" book. Through your cell phone display, the system tells you that you would be particularly interested in section 3 because it is relevant to your current research topics. It would tell you that your friends Henry and Barbara listed this book among their favorites, and that the author's expressed opinions seem sympathetic to your own, based on semantic analyses of both your writings. The system can indicate that you would find the book tasteful because it can use taste fabric to detect that it is indeed within close proximity to your taste ethos, translating to a strong taste-based recommendation.

Exposing shared taste-context between two strangers. The second use case concerns the system facilitating social introductions by breaking the ice. This scenario demonstrates using the taste fabric for the quantification and qualification of the taste-similarity between two strangers. First, a scenario. You are at a business networking event where Ambient Semantics wristwatches have been given to the attendees. You are tired of the same old conversation starters — what's your name — who do you work for — how do you like it here? — so you head to the Ambient Semantics kiosk where people are meeting each other in a new way. You introduce yourself to a lady standing next to you. By virtue of your handshake, the physical surroundings are transformed. The music and lighting in the area change to suit the shared aspects of yours and the lady's tastes. Some graphics of kayaking are thrown up on the kiosk display, as well as the faces of some people. The lady says to you, 'so you know Bob and Terry too? Are you in the Boston Outdoor Society too?'

Calculating taste-similarity: quantitatively vs. qualitatively. There is more than one good way to use taste fabric to calculate the taste-similarity of two people. The more direct way is to measure the intersection of two spread activations.

Taking each person's seed profile of interests and mapping it into the taste fabric, we arrive at an initial configuration. Spreading activation outward from this configuration defines a semantic neighborhood, which earlier in the paper we referred to as a person's taste ethos. Taking the semantic intersection of two or more persons' ethoi, we arrive at the quantitative calculation of taste-similarity.

However, another intriguing possibility is to make a qualitative calculation about taste-similarity. Although the intersection of two taste ethoi is mathematically satisfying, it is not easily explainable and articulated. In other words, having the system explain that "the two of you share taste because you both have interests x, y, and z in your spreading activation clouds" is inappropriate. More articulate would be to cite a shared habitation of taste neighborhoods, for example, this explanation — "the two of you share taste because both of you are adventurers and lovers of wine." Here, the mechanism of the recommendation feels more transparent. To calculate qualitative similarity, each person's taste ethos would be used to score the degree of a person's habitation across the various taste neighborhoods, which as you recall, are centered around identity nodes. Like the classic k-nearest neighbors classification scheme, here we classify persons by their k-nearest taste neighborhoods. Having completed this mapping, the subset of neighborhoods shared among the two or more persons become those persons' shared situation. To communicate shared neighborhoods to the persons, the neighborhoods could be effectively visualized on a screen, or, neighborhoods are safely summarized by stating the identity nodes which live within that neighborhood.

IdentityMirror

What if you could look in the mirror and see not just what you look like, but also who you are? Identity mirror (Figure 6) is an augmented evocative object that reifies its metaphors in the workings of an ordinary mirror. When the viewer is distant from the object, a question mark is the only keyword painted over his face. As he approaches to a medium distance, larger font sized identity keywords such as "fitness buffs", "fashionistas", and "book lovers" identify him. Approaching further, his favorite book, film, and music genres are seen. Closer yet, his favorite authors, musicians, and filmmakers are known, and finally, standing up close, the songs, movies, and book titles become visible.

Figure 6. Three screenshots of one of the authors gazing into the IdentityMirror. (left) Far away, only general identities can be seen; (center) at mid-distance, favorite music, book, and film genres emerge; (right) finally, up-close, all of the details and specific interests in the viewer's taste ethos become visible.

The Identity Mirror learns and visualizes a dynamic model of a user's identity and tastes. Looking into it, the viewer's face is painted over with identity and keywords, sourced from this dynamic user model. Taste fabric is used to interpret an initial seed profile into a semantic situation within the fabric. For instance, the viewer specifies that he listens to "Kings of Convenience" and enjoys the fiction of Vladmir Nabakov, and using this, taste fabric situates the viewer within its multiple neighborhoods of taste. The keywords which paint over the viewer's face represent his context within taste-space.

Dynamic model of taste. The richness of connections in the taste fabric allow for a truly dynamic model of a user's taste — one that can evolve over time, and can absorb the influence of each morning's world events. First, we explain how world events effect the dynamic user model. In Liu (2003), one of the authors gave a model of context-sensitive semantic interpretation for noun phrases. The phrase "fast car," under a default context, would mean "a car that is moving fast," but uttered at a carwash, it could also mean "a car that is washed fast." Similarly, a person's identity can be interpreted differently based on each morning's news. For example, supposing that the morning news reveals an international conspiracy, that event could tease out from the user's taste ethos her one-time penchant for Tom Clancy mystery and suspense novels, even though on any other day, that part of her taste would not have been visible. IdentityMirror implements a feature to allow world events to bias who you look like. It operationalizes this by parsing each morning's news feeds for major topics, and activating those topics in the taste fabric as contextual biases. When the user's taste ethos is generated by spreading activation away from a starting configuration, the activation would now flow in an unusual way because of the new contextual biases. Thus, the image of the user's identity has been biased by world events.

Second, we explain how the user's model can evolve over time by recording the history of changes that a viewer makes to himself in the mirror. By gazing into IdentityMirror, a viewer can glean his identity-situation. Is his hair out of place? Are one of his *interests* out of place? How do his facial features combine to compose a gestalt? How do his various interests come together to compose an identity or *aesthetic gestalt*? We implement a feature called Identity Fixing which allows a viewer to "fix" himself as he would fix his hair. Keywords are distributed between a hearth (keywords that are taste-cohesive) and a periphery (outlier keywords seemingly out-of-place about a person); the hearth covers the face, the periphery covers the hair. A person with a strong degree of taste-coherence has ruly hair, whereas a postmodernist with scattered interests has unruly hair. The viewer can use his hands to adjust his hair — he can dishevel those unwanted peripheral keywords, or accept them by packing them into his hair. In the user model, rejecting a keyword de-energizes that keyword in the user's taste ethos, whereas affirming the keyword energizes that keyword in the user's taste ethos. As world events tease out new and hidden aspects to the viewer's taste over time, and as the viewer continues to fix his identity, over time, the viewer's identity will be well groomed and even well vetted.

ADVANCED DISCUSSION

In this section, we present an evaluation of the taste fabric, present related work, and discuss other ways in which this work is of consequence to the semantic mining and Semantic Web communities.

Evaluation

We evaluate the quality of the taste fabric apropos a *telos* of recommendation, scrutinizing the performance of recommending interests via spreading activation over the taste fabric, as compared with a classic collaborative filtering recommender. Much of this discussion is adapted from (Liu & Maes, 2005a).

In this evaluation, we introduced three controls to assess two particular features: (1) the impact that identity hubs and taste cliques have on the quality of recommendations; and (2) the effect of using spreading activation rather than a simple tally of PMI scores. Notably absent is any evaluation for the quality of the produced taste neighborhoods, because here we consider only quantitative and not qualitative recommendation. Qualitative recommendation is not claimed to outperform quantitative recommendation in terms of accuracy — our suggestion was that linguistically identifying and visually illustrating two persons' cohabitations of taste neighborhoods should facilitate trust and transparency in the recommender's process.

In the first control, identity descriptor nodes are simply removed from the network, and spreading activation proceeds as usual. In the second control, identity descriptor nodes are removed, and n-cliques[9] where $n>3$ are weakened[10]. The third control does not do any spreading activation, but rather, computes a simple tally of the PMI scores generated by each seed profile descriptor for each of the 11,000 or so interest descriptors. We believe that this successfully emulates the mechanism of a typical non-spreading activation item-item recommender because it works as a pure information-theoretic measure.

We performed five-fold cross validation to determine the accuracy of the taste fabric in recommending interests, versus each of the three control systems. The corpus of 100,000 normalized and metadata-expanded profiles was randomly divided into five segments. One-by-one, each segment was held out as a test corpus and the other four used to train a taste fabric using PMI correlation analysis. The final morphological step of neighborhood discovery is omitted here.

Within each normalized profile in the test corpus, a random half of the descriptors were used as the "situation set" and the remaining half as the "target set." Each of the four test systems uses the situation set to compute a *complete recommendation* — a rank-ordered list of all interest descriptors; to test the success of this recommendation, we calculate, for each interest descriptor in the target set, its percentile ranking within the complete recommendation list. As shown in (2), the overall accuracy of a complete recommendation, $a(CR)$, is the arithmetic mean of the percentile ranks generated for each of the k interest descriptors of the target set, t_i.

$$a(CR) = \frac{1}{k} \sum_{i=1}^{k} percentile(t_i, CR)$$

$$(2)$$

We opted to score the accuracy of a recommendation on a sliding scale, rather than requiring that descriptors of the target set be guessed exactly within n tries because the size of the target set is so small with respect to the space of possible guesses that accuracies will be too low and standard errors too high for a good performance assessment. For the TASTEFABRIC test system and control test systems #1 (Identity OFF) and #2 (Identity OFF and Taste WEAKENED), the spreading activation discount was set to 0.75). The results of five-fold cross validation are reported in Figure 7.

The results demonstrate that on average, the full taste fabric recommended with an accuracy of 0.86. In control #1, removing identity descriptors from the network not only reduced the accuracy to 0.81, but also increased the standard error by 38%. In control #2, removing identity descriptors and weakening cliques further deteriorated accuracy slightly, though insignificantly, to 0.79. When spreading activation was turned off, neither identity hubs nor taste cliques could have had any effect, and we believe that is reflected in the lower accuracy of 73%. However, we point out that since

Figure 7. Results of five-fold cross-validation of taste-fabric recommender and three control systems on a graded interest recommendation task.

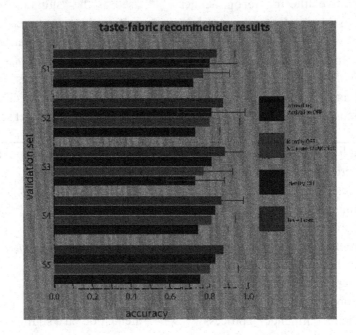

Related Works

control #3's standard error has not worsened, its lower accuracy should be due to overall weaker performance across all cases rather than being brought down by exceptionally weak performance in a small number of cases.

We suggest that the results demonstrate the advantage of spreading activation over simple one-step PMI tallies, and the improvements to recommendation yielded by identity and taste influences. Because activation flows more easily and frequently through identity hubs and taste cliques than through the typical interest descriptor node, the organizational properties of identity and taste yield proportionally greater influence on the recommendation process; this of course, is only possible when spreading activation is employed.

A cultural metadata approach to musical taste. Whitman and Lawrence (2002) developed a metadata model for characterizing the taste coherence of musical genres. Mining adjectival and noun phrases collocated with musical artist discussions in newsgroups and chatrooms, they applied machine learning to automatically annotate music artists with what they termed "community metadata." Then Whitman and Smaragdis (2002) applied community metadata to build cultural signatures for music genres that could be used, in conjunction with the auditory signal, to classify unknown artists based on style similarity. Their notion of a metadata signature for musical styles is sympathetic to our notion of taste ethos and taste neighborhood, and both systems take a bottom-up metadata-driven view of meaning definition. A chief difference between our two works is that taste knowledge is located in descriptive word-choice in their system (e.g., "wicked," "loud"), and located in interest-choice in our system, that is, the choices of what people consume (e.g., "Britney Spears", "Oreo cookies").

Social information filtering. In prior work, one of the authors co-developed a well-known technique for item recommendation based upon nearest taste-neighbor, the approach known variously as social filtering, or collaborative filtering. Shardanand and Maes (1995) represent users as vectors of (item, rating) pairs, and compute taste-similarity as statistical correlation between user vectors, or alternatively as cosine similarity of vectors in n-dimensional item space. In their Ringo social music browsing system, users were recommended a list of potential 'tastemates' on the basis of taste-similarity. One difference between our two approaches is that social filtering maintains distinct user profiles, whereas taste fabrics dissolves user boundaries, and is, in their terminology, a 'content-based filtering' approach. In distilling a reusable knowledge resource out of social network profiles that can be reappropriated for a variety of other purposes not concerned with the original social network community, it is necessary to protect the privacy of the original users, and we suggest that taste fabrics serves as a model for doing so. Also relevant is Sarwar et al.'s (2001) item-based collaborative filtering approach to recommendation, which, like taste fabrics, relies upon item-item correlation rather than user-user correlation. Taste fabric exceeds item-based filtering by use of extensive metadata to 'relax' the meaning from the item itself, by defining identity descriptors as supernodes, and by representing users as k-nearest neighborhoods. In general, collaborative filtering is more representation-opaque whereas spreading activation over neighborhoods can be visualized and more easily debugged.

Social network analysis and relational mining. Much research has examined the explicit structure of social networks, and studied their topologies via graph theory. Newman (2001) mined scientific coauthorship networks and found that collaborations 'funneled' through gatekeeper scientists. In taste fabrics, identity hubs, and hubs created around particularly salient interest descriptors constitute a similar topological feature. Jensen and Neville (2002) mined structured metadata relations from the Internet Movie Database (imdb.com) called 'schema' and learned a Bayesian network model to represent and predict item distances probabilistically. They also model the relational semantics of social network relations implied between movie actors from the Internet Movie Database and the Hollywood Stock Exchange (www.hsx.com). Finin et al. (2005) examine how the FOAF ("friend-of-a-friend") ontology applies Semantic Web concepts to enable efficient exchange of and search over social information, illustrating how social networks could develop with its semantics already explicit. Finally one work which considers the semantic content entailments of social network users is McCallum, Corrada-Emmanuel, and Wang's (2005) modeling of Author-Recipient-Topic correlations in a social network messaging system. Given the topic distributions of email conversations, the ART model could predict the role-relationships of author and recipient. The work considers group clusters and dyadic relationship dynamics but does not consider cultural aggregates as is the concern of our present work.

Large-scale commonsense knowledge networks. Taste fabrics are a rich tapestry which define the meaning space of taste and interests. They are represented as semantic networks and reasoning is performed via spreading activation over this network. This approach to knowledge representation and reasoning builds upon previous work in large-scale semantic knowledge bases such as WordNet (Fellbaum, 1998) and ConceptNet (Liu & Singh, 2004). WordNet is a semantic network whose nodes are words, and edges are various nymic lexical relations between the words, e.g. a "dog" has the hypernym of "canine." ConceptNet is a semantic network of commonsense knowledge whose 200,000 nodes are verb phrases ("eat burger", "take shower"), and 1.6 million edges are one of 20 kinds of world semantic relations (e.g., "EffectOf," "PropertyOf," "DesireOf"), e.g., (EffectOf "be hungry" "cook food"). ConceptNet and taste fabrics reason similarly by activating a seed configuration of nodes, and spreading activation outward to define a semantic context. Both resources are densely connected, semantically extensive within their respective domains, and allow for improvisational manipulations of meaning to take place atop them.

Reusable Methodologies

Sanitary semantic mining. The sanitariness of a mined knowledge resource is the degree to which it is purged of idiosyncrasy, especially idiosyncratic traces of user-specific information, and also idiosyncrasies which implicate the original application domain from which the resource was mined. When a knowledge resource is sanitary, assurances can be made that private user data is not recoverable, and that the resource is sufficiently context-free so that it could potentially be used to solve problems across a variety of domains. Taste fabrics are an illustration of how a sanitary knowledge resource can be mined out of a highly idiosyncratic and application-specific data source such as self-descriptive social network profiles. Because it is sanitized, taste fabrics can be publicly distributed and used to power applications living in other domains.

When mining social network data, concern for privacy and copyrights of user data make derivative works especially problematic; yet there is a great need and opportunity to infer valuable semantic knowledge from these sources. Ensuring data anonymity in the produced knowledge resource is a particularly sensitive issue. An early

phase of the taste fabric construction process is to normalize the casually-stated keywords and phrases into formal ontologies of non-idiosyncratic form (e.g., "Nietzsche" into "Friedrich Nietzsche", "dogs" appearing under the "passions" category into "Dog Lover"). Already, the unrestricted idiosyncratic language which bears traces of an authorship are beginning to be wiped away. In contrast, collaborative filtering systems maintain ratings for each user, and while users do not have to be named, even unnamed users are not anonymous, they are only pseudonymous. A user's name is simply wiped away and replaced with a unique id (renamed from "John Smith" to "User #123"), but the profile's integrity is intact. Because the number of instances is quite large in the space of tastes, it may be possible to recover the identities of pseudonymized users because the constitution of profiles are quite unique. At the very least, maintaining any information structured around the notion of a user lends itself to the perception that privacy of the source data may be violated.

Rather than preserving individual profiles, the taste fabric simply uses these profiles to learn the strengths of connections on a network whose nodes already exist (they are simply an exhaustively enumeration of all features in the ontology). The method of the learning is nonlinear so explicit frequency counts cannot easily be recovered. Thresholding and neighborhood definition are further lossful transformations which make details of the original application data virtually unrecoverable. The final structure is sanitary — it assures the anonymity of the data source, and is much easier to distribute.

Instance-based semantic webs and ethotic representation. In the Semantic Web community, ontology and metadata systems are often seen as top-down and bottom-up approaches to knowledge representation, respectively. To draw parallels with the artificial intelligence literature, ontology is a category-based representation, and metadata is a feature-based representation. However, taste fabrics introduces the notion of an instance-based representation, which we feel to be a promising methodology for the Semantic Web community that warrants further study, especially into the issue of scalability. An instance-based representation lacks categories or features, having only items and dense numerical connections between them. Knowledge is thus unpacked from the linguistic symbolism of a category or feature's name, and instead, is found in connectionism — the flow of semantics through a graph of items. The shift from symbolic interpretation toward continuous interpretation parallels Zadeh's efforts in attempting to soften the bivalence of logic representation by giving a fuzzier, more continuous account of meaning (Zadeh, 2004).

Instance-based representations are more appropriate for semantic recognition and semantic mediation because they offer continuous numerical interpretation of entity similarity. In taste fabrics, users, groups of users, and cultures can all be represented uniformly as clouds of node activations in the fabric. A taste fabric allows the meaning of a user's keyword profile to be 'relaxed' into a semantic cloud which we term an ethos. Using ethotic representation, semantic mediation between two users or entities in the fabric can be computed quite easily as shared activation, and even effectively visualized. By interpreting an ethos as a membership into k-neighborhoods, the resource can be used to classify users or entities into an ontology of neighborhoods (the organizing force of ontology, in fact, is still present in the resource via neighborhoods and identity descriptors). Instance-based representations and ethotic representations would be well-suited for semantic resources meant for mediation and classification in the Semantic Web.

CONCLUSION

This paper presented a theory and implementation of taste fabrics — a semantic mining approach to the modeling and computation of personal tastes for lifestyle, books, music, film, sports, foods, and television. Premised on philosophical and sociological theories of taste and identity, 100,000 social network profiles were mined, ontologically-sanitized, and a semantic fabric of taste was weaved. The taste fabric affords a highly flexible representation of a user in taste-space, enabling a keyword-based profile to be 'relaxed' into a spreading activation pattern on the taste fabric, which we termed a *taste ethos*. *Ethotic representation* makes possible many improvisational manipulations of meaning, for example, the taste-similarity of two people can be computed as the shared activation between two ethoi. Taste-based recommendation is already implied by a taste ethos, as all items within an ethos are intrinsically relevant to the taste of the individual. Indeed, an evaluation of recommendation using the taste fabric implementation shows that it compares favorably to classic collaborative filtering recommendation methods, and whereas collaborative filtering is an opaque mechanism, recommendation using taste fabrics can be effectively visualized, thus enhancing transparency and cultivating user trust.

Two models of taste-based recommendation —one quantitative based on shared activation, and one qualitative based on *k-nearest neighborhoods* — were presented. Recommendation, time and world-sensitive user representation, and interpersonal taste-similarity, were illustrated within a survey of three applications of taste fabrics.

This paper makes three contributions to the literature. First, it presents a novel mechanism for mining and modeling the taste-space of personal identities and interests. Second, the mining and weaving of taste fabrics from idiosyncratic social network profiles raises the issue of *sanitation* of knowledge resources, and this paper illustrated how ontology and non-linear correlation learning can be used to purge idiosyncrasy and prepare a general-purpose grade knowledge resource. Finally and third, in addition to ontology-based and metadata-based knowledge resources, taste fabrics introduces a novel third approach to the literature — instance-based fabrics, where the notion of 'knowledge' is a purely relational one. Fabrics, we suggest, excel at semantic mediation, contextualization, and classification, and may play a valuable role as a context mediator in a recently complicated Semantic Web of formal, semi-formal, and now, informal, entities.

ACKNOWLEDGMENTS

This research was supported by a British Telecom Fellowship, an AOL Fellowship, and by the research consortia sponsors of the MIT Media Lab.

REFERENCES

Aberer K., et al. (2004). Emergent semantics. *Proc. of 9th International Conference on Database Systems for Advanced Applications (DASFAA 2004)*, LNCS 2973 (pp. 25-38). Heidelberg.

Aristotle. (350 BCE). *Nichomachean Ethics.*

Boyd, D. (2004). Friendster and publicly articulated social networks. *Conference on Human Factors and Computing Systems (CHI 2004)*. ACM Press.

Brin, S., & Page, L. (1998). The anatomy of a large-scale hypertextual Web search engine. *Computer Networks and ISDN Systems, 30*(1-7), 107-117.

Church, K.W., & Hanks, P. (1990). Word association norms, mutual information, and lexicography. *Computational Linguistics, 16*(1), 22-29.

Collins, A.M., & Loftus, E.F. (1975). A spreading-activation theory of semantic processing. *Psychological Review, 82*, 407-428.

Csikszentmihalyi, M., & Rochberg-Halton, E. (1981). *The meaning of things: Domestic symbols and the self.* Cambridge, UK: Cambridge University Press.

Deane, P. (2005). A nonparametric method for extraction of candidate phrasal terms. *Proceedings of ACL2005.*

Fellbaum, C. (Ed.). (1998). *WordNet: An electronic lexical database.* MIT Press.

Finin, T., Ding, L., Zhou, L., & Anupam J. (2005) Social networking on the Semantic Web. *The Learning Organization: An International Journal, 12*(5), 418-435.

Goffman, E. (1959). *The presentation of self in everyday life.* Garden City, NY: Doubleday.

Haralick, R.M., Sternberg, S.R., & Zhuang, X. (1987). Image analysis using mathematical morphology. *IEEE Transactions on Pattern Analysis and Machine Intelligence, 9*(4), 532-550.

Herlocker, J., Konstan J., & Riedl, J. (2000). Explaining collaborative filtering recommendations. *Conference on Computer Supported Cooperative Work* (pp. 241-250).

Jensen, D., & Neville, J. (2002). Data mining in social networks. *National Academy of Sciences Symposium on Dynamic Social Network Analysis.*

John, O.P. (1990). The "Big Five" factor taxonomy: Dimensions of personality in the natural language and in questionnaires. In L. A. Pervin (Ed.), *Handbook of personality: Theory and research* (pp. 66-100). New York: Guilford.

Landauer, T.K., Foltz, P.W., & Laham, D. (1998). An introduction to latent semantic analysis. *Discourse Processes, 25*, 259-284.

Levenshtein, V. (1965/1966). Binary codes capable of correcting deletions, insertions, and reversals, *Doklady Akademii Nauk SSSR, 163*(4), 845-848,

1965 (Russian). English translation in *Soviet Physics Doklady, 10*(8), 707-710.

Liu, H. (2003). Unpacking meaning from words: A context-centered approach to computational lexicon design. In Blackburn et al. (Eds.), *Modeling and Using Context, The 4th International and Interdisciplinary Conference, CONTEXT 2003*, LNCS 2680 (pp. 218-232). Springer.

Liu, H., & Maes, P. (2005a, Jan 9). InterestMap: Harvesting social network profiles for recommendations. *Proceedings of IUI Beyond Personalization 2005: A Workshop on the Next Stage of Recommender Systems Research*, San Diego, CA (pp. 54-59).

Liu, H., & Singh, P. (2004). ConceptNet: A practical commonsense reasoning toolkit. *BT Technology Journal, 22*(4), 211-226.

Maes, P., et al. (2005). Ambient semantics and reach media. *IEEE Pervasive Computing Magazine*. Submitted.

McCallum, A., Corrada-Emmanuel, A., & Wang, X. (2005). Topic and role discovery in social networks. *Proceedings of 19th International Joint Conference on Artificial Intelligence* (pp. 786-791).

McCracken, G. (1991). *Culture and consumption: New approaches to the symbolic character of consumer goods and activities*. Indiana University Press.

McCracken, G. (1997). *Plenitude*. Toronto: Periph: Fluide.

Newman, M. (2001). Who is the best connected scientist? A study of scientific coauthorship networks. *Phys. Rev., E 64*.

Sarwar, B.M., et al. (2001). Item-based collaborative filtering recommendation algorithms. *The 10th Int'l World Wide Web Conference* (pp. 285-295). ACM Press.

Saussure, Ferdinand de (1915/1959). *Course in general linguistics* (W. Baskin, Trans.). New York: McGraw-Hill.

Schleiermacher, F. (1809/1998). General hermeneutics. In A. Bowie (Ed.), *Schleiermacher: Hermeneutics and criticism* (pp. 227-268). Cambridge University Press.

Serra, J. (1982). *Image analysis and mathematical morphology*. London: Academic Press.

Shardanand, U., & Maes, P. (1995). Social information filtering: Algorithms for automating 'word of mouth'. *Proceedings of the ACM SIGCHI Conference on Human Factors in Computing Systems* (pp. 210-217).

Sheth, A., Ramakrishnan, C., & Thomas, C. (2005). Semantics for the Semantic Web: The implicit, the formal and the powerful. *International Journal on Semantic Web and Information Systems, 1*(1), 1-18.

Simmel, G. (1908/1971). How is society possible? In D. N. Levine (Ed.), *On individuality and social forms: Selected writings*. University of Chicago Press.

Staab, S., Santini, S., Nack, F., Steels, L., & Maedche, A. (2002). Emergent semantics. *IEEE Intelligent Systems, 17*(1), 78-86.

Wasserman, S. (1994). *Social network analysis: Methods and applications*. Cambridge University Press.

Wheeless, L., & Grotz, J. (1977). The measurement of trust and its relationship to self-disclosure. *Communication Research, 3*(3), 250-257.

Whitman, B., & Lawrence, S. (2002). Inferring descriptions and similarity for music from community metadata. In *"Voices of Nature," Proceedings of the 2002 International Computer Music Conference* (pp. 591-598).

Whitman, B., & Smaragdis, P. (2002). Combining musical and cultural features for intelligent style detection. *Proceedings of the 3rd International Conference on Music Information Retrieval.*

Zadeh, L.A. (2004, Fall). Precisiated natural language. *AI Magazine.*

ENDNOTES

[1] http://www.dmoz.org
[2] http://www.imdb.com
[3] http://tvtome.com
[4] http://tvguide.com
[5] http://www.wikipedia.org
[6] http://www.allmusic.com
[7] http://allrecipes.com
[8] http://www.foodsubs.com
[9] A qualifying clique edge is defined here as an edge whose strength is in the 80th percentile, or greater, of all edges.
[10] By discounting a random 50% subset of the clique's edges by a Gaussian factor (0.5 mu, 0.2 sigma).

This work was previously published in the International Journal on Semantic Web & Information Systems, edited by A. Sheth and M. Lytras, Volume 2, Issue 1, pp. 42-71, copyright 2006 by IGI Publishing, formerly known as Idea Group Publishing (an imprint of IGI Global).

Chapter XVI
Mobile Phone Use Across Cultures:
A Comparison Between the United Kingdom and Sudan

Ishraga Khattab
Brunel University, UK

Steve Love
Brunel University, UK

ABSTRACT

Recently, the ubiquitous use of mobile phones by people from different cultures has grown enormously. For example, mobile phones are used to perform both private and business conversations. In many cases, mobile phone conversations take place in public places. In this article, we attempt to understand if cultural differences influence the way people use their mobile phones in public places. The material considered here draws on the existing literature of mobile phones, and quantitative and qualitative work carried out in the UK (as a mature mobile phone market) and the Sudan (that is part of Africa and the Middle East culture with its emerging mobile phone market). Results indicate that people in the Sudan are less likely to use their mobile phones on public transport or whilst walking down the street, in comparison to their UK counterparts. In addition, the Sudanese are more willing to switch off their mobile phones in places of worship, classes, and meetings. Implications are drawn from the study for the design of mobile phones for different cultures.

INTRODUCTION

Economic globalization and the widespread use of mobile phones have changed the way people live and manage their lives, and cut down the virtual distance between countries, regions, and time zones. New ways of using mobile phones are constantly emerging (e.g., downloading music to listen to on the train), and the pervasive use of mobile phones in public places for private talk (both business- and socially-oriented) is a clear example of how mobile phones are changing our economic and social lives. As a result of this, there is an emergent body of research on the use of mobile phones in social spaces. For example, Ling (2004) highlights how their use in public places has raised questions of what the appropriate or inappropriate behaviour is in public places. In this study, he found that people perceived mobile phone use in places such as restaurants as unacceptable, partly because mobile phone users tend to talk louder than usual so that people nearby feel intruded upon, embarrassed, and have a sense of being coerced into the role of eavesdropper on a private conversation.

Research has also shown that mobile phones can occupy concurrent social spaces, spaces with behavioural norms that sometimes conflict, such as the space of the mobile phone user, and the virtual space where the conversation takes place (Palen, Salzman, & Youngs, 2000). This feeling of conflict has led researchers in this area to propose that the use of mobile technology in public places is creating a new mixture of public and private space that has yet to be accommodated by for users of mobile technology and bystanders in terms of what is acceptable or unacceptable behaviour.

This phenomenon has been analysed predominately using concepts drawn from Goffman's analysis of social interaction in public places (Goffman, 1963). In this work, Goffman suggested that people have specific "public faces" and personas for different public social locations. The idea behind this is that individuals have rules that determine their behaviour in public places, or what Burns (1992) refers to as the "observance of social propriety." For example, Murtagh (2001) presented findings from an observational study of the nonverbal aspects of mobile phone use in a train carriage. Murtagh found that changing the direction of one's gaze—turning one's head and upper body away from the other people sitting next to you in the carriage—was a common feature of mobile phone behaviour on trains. These behavioural responses were seen as being indicative of the subtle complexities involved when using mobile phones in public locations. This study suggests that mobile phone users are actively engaged in trying to distance themselves from their current physical location in order to enter a virtual environment with the person they are having a mobile phone conversation. In relation to this, Love and Perry (2004) used role-play experiments to investigate the behaviour and attitudes of bystanders to a mobile phone conversation. They found that participants had strong views on embarrassment, discomfort, and rudeness. They also report that the actions of those who were put in the position of overhearers followed a pattern: they acted as though they were demonstrably not attending, even though they were all able to report accurately on the content of the conversation.

However, to date, most of the research reported in this area has tended to focus on what is termed the developed world. Mobile phones are also transforming people's lives in the developing world. In Africa, the unreliable and inefficient landline telecommunication infrastructure has made the mobile phone the solitary available communication tool for many people (BBC, 2003). However, as mobile phone use in Africa continues to grow, there is a need for mobile phone companies who are entering this market to consider the possible impact of cross-cultural differences in people's attitude towards mobile phone and service applications.

This article first briefly reviews relevant literature about the use of mobile phones in public places. The concept of culture and cultural models are explored in th second section. In the third section, the methods of this study are presented. Techniques of collecting the data and the procedure of this study are presented in the fourth and fifth sections, respectively. Some key findings from the study are presented and discussed in the sixth and seventh sections with reference to how cultural differences might affect mobile phone use in public places. Finally, the conclusion of this study is presented in the last section.

WHAT IS CULTURE?

Culture is a complicated paradigm that is difficult to accurately define. According to some researchers, culture must be interpreted (van Peursson, in Evers & Day, 1997). Hofstede (1980) conceptualized culture as "programming of the mind," suggesting that certain reactions were more likely in certain cultures than in others, based on differences between the basic values of the members of different cultures (Smith, Dunckley, French, Minocha, & Chang, 2004). Culture can also be seen as a collection of attributes people acquire from their childhood training. These attributes are associated with their environment, surroundings that influence the responses of people in that culture to new ideas, and practices and use of new technology (such as mobile phones). Given that culture may affect the way people behave and interact in general, Ciborowski (1979) identified a close link between knowledge and culture. In the context of mobile phone communication, it may be argued that culture influences knowledge—or the individual's general experience—therefore affecting, in this instance, their attitude towards mobile phone use in public places.

Another explanation of culture has been offered by Hofstede (1980). He produced a cultural model that focuses on determining the patterns of thinking, feeling, and acting that form a culture's "mental programming." This model has been adopted for the study reported in this article, as researchers in the area of cross-cultural differences and technology use consider it a valid and useful measure of systematic categorization (e.g., De Mooij, 2003; Honald, 1999). In addition, it is also considered to be directly related to the relationship between product design and user behaviour (De Mooij & Hofstede, 2002). An explanation of Hofstede's cultural dimensions is as follows:

- **Power distance:** the extent to which less powerful members expect and agree to unequal power distribution within a culture. The two aspects of this dimension are high and low power distance.

- **Uncertainty avoidance:** discusses the way people cope with uncertainty and risk. The two faces of this dimension are high uncertainty avoidance and low uncertainty avoidance.

- **Masculinity vs. femininity:** refers to gender roles, in contrast to physical characteristics, and is usually regarded by the levels of assertiveness or tenderness in the user. The two aspects of to this dimension are masculinity and femininity.

- **Individualism vs. collectivism:** deals with the role of the individual and the group, and is defined by the level of ties between an individual in a society. The two aspects of this dimension are individualism and collectivism.

- **Time orientation:** deals with the extent to which people relate to the past, present, and future. The two aspects of this dimension are short-term orientation and long-term orientation.

A number of cross-cultural studies have investigated differences in attitudes towards new technology. Smith, French, Chang, and McNeill (2001) carried out a study using Hofstede's model. They adapted the Taguchi method—a partial factorial experimental design method—in order to investigate differences between British and Chinese users' satisfaction and preferences for Web sites. They found significant differences between British and Chinese users in their preference of detailed e-finance product information. For example, Chinese users tended to adopt a more holistic approach to viewing Web content, as compared to British users.

In another study, Honald (1999) found that German mobile phone users preferred clearly-written and inclusively rich user manuals, whereas Chinese mobile phone users focused on the quality of the pictorial information.

Evers and Day (1997) found that there are clear cultural differences between user acceptance of interfaces for different cultural groups. In their study, they found differences between Chinese and Indonesian users. Indonesians were found to like soft colours, black and white displays, and pop-up menus more than Chinese users. Also, Indonesians seemed to prefer alternative input and output modes (e.g., sounds, touch screens, data gloves, and multimedia) in comparison to the Chinese who preferred the use of many different colours for the interface design.

Despite the importance and the relevance of cultural factors and its impact on the use of global products and services (such as mobile phones), little research has compared the effect of cultural differences on issues such as social usability of mobile phone use in the developing and the developed world. Sun (2003) argues that variation in cultural states will cause different attitudes or ways of using mobile phones.

The practice of the "missed call" is a clear example of how users from different cultures develop their own usage style. The missed call is when the caller places a mobile phone call and purposely hangs up before the recipient can answer the call. Donner (2005) investigated the phenomenon in Sub-Saharan Africa where the missed call is known as "Beeping." He found that users have produced elaborated codes and social messages to be exchanged over the network without bearing any cost—or at least not from those who are in a less secure financial situation.

Another exclusive mobile phone cultural attitude is evident in Bangladesh, Uganda, and Rwanda, where a woman, for example, borrows money to buy a special mobile phone designed for multiple user accounts and rural access. After this, she then buys minutes in bulk and resells them to customers in her village. This programme is funded by the Grameen Bank mainly for use in rural areas (Bayes, von Braun, & Akhter, 1999).

The same idea has mutated slightly in the big cities of Egypt and the Sudan where vendors who own fixed contract mobile phones buy a bulk of talk minutes and resell them in smaller chunks to individuals in order to make a profit. This practice is accommodated by their national phone service providers and is known as "balance transfer." Obviously, this practice cannot be seen in London or any of the developed world cities.

If mobile phone users have different usage patterns, the question that the study in this article addresses is: can we assume that people from different countries use mobile phones in the same way? Thus the question arises: are there any roles for cultural differences in the way people use their mobile phones in public places? Therefore, the attitude of the British (a mature mobile phone user market) and the Sudanese (an emerging mobile phone user market) were examined in relation to their attitudes towards the use of mobile phones in public places.

METHODOLOGY

Participants

88 participants took part in the study: 43 British (22 male, 21 female) and 45 Sudanese (20 male, 25 female), ranging in age from 15 to 63 years old, with the average age of 30 years. All participants were mobile phone users. The range of mobile phone use for the Sudanese participants was from 2-5 years, whereas the British participants had used mobile phones for 4-12 years.

Data Collection

Data was collected in this study using a questionnaire and an interview. The development of the questionnaire went through several stages. First, the generation of the questionnaire was collated by employing an exhaustive review of the literature generally on mobile phones, human-computer interaction (HCI), and cultural issues in mobile phone use. Second, an in-depth session was conducted with participants from both countries (the UK and the Sudan) to develop the questionnaire. Initially, a total of nine Likert-type questions were developed. The scale was then tested for content validity, which can be defined as the extent to which a test actually measures what it is supposed to measure (Rust & Golombok, 1989). This was undertaken using what is known as the judgemental approach, with three mobile HCI experts.

As a result of this process, the questionnaire was subsequently revised to consist of six Likert-type questions. The six Likert statements focused on attitudes towards the use of mobile phones in public places. An example of the Likert statement used in this study is as follows:

Mobile phones should not be switched off during meetings:

- ☐ Strongly agree
- ☐ Agree
- ☐ Neutral
- ☐ Disagree
- ☐ Strongly disagree

The attitude scale had a combination of positive and negative statements in order to control for any possible acquiescence effect from participants when they were completing the attitude questionnaire. This is a phenomenon whereby participants in a study may unwittingly try to respond positively to every question in order to help the investigator with their study. This type of questionnaire format is one of the most common methods used to elicit attitudes from users in HCI research (Love, 2005).

In addition to the questionnaire, a semistructured interview was carried out. The interview questions included open-ended and closed questions, and were designed to gather information on the use of mobile phones in public places, the practice of the missed call, and other features such as the use of mobile phone caller ID. The main points that were covered in the interview were:

1. Attitude towards the use of mobile phones in public places.
2. The use of the missed calls types in the two cultures. For example, the type of missed calls used and the social messages sent through the missed call, and how recipients differentiate between these types of missed calls.

Examples of questions covered in the interview were:

How do you feel about using mobile phones on public transport?
How do you feel about using mobile phones in school during classes?
How do you feel about using mobile phones in restaurants?

PROCEDURE

Participants were chosen from an opportunistic sample in both the UK and Sudan and asked to complete the questionnaire and return them to the researcher once they had completed them.

The questionnaires took approximately 15 minutes to complete. At this point, an arrangement was made to interview a subset of the participants who had been selected randomly and volunteered to answer the interview questions. Participants were informed from the outset that the results of the study would be anonymous, and they would be able to obtain the results of the study from the researcher on request.

RESULTS

An independent sample T test was carried out to compare attitudes towards using mobile phones in

Table 1. Attitudes towards the use of mobile phones in public places in the UK and the Sudan

	COUNTRY	N	Mean	Std. Deviation	Std. Error Mean	t	df	P Value Sig 2 tailed	
I would be comfortable using my mobile phone in restaurants	British	42	2.83	1.146	.177	1.325	70.241	.189	
	Sudan	45	2.56	.755	.113				
I would not be comfortable using my mobile phone on public transport	British	42	3.29	1.175	.181	5.925	69.046	.000	***
	Sudan	45	2.02	.753	.112				
I would be comfortable using my mobile phone whilst walking down the street	British	42	3.69	1.070	.165	3.884	82.171	.000	***
	Sudan	45	2.84	.952	.142				
Mobile phones should be switched off in places of worship	British	42	4.45	.861	.133	3.094	51.314	.003	**
	Sudan	45	4.89	.318	.047				
Mobile phones should not be switched off during meetings	British	42	3.88	.968	.149	2.316	69.411	.023	*
	Sudan	45	4.29	.626	.093				
Mobile phones should be switched off in schools during classes	British	42	4.00	1.307	.202	2.552	61.278	.013	*
	Sudan	45	4.58	.690	.103				

*P<0.05
**P<0.01
***P<0.001

public places in the UK and the Sudan. There was a significant difference found in the attitudes for using mobile phones in public transport between the British and the Sudanese (t=5.99, p<0.001).

The British were more willing to use it on public transport than the Sudanese.

Another significant difference was noted between the two countries towards using mobile

Table 2. Attitude difference between the Sudanese males in using mobile phones in public places and the British males

	Gender	N	Mean	Std. Deviation	Std. Error Mean	t	df	P value sig 2 tailed	
Mobile phones should be switched off in places of worship	Sudanese Male	20	4.90	.308	.069				
	British Male	23	4.43	.992	.207	2.134	26.761	.042	
Mobile phones should be switched off during meetings	Sudanese Male	20	4.20	.523	.117				
	British Male	23	3.83	1.154	.241	1.397	31.583	.172	***
Mobile phones not to be switched on in schools during classes	Sudanese Male	20	4.50	.827	.185				
	British Male	23	4.17	1.403	.293	.942	36.374	.352	
I would be happy using mobile phones in restaurants	Sudanese Male	20	2.50	.688	.154				
	British Male	23	2.70	1.105	.230	-.706	37.389	.485	*
I would not be comfortable using a mobile phone on public transport	Sudanese Male	20	2.25	.786	.176				
	British Male	23	3.13	1.180	.246	-2.912	38.570	.006	**
I would be comfortable using a mobile phone whilst walking on the street	Sudanese Male	20	3.15	.813	.182				
	British Male	23	4.04	.825	.172	.869	40.330	.001	**

*P<0.05

**P<0.01

***P<0.001

phones whilst walking on the street. Again, the British were more favourable towards this than the Sudanese (t=3.884, p<0.001). The Sudanese were found to be more willing to switch off their

mobile phones in places of worships, meetings, and in schools during classes. Please see Table 1 for a summary of the main results.

Table 3. Attitude differences between females in the UK and the Sudan

	Gender	N	Mean	Std. Deviation	Std. Error Mean	t	df	P value sig 2 tailed	
Mobile phones should be switched off in places of worship	Sudanese Female	25	2.60	.816	.163				
	British Female	19	3.00	1.202	.276	-1.248	30.068	.222	
Mobile phones should be switched off during meetings	Sudanese Female	25	1.84	.688	.138				
	British Female	19	3.47	1.172	.269	-5.408	27.256	.000	***
Mobile phones should not be switched in schools during classes	Sudanese Female	25	2.60	1.000	.200				
	British Female	19	3.26	1.195	.274	-1.955	34.863	.059	
I would be happy to use my mobile phone in a restaurant	Sudanese Female	25	4.88	.332	.066				
	British Female	19	4.47	.697	.160	2.348	24.196	.027	*
I would not be comfortable using a mobile phone on public transport	Sudanese Female	25	4.36	.700	.140				
	British Female	19	3.95	.705	.162	1.929	38.758	.061	
I would be comfortable using a mobile phone whilst walking on the street	Sudanese Female	25	4.64	.569	.114				
	British Female	19	3.79	1.182	.271	2.892	24.322	.008	**

*P<0.05
**P<0.01
***P<0.001

In terms of differences between the attitude of the British and the Sudanese males, an unrelated T test revealed that the British males are more willing to use mobile phones on public transport and when walking on the street than the Sudanese males (t=-2.912, t=.869, p<.001). Please see Table 2 for a full summary of the results.

Comparing the attitudes of the British and the Sudanese females towards the use of mobile phones in public places—an unrelated T test revealed the British females are more relaxed using mobile phones in public transport than the Sudanese females (t=2.348,p<.001). Please see Table 3 for a full summary of the results.

INTERVIEW RESULTS

The interview results corresponded with the questionnaire data, indicating that there is a difference between the British and the Sudanese attitudes towards the use of mobile phones in public places. Sudanese were found to be less willing to use mobile phones in public places than their British counterparts. In the interview, Sudanese participants revealed various reasons for their uncomfortable attitude towards the use of mobile phones in public places. For example, some of the participants felt that the use of mobile phones in public transport is unacceptable because it can be disturbing to other people in close proximity to the mobile phone user. As one of the Sudanese interviewees commented:

Using a mobile phone in public places, especially on public transport where you are closely surrounded by people, is not something that you can do comfortably. It is viewed as improper and unacceptable, as it disturbs others.

Another Sudanese interviewee added:

The use of mobile phones on public transport may be considered as a sign of disrespect to others. In particular, to older passengers who you have to respect and act quietly around them.

An added justification that was revealed by Sudanese participants for not feeling comfortable using mobile phones in public places was related to their tight rules in keeping private issues private, as one of the interviewees commented:

The use of mobile phones in public places to discuss private matters can put you in an awkward situation; because most of the people surrounding you will hear your conversation and this attitude in itself is not acceptable in our community. People are not expected to discuss private issues so publicly.

On the other hand, British participants were found to be more comfortable using mobile phones in public places as one of the interviewees commented:

I have no problems using my mobile phone in public places and especially on public transport, as I can make use of time while sitting there doing nothing.

Another British interviewee added:

I use my mobile phone in public places all the time and it does not bother me at all that people are listening to my mobile phone conversations. I do not know them and it is unlikely they are going to know more details about the topic I am discussing.

The results of this study also indicated that Sudanese females were less willing to use mobile phones in public places than British females. Sudanese females felt that the use of mobile phones in public places, especially on public transport, could attract unwanted attention to them in a society that expects females to keep a low profile. This was echoed in one of the Sudanese female interviewee's comments:

I do not like using my mobile phone in public places at all as it only magnetizes others' attention towards me. If you are on the mobile phone in a public place, people start gazing at you unappreciatively.

Another Sudanese female interviewee added:

Usually, I do not use my mobile phone in public places, I prefer to keep a low profile. For me, this attitude is a sign of respect for my self and others.

British females appeared to have different view—most of the interviewees were found to feel more comfortable using their mobile phones in public places. As one of the British interviewees commented:

I prefer to use my mobile phone in public places; it keeps me busy and in a way safe, for example when I want to get my car from the car park when it is dark, I always make sure that I am talking to one of my friends on the mobile phone just in case something happens.

DISCUSSION

The results from the study were interpreted in the light of Hofstede's cultural dimensions to try and gain some insight into the way culture may influence the use of mobile phones in public places.

It appears from the results that the British generally are more comfortable using mobile phones in public places than their Sudanese participants, who are more reluctant to use mobile

phones in contexts such as public transport and whilst walking along the street.

The collectivistic culture to which the Sudan belongs to (using Hofstede's criteria) indicates an inclination toward a tightly-knit social framework (Hofstede, 1980). The priority is for the groups' needs, rather than the individual wishes. Therefore, perhaps the use of mobile phones in public places for private talks can be seen as a self-centred act, and quite impertinent for the group needs. The group expects the individual to be considerate to the established social etiquette. The mobile phone user in public transport is expected to adhere to the social protocol and to respect other people's privacy.

Another reason for the British comfortable attitude to mobile phone use in public places may be due to bystanders' nonverbal communication attitude. This concept is highlighted by Goffman (1963) where he refers to it as "civil inattention." Civil inattention refers to the ways in which people acknowledge the existence of others without paying them extra attention; he regarded this as a gesture of respect required from strangers. Lasen (2002a) found that "civil inattention" is clearly present in UK culture: the British tend to avoid open and straightforward looking at other people, and keep away from paying direct attention to others, especially on public transport, such as the Underground. He suggested that this attitude may encourage British mobile phone users to talk more freely outdoors without being concerned about others watching them.

In contrast, in the Sudan, it was noted that "civil inattention" is not clearly evident. Sudanese people tend to look at each other directly. Lasen (2002a) suggested that a lack of proper gaze in certain cultures where "civil inattention" does not rule may be viewed as a lack of respect or ignorance. This lack of civil inattention perhaps justifies the reason behind the Sudanese unwillingness to use their mobile phones in public places, as they are influenced by bystanders' nonverbal communication attitude. One can say the more civil inattention paid to others, the more free and relaxed they might feel towards using their mobile phones, and vice versa.

Another justification for not using mobile phones in public places might be due to the high score that the Sudan attained on Hofstede's uncertainly avoidance dimension. According to Hofstede, cultures with high uncertainty avoidance scores tend to be expressive—people talk with their hands, raise their voices, and show emotions. These characteristics can play a role in decreasing the need to carry out private conversations in public places because people in these cultures know that they tend to talk loudly and expressively, which attract bystanders' attention, plus there is a high risk of being known to people around you. Another important point is that as Sudanese people in general talk loudly and in an expressive way, this tends to increase the level of external noise for mobile phone users. Therefore, people talking on mobile phones need to raise their voices more to win over competitive speakers. This loud talking may attract bystanders' attention and invite eavesdroppers, which can cause a feeling of embarrassment on the part of the mobile phone user. In addition, mobile phone users may feel that bystanders might disrespect them if they discuss their private matters publicly.

Additionally, the Sudanese attitude might be related to the high score obtained on Hofstede's power distance dimension, where a tight set of social rules are established, and people are expected to follow and respect these rules. For example, the social protocol for behaviour in public places is well recognized in the Sudan, and people are expected to behave in certain ways and not to speak loudly in front of others (especially older people). Private issues should be kept private and dealt with in a private manner and in private settings. It is considered improper to breach these norms. Although in the UK, a social protocol for behaviour in public places also exists, the maturity of the UK mobile phone market may have relaxed or altered people's expectations and

acceptance behaviour in public places. Palen et al. (2000) found that a person's attitude towards public mobile phone use changes (becomes more accepting) as their mobile use increases. In addition, Palen (2002) predicted that as adoption of mobile phones increases, people will be less disturbed about proper use, but will still prefer to have "mobile free" zones.

In terms of specific gender differences, Sudanese females were found to be more uncomfortable about using mobile phones in public places in comparison to British females. This attitude fits in with the "feminine" attribute of the Sudan culture suggested by Hofstede (1980), where the prevailing value is caring for others. The UK, in contrast, is judged by Hofstede to be more masculine-oriented, and the dominant values are achievement and success.

Although the Sudanese females practice all their rights in terms of education, work, leisure, and the like, they are looked after and cared for by the whole society. As a result of this caring perception towards females in the Sudanese culture, their attitudes and behaviours are more controlled and guarded as they are expected to follow social protocols more than men. For example, Sudanese females are expected to keep a low profile and deflect attention from themselves by talking quietly—and preferably avoid talking—in public spaces.

On the other hand, according to the results of this study, British females are more comfortable using mobile phones in public places. This may be due to the feminine attribute of the UK suggested by Hofstede (1980) where women are seen as equal to men, and they are expected to look after and guard themselves more autonomously. In contrast to the Sudanese females, British females can use mobile phones in public places as "symbolic bodyguards" (Lasen, 2002b). In this context, mobile phones are used as a technique to defend your private space within areas that are heavily populated with unknown strangers (Cooper, 2000; Haddon, 2000). As Goffman

(1963) has remarked, women especially do not like to show themselves alone in public places, because this may indicate that they are not in a relationship: a condition which (1) provides a bad impression of their social status and (2) leaves them in a vulnerable situation which can be acted upon by unknown males. To deal with these situations, the mobile phone is quite useful, as it works as a safety net and indicates that this person has their social networks and is not isolated (Plant, 2002).

The other significant result reported in this study is that the Sudanese are more likely to switch off their mobile phones in places of worship. Measuring these results against the Hofstede typology, the Sudanese score high on uncertainty avoidance scale—religion is valued and greatly respected. People's attitude towards switching off mobile phones in places of worship in the Sudan is therefore expected. It is also related to the high scores Sudan has on power distance, as roles are set, and religious men are very much valued and respected in the society, so both the Muslim and the Christians in the Sudan tend to be aware of the importance of switching off their mobile phones in places of worship. This result could also be related to the reduced number of people in the UK attending places of worship.

The Sudanese also appear more willing to switch off their mobile phones during meetings than the UK participants. This attitude may be related to their high score in the power distance dimension where people are expected to respect the structure, rules, and the norms of the setting where they are currently present.

As for the British disinclination to switch off their mobile phones during meetings, it might be related to the individualistic feature of the British society, where time is valued, and there is a push for making good use of it. It may also be related to the maturity of British mobile phone adoption where mobile phones have blurred the borders between business and social rules. In relation to this, Churchill (2001) found that the mobile phones in the UK are used to form and maintain both work and leisure relationships.

CONCLUSION

The increased use of mobile phones by people from different cultural backgrounds has become an integral part of our world phenomena, yet to date the impact of cultural differences on the way people use their mobile phones—and its implications on mobile phone design—has failed to be investigated comprehensively. As this article illustrates, mobile phone users with cultural differences were found to use their mobile phones in different ways, and their attitudes may have been influenced by their cultural norms. Although one can argue that cultural norms can be reshaped by technology, results obtained from this study indicate that cultural heritage would appear to influence users' mobile phone behaviour. The results obtained from this study also suggest that mobile phone designers need to develop a richer understanding of culture in order to develop mobile phones that satisfy culturally specific needs, and thus support mobile phone users' in their current and potential future communication activities. This is an issue we intend to explore in the next phase of our research.

REFERENCES

Bayes, A., Von Braun, J., & Akhter, R. (1999). *Village pay phones and poverty reduction: Insights from a Grameen bank initiative in Bangladesh.* Bonn: Center for Development Research, Universitat Bonn.

BBC. (2003). *A report by the Worldwatch Institute in Washington. Mobile phone use grows in Africa.* Retrieved October 9, 2007, from http://news.bbc.co.uk/1/hi/world/africa/3343467.stm

Burns, T. (1992). *Erving Goffman*. London: Routledge.

Churchill, E. (2001). *Getting about a bit: Mobile technologies & mobile conversations in the UK* (FXPL International Tech. Rep. No. FXPAL. TR.01-009).

Ciborowski, T.J. (1979). Cross-cultural aspects of cognitive functioning: Culture and knowledge. In A.J. Marsella, R.G. Tharp, & T.J. Ciborowski (Eds), *Perspectives on cross-cultural psychology*. New York: Academic Press Inc.

Cooper, G. (2000). *The mutable mobile: Social theory in the wireless world*. Paper presented at the Wireless World Workshop, University of Surrey.

De Mooij, M. (2003). *Consumer behavior and culture. Consequences for global marketing and advertising*. Thousand Oaks, CA: Sage Publications Inc.

De Mooij, M., & Hofstede, G. (2002). Convergence and divergence in consumer behavior: Implications for international retailing. *Journal of Retailing, 78*, 61-69.

Donner, J. (2005). *The rules of beeping: Exchanging messages using missed calls on mobile phones in Sub-Saharan Africa*. Paper presented at the 55th Annual Conference of the International Communication Association: Questioning the Dialogue, New York.

Evers, V., & Day, D. (1997). The role of culture in interface acceptance. In M.S. Howard, J. Hammond, & G. Lindgaard, *Proceedings of the Human Computer Interaction INTERACT'97 Conference* (pp. 260-267). Sydney: Chapman and Hall.

Goffman, E. (1963). *Behaviour in public places. Notes on the social organization of gatherings*. Free Press.

Haddon, L. (2000). *The social consequences of mobile telephony: Framing questions*. Paper presented at the seminar Sosiale Konsekvenser av Mobiltelefoni, organised by Telenor, Oslo.

Hofstede, G. (1980). *Culture's consequences: International differences in work-related values*. Beverly Hills: Sage Publications.

Honold, P. (1999). Learning how to use a cellular phone: Comparison between German and Chinese users. *Jour Soc. Tech. Comm, 46*(2), 196-205.

Lasen A. (2002a). *The social shaping of fixed and mobile networks: A historical comparison*. DWRC, University of Surrey.

Lasen, A. (2002b). *A comparative study of mobile phone use in London, Madrid and Paris*.

Ling, R. (2004). *The mobile connection the cell phone's impact on society*. San Francisco: Morgan Kaufmann.

Love, S. (2005). *Understanding mobile human-computer interaction*. Elsevier Blueworth Heinemann: London.

Love, S., & Perry, M. (2004). Dealing with mobile conversations in public places: Some implications for the design of socially intrusive technologies. *Proceedings of CHI 2004*, Vienna (pp. 24-29).

Murtagh, G.M. (2001). Seeing the rules: Preliminary observations of action, interaction and mobile phone use. In B. Brown, N. Green, & R. Harper (Eds.), *Wireless world. Social and interactional aspects of the mobile age* (pp. 81-91). London: Springer-Verlag.

Palen, L. (2002). Mobile telephony in a connected life. *Communications of the ACM, 45*(3), 78-82.

Palen, L., Salzman, M., & Youngs, E. (2000). Going wireless: Behaviour and practice of new mobile phone users. In *Proceedings of the Conference on Computer Supported Cooperative Work (CSCW'00)* (pp. 201-210).

Plant, S. (2002). *On the mobile: The effects of mobile telephones on social and individual life*.

Motorola, London. Retrieved October 9, 2007, from http://motorola.com/mot/doc/0/267_Mot-Doc.pdf

Rust, J., & Golombok, S. (1989). *Modern pychometrics: The science of psychological assessment.* New York: Routledge.

Smith, A., Dunckley, L., French, T., Minocha, S., & Chang, Y. (2004). A process model for developing usable cross-cultural Websites. *Interacting with Computers, 16*, 63-91.

Smith, A., French, T., Chang, Y., & McNeill, M. (2001). E-culture: A comparative study of efinance Web site usability for Chinese and British users. In D. Day & L. Duckley (Eds.), *Designing for global markets. Conference (6th. 2001). Proceedings of the Third International Workshop on Internationalisation of Products and Systems* (pp. 87-100). Buckinghamshire: The Open University.

Sun, H. (2003). *Exploring cultural usability: A localization study of mobile text messaging use.* Paper presented at CHI 2003, Ft. Lauderdale, FL.

This work was previously published in the International Journal of Technology and Human Interaction, edited by B. C. Stahl, Volume 4, Issue 2, pp. 35-51, copyright 2008 by IGI Publishing, formerly known as Idea Group Publishing (an imprint of IGI Global).

Chapter XVII
The Internet, Health Information, and Managing Health:
An Examination of Boomers and Seniors

Christopher G. Reddick
The University of Texas at San Antonio, USA

ABSTRACT

This article examines the use of the Internet for gathering health information by boomers and seniors. This study attempts to determine whether online health seekers (individuals that have Internet access and have searched for health information online) have changed their behaviors from the information they found online. Essentially, has online health information helped them to manage their health more effectively? This research analyzes the Kaiser Family Foundation e-Health and the Elderly public opinion dataset of access by boomers and seniors to online health information. The major results indicate that boomers marginally use online health information more than seniors for the management of their health. The most significant results indicated that boomers

and seniors who are more aware and have positive feelings toward online health information would use it more to manage their health.

INTRODUCTION AND BACKGROUND

For baby boomers, the Internet has become the most important source of health information other than consultation with their family doctor (Kaiser Family Foundation, 2005). The focus of this article is on both baby boomers, those in the age range of 50 to 64, and seniors, or those 65 and older.[1] This study examines the use of online health information by baby boomers and seniors and how they use the information for managing their health. The primary objectives of this article are to examine the differences in behavior between boomers and seniors and to test for the presence of a variety of associations among their characteristics and a number of management of health variables.

This study explores five specific questions. First, are there any differences between boomers and seniors and their access to health information for managing health? Second, will healthier boomers and seniors rely less on online health information in order to manage their health because they would have less need? Third, will the presence of boomers and seniors that have more experience and familiarity with the Internet lead to greater use of online health information to manage health? Fourth, will individuals who are in a lower sociodemographic status rely less on online health information because of lack of resources to access this information? Finally, will avid Internet users use online health information more often to manage their health because they would have greater access to and familiarity with the Internet?

The American health care system is different from many Western countries, since it is administered primarily by the private marketplace. The majority of the United States population contracts with a private provider for his or her health insurance coverage. Medicare is a federal health insurance program for people age 65 and older. In addition, Medicaid, a program sponsored by the federal government and administered by states, is intended to provide health care and health-related services to low-income individuals. However, there are millions of Americans who do not fit into either the Medicare or Medicaid plans and, essentially, remain uninsured. Online health information is especially important, given the millions of uninsured Americans trying to get information on their health situation. Individuals can use this online health information to make informed choices on their health care needs. They potentially can use information on the Internet to better manage their health.

Essentially, has online health information influenced the behaviors of boomers and seniors with respect to their health care needs? This influence could be as extensive as visiting a doctor or simply talking to family or friends about health information that a boomer or senior found online.

Access to timely and reliable information on health and health care long has been a goal for seniors, who face a greater number of health conditions and use prescription drugs and health care services at a higher rate than younger adults (Kaiser Family Foundation, 2005). However, the online behavior of seniors has not been studied as closely as that of health information searches of adolescents (Gray, Klein, Noyce, Sesselberg, & Cantrill, 2005), women (Pandey, Hart, & Tiwary, 2003), cancer patients (Eysenbach, 2003; Ziebland, 2004), those affected by the digital divide (Skinner, Biscope, & Poland, 2003), and those that compare online and off-line behavior (Cotton & Gupta, 2004). There is little empirical research that examines whether online health searches affect the management of health (Lueg, Moore, & Warkentin, 2003; Nicholas, Huntington, Williams, & Blackburn, 2001), one of the two objectives of this study. This study measures whether Internet health information changed the self-reporting behavior of boomers and seniors and does not specifically address change in health outcomes.

There are two reasons why this study does a comparison of both boomers and seniors. First, baby boomers represent future seniors, and by examining this age group, this study can provide some indication about what the future holds for the Internet and health information. Second, both boomers and seniors are in the greatest need of health information, since they are more prone to have health problems than other age groups.

This study is different from existing works of Nicholas et al. (2001), Lueg et al. (2003), and Huntington et al. (2004), since it focuses on the use of online health information in the management of health. This study focuses especially on comparing two groups, boomers and seniors, while the existing empirical work examines the entire Internet population. This study is different from studies that conduct a meta-analysis, which combine published results from different sources (Eysenbach, 2003). This research performs a statistical analysis that leads to conclusions that are different from the original dataset (Kaiser Family Foundation, 2005). The aim of this study is not just to learn about the differences between boomers and seniors and access to online health information; it is to discern the magnitude of differences between these groups and the impact of factors such as awareness and feelings on health management.

In order to accomplish the goal of examining online health information and the management of boomers' and seniors' health, this article is divided into several sections. First, this research examines the literature on the use of the Internet as a health information source. Second, this article outlines how the literature can be summarized into hypotheses that model the most probable impacts on management of boomers' and seniors' health. Third, this research provides details of the Kaiser Family Foundation's e-Health and the Elderly dataset that is used to model public opinion data of online health information (Kaiser Family Foundation, 2005). The fourth and fifth sections discuss the models and results of tests on the use of online health information for health

care management. The sixth section provides a discussion that outlines how the test results confirm or deny the specified hypotheses and shows the broader significance of this work. The last section provides avenues for future research and presents limitations of this study.

LITERATURE REVIEW

The following section outlines the common themes found in the literature on the Internet and health information and the management of health. They can be divided into the factors of differences between age groups, the health of the individual, online proficiency, sociodemographic characteristics, and awareness and feelings about online health information. Existing research shows that little is known about how Internet usage, health status, and sociodemographic characteristics affect health information seeking (Cotton & Gupta, 2004).

Eysenbach (2003) provides a conceptual framework of the possible link between Internet use and cancer. Some of the important factors, according to that author's meta-analysis, indicate that Internet use is related to communication, community, and content, leading to an impact on cancer outcomes. In a similar line of inquiry, a study by Lueg et al. (2003) provided a conceptual framework of Internet searches for online health information.

Figure 1. Conceptual framework of access to online health information by boomers and seniors

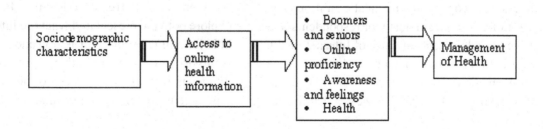

These authors examine the situations with which individuals find themselves confronted in terms of health needs and frequency of use, predicting access to health information. Eysenbach's (2003) conceptual framework is different from Lueg et al. (2003), in that the former examines the social aspects of Internet use and health information, while the latter study focuses on the situation involvement and the frequency of Internet use. The conceptual framework of this study is similar to Eysenbach (2003) and Lueg et al. (2003) but differs, in that it examines boomers and seniors and factors such as frequency and satisfaction having an influence on the management of health (Figure 1).

Online Health Information and Managing Boomers' and Seniors' Health

If the Internet can be used to change the behavior of individuals, this is one assessment of the long-term utility of this information resource. If individuals just look at information online and do not use it in any substantial way, it does not make much sense to invest in Internet health resources. The Internet suggests a remarkable change from the traditional doctor-knows-best approach (Eysenbach & Jadad, 2001). The Internet can be seen as challenging hierarchical models of information sharing, in which the provider of the information decides how the information should be delivered (Ziebland, 2004).

For example, existing research in a 2001 survey showed that 44% of online health information seekers said that the information they found online affected a decision about how to treat an illness or to cope with a medical condition (Fox & Rainie, 2002). A majority of respondents to a survey of adolescents and use of Internet health information reported that it helped them to start a conversation with a lay or professional medical person (Gray et al., 2005). Online health informa-

tion seekers mostly are going online to look for specific answers to targeted questions (Fox & Rainie, 2000). In addition, four out of 10 young people say that they have changed their personal behaviors because of health information that they obtained online (Rideout, 2002). In an Internet survey, more than one-third of the respondents said that their conditions had improved after having visited a Web site, and more than one in four said that the Web information had resulted in a deferred visit or had actually replaced a visit to the doctor (Nicholas et al., 2001). Therefore, the existing research has examined adolescents' and all age groups' behavioral changes but has not focused on seniors and their use of the Internet for managing health. There are five factors outlined in the literature, which are differences between boomers and seniors, the health of boomers and seniors, their online proficiency, their sociodemographic characteristics, and awareness and feelings toward online health information that are predicted to have an impact on whether online health information is used.

Boomers' and Seniors' Differences

Existing empirical evidence shows that health seekers are proportionately more middle-aged than very young or old, with the highest proportion of usage witnessed in those between the ages of 30 and 64 (Fox & Rainie, 2000). A more recent survey indicates that 70% of baby boomers has gone online in 2004, while only 31% of seniors has gone online (Kaiser Family Foundation, 2005). Boomers will retire shortly, and the amount of online health information for which they will search should increase dramatically compared to what seniors are currently consuming. In order to explore both the present and what the future will hold for online health information and seniors, it is important to compare both age groups. In addition, individuals over the age of 50 may have a greater need for more information on health care than someone much younger because of the greater chance of facing health problems (Brodie et al., 2000).

Health of Boomers and Seniors

The literature also mentions that individuals who are in worse health will want to search more for online health information. The Internet becomes an additional tool in order for them to search for health information. Empirical evidence shows that there is a link between an individual's health and his or her need for online health information. Less healthy individuals are more likely to explore different aspects of a Web site and to use more health-related interactive features and, in doing so, improve their well being (Lueg et al., 2003). Individuals who were suffering with an illness were two and half times as likely, compared to respondents without a standing illness, to say that they had used information from the Internet as an alternative to seeing their general practitioner (Nicholas et al., 2001). In many cases, information seekers were acting on behalf of others, such as family and friends. However, access to online health information also should be related to the consumer's ability to use the Internet, not just on whether they are healthy.

Online Proficiency

The ability to use the Internet also should have an impact on whether boomers and seniors use online health information to manage their health. Individuals who use Internet information more to manage their health have broadband Internet access, are frequently online, spend many hours online, and search for information on many different topics. Research shows that individuals using a Web site regularly were more likely to have said that the information was helpful (Nicholas et al., 2001). A survey of adolescents shows that there are issues of the disparity of Internet access

and quality of Internet access such as dial-up vs. broadband connection (Skinner et al., 2003).

Sociodemographic Characteristics of Online Health Seekers

Another factor explored in the literature that should have an impact on access to online health information is the sociodemographic characteristics of the individual. There is research on the digital divide, between the haves and the have-nots of Internet access. This research predicts that those who have greater access to the Internet would have more resources in society. For instance, those groups of individuals who are more disadvantaged economically in the United States would have less access to the Internet and online health resources. Hispanics, the largest minority group in the United States, traditionally have had less Internet access (Fox & Rainie, 2000). Those with medium to high family incomes should be able to access the Internet more for health information because of greater resources.

Existing research shows that individuals who are older, have lower incomes, are minorities, are less educated, and are males will be less likely to use the Internet for health information seeking (Cotton & Gupta, 2004; Anderson, 2004). In contrast, women increasingly rely on the Internet to supplement health information received from traditional sources (Pandey et al., 2003) and are more likely than men to seek online health information (Fox & Rainie, 2000; Nicholas et al., 2001). Awareness and feelings toward online health information also should have an impact on using this information to manage consumers' health.

Awareness and Feelings Toward Online Health Resources

A final factor that should explain access to Internet health information is the awareness and feelings of the individual toward online health information. If boomers and seniors have more positive feelings about the Internet as a health information resource, they will utilize it more often than someone who harbors more negative feelings toward the Internet. In addition, individuals who go online for health information frequently should use it more to manage their health. If a boomer's or senior's doctor or medical professional recommends or uses the Internet as a communication device, the patient is more likely to use it to manage his or her health. In summary, the prediction is that boomers and seniors who are more aware of online health resources should use these resources more to manage their health. In addition, boomers and seniors who have positive feelings about the benefits of online health information will use this resource more to manage their health.

Empirical evidence shows that there is a relationship between using the Internet more often and accessing health information (Lueg et al., 2003). Those using the Web once a day were twice as likely to report that it helped a lot in terms of being better informed from health information found on the Web (Nicholas et al., 2001). E-mail is still a new medium for obtaining access to consumer health information and also is explored in the research as a way to manage a consumer's health (Huntington et al., 2004). The literature just outlined can be formally specified with the following hypotheses that demonstrate the relationship between boomers and seniors, the Internet, and the management of health.

HYPOTHESES

In order to examine whether online health information has affected the choices that individuals make in managing their health and the differences between boomers and seniors, several hypotheses are tested in this article. These hypotheses are derived from the literature mentioned in the previous section and are divided into five areas:

Boomers' and Seniors' Differences

Hypothesis 1: Online health seekers who are baby boomers are more likely to believe that online health information has helped them to manage their health better compared with seniors.

Health of Boomers and Seniors

Hypothesis 2: Online health seekers who are healthy or who have family and friends that are healthy will rely less on online health information because of lack of need.

Online Proficiency

Hypothesis 3: Online health seekers who have broadband Internet access will go online more for health information to manage their health.

Hypothesis 4: Online health seekers who go online more often and conduct many online activities will use Internet health information more to manage their health.

Sociodemographic Status

Hypothesis 5: Boomers and seniors who are females will rely more on online health information.

Hypothesis 6: Boomers and seniors who are college educated will rely more on online health information.

Hypothesis 7: Boomers and seniors who are Hispanics will go online less for health information.

Hypothesis 8: Boomers and seniors who have family income above $75,000 will go online more for health information.

Awareness and Feelings Toward Online Health Resources

Hypothesis 9: Online health seekers who most of the time and always look to see who provides medical information on the Internet will use online health information more to manage their health.

Hypothesis 10: Online health seekers who access health information online once or twice a month will have a greater likelihood of using online health information to manage their health.

Hypothesis 11: If a doctor has recommended a Web site to an online health seeker, he or she is more likely to use health information to manage his or her health.

Hypothesis 12: If an online health seeker has communicated with his or her doctor via e-mail, he or she is more likely to use online health information to manage his or her health.

Hypothesis 13: Online health seekers that have more positive feelings about looking for health information on the Internet are more likely to use this information to manage their health.

These hypotheses are examined with a dataset that surveyed public opinion of both baby boomers and seniors on their use and acceptance of online health information.

DATASET AND METHODS

The e-Health and the Elderly dataset is a nationally representative random digit dial telephone survey of 1,450 adults age 50 and older.[2] Included in this sample were 583 respondents age 65 and older. The survey was designed by Kaiser Family Foundation (KFF) (2005) in consultation with Princeton Survey Research Associates (PSRA), and the survey was administered in the field by PSRA. The survey interviews were conducted between March 5 and April 8, 2004. The entire dataset of 1,450 respondents was first examined to determine the characteristics of boomers and seniors and access to online health information.

Out of the 1,450 responses to the survey, this study also has taken a subsample of 628 respondents, of which there were 464 boomers and 164 seniors surveyed. Therefore, the original dataset was split, and the sample sizes differ for both age groups. The 628 boomers and seniors represent those individuals who are called online health seekers. They both have Internet access and have looked for online health information. This group is of interest, since in this study, there is a comparison of the characteristics of those that actually look up online health information.

In this study, we use a consumer survey to explore the differences between boomers and seniors and their use of online health information to manage health. This research uses both descriptive statistics and logistic regression to explore differences in access to online health information between boomers and seniors.[3]

DESCRIPTIVE STATISTICS OF BOOMERS AND SENIORS AND ONLINE HEALTH INFORMATION

In order to model the relationship between seniors and boomers, online health information, and its impact on managing health care needs, this study has specified the following variables that will comprise the models tested.

Table 1 provides information on boomers and seniors who go online for health information. Boomers that go online for health information represent 78.2%, while seniors that go online for health information represent just over 21% of those surveyed in this category. This table

Table 1. Boomers and seniors who go online for health information

Go online for health information (Yes or No)	Age group	Frequency	Percent
No	50-64	335	42.5
	65+	454	57.5
	Total	789	100
Yes	50-64	464	78.2
	65+	129	21.8
	Total	593	100

generally supports the notion that boomers tend to go online more for health information than seniors. Boomers that do not go online for health information represent 43%, and seniors that do not go online represent 58% of those surveyed in this category.

Table 2 outlines demographic information of boomers and seniors that go online and do not go online for health information. The digital divide is very evident with the data presented in this table. For instance, 43% of college-educated individuals go online for health information compared with only 15% who are college-educated that do not go online for health information. Among females and Hispanics, there is not much of a difference in the percentage who go online and do not go online for health information. However, boomers and seniors that have a family income above

Table 2. Demographic information of boomers and seniors and going online for health information

Go online for health information (Yes or No)		N	Mean	Standard Deviations
No	College educated	822	0.15	0.36
	Gender is female	822	0.65	0.48
	Race is Hispanic	822	0.03	0.18
	Family income 2003 above $75,000	822	0.07	0.25
	Age	822	68.79	12.41
Yes	College educated	628	0.43	0.50
	Gender is female	628	0.61	0.49
	Race is Hispanic	628	0.03	0.17
	Family income 2003 above $75,000	628	0.27	0.45
	Age	628	60.88	11.81

$75,000 in 2003 were more likely to go online for health information. Finally, age seems to have an impact on accessing online health information. The mean age was 61 years for individuals that go online and 69 years for consumers who do not go online for health information. Higher income implies greater use of online health information, and having a college education means a greater likelihood of going online for health information. This finding also indicates that boomers are more likely to go online for health information, since the average age range was just over 61 years old.

Logistic regression is used to test whether sociodemographic variables predict whether boomers or seniors go online for health information. Logistic regression was used, since this study models dependent variables that are binary, represented by either a 1 or 0 (Nicholas et al., 2001; Lueg et al., 2003). The odds ratio can be used to interpret the relative impact of the observance of a 1 in the dependent variable. Table 3 shows that almost all of the sociodemographic variables help to explain whether someone goes online for health information, with the only exception being Hispanic. For instance, having a college education means that a boomer or senior is four times

more likely to go online for health information. Having a higher income indicates that boomers and seniors are two times more likely to go online for health information. However, as the age of the respondent increases, this marginally decreases the likelihood of someone going online for health information.

Dependent Variables

Table 4 provides a list of the dependent and predictor variables and also demonstrates whether there were differences between boomers and seniors in these variables. Perhaps the most important dependent variable is whether "somewhat" or "a lot" of information on the Internet has helped to take care of a senior's or a boomer's health. The mean score indicates that 59% of boomers and 46% of seniors believed that the Internet has helped them to take care of their health, demonstrating some impact on the management of their health.

The second dependent variable measures whether online health seekers had a conversation with family or friends about health information that they found online (Table 4). Family and friends who go online for health information may guide

Table 3. Logistic regression results of sociodemographic variables predicting going online for health information

Dependent Variable	Go Online for Health Information		
Predictor Variables	Odds Ratio	Wald Statistic	Prob. Sig.
Age	0.95	(301.47)***	0.00
College educated	4.05	(300.72)***	0.00
Gender is female	1.25	(11.49)***	0.00
Race is Hispanic	1.06	0.26	0.61
Family income 2003 above $75,000	2.25	(63.38)***	0.00
Constant	11.34	(139.67)***	0.00
Nagelkerke R-Square	0.25		
Note: *** significant at the 0.01 level.			

Table 4. Difference of means tests of dependent and predictor variables for online health seekers; boomers are significantly different from seniors

Variable Name	Mean of Boomers	Standard Deviations Boomers	Mean of Seniors	Standard Deviations Seniors	Probability Significantly Different Boomers and Seniors
Dependent Variables					
Somewhat and a lot of information on Internet helped take care health	0.59	0.49	0.46	0.50	0.07
Had a conversation family or friend about online health information	0.66	0.47	0.48	0.50	0.00
Online health information changed behavior	0.36	0.48	0.25	0.43	0.00
Made a decision about how to treat an illness because of online health information	0.34	0.48	0.26	0.44	0.00
Visited a doctor because of information found online	0.16	0.37	0.13	0.34	0.07
Predictor Variables: Health					
Excellent or very good health	0.58	0.49	0.52	0.50	0.07
Health problems index	3.95	2.45	3.80	2.41	0.48
Predictor Variables: Online Proficiency					
Broadband Internet access	0.43	0.50	0.29	0.45	0.00
Online more than 10 hrs week	0.28	0.45	0.23	0.42	0.00
Online every day	0.57	0.50	0.51	0.50	0.08
Online activities index	2.86	0.97	2.45	1.14	0.00
Predictor Variables: Online Health Information					
Most of the time and always look to see who provides medical information on Internet	0.40	0.49	0.24	0.43	0.00
Access health information online once or twice a month or greater	0.38	0.49	0.34	0.48	0.04
Doctor recommended a health or medical Website	0.06	0.23	0.04	0.20	0.13
Communicated with doctor or other health care provider through email	0.12	0.32	0.11	0.31	0.55
Positive feelings about looking for health information on the Internet Index	2.59	0.73	2.23	0.94	0.00
Negative feelings about looking for health information on the Internet	0.68	0.78	0.71	0.81	0.25

Notes: The number of observations are 464 for boomers and 164 for seniors.

someone else as to whether they should see a doctor because of this information (Eysenbach, 2003). The results indicate that 66% of boomers said that

they had a conversation with family members or friends, and only 48% of seniors said that they had this conversation about the information they saw online. There were statistically significant differences between seniors and boomers for this question with the reported F-statistic being significant at the 0.01 level, meaning that boomers were more likely to have a conversation with family and friends about health information that they found online.

The third dependent variable measures whether online health information changed the behavior of boomers and seniors (Table 4). Thirty-six percent of boomers' behaviors changed as a result of online health information, compared with 25% of seniors. This result also was shown to have a statistically significant difference between boomers and seniors at the 0.01 level. Around one-third of boomers changed their behaviors, which is a good indication that the information that they are finding is affecting their health.

A fourth management of health issue was whether boomers or seniors made a decision on treatment of an illness as a result of the information they found online (Table 4). The results showed that 34% of boomers believed that they made a decision about how to treat an illness because of information they found online, while only 26% of seniors made a decision on treatment. This result also showed a statistically significant difference between the two age groups at the 0.01 level.

Another dependent variable was visiting a doctor as a result of the health information found online (Table 4). Only 16% of boomers visited a doctor as a result of health information they found online, while 13% of seniors visited a doctor. Visiting a doctor was the least utilized change in behavior as a result of online health information.

Referring back to Hypothesis 1 on whether online health information has been used to manage a boomer's or a senior's health, this study has found that overall, there were differences between both groups of online health seekers (Table 4). The mean values for all five dependent variables were higher for boomers compared with seniors. In addition, three out of the five dependent

variables showed statistically significant differences between boomers and seniors at the 0.01 level. With these dependent variables outlined, this research also should describe the predictor variables and their characteristics.

Predictor Variables

The predictor variables used to explain how the Internet has managed the health care of boomers and seniors also are presented in Table 4. Many of the predictor variables are represented in terms of binary numbers in order to capture the specific impacts on the dependent variables. As previously noted, this study has divided the hypotheses into the differences between boomers and seniors, the relative health of the individual, his or her online proficiency, and how active he or she is at seeking online health information. This study discerns the impact that these factors have on the management of the health care of boomers and seniors.

To see all of the predictor variables, refer to Table 4. We will only mention a few of them in this section. For instance, an index was created of the health problems that boomers and seniors or someone they know have faced in the past year. An individual who has more health problems or is concerned with someone else's health problems would score higher on the index. The health problems index indicates less than four issues that they or someone they know faced, indicated by online health seekers (out of nine possible health problems). The nine possible health problems listed were cancer, heart disease, obesity and weight loss, arthritis, diabetes, Alzheimer's, high cholesterol, osteoporosis, and mental health.

The online activities index measures the amount of activities that boomers and seniors conduct online, and the average is around two activities (Table 4). The prediction is that health seekers who conduct more online activities have a greater likelihood of using health information to manage their health because of their familiarity and comfort with the Internet. The four online activities that comprised the index were using instant messaging, reading news, buying a product, and checking the weather.

The online health information predictor variables also show the capacity of the individual to look up health information on the Internet (Table 4). Seniors are more trusting of the health information that they read online, with only 24% of seniors "most of the time" and "always" looking to see who provides medical information on the Internet. On the other hand, 40% of boomers are looking to see who provides the online health information. This difference was also statistically significant at the 0.01 level. In addition, boomers are more frequent consumers of online health information, using it at least once or twice a month, as represented by 38% of the sample. Seniors consume online health information marginally less frequently with 34% doing so.

With regard to overall positive feelings toward the Internet, there was an average score of two on an index scaled from zero to three, indicating that boomers and seniors have overall positive feelings toward the Internet as a source of health information. The index was calculated by adding up the specific responses to whether the online health seeker agreed that online health information gave them information quickly, whether it helped them feel more informed when they go to the doctor, and whether it allows them to get information from a lot of different sources.

On an index of zero being the lowest and two being the highest, less than one was found, indicating that very few online health seekers harbor negative feelings toward the Internet as a source of health information. Having positive feelings about online health information also showed a statistically significant difference between boomers and seniors at the 0.01 significance level. Similarly, this negative feelings index was calculated by adding the individual responses, if they agreed that online health information was frustrating because it is hard to find what they were searching for and if it is confusing because there is too much informa-

tion. The following section tests the relationship between accessing online health information and managing a boomer's and a senior's health.

RESULTS OF LOGISTIC REGRESSION MODELS OF ONLINE HEALTH INFORMATION MANAGING HEALTH

This study uses logistic regression with five separate management-of-health dependent variables. A "1" was recorded for each of the five dependent variables if (1) the online health seeker said "somewhat" or "a lot" of information on the Internet helped them to take care of their health; (2) they had a conversation with family or friend about online health information; (3) online health information changed their behavior; (4) they made a decision about how to treat an illness because of online health information; and (5) they visited a doctor because of information found online. A "0" was recorded for each of the five dependent variables if this was not the case.

The results in Table 5 indicate that for four of the five dependent variables, boomers were slightly more likely to use the Internet to manage their health. For instance, an odds ratio of 1.31 for the dependent variable of "somewhat" or "a lot" of information on the Internet has helped to take care of the online health seekers' problems implies that consumers are around one and one-third times more likely to say that this is the case, if they are a boomer rather than a senior.

Changing behavior for boomers because of information found online registered an odds ratio of 1.71, having a conversation with family or friend about online health information had an odds ratio of 1.49, and making a decision about how to treat an illness had an odds ratio of 1.66 (Table 5). Overall, the results showed that boomers are around one and one-half times more likely than seniors to change their behavior and to use online health information to manage their health, which

Table 5. Logistic regression of factors predicting whether online health information has managed a boomer's or a senior's health

Dependent Variables → Independent Variables ↓	Somewhat and a lot of information on Internet helped take care health		Had a conversation family or friend about online health information		Online health information changed behavior		Made a decision about how to treat an illness because of online health information		Visited a doctor because of information found online	
	Odds Ratio	Wald Statistic	Odds Ratio	Wald Statistic	Odds Ratio	Wald Statistic	Odds Ratio	Wald Statistic	Odds Ratio	Wald Statistic
Boomers = 1 (age between 50 to 64)	1.31	(4.49)**	1.49	(10.67)***	1.71	(14.99)***	1.66	(12.63)***	0.90	(0.36)
Health										
Excellent or very good health	1.11	(0.88)	1.64	(21.39)***	1.21	(3.06)	1.36	(7.09)***	1.10	(0.41)
Health problems index	0.99	(0.36)	1.14	(34.51)***	1.04	(3.40)	1.00	(0.00)	1.04	(1.35)
Online Proficiency										
Broadband Internet access	0.82	(2.79)	0.63	(15.51)***	0.90	(0.80)	0.68	(9.37)***	0.89	(0.51)
Online every day	1.55	(13.13)***	1.31	(5.01)**	1.82	(22.22)***	1.43	(7.15)***	1.41	(3.99)**
Online more than 10 hrs week	0.65	(9.62)***	0.89	(0.71)	0.97	(0.05)	1.46	(7.26)***	0.81	(1.39)
Online activities index	1.01	(0.01)	0.93	(1.50)	0.95	(0.55)	0.92	(1.83)	0.80	(7.75)***
Online Health Information										
Access health information online once or twice a month or greater	3.51	(115.95)***	1.59	(17.35)***	2.29	(54.99)***	3.11	(95.83)***	1.82	(16.15)***
Communicated with doctor or other health care provider through email	0.91	(0.28)	1.95	(12.45)***	1.58	(7.28)***	2.83	(35.37)***	1.86	(9.94)***
Doctor recommended a health or medical Website	0.76	(0.97)	0.91	(0.10)	1.17	(0.31)	2.13	(7.10)***	3.68	(22.13)***
Positive feelings about looking for health information on the Internet Index	2.46	(119.44)***	1.63	(46.32)***	1.85	(42.97)***	1.70	(31.68)***	1.84	(19.73)***
Most of the time and always look to see who provides medical information on Internet	1.31	(4.86)**	2.80	(63.13)***	1.61	(15.80)***	1.57	(13.23)***	1.69	(11.21)***
Negative feelings about looking for health information on the Internet	0.75	(16.82)***	0.81	(10.16)***	0.71	(21.06)***	0.70	(20.83)***	0.77	(6.21)***
Constant	0.08	(89.93)***	0.13	(65.14)***	0.03	(122.43)***	0.04	(103.03)***	0.03	(66.25)***
Nagelkerke R-Square	0.27		0.22		0.22		0.26		0.13	

Notes: ** significant at the 0.05 level and *** significant at the 0.01 level.

is not that high, given the attention placed on the differences between these age groups (Kaiser Family Foundation, 2005).

In terms of online proficiency, those who had broadband Internet access were less likely to have a conversation with a family member or a friend about what they saw online and less likely to make a decision about how to treat an illness. However, for those online health seekers who are online every day, this had a consistent impact across all five dependent variables, if they used online health information to manage their health. For instance, there was a 1.82 times greater chance that daily online users changed their behavior because of online health information. In addition, individuals who go online every day were 1.41 times more likely to visit a doctor because of information that they found online. In terms of being online more than 10 hours a week, this had a negative likelihood for the dependent variables "somewhat" or "a lot" of information on the Internet helped to take care of their health, but had a positive impact with an odds ratio of 1.46 for making a decision on how to treat an illness. Overall, there was no overwhelming support that being more proficient with the Internet had a substantial impact on using health information to manage an online health seeker's health. The only consistently significant variable that had an impact on managing health was being online every day.

Boomers and seniors who had excellent or very good health were 1.64 times more likely to have a conversation with a family member or a friend about online health information. In addition, the boomer or senior who had more health problems or who knew someone who was experiencing health problems was 1.14 times more likely to have a conversation with family or friends about online health information. Individuals who were in excellent and very good health were 1.36 times more likely to use online health information to make a decision about how to treat an illness because of online health information. Gener-

ally, the health of the individual was not a strong predictor of using health information to manage a boomers' or seniors' health.

The strongest predictors of using health information to manage health were for the online health information awareness and feelings variables. Frequent consumers of online health information were 3.51 times more likely to use the Internet to take care of their health. It has become a valuable tool for their health care management needs. There was also a 3.11 greater likelihood of someone making a decision about treating an illness to use the Internet more than once a month for health information. In fact, frequently accessing health information registered an impact for all of the dependent variables.

Individuals who had positive feelings about online health information were more likely to use online health information to manage their health. Boomers and seniors who had more negative feelings toward online health information were less likely to use it for health management. This finding was consistently found across all five of the dependent variables. Online health seekers who usually looked to see who provided the health information were more likely to use this to manage their health. For instance, individuals who looked to see who provided the health information were 2.80 times more likely to have a conversation with family or friends about the information that they saw online. If a doctor recommended a health or medical Web site, online health seekers were 2.13 times more likely to make a decision about how to treat an illness because of online health information, and they were 3.68 times more likely to visit a doctor because of information they found online. In addition, individuals who communicated with a doctor or a health care provider via e-mail were 1.95 times more likely to have a conversation with a family member or a friend about health information that they found online. Overall, the logistic regression results indicate the most consistent and highest support for increased awareness and positive feelings toward online health information as a driver for helping to manage boomers' and seniors' health.

CLASSIFICATION TREES ANALYSIS OF TAKING CARE OF BOOMERS' AND SENIORS' HEALTH

Another way to examine the relationship between boomers and seniors and online health information is a classification tree analysis. Classification trees are used to predict membership of cases or objects in the classes of a categorical dependent variable from their measurements on one or more predictor variables. Classification tree analysis is a common data mining technique. Figure 2 shows that the taking care of health variable is related to boomers and seniors having positive feelings toward looking for online health information. In addition, having positive feelings about online health information is related to accessing health information online once or twice a month or more. These findings reinforce the logistic regression results that awareness and feeling toward online health information helps in the management of a boomer's or a senior's health. How do these findings relate to the hypotheses outlined in the beginning of this article?

DISCUSSION OF RESULTS AND HYPOTHESES

This section will discuss how the empirical results of this study confirm or deny the hypotheses (see Table 6). First, the evidence shows through the difference of means tests that boomers and seniors are different in terms of their use of online health information in the management of their health. The mean values scored higher for boomers in using online health information to take care of their health, having a conversation with a family

or a friend about the health information found online, changing their behavior because of online health information, and making a decision about treating an illness because of online health information. There is some evidence that boomers will use more online health information to manage their health, supporting Hypothesis 1. However, there is no overwhelming support for differences between boomers and seniors and using health information to manage their health, with boomers only utilizing this information one and one-half times more than seniors.

The health of the individual, or Hypotheses 2, only predicted the use of online health information to manage a boomer's and a senior's health when they had a conversation with a family member or a friend about online health information and when they made a decision about how to treat an illness. In addition, the health variable predicted a boomer's and a senior's behavior when he or she talked to his or her doctor about information that he or she found online. Overall, there was not overwhelming support that the health of the boomer or senior had an impact on use of online health information to manage his or her health.

Hypotheses 3 and 4 examine whether being more proficient online means that the online health seeker will use the Internet more to manage his or her health. The results consistently showed that those who go online every day were more likely to use the Internet to manage their health. There was not much support that being more proficient with the Internet meant that boomers and seniors would use it more often for health information, since many of the other independent variables in this category were not statistically significant. This is most likely explained by what these online health seekers are doing on the Internet; they are looking for information, which does not require, for instance, broadband Internet access, since a standard dial-up connection will suffice. Therefore, this research cannot confirm that being more proficient with the Internet means that

Figure 2. Classification tree of impact of online health information taking care of a boomer's and a senior's health

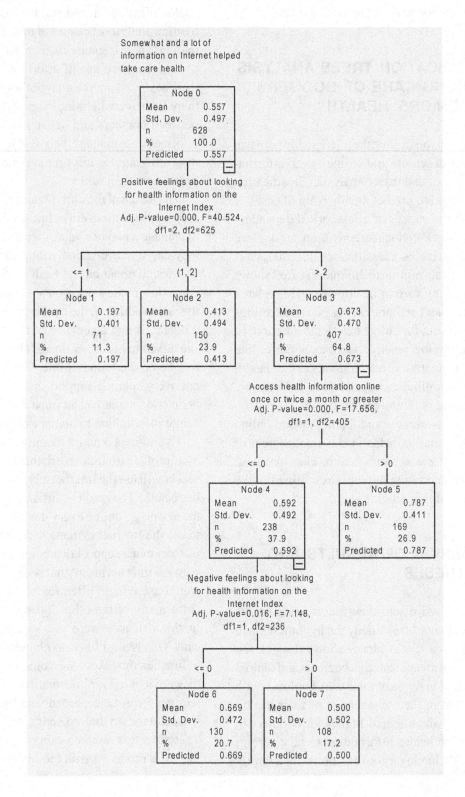

Table 6. Support for hypotheses of boomers and seniors and online health information

Hypotheses	Supported? (Yes, No, or Partially)	Major Test(s) Performed
Hypothesis 1: Online health seekers who are baby boomers are more likely to believe that online health information has helped them manage their health better compared with seniors.	Yes	Descriptive statistics, difference of means tests, and logistic regression
Hypothesis 2: Online health seekers who are healthy or who have family and friends that are healthy will rely less on online health information because of lack of need.	Partially	Logistic regression
Hypothesis 3: Online health seekers who have broadband Internet access will go online more for health information to manage their health	No	Logistic regression -Evidence found in the opposite direction
Hypothesis 4: Online health seekers who go online more often and conduct many online activities will use Internet health information more to manage their health.	Yes	Logistic regression
Hypothesis 5: Boomers and seniors who are females will rely more on online health information.	Yes	Logistic regression
Hypothesis 6: Boomers and seniors who are college educated will rely more on online health information.	Yes	Logistic regression
Hypothesis 7: Boomers and seniors who are Hispanics will go online less for health information.	No	Logistic regression -No support found in logistic regression
Hypothesis 8: Boomers and seniors who have family income above $75,000 will go online more for health information.	Yes	Logistic regression
Hypothesis 9: Online health seekers who most of the time and always look to see who provides medical information on the Internet would use online health information more to manage their health.	Yes	Logistic regression
Hypothesis 10: Online health seekers who access health information online once or twice a month would have a greater likelihood of using online health information to manage their health.	Yes	Logistic regression
Hypothesis 11: If a doctor has recommended a Website to an online health seeker he or she is more likely to use health information to manage their health.	Partially	Logistic regression
Hypothesis 12: If an online health seeker has communicated with his or her doctor via email he or she is more likely to use online health information to manage their health.	Yes	Logistic regression
Hypothesis 13: Online health seekers that have more positive feelings about looking for health information on the Internet are more likely to use this information to manage their health.	Yes	Logistic regression

online health seekers will use this communication media to manage their health more than those who are not as proficient. However, this could change with greater availability of streaming video health information, which is much more suited to a broadband Internet connection.

Boomers and seniors of higher sociodemographic status use the Internet for health information much more than lower sociodemographic status individuals (Hypotheses 5-8). Therefore, this research confirms that there is a digital divide in access to online health information, and public policy should attempt to address this issue. It should be noted that one-third of the United States adult population has not gone online and, therefore, would not be able to benefit from online health information (Pew Internet & American Life, 2005).

Hypothesis 10 was confirmed in the logistic regression results that those who are frequent patrons of online health information actually will use it more often to manage their health. The results showed that health seekers who are accessing health information online once or twice a month or more will be more likely to actually use this information to manage their health. Therefore, these individuals are not just searching for information; they actually are using some of what they find online. Individuals who have positive feelings about online health information also will use it more often to manage their health, and individuals that harbor more negative feelings will use it less often (Hypothesis 13). Online health seekers who are very aware of who provides the medical information on the Internet are more likely to use this information to manage their health (Hypothesis 9). Finally, where there is communication with their doctor via e-mail or at the doctor's office about online health information, boomers and seniors are more likely to use online health information to manage their health (Hypothesis 12). Awareness and feelings toward online health information generally were well-supported predictor variables (Hypotheses 9-13), having an impact on a boomer's or a senior's use of this information to manage his or her health care needs.

RECOMMENDATIONS, LIMITATIONS, AND FUTURE RESEARCH

This article examined the use of the Internet for accessing health information by boomers (age 50 to 64) and seniors (age 65 and over). Boomers generally use Internet health information to manage their health more than seniors. However, there was no overwhelming differences between boomers and seniors, which is the main difference in the finding from another study (Kaiser Family Foundation, 2005). For instance, boomers are much more likely to talk to a doctor about health information that they saw online. Boomers are around one and one-half times more likely than seniors to use online health information to manage their health. This study found that awareness and feelings toward online health information provided the best explanation of health information for management of boomers' and seniors' health.

Since boomers were found to use online health information marginally more than seniors, what are the implications of this observation? Will seniors of tomorrow be similar to seniors of today? Perhaps boomers will continue to seek online health information as they get older. The implication that boomers and seniors may be in the greatest need of health information may not be true in the future with the growing obesity epidemic in the United States, which affects all age groups.

Some policy recommendations should be noted in order to bring more seniors online and to enhance the quality of Internet health resources. Health care professionals should recommend Web sites, promote more effective search and evaluation techniques, and be more involved in developing and promoting uniform standards for health Web sites (Morahan-Martin, 2004). Since only a minority of seniors has ever gone online, this represents a significant digital divide. These findings confirm that for the foreseeable future, the Internet is less likely to be a primary source of information for most seniors, which suggests a need to invest more heavily in education and outreach strategies. This is especially the case for seniors with low or modest incomes, who are least likely to go online for this information. These recommendations could make seniors more aware and could create a positive experience when going online for health information.

In the near future, the Internet will become a decision-making tool for seniors, who will need to make choices about the Medicare prescription drug benefits. They will need to decide which plan has the most attractive premium and to determine whether it will cover the medications they take and will work with the pharmacy they use. Seniors also will need to manage the Internet to make these important decisions. Web site design is part of the solution, since seniors have problems scrolling on Web sites and remembering Web pages (Voelker, 2005).

There are some limitations of this research. With any type of public opinion data, especially when asking subjective questions about sensitive topics of consumers' health, respondents may not be as forthcoming with information. Another limitation is that of the general applicability of the results, given that the proportion of the sample is different for seniors and boomers. In addition, there is no question that specifically addressed whether there was an improvement in the health outcome, just that people felt better informed. Future research could do a longitudinal follow up of this dataset, which might reveal shifts in the use of Internet health information for managing health with boomers and seniors, looking at other measures to see if there is an impact on change in the person's health.

REFERENCES

Anderson, J. G. (2004). Consumers of e-health: patterns of use and barriers. *Social Science Computer Review, 22*(2), 242-248.

Brodie, M., Flournoy, R. E., Altman, D. E., Blendon, R. J., Benson, J. M., & Rosenbaum, M. D. (2000). Health information, the Internet, and the digital divide. *Health Affairs, 19*(6), 255-265.

Cotton, S. R., & Gupta, S. S. (2004). Characteristics of online and offline health information seekers and factors that discriminate between them. *Social Science & Medicine, 59*(9), 1795-1806.

Eysenbach, G. (2003). The impact of the Internet on cancer outcomes. *CA A Cancer Journal for Clinicians, 53*(6), 356-371.

Eysenbach, G., & Jadad, A. R. (2001). Evidence-based patient choice and consumer health informatics in the Internet age. *Journal of Medical Internet Research, 3*(2), e35.

Fox, S., & Rainie, L. (2000). *The online health care revolution: How the Web helps Americans take better care of themselves.* Washington, DC: Pew Internet & American Life.

Fox, S., & Rainie, L. (2002). *Vital decisions: How Internet users decide what information to trust when they or their loved ones are sick.* Washington, DC: Pew Internet & American Life.

Gray, N. J., Klein, J. D., Noyce, P. R., Sesselberg, T. S., & Cantrill, J. A. (2005). Health information-seeking behavior in adolescence: The place of the Internet. *Social Science & Medicine, 60*(7), 1467-1478.

Huntington, P., Nicholas, D., Homewood, J., Polydoratou, P., Gunter, B., Russell, C., et al. (2004). The general public's use of (and attitudes towards) interactive, personal digital health information and advisory services. *Journal of Documentation, 60*(3), 245-265.

Kaiser Family Foundation. (2005). *E-health and the elderly: How seniors use the Internet for health information.* Washington, DC: Kaiser Family Foundation.

Lueg, J. E., Moore, R. S., & Warkentin, M. (2003). Patient health information search: An explanatory model of Web-based search behavior. *Journal of End User Computing, 15*(4), 49-61.

Morahah-Martin, J. M. (2004). How Internet users find, evaluate, and use online health information: A cross-cultural review. *CyberPsychology & Behavior, 7*(5), 497-510.

Nicholas, D., Huntington, P., Williams, P., & Blackburn, P. (2001). Digital health information provision and health outcomes. *Journal of Information Science, 27*(4), 265-276.

Pandey, S. K., Hart, J. J., & Tiwary, S. (2003). Women's health and the Internet: Understanding emerging trends and implications. *Social Science & Medicine, 56*(1), 179-191.

Pew Internet & American Life. (2005). *January 2005 Internet tracking survey.* Retrieved May 10, 2005, from http://www.pewinternet.org

Rideout, V. (2002). Generation Rx.com: What are young people really doing online? *Marketing Health Services, 22*(1), 27-30.

Skinner, H., Biscope, S., & Poland, B. (2003). Quality of Internet access: Barrier behind Internet use statistics. *Social Science & Medicine, 57*(5), 875-880.

Voelker, R. (2005). Seniors seeking health information need help crossing the "digital divide." *JAMA, 293*(11), 1310-1312.

Ziebland, S. (2004). The importance of being expert: The quest for cancer information on the Internet. *Social Science & Medicine, 59*(9), 1783-1793.

ENDNOTES

[1] In this study, for simplicity, baby boomers are classified as those individuals between the ages of 50 and 64, and seniors are classified as 65 and older.

[2] This author would like to thank Victoria Rideout, M.A., Vice President and Director, Program for the Study of Entertainment Media and Health, Kaiser Family Foundation (KFF), for the dataset and documentation used in the statistical analysis of this study. I would also like to thank Virginia Rodgers for her editorial assistance.

[3] For the data analysis, the software package used was SPSS version 13.0.

This work was previously published in the International Journal of Healthcare Information Systems and Informatics, edited by J. Tan, Volume 1, Issue 2, pp. 20-38, copyright 2006 by IGI Publishing, formerly known as Idea Group Publishing (an imprint of IGI Global).

Chapter XVIII
Insights into the Impact of Social Networks on Evolutionary Games

Katia Sycara
Carnegie Mellon University, USA

Paul Scerri
Carnegie Mellon University, USA

Anton Chechetka
Carnegie Mellon University, USA

ABSTRACT

In this chapter, we explore the use of evolutionary game theory (EGT) (Nowak & May, 1993; Taylor & Jonker, 1978; Weibull, 1995) to model the dynamics of adaptive opponent strategies for a large population of pl
ion propagation through social networks in evolutionary games. The key underlying phenomenon that the information diffusion aims to capture is that reasoning about the experiences of acquaintances can dramatically impact the dynamics of a society. We present experimental results from agent-based simulations that show the impact of diffusion through social networks on the player strategies of an evolutionary game and the sensitivity of the dynamics to features of the social network.

INTRODUCTION

We use EGT (Cabrales, 2000; Hofbauer & Sigmund, 2003; Weibull, 1995) to model the dynamics of adaptive opponent strategies for a large population of players. Previous EGT work has produced interesting, and sometimes counter-intuitive results about how populations of self-interested agents will evolve over time (d'Artigues & Vignolo, 2003; Frey & Luechinger, 2002).

In our model, at each stage of the game, boundedly rational players observe the strategies and payoffs of a subset of others and use this information to choose their strategies for the next stage of the interaction. Building on EGT, we introduce a model of interaction where, unlike the standard EGT setting, the basic stage game changes over time depending on the global state of the population (state here means the strategies chosen by the players). More precisely, each player has three strategies available (cooperate *C*, defect *D,* and do-nothing *N*), and the payoffs of the basic stage game are re-sampled when the proportion of the players playing *D* crosses a certain threshold from above. This feature requires long-term reasoning by the players that is not needed in the standard EGT setting. A possible example of a similar real-world situation is a power struggle between different groups. When cooperation drops sufficiently and there are many defections—the situation turns to chaos. When order is restored, that is, when cooperation resumes, the power structure and thus, the payoffs, will likely be different than before the chaos. The payoffs are kept constant while most of the players *C*ooperate (support the status quo) or do-*N*othing, but when enough players are unhappy and choose to *D*efect, the power balance breaks and a radically different one may emerge afterwards.

The available strategies were chosen to abstractly capture and model violent uprisings in a society. Players playing *C* cooperate with the current regime and receive reward when interacting with others playing *C*. If a player has a good position in a regime, it has a large incentive to continue playing *C*. *D* is a strategy played to change the payoffs over a long term, but at an unavoidable immediate cost. Intuitively, it resembles resorting to insurgency or other violent tactics to overthrow a regime. When many players play *D*, playing *C* can lead to very low payoffs. For example, one can imagine a person trying to run a small business during a violent uprising. If these costs are too high, but the player has no

incentive to change the regime, playing *N* can limit payoffs—both negative and positive, until the situation stabilizes. Intuitively, this might correspond to going into hiding or temporarily leaving the conflicted area.

Similar to Nowak and May (1993) and Killingback and Doebeli (1996), we investigate the spatial aspect of the interaction. Previous work has shown that spatial interaction can change which strategies are most effective, for example, in Brauchli, Killingback, and Doebeli (1999) an interaction lattice changed which strategies were most effective in an iterative prisoner's dilemma game. In our model, the players are connected into a *social network*, through which the rewards are propagated (Travers & Milgram, 1969; D. J. Watts, Dodds, & Newman, 2002). Thus the players can benefit (or suffer) indirectly depending on how well off their friends in the network are. We show empirically that the connectivity pattern of the network, as well as the amount of information available to the players, have significant influence on the outcome of the interaction. In particular, the presence of a dense scale-free network or small-world network led to far higher proportions of players playing *C* than other social network types.

GAME DETAILS

We consider a finite population X of players. At each stage all the players are randomly matched in triples to play the basic stage game. Each player thus participates in every stage. Each player has three strategies available: cooperate (*C*), defect (*D*), and do-nothing (*N*) (one can interpret these choices as participating in democratic process, resorting to insurgency, and minimizing interactions with the outer world correspondingly). The payoff $p_i(k)$ of the stage k game to player x_i is ($\#_i(N)$ means the number of agents playing *N*)

		0 opponents play D	1 or 2 opponents play D
x_i's strategy	C	$cc_i - \#_i(N)$	cd
	D	dc	dd
	N	n	

where $cc_i - 2 > n > dc > dd > cd$. Here is a simple rule for distinguishing between these four variables: the first letter corresponds to x_i's strategy, the second letter is c if both of the x_i's opponents play C and d otherwise. For example, cd is the payoff of playing C given that at least one of the opponents plays D. Note that the payoff matrices for different players can only differ in the value of cc_i. All the other payoffs are constant across the population.

Denote $SD(k)$ the proportion of the population that defected during stage k:

$$SD(k) = \frac{\text{number of players that played } D \text{ during stage } k}{|X|},$$

Before the start of the first stage, c_i are sampled uniformly from an interval $[CC_{min}, CC_{max}]$. If during stage k^* the series $SD(k)$ crosses a fixed threshold (see the end of this section for the interpretation of the threshold) $T \in (0,1)$ from above, that is,

$$SD(k^* - 1) > T \text{ and } SD(k^*) < T,$$

then all cc_i are re-sampled. Otherwise they stay the same as for previous stage. For example, in an individual run plotted in Figure 1, the values of cc_i would be re-sampled only at point B.

One can interpret the previous interaction as a power struggle: If the proportion of players supporting status quo (i.e., cooperating or doing nothing) is high enough, the payoffs for each individual players do not change. When enough players defect, the system "falls into chaos" and after it emerges back from this state, a new power

Figure 1. An example trace of an individual run of the system. x-axis is the stage number ("time step"), y-axis is the proportion SD of the population playing D. The level of threshold T is also plotted for a reference.

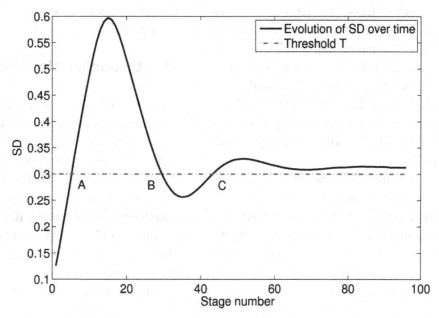

balance is formed and the payoffs change correspondingly. Threshold T in this interpretation is the minimum number of defectors that brings the system into chaos.

Impact of Social Networks

A social network for finite population X is an undirected graph $<X,E>$. Two players i and j are neighbors in the network if and only if $(x_i, x_j) \in E$. We investigate the effect of reward sharing in social networks. After each stage k every player x_i obtains in addition to its own payoff p_i a shared payoff ps_i:

$$ps_i(k) = a \sum_{x_j \in neighbors(x_i)} p_j(k),$$

where $\alpha \in [0,1]$ is a parameter of the system.

Notice that this does not incur payoff redistribution: The shared payoff is not subtracted from payoffs of the players that cause it. One can interpret this phenomenon as players being more happy when their friends are happy.

Social Network Type

The *small-world property* of the network means that the average distance between two nodes in the network is small. It has been shown (D. Watts & Strogatz, 1998) that regular non-small-world networks, such as grids, may be transformed to small-world ones by changing only a small fractions of edges. We followed the algorithm from D. Watts and Strogatz to generate the networks with probability 0.1 of rewiring any edge of the regular structure.

In scale-free networks (Barabási & Albert, 1999) the number of neighbors of a vertex is distributed according to a scale-free power law, therefore few highly connected vertices dominate the connectivity. Many real-world networks possess the small-world and/or scale-free properties (Barabási & Albert, 1999; D. Watts & Strogatz, 1998).

The impact of both small-world and scale-free networks are explored next.

PLAYER REASONING

Information Available to Players

Before describing the player reasoning algorithm one has to define what information is available to the player, that is, define an observation model. We assume that the players are aware of the overall behavior of the game, but may not be aware of the true values of parameters, such as the proportion $SD(k)$ of the population that played D at stage k. The players only observe the actions of their opponents for the given stage, as opposed to observing the whole population. Therefore, the observations available to i after stage k are its payoff $p_i(k)$, shared payoff $ps_i(k)$, and proportion $SC_i^{obs}(k), SD_i^{obs}(k), SN_i^{obs}(k) \in \{0, 0.5, 1\}$ of its direct opponents playing C, D and N during the kth stage.

Note that the information about the global properties of social network connectivity, such as density or whether the network is small worlds or scale free, is not available to players. Therefore, this global information is not used in the reasoning algorithm.

The Reasoning Algorithm

It is easy to see that for any triple of players, a single-stage game has 2 Nash equilibria in pure strategies: everybody cooperating and everybody defecting. The cooperative equilibrium Pareto-dominates the "all-defect" equilibrium. Therefore, if the "all-cooperate" payoffs cc_i were always held constant across the stages, one would expect a population of rational players to always play C. However, the payoffs are re-sampled once the proportion of players playing C drops below T and then grows above T again. This provides an incentive for the players that happened to receive relatively low values of cc_i, to play D for some period of time in order to try and cause the re-sampling of payoffs. On the other hand, if a significant share of the players play D, some of the players may decide to play N, which guarantees a fixed payoff and provides an opportunity to "wait until the violence ends."

A natural way for a player to choose a strategy for the next stage is to compare the (approximate) cumulative future expected payoffs resulting from different strategies. Denote $EP_i(X)$ the approximate cumulative future expected payoff for player i and strategy X. Let $SX_i(k)$ be i's estimate of the share of population playing X on time step k. Then the action selection for step $k+1$ is as follows. If $SD_i(k) > T$, player i chooses action $\arg\max_{X=C,N} EP_i(X)$. Otherwise it chooses $\arg\max_{X=C,D,N} EP_i(X)$. The reason for treating situation $SD_i(k) > T$ specially is that once the share of defectors reaches the threshold, reducing the share of players below T is in common interest of all the players, and the approximate computations of expected utilities do not always capture this feature.

The previous paragraph assumed $EP_i(X)$ to be known. We now turn to their approximate computation.

First consider $EP_i(D)$. The only incentive for a player i to play D is to try to bring the system into chaos in hopes that, when the system emerges from chaos, the re-sampled all-cooperate payoff cc_i for that player will be higher than it is now. Denote TTC_i the i's estimate of the number of stages that it will need to play D before the share of those playing D is higher than T, TC_i—estimate of the number of stages that the system will spend above the threshold and finally, TS_i the length of the following "stability period." Then

$$EP_i(D) \approx (TTC_i + TC_i)E[p_i(D)] + TS_iE[cc_i^{new}]$$
$$= TTR_iE[p_i(D)] + TS_i\frac{CC_{min} + CC_{max}}{2},$$

$$(1)$$

where $TTR_i \equiv TTC_i + TC_i$ is "time to re-sampling" and

$$E[p_i(D)] = P(\#_i(D) = 0)dc + P(\#_i(D) > 0)dd.$$

Expected payoff for action C over the time period is approximated as

$$EP(C) \approx TS_i(p_i(C) + ps_i) + TTC_iE[p_i(c)]$$
$$+ TC_i(P(\#_i(D) > 0)cd + P(\#_i(D) = 0)(p_i(C) + ps_i))$$

$$(2)$$

where $P(\#_i(D) > 0) = 1 - (1 - T)^2$ and

$$E[p_i(C)] = P(\#_i(C) = 2)cc_i + P(\#_i(C) = 1, \#_i(N) = 1)(cc_i - 1)$$
$$+ P(\#_i(N) = 2)(cc_i - 2) + P(\#_i(D) > 0)cd$$

(note that the probabilities here sum to one).

Finally, expected payoff for N over the same time interval is

$$EP(H) = (TTC_i + TC_i + TS_i)n.$$

One can see that a player only expects to get the shared payoff in case of all-cooperative outcomes.

In our model, time of stability TS_i and time in chaos TC_i are system constants that do not differ across the population.

The belief $SX_i(k)$ about the proportion of players playing X at stage k is maintained by each player individually. After each stage each player learns about the strategies of its opponents for that stage. SX_i is then updated according to

$$SX_i(k+1) = \gamma SX_i^{obs}(k+1) + (1-\gamma)SX_i(k)$$

$$(3)$$

where $\gamma \in (0,1]$ is learning rate. Each player also maintains $\delta SX_i(k)$, an estimate of

$$\delta SX(k) \equiv SX(k) - SX(k-1),$$

using an expression analogous to Equation 3 to update it. In the expressions (1-2) $P(\#_i(X))$ are approximated straightforwardly using SX_i, for example

$$P(\#_i(C) = 2) \approx SC_i^2(k)$$

Having SX_i and dSX_i, each player can estimate TTC_i using a linear approximation. For $SD_i < T$, we have (TTC is a system-wide constant)

$$TTC_i = \begin{cases} TTC, & \delta SD_i \leq 0 \\ \dfrac{T - SD_i}{\delta SD_i}, & \delta SD_i > 0 \end{cases}$$

For $SD_i^3 T$, $TTC_i = 0$.

EXPERIMENTAL RESULTS

In our experiments the population size was fixed to 1,000 players. The numerical values of payoff constants were

$$dc = -1, dd = -3, cd = -5, CC_{min} = 3, CC_{max} = 10$$

Estimated time of stability was fixed to $TS_i = TS = 50$ stages, "chaos threshold" $T=0.3$. Initial player-specific values were $SC_i(0) = 1$, $\delta SC_i = -0.02$. For each set of specific parameter values the results were averaged over 500 runs. Unless otherwise noted, the players were connected via a scale-free network with average density of 8.

We were primarily interested in how different parameters of the model affect the evolution of proportion of players playing C over time. On all graphs x-axis denotes the stage of the interaction, y-axis denotes SC, SD, and SN. In a previous work (Sycara, Scerri, & Chechetka, 2006), we presented results for the case where action N was not available to the players. In each of the following figures we contrast the results when N is and is not available to the players.

Note that because the plotted results are averages over 100 runs, averages provide more meaningful information about the influence of the parameters values on the system, than do in-

dividual runs which can vary distinctly from run to run. Most parameter values allow the SC to fall below T on some occasions, but what varies is how often this occurs, how rapidly changes happen, and how quickly cooperation resumes. These effects are more clearly seen on graphs of averages than many individual runs superimposed on a single graph. Notice that the fact that the value of SD on the plots rarely rises above T does not mean that payoffs are almost never re-sampled—individual runs have much more variance and re-sampling happens quite often. It simply means that on average SD is below T.

Figure 2 shows the baseline configuration, with 2(a) showing the case where N is available and 2(b) showing the case where it is not. In both cases, early in the game many players choose D to either try to change the payoffs or protect against losses. When N is available to the players, many choose this action in response to others playing D. Eventually this discourages the use of D and an equilibrium settles in. While the initial dynamics in both cases are similar, notice that over time the proportion of C is far higher in the case where N is available than when it is not. This may indicate that if players are able to avoid spasms of violence without getting hurt, the outcome for all will be better.

Figure 3 shows the impact of setting the network density to 2, 4, 8, and 16. In general, the higher the average network degree, the more players played C and the more quickly players stopped playing D. For the less dense networks, players often chose D early on, but in the most dense network, the lure of shared rewards was too high for players to have incentive to try to move the system towards chaos. In the less dense networks, the availability of the N action allowed the system to move toward all playing C, but as in the baseline case, without the N action, some level of SD persisted. When the average network density was 4, the system moved back towards $SC=1$ faster than when the network density was

Figure 2. Baseline configuration (scale-free network with density 8) with available action N (a) and with N not available (b).

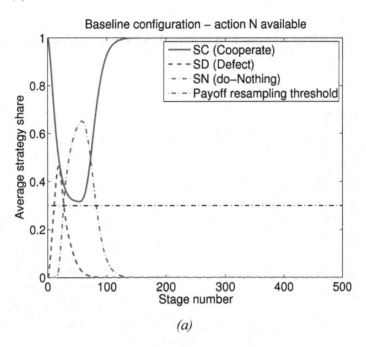

(a)

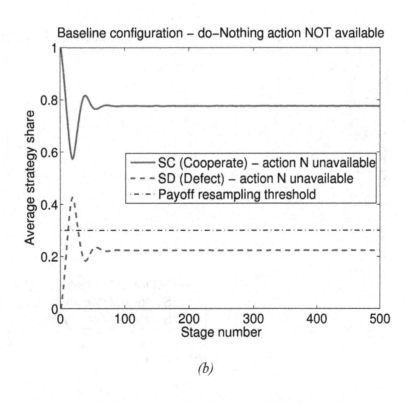

(b)

Figure 3. Impact of network density on the players' strategies. In the top row, the share of players playing cooperate, in the bottom—defect. On the left, the action N is available to the players, on the right—not available.

SC: Social network density impact with do-Nothing action available

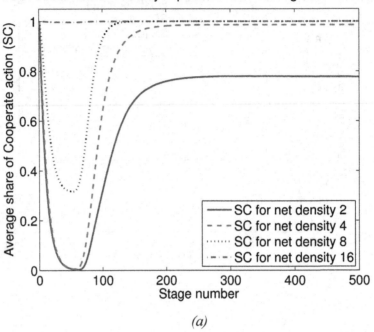

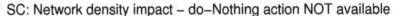

(a)

SC: Network density impact – do-Nothing action NOT available

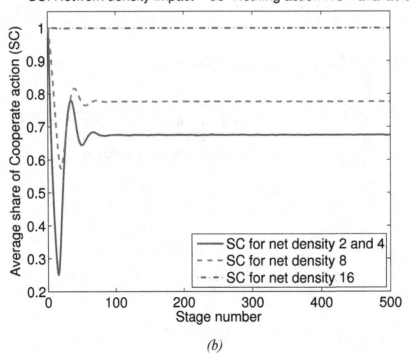

(b)

Figure 3. continued

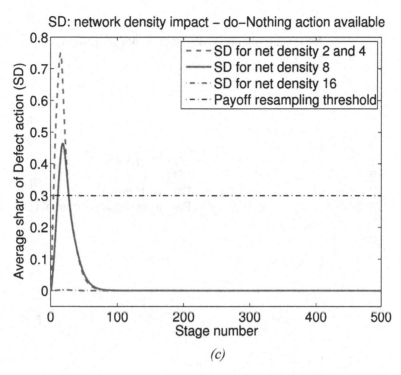

(c)

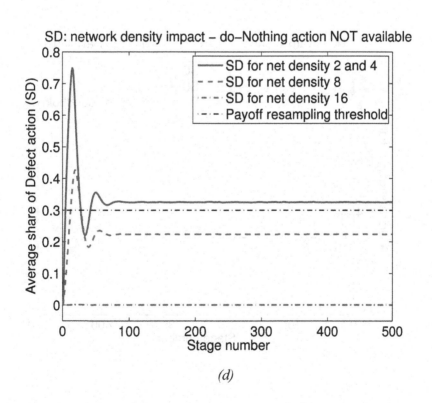

(d)

Figure 4. Results with reward sharing disabled with available action N (a) and with N not available (b)

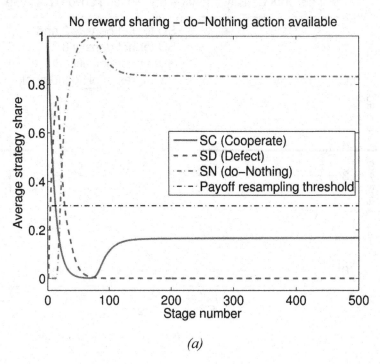

(a)

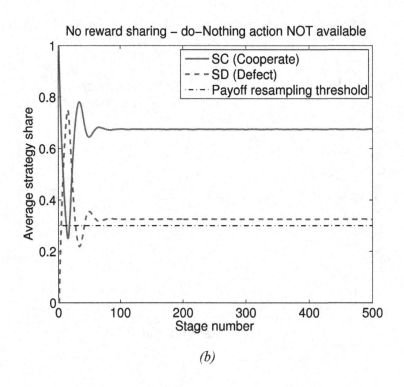

(b)

Figure 5. Impact of learning rate on the players' strategies. In the top row, the share of players playing cooperate, in the bottom—defect. On the left, the action N is available to the players, on the right—not available.

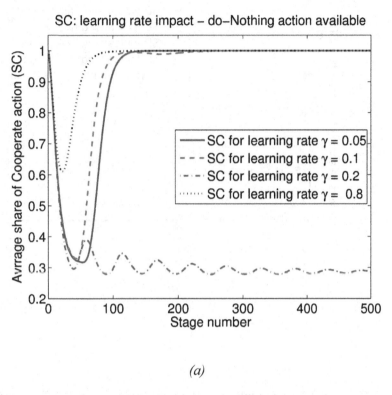

(a)

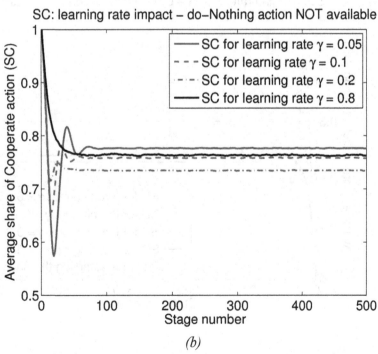

(b)

Figure 5. continued

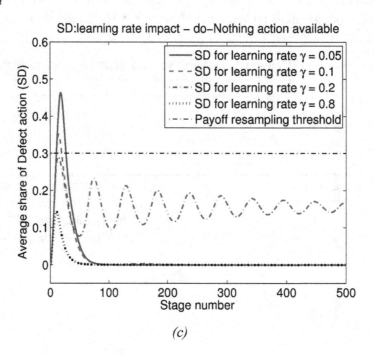

(c)

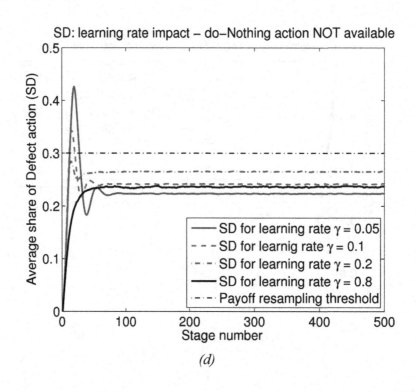

(d)

2. This result may indicate that dense social networks are critical to stable societies.

Figure 4 shows what happens when there is no sharing across the social network. The sharp early peak in *SD* is similar to the sparse network shown above. This is one of the few cases where the availability of the *N* action leads to a lower *SC* over the course of the game. However, the option to play *N* is extensively used and *SD* is reduced to 0. Over an extended period of time, *SC* does rise to 1, but *N* dominates for a long time.

If the type of the network is set to small-world instead of scale-free (with the average of four neighbors), *SC* stays very close to 1 regardless of the availability of *N* to the players (there is no plot for this case, because the results are so trivial). This remarkable relative stability is likely due to the very even sharing of reward across all members of the team, reducing the possibility of a cascade towards chaos. This result may suggest that human societies that have a more scale-free nature will be more likely to descend into chaos.

Figure 5 shows the result as the learning rate is set to 0.05, 0.1, 0.4, and 0.8. Smaller learning rate means that the players are reluctant to change their estimates of the parameters; the closer the learning rate to 1, the more importance is attributed to the most recent observations.

Several interesting effects occur due to the learning rate. Firstly, an intermediate learning rate induces an oscillation in behavior with increasing and decreasing *SD*. Higher or lower learning rates induce different behavior. A high learning rate quickly settles the population down to playing *C*, because the players are better able to estimate future rewards which are maximized by a stable society. A low learning rate eventually allows a stable society but not before a large *SD* has occurred. Interestingly, none of these effects were observed when the *N* action was not available to the players. With learning eventual behavior (except for the intermediate learning rate) *SC* was higher when *N* was available.

CONCLUSIONS AND FUTURE WORK

This chapter presented an evolutionary game with players connected into a social network, sharing payoffs with their neighbors in that network. If individual players reason that increased long-term payoffs might be higher if the whole society can be forced into chaos, they will accept significant short-term costs and risk, to bring that situation about. The key conclusion from this game is that a society of *rational* agents who will all gain if they all play cooperative strategies can easily be induced to play strategies that are guaranteed to lead to a negative payoff.

Our experiments show that the existence and nature of a social network makes a dramatic difference to the evolution and conclusion of the game. Very dense networks or small-world networks had far higher proportions of players playing cooperative strategies than when there is a sparse scale-free network. This result has implications for all EGT where interaction occurs between players, but only simple social networks are used. It is possible that such results will change if different interaction networks are used.

REFERENCES

Barabási, A.-L., & Albert, R. (1999). Emergence of scaling in random networks. *Science, 286*.

Brauchli, K., Killingback, T., & Doebeli, M. (1999). Evolution of cooperation in spatially structured populations. *Journal of Theoretical Biology*.

Cabrales, A. (2000). Stochastic replicator dynamics. *International Economic Review, 41*(2).

d'Artigues, A., & Vignolo, T. (2003). Why global integration may lead to terrorism: An evolutionary theory of mimetic rivalry. *Economics Bulletin, 6*(11).

Frey, B. S., & Luechinger, S. (2002). Terrorism: Deterrence may backfire. *European Journal of Political Economy, 20*(2).

Hofbauer, J., & Sigmund, K. (2003). Evolutionary game dynamics. *Bulletin of the American Mathematical Society, 40*(4).

Killingback, T., & Doebeli, M. (1996). Spatial evolutionary game theory: Hawks and doves revisited. In *Proceedings of The Royal Society (Biological Sciences)*.

Nowak, M., & May, R. (1993). The spatial dilemmas of evolution. *International Journal of Bifurcation and Chaos, 3*.

Sycara, K., Scerri, P., & Chechetka, A. (2006). Evolutionary games and social networks in adversary reasoning. In *Proceedings of the international conference on complex systems*. Boston.

Taylor, P., & Jonker, L. (1978). Evolutionary stable strategies and game dynamics. *Mathematical Biosciences, 40*.

Travers, J., & Milgram, S. (1969). An experimental study of the small world problem. *Sociometry, 32*, 425-443.

Watts, D., & Strogatz, S. (1998). Collective dynamics of small-world networks. *Nature, 393*.

Watts, D. J., Dodds, P. S., & Newman, M. E. J. (2002). Identity and search in social networks. *Science, 296*(5571), 1302-1305.

Weibull, J. (1995). *Evolutionary game theory*. Cambridge, MA: MIT Press.

Section V
Critical Issues

Chapter XIX
Information–Communications Systems Convergence Paradigm:
Invisible E–Culture and E–Technologies

Fjodor Ruzic
Institute for Informatics, Croatia

ABSTRACT

This chapter is on cultural aspects of information-communications systems embedded into new media environment and invisible e-technologies, and on a new age of social responsibility for information technology professionals. Besides the key issues in information technology development that create smart environment and ambient intelligence, the chapter also discusses digital e-culture and the new media role in cultural heritage. From the viewpoint of information technology, the current information-communications systems converge with media. This convergence is about tools-services-content triangle. Thus, we are confronted with a new form of media mostly presented with the term digital, reshaping not only media industry but also a cultural milieu of an entire nation on a regional and global basis. The discussion follows on the World Library idea that is rebuilding with new form of World Memory (World Brain), the shift from visible culture domination to the domination of invisible culture in the world of e-technologies predominance. From this scenario, information technology professionals coping with information systems projects, e-services development, and e-content design have more cultural responsibility than in the past when they worked within closer and inner cultural horizons and when their misuse of technologies had no influence on culture as a whole.

INTRODUCTORY REMARKS

The information society is, above all, an economic concept but with important social and cultural implications. The new forms of direct access to information and knowledge create new forms of e-culture. E-culture is a part of a culture. It not only concerns users but the community of information professionals as well. When one speaks of information technology, it is always from the Western point of view, whereas e-technology (especially its applications) takes place throughout the world, and every culture has a different understanding of it. The shift to an e-culture at the level of society in general is translated to the individual level, enabling cultural change to be described empirically. The term *e-culture* refers to the diffusion of new technology, its application for various purposes (especially information and communication), and shifts in related attitudes, values, and norms. E-technology may not be gnawing at the roots of our culture, but those roots are gradually absorbing it. As with all innovation, cultural or otherwise, this technology will reinvigorate, transform, and inspire older cultural forms. We are living in the era of globalization, the information economy, with borderless communities and multiple citizenships. E-culture literacy and attainment will require serious attention to new infrastructure, to the building blocks and platforms for e-culture. These are critical issues for the pursuit of information professionals' excellence, for creativity in an information society, as well as for fundamental imperatives for commerce and trade in a new media environment.

The main notion of the following text is on cultural aspects of information-communications systems embedded into a new media environment, on invisible technologies, and on a new age of cultural responsibility for information technology professionals. The key issues in information technology development that create invisible e-technologies and smart environments are under e-culture influence. From the viewpoint of information technology, the current information-communications systems converge with media. This convergence is about tools-services-content triangle. Thus, we are accepting a new form of media mostly presented with the term *digital*,

reshaping not only media industry but also a cultural milieu of an entire nation on a regional and global basis. The discussion follows on the new e-technology and information-communications systems convergence as the basis for defining pervasive computing and positive e-technologies. The findings at the end of this chapter explain the process of a fundamental cultural shift from the computer-based information technology to the computerless (invisible) e-technologies in which the e-culture is the essential factor of the success. The discussion section is about the role of information technology professionals coping with information systems projects, e-services development, and e-content design. They have more social responsibility than in the past when they worked within closer and inner cultural horizons and when their misuse of technologies had no influence on culture as a whole.

BACKGROUND ON INFORMATION COMMUNICATIONS SYSTEMS AND NEW MEDIA

One of the most valuable and essential processes that humanity can engage in and which is, therefore, essential to look at in terms of information technologies, is the process of self-determination. The principal of self-determination of people was embodied as a central purpose of the United Nations in its 1945 charter. The purposes of the United Nations are to develop friendly relations among nations based on respect for the principle of equal rights and self-determination of nations, and to take other appropriate measures to strengthen universal peace. Resolution 1514 (XV) of December 14, 1960, containing the Declaration on the Granting of Independence to Colonial Countries and Peoples, stated that all nations have the right to self-determination; by virtue of that right, they freely determine their political status and freely pursue their economic, social, and cultural development (United Nations, 1960). In the 1990s, these issues continued to be highly relevant as numerous people around the world strove for the fulfillment of this basic right of self-determination. The UN General Assembly in 1995 again adopted a resolution regarding the universal realization of the right of nations to self-determination. Thus, the General Assembly reaffirmed the importance for the effective guarantee and observance of human rights and of the universal realization of the right of nations to self-determination (United Nations, 1995). By this, we see that self-determination is tied to all aspects of life: political, economic, social, and cultural. It is ultimately about how we choose to live and allow others to live together on this planet. Furthermore, information technology plays a key role in current economic and social affairs, so the information technology specialists/professionals have much more social responsibility than other professions. Information and communication technologies and networking infrastructures are playing an expanding role in supporting the self-determination of people and emergent nations. Access to information and the facilitation of communication provides new and enhanced opportunities for participation in the process of self-determination. It gives the potential to enhance political, economic, social, educational, and cultural advancement beyond the scope of traditional institutions and forms of governance.

The next step in recognizing cultural and social dimensions of information technology on the international scene is regarding the Council of Europe document, Declaration of the Committee of Ministers on human rights and the rule of law in the information society (Council of Europe, 2005). The Declaration recognizes that information and communication technologies are a driving force in building the information society with the convergence of different communication media. It also stressed that building societies should be based on the values of human rights, democracy, rule of law, social cohesion, respect for cultural diversity, and trust between individuals and be-

tween nations, and their determination to continue honoring this commitment as their countries enter the Information Age.

Vannevar Bush (1945) predicted that the advanced arithmetical machines of the future would be (a) electrical in nature, (b) far more versatile than accounting machines, (c) readily adapted for a wide variety of operations, (d) controlled by instructions, (e) exceedingly fast in complex computation, and (f) capable of recording results in reusable form. The new computer devices as smart devices, linked through communications systems, are creating new forms of information-communications systems. Thus, the new form of information appliances and ubiquitous information technology creates the basis for the concept of an information-processing utility. Based on interactive and ubiquitous carriers of information, the first generation of new information systems evolved to provide easy communication over time and space barriers. Thus, the new information systems are media. They are virtual communication spaces for communities of agents interested in the exchange of goods and knowledge in a global environment. Further promising technologies are pervasive computing and augmented reality. The vision of pervasive computing is, to some extent, a projection of the future fusion of two phenomena of today: the Internet and mobile telephony. The emergence of large networks of communicating smart devices means that computing no longer will be performed by just traditional computers but rather by all manners of smart devices. From these notions, it is evident that information-communications systems open the way to information society development. The information society is based on the new (digital) media that provides vast opportunities for information/content networking. New organizational networks are built, cutting across national borders and interests. The networks themselves increasingly may take precedence over nation-states as the driving factor in domestic and foreign affairs. At the same time, native communities have been actively engaged in creating and utilizing such networks with increasing participation and sophistication.

We are entering the era of new media. New media are tools that transform our perception of the world and, in turn, render it invisible or visible. Information technology (IT) professionals must understand new problems, considering the role of e-technologies in the integration and interaction between cultures. It is apparently true with tera architecture of the sensor networks that will transform business, healthcare, media, and e-culture itself. A new form of information-communications systems boosts intelligent networks with the majority of computers that are invisible and disposable. The IT professionals have the challenge in turning all that data into useful and meaningful information and in resolving cultural and privacy issues that accompany pervasive networked computing and ambient intelligence. IT professionals are confronted with the stage when e-technologies extract analytic values from social networks turning information issued by sensors and other data sources into knowledge management systems.

Defining new media is hard work. If we begin to use voice or books in an innovative fashion, we have just made old media into new media. Whatever we define as new media now would be old media as soon as we add innovations. We cannot define new media strictly based on the use of new technology for distance communication, since technology is always changing. What is new media today will be passé tomorrow. If we try to define new media by process rather than by structure, we are still in trouble. Whatever we define new media as today no longer will be valid tomorrow as technology changes the structures and processes. Trying to define the limits of change is a futile effort due to the very nature of change. This means that the regulation of new media is also an exercise in utility. The experiences with first-generation media platforms showed that in order to take advantage of the potentials and chances offered by new media, we need to explore their

features and learn how to use them effectively and to build them efficiently. In short, we need to develop innovative concepts, frameworks, and methodologies for the design, realization, and management of the new media. The new media offer unprecedented opportunities and potentials for positively changing almost any aspect of our lives. The growing importance of new media and the demand for appropriate platforms have given rise to the development of innovative technologies and components for such media. Consequently, we can now observe the first generation of media platforms and the first management approaches for such platforms.

The evolution in convenient, high-capacity storage of digital information is one of the enabling technologies for new media. Disk drives that allow local storage, retrieval, and manipulation of digital content are increasing in capacity and falling in price. The current TV experience will evolve into a highly personalized process. Consumers have access to content from a wide variety of sources tailored to their needs and personal preferences. New business models and opportunities for the various providers in the value chain will evolve in an organic market focused on addressing individuals directly with new services. This will allow content providers to respond more effectively to audience needs. Digital media and the emerging communication technologies have created an overabundance of programs and information available from which each consumer can choose. The consumer will need new solutions enabling smart and active decision making over viewing preferences, such as a personal filter for the multitude of choices, dynamically adapting to changing needs and preferences.

Communications technology is available for the support of highly complex interenterprise service networks that support new services (Negroponte, 1996). Altogether, this creates a new view on the product, emphasizing the utility of the package (product and services) instead of the product itself. Analyzing the lifecycle of a product is crucial for synthesizing and specifying new types of benefits for a customer. Therefore, modern manufacturers have to provide benefits to customers. Questions are what could be the benefits and what kind of utility may be beneficial for the customer. Based on that exercise, they have to come up with appropriate business concepts based on new media e-culture.

THE CULTURE AND INVISIBLE CULTURE

To cope with the new culture space in the context of information-communications systems embedded into new media environment, there is a need for basic definitions on culture, new media, and digital e-technologies. The great advances in culture come not when people tried to impose the values of one culture to the exclusion of all others, but rather when modern individuals try to create structures that are more exciting by combining elements from different cultures. The current information technology is capable of recording universal standards and particulars around the world, and it opens new ways and sources for creativity and global cultural heritage. Hence, information technology must reflect the full range of human existence, the values, the culture, and the entire knowledge. At the same time, the new e-culture is born interacting with e-technologies,

and it exists in new cultural ecology. This new cultural ecology stimulates the development of a new trio (triple convergence) consisting of e-technologies, e-culture, and e-society.

The culture is a shared set of manifest and latent beliefs and values (Sackmann, 1991). It helps people to categorize and predict their world by teaching them about habits, rules, and expectations from the behaviors of others. Culture also molds the way people think—what their motivations are, how they categorize things, what inference and decision procedures they use, and the basis on which they evaluate themselves. Most of other definitions are too narrow. Sociologists have focused on behaviorist definitions of culture as the ultimate system of social control. In this system, people act appropriately and monitor their own standards and behaviors. Thus, the culture consists of the learned ways of group living and group responses to various stimuli; sociologists describe the content of the culture as the values, attitudes, beliefs, and customs of a society. Media theorists have explored the interplay of culture and technology, which has led to an emphasis on some aspects of culture. The new approaches are considering cultural ecology as consisting of new media in which various types of media are translated into a common digital form that is accessible within a single framework.

Today's networked media allow each user to participate actively in the creation of cultural

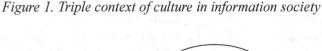

Figure 1. Triple context of culture in information society

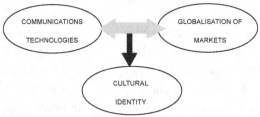

expressions, which we perceive simultaneously and with immediate proximity. The new culture is emerging due to the use of digital technology (e-technology). At the same time, there is a strong relation between values promoted by the new digital e-culture and the traditional moral values created by the major world cultures. These notions open the new contextual approaches on culture in the information society. The culture related to the information society is about three contextual elements (Figure 1.)

The forces of globalization and technology development are paradoxical by nature, offering both threats and opportunities for cultural diversity. Yet, the information society is currently perceived only as an economic imperative in a new environment shaped by rapid information technology developments, based on visions shaped primarily by technologist and business concerns and priorities. The prevailing options embedded in these visions, such as globalization based on cultural homogenization, are questionable not only from a political and social standpoint but also in economic terms. Citizens around the world are becoming increasingly concerned about the way accelerating processes of globalization and

technological innovation are leading to cultural homogenization and immense concentrations of financial power. Globalization generally is seen to be a phenomenon driven primarily by economic interests. As such, it has neither moral content nor values. Therefore, it could be independent from culture.

Cultural Diversity and the Information Society

Cultural diversity potentially can become a key asset in the information society, despite the fact that the culture could be defined as an obstacle. It is clear from the previous discussion on globalization that the economic forces of globalization pose a serious threat to cultural identity. Information technologies are not only the tools that accelerate the pace of globalization, but they are also becoming the key means of access to any good or service. One could thus argue that cultural diversity is an obstacle. Cultural diversity is essentially a question of communication, both internally to one's own culture and externally with distributed cultures. Thus, one of the central issues is not only access to new e-technologies but

Figure 2. Tools-services-content triangle as the basis for information society

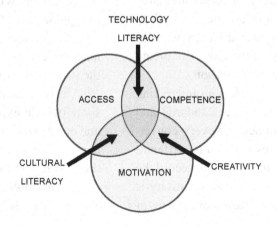

also the capability of manipulating new media in order to participate actively in communicational exchanges.

Technology literacy is needed to operate IT effectively. Cultural literacy refers to the ability of an individual (or community) to relate to the services made by one's own cultural heritage and with access to another culture in a positive way. This means learning from both similarities and differences, being able to reject some aspects, and accepting others. Cultural literacy thus lies at the heart of the possibility of communication in a context of cultural diversity. Content is about Creativity. Creativity is the factor lying at the intersection of motivation and competence, and it covers both the individual and the collective levels. Collective creativity is of greater importance if we are aiming for a shift toward an information society in which a given community will depend on the collective creativity of its social and economic individuals and organizations (with accepting collective memory and brain).

Visible Culture

Western culture has had a strong bias toward the so-called fine arts, such as painting and sculpture. These expressions of culture, which are continuously visible, were more significant than the performance arts (theatre, film, music), which are only visible when they are being played. One of the key elements of great visible culture is uniqueness. Thus, the challenge of universal standards has brought the question of uniqueness back to the fore. To communicate internationally, we need global standards that bring the risk of reducing everything to one mode of expression.

The world of telephony offers an interesting case in point. We clearly need standards and uniform rules for telephones, yet every conversation on those telephones still can be different (Veltman, 1997). In this imperative to record the particular as well as the universal, creativity is only one essential element. The major cultures of

the world owe much of their greatness to the fact that they have a recorded tradition, which stabilizes the corpus but also ensures the possibility of a cumulative dimension, which is reflected in terms such as cultural heritage. Even so, there are many skills in the craft tradition relating to culture that remain oral and invisible.

Invisible Culture

Many people favor material culture because it is visible and easily recognized. Culture is about more than objects in visible and tangible places. For example, many computer users are accustomed to thinking of computers as tools for answering questions. We need to think of them as tools for helping us to understand which questions can be asked, to learn about contexts when and where questions are not asked, of knowing that there are very different ways of asking the same thing. If software continues to be dominated by one country and if the so-called wizards of those programs all rely on the questions of that single country, then many potential users of computers inevitably will be offended, and it is likely that they will not use the programs.

The base assumption is that culture for us is invisible (invisible culture). As workers do not know that they are participants accepting entire organization values, the culture of an organization is invisible (Cooke & Lafferty, 1989). Yet, it is all-powerful. Therefore, this assumption is important for invisible e-culture. We are working in organizations that actually drive our behavior and performance in a way that most of the time is not visible to us. A definition of culture includes the way we do things.

A way to look at culture is actually to have some outside expert or outside person come in and question the way things are going, which can begin to give some insight to the people inside the organization about their own culture (Cleary & Packard, 1992). However, the culture is also considering exchange of ideas, thoughts, and beliefs, and it helps people realize that things can be done differently somewhere else. The success in one culture does not mean success in another culture, and there are actually many ways to succeed, change, and live. People realize that they can act on some other level of culture and act on their own culture.

E-Culture

We could define culture as the beliefs, behaviors, languages, and entire way of life of a particular time or group of people. Culture includes customs, ceremonies, art, inventions, technology, and traditions. The term also may have a more specific aesthetic definition and can describe the intellectual and artistic achievements of a society. The new world economy develops in e-culture and characterizes with the fast, open access to information and the ability to communicate directly with nearly anyone anywhere (Kanter, 2001). This sets e-culture apart from traditional environments.

In a first approximation, one could say that an e-culture is emerging from the convergence of communication and computing along with globalization and the penetration of e-technology in the smallest corners of our lives. The advent of information and communication technology goes hand in hand with changes in attitudes, skills, and behaviors that play a central role in daily life. The advent of an e-culture is correlated with terms of a broad definition of culture. This concerns the culture of a society with both invisible and material characteristics. E-technology as a part of the cultural information may be classified as e-invisible culture, but the outputs of that technology (information appliances) may range among the material (visible) cultural products.

The shift to an e-culture at the level of society is translated to the individual level enabling cultural change to be empirically described. The term *e-culture* refers to the diffusion of new technology; its application for various purposes (especially information and communication); and shifts in related attitudes, values, and norms. The human thinking and behavior are changing gradually by information and communication technology. E-technology may not be gnawing at the roots of our culture, but those roots gradually are absorbing it. As with all innovation, cultural or otherwise, this technology will reinvigorate, transform, and inspire older cultural forms. We are living in the era of globalization, the information economy, with borderless communities and multiple residencies. E-culture literacy and attainment will require serious attention to new infrastructure and to the building blocks and platforms for e-culture. These are critical issues for the pursuit of information professionals' excellence, for creativity in an information society, as well as for fundamental imperatives for commerce and trade in new media environments.

E-TECHNOLOGIES AND UBIQUITOUS INFORMATION (DIGITAL) APPLIANCES

The Internet is without precedent because of two key features: its interactive and communicative natures. It is not a commodity in the sense that you can go out and buy a TV. You cannot go out and buy a net. The key word here is interactivity. Interactivity implies a dialogue of some kind, a changing response based on changing stimuli. There is much talk of interactive Web sites, but even the best of these choose from a preprogrammed set of possibilities in order to give the illusion of being interactive. You have interactivity over the telephone, and you have interactivity in a face-to-face dialogue. However, you do not have interactivity in traditional analogue television. The prosperity of the net is that it permits simultaneous interactivity with thousands and, perhaps, millions of people worldwide. This is a first in the history of humankind.

With the new and upcoming information-communications systems with pervasive and personal appliances, there will be a huge number of networked intelligent devices and information appliances functioning as self-organizing and managed networks (Figure 3).

In the near future, information communications systems with invisible networked devices, sensors, and appliances will transform businesses, public administration, public services, and the way we communicate within digital networks. Digital networks through the new form of information transport by ultra wideband and WiMax technologies will boost the intelligent networks development around the entire globe. The computer is becoming invisible and everywhere simultaneously. This is the beginning of the invisible computer era.

Parallel to this development is that of networking, which conceivably could result in all the invisible computers in the world being networked into a single virtual computer. This would lead to the evolution of a computer that would be everywhere and nowhere at the same time. Technology itself and on its own is not a cultural determinant. Technology is the invention of a particular culture—a cultural expression. The relationship between culture and technology is not linear and monodirectional but rather multidimensional and hyperspatial. Ten years from now, the computer as we know it today will be an anachronism, a device consigned to museums. Instead, the digital information and services once delivered via conventional computers will be available through almost everything we touch. At the heart of this next generation of computing is the network. It will be pervasive and personal. Looking out a decade or two, every person and thing could be instrumented with sensors that feed data into the content base and take actions on behalf of the client.

The new term, *speckled computing*, goes in that way. It offers a radically new concept in information technology that has the potential to revolutionize the way we communicate and exchange information (Arvind, 2005). Computing with Specknets will enable linkages between the material and digital worlds, and it is the beginning of truly ubiquitous computing. As the once-separate worlds of computing and wireless communications collide, a new class of information appliances will emerge. Where once they are

Figure 3. Scenario of universal personal information appliance

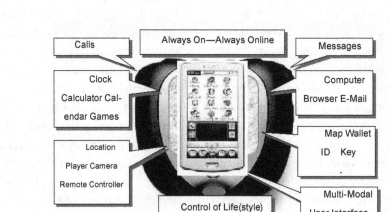

used regularly, the post-modern equivalent might not be explicit after all. Rather, data sensing and information processing capabilities will fragment and disappear into everyday objects and the living environment. At present, there are sharp dislocations in information processing capability—the computer on a desk, the PDA/laptop, the mobile phone, smart cards, and smart appliances. However, Speckled Computing, the sensing and processing of information, will be highly diffused. The person, the artifacts, and the surrounding space become computational resources and interfaces to those resources. Surfaces, walls, floors, ceilings, articles, and clothes will be invested with a computational activity for rich interactions with the computational resources.

The information appliance is the natural outcome in the evolution of information processing. That is why they were foreseen a long time ago. Digital computers started out as expensive mainframes accessible to a few. The next step was the personal computer that individuals could own, and it was incorporated into everyday human activities. Thus, it was essential to have as much functionality in the personal computer as possible. Information technology is making feasible small and inexpensive devices that are smart. This helps to push intelligence closer to the people, the ultimate customers of information technology that accept some of the hidden cultural attributes of the entire community.

In a smart environment, the interaction end points simply could not be cognitively or physically visible. In essence, the user may have no idea that they are engaging in a computer-mediated communication. A smart environment is a composite space made from many individual objects. These objects are either fixed or mobile. The term *invisible* means that a technology has become so natural (common) and so comfortable that we use it all the time without ever thinking of it as a technology or a number of linked technologies. These invisible technologies are taken for granted. Since they are no longer technological,

we can afford to think of them as customary, as the day-to-day workings of our world. As it continues to become more acceptable and as people come into the any-information system more proficient with these new tools, computer technologies will become increasingly invisible.

The exact example of the ubiquitous e-technologies environment is under way through the ubiquitous city in South Korea. New Songdo City (U-city), being built on a manmade island, will feature pervasive computer technology throughout, driven by RFID tags and CDMA wireless communication. Although many Western observers would find the lack of privacy disquieting, Asian countries are more interested in the technological potential of such environments. U-life will become its own brand, its own lifestyle. Residents will enjoy full videoconferencing calls between neighbors, video on demand, and wireless access to their digital content and property from anywhere in Songdo. At the same time, privacy is also encountered: all information services will be anonymous, and they will not be linked to user identity.

INVISIBLE E-TECHNOLOGIES' INTERACTION WITH INVISIBLE E-CULTURE

Our relationship with the manmade world is dominated by the paradigm of the device. This paradigm creates an illusory separation between the technological means (the machinery, the medium) and the technological ends (the commodity, the message). Technological progress generally is devoted to increasing the availability of technological goods, to make them everywhere available instantly without risk or hassle. At the same time, we want the machinery to become invisible. For various reasons, we repress ourselves from seeing the machinery and our dependence upon it. Our conscious awareness focuses on the message, and we refuse to acknowledge the medium (Pribram,

1971). Our perception of the world and our place in it are inextricably mediated through technology and the device paradigm. Our discovery of ourselves (identity through self-determination) is technical and complicated.

We are entering a new era of computing, often referred to as ubiquitous or pervasive computing. Ubiquitous computing consists of information appliances, specialized and easy-to-use devices that avoid the complexity of the computer. The future belongs to information appliances. When technology changes rapidly, greater ease of use serves to attract more users and developers, creating new frustrations. The most we can do is ameliorate the spread of the information appliance products and services. To do this, it appears necessary to recognize that flexibility and ease of use are in an unavoidable conflict and that the optimal balance between those two factors differs among users. Therefore, systems should be designed to have degrees of flexibility that can be customized for different people. Information appliances will be popular, since they will provide many new services for which the desktop computer is ill-suited and will do so in user-friendly ways. However, they will introduce their own complexity, and the level of frustration with information technology will not decrease. This is a result of the conflict between usability and flexibility. The information appliance market will be anything but mature for a long time to come. The emphasis in information processing has been and is likely to continue to be on development of novel applications. When the available information is stored on computers, it is important for information management applications to be able to model users' interpretations of their data and to capture the possibly different meanings, semantics links, and relationships with which users associate the information units available. This is in correlation to one's personal culture. For this purpose, various Personal Information Management tools are being developed to assist the user with navigation/browsing over various

forms of personal digital data. As an example of capturing, organization, and archiving new media content, the MyLifeBits project is very explanatory. MyLifeBits has the aim to store in digital form everything related to the activities of an individual, providing full-text search, text and media annotations, and hyperlinks to personal data (Gemmell, Aris, & Lueder, 2005).

Information technology should mature to the humane technology of appliances in which the technology of the computer disappears behind the scenes into task-specific devices that maintain all the power without the difficulties. This could be explained by the technology of radio. Thus, computers should evolve the way radio receivers did (Norman, 1998). However, there is a problem of motivation, beliefs, knowledge, and frustration dealing with the information technology. This is considering culture (dominantly invisible culture). The problem is that with information appliances and by invisible technologies, we are confronted with the services that must be wel- understood and stable. We will not see this scenario with information appliances, not for a long time. In a world with a huge potential in services, content, and navigation, we cannot know how people will want to use information appliances.

Careful design that is focused on human factors and incorporates powerful processors and software can provide information appliances that are a delight to use. However, once the number of devices to be connected increases and wireless communication with WiFi networks expands, the difficulties will increase. Building complicated systems that work is hard. Building ones that work and are user-friendly is much harder. Further, it is necessary to balance the demand for user friendliness with the demand for more features. A tradeoff between flexibility and ease of use is unavoidable. The problem is that we should not be thinking just of individual information appliances. We have to be concerned with the whole system, which is likely to be complex. The problem is also how to balance flexibility and ease of use in a way that can be customized for people with different needs. This problem is especially focused on multimedia home systems. The home information appliance environment is likely to be more complicated than the office environment today. In addition, many users will be less knowledgeable about information technology than the typical office worker will (Ronfeldt, 1992). Therefore, it will be essential to outsource the setup and maintenance of home computing and electronics to experts. This notion opens new ways for information technology professionals that are accessing information appliances environment (this environment asks for new interface design, navigation methods, and computational power over networked appliances). Hence, there is convergence of culture and technology in use, be they visible or invisible.

Positive E-Technologies

Rheingold (2000) argues that the technology that makes virtual communities possible has the potential to empower ordinary citizens at a relatively small cost. E-technology potentially can provide citizens and professionals advantage and power, which is intellectual, social, commercial, and political. At the same time, civil and informed people must understand the advantages that e-technology provides. They must learn to use it wisely and constructively, as it cannot fulfill its positive potential by itself. Thus, the positive e-technologies should be developed as reduction technologies that make target behaviors easier by reducing a complex activity to a few simple steps. One of the most explicit theories that attempts to describe our natural inclination to do a cost/benefit assessment is expectancy theory. This theory posits that behavior results from expectations about what alternatives will maximize pleasure and minimize pain. E-technologies also should be self-monitoring technologies to perform tedious calculations or measurements, helping people achieve goals or outcomes. Ideally, these technolo-

gies work in real time, giving users immediate feedback on a performance or status. When people can take immediate action on a persuasive message, psychologists have found the message more persuasive than when presented at other times. The recent effort on real-time speech translation is an obvious example of these notions. Researchers from the International Center for Advanced Communication Technologies (interACT), a joint venture of Carnegie Mellon and the University of Karlsruhe, have developed a wearable system that allows real-time speech translation. The system consists of sensors that detect mouth muscle movements, translates that to a spoken language, and then retranslates that into other languages. It will make communication and cultural learning more likely, since people using this technology will be empowered to come together when they otherwise would not interact.

Culture is omnipresent in all technological advancements over the course of history, whether it is the result of intrinsic societal dynamics or the extrinsic factors of the environment. As history clearly documents, whenever technology changes, some pressing force of culture has had an effect on it. Moreover, there is a sort of invisible complimentary system between culture and technology; that is, whenever technology changes, the culture will adapt its way of life to fit the technology. For example, with the invention of the technology necessary for agriculture, cultures worldwide changed their hunting and gathering way of life in order to use the new technology and expand its horizons. This would be expected with the information technology, too. In essence, culture indeed influences human technology, but technology also simultaneously molds the way in which cultures function.

PERSUASIVE AGENDA

Like human persuaders, persuasive interactive technologies can bring about positive changes in many domains, including health, business, safety, and education (Dillard & Pfau, 2002). With such ends in mind, the new area of information technology development is created under the term *captology*. Captology focuses on the design, research, and analysis of interactive computing products created for the purpose of changing people's attitudes and behaviors. The fact that people respond socially to computer products has significant implications for persuasion. It opens the door for computers to apply a host of persuasion dynamics that are described collectively as social influence. These dynamics include normative influence and social comparison as well as less familiar dynamics such as group polarization and social facilitation.

Just as the term *software* shifts the emphasis from media/text to the user, the term *information behavior* also can help us to think about the dimensions of cultural communication, which previously went unnoticed. These dimensions always have been there, but in an information society, they have rapidly become prominent in our lives and, thus, intellectually visible. Today, our daily life consists of information activities in the most literal way: checking e-mail and responding to e-mail, checking phone messages, organizing computer files, using search engines, and so forth. In the simplest way, the particular way people organize their computer files, use search engines, or interact on the phone can be thought of as information behavior. Of course, according to a cognitive science paradigm, human perception and cognition, in general, can be thought of as information processing. While every act of visual perception or memory recall can be understood in information processing terms, today there is much more to see, filter, recall, sort through, prioritize, and plan. In other words, in our society, daily life and work largely revolve around new types of behavior activities that involve seeking, extracting, processing, and

communicating large amounts of information. Information behaviors of an individual form an essential part of individual identity. They are particular tactics adopted by an individual or a group to survive in information society. Just as our nervous system has evolved to filter information existing in the environment in a particular way that is suitable for information capacity of a human brain, so we evolve particular information behaviors in order to survive and prosper in an information society. In today's world of information, people suddenly are shifting their attention to the Web for their computing needs.

Levy (1998) contends that communication in the virtual world can cultivate collective intelligence, which can encourage the development of intelligent communities. He states that sharing of information, knowledge, and expertise in e-communities can promote a kind of dynamic, collective intelligence, which can affect all spheres of our lives. He contends that the virtual world can foster positive connections, cooperation, bonds, and civil interactions. In e-groups or e-communities, which are flexible, democratic, reciprocal, respectful, and civil, this collective intelligence can be enhanced continually. Researchers in science, education, business, and industry are pooling their collective intelligence, knowledge, and data in collaborative memories. These are virtual centers in which people in different locations work together in real time, as if they were all in the same place. Science, education, commerce, and industry have become increasingly global. Collaboration, which is efficient, maximizing, and timesaving among distance researchers in these fields, has become more critical.

This new e-culture paradigm within the Web users' community opens the ways for Web 2.0 e-technologies platform comprising the set of principles and practices based dominantly on the user behavior and cultural values of collaboration. Most users find that Web 2.0 sites are extremely useful, because they are always available (whenever they need it and anywhere they go) with their information. Web 2.0 is the network as platform, spanning all connected devices. Web 2.0 applications are those that make the most of the intrinsic advantages of that platform:

- Delivering software as a continually updated service that gets better, the more people use it.
- Consuming and remixing data from multiple sources, including individual users, while providing their own data and services in a form that allows remixing by others.
- Creating network effects through architecture of participation.
- Going beyond the page metaphor of Web 1.0 to deliver rich user experiences.

One of the key aspects of Web 2.0 is that it connects people so that they can participate effortlessly in fluid conversations and dynamic information sharing. At the same time, information appliances and computing devices are giving people permapresence on the Web. Before now, the user consciously had to go to cyberspace by sitting at a desktop computer and looking at it through a display. Web 2.0 applications will become invisible as they become more popular, and there also would not be such a phrase as "going on the Web." Moreover, if the network is omnipresent and invisible, we do not need the term *cyberspace* anymore. Web 2.0 is also more human and a social one labeled with social interactions like conversation, sharing, collaboration, publishing, which could be supported by the corresponding processes (blogging, tagging, sharing, publishing, networking) and content formats (blogs, wikis, podcasts, folksonomies, social software). In addition, Johnson and Kaye (2004) stated that the Web would become a trustworthy place and the users would take it with much more reliance and credibility.

Computers Influence our Thoughts and Actions

Although culture is mostly learned, it is bound by necessity to a particular setting or context of its behavioral and material articulation. Culture is both conservative and adaptable. Culture is articulated symbolically and has the function of symbolically integrating the diverse moments and spaces of culture into a coherent sense of order. This format is emerging throughout the social field as a format of technology (the point-to-point Internet, file sharing, grid computing, blogs), and as a third mode of production producing hardware, software (often called open sources software) and intellectual and cultural resources (wetware) that are of great value to humanity (GNU/Linux, Wikipedia).

Cognitive scientist Clark (2003) believes that we are liberating our minds, thanks to our penchant for inventing tools that extend our abilities to think and communicate, starting with the basics of pen and paper and moving on to ever more sophisticated forms of computers and e-technologies. He declares that we are, in fact, human-technology symbionts, or natural-born cyborgs, always seeking ways to enhance our biological mental capacities through technology. The persuasive e-technologies are in front of us to solve the problem of difficulties in utilization of the computer, which complexity is fundamental to its nature. We have to start over again to develop information appliances that fit people's needs and lives (Norman, 1998). In order to do this, companies must change the way they develop information system products. They need to start with an understanding of people: user needs first, technology last. Companies need a human-centered development process, even if it means reorganizing the entire company.

People are more readily persuaded by computing technology products that are similar to them in some way (Fogg, 2003). Although people respond socially to computer products that convey social cues, in order to be effective in persuasion, hardware and software designers must understand the appropriate use of those cues. If they succeed, they make a more powerful positive impact. If they fail, they make users irritated or angry. With that in mind, when is it appropriate to make the social quality of the product more explicit? In general, it is appropriate to enhance social cues in leisure, entertainment, and educational products, especially with smart mobile devices (Rheingold, 2002). Users of such applications are more likely to indulge, accept, and perhaps even embrace an explicit cyber social actor. When perceived as social actors, computer products can leverage these principles of social influence to motivate and persuade.

DISCUSSION ON NEW FORMS OF CULTURAL RESPONSIBILITY OF IT PROFESSIONALS

Culture and ethics are a very important part of our everyday life in information society. The invention of new e-technologies tends to bring many different dilemmas into the lives of the creators and the people who use them. Some technologies have been created without choice, and we must make sure we fully understand how to use them properly. The introduction and use of new technologies require a check against the moral structure of the society and the ethical beliefs of the individuals that will feel the effects of such an addition to their lives (Postman, 1992). This belief should be the foundation of innovation so that members of the society can have a strong, viable, and ethical solution to satisfy their wants and needs and to extend their capabilities. Ubiquitous computing and smart environments will be characterized by massive numbers of almost invisible miniature sensing devices that potentially can observe and store information about our most personal and intimate experiences.

The new forms of direct access to information and knowledge create new forms of e-culture. It concerns not only users but the community of information professionals as well.

Technology can be a powerful tool for change, especially when used responsibly. Responsible IT management should be an important part of any socially responsible enterprise's strategies, policies, and practices. Users should have information technology choices that can and should reflect organizational, community, and national values and social responsibility. These notions are considering IT professionals' activities; they should create applications that guarantee accessibility. Accessibility to information via the information-communications systems should not be inhibited by disability or resource limitations, and the design solutions should be for the user experience. Usability of information technology solutions requires attention to the needs of the user (information consumer). The information-communications systems create new psychological demands from human. They ask us to bring a greater capacity for innovation, self-management, and personal responsibility. They also demand social responsibility of information technology professionals. Information technology is the wave of today and the future. Society must adapt to it by creating responsible rules, norms, ethics, and knowledge workers that will enhance its rapid growth.

Many firms acting on the global scene via information-communications systems are committed to incorporating socially responsible projects into their policies and activities. Corporate social responsibility is a development that is here to stay for the long term as a part of corporate policy influencing the company's involvement in the well being or development of local as well as global communities (Furnham & Gunter, 1993). Information technology firms are in a unique position to distribute their high-tech expertise and cultural values in development projects. The new information society environment poses a new relation between values promoted by the new digital civilization and the traditional moral and cultural values created by the major world civilizations. Computer technology and ethical egoism are the products of secular research within a free market capitalist society. The majority of non-Western societies and some Western, as well, follow ethical rules created within traditional culture. These rules are centered on guiding the individual in properly fulfilling his or her role within the society, which means the superiority of the society over the individual. The changes that information technology is bringing to people's lives are revolutionary, and one of the features of every revolution is that it is at the same time both a process of creation and of destruction. The revolutionary process itself is a very rapid one, which means that there is little or no time for a methodical and deep reflection on it while the process is actually in progress. These points ask for more attention from information technology professionals to cope with the culture exposed through the visible objects. They also should implement invisible culture elements when designing new information services. One possible way of minimizing the harm could be through incorporating the experiences of the process of intercultural dialogue into the process of creating a global e-culture of the information society.

REFERENCES

Arvind, D. K. (2005). Speckled computing. In *Proceedings of Nanotech 2005, Anaheim, CA* (Vol. 3, pp. 351-354). Cambridge, MA: Nano Science and Technology Institute.

Bush, V. (1945). As we may think. *The Atlantic Monthly, 176*(1), 101-108.

Clark, A. (2003*). Natural-born cyborgs: Minds, technologies, and the future of human intelligence*. Oxford, UK: Oxford University Press.

Cleary, C., & Packard, T. (1992). The use of metaphors in organizational assessment and change. *Group and Organizational Management, 17*, 229-241.

Cooke, R., & Lafferty, J. (1989). *Organizational culture*. Plymouth, MI: Human Synergistics.

Council of Europe. (2005). *Declaration of the committee of ministers on human rights and the rule of law in the information society*. Strasbourg, France: Office of Publications.

Dillard, J. P., & Pfau, M. (2002). *The persuasion handbook: Developments in theory and practice*. London: Sage Publications.

Fogg, B. J. (2003). *Persuasive technology: Using computers to change what we think and do*. San Francisco: Morgan Kaufmann Publishers.

Furnham, A., & Gunter, B. (1993). Corporate culture: Definition, diagnosis, and change. *International Review of Industrial and Organizational Psychology, 8*, 233-261.

Gemmell, J., Aris, A., & Lueder, R. (2005). Telling stories with MyLifeBits. In *Proceedings of the IEEE International Conference on Multimedia 2005*, Amsterdam, The Netherlands (pp. 1536-1539). Piscataway, NJ: IEEE Publications.

Johnson, T. J., & Kaye, B. K. (2004). For whom the Web toils: How Internet experience predicts Web reliance and credibility. *Atlantic Journal of Communication, 12*(1), 19-45.

Kanter, R. M. (2001). *Evolve: Succeeding in the digital culture of tomorrow*. Boston: Harvard Business School Press.

Levy, P. (1998). *Becoming virtual: Reality in the digital age*. New York: Plenum Publishing.

Negroponte, N. (1996). *Being digital*. London: Coronet.

Norman, D. (1998). *The invisible computer: Why good products can fail, the personal computer is so complex, and information appliances are the solution.* Cambridge, MA: MIT Press.

Postman, N. (1992). *Technopoly: The surrender of culture to technology.* New York: Alfred A. Knopf.

Pribram, K. (1971). *Languages of the brain.* Englewood Cliffs, NJ: Prentice-Hall.

Rheingold, H. (2000). *The virtual community: Homesteading on the electronic frontier.* Cambridge, MA: MIT Press.

Rheingold, H. (2002). *Smart mobs: The next social revolution.* Cambridge, MA: Perseus Publishing.

Ronfeldt, D. (1992). *Cyberocracy is coming.* London: Taylor & Francis.

Sackmann, S. A. (1991). Uncovering culture in organizations. *Journal of Applied Behavioral Science, 27,* 295-317.

United Nations. (1960). *General assembly resolution 1514 (XV), declaration on the granting of independence to colonial countries and peoples.* 947th Plenary Meeting. New York: UN Publishing Office.

United Nations. (1995). *General Assembly resolution 49/148, universal realization of the right of peoples to self-determination.* Forty-Ninth Session. New York: UN Publishing Office.

Veltman, K. H. (1997). Why culture is important in a world of new technologies. In *Proceedings of the Panel on Cultural Ecology, 28th Annual International Institute of Communications Conference,* Sydney, Australia. Sydney: International Institute of Communications.

Chapter XX
The Impact of Ideology on the Organizational Adoption of Open Source Software

Kris Ven
University of Antwerp, Belgium

Jan Verelst
University of Antwerp, Belgium

ABSTRACT

Previous research has shown that the open source movement shares a common ideology. Employees belonging to the open source movement often advocate the use of open source software within their organization. Hence, their belief in the underlying open source software ideology may influence the decision making on the adoption of open source software. This may result in an ideological—rather than pragmatic—decision. A recent study has shown that American organizations are quite pragmatic in their adoption decision. We argue that there may be circumstances in which there is more opportunity for ideological behavior. We therefore investigated the organizational adoption decision in Belgian organizations. Our results indicate that most organizations are pragmatic in their decision making. However, we have found evidence that suggests that the influence of ideology should not be completely disregarded in small organizations.

INTRODUCTION

The free software movement—led by Richard M. Stallman—has always taken an ideological, political view on software. Adherents to the free software movement advocate that all software should be free, in the sense that it should be free to read, modify, and distribute. The open source movement on the other hand was created in order to facilitate the introduction of free software in organizations and takes a more pragmatic stance in its efforts to market open source software (OSS). Previous research has shown that the open source movement is characterized by a shared, underlying ideology (e.g., Ljungberg, 2000; Bergquist & Ljungberg, 2001). Lately, an increasing number of developers are hired by commercial organizations to work on OSS projects. These developers may or may not share the OSS ideology. Nevertheless, many adherents to the open source movement still feel connected to the OSS ideology. Moreover, commercial organizations still need to find a balance between their commercial objectives and the traditional values of the open source movement (Fitzgerald, 2006).

Many organizations have already adopted OSS, especially mature server software such as Linux and Apache. Research on the organizational adoption of OSS has shown that its use was frequently a bottom-up initiative, suggested by technical employees within the organization who are an adherent to the open source movement (Dedrick & West, 2003; West & Dedrick, 2005; Lundell, Lings, & Lindqvist, 2006). In some cases, decision makers could also be considered an adherent to the open source movement. These employees will take on the role of *boundary spanners* in their organization, bringing the organization in contact with new innovations (Tushman & Scanlan, 1981). West and Dedrick (2005) have found in their study on American organizations that although such employees try to ensure that an open source alternative is considered in the decision making, the final decision is made on pragmatic grounds (i.e., based on characteristics of the software such as cost, reliability, and functionality), and not based on ideological feelings towards OSS. The organizations included in their study are rather large,[1] which may have had an impact on their results.

We argue that it is useful to perform a similar study in a context in which there is more opportunity for ideological behavior. We expect that this might be the case in smaller organizations. In order to investigate whether decision making in small organizations is ideological, we have conducted 10 case studies in Belgian organizations to investigate the organizational adoption

of OSS. The article is structured as follows. We will start by discussing the theoretical background of this study. Next, we will discuss our research design. Subsequently, we will present the results of our study, focusing on three organizations that used fairly ideological decision making. This is followed by a discussion of our findings. Finally, we will offer our conclusions.

THEORETICAL BACKGROUND

OSS Ideology

Numerous definitions have been proposed in literature for the term "ideology." Usually, the term is used in a pejorative meaning. Such use implies that an ideology is based on false beliefs of reality. Several authors however recommend against using such a perspective (e.g., Hamilton, 1987). The definition of ideology that we will use in this article is proposed by Hamilton (1987, p. 38):

"An ideology is a system of collectively held normative and reputedly factual ideas and beliefs and attitudes advocating a particular pattern of social relationships and arrangements, and/or aimed at justifying a particular pattern of conduct, which its proponents seek to promote, realise, pursue or maintain."

This definition is non-judgmental, and as a result we do not make any pronouncements with respect to the correctness of the beliefs, values, and norms that characterize an ideology. Hence, acting according to an ideology will not necessarily have negative consequences for the organization.

Previous research has described several ideological principles of the open source movement (e.g., Markus, Manville, & Agres, 2000; Ljungberg, 2000; Stewart & Gosain, 2006). This ideology has been shown to enhance the effectiveness of the OSS community (Stewart & Gosain, 2006).

Stewart and Gosain (2006) identified a number of underlying norms, beliefs, and values of the open source movement (see Table 1). These norms, beliefs, and values are proposed as the tenets of the OSS ideology.

The tenets listed in Table 1 are used to describe the attitudes of developers within the OSS community. We argue however that some of the OSS beliefs and values (i.e., tenets 4–15 in Table 1) can also be shared by technical employees and decision makers in organizations. Hence, it is interesting to investigate whether decision makers who share these ideological ideas of the open source movement make an ideological—rather than pragmatic—decision. Although the study of West and Dedrick (2005) has shown that decision making on OSS is pragmatic, we believe that this may be different in small organizations. Some authors have pointed out that decision making with respect to IT in small organizations

is often the responsibility of a single individual (Harrison, Mykytyn, & Riemenschneider, 1997; Riemenschneider, Harrison, & Mykytyn, 2003). We argue that the impact of the OSS ideology will be greater if a single decision maker—who can be considered an OSS advocate—is present in the organization. In such situations, the adoption decision may be ideological since personal traits and beliefs of the decision maker are more likely to impact the final decision than in larger organizations.

Mindful Innovation

Nowadays, many things require the attention of managers, making their attention a scarce resource (Hansen & Haas, 2001; Swanson & Ramiller, 2004). One of the consequences is that much innovation in organizations is actually driven by bandwagon phenomena, in which organizations

Table 1. Tenets of open source ideology (Stewart & Gosain, 2006, pp. 294–295)

OSS Norms	OSS Beliefs	OSS Values
(1) *Forking*—There is a norm against forking a project, which refers to splitting the project into two or more projects developed separately. (2) *Distribution*—There is a norm against distributing code changes without going through the proper channels. (3) *Named Credit*—There is a norm against removing someone's name from a project without that person's consent.	(4) *Code Quality*—Open source development methods produce better code than closed source. (5) *Software Freedom*—Outcomes are better when code is freely available. (6) *Information Freedom*—Outcomes are better when information is freely available. (7) *Bug Fixing*—The more people working on the code, the more quickly bugs will be found and fixed. (8) *Practicality*—Practical work is more useful than theoretical discussion. (9) *Status Attainment*—Status is achieved through community recognition.	(10) *Sharing*—Sharing information is important. (11) *Helping*—Aiding others is important. (12) *Technical Knowledge*—Technical knowledge is highly valued. (13) *Learning*—There is a value on learning for its own sake. (14) *Cooperation*—Voluntary cooperation is important. (15) *Reputation*—Reputation gained by participating in open source projects is valuable.

mimic the adoption behavior of other organizations and do not properly evaluate alternatives (Abrahamson, 1991; Swanson & Ramiller, 2004). Recently, the bandwagon phenomenon has been framed into the broader context of *mindful innovation* (Swanson & Ramiller, 2004; Fiol & Connor, 2003). The concept of mindfulness originated in psychology and denotes a state of an individual involving: (1) openness to novelty; (2) alertness to distinction; (3) sensitivity to different contexts; (4) implicit, if not explicit, awareness of multiple perspectives; and (5) orientation in the present (Sternberg, 2000). Decision makers in organizations who are mindful have a "watchful and vigilant state of mind" (Fiol & Connor, 2003). An organization that innovates mindfully with IT will therefore not take generalized claims about advantages for granted, but will critically examine their relevance and validity in the organization-specific context (Fiol & Connor, 2003). Mindless innovation, on the other hand, is characterized by "...acting on automatic pilot, precluding attention to new information, and fixating on a single perspective" (Fiol & Connor, 2003; Weick, Sutcliffe, & Obstfeld, 1999).[2] Such innovation may result in making premature decisions based on beliefs that do not necessarily accurately reflect reality (Butler & Gray, 2006). Hence, a dogmatic belief in the OSS ideology may lead to mindless adoption, in which no proprietary alternatives are considered.

Swanson and Ramiller (2004) note that boundary-spanning activities are important for mindful organizational decision making, in order to obtain information on the innovation. We argue that in the case of OSS, this information may be ideologically colored. As a result, the presence of boundary spanners in the adoption of OSS may actually lead to ideological (mindless) behavior instead, especially if decision makers share the OSS ideology. There are at least two factors that can facilitate ideological behavior in such context. First, decision structures in small organizations tend to be less formal (bureaucratic) than in large

organizations. Fiol and Connor (2003) argue that underspecified decision structures may encourage further mindless behavior, if decision making was mindless to begin with. Second, Swanson and Ramiller (2004) point out that although personal mindfulness with respect to innovation does not necessarily equate to organizational mindfulness, it will definitely have an impact on it.

Ideology vs. Pragmatism

In order to investigate whether decision making in organizations exhibits ideological characteristics, we need to determine how ideological behavior can be identified. Based on the work of Stewart and Gosain (2006), we determine whether decision makers and other employees shared some of the beliefs and underlying principles (tenets) of the free and open source movements (see Table 1), *and* did not properly assess their relevancy for the organization. For example, proponents may argue that software should be free (similar to the views of the FSF), may have a negative attitude towards proprietary software, or may be convinced that OSS delivers software of a higher quality (Stewart & Gosain, 2006; Ljungberg, 2000). Consequently, decision makers may have a strong preference for using OSS, without (properly) considering proprietary alternatives. Such decision making may result in a less than optimal solution for the organization. In fact, decision makers are in that case rather mindless in their decision making. Mindless organizations will pay little attention to the organization's specifics or to studying new innovations. This will result in making decisions on "autopilot," using a single perspective (Swanson & Ramiller, 2004; Fiol & Connor, 2003). This means that the beliefs of the OSS ideology are taken for granted, without considering their suitability in the organization-specific context.

On the other hand, we consider an organization to be pragmatic in its decision making when the organization does not exhibit any of the tenets of the OSS ideology, or when decision makers do not take any claims of the OSS ideology for granted, but carefully examine their implications in the organization-specific context. Such organizations are mindful in their decision making. This means that decision makers base their decision on the characteristics of the innovation itself and consider how well the innovation fits within the organization. Pragmatic decision makers will probably consider both proprietary and OSS alternatives, outweigh the benefits of all alternatives, and choose the best solution based on factors such as cost and product features. In this case, no favoritism towards using OSS should be present.

It must be noted that ideological and pragmatic decision making is not a black and white phenomenon. In practice, we expect organizations to exhibit some ideological and some pragmatic characteristics. This is consistent with Geuss (1994), who remarks that an ideology is generally not only composed of the beliefs and values that are shared by *all* members of a group. Consequently, not all adherents to the open source movement will share *all* values proposed by the OSS ideology. This is similar to the statement of Ljungberg (2000) who suggests that developers vary in their adherence to the OSS ideology. Hence, there are many shades of gray in this classification. In this article, we will discuss decision making in three organizations in our sample which clearly exhibited ideological behavior.

RESEARCH DESIGN

To investigate whether decision making is ideological or pragmatic, we studied the organizational adoption of OSS in Belgian organizations. In this study, decision makers were questioned about the reasons for using OSS and their attitudes towards the open source movement. Based upon the information obtained from these organizations, we were able to determine whether their

decision making was either pragmatic or rather ideological.

Scope

We decided to focus mainly on the adoption of open source *server* software. We use the term open source server software to refer to both open source operating systems (such as Linux and FreeBSD) and other OSS for server use (for example, the Apache Web server or the Bind name server). This choice is motivated by the fact that this type of OSS is generally considered to be stable and mature, and is already in use by a significant number of organizations. A similar research approach has been undertaken by other researchers (e.g., West & Dedrick, 2005). On the other hand, we also gathered information on other OSS that was being used in the organizations (such as desktop software, development, and networking tools).

Methodology

We used the exploratory case study approach to study the organizational adoption decision on open source server software. The case study approach is well suited to study a contemporary phenomenon in its natural setting, especially when the boundaries of the phenomenon are not clearly defined at the start of the study (Yin, 2003; Benbasat, Goldstein, & Mead, 1987). We conducted a series of in-depth face-to-face interviews with informants from 10 Belgian organizations to identify the factors that influence the decision to use open source server software as well as their attitudes towards the open source movement. Organizations were selected from the population of all Belgian organizations and were sampled on the basis of two criteria: the size of the organization measured by the number of employees and the sector in which the organization operated. Organizations were only included in our sample if they were using open source server software at the time of our study. Informants within each organization were selected using the *key informant method.* Since the use of a single informant has been shown to give inconsistent results (Phillips, 1981), we tried to speak to both a senior manager (e.g., the IT manager) and a technical person (e.g., the system administrator) whenever possible.

The interviews took place between July and November 2005. An overview of the cases in our study is shown in Table 2. As can be seen from this table, the organizations in our sample are considerably smaller than those in the study of West and Dedrick (2005).[3] In each organization, we have conducted a single interview during which all informants in the organization were present. The interviews were semi-structured, and the format was revised after each interview to incorporate new findings (Benbasat et al., 1987). In the first part of the interview, informants were asked to freely discuss their reasons for adopting OSS. In the second part of the interview, we probed for specific factors that were found relevant in previous studies, as well as the informants' perceptions of the free and open source movements. Each interview lasted 45-90 minutes, was recorded and transcribed verbatim. In order to increase the validity of our findings, informants were sent a summary of the interview and were requested to suggest any improvements if necessary. Follow-up questions were asked by telephone or via e-mail. The transcripts were coded and then further analyzed using procedures to generate theory from qualitative data, as described in the literature (e.g., Benbasat et al., 1987; Eisenhardt, 1989; Dubé & Paré, 2003). Various data displays were used to visualize and further analyze the qualitative data (Miles & Huberman, 1994; Eisenhardt, 1989).

EMPIRICAL FINDINGS

The dominant attitude towards OSS in seven organizations in our sample was pragmatism. These organizations did not exhibit any of the tenets of the OSS ideology, or their decision makers considered how the advantages of OSS could be realized in their organization. Consequently, these organizations could be considered pragmatic (and mindful) in their decision making with respect to the adoption of OSS. The most commonly cited

Table 2. Overview of the organizations in our study

Name	Sector	Employ-ees	Infor-mants	Extent of adoption
OrganizationA	Audio, video, and telecommunications	11	2	moderate
OrganizationB	Machinery and equipment	749	2	extensive
OrganizationC	Telecommunications	1346	1	limited
OrganizationD	Publishing and printing	31	1	extensive
OrganizationE	Food products and beverages	204	2	moderate
OrganizationF	Research and development	152	2	extensive
OrganizationG	Information technology	583	1	moderate
OrganizationH	Chemicals	4423	1	moderate
OrganizationI	Education	3303	3	limited
OrganizationJ	Publishing and printing	12	1	extensive

advantages—and reasons for the adoption—of OSS were *cost* and *reliability*. In general, decision makers tended to consider both proprietary and OSS alternatives, and based their decision on the cost and functionality offered by the various alternatives. Some organizations even explicitly mentioned that they made a pragmatic adoption decision. These seven organizations did not have a preference for using OSS over proprietary software, except OrganizationB where a slight preference for OSS was present. Although they would accept a minor workaround in order to be able to use OSS, this effort should be limited. Or, as expressed by an informant:

We are not going to program around something, because we really want to use that [open source] component. But if there is a little workaround, we will certainly take it.

The other six organizations were quite agnostic about using OSS. One informant in OrganizationF expressed this as:

[The fact that the software is open source] does not really matter for a company.

Some of the technical employees who served as informants in our study had a background in OSS. Although some indicated that they did suggest the use of OSS when appropriate, they did not try to force its use and remained pragmatic. Nevertheless, many OSS development and networking tools (e.g., Nagios, Eclipse, and Maven) were being used by the organizations in our sample.

The results obtained from these seven organizations are quite consistent with the results obtained by West and Dedrick (2005). On the other hand, we observed a different behavior in the three very small organizations in our sample (OrganizationA, OrganizationD, and OrganizationJ) consisting of less than 50 employees. In those organizations, we were able to detect several characteristics of ideological behavior.

In the remainder of this section, we will discuss these three cases in more detail.

OrganizationA

OrganizationA specialized in telecommunication devices. It originally started as a research and development company. Initially, all projects within the organization aimed to gather knowledge and experience in order to develop the initial product. Developers were free in their decision making on which products to incorporate into the final product. Consequently, decision making was significantly influenced by the personal experience of developers.

Our informants indicated that at the time of the organization's founding, many employees—including the organization's founders and the CIO—shared the same background, were very familiar with Linux, and shared the philosophical ideas of the open source movement. These employees had a "firm conviction" in OSS:

The firm conviction was coming from a number of people who said: 'It must be [OSS], we do not want anything else!'...The choice for using OSS was...just a conviction, rather than the result of a comparative assessment.

As a result, most software that was used in the organization was OSS. During package selection, no objective evaluation of (proprietary) alternatives was performed. Although some proprietary software was used, this was either on demand of a customer, or the software was eventually replaced by an OSS alternative.

The choice for OSS at that time was primarily motivated by the lower or non-existing license cost, the fact that there was more confidence in OSS, and the fact that OSS provides access to the source code. Our informants however admitted that these reasons were influenced by the philosophical view towards OSS and that this view on OSS dominated the adoption decision. They were for example aware that using OSS includes additional costs (e.g., packaging and updates), which makes it less clear whether OSS really offers a cost advantage. Such considerations were however not taken into account at that time.

Another factor that has influenced the decision is the avoidance of vendor lock-in. The open source movement generally depicts Microsoft as their common "enemy." This feeling was also present in the organization at that time. Vendor lock-in with Microsoft was feared, partly due to negative experiences in the past. The adoption decision appeared to be anti-Microsoft oriented. As expressed by one informant:

If you mentioned Microsoft, things exploded!

The organization also initiated its own OSS project. It consisted of a Java virtual machine for embedded devices. This project was started to try to benefit from the OSS community model (cf. tenets 4–15). This project was in fact quite successful, and the organization took the role of project maintainer. In the course of time, the project became less interesting for the community (as the product further matured) and participation of the community declined. The software is however still used in the organization's products.

As illustrated, the choice for using OSS was quite ideological in the early years of the organization. Interesting to note is that over the years, several employees of the organization who were adherents to the open source movement, and who advocated the use of OSS, left the organization. As a result, the choice for OSS became much more pragmatic. Another factor that may have influenced this evolution is that the organization finished its software products, gradually became less of an R&D organization, and other goals such as efficiency started to become more important.

At the time of our study, a slight preference for OSS still existed. One informant stated:

Our choice will in the first place go to open source or Linux, but less fanatical than in the past.

Furthermore, the organization seemed to be less willing to take risks in using OSS, or to invest additional effort to get OSS working. This was expressed by an informant as:

I think we are looking rather quickly towards open source products. But if it looks that it will deliver us more worries than it yields advantages, we will not doubt to use a commercial product.

Hence, the organization will only consider using OSS if the product complies with the requirements. The "firm conviction" that was present in the organization has now faded away. The choice for OSS is now mainly based on the potential cost advantages.

Nevertheless, it appears that the organization still felt connected to the principles of the open source movement. When asked whether the organization contributed back any modifications they made to OSS, one informant appeared to feel guilty about not contributing:

...we did contribute quite little, rather naughty, isn't it?

He further noted that the organization tried to participate in OSS projects in other ways, for example by filling in bug reports or by participating in mailing lists (cf. tenets 10–15).

OrganizationD

OrganizationD was active in the publishing and printing sector. The organization had a single person responsible for decision making on IT, and had no internal IT staff. The organization used OSS on a variety of systems (i.e., one Internet gateway, two file servers, and one intranet server). The organization also had 3 LAMP (Linux–Apache–MySQL–PHP) servers, running custom-developed software for time registration. Finally, three desktops were equipped with the Linux operating system in the offices, and an additional 11 PCs function as terminals for the time registration system. The main reason for choosing OSS was to reduce vendor lock-in and maximize the freedom of the IT infrastructure. Consequently, the decision maker investigated OSS solutions without considering proprietary alternatives. Other reasons for using OSS were an increased control over the software, cost advantages, and an increased flexibility. These factors are consistent with the advantages proposed by the OSS community. We were able to detect a few additional ideological characteristics, although they were not that strong.

Our informant indicated that his extensive personal experience with Linux influenced his decision to start using OSS within the organization:

Following [new evolutions] is not enough: you try out software, and free software has the advantage that it is much easier to try out. And of course, since you have tried it yourself, it did influence the [organizational] decision.

His decision to start using OSS within the organization was also influenced by some negative experiences with proprietary software in the past (including vendor lock-in). For example, some proprietary application the organization was using contained a bug which the vendor refused to resolve. As a result, our informant tried to remain in full control over his IT infrastructure. He therefore wanted to maximize the degree of freedom in the IT infrastructure, not only by using open standards, but by using OSS as well: "I wanted to go a step further: not only by using open standards, but also by using open source

applications to have full insurance" (cf. tenets 5–6). He felt that by having access to the source code of OSS, he had maximum control over his applications.

The organization was remarkably committed to its pursuit of freedom. This commitment has moved the organization to start its own OSS project, namely a time registration system for employees. Existing software either did not satisfy all requirements, or was too expensive and did not allow for customizing the software. Hence, the software needed to be custom developed. The decision maker did not want to become dependent on an external organization—not even on the external programmer who develops the software. Instead of performing in-house development or closing an escrow agreement, the organization has chosen a different path. The organization has hired a programmer from an external organization to develop the software, and our informant decided to release the software under an OSS license (the GPL) to ensure that the software would remain completely free (cf. tenet 5). This way, the organization aimed to remain in control over the application, avoid vendor lock-in, and be allowed to make modifications to the software at a later time. The software is being developed as a cooperation between our informant (who is mainly responsible for the analysis) and the paid external programmer. It was the intention of our informant to eventually share this application with other organizations in the same sector. He strongly valued the ability to cooperate with other organizations, and hoped that he would be able to leverage the OSS development model (cf. tenets 4–15) and to receive comments, bug fixes, and maybe even new code submissions.

Interestingly, he was the only informant in our sample who deliberately used the term *free software.*[4] He preferred this term since—in his experience—the term OSS is misused by some vendors to refer to software of which the source code is available, but whose license is still proprietary and does not offer the same freedom as OSS licenses. He felt that the Dutch term for *free software* did not suffer from the confusion in English, and that it better articulated the spirit of the open source movement (cf. tenet 5).

OrganizationJ

The most prominent form of ideological behavior was found in OrganizationJ. Our informant was the IT and business manager of the organization, who was the only one responsible for the IT infrastructure. No internal IT staff was present. The complete IT infrastructure of the organization was based on OSS. This included two important servers: an intranet server running ERP software and an Internet server running the e-commerce site of the organization. Recently, all desktops in the organization were migrated from MS Windows to Linux. The desktops consisted of lightweight terminals which booted from a server. All applications ran on the server, which placed very low demands on the desktop itself. All administration could be performed on the server. The desktops were running the XFCE desktop environment and OpenOffice.org was used as the office suite.

Our informant had a technical background and was an experienced programmer. In fact, he developed his own e-commerce application and was currently rewriting his own ERP software. His personal experience with Linux dates back from 1999. Based on this personal experience, he decided to migrate his Unix-based server to Linux when he was experiencing difficulties with that server.

Similar to our informant in OrganizationD, the IT manager wanted to remain in control of his IT infrastructure (cf. tenets 5–6). Consequently, he tried to make exclusive use of open standards. Moreover, he stated that he only considered using OSS (except for one PC running Microsoft Windows on which specific banking software was

installed that is unavailable for Linux). He also did not want to pay for software, hence he did not use any of the commercial Linux distributions.

Similar to the other two organizations, our informant indicated that his organization had bad experiences with proprietary vendors in the past. In fact, when migrating the server that ran the ERP software, the organization faced huge switching costs when transferring the software from the Unix-based system (developed by a small company) to Linux. He was also suspicious of proprietary software, because it could contain hidden features. This prevented him from having total control over the software. OSS was believed to be more secure, thanks to the availability of the source code: "I think there are thousands, ten thousands or millions of people who use and study it, so I don't have to worry" (cf. tenets 4 and 7).

As a result, he had a rule that proprietary software should not be used under Linux. Proprietary software was simply not considered as an alternative during decision making. This non-pragmatic decision making can be illustrated with two examples. First, the organization recently acquired a new printer/copier. Although the manufacturer provided drivers for Linux, they were proprietary; and the source code of the drivers was not provided. Consequently, the drivers were not installed on the Linux desktops. This means that default Postscript and PCL drivers were used. If specific features would be required, the IT manager stated that he would rewrite the drivers, based on the Postscript definition. He motivated his choice as follows:

Nothing is installed from which the source code is not available: I need control. ... [The manufacturer of the printer] will probably have no bad intentions, probably, but nowadays you never know.

Second, when the IT manager decided that the ERP software needed replacement, he reviewed some OSS alternatives. One of the reasons why

Compiere was not properly examined as an alternative, was that it required the Oracle database server.[5]

The IT manager also started a small OSS project. It consisted of a Perl module to create OpenOffice.org documents. He also indicated that he valued the OSS development model. Two important advantages of this model were the peer review process (see supra) and that it offers more continuity. Although his ERP software was using a graphical library that was maintained by a single person, he was not afraid of becoming too dependent. If the maintainer would quit, our informant was convinced that other people would take over the project. Otherwise, he would still have access to the source code of the library and make any required changes himself (cf. tenets 5 and 14).

DISCUSSION

As can be gathered from our findings, ideological or pragmatic decision making is not a binary variable. Instead, decision making will exhibit both ideological as well as pragmatic character-

Table 3. Ideological characteristics in the decision making of organizations in our sample

OrganizationA:
- Employees, including the organization's founders, shared the philosophical and cultural views of the OSS movement.
- A strong anti-Microsoft sentiment was present.
- Vendor lock-in was feared.
- The organization started its own OSS project to benefit from the OSS development model.
- All software that was used had to be OSS.
- The adoption decision was based on a "firm conviction" in OSS, not on an objective evaluation of alternatives.

OrganizationD:
- The IT manager strives to maximize the freedom in the IT infrastructure by using open standards and OSS.
- Extensive personal experience of the IT manager with Linux influenced the organizational adoption decision.
- The organization started its own OSS project to ensure that the software would remain totally free.
- Driven to OSS by negative experiences (including vendor lock-in) with proprietary software in the past.
- The IT manager uses the term "free software."

OrganizationJ:
- The IT manager does not want to pay for software, including application software.
- The switch to Linux was influenced by personal experience with Linux.
- All software that was used had to be OSS.
- Proprietary printer drivers were not used, even if this means that a work-around must be devised.
- Commercial software is not trusted because the source code is not available.
- Driven to OSS by negative experiences (including vendor lock-in) with commercial software in the past.
- The OSS development model is valued, because thousands of developers are reading the source code, correcting bugs, and ensuring the continuity of the project.
- The complete IT infrastructure was migrated to OSS.
- The IT manager started his own OSS project.

istics, which places the organization's decision making on a continuum between both extremes. In practice, most organizations clearly use a pragmatic decision-making process with respect to the use of OSS. Nevertheless, we were able to detect rather ideological decision making in three small organizations in our sample. The degree of ideology varied between these three cases. A summary of the ideological characteristics in the decision-making process of these organizations is shown in Table 3.

Identifying Ideology

There were clear distinctions between the seven organizations that we labeled "pragmatic" and the three we identified as "ideological." First, within the three latter organizations, there was a clear push behind—or favoritism towards—using OSS. This was caused by the fact that decision makers were adherents to the open source movement and wanted to use OSS as much as possible, or even exclusively. Their personal experience and background was a major factor in this decision. The other seven organizations did consider OSS as one of the alternatives, but would not give preferential treatment to OSS.

Second, the tenets of the OSS ideology were only present in the three organizations. Among the tenets that were most prominently present were software freedom (tenet 5), information freedom (tenet 6), and cooperation (tenet 14).[6] These tenets are indeed central to the OSS ideology. The other seven organizations were rather agnostic about the values and beliefs of the open source movement and considered the OSS character irrelevant during decision making.

Third, several of the factors that influenced the adoption decision are consistent with the advantages put forward by the open source movement. Evidently, this is not sufficient to claim that these organizations shared the OSS ideology. However, there are indications (particularly in Organization A and Organization J) that the perceptions with respect to these adoption factors are influenced by the belief in the OSS ideology, and that their relevancy in the organization-specific environment were not or insufficiently evaluated. This indicates mindless decision making.

Finally, these three organizations were the only ones in our sample that initiated their own OSS projects. Organization A and Organization D clearly indicated that by starting their own OSS projects they wanted to try to leverage the OSS community model. This indicates a belief in the underlying principles of the open source movement (cf. tenets 10–15). If organizations would not be convinced of the advantages of the OSS development model, it seems likely that they would not initiate an OSS project and they would simply develop the software in-house. Nevertheless, principles such as sharing (tenet 10) and cooperation (tenet 14) were deemed quite important by the three organizations.

The previous four points demonstrate that the three organizations discussed in this article exhibited some form of ideological behavior. It is however not trivial to identify ideological tenets in organizations, since the ideas and beliefs of the OSS ideology are not explicitly formulated, as is often the case with ideologies (Hamilton, 1987). A second difficulty is that the presence of one of these characteristics by itself does not automatically lead to ideological decision making. A good example is the avoidance of vendor lock-in. All three organizations indicated having had bad experiences with proprietary vendors in the past and wished to minimize vendor lock-in. The desire to avoid vendor lock-in can be a pragmatic reason for choosing OSS. It may however also lead to a situation in which the decision maker—based on negative experiences with some vendors in the past—only wants to use OSS without considering proprietary alternatives, leading to an ideological position towards OSS. Similarly, the list of characteristics in Table 3 is not exhaustive, and there may be other indicators of ideological behavior. A third issue is that there may be "instances where actors, genuinely or otherwise, do not interpret their behavior in terms of any commitment to a set of beliefs but as simply pragmatic, but where it is clear to the observer that it is, in fact, in conformity with such a set of beliefs" (Hamilton, 1987, p. 21). Nevertheless, the evidence presented in this article and the impression of the decision makers obtained during the interview allowed us to identify ideological characteristics in the decision making of these three organizations. These characteristics had a clear impact on the adoption decision on OSS, resulting in a strong favoritism towards OSS. The attitude in these three organizations was fundamentally different from the other seven organizations in our sample.

Limitations

This study has a number of limitations. First, we used a qualitative approach consisting of 10 case studies. Although we have found that small organizations may engage in ideological decision making, a large-scale quantitative study could provide more insight into the generalizability of this result.

Second, we only included organizations that have adopted OSS. Future research may provide more insight into the attitudes of non-adopters. We can make a meaningful distinction between two groups of non-adopters. On the one hand, there can be organizations that have considered using OSS, but decided not to adopt. The experiences of these organizations may provide more insight into the main drawbacks of using OSS. On the other hand, there are organizations that did not consider OSS as one of the alternatives. Such organizations may have negative perceptions towards OSS and did not further investigate them. For example, organizations may be convinced that OSS costs more in maintenance or is unreliable. Similarly, organizations may also have unverified ideas with respect to proprietary software. They may believe that using proprietary software is less expensive or may place more trust in a closed, proprietary software model. In the most extreme case, organizations may even only consider using software from one specific vendor. In either case, decision making will not be mindful, as not all alternatives are being considered.

Another interesting avenue for future research is to investigate whether decision making on OSS will become less ideological. Since the adoption of OSS is still a relatively recent phenomenon, less information is available on OSS than on proprietary software. It can be expected that as time passes, more information on an innovation becomes available, and decision makers will be able to make better informed choices. On the other hand, Swanson and Ramiller (2004) point out that later adoption can also be driven by diffusion itself, making later adoption not necessarily more mindful than early adoption.

A final topic for further investigation concerns situations in which the decision to start using OSS is triggered by the mere availability of OSS, rather than a concrete problem situation that gives rise to a search, evaluation, and decision-making process. This process resembles the *garbage can model* of decision making (Cohen, March, & Olsen, 1972). Hence, future research could investigate the applicability of this theory in situations in which decision makers share the OSS ideology.

CONCLUSION

The contribution of this article is that we were able to identify ideological characteristics in the decision making on OSS in very small organizations. This result further elaborates on the study of West and Dedrick (2005), who did not detect such behavior in their sample. We argue that while medium to large businesses are likely to be pragmatic in their decision making, the influence of ideological beliefs should not be completely disregarded in small organizations.

Although a minority of organizations in our sample has exhibited ideological behavior, it is remarkable that all three very small organizations in our sample—with a single decision maker—did to some degree. If that decision maker can be considered an open source advocate—which was definitely the case in OrganizationA and OrganizationJ—it is more likely that personal beliefs and values of the decision maker have an impact on the final decision making. Hence, the adoption decision with respect to OSS is more likely to be ideological. This is consistent with the observation of Fiol and Connor (2003) who argue that mindlessness in combination with the absence of formal procedures will further enable mindlessness. In larger organizations, decision making is more likely to be pragmatic, since there are more decision makers and procedures involved in the OSS adoption decision.[7] Ideological decision making is however not necessarily a static phenomenon. Since it appears that ideological decision making is closely related to a single decision maker, the situation may change if that person leaves the organization, or if other decision makers join the organization. This could be observed in OrganizationA.

The definition of ideology we have used in this article is non-judgmental. Consequently, we do not want to make any claims with regard to whether the organizations have made a wrong decision in choosing for OSS. We have found no evidence to suggest that the decision has had a negative impact on the organizations. In fact, OrganizationA actually seemed to be able to innovate by using OSS and proved to be quite successful. On the other hand, it could be established that OrganizationA (at the time of founding) and OrganizationJ were not sufficiently mindful in their decision. These organizations only considered using OSS and did not properly investigate alternatives. Such mindless behavior always entails the risk that the organization does not properly reflect on whether the innovation is suitable within the organization, resulting in a less-than-optimal solution for the

organization (Swanson & Ramiller, 2004). A mindful organization that adopts OSS should not take the claims proposed by the OSS ideology for granted. Instead, it should investigate the implications of using OSS in the organization-specific environment. This is important since this situational context can be complex, rendering some claims irrelevant for the organization.

Swanson and Ramiller (2004) however point out that notwithstanding the risks, mindless decision making can have its merits for organizations. This can be the case when the rewards are likely to outweigh the risks, or when time limitations do not allow for a thorough decision-making process. Hence, mindless decision making can be a valid strategy for routine decisions and does not necessarily imply ideological decision making. However, we were able to exclude this possibility in the three small organizations in our sample by investigating the background of the decision-making process. In all three organizations, the adoption of OSS constituted an important change that concerned the replacement of existing proprietary software or the use of a new type of software. Therefore, no similar evaluation of OSS was previously undertaken, and decision making was indeed ideological.

REFERENCES

Abrahamson, E. (1991). Managerial fads and fashions: The diffusion and refection of innovations. *Academy of Management Review, 16*(3), 586–612.

Benbasat, I., Goldstein, D.K., & Mead, M. (1987). The case research strategy in studies of information systems. *MIS Quarterly, 11*(3), 368–386.

Bergquist, M., & Ljungberg, J. (2001). The power of gifts: Organizing social relationships in open source communities. *Information Systems Journal, 11*(4), 305–315.

Butler, B.S., & Gray, P.H. (2006). Reliability, mindfulness, and information systems. *MIS Quarterly, 30*(2), 211–224.

Cohen, M.D., March, J.G., & Olsen, J.P. (1972). A garbage can model of organizational choice. *Administrative Science Quarterly, 17*(1), 1–25.

Dedrick, J., & West, J. (2003). Why firms adopt open source platforms: A grounded theory of innovation and standards adoption. In J.L. King & K. Lyytinen (Eds.), *Proceedings of the Workshop on Standard Making: A Critical Research Frontier for Information Systems* (pp. 236–257), Seattle, WA.

Dubé, L., & Paré, G. (2003). Rigor in information systems positivist case research: Current practices, trends, and recommendations. *MIS Quarterly, 27*(4), 597–635.

Eisenhardt, K.M. (1989). Building theories from case study research. *Academy of Management Review, 14*(4), 532–550.

Fiol, C.M., & Connor, O.J. (2003). Waking up! Mindfulness in the face of bandwagons. *Academy of Management Review, 28*(1), 54–70.

Fitzgerald, B. (2006). The transformation of open source software. *MIS Quarterly, 30*(3), 587–598.

Geuss, R. (1994). Ideology. In T. Eagleton (Ed.), *Ideology* (pp. 260–278). Essex, UK: Longman Group.

Hamilton, M.B. (1987). The elements of the concept of ideology. *Political Studies, 35*(1), 18–38.

Hansen, M.T., & Haas, M.R. (2001). Competing for attention in knowledge markets: Electronic document dissemination in a management consulting company. *Administrative Science Quarterly, 46*(1), 1–28.

Harrison, D.A., Mykytyn, P.P. Jr., & Riemenschneider, C.K. (1997). Executive decisions about adoption of information technology in small business: Theory and empirical tests. *Information Systems Research, 8*(2), 171–195.

Ljungberg, J. (2000). Open source movements as a model for organizing. *European Journal of Information Systems, 9*(4), 208–216.

Lundell, B., Lings, B., & Lindqvist, E. (2006). Perceptions and uptake of open source in Swedish organizations. In E. Damiani, B. Fitzgerald, W. Scacchi, M. Scotto, & G. Succi (Eds.), *IFIP international federation for information processing: Volume 203—open source systems* (pp. 155–163). Boston: Springer.

Markus, M.L., Manville, B., & Agres, C.E. (2000). What makes a virtual organization work? *Sloan Management Review, 42*(1), 13–26.

Miles, M.B., & Huberman, A.M. (1994). *Qualitative data analysis: An expanded sourcebook* (2nd ed.). Thousand Oaks, CA: Sage.

Phillips, L.W. (1981). Assessing measurement error in key informant reports: A methodological note on organizational analysis in marketing. *Journal of Marketing Research, 18*(4), 395–415.

Riemenschneider, C.K., Harrison, D.A. & Mykytyn, P.P. Jr. (2003). Understanding IT adoption decisions in small business: Integrating current theories. *Information & Management, 40*(4), 269–285.

Sternberg, R.J. (2000). Images of mindfulness. *Journal of Social Issues, 56*(1), 11–26.

Stewart, K.J., & Gosain, S. (2006). The impact of ideology on effectiveness in open source software development teams. *MIS Quarterly, 30*(2), 291–314.

Swanson, E.B., & Ramiller, N.C. (2004). Innovating mindfully with information technology. *MIS Quarterly, 28*(4), 553–583.

Tushman, M.L., & Scanlan, T.J. (1981). Characteristics and external orientations of boundary spanning individuals. *Academy of Management Journal, 24*(1), 83–98.

Weick, K.E., Sutcliffe, K.M., & Obstfeld, D. (1999). Organizing for high reliability: Processes of collective mindfulness. In R.I. Sutton & B.M. Staw (Eds.), *Research in organizational behavior* (vol. 21, pp. 81–123). Greenwich, CT: JAI Press.

West, J., & Dedrick, J. (2005). The effect of computerization movements upon organizational adoption of open source. *Proceedings of the Social Informatics Workshop: Extending the Contributions of Professor Rob Kling to the Analysis of Computerization Movements,* Irvine, CA.

Yin, R.K. (2003). *Case study research: Design and methods* (3rd ed.). Newbury Park, CA: Sage.

ENDNOTES

[1] These organizations had on average 41,885 employees (25,529 when only counting the unit studied in the organization).

[2] The term "mindless" generally has a pejorative meaning, such as "unintelligent." In academic literature however, the term is used to refer to automatic or inattentive behavior (e.g., Swanson & Ramiller, 2004; Fiol & Connor, 2003; Butler & Gray, 2006; Sternberg, 2000). We use the term "mindless" in the second sense. Hence, we do not wish to imply any negative connotations.

[3] The organizations in our case studies have on average 1,081 employees.

[4] Actually, the Dutch equivalent was used, namely "*vrije* software," which is similar in meaning as the French term *libre* software and refers to "freedom" rather than "free of charge."

[5] Other reasons were that it used Java (which the IT manager did not like very much), and the fact that he preferred using custom-developed software that fits his business.

[6] This may indicate that these organizations preferred to cooperate with other organizations within the same industry in order to extend their own capabilities, rather than to outsource development to an external firm.

[7] On the other hand, Fiol and Connor (2003) have noted that formal procedures may also lead to mindlessness (i.e., when decision makers follow procedures without critically considering them).

This work was previously published in the Journal of Database Management, edited by K. Siau, Volume 19, Issue 2, pp. 58-72, copyright 2008 by IGI Publishing, formerly known as Idea Group Publishing (an imprint of IGI Global).

Chapter XXI
The Paleolithic Stone Age Effect?
Gender Differences Performing Specific Computer–Generated Spatial Tasks

Geoffrey S. Hubona
Georgia State University, USA

Gregory W. Shirah
National Aeronautics and Space Administration, USA

ABSTRACT

Most computer applications feature visual user interfaces that assume that all users have equivalent propensities to perceive, interpret, and understand the multidimensional spatial properties and relationships of the objects presented. However, the hunter-gatherer theory (Silverman & Eals, 1992) suggests that there are modern-day differences between the genders in spatial and cognitive abilities that stem from differentiated prehistoric sex roles. If true, there may be discrepancies in how males and females differentially utilize particular spatial visual cues and interface features. We report three experiments in which participants engage in visual spatial tasks using 2D and 3D virtual worlds: (1) matching object shapes; (2) positioning objects; and (3) resizing objects. Female subjects under-perform male subjects in the matching and positioning experiments, but they outperform male subjects in the resizing experiment. Moreover, male subjects make more use of motion cues. Implications for the design of gender-effective user interfaces and virtual environments are considered.

INTRODUCTION

A perennial trend in the evolution of computer technology relates to the ever-increasing power of hardware and the resulting burgeoning possibilities to develop more complex software. These trends have enabled the proliferation of more specialized and powerful computer applications that support users in a wide variety of personal and professional tasks. Associated with these trends are multiple challenges: (1) to make the presentation of geometrically increasing amounts of data ever more concise; and (2) to condense, convey, and present larger and larger volumes of useful information using smaller and smaller spaces. To meet these challenges, new and creative approaches to the design of visual user interfaces have emerged, many that present complex, multidimensional data sets and relationships into condensed visual forms and spaces.

Unfortunately, an implicit assumption in the design of commonplace visual user interfaces is that preponderant portions of the existing user population have similar abilities to cognitively perceive, process, interpret, and ultimately understand the intended visual and spatial properties of the objects presented. Yet, it is known that certain measures of spatial cognition are correlated with performance in user interface tasks (Cockburn, 2004). As an example of how individual perceptual differences can affect user interface design, professional Web designers are aware of color blindness patterns[1] in the general population that affect the ability to correctly perceive color-encoded information. As a result, professional designers of high-traffic Internet Web sites avoid these color blindness traps in order to enhance the universal usability of the sites.

Clearly, the assumption of equivalent user capabilities runs the risk of impairing the usability of visual interfaces that ignore broad, existing population anomalies in spatial cognitive and task performance abilities. Through the process of evolutionary natural selection, the hunter-gatherer theory (Silverman & Eals, 1992) ties modern-day, gender-based differences in certain cognitive, spatial abilities back to sharply differentiated sex roles from prehistoric times. Also, it is recognized in behavioral research communities that there are innate differences between the male and female genders related to cognitive spatial abilities (Kimura, 2000; Linn & Petersen, 1985; Voyer, Voyer, & Bryden, 1995). These gender differences may directly impact the ability to perceive, interpret, and cognitively process spatial properties and spatial relationships of multiple visual objects presented on a computer screen. Thus, there may be fundamental differences between the genders with respect to the ability to use certain visual user interface features, particularly when these features relate to the perception of depth and to the spatial relationships of objects and scenes presented at varying levels of intended depth.

In this article, we review theory and empirical studies relating to (1) gender and human computer interaction and (2) gender differences in innate spatial cognitive and task performance abilities. We then describe three experiments that examine gender-based performance differences in object matching, positioning, and size estimation tasks using two-dimensional (2D) and three-dimensional (3D) virtual worlds. The observed gender performance differences are discussed with respect to applicable theory and with respect to the design of gender-neutral user interfaces and virtual environments.

THEORY AND BACKGROUND

Gender and Human-Computer Interaction

Researchers long have acknowledged the relevance of gender as impacting human computer interaction. Gender has been noted as a broad issue affecting computer skills and computer design issues (Balka, 1996). Gender has been recognized as an important consideration for the design of user interfaces (Leventhal, Teasley, & Stone, 1994) and display techniques (Shneiderman, 1990) and as an issue relevant to achieving universal usability among diverse users of Web-based computer services (Shneiderman, 2000). Gender has been related to the process of decision making, to preferences for investment models, and consequently, as an important consideration in the design of financial (Palma-dos-Reis & Zahedi, 1999) and organizational decision support systems (Powell & Johnson, 1995) for men and women. It has been shown that there are different perceptions and preferences between men and women with respect to the use and satisfaction with different features of electronic commerce Web sites (Simon, 2001).

Numerous researchers have noted differences between the genders while interacting with computers. For example, it has been shown that boys and girls think differently about computers (Hall & Cooper, 1991; Wilder, Mackie, & Cooper, 1985), and that boys and girls have different motivations for using computers (Inkpen et al., 1994; Upitis & Koch, 1996). Moreover, gender-specific preferences for computer interface features and usage styles also have been documented (Lockheed, 1985). Hinckley, Pausch, Proffitt, and Kassell (1998) reported that females were faster than males performing a two-handed, 3D neurosurgical visualization (manipulation) task, and it has been suggested that females outperform males at certain dexterity tasks (Halpern, 1986; Hinckley, Pausch, Proffitt, Patten, & Kassell, 1997).

However, some studies have found no gender differences while interacting with computers. For example, Inkpen (2001) found no boy-girl differences in children's interaction styles with point-and-click as compared to drag-and-drop interfaces. In addition, Rieman (1996) found no significant gender impact on the number of reported exploratory learning discoveries using new systems.

One area of HCI that has examined closely the gender performance differences is with respect to the exploration, use, and navigation of virtual reality (VR) and virtual environment (VE) applications. Investigating gestural input techniques for multimodal and virtual environment applica-

tions, Wexelblat (1995) reported that gender was not a reliable predictor of gesture frequency for subjects describing movie scenes. Basdogan, Ho, Srinivasan, and Slater (2000) found that female subjects engaged in haptic communication in shared virtual environments (SVEs) reported higher levels of sense of togetherness in performing a collaborative task with an unseen partner than did male subjects. Kauppinen, Kivimaki, Era, and Robinson (1998) argued that gender differences in interacting with others in Collaborative Virtual Environments (CVEs) can be traced to broader, societal-driven, gender-specific, identity distinctions that are also witnessed in natural, non-computer-mediated interactions.

Waller, Hunt, and Knapp (1998) suggested that the transfer of spatial knowledge in virtual environment training is responsible for males outperforming females in computer-generated environments. Similarly, other studies have reported men outperforming women (Astur, Ortiz, & Sutherland, 1998) and making use of different cues than women (Sandstrom, Kaufman, & Huettel, 1998) in navigating virtual worlds. Tan, Robertson, and Czerwinski (2001) reported that men completed 3D virtual environment navigation tasks more quickly than women while using smaller, 15-inch displays, but that this male performance advantage disappeared when using larger, 39-inch displays. Subsequently, Czerwinski, Tan, and Robertson (2002) extended this work with two navigation studies. The first study replicated their findings that a wider field of view combined with a large display reduces gender performance biases. Their second study demonstrated that wider fields of view assist females' performances in navigating virtual worlds that are densely populated with objects.

Gender Differences in Spatial Abilities

Innate gender differences in mental spatial abilities generally are identified as the basis for gender disparities in performing spatial tasks (Kimura, 2000; Linn & Petersen, 1985; Voyer et al., 1995). Certain meta-analytic studies (Linn & Petersen, 1985; Voyer et al., 1995) do indicate a male advantage on particular cognitive spatial tests, but individual studies' results are inconsistent in this regard. Further, the different studies often use varying test instruments to measure spatial abilities. Linn and Petersen (1985) categorized the various instruments reported in the literature into three distinct groups: those that measure (1) spatial perception, (2) mental rotation, and (3) spatial visualization. Spatial perception is described as the ability to determine spatial relations despite distracting information. Mental rotation refers to the ability to rotate quickly and accurately two- or three-dimensional figures in imagination. Spatial visualization is the ability to manipulate complex spatial information when several stages are needed to produce the correct solution. These meta-analyses (Linn & Petersen, 1985; Voyer et al., 1995) conclude that men score higher than women on spatial perception and mental rotation cognitive tests, but that neither gender has higher scores on spatial visualization cognitive tests.

The hunter-gatherer theory of the origin of sex-specific spatial attributes (Silverman & Eals, 1992) is one prominent theory that offers an evolutionary perspective on gender differences in modern-day spatial abilities. This theory suggests that men and women have different present-day cognitive skill predispositions that relate to handling differentiated sex role aspects from prehistoric times. Prehistoric females, or *gatherers*, who could effectively forage for food, and who were successful at keeping track of relationships, activities, objects, locations, and landmarks near their habitats, were superior at acquiring resources for bearing and raising offspring. On the other hand, prehistoric males, or *hunters*, who could travel better in unfamiliar territory, estimate distance, and navigate with a bird's-eye view orientation, were, as a consequence, more successful at hunt-

ing, competing with other males, finding mates, and, thus, fathering offspring.

The hunter-gatherer theory suggests that these male-female cognitive predispositions persist today through the process of natural evolutionary selection. As evidence supporting this theory, it has been shown that contemporary females outperform men on spatial tasks related to foraging-related activities, such as remembering the location of objects (e.g., landmarks) in their environment (Dabbs, Chang, Strong, & Milun, 1998). Moreover, it has been demonstrated that women outperform men at keeping track of objects and in finding objects that are lost (Eals & Silverman, 1994; Silverman & Eals, 1992). In addition, studies have shown that women remember the locations of previously viewed items better than men (McBurney, Gaulin, Devineni, & Adams, 1997), and that women outperform men remembering the locations of specific objects (James & Kimura, 1997). In contrast, men typically outperform women at spatial tasks manipulating objects in space (Collins & Kimura, 1997; Goldstein, Haldane, &Mitchell, 1990; Kimura, 1983; Kolb & Whishaw, 1990; Linn & Petersen, 1985; Lohman, 1986; Maccoby & Jacklin, 1974). Other studies have demonstrated that men have more adept mental rotation spatial abilities than women (Dabbs et al., 1998; Silverman, Choi, Mackewn, Fisher, Moro, & Olshansky, 2000), purportedly as an evolutionary artifact of the ability to pursue an animal through unfamiliar terrain and then expeditiously find their way home.

METHOD

Hypotheses and Experimental Tasks

We report three experiments performing spatial tasks using 2D and 3D virtual worlds: object matching, object-positioning, and object resizing. The object-matching experiment was designed largely to tap mental rotation abilities (Linn & Petersen, 1985). The object-positioning and resizing experiments were designed to tap spatial visualization abilities (Linn & Petersen, 1985). Commensurate with the spatial abilities literature, we expect men to outperform women in the object-matching task, but there should be no male-female performance differences in the object-positioning/resizing tasks. Consequently, we propose the following two hypotheses:

H1: Male subjects will outperform female subjects matching objects using a mental rotation paradigm.

H2: Male and female subjects will exhibit equivalent performances positioning and resizing objects.

Object-Matching Experiment. The object-matching experiment was based on the mental rotation paradigm first developed by Shepard and Metzler (1971). Viewing successive pairs of object images presented from different angles, the task was to judge as accurately and as quickly as possible whether the two images represented identical or different objects. For example, Figure 1 shows a typical object-matching image pair. As quickly as the subject could judge whether the split-screen image pair represented the same or different objects, she or he clicked a corresponding *same* or *different* button on the interface, causing the next image pair trial to be presented. Exactly one-half of the 208 randomly presented image pairs represented identical objects, and the other half showed non-identical objects in the pair.

One-half of all trials were viewed by the men and women subjects in stereo, using 3D Crystal-Eyes™ glasses. The remaining trials were viewed in 2D (monoscopically). The left object image in each trial was always stationary, while the right image was always capable of motion and, specifically, two kinds of motion: (1) in one-half of the trials, subjects could control the motion of the right object image by rotating it in any direction for 360 degrees around the center; and (2) in the remaining trials, the right object always rotated automatically in a fixed and random direction about the center point, rotating at a constant speed of approximately 18 degrees per second. The measured performance variables included

Figure 1. Object-matching image pair

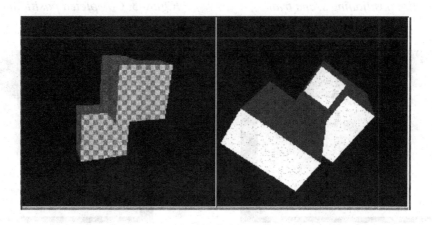

error rate, the percentage of incorrect matching responses, and *response time*, measured in milliseconds.

Seventeen males and 14 female subjects volunteered to participate in the object-matching experiment. All subjects were employees or contractors of the Goddard Space Flight Center in Greenbelt, Maryland. Subjects with corrected vision wore their eyeglasses underneath the stereoscopic viewing glasses. All subjects had professional occupations and included engineers, computer programmers, and computer scientists. The mean age of the subjects was 34.97 years with 4.48 mean years of education beyond high school, 17.03 mean years of computer experience, and 12.65 mean years of professional work experience.

Object-Positioning Experiment. The object-positioning task consisted of subjects viewing computer-generated virtual worlds containing three identically sized spherical objects suspended in 3D space (see Figures 2 and 3). As quickly and accurately as possible, subjects were asked to reposition a target object in order to complete a straight line vector configuration defined by three spheres positioned at equal distances from each other. For example, Figure 2 shows a typical initial scene presented at the beginning of a positioning trial.

Subjects would *fly* the object to be repositioned within the virtual world using a (six-degrees-of-freedom) spaceball input device. When satisfied that they had correctly positioned the misplaced object, they pressed a button on the spaceball that recorded their performance data in an output file and caused the next world to appear immediately. Figure 3 shows the correct (solution) placement of the spheres for the initial trial scene presented as Figure 2. Note that correctly performing the positioning task required subjects to locate the displaced object in three dimensions: x (left and right); y (up and down); and z (toward and away from the viewer). One hundred and forty-four unique worlds were presented to each subject in random order.

Thirty volunteer subjects, 14 female and 16 male, participated. All had professional occupations as computer programmers, analysts, and scientists at the Goddard Space Flight Center. The subjects' mean age was 35.03 years, with 5.53 mean years of education beyond high school, 17.07 mean years of computer experience, and 13.12 mean years of professional work experience.

One-half of all positioning trials was viewed stereoscopically using 3D CrystalEyes™ glasses, while the remaining trials were viewed in 2D

Figure 2. Initial positioning scene trial

Figure 3. Completed positioning scene trial

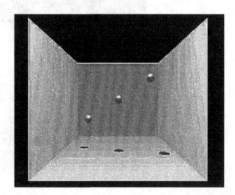

(monoscopically) without wearing the glasses. Because subjects wore the glasses to view scenes in 3D, the stereo and mono trials were presented in cohesive blocks of 72 scenes each. The starting order for presenting the stereo and mono blocks was alternated between subjects.

The measured performance variables included distance error magnitude, response time, and rotational distance magnitude. Distance error magnitude was defined as the Euclidean summation of the three directional errors in the x, y, and z dimensions, or $((e^2_x + e^2_y + e^2_z)^{1/2})$. Thus, this metric measured the exact absolute distance of the repositioned target object from its correct location in three-dimensional space. Response time again was measured in milliseconds. Also, subjects were able to voluntarily rotate the world left or right a total of 45 degrees from the center in either direction, using the left and right arrow keys on the keyboard. The total number of degrees in which the world was rotated in both the left and right directions was captured as a performance *rotational distance* metric. In addition to positioning distance accuracy and response latency, we were particularly interested in observing mean variances in rotational distance as a function of gender. We introduced the ability for the subjects

to rotate the worlds for two predominant reasons: (1) to extract another dependent variable performance measure in addition to standard accuracy and response time measures; and (2) to provide an additional motion-related cue and to see if the male and female subjects would use this cue differentially.

Object-Resizing Experiment. The object-resizing task consisted of subjects viewing virtual worlds containing two differently sized spherical objects suspended in 3D space and displaced at different depths from the viewer (see Figures 4 and 5). Unlike the positioning task, the resizing objects were fixed in position. The task was to adjust the size of a target object in order to correspond with the apparent size of a referent object. Figures 4 and 5 show a typical set of starting and correctly resized ending virtual worlds. One hundred forty-four unique worlds again were displayed in random order to each subject within alternating blocks, consisting of 72 2D (monoscopic) or 3D (stereoscopic) scenes. Each subject viewed the same 144 worlds (although in a random order); thus, the average target and referent ball sizes across all scenes were equivalent and, therefore, the same for all males and females.

Figure 4. Initial resizing scene trial

Figure 5. Completed resizing scene trial

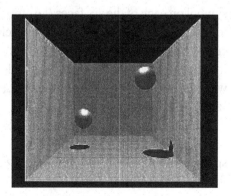

The same 30 subjects from the object-positioning experiment participated in the object-resizing experiment. The measured performance variables included radius error percentage in addition to response time and rotational distance magnitude. Specifically, radius error percentage was defined as the absolute value of the difference between the correct (e.g., referent sphere) radius length and the final resized (e.g., target sphere) radius length divided by the radius length of the referent sphere, or $(((\text{CORRECT}_{RL} - \text{FINAL}_{RL})^2)^{1/2} \div \text{CORRECT}_{RL})$. An accuracy measure relative to the size of the referent object was used, because the referent objects randomly varied in size from large to very small. The response time and rotational distance performance metrics were identical to those used in the positioning experiment.

Assessing Gender Differences in Cognitive Spatial Abilities

Gender-based differences in subjects' mental (cognitive) spatial abilities were assessed using the factor-referenced cognitive tests (Ekstrom, French, Harman, & Dermen, 1976) developed by the Office of Naval Research (ONR) and licensed for research use through the Educational Testing Service (ETS). In all three experiments, subjects were administered the cube comparisons and paper-folding cognitive tests. The ETS cube comparisons test assesses mental rotation cognitive ability. In this timed test, subjects were presented with image pairs of wooden cubes, or blocks. Each cube had a different letter, number, or symbol on each of the six faces (i.e., top, bottom, four sides) of the cube. However, in each pair of cubes presented, only three (of the six) sides of the cube were visible. The task was to determine whether the pair represented identical (e.g., the same) or different cubes.

Unlike cube comparisons, which assess mental rotation ability, the ETS paper-folding test assesses spatial visualization ability. In the timed paper-folding test, subjects had to imagine correctly the folding and unfolding of pieces of paper with holes punched through them. According to ETS, cube comparisons require only the mental rotation of the cube configurations, whereas paper folding requires both rotation and visualization, defined as performing serial operations on the configuration. Since both cube comparisons and object-matching task performances are based on the mental rotation process, as described by Shepard and Metzler (1971), cube comparison ability should correspond with object-matching task performances. Similarly, paper-folding skill should correspond to task performances in the object-positioning and resizing experiments, since all are based on spatial visualization ability.

Results

Cognitive Abilities Test Scores. Tables 1 and 2 reflect the mean scores of the male and female subjects by experiment on the cube comparisons and paper-folding cognitive abilities tests. According to Dr. Ruth Ekstrom (by personal correspondence), the appropriate approach to assess these test results is to consider separately for each test the total number of items answered correctly, the number answered incorrectly, and the number omitted, or unanswered. As indicated in Table 1 (and after checking for equal variances in the male-female scores populations[2]), t-test comparisons of male-female scores on each test indicated that for the object-matching subjects, female subjects answered incorrectly significantly more cube comparison items than males. However, there were no male-female differences in the number of cube comparison items answered correctly or in the number omitted. Moreover, for the paper-folding test, there were no significant male-female differences in the number of items answered correctly, answered incorrectly, or omitted. By answering significantly fewer cube comparison items incorrectly, there is at least some evidence that the male subjects in the object-matching experiment had an advantage over the

Table 1. *Mean cube comparisons and paper folding test scores by gender for subjects in the object-matching experiment*

Object Matching Subjects	Cube Comparisons Test (Mental Rotation)		Paper Folding Test (Spatial Visualization)	
Number of Test Items:	Males	Females	Males	Females
Answered Correctly	**26.65**	**26.00**	**13.29**	**13.57**
Answered Incorrectly	**3.47***	**6.07***	**2.71**	**2.57**
Omitted (Unanswered)	**11.29**	**9.93**	**4.00**	**3.93**

* *Bolded test scores indicate significantly different (at p < 0.05) male-female scores.*

Table 2. *Mean cube comparisons and paper-folding test scores by gender for subjects in the object-positioning and resizing experiments*

Object Positioning/ Resizing Subjects	Cube Comparisons Test (Mental Rotation)		Paper Folding Test (Spatial Visualization)	
Number of Test Items:	Males	Females	Males	Females
Answered Correctly	**28.25***	**21.43***	13.06	10.36
Answered Incorrectly	**2.38***	**5.79***	2.31	4.00
Omitted (Unanswered)	11.38	14.64	4.63	5.64

* *Bolded test scores indicate significantly different (at p < 0.05) male-female scores.*

females in innate mental rotation cognitive ability. However, the paper-folding test scores indicate no significant male-female differences in innate spatial visualization cognitive abilities.

As indicated in Table 2, t-test comparisons of male-female cube comparison test scores for subjects in the object-positioning and resizing experiments indicate that male subjects answered (1) significantly more items correctly than females and (2) significantly fewer items incorrectly than females. However, there were no significant male-female differences in the number of items omitted in the cube comparisons test. Moreover, there were no significant male-female differences in the number of paper-folding test items

answered correctly, answered incorrectly, or omitted. Thus, in the object-positioning and resizing experiments, there again is evidence that males compared to females had superior innate mental rotation cognitive abilities. However, similar to the cognitive test data for subjects in the object-matching experiment, there again is no evidence of significant male-female differences in innate spatial visualization cognitive abilities.

Object-Matching Experiment Results. The object-matching data were fitted to a repeated measures multivariate analysis of variance model (MANOVA). There were significant differences in both error rate (p < 0.0001) and response time (p < 0.0001) as a function of gender. Males were more accurate at judging whether the objects were identical or different (see Figures 6 and 7). The overall mean male error rate was 9.39%, whereas the overall mean female error rate was 13.05%. Furthermore, the male subjects were faster at making these object comparisons (see Figures 8 and 9). Males exhibited an overall mean response time of 12.53 seconds, whereas females responded in an overall mean time of 13.58 seconds.

To further investigate the gender-based impact of the viewing and motion conditions on object-matching performances, the sample then was split by gender and tested for the effects of viewing mode and type of motion on the object-matching error rates and response times for each gender. The data are presented in tabular form in Table 3. Figures 6, 7, 8, and 9 present these data using line graphs that indicate the minimum significant

Table 3. Mean object-matching error rates and response times by gender* for the viewing and motion conditions

Object Matching	Error Rate (%)		Response Time (seconds)	
Conditions:	Males	Females	Males	Females
Stereo Viewing	6.79	10.10	11.75	12.88
Mono Viewing	11.99	16.00	13.32	14.28
Controlled Motion	7.07	11.95	12.87	13.98
Uncontrolled Motion	11.71	14.15	12.20	13.18

* The minimum significant performance differences (at $p < 0.05$) between the genders for the object-matching task are (1) mean error rate: 1.51%; (2) mean response time: 0.43 seconds.

Figure 6. Object-matching error rate by gender by viewing mode

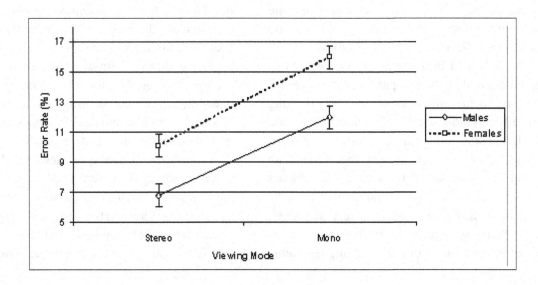

Figure 7. Object-matching error rate by gender by type of motion

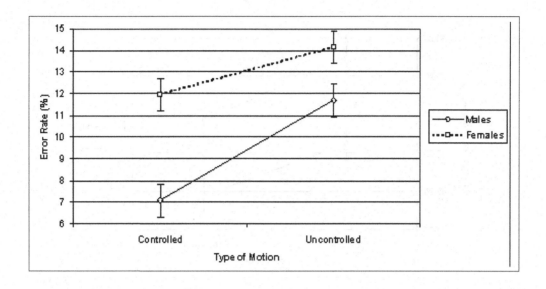

Figure 8. Object-matching response time by gender by viewing mode

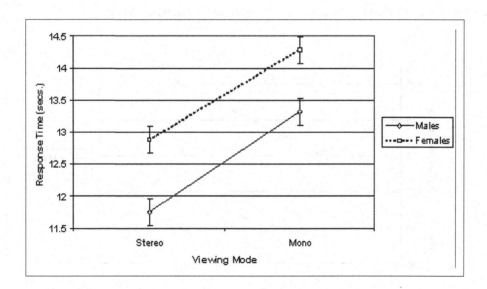

Figure 9. Object-matching response time by gender by type of motion

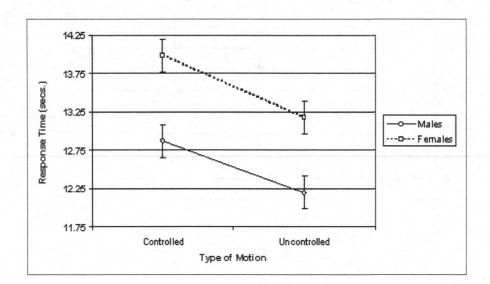

Figure 10. Object-positioning distance error by gender by viewing mode

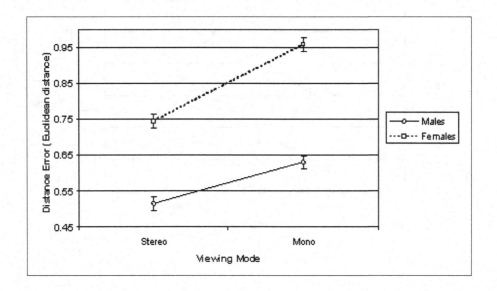

*Table 4. Mean object-positioning distance errors, response times, and rotational distances by gender[*]
for the viewing conditions*

| | Object Positioning Performance Measures | | | | | |
| | Distance Error (Euclidean distance) | | Response Time (seconds) | | Rotational Distance Magnitude (degrees) | |
Viewing Conditions:	Males	Females	Males	Females	Males	Females
Stereo Viewing	0.515	0.745	17.71	19.44	140.63	142.43
Mono Viewing	0.631	0.957	22.49	20.80	203.36	159.13

[*] *The minimum significant performance differences (at p < 0.05) between the genders for
the object-positioning task are (1) mean Euclidean distance error: 0.0377 units; (2) mean
response time: 0.78 seconds; and (3) mean rotational distance: 9.62 degrees.*

Figure 11. Object-positioning response time by gender by viewing mode

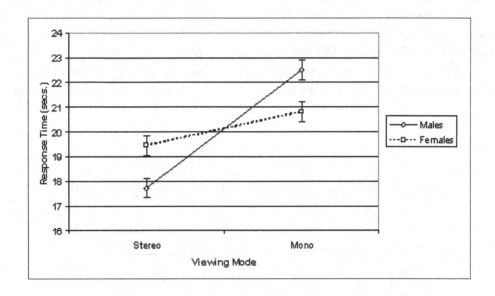

differences (at p < 0.05) between the genders for object-matching error rate and response time (noted in Table 3).

Both male and female subjects were more accurate and faster at matching objects when viewing the object pairs in stereo (see Figures 6 and 8). When the males controlled the motion of the right-hand object image, also called the comparison object (recall that the left image was always stationary), they were more accurate than when they did not control this motion (see Figure 7). For females, there was no significant difference in object-matching accuracy whether they controlled the motion of the comparison object or not (see Figure 7). However, both males and females took longer to judge whether the objects were identical or different when they were controlling this motion (see Figure 9).

Object-Positioning Experiment Results. The positioning data were also fitted to a MANOVA model. There were significant differences in distance error magnitude ($p < 0.0001$) and in rotational distance magnitude ($p < 0.0001$) as a function of gender. The male subjects were more accurate in the positioning task (see Figure 10). The overall mean male distance error was 0.573 units, whereas the overall mean female distance error was 0.851 units. Furthermore, the male subjects rotated the positioning scenes to a greater extent than did the females (see Figure 12). The overall mean male rotational distance was 171.99 degrees, whereas the overall mean female rotational distance was 150.78 degrees. The difference in positioning response time as a function of gender was not significant ($p = 0.97$). Both males and

females exhibited a mean positioning response time of 20.1 seconds (see Figure 11).

To further investigate the gender-based impact of the viewing conditions on object-positioning performances, the sample again was split by gender and tested for the effects of mono and stereo viewing on positioning accuracies, response times, and rotational distances for each gender. The data are presented in tabular format in Table 4. Figures 10, 11, and 12 present these data using line graphs that indicate the minimum significant differences (at $p < 0.05$) between the genders for object-positioning radius error, response time, and rotational distance (noted in Table 4). Both males and females were more accurate and faster at positioning objects in stereo (see Figures 10 and 11). Stereo viewing particularly improved the positioning response time for males more than for females (see Figure 11). Furthermore, both males and females used less rotational distance positioning objects when viewing the objects in stereo, although males exhibited more of this effect than did the females (see Figure 12).

Figure 12. Object-positioning rotational distance by gender by viewing mode

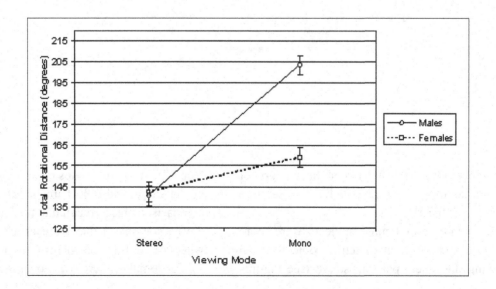

Object Resizing Experiment Results. In the resizing task, there were significant differences in radius error percentages (p < 0.027) and rotational distance magnitudes (p < 0.006) as a function of gender. The male subjects were less accurate resizing the objects than were the females (see Figure 13). The overall mean male radius error percentage was 15.14%, whereas the overall mean female radius error percentage was 14.05%. However, the male subjects rotated the resizing scenes to a greater extent than did the females (see Figure 15). The overall mean male

Table 5. Mean object resizing radius error percentages, response times, and rotational distances by gender* for the viewing conditions

| | Object Resizing Performance Measures | | | | | |
| | Radius Error (%) | | Response Time (seconds) | | Rotational Distance Magnitude (degrees) | |
Viewing Conditions:	Males	Females	Males	Females	Males	Females
Stereo Viewing	14.61	13.53	9.87	10.05	100.05	98.46
Mono Viewing	15.66	14.57	11.49	11.90	125.32	112.39

* *The minimum significant performance differences (at p < 0.05) between the genders for the object resizing task are (1) mean radius error percentage: 0.96%; (2) mean response time: 0.64 seconds; and (3) mean rotational distance: 5.20 degrees.*

Figure 13. Object resizing radius error by gender by viewing mode

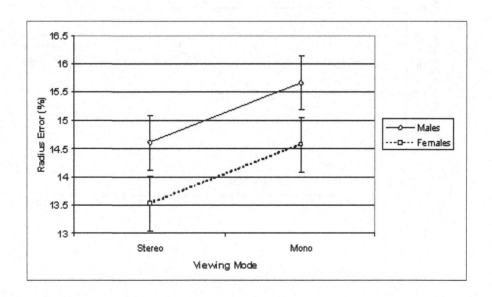

Figure 14. Object resizing response time by gender by viewing mode

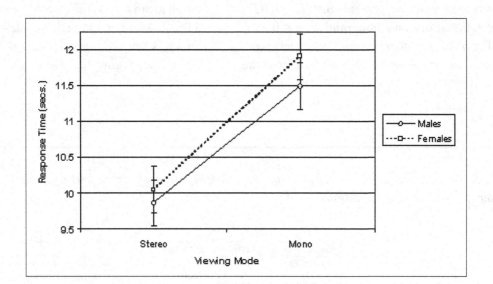

Figure 15. Object resizing rotational distance by gender by viewing mode

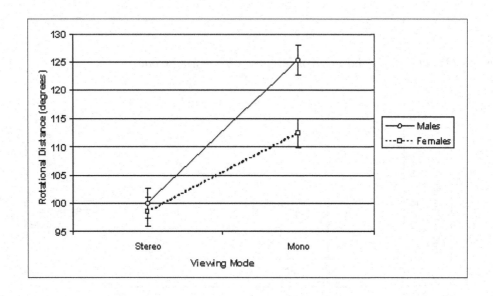

rotational distance was 112.68 degrees, whereas the overall mean female rotational distance was 105.43 degrees. Furthermore, males and females were equally fast at performing the resizing task (see Figure 14). The difference in resizing response time as a function of gender was not significant (p = 0.37). The mean male response time was 10.68 seconds, and the mean female response time was 10.98 seconds.

The resizing data sample also were split by gender and tested for the effects of mono and stereo viewing on resizing accuracies, response times, and rotational distances for each gender. The data are presented in tabular format in Table 5. Figures 13, 14, and 15 present these data using line graphs that indicate the minimum significant differences (at p < 0.05) between the genders for object resizing radius error, response time, and rotational distance (noted in Table 5). Viewing the worlds in stereo compared to mono had no significant effect on the mean resizing accuracy for either gender (see Figure 13), although it did reduce mean response times for both genders (see Figure 14). Similar to the results from the positioning task, both males and females rotated the scenes less while resizing objects viewed in stereo compared to mono viewing, although the males

reduced this stereo-viewed rotational distance more than the females (see Figure 15).

SUMMARY OF FINDINGS

Table 6 summarizes relative task performance differences by gender with each experiment. The spatial abilities literature indicates a robust male performance advantage in mental rotation tasks but no clear advantage for either gender in spatial visualization tasks. Indeed, the ETS factor-referenced cognitive tests administered to our subjects generally corroborate the existing literature. The male subjects answered significantly fewer cube comparisons (mental rotation) test items incorrectly than the females, but there were no differences in male-female paper folding (spatial visualization) test scores.

We hypothesized a male performance advantage in the (mental rotation) object-matching experiment (H1) but no advantage for either gender in the (spatial visualization) object-positioning and resizing experiments (H2). Consistent with the prediction of hypothesis H1, males did exhibit more accurate and faster performances than females in the object-matching experiment. As this

Table 6. Summary of gender-based differences in accuracy, response time, and rotational distance performances for object matching, positioning, and resizing experiments

Experiment:	Accuracy/Gender:	R T/Gender:	Rot. Dist./Gender
Object Matching	Males more accurate	Males faster	Not Applicable[*]
Object Positioning	Males more accurate	No M/F difference	Males use more
Object Resizing	Females more accurate	No M/F difference	Males use more

[*] *There was no formal rotational distance dependent variable performance measure in the object-matching experiment. However, when males controlled the motion of the comparison object, they were more accurate (unlike the females) in their object-matching performances.*

task was based on a mental rotation paradigm (Shepard & Metzler, 1971) and coupled with spatial literature meta-analyses indicating male advantages in mental rotation tasks and cognitive tests, it is not surprising that the male subjects outperformed the female subjects in the accuracy and speed of matching objects. Moreover, controlling the motion of the right-hand comparison object image significantly improved (i.e., reduced) male object-matching error rates but had no effect on female error rates. Since controlling the motion facilitated the mental rotation task in general, and since males typically outperform females at mental rotation tasks (Dabbs et al., 1998; Silverman et al., 2000), this could explain why males made more effective use of this motion cue.

However, contrary to the prediction of hypothesis H2, in the object-positioning and resizing (spatial visualization) experiments, the relative gender performances were mixed; males were more accurate at positioning objects, whereas females were more accurate at resizing objects. Moreover, the male subjects made more use of the rotational distance feature in both the positioning and resizing tasks. Note that the rotational distance feature, by nature, is a type of motion cue. That is, by rotating the virtual world left or right, the viewer is able to adjust the locations and displacements of the objects in relation to the other objects and in relation to the viewer. The males evidently found this rotating feature to be more useful than females in attempting to position and resize objects in the virtual worlds.

To understand why males were more accurate at positioning objects and why females were more accurate at resizing objects, it is worthwhile to scrutinize the elements of each task. In this regard, object motion was a critical attribute for successfully positioning objects but not for resizing objects. Accurately positioning the target object in a straight line segment required flying the object around the visual space. This essential motion attribute may have contributed to a male

performance advantage at positioning objects and is consistent with previous findings that men typically outperform women in tasks manipulating objects in space (Collins & Kimura, 1997; Goldstein et al., 1990; Kimura, 1983; Kolb & Whishaw, 1990; Linn & Petersen, 1985; Lohman, 1986; Maccoby & Jacklin, 1974).

However, the females were more accurate than the males at resizing the target object to match the apparent size of the referent object. The females evidently had a better sense of the relative comparative sizes of the two objects that were displaced in distance but otherwise fixed in position. It has been demonstrated that females, compared to men, rely more on landmarks for way finding (McGuiness & Sparks, 1983; Miller & Santoni, 1986) and refer to landmarks when giving directions (Miller & Santoni, 1986). The literature also indicates that females outperform males in remembering the location of objects that are fixed in space (Dabbs et al., 1998; McBurney et al., 1997). Accurately resizing the target object required the cognitive calibration of the relative apparent sizes of two objects that were displaced in distance from the viewer but otherwise fixed in position. We speculate that the female resizing accuracy advantage could be related to a female propensity to recognize better the locations of landmark objects that are fixed in position (Eals & Silverman, 1994; Silverman & Eals, 1992).

CONCLUSION AND DISCUSSION

In general, the results of these experiments indicate the following:

1. Males outperform females at matching abstract, visual objects using mental rotation in computer-generated virtual worlds.
2. Males make more use of certain motion-related cues in performing visual tasks in computer-generated virtual worlds.

3. Males are more accurate at moving and positioning objects in computer-generated virtual worlds.
4. Females are more accurate at estimating the relative sizes of objects displaced in depth but fixed in position in computer-generated virtual worlds.

How do these findings suggest approaches to developing gender-neutral visual interfaces? The ideal goal in this regard is to move toward the design of user interfaces that will improve usability for both genders and, particularly, to mitigate the postulated female handicap with mental rotation and motion cues. Simply adding a third dimension to an otherwise 2D display does not guarantee improved task performances (Cockburn & McKenzie, 2002). One suggestion is to add meaningful landmarks and to decrease user reliance on mental rotation ability. For example, visual interfaces that allow the stationary user to look right or look left (or up, down, backward, etc.) for familiar landmarks may prove to be an effective, gender-neutral alternative to the use of typical motion cues such as flying around virtual spaces. Our research suggests that the reliance on motion cues, in particular, to extract information can be especially problematic and can lead to a male performance advantage.

An evolving area of visual computing technology to which these findings are relevant is computer-generated virtual environments (VEs). The spatial structure of a VE and the objects that are visible sometimes are used to represent information. According to Vinson (1999), "a VE could contain objects whose spatial properties (e.g. shape, position, size) represent data values on different dimensions. Here, it is necessary for the navigator to quickly develop accurate representations of those spatial properties in order to understand the relationships in the data" (p. 279). These spatial properties (i.e., shape, position, and size) correspond with the three spatial

task manipulations analyzed in our studies. To the extent that there are gender biases when cognitively processing and understanding these spatial properties, then these biases likely would extend to understanding the corresponding data relationships in VEs.

Although the tasks analyzed in our studies are not navigation tasks per se, the findings, nevertheless, have implications for the design of navigable VEs, since recognizing object shape and estimating the size and distance of objects are intrinsic activities of successful VE navigation (Vinson, 1999). Navigation is a process of tracking one's position in an environment in order to arrive at a desired destination. Doing so requires knowledge about positional, velocity, and acceleration attributes, which are derived from location, depth, and motion cues (Cutmore et al., 2000). Location information comes from landmarks and other fixed, distant features in the environment. The ability to recognize object shapes and to estimate their relative distances (or positions) is necessary in order to acquire basic location information that is a foundation of successful navigation. Moreover, correctly estimating the relative size of a landmark directly relates to understanding its distance and also promotes successful navigation.

Previous studies have indicated male performance advantages when navigating virtual worlds (Astur et al., 1998; Sandstrom et al., 1998; Waller et al., 1998). However, other researchers have noted that the apparent male navigation superiority is mitigated when the virtual worlds are presented to users with wider fields of view and larger display screens (Czerwinski et al., 2002; Tan et al., 2001). Indeed, both genders benefit under these conditions. Tan, Gergle, Scupelli, and Pausch (2003) reported that using larger displays improved both male and female performances in a static, 2D, mental rotation task[3], but there was no corresponding performance benefit in a reading comprehension task. Subsequently, Tan, Gergle, Scupelli, and Pausch (2004) also demonstrated that users are more effective when performing 3D virtual navigation tasks on larger displays. They noted that when navigating, users continually update their mental sense of position and orientation within the environment (termed *spatial updating*) using two basic strategies: (1) piloting, or using external landmarks to position themselves within the environment; and (2) path integration, or sensing self-velocity and acceleration to determine their position relative to some starting point. There is evidence that women rely more heavily on the piloting strategy (Czerwinski et al., 2002; Golledge, 1999).

Cockburn (2004) suggested that human spatial capabilities could be leveraged while interacting with computer-generated 3D scenes if the scenes were presented in ways "that better reflect the way we perceive our natural environment" (p. 25). We submit that user interface technology will best support all users to effectively navigate virtual worlds when those worlds are presented to user groups in ways that most closely mirror how users typically and best navigate in natural environments. Flying around over terrain that is visually presented on a limited 2D display screen is not a natural approach for ordinary human navigation. Extending the wider field of view and wider display arguments of Czerwinski et al. (2002), we suggest that the total immersion of users navigating a pedestrian and, apparently, terrestrial virtual world can better support individual human navigation in those worlds. Spatial navigation is improved with an increased sense of presence, or being *in* the virtual environment, which is a direct outcome of immersion (Tan et al., 2003). For women, these worlds perhaps would be designed best using highly visible and easily recognizable landmarks[4] that are stationary in position and visible within a 360° field of view. That is, women users should be able to look around the virtual landscapes in all directions. Furthermore, the mode of navigating, or movement, should be along the surface of the virtual landscape, especially with alignment and

orientation to and from those salient landmarks. For men, cues that further suggest Euclidean distance and direction also should be helpful. Virtual worlds that support both genders' existing propensities to navigate would be most effective for the majority of users.

Limitations

The results of this study should not be interpreted as suggesting that either gender is superior in terms of spatial abilities. Rather, the study suggests (and the reported findings confirm) that there are *differences* in relative male and female performances on particular spatial processing tasks. Some of these differences are explored in this study. Many others are well-documented in the gender-specific mental abilities literature. In point of fact, both males and females have performance advantages in particular cognitive tasks.

The domain of this study is limited. It focuses on the gender-effective use of abstract visualizations and visual tasks that may relate to particular attributes of visual user interfaces. For example, visual user interface domains that involve the mental rotation of objects or the user-controlled motion, orientation, or resizing of objects, particularly in scenes representing three-dimensional space, are germane. However, domains relating to typical two-dimensional point-and-click activities or to the user interpretation of textual information are not addressed in this study.

In terms of methodology, a limitation of this study is that there was a separate set of subjects in the mental rotation experiment compared to the positioning and resizing experiments. As a result, there was a combination of within- and between-subject comparisons pertinent to the findings and related discussions. However, because these experiments were conducted over a period of time, the attrition of some subjects was unavoidable.

Further, in generalizing these findings, we note that these subjects likely have heightened spatial abilities relative to the general population. They were all working professionals in a premier scientific governmental organization, many holding advanced degrees. Therefore, whether these findings generalize to the population at large is debatable. However, one could argue that any performance effects fostered by the spatial cues would be more pronounced within this group than within the general population. That is to say, if there were no observable effects with these select subjects, then there likely would be no effect within the general population.

Finally, we mention one additional limitation. Egocentric motion tasks, for example, physically walking through a 3D environment, and finding one's way along a route and/or to and from landmarks have additional perceptual dimensions than do the tasks in our study. However, some elements of egocentric way-finding are embedded in our tasks, such as recognizing the relative shapes, orientations, distances, and sizes of objects in the visual field. Additionally, we did incorporate aspects of egocentric motion skills by enabling the rotation of objects and the rotation of the scenes left and right. However, these tasks do not capture completely all of the perceptual cues and sensory elements inherent in egocentric motion tasks.

Considerations for Future Research

There are large segments of the general population that are characterized by differing opportunities, propensities, and abilities to access and make effective use of computer technologies. For example, the very young, the elderly, and the handicapped all have particular impediments to using computer technologies that most people take for granted. As computer applications become increasingly prevalent in everyday life, it is a worthwhile goal to try to mitigate intrinsic barriers and to equalize access and opportunities in order to make effective use of computer technologies.

In terms of gender differences in using visual interfaces, this research is an attempt to identify and highlight broad categories of disparities in male-female abilities to interpret and to manipulate visual abstractions. The intent is to work toward the development of gender-neutral guidelines for effective visual user interfaces and virtual environments. Future research should explore the relative efficacies of different approaches of augmenting computer-generated visualizations so as to promote equal understanding and effective interfaces for different user groups. To this end, investigating approaches that do not rely strictly on abstract visualizations to convey information is warranted. Although it has been demonstrated that visual abstractions effectively can condense and convey large volumes of tabular, multi-dimensional (2D and 3D) data, the combination of visual with, in some cases, textual as well as multi-modal approaches likely will lead to more effective user interfaces across a larger number of user groups. Furthermore, investigating the design of virtual worlds that most closely mimic how men and women navigate real worlds likely would benefit the largest share of all users.

REFERENCES

Astur, R. S., Ortiz, M. L., & Sutherland, R. J. (1998). A characterization of performance by men and women in a virtual Morris water task: A large and reliable sex difference. *Behavioural Brain Research, 93*(1-2), 185-190.

Balka, E. (1996). Gender and skill in human-computer interaction. In *Proceedings of the CHI 1996* (p. 325). New York: ACM Press.

Basdogan, C., Ho, C., Srinivasan, M., & Slater, M. (2000). An experimental study on the role of touch in shared virtual environments. *ACM Transactions on Computer-Human Interaction, 7*(4), 443-460.

Cockburn, A. (2004). Revisiting 2D vs. 3D implications on spatial memory. In *Proceedings of the*

Fifth Conference on Australasian User Interface (pp. 25-31), Darlinghurst, Australia: Australian Computer Society, Inc.

Cockburn, A., & McKenzie, B. (2002). Evaluating the effectiveness of spatial memory in 2D and 3D physical and virtual environments. In *Proceedings of the CHI 2002* (pp. 203-210). New York: ACM Press.

Collins, D. W., & Kimura, D. (1997). A large sex difference on a two-dimensional mental rotation task. *Behavioral Neuroscience, 111*(4), 845-849.

Cutmore, T. R. H., Hine, T. J., Maberly, K. J., Langford, N. M., & Hawgood, G. (2000). Cognitive and gender factors influencing navigation in a virtual environment. *International Journal of Human-Computer Studies, 53*(2), 223-249.

Czerwinski, M., Tan, D. S., & Robertson, G. G. (2002). Women take a wider view. In *Proceedings of the CHI 2002* (pp. 195-202). New York: ACM Press.

Dabbs, J. M., Chang, E.-L., Strong, R. A., & Milun, R. (1998). Spatial ability, navigation strategy, and geographic knowledge among men and women. *Evolution and Human Behavior, 19*(2), 89-98.

Eals, M., & Silverman, I. (1994). The hunter-gatherer theory of spatial sex differences: Proximate factors mediating the female advantage in recall of object arrays. *Ethological Sociobiology, 15*, 95-105.

Ekstrom, R. B., French, J. W., Harman, H. H., & Dermen, D. (1976). *Manual for kit of factor-referenced cognitive tests*. Princeton, NJ: Educational Testing Service.

Goldstein, D., Haldane, D., & Mitchell, C. (1990). Sex differences in visual-spatial ability: The role of performance factors. *Memory & Cognition, 18*(5), 546-550.

Golledge, R. G. (Ed.). (1999). *Wayfinding behavior: Cognitive mapping and other spatial processes*. Baltimore, MD: John Hopkins University Press.

Hall, J., & Cooper, J. (1991). Gender, experience and attributions to the computer. *Journal of Educational Computer Research, 7*(1), 51-60.

Halpern, D. F. (1986). *Sex differences in cognitive abilities*. Hillsdale, NJ: Lawrence Erlbaum Associates.

Hinckley, K., Pausch, R., Proffitt, D., & Kassell, N. (1998). Two-handed virtual manipulation. *ACM Transactions on Computer-Human Interaction, 5*(3), 260-302.

Hinckley, K., Pausch, R., Proffitt, D., Patten, J., & Kassell, N. (1997). Cooperative bimanual action. In *Proceedings of the CHI 1997* (pp. 27-34). New York: ACM Press.

Hubona, G. S., & Shirah, G. W. (2004, January 5-8). The gender factor performing computer tasks on computer media. In *Proceedings of the 37th Hawaii International Conference on System Sciences* (CD/ROM). Computer Society Press.

Inkpen, K. (2001). Drag-and-drop versus point-and-click mouse interaction styles for children. *ACM Transactions on Computer-Human Interaction, 8*(1), 1-33.

Inkpen, K., Klawe, M., Lawry, J., Sedighian, K., Leroux, S., Hsu, D., et al. (1994). We have never-forgetful flowers in our garden: Girls' responses to electronic games. *Journal of Computers in Math and Science Teaching, 13*(4), 383-403.

James, T. W., & Kimura, D. (1997). Sex differences in remembering the locations of objects in an array: Location-shift versus location-exchanges. *Evolution and Human Behavior, 18*(3), 155-163.

Kauppinen, K., Kivimaki, A., Era, T., & Robinson, M. (1998). Producing identity in collaborative virtual environments. In *Proceedings of the ACM Symposium on Virtual Reality Software and Technology* (pp. 35-42). New York: ACM Press.

Kimura, D. (1983). Sex differences in cerebral organization for speech and praxis functions. *Canadian Journal of Psychology, 37*, 19-35.

Kimura, D. (2000). *Sex and cognition.* Cambridge, MA: MIT Press.

Kolb, B., & Whishaw, I. (1990). *Human neuropsychology.* New York: Freeman.

Leventhal, L., Teasley, B., & Stone, D. (1994). Designing for diverse users: Will just a better interface do? In *Proceedings of the CHI 1994* (pp. 191-192). New York: ACM Press.

Linn, M. C., & Petersen, A. C. (1985). Emergence and characterization of sex differences in spatial ability: A meta-analysis. *Child Development, 56*, 1479-1498.

Lockheed, M. (1985). Women, girls and computers: A first look at the evidence. *Sex Roles, 13*(3/4), 115-122.

Lohman, D. F. (1986). The effect of speed-accuracy tradeoff on sex differences in mental rotation. *Perception and Psychophysics, 39*, 427-436.

Maccoby, E. E., & Jacklin, C. N. (1974). *The psychology of sex differences.* Stanford, CA: Stanford University Press.

McBurney, D. H., Gaulin, S. J. C., Devineni, T., & Adams, C. (1997). Superior spatial memory of women: Stronger evidence for the gathering hypothesis. *Evolution and Human Behavior, 18*(3), 165-174.

McGuiness, D., & Sparks, J. (1983). Cognitive style and cognitive maps: Sex differences in representations of familiar terrain. *Journal of Mental Imagery, 7*(1), 91-100.

Miller, L. K., & Santoni, J. (1986). Sex differences in spatial abilities: Strategic and experimental coordinates. *Acta Psychologica, 62*(3), 225-235.

Palma-dos-Reis, A., & Zahedi, F. (1999). Designing personalized intelligent financial decision support systems. *Decision Support Systems, 26*(1), 31-47.

Powell, P. L., & Johnson, J. E. V. (1995). Gender and DSS design: The research implications. *Decision Support Systems, 14*(1), 27-58.

Rieman, J. (1996). A field study of exploratory learning strategies. *ACM Transactions on Computer-Human Interaction, 3*(3), 189-218.

Sandstrom, N. J., Kaufman, J., & Huettel, S. A. (1998). Males and females use different distal cues in a virtual environment navigation task. *Cognitive Brain Research, 6*(4), 351-360.

Shepard, R. N., & Metzler, J. (1971). Mental rotation of three-dimensional objects. *Science, 171*(972), 701-703.

Shneiderman, B. (1990). Human values and the future of technology: A declaration of empowerment. In *Proceedings of the Conference on Computers and the Quality of Life* (p. 16). New York: ACM Press.

Shneiderman, B. (2000). Universal usability. *Communications of the ACM, 43*(6), 85-91.

Silverman, I., & Eals, M. (1992). Sex differences in spatial abilities: Evolutionary theory and data. In J. H. Barkow, L. Cosmides, & J. Tooby (Eds.), *The adapted mind: Evolutionary psychology and the generation of culture* (pp. 531-549). New York: Oxford Press.

Silverman, I., Choi, J., Mackewn, A., Fisher, M., Moro, J., & Olshansky, E. (2000). Evolved mechanisms underlying wayfinding: Further studies on the hunter-gatherer theory of spatial sex differences. *Evolution and Human Behavior, 21*(3), 201-213.

Simon, S. J. (2001). The impact of culture and gender on Web sites: An empirical study. *The DATA BASE for Advances in Information Systems, 32*(1), 18-37.

Tan, D. S., Czerwinski, M., & Robertson, G. (2003). Women go with the (optical) flow. In *Proceedings of the CHI 2003* (pp. 209-215). New York: ACM Press.

Tan, D. S., Gergle, D., Scupelli, P. G., & Pausch, R. (2003). With similar visual angles, larger displays improve spatial performance. In *Proceedings of the CHI 2003* (pp. 217-224). New York: ACM Press.

Tan, D. S., Gergle, D., Scupelli, P. G., & Pausch, R. (2004). Physically large displays improve path integration in 3D virtual navigation tasks. In *Proceedings of the CHI 2004* (pp. 439-446). New York: ACM Press.

Tan, D. S., Robertson, G. G., & Czerwinski, M. (2001). Exploring 3D navigation: Combining speed-coupled flying with orbiting. In *Proceedings of the CHI 2001* (pp. 418-425). New York: ACM Press.

Upitis, R., & Koch, C. (1996). Is equal computer time fair for girls? In *Proceedings of the 6th Conference of the Internet Society on INET '96*, Montreal, Quebec, Canada.

Vinson, N. G. (1999). Design guidelines for landmarks to support navigation in virtual environments. In *Proceedings of the CHI 1999* (pp. 278-285). New York: ACM Press.

Voyer, D., Voyer, S., & Bryden, M. P. (1995). Magnitude of sex differences in spatial abilities: A meta-analysis and consideration of critical variables. *Psychological Bulletin, 117*, 250-270.

Waller, D., Hunt, E., & Knapp, D. (1998). The transfer of spatial knowledge in virtual environment training. *Presence: Teleoperators and Virtual Environments, 7*(2), 129-143.

Wexelblat, A. (1995). An approach to natural gesture in virtual environments. *ACM Transactions on Computer-Human Interaction, 2*(3), 179-200.

Wilder, G., Mackie, D., & Cooper, J. (1985). Gender and computers: Two surveys of computer-related attitudes. *Sex Roles, 13*(3/4), 215-228.

ENDNOTES

[1] http://www.webaim.org estimates that as many as 10% of all males and 0.5% of all females are characterized by patterns of color blindness that affect their ability to understand certain shades of color-encoded information.

[2] Pooled t-test method was utilized with equal population variances; satterthwaite t-test method was utilized with unequal population variances.

[3] Specifically, they used the Guilford-Zimmerman spatial orientation task. Please see Tan et al. (2003) for more detailed information.

[4] For a complete discussion of guidelines for designing landmarks to support navigation in VEs, please see Vinson (1999).

This work was previously published in the International Journal of Technology and Human Interaction, edited by B. C. Stahl, Volume 2, Issue 2, pp. 24-48, copyright 2006 by IGI Publishing, formerly known as Idea Group Publishing (an imprint of IGI Global).

Chapter XXII
Computer and Stress in Social and Healthcare Industries

Reima Suomi
Turku School of Economics and Business Administration, Turku

Reetta Raitoharju
Turku School of Economics and Business Administration, Turku

ABSTRACT

Social and healthcare industries offer demanding occupations, as they are very human-contact intensive workplaces and, moreover, the customers are usually met in critical and not-wished-for situations. Possible actions are many, and seldom are there clear procedures on how to continue: Each customer contact is a place for genuine decisions. Add to this deliberate service situation a computer, and you can count on difficulties. Our focus is on how information systems affect the stress levels of health and social-care workers. Our empirical study shows–among many other factors–strong correlation between the use of computers and stress levels in the healthcare professions: The more computer use, the more stress. We discuss what could be done to manage stress levels in relationship to computer use in health and social-care industries. In conclusion, we wrap the research findings together and propose our extensions to the current knowledge on the relationship between stress and information systems in health care. Our most important finding is that when users understand the total collaborative work setting, computer work obtains meaning, and stress levels reduce.

INTRODUCTION

Knowledge or computer work and healthcare work are professional areas that spread out in modern society. Unfortunately, workers in both sectors are prone to suffer from stress. As we combine healthcare work and computers in the same environment, the situation becomes even more problematic. That is why we want to study the way in which computers cause stress in healthcare professions. Some of the factors that increase stress levels in both industries are summarized in Table 1.

Table 1. Work stressors in healthcare and computer industries

Healthcare
    Intensive human contact
    Customer interaction, often in a crisis situation
    Decision-making pressure under insufficient information
    Area's total professional knowledge growing fast, information overload

Computer industry
    Work often performed by virtual teams
    Area's total professional knowledge growing fast, information overload
    Constant change of the discipline
    Work with abstract entities
    Need for networking

Research on stress and related phenomena has deep roots both in computer and information research as well as in healthcare research. In the field of computing, dominant topics seem to be those of information overload (Edmunds & Morris, 2000; Laskin, 1994; Levinson, 1970; Maes, 1994), coping with constant change (Thong & Yap, 2000; van Rooyen, 2000; Wastell & Newman, 1996) and problems of working in groups and virtual organizations (Anonymous, 1996; Armour, 1995; Kokko, Vartiainen, et al., 2004; Schill, Toves, et al., 1980; Trent, Smith, et al., 1994).

Our research questions include the following:

1. How do computers affect workers' stress levels in health and social care industries,?
2. What kinds of effects does information technology have on work?
3. What can be done to manage stress levels in the healthcare industries?

Methodologically, our research was very classical. First, we ran through a literature study on stress in general and specifically in the healthcare and computer industries. Second, 5,000 Finnish healthcare professionals were given a comprehensive survey on their working conditions; the relationship between information technology (IT) and work was one of the topics discussed. This survey was originally administered by Statistics Finland on the order of the Finnish Institute for Occupational Health.

The chapter unfolds as follows: In the first section, we define the terms used (among others, *stress*), and briefly discuss why stress is very much present in health and social-care industries. In next section, we review the current literature on the relationship between stress, computers, and information systems. As stress is a usual phenomenon, in the following section we review how to manage stress levels in organizational work settings. Section 4 reviews results from a survey that got responses from 3,072 social and healthcare professionals in Finland. Finally, in the next section we discuss what could be done to reduce computer-based stress in the social- and healthcare industries. In the final section we discuss conclusions.

COMPUTERS AS A SOURCE FOR STRESS

Defining Stress

Stress is a meaningful concept in many disciplines and has hundreds of definitions. For example, in physics stress is defined as "the force per unit area resulting from the application of a load" (SGIA, 2004). In fonetics and music, stress is defined as follows: "the relative prominence of a syllable or musical note (especially with regard to stress or pitch)... he put the stress on the wrong syllable" (WordNet, 2004). Stress can also be seen as just a biological phenomenon: "Stress is the sum of the biological reactions to any adverse stimulus, physical, mental or emotional, internal or external, that tends to disturb a person's normal state of well-being" (MedSearch, 2004). A very general and widely usable definition is "mental or physical tension that results from physical, emotional, or chemical causes" (ViaHealth, 2004). For our purposes in this chapter, the definition for stress describing "difficulty that causes worry or emotional tension" (WordNet, 2004) is very suitable. We can see that even though the basic prequisities differ, the definitions are related.

Scanning through the definitions, we can see that *stress* is a neutral term: It is per se neither bad nor good; everything depends on the context. Especially, we want to stress that stress is not solely a negative phenomenon but can have positive effects, even in the field of psychology. As the World Federation for Mental Health (WFMH) has defined, "Stress is not necessarily negative. Some stress keeps us motivated and alert, while too little stress can create problems. However, too much stress can trigger problems with mental and physical health, particularly over a prolonged period of time" (WFMH, 2004). The National Institute for Occupational Safety (NIOSH) defined positive stress as challenge:

The concept of job stress is often confused with challenge, but these concepts are not the same. Challenge energizes us psychologically and physically, and it motivates us to learn new skills and master our jobs. When a challenge is met, we feel relaxed and satisfied. Thus, challenge is an important ingredient for healthy and productive work. The importance of challenge in our work lives is probably what people are referring to when they say "a little bit of stress is good for you." (NIOSH, 2004)

In biology, stress is often connected to the following phenomena:

Stress is defined as a nonspecific response of the body to any demand made upon it which results in symptoms such as rise in the blood pressure, release of hormones, quickness of breath, tightening of muscles, perspiration, and increased cardiac activity. (WFMH, 2004)

Similarly, we often define that computer systems can be stressed. For example, a computer, a database management system, or a network connection can be stressed. Similarly, as in the case of the human body, we want to tell that the systems are overloaded by an external force.

Biologically, job stress can lead to loss of health or even to death. Typical biological disorders based on job stress follow (NIOSH, 2004):

- **Cardiovascular Disease:** Many studies suggest that psychologically demanding jobs that allow employees little control over the work process increase the risk of cardiovascular disease.
- **Musculoskeletal Disorders:** It is widely believed that job stress increases the risk for development of back and upper extremity musculoskeletal disorders.
- **Psychological Disorders:** Several studies suggest that differences in rates of mental

health problems (such as depression and burnout) for various occupations are due partly to differences in job stress levels. (Economic and lifestyle differences between occupations may also contribute to some of these problems.)

- **Workplace Injury:** Although more study is needed, there is a growing concern that stressful working conditions interfere with safe work practices and set the stage for injuries at work.
- **Suicide, Cancer, Ulcers, and Impaired Immune Function:** Some studies suggest a relationship between stressful working conditions and these health problems.

There is too a specific literature on job or occupational stress. WFMH (2004) defined job stress and discussed its main outcomes as follows:

Job stress can be defined as the harmful physical and emotional response that occurs when the requirements of the job do not match the capa-bilities, resources, or needs of the worker. Job stress can lead to poor health and even injury. Long-term exposure to job stress has been linked to an increased risk of musculoskeletal disorders, depression, and job burnout, and may contribute to a range of debilitating diseases, ranging from cardiovascular disease to cancer. Stressful working conditions also may interfere with an employee's ability to work safely, contributing to work injuries and illnesses. In the workplace of the 1990s, the most highly ranked and frequently reported organizational stressors are potential job loss, technological advances, and ineffective top management. At the work unit level, work over-load, poor supervision, and inadequate training are the top-ranking stressors.

Computers and Stress

Thong and Yap (2000) defined what a theoretical framework on occupational stress should include (their framework is depicted in Figure 1). We structure our discussion on computers or infor-

Figure 1. Key points for a theoretical framework on computers and stress (adapted from Thong & Yap, 2000)

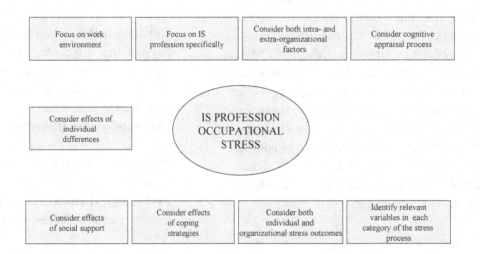

mation systems as related to stress, according to their framework.

When Thong and Yap (2000) talk about the importance of focus on work environment, they mean that occupational stress should always be understood and studied in a defined environment. Occupational stress, for example, in the computer industry, is different from occupational stress in the healthcare industry.

Focus on IS profession specifically means that a occupational health model for the IS profession should be specific to that profession. Similarly, we can infer that an occupational health model for health professionals should be specific to them.

Intra- and extra-organizational factors refer to the stress-causing factors, stressors. They are born both within and outside organizations. Intra-organizational factors can be affected by the organization's management, but extra-organizational factors are beyond their control. We discuss four major stressors supported by computerization, namely those of:

1. information overload,
2. the need to maintain different virtual organizations and social networks,
3. constant change, and
4. the built-in conflict in formal organizations and in virtual organizations.

A major stressor in work related to information systems, as already defined in Table 1, is that of information overload. Information overload is a major burden for information workers (Edmunds & Morris, 2000). Actually, knowledge workers tend to collect more data and information than what is actually needed. Butcher (1998) cited some reasons why managers and information workers tend to collect and use more information than what would actually be needed:

- They collect information to indicate a commitment to rationalism and competence that they believe improves decision making.

- They receive enormous amounts of unsolicited information.
- They seek more information to check out the information already acquired.
- They need to be able to demonstrate justification of decisions.
- They collect information just in case it may be useful.
- They play safe and get all information possible.
- They like to use information as a currency and not get left behind their colleagues.

Information overload can be limited in several ways. One revolution happened when reading habits shifted from intensive reading to extensive reading: "One historian has claimed that a 'reading revolution' took place in the later eighteenth century, and the sense of a shift from intensive to extensive reading" (Burke, 2000). In a similar way, we can say that a lot of work in organizations has turned from "intensive" to "extensive."

Maintaining social networks is a hard task needing a lot of effort. Especially, failures in establishing a social network can result in increased stress. (Cross, Nohria, et al., 2002) identify following myths as it comes to the building and maintaining of networks.

- The more communication the better.
- Everyone should be connected to everyone.
- We can not do much to aid informal networks.
- How people fit into networks is a matter of personality (which can not be changed).
- Central people who have become bottlenecks should make themselves more accessible.
- I already know what is going on in my network.

Change means that leaving something that is safe and known also causes stress. To the computer profession is tied the concept of seeking for the new. For example, the business process redesign metaphor supports this kind of thinking. The same is true for the search for competitive advantage. Levinson (1970) nicely described the connection between stress and seeking for new innovations, in this example of scientists:

Unlike most other people, who much prefer to accept what they find around them and who therefore are uneasy with people who question the status quo, the scientist built up a tolerance for the anxiety which comes from seeking out the new and unfamiliar. Once a man takes on a scientific career, he has, in essence, identified himself with a group whose whole rationale is tied up with intellectual rebellion, embodied in the rejection of old knowledge and a courageous search for the new. (Levinson, 1970)

Working in formal organizations always builds in conflict and stress. Pondy (1967) defined the following sources of conflict in formal organizations:

- Bargaining conflict occurs among parties who have an interest in maintaining and encouraging a shared relationship.
- Bureaucratic conflict occurs between two or more parties where some form of power relationship (superior/subordinate) exists
- Sytematic conflict occurs among parties as a part of lateral or working relationships

This source of stress might be a reason why less formal virtual organizations gain ground, even though they surely have their sources of stress.

Recent studies have shown that even virtual organizations can be stressful (Kokko et al., 2004; Kurland & Egan, 1999; Markus, Manville, et al., 2000; Suomi 2000; Walsham, 1994). Virtual organizations have the following characteristics that easily cause stress for workers (Gristock, 1997):

- Mediated interaction
- Geographical dispersion
- Mobility
- Diversity of actors
- Asynchronous work time
- Temporary structure

Cognitive appraisal processes refer to the ways on how individuals develop their understanding and awareness of their and their co-workers' stress. As with other diseases, this is connected to the phenomenon of health deficit. Individuals live through three phases when struggling with their health problems: In the first phase, the disease is not identified. In the second phase, the disease is diagnosed but not taken care of. In the third and last phase, the diseases is diagnosed and taken care of as well as possible (Bonaccorso & Sturchio, 2002).

Individual differences materialize when identifying stress, reacting to work stressors, and coping with them. Most likely in any profession a part of the professional development is the capacity to handle stress. As professionals develop, they most likely develop better skills to manage stress. Dreyfus (1992) defined the following categories of professionalism:

- Blind person
- Jerk
- Novice
- Advanced beginner
- Professional
- Proficient professional
- Expert
- Master
- Legend

There is also some discussion hinting that women and men might feel stress in a different way (Meyerson, 1998).

Social support can help in handling stress. Social support can come from supervisors, colleagues, friends, relatives, and spouses (Thong & Yap, 2000). Unfortunately, work with information systems, especially if innovation is looked for, necessitates some conflict, as is documented in recent literature. Working in groups connected to the search for innovation fosters built-in conflict and stress situations:

There is a diminished benefit for working together in teams if this does not create some level of conflict. Group work provides one means of bringing multiple perspectives to be a on a common problem. A lack of conflict among team members is often called "group-think" and the literature provides several examples of poor decisions from groups with too little conflict. (Sawyer, 2001)

Robey (1984) visualized the factors that lead to conflict and stress in computer-focused group work, as in Figure 2.

Social support from the colleagues is important, but a lot can be done by the formal management. Good human resource management practices play a key role (Holm, Lähteenmäki, et al., 2002). Agarwal and Ferratt (2002) define

good management of IT-professionals as having five components:

- Recruiting Posture
- Career Development and Security
- Compensation
- Concern for Individual
- Concern for Productivity

Their star-model of good management of IT-professionals is summarized in Figure 3.

Coping strategies refer to the ways in which individuals manage stress. We would like to take a closer study of two major universal coping strategies:

1. avoidance of role conflicts
2. building of trust in the workplace

In formal organizations, individuals suffer from stress if they suffer from imbalance between their behavior and their expected roles. According to Kallinikos (2004), bureaucratic order, also the basis of modern organizations, rests on the following principles:

Figure 2. Conflict factors in teamwork (Adopted from Robey, 1984)

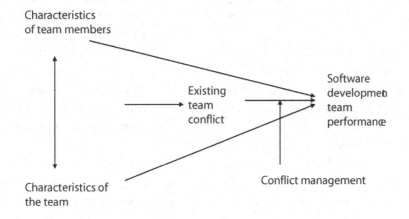

Figure 3. The components of good management for IT-professionals (Adopted by Agarwal & Ferratt, 2002)

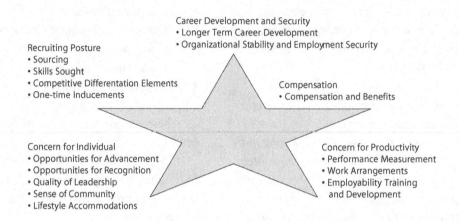

- **Selectivity:** Individuals taking organizational roles are expected to suspend nonrole demands and act on the basis of a well-specified and delimited set that constitutes the role.
- **Mobility:** A role, being and abstract set of functional requirements, can be unleashed from the particular circumstances into which it is embedded, and be transferred across various organizational contexts.
- **Reversibility:** Jobs can be altered or redesigned and the organizational sanctioning of job positions modified or even withdrawn.

Especially, selectivity is a root cause for stress. Individuals are not allowed to act naturally, but they are expected to adopt unnatural roles, where they have to suspend their normal personal characteristics.

Working in workplace where you can trust others and where you feel trusted is a major benefit that reduces stress. Lack of mutual trust is a major stress factor in organizations. Luo and

Najdawi (2004) identified five measures through which trust can be built:

1. **Calculative process:** A trustor develops trust based on a calculation of the costs and rewards a trustee to cheat or cooperate in a relationship.
2. **Prediction process:** A trustor develops trust by predicting a trustee's future actions based on his or her past behavior.
3. **Intentionality process:** A trustor develops trust based on his or her prediction of the intentions of the trustee.
4. **Capability process:** A trustor develops trust based on an evaluation of the trustee's ability to perform his promises.
5. **Transference process:** A trustor develops trust based on transferring trust from a known entity to an unknown entity.

The characteristics an individual can develop in order to maintain trust are the following (Luo & Najdawi, 2004):

- **Ability** refers to whether and individual has a set of skills and competencies that would enable him or her to perform the promises.
- **Benevolence** is the extent to which an individual is perceived to have good intention toward others without profit motive.
- **Integrity** refers to whether an individual adheres to a set of principles that are acceptable to those who may trust him.

Bashein and Markus (1997) deliver a list of characteristics of a person that instill trustworthiness:

- Similarity and likability
- Prolonged interaction
- Appropriate behavior
- Consistent behavior

Individual and organizational stress outcomes vary a lot. Usually, the focus on stress studies is on individuals, but the organizational dimension should not be forgotten. An interesting stream of literature is that compares organizational malfunctions with those of traditional diseases of humans. We have identified four entities in this discussion:

- Paranoia
- Autism
- Attention Deficit Disorder
- Web Addiction

Paranoia is a psychological disorder characterized by delusions of persecution or grandeur (WordNet, 2004). Both organizations and humans can manifest paranoia. Uneasiness and stress in a workplace can have its roots in suspicion about the behavior of others. Again, however, a sensible amount of suspicion can be a good characteristics of a human. Kramer (2002) calls this type of suspicion *prudent paranoia*: Prudent paranoia is a form of constructive suspicion regarding the intentions and actions of people and organizations.

An interesting theory is that the modern information society has characteristics of autism, a mental health disorder connected to behavioral difficulties. According to Beruch (2001), an autistic society and a person with autism both have the following characteristics:

- Profound lack of affective emotional contact
- Intense insistence on sameness
- Bizarre and elaborate repetitive routines
- Being mute or having a marked abnormality of speech
- Fascination with and dexterity in manipulating objective, high levels of visuo-spacial skills or rote memory
- Learning difficulties in other areas
- Attractive, alert, and intellectual appearance

Attention deficit/hyperactivity disorder (ADD/ADHD) is a disease in which individuals find it difficult to concentrate. It is defined as follows:

Attention Deficit Hyperactivity Disorder (ADHD) is a condition that becomes apparent in some children in the preschool and early school years. It is hard for these children to control their behavior and/or pay attention. It is estimated that between 3 and 5 percent of children have ADHD, or approximately 2 million children in the United States. This means that in a classroom of 25 to 30 children, it is likely that at least one will have ADHD. (NIMH, 2004)

The importance of attention was brought to the knowledge of the IS community by Davenport, in his classic article (Davenport & Beck, 2000). The message was that modern society is rich in information; the scarce resource is human attention. So we can speak of an attention economy.

Again, both individuals and organizations can have difficulties in concentrating effort and attention on important things.

Computers can cause stress, even in leisure time. One difficult condition is that of Web addiction. Young (1996) defined the symptoms of Web addiction as follows:

- Staying online for 38 hours a week or more in leisure time
- Lying to family or colleagues about time spent on the Internet
- Restlessness
- Irritability and anxiety when not engaged in computer activities
- Neglect of social obligations
- Consistent failure to quit computer activities

Finally, Thong and Yap (2000) underscored that in order to perform quantitative research on stress, there is a need of identifying relevant variables. Without distinct and clear variables, testable and predictable hypotheses can not be built and tested.

ELIMINATING STRESS: USUAL TOOLS

Because stress is mostly conceived as negative, action should be taken to eliminate it. As stress is cause by a mismatch between the individual and his or her environment, activities on both sides can be beneficial. As discussed earlier, humans feel stress in very different ways, and their stress management capabilities greatly vary. Here we concentrate more on activities organizations and working environments can take to reduce risks.

According to Price et al. (1988), three types of health prevention can be identified: primary, secondary, and tertiary.

1. Primary prevention aims to eliminate causal factors in the development of problems. Theoretically, opportunities to improve psychological well-being could include reducing workloads or increasing employees' control over their work.
2. Secondary prevention aims to reduce the severity or duration of disorders and thus avoid the development of more serious, chronic, or disabling conditions. Occupational stress interventions of this form could include stress management training programs, where the employees can be taught how to handle stress in their work environment.
3. Tertiary prevention deals directly with existing disorders or problems. The aim of tertiary activities may be either to cure or restrict the disorder to the extent whereby the employee is restricted by the disability. This can include services such as counselling and psychotherapy.

Also, Cooper and Cartwright (1997) use a three class classification:

1. **Stressor reduction:** Taking action to modify or eliminate sources of stress at work and thus reduce the negative impact on the individual. The focus is in adapting the environment to fit the individual.
2. **Stress management:** Prompt detection and management of stress by increasing awareness and improving management skills of the individual through training and education. This prevention can help individuals to recognize the symptoms of the stress and improve relaxation techniques and work modification skills.
3. **Employee assistance programs:** Concerned with the treatment, rehabilitation, and recovery process to individuals who are suffering from ill health as a result of stress. This level activities typically involve the provision of counseling services.

Stressor Reduction

Prevention tools to eliminate stress consist of both organizational changes and individual targeted operations. Sauter, Murphy, et al. (1990) defined the following general guidelines for preventing negative stress from occurring:

1. Ensure that the workload is in line with workers' capabilities and resources.
2. Design jobs to provide meaning, stimulation, and opportunities for workers to use their skills.
3. Clearly define workers' roles and responsibilities.
4. Give workers opportunities to participate in decisions and actions affecting their jobs.
5. Improve communications, reduce uncertainty about career development and future employment prospects.
6. Provide opportunities for social interaction among workers.
7. Establish work schedules that are compatible with demands and responsibilities outside the job.

Elkin and Rosch (1990) stated a slightly different list concerning the same subject:

1. Redesign the task.
2. Redesign the work environment.
3. Establish flexible work schedules.
4. Encourage participative management.
5. Include the employee in career development.
6. Analyze work roles and establish goals.
7. Provide social support and feedback.
8. Build cohesive teams.
9. Establish fair employment policies.
10. Share the reward.

Tsutsumi and Kawakami (2005) presented effort–reward-based guidelines to prevent occupational stress:

Extrinsic Effort

- Even distribution of workload
- Reduction of long overtime work; secure rests or holidays

Extrinsic Rewards

- Monetary and nonmonetary compensatory reward
  - Encouraging praise for good work
  - Introduction of additional reward system such as welfare facilities and retirement benefits
- Esteem reward
  - Skill up of supervisors–managers for interpersonal relationship and social skill
- Career opportunity
  - Clear distinctions of the stages of promotion
  - Appropriate training for career development
- Other organizational system relevant to rewards (target dimensions)
  - Better information (sense of fairness)
  - Assessment of an employee's performance with her or his consent (sense of fairness)
  - Developing social support at or beyond the workplace (esteem and buffering of effort–reward imbalance)
  - Mentoring system (esteem and career opportunity)

Primary intervention strategies to reduce stress demand often cultural change. To find out the crucial stressors an organization should define them by some prior diagnosis (Cooper & Cartwright, 1997). This can be done by using risk assessment to identify the organizational stressors responsible for employee stress.

Stress Management

Stress management training aiming to educate employees about the impact of stress and teaching skills to cope with work demands is one of the most evaluated training programs (Reynolds, 1997). Psychological well-being appears to depend on a vast number of related factors, some of which work or employment cannot have any impact on, such as temperament and early experiences (Reynolds, 1997). On a study of job stress management and its effects on stress symptoms (Feuerstein et al. 2004) found significant decreases in pain, symptoms, and functional limitations. The role of these secondary preventive actions is essentially damage limitation addressing the consequences rather than the sources of stress (Cooper & Cartwright, 1997). These kind of actions implicitly assume that the organization will not change but continues to be stressful, and therefore the individual has to develop resistance and coping skills with stress.

Employee Assistance Program

Evidence has been found that counseling and other employee assistance programs are effective in improving the psychological well-being of employees (Cooper & Cartwright, 1994). These kinds of actions have also been suggested to have considerable cost benefits. For example, a counseling program in the U.K. Post Office resulted in a reduction in absenteeism in one year by approximately 60% (Cooper & Sadri, 1991). In this study, some significant improvements in mental health and self-esteem were found.

According to the findings of Cooper and Cartwright (1997), the reasons that stress management and employee assistance programs are more popular in organizations than stress prevention actions can be listed as follows:

- There is relatively more published data available on the cost-benefit analysis of such programs
- The counselors, physicians, and clinicians responsible for healthcare feel more comfortable with changing individuals than with organizations
- It is considered easier and less disruptive for a business to change the individual
- The organization looks like it is taking an action to safeguard employee's health

However, reducing stressors before stress even occurs can not only be more cost effective than curing actions but also reduce absenteeism and improve organization performance, not to mention the human benefits.

EMPIRICAL FINDINGS

In order to empirically examine the influence of IT to stress, a data analysis was made. The purpose was to test if the use of IT had some kind of relation to different factors causing stress in the healthcare environment.

Sample

Questionnaires were mailed to 5,000 social and healthcare employees in Finland. A total 3,072 returned questionnaires were accepted. The response rate was 72.2%. The sample did not reach new or temporary social- or healthcare employees because the sample was taken from a register that was two years old. A summary of the demographic characteristics of the sample is presented in Table 2. The data were collected by the Finnish Institute of Occupational Health.

Thirty-one percent of respondents did not use IT at their work at all. 20% used just a little IT, 22% used IT sometimes, and 27% used a lot.

Table 2. Sample demographics

Gender	%
Male	10
Female	90
Age	
-25	2
26-35	35
36-45	36
46-55	17
55-	10
Work experience	
-5	11
6-15	30
16-25	34
26-	19

39% of respondents considered their IT skills to be insufficient, 42% thought they had reasonable IT skills, and 19% answered they had good IT skills.

Analysis of Data

The data were analyzed using the SPSS program, Version 5.0. Cross tabulation was used in order to find relations between different factors. Significance rate was set to 0,05. For those job satisfaction

Figure 4a. Use of IT

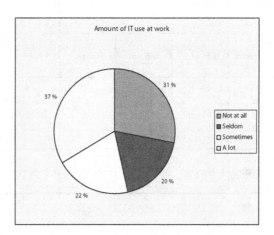

Figure 4b. IT skills

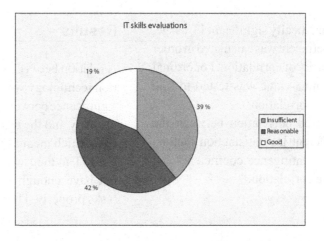

Table 3. Results of the study (+) = the direction of correlation is positive; (-) = the direction of correlation is negative; X= no statistically significant correlation.)

	How much IT used at work?	Personal skills to use IT	Way the use of IT is experience d	Estimate how much use of I T will increase i n the future	Estimate the increase of IT influence at wor k
Amount of extr a work without compensation	0, 203 (+)	0, 176 (+)	0, 151 (-)	0, 179 (+)	0, 155 (-)
Lack of time to accomplish the work tasks properly	0, 143 (+)	X	0, 138 (+)	0, 224 (+)	0, 177 (+)
Continuous stress and pressure of unfinished wor k	0, 184 (+)	X	0, 147 (-)	0, 217(+)	0, 155 (+)
Several interruptions and disturbanc es at work	0, 263 (+)	0, 170 (+)	0, 159 (-)	0, 258 (+)	0, 153 (+)
Ability to manage curren t work tasks	0, 174 (+)	0, 208 (+)	0, 199 (-)	0, 153(-)	0, 137(-)
Possibilities to influence the planning of changes at the workplace	0, 158 (-)	0, 148 (-)	0, 160 (+)	0, 160 (-)	0, 210 (+)
Other educatio n during the last 12 months	0, 250 (+)	0, 212(+)	0, 211(-)	0, 236(+)	0, 141 (-)

factors that had statistically significant IT usage, the contingence coefficient was calculated in order to find out the intensity of correlation. For ordinal scaled factors, gamma-value was tested to find out the direction of correlation.

The result showed correlation between the use of IT and different job-satisfaction factors. In Table 3 are the contingence coefficients and the direction of the correlation.

Results

A relation between stress and the use of information technology was found. There was statistical significance between enough time to do work tasks properly and the use of IT. Correlation was positive, which means that the more the respondents used IT in their work the more they felt they did not have enough time to carry out their work tasks properly. There was also a correlation with the amount of use and how much interruption the respondents had in their work. This correlation was also positive: The more the respondents used IT in their work the more interruptions they felt they had. Also, the expectations of increasing the use of IT in work correlated with the amount of interruptions. Respondents that had most interruption in their work were the ones that most expected the use of IT to increase in their work.

Possibilities to have influence over work tasks had a correlation with the extent of use and the expectations of IT. Employees that were using more IT thought they had fewer possibilities to influence their work. Also, the employees that expected the IT to increase more were those who thought they had less power over their work. This can result from the routines IT brings to work. The ways the tasks are made have to be standardized, and therefore employees cannot work as freely in their own way as they used to.

Employees that used more IT in their work seemed to make more work without compensation. Also, the more skilled the employees were in using IT, the more they answered they work extra hours without compensation.

Even though the purpose of IT is to improve work processes and therefore decrease work stress, it seems that it may not be the reality in the social and healthcare areas. According to the results, the most stressed workers were those using the most IT in their work. This can be due to lack of IT skills; not knowing how to use IT properly can cause additional work. Another explanation could be that the tasks requiring the use of IT have been given to those people already most stressed. It can also be that there is more stress in the sectors that use IT the most.

Education seems to have a positive correlation with the use of IT and IT skills. Employees with the most education in work managed IT better in work. Respondents that used more IT in their work think they have more possibilities to participate in changes in their work.

Table 4. Impacts of IT

The more IT usage, the more
1. extra work without compensation
2. pressure of unfinished work
3. disturbance and interruptions at work
4. capability to manage current tasks
5. possibilities to influence work

The ability to manage current work tasks correlated with the use of IT and IT skills. Employees that used more IT thought they could manage well with their current work tasks or even more challenging tasks in the future. Some factors that had a correlation with IT use are summarized in Table 4.

The results indicate that IT use in health and social-care environment can have more of an impact on work than purely positive or negative. IT use can cause stress by disturbing other work tasks by taking extra time. Also, disturbance and interruptions at work relate to IT use, which can indicate that IT skills of personnel are not sufficient or that the applications used are not sophisticated enough. Also, poor IT skills of colleagues can lead to interruptions if assistance is often needed to solve other's computer-related problems. However, the effects of IT need not only be negative. Capability to manage current tasks and possibilities to influence one's work relate to higher rates of IT use.

What Can Be Done in the Health and Social-Care Industries to Eliminate IT-Based Stress?

As factors affect stress in the healthcare sector, these factors are also used to discuss the ways of eliminating direct negative effects of IT in health and social-care industries. Most approaches to stress reduction in the workplace focus on individuals (van der Hek & Plopm, 1997) still more permanent and efficient effects are anticipated from organization focused interventions (Karasek, 1997). Using parts of the guidelines presented previously (Sauter, Murphy, et al., 1990), we define the following general guidelines for preventing negative IT stress from occurring in healthcare.

- **Ensure that the workload is in line with workers' capabilities and resources:** It is highly important to take into consideration that learning to use new IT demands time and effort. Employees should also have the possibility to be trained properly in order to be able to get the capabilities to use the new technology. The workload should be adjusted according to estimations of the effort needed to use the new IT. This is especially important in a hectic healthcare environment, where the employees already are under a large workload.

- **Clearly define workers' roles and responsibilities:** It is important to clarify the importance of IT for the whole organization. Proper information should be filed in the systems from the beginning in order to avoid mistakes and misinterpretations at a later stage. Healthcare tasks such as filling in patient records are often delegated from doctors to secretaries. This can lead to mistakes and to the disappearance of important information.

- **Give workers opportunities to participate in decisions and actions affecting their jobs:** When designing a new information system, the role of the end users in health and social care should be more diverse. Participation in designing phase can make the launching and use easier and at the same time motivate the users. Although employees

in the healthcare are not experts in IT they are experts in their own field. This knowledge should be moved into the IT as well in order to create better systems and to get users involved with IT.

- **Provide opportunities for social interaction among workers:** IT use should not alienate colleagues from each other. Even if more IT is used for communication and distance working, personal meetings are vital in the health and social-care environment. Also, effort reward-based guidelines (Tsutsumi & Kawakami, 2004) can be used to find way to reduce IT-based stress.

Extrinsic Effort

Use of IT should be distributed evenly. No group of professionals should allocate the use of IT to other groups. Information should be placed in the information systems at the point it is born.

Extrinsic Rewards

- Monetary and nonmonetary compensatory reward
  - Encouraging praise for good work could also include rewards for training to use new IT. Some monetary reward system concerning the use of IT could be presented to motivate the users.
- Esteem reward
  - The managers should be trained to value and encourage the employees to use IT.
- Other organizational system relevant to rewards
  - Better information about new IT projects and plans should be distributed.
  - Mentoring system for using IT for new employees.

The most important indirect effects of IT use in the healthcare sector that we found in our em-

Table 5. Eliminating stress in healthcare

Problem:	Cure:
Extra work without compensation	IT training Reward system Adjustment of workload
Pressure of unfinished work	IT training IT support Even distribution of IT tasks
Disturbance and interruptions at work	IT training IT support Participative design

pirical study were listed in Table 2. Eliminating these indirect effects is both an organizational- and individual-level task. To reduce stress caused by these factors, some guidelines of usual stress elimination tools were used to create Table 5.

Guidelines to Prevention of IT-Based Stress in the Healthcare Environment

As a summary, we use the classification of Price. Health prevention among healthcare workers in computer-use related stress could go as follows:

Primary Prevention

- Cooperation on designing and launching new IT
- Training to use IT; not only one application
- Showing the whole chain of IT use, not only one part, without understanding where to go
- Sufficient IT support

Secondary and Third Prevention

- Job stress-management programs should include a discussion about IT. Discussion and training can be helpful in this situation.
- Meetings can change negative attitudes by showing the whole chain of information.

CONCLUSIONS

Occupational health is increasingly more threatened by mental problems than by physical accidents. Inability to work is often a result of mental problems, and a factor of mental problems is stress. Stress is born out of haste, overburden with work, and missing or insufficient resources to handle the workload. Fragmentation of working time is one important cause of stress.

We conducted a literature study about the connections between IT use and stress at work. The reasons computers and applications cause stress were discussed, and a list of approaches that can alleviate stress in computer work was presented.

However, we did not conclude that stress is bad: A managed level of stress can increase productivity and in total boost work performance at the individual and organizational levels. Stress can be manifested in several ways: It can be healthy and productivity-enhancing, it can be harmful, or it can develop into a disease or increase the development of other diseases.

We found that stress is a very meaningful and usual concept in almost any scientific discipline. At a very general level, it means external pressure towards an entity. One can clearly see that human stress can be included into this definition. Occupational stress is one subcategory of stress. Stressors from work and other factors have an complex interplay, and the total load on the individual as related to his or her stress carrying capacity is the important issue.

We used the framework of Thong and Yap (2000) to discuss the relationship between computers and stress. It can be interpreted that the connection between computers and stress is multilevel. Computers and information systems as such cause stress. More important, however, is that the governance structures, work processes, and working habits they enable can be more stressful than earlier, noncomputerized processes. On the other hand, computers could be implemented in a way that reduces risk. We would like to conclude that computers at the very least are risk-neutral devices: Stress outcomes materialize because of their unskilled implementation and wrong working habits developed by individuals and organizations.

An interesting genre of research is that in which problems and malfunctions in organizations are compared to known human diseases. The cases of paranoia, autism, ADHD, and Web addiction are interesting examples of this type of discussion.

Three types of health prevention can be identified: primary, secondary, and tertiary. The earlier that stress is identified and treated, the easier and cheaper the task is. This is very similar to the tracking of mistakes and malfunctions in information systems: The earlier they can be tracked down and eliminated in the system life cycle, the better.

Our empirical study found relationships between computer usage and the following issues in the healthcare industry:

1. extra work without compensation
2. pressure of unfinished work
3. disturbance and interruptions at work
4. capability to manage current tasks
5. possibilities to influence work

Even here, we see that computer usage had positive effects (points 4 and 5). One of our conclusions is that computer application is not always meaningful for healthcare staff, as they do not understand the total work process they are a part of and to which the computer system should give support. Educating them and giving a stronger motivation to use computers would be one thing eliminating stress in healthcare professions.

REFERENCES

Agarwal, R., & Ferratt, T. W. (2002). Enduring practices for managing IT professionals. *Communications of the ACM, 45*(9), 73-79.

Anonymous. (1996). Aluminum labor pact stresses teamwork. *Purchasing, 120*(11), 48B22.

Armour, N. L. (1995). The beginning of stress reduction: Creating a code of conduct for how team members treat each other. *Public Personnel Management, 24*(2), 127-132.

Bashein, B. J., & Markus, M. L. (1997). A credibility equation for IT specialists. *Sloan Management Review, 38*(4), 35-44.

Beruch, Y. (2001). The autistic society. *Information & Management, 38,* 129-136.

Bonaccorso, S. N., & Sturchio, J. L. (2002, April). Direct to consumer advertising in medicalising normal human experience. *British Medical Journal, 324,* 910-911.

Burke, P. (2000). *A social history of knowledge: From Gutenberg to Diderot.* Polity Press.

Butcher, H. (1998). *Meeting managers' information needs.* London: Aslib.

Cross, R., N., Nohria, et al. (2002, Spring). Six myths about informal networks and how to overcome them. *Sloan Management Review,* 67-75.

Davenport, T., & Beck, J. C. (2000, September-October). Getting the attention you need. *Harvard Business Review,* 119-126.

Dreyfus, H. L. (1992). *What machines still can't do.* Cambridge, MA: MIT Press.

Edmunds, A., & Morris, A. (2000). The problem of information overload in business organizations: A review of literature. *International Journal of Information Management, 20*(1), 17-28.

Gristock, J. (1997). Communications and organizational virtuality. *Electronic Journal of Organizational Virtualness.*

Holm, J., Lähteenmäki, S., et al. (2002). Best practices of ICT workforce management: A comparatible research initiative in Finland. *The Journal of European Industrial Training, 26*(7), 333-341.

Kallinikos, J. (2004). The social foundations of the bureaucratic order. *Organization, 11*(1), 13-36.

Kokko, N., Vartiainen, M., et al. (2004). Work stressors in virtual organizations. *International Congress New Work 2004.* Heraklios, Greece.

Kramer, R. M. (2002, July). When paranoia makes sense. *Harvard Business Review,* 62-69.

Kurland, N. B., & Egan, T. D. (1999). Telecommuting: Justice and control in the virtual organization. *Organization Science, 10*(4), 500-513.

Laskin, D. (1994). Dealing with information overload. *Journal of Oral Maxillofacial Surgery, 47*(7), 661.

Levinson, H. (1970). *Executive stress.* London: Harper & Row.

Luo, W., & Najdawi, M. (2004). Trust-building measures: A review of consumer health portals. *Communications of the ACM, 47*(1), 109-113.

Maes, P. (1994). Agents that reduce work and information overload. *Communications of the ACM, 37*(7), 31-146.

Markus, M. L., Manville, B., et al. (2000, Fall). What makes a virtual organization work. *Sloan Management Review,* 13-26.

MedSearch. (2004). MedSearch: Medical reference for Gulf-War related research. From *http://www.gulflink.osd.mil/medsearch/glossary/glossary_s.shtml*

Meyerson, D. E. (1998). Feeling stressed and burned out: A feminist reading and re-visioning of stress-based emotions within medicine and organization science. *Organization Science, 9*(1), 103-118.

National Institute for Occupational Safety and Health. (2004). *Stress at work.* Washington, DC: Author.

NIMH. (2004). National Institute of Mental Health: Attention Deficit Hyperactivity Disorder. From *www.nimh.nih.gov/publicat/adhd.cfm*

Pondy, L. R. (1967). Organizational conflict: Concepts and models. *Administrative Science Quarterly, 12,* 296-320.

Robey, D. (1984). Conflict models for implementation research. *Applications of Management Science* (Suppl. 1), 89-105.

Sauter, S. L., Murphy, L. R., et al. (1990). Prevention of work-related psychological disorders. *American Psychologist, 45*(10), 1146-1158.

Sawyer, S. (2001). Effects of intra-group conflict on packaged software development team performance. *Information Systems Journal,* (11), 155-178.

Schill, T., Toves, C., et al. (1980). Interpersonal trust and coping with stress (Pt. 2). *Psychological-Reports, 47*(3), 1192.

SGIA. (2004). SGIA's (specialty graphic imaging association) glossary of terms. From *http://www.sgia.org/glossary/Ss.cfm*

Suomi, R. (2000). *Different conceptual approaches to virtual organization*. The 5th International Telework Workshop, Stockholm, Sweden.

Thong, J. Y. L., & Yap, C. S. (2000). Information systems and occupational stress: A theoretical framework. *Omega, 28,* 681-692.

Trent, J. T., Smith, A. L., et al. (1994). Telecommuting: Stress and social support. *Psychological Reports, 74,* 1312-1314.

Walsham, G. (1994). Virtual organization: An alternative view. *Information Society, 10*(4), 289-292.

Van Rooyen, E. (2000). A comprehensive change management framework for information technology-driven change in organisations. *Proceedings of the 8th European Conference on Information Systems*, Vienna, Austria.

Wastell, D., & Newman, M. (1996). Information system design, stress and organizational change in the ambulance services: A tale of two cities. *Accounting, Management and Information Technologies, 6*(4).

WFMH. (2004). *World Federation for Mental Health: The world mental health day project: glossary.* From *http://www.wfmh.org/wmhday/sec3_pt3_4_glossary.html*

ViaHealth. (2004). *ViaHealth disease and wellness information.* From *http://www.viahealth.org/disease/cardiac/glossary.htm#Glossary%20of%20Cardiac%20Terminology*

WordNet. (2004). *WordNet: A lexical database for the English language.*

Young, K. S. (1996). *Caught in the net.* New York: Wiley.

This work was previously published in E-Health Systems Diffusion and Use: The Innovation, the User and the USE IT Model, edited by T. A. M. Spil and R. W. Schuring, pp. 61-92, copyright 2006 by IGI Publishing, formerly known as Idea Group Publishing (an imprint of IGI Global).

Section VI
Emerging Trends

Chapter XXIII
Neo–Symbiosis:
The Next Stage in the Evolution of Human Information Interaction

Douglas Griffith
General Dynamics Advanced Information Systems, USA

Frank L. Greitzer
Pacific Northwest National Laboratory, USA

ABSTRACT

The purpose of this article is to re-address the vision of human-computer symbiosis as originally expressed by J.C.R. Licklider nearly a half-century ago and to argue for the relevance of this vision to the field of cognitive informatics. We describe this vision, place it in some historical context relating to the evolution of human factors research, and observe that the field is now in the process of re-invigorating Licklider's vision. A central concept of this vision is that humans need to be incorporated into computer architectures. We briefly assess the state of the technology within the context of contemporary theory and practice, and we describe what we regard as this emerging field of neo-symbiosis. Examples of neo-symbiosis are provided, but these are nascent examples and the potential of neo-symbiosis is yet to be realized. We offer some initial thoughts on requirements to define functionality of neo-symbiotic systems and discuss research challenges associated with their development and evaluation. Methodologies and metrics for assessing neo-symbiosis are discussed.

BACKGROUND

In 1960, J.C.R. Licklider wrote in his paper "Man-Machine Symbiosis,"

The hope is that in not too many years, human brains and computing machines will be coupled together very tightly, and that the resulting partnership will think as no human brain has ever thought and process data in a way not approached by the information-handling machines we know today (p. 5).

This statement is breathtaking for its vision — especially considering the state of computer technology at that time, that is, large mainframes, punch cards, and batch processing. The purpose of this article is to re-address Licklider's vision and build upon his ideas to inform contemporary theory and practice within the broader field of human factors as well as to offer a historical perspective for the emerging field of cognitive informatics.

It is curious to note that Licklider did not use the term symbiosis again, but he did introduce more visionary ideas in a symbiotic vein. A paper he co-authored with Robert Taylor, titled "The Computer As a Communication Device," made the bold assertion, "In a few years, men will be able to communicate more effectively through a machine than face to face" (p. 21). Clearly the time estimate was optimistic, but the vision was noteworthy. Licklider and Taylor described the role of the computer in effective communication by introducing the concept of "On-Line Interactive Vicarious Expediter and Responder" (OLIVER), an acronym that by no coincidence was chosen to honor artificial intelligence researcher and the father of machine perception, Oliver Selfridge. OLIVER would be able to take notes when so directed, and would know what you do, what you read, what you buy and where you buy it. It would know your friends and acquaintances and would know who and what is important to you. This paper made heavy use of the concept of "mental models," relatively new to the psychology of that day. The computer was conceived of as an active participant rather than as a passive communication device. Remember that when this paper was written, computers were large devices used by specialists. The age of personal computing was off in the future.

Born during World War II, the field of human factors engineering (HFE) gained prominence for its research on the placement of controls — commonly referred to as knobology within the field of HFE, which was an unjust characterization. Many

important contributions were made to the design of aircraft, including controls and displays. With strong roots in research on human performance and human errors, the field gained prominence through the work of many leaders in the field who came out of the military: Alphonse Chapanis, a psychologist and a Lieutenant in the U.S. Air Force; Alexander Williams, a psychologist and naval aviator; Air Force Colonel Paul Fitts; and J.C.R. Licklider. Beginning with Chapanis, who realized that "pilot errors" were most often cockpit design errors that could be corrected by the application of human factors to display and controls, these early educators were instrumental in launching the discipline of aviation psychology and HFE that led to worldwide standards in the aviation industry. These men were influential in demonstrating that the military and aviation industry could benefit from research and expertise of the human factors academic community; their works (Fitts, 1951a) were inspirational in guiding research and design in engineering psychology for decades. Among the most influential early articles in the field that came out of this academic discipline was George Miller's (1956) "The Magical Number Seven, Plus or Minus Two: Some Limits on Our Capacity to Process Information," which heralded the field of cognitive science and application of quantitative approaches to the study of cognitive activity and performance.

An early focus of HFE was to design systems informed by known human information processing limitations and capabilities — systems that exploit our cognitive strengths and accommodate our weaknesses (inspired by the early ideas represented in the Fitts' List that compared human and machine capabilities; Fitts, 1951b). While the early HFE practice emphasized improvements in the design of equipment to make up for human limitations (reflecting a tradition of *machine centered computing*), a new way of thinking about human factors was characterized by the design of the human-machine system, or more generally, *human-* or *user-centered computing* (Norman &

Draper, 1986). The new subdiscipline of interaction design emerged in the 1970s and 1980s that emphasizes the need to organize information in ways to help reduce clutter and "information overload" and to help cope with design challenges for next-generation systems that will be increasingly complex while being staffed with fewer people. Emphasis on human cognitive processes, and on the need to regard the human-machine system as a joint cognitive system, represented a further refinement that has been called *cognitive systems engineering* (Hollnagel & Woods, 1983).

Fundamental to all of these approaches and perspectives on HFE is the overriding principle to "know your user." In a recent critical essay, Don Norman (2005) asks us to re-assess the human-centered design perspective: Developed to overcome the poor design of software products, human-centered design emphasized the needs and abilities of users and improved the usability and understandability of products. But despite these improvements, software complexity is still with us. Norman goes on to ask why so many designs of everyday things work so well, even without the benefit of user studies and human-centered design. He suggests that they all were "developed with a deep understanding of the activities that were to be performed (p.14)." Successful designs are those that fit gracefully into the requirements of the underlying activity. Norman does not reject human-centered design, but rather encompasses it within a broader perspective of *activity-centered design*. Further, he questions a basic tenet of human centered design that technology should adapt to the human, rather than *vice versa*. He regards much of human behavior as an adaptation to the "powers and limitations of technology." Activity-centered design aims to exploit this fact.

Other perspectives suggest that the focus of design should be on human-information interaction rather than human-computer interaction. Gershon (1995) coined the term Human-Information Interaction (HII) to focus attention on improving the way people "find, interact with, and understand information." As such, HII includes aspects of many traditional research efforts, including usability evaluation methods and cognitive task analysis, but also design concepts that address the ethnographic and ecological environment in which action takes place. Examples of work in this area include distributed cognition (Zhang & Norman, 1994), naturalistic and recognition-primed decision making (Zsombok, 1997); and information foraging and information scent (Pirolli & Card, 1999).

In summary, over the last half century or so, the field of human factors has evolved through a series of modest perspective shifts and insights that have yielded a fair degree of success in approaches, methods, and techniques for design and evaluation of systems that are created to support and enhance human-information interaction. The many labels that have been applied to the field (cognitive engineering, human-centered computing, participatory design, decision centered design, etc.) are all "differently hued variants of the same variety" (Hoffman, Feltovich, Ford, Woods, Klein & Feltovich, 2002).

Engineering psychology and human factors are moving to a more encompassing scope of the field. Raja Parasuraman (2003) married neuroscience with ergonomics and termed it neuroergonomics. Don Norman (2004) incorporated affect (emotion) into the field with his book, *Emotional Design: Why We Love (or Hate) Everyday Things*. Hancock, Pepe and Murphy (2005) are developing the concept of hedonomics. They have developed a hierarchy of ergonomics and hedonomic needs derived from Maslow's (1970) hierarchy of needs: safety, the prevention of pain, forms the foundation of this pyramid; next comes functionality, the promulgation of process; then usability, the priority of preference (the transition from ergonomics to hedonomics begins at the usability layer); the next layer is pleasurable experience; and the apex of the pyramid comprises individuation and personal perfection. So the field is beginning to address the enhancement of individual potential.

Recent research in the emerging field of cognitive informatics (Wang, 2005a, b) addresses Maslow's hierarchy of needs within a formal model that attempts to capture the relationships among human factors and basic human needs.

Recently a new research thrust has emerged that aims to shift the focus once more to not only enhancing the interaction environment, which is the aim of cognitive systems engineering, but also to enhance the cognitive *abilities* of the human operators and decision makers themselves. The Augmented Cognition program (Schmorrow & Kruse, 2004) within the DARPA Information Processing Technology Office (IPTO) aims to monitor and assess the user's cognitive state through behaviorally and neurologically derived measures acquired from the user while interacting with the system and then to adapt or augment the computational interface to improve performance of the user-computer system. Schmorrow and McBride (2005) explain that this research is based on the view that the weak link in the human-computer system may be attributed to human information processing limitations, and that human and computer capabilities are increasingly reliant on each other to achieve maximal performance. Much of the research within the augmented cognition program seeks to further our understanding of how information processing works in the human mind so that augmentation schemes might be developed and exploited more effectively — in a variety of domains from clinical restoration of function to education to worker productivity to warfighting superiority. Thus, as described by Schmorrow and McBride: "the DARPA Augmented Cognition program at its core is an attempt to create a new frontier, not by optimizing the friendliness of connections between human and computer, but by reconceptualizing a true marriage of silicon- and carbon-based enterprises [International of Journal Human Computer Interaction, p. 128]."

While augmented cognition exploits neuroscience research as a path toward symbiosis of humans and machines, research in cognitive informatics embraces neuroscience research as a potential model and point of departure for "brain-like" machine-based cognitive systems that may someday exhibit human-like properties of sensation, perception, and other complex cognitive behaviour (Anderson, 2005a, b). We believe that neo-symbiosis provides a strong contextual framework to organize and guide research in cognitive informatics.

NEO-SYMBIOSIS

Once more, then, we are on the threshold of resurrecting a vision of symbiosis – but today we have the advantage of far greater computational resources and decades of evolution in the field of human factors/cognitive engineering. Licklider's notion of symbiosis does require updating. First, the term "man/machine symbiosis" is politically incorrect and would be more appropriately termed "human/machine symbiosis." Then there is a problem with the term symbiosis itself. Symbiosis implies *co-equality* between mutually supportive organisms. However, we contend that the human must be in the *superordinate* position. The Dreyfuses (Dreyfus, 1972, 1979, 1992; Dreyfus & Dreyfus, 1986) have made compelling arguments that there are fundamental limitations to what computers can accomplish, limitations that will never be overcome (Dreyfus & Dreyfus, 1986). In this case, it is important that the human remain in the superordinate position so that these computer limitations can be circumvented. On the other hand, Kurzweil has argued for the unlimited potential of computers (Kurzweil, 1999). But should it be proven that computers do, indeed, have this unlimited potential, then some attention needs to be paid to Bill Joy and his nightmarish vision of the future should technology go awry (Joy, 2000). In this case, humans would need to be in the superordinate position for their own survival. Griffith (2005a) has suggested the term neo-symbiosis for this updated vision of symbiosis.

The augmented cognition research community is taking Licklider's vision quite literally in exploring technologies for acquiring, measuring, and validating neurological cognitive state sensors to facilitate human-information interaction and decision-making. Neurobiologically inspired forms of symbiosis, while consistent with the metaphor that Licklider used, were not a focus of Licklider's vision; but the possibilities for enhanced cognitive performance are enticing. Clearly, however, much work is required to achieve a brain-computer interface that might be called neo-symbiotic. Much of the effort in this field to date has focused on cognitive activity that tends to be more oriented toward attention and perception processes, and less toward decision making and thinking. In this sense, augmented-cognition neurological inputs can help to approach neo-symbiosis by providing information to the computer that can in turn be fed back to the human in the form of adaptive displays and interactions or other functions aimed to mitigate the effects of stress or information overload. More ambitious goals of increasing total cognitive capacity through augmented cognition technologies are still on the horizon of this research program and recent offshoots of augmented cognition R&D such as DARPA's Neurotechnology for Intelligence Analysts program[1]. Our interest, similarly, is in the current potential for enhanced human-computer collaboration that will achieve a level of performance that is superior to either the human or the computer acting alone.

The principal reason that the beginning of the 21st century is so propitious for the reinvigoration of Licklider's vision is the result of advancements in computer technology and psychological theory. Therefore, one of our major objectives is to increase the human's understanding, accuracy, and effectiveness by supporting the development of creative insights. Understanding involves learning about the problem area and increasing the variety of contexts from which the problem can be understood. Enhanced accuracy/effectiveness can be achieved by endowing the computer with a variety of means to support the task or activity. Revisiting thoughtful prescriptions for such computer-based intelligent support capabilities from two decades ago, we find examples such as knowledge of the user's goals and intentions, contextual knowledge (Croft, 1984). and "cognitive coupling" (Fitter & Sime, 1980) functions that include (Greitzer, Hershman & Kaiwi, 1985) the ability to inform the user about the status of tasks, remind the user to perform certain tasks, advise the user in selecting alternative actions, monitor progress toward the goal, anticipate requests to display or process information, and test hypotheses. In the context of information analysis tasks, examples of such neo-symbiotic contributions by the computer include considering alternative hypotheses, assessing the accuracy of intelligence sources, and increasing the precision of probability estimates through systematic revision. These types of activity-based support functions, enhanced by cognitive models, are the concepts that we believe will put us more solidly on the path to the original vision of Licklider, a neo-symbiosis where there is a greater focus on cognitive coupling between the human user and the computer.

NEO-SYMBIOSIS RESEARCH AGENDA

Requirements: Implementing Neo-Symbiosis

How should neo-symbiosis be implemented? Fortunately, Kahneman (2002, 2003) and Kahneman and Frederick (2002) has provided guidance through a theoretical framework. In his effort to organize seemingly contradictory results in studies of judgment under uncertainty, he has advanced the notion of two cognitive systems introduced by Sloman (1996, 2002) and others (Stanovich, 1999; Stanovich & West, 2002). System 1, termed Intuition, is fast, parallel, automatic, effortless, associative, slow learning, and emotional. System 2, termed Reasoning, is slow, serial, controlled, effortful, rule-governed, flexible, and neutral. The cognitive illusions, which were part of the work for which he won the Nobel Prize, as well as perceptual illusions, are the results of System 1 processing. Expertise is primarily a resident of System 1. So are most of our skilled performance such as recognition, speaking, driving, and many social interactions. System 2, on the other hand, consists of conscious operations, such as what is commonly thought of as thinking. Table 1 summarizes these characteristics and relationships. The upper portion of the table describes human information processing characteristics and strengths, interpreted within Kahneman's (2003) System 1/System 2 conceptualization. The bottom portion of the table represents an update of traditional characterizations of functional allocation based on human and computer capabilities, such as the original Fitts' List (Fitts, 1951b), cast within the System 1/System 2 framework.

System 1 is effective presumably due to evolutionary forces, massive experience, and by constraining context. Most of the time, it is quite effective. System 1 uses nonconscious heuristics to achieve these efficiencies, so occasionally it errs and misfires. Such misfires are responsible for perceptual and cognitive errors. One of the roles of System 2 is to monitor the outputs of System 1 processes. It is the System 2 processes that require computer support, not only with respect to the pure drudgery and slowness of human System 2 processes, but also with respect to the monitoring of System 1 processes. In most cases, however, it is a mistake to assign System 1 processes to the computer. This was the fundamental error in many automatic target recognition and image interpretation algorithms that attempted to automate the human out of the loop. Even to this day, computer technology has been unsuccessful in modeling human expertise in System 1 domains[2]. The perceptual recognition processes of most humans are excellent. System design should capitalize upon these superb processes and provide support to other areas of human information processing such as search (there is a tendency to overlook targets); interpretation keys to provide a check and support for the recognition process; analysis and synthesis (e.g., to augment reasoning processes); support to facilitate adjusting to changes in context (e.g., to maintain situational awareness); and computational support (e.g., to make predictions). The bottom portion of Table 1 exhibits examples of how human and computer contributions can be allocated to System 1 and System 2 processing in a neo-symbiotic system.

Greitzer (2005b) has discussed the importance of identifying cognitive states in real-world decision-making tasks. A critical question here is, what are the cognitive states that need to be measured? What are the cognitive states that, if identified and measured, could enhance neo-symbiosis? Clearly it would be beneficial to identify neurological correlates for System 1 and System 2 processes. It would be especially beneficial to identify neurological correlates of System 2 while monitoring System 1 processing. Perhaps there is a neurological signature when potential errors are detected in System 1 processing. It is conceivable that some of these errors remain below the threshold of consciousness. If these errors were detectable in the neurological stream, computers could assist in this error monitoring process.

As was mentioned previously, the identification of neurological correlates is not a requirement, nor is it the only enabler for neo-symbiosis. Griffith (2005b) has argued that neo-symbiosis can be achieved over a wide range of technological sophistication. Overviews and tutorials can be presented on basic human information processing capabilities, limitations, and biases. A software agent, or avatar, can pop up at strategic times with reminding prompts or checklists. Of course, the capability to monitor the human's cognitive state through neurological correlates will enhance the ability of the avatar to pop up at strategic times. It might also be possible to monitor the content

Table 1. System 1 and System 2 processes

Human Processes		
	System 1: Intuition	**System 2: Reasoning**
Processing Characteristics[a]:	o Fast o Parallel o Automatic o Effortless o Associative o Slow-Learning o Emotional	o Slow o Serial o Controlled o Effortful o Rule-governed o Flexible o Neutral
Type of Processing (Examples of Human Information Processing Strengths)	o Expertise o Skilled Performance o Most Perception	o Thinking o Goal-driven Performance o Anomaly and Paradox Detection
Neo-Symbiotic Functions		
	System 1: Intuition	**System 2: Reasoning**
Examples of Human Contributions	o Providing Context o Detecting Contextual Shifts o Intuition o Pattern Recognition o Creative Insights	o Supervision/Monitoring o Inductive Reasoning o Adaptability to Change o Contextual Evaluations o Anomaly Recognition/ Detection o Goal-Driven Processes/ Planning o Creative Insights
Examples of Computer Contributions	o Recognize Cognitive State Changes o Adapt Displays/ Interaction Characteristics to Human's Cognitive State	o Deductive Reasoning o Search o Situational Awareness o Analysis/Synthesis o Hypothesis Generation/ Tracking o Computational Support o Information Storage/ Retrieval o Multiprocessing o Update Status of Tasks o Advise on Alternatives o Monitor Progress o Monitoring System 1 Processes

[a] *This portion of the table based on Kahneman (2003)*

of the interactions with the computer to identify potential processing problems. Differences in processing time present is yet another potential source of information for detecting errors and biases.

In our view, the thrust of the HII research agenda should be targeted at enhancing neo-symbiosis. A major focus of HII research today is aimed at visualization technology that processes and seeks to represent massive data in ways that facilitate insight and decision making. Data visualization technology seeks to facilitate visual thinking to gain an understanding of complex information, and perhaps most particularly to gain insights that would otherwise not be apparent from other data representations. A famous example of a successful visualization is the periodic table of elements (conceived by Mendeleev and published in 1869), which not only provided a simple display of known data but also pointed out gaps in knowledge that led to discoveries of new elements. However, creating novel visualizations of complex data (information visualization) does not guarantee success; there are arguably more examples of visualizations that have not lived up to expectations than success stories. A leap of faith is required to expect that a given scientific visualization will produce the "aha!" moment that leads to an insightful solution to a difficult problem. We assert that the key to a successful scientific visualization is its effectiveness in fostering new ways of thinking about a problem — in the System 1 sense as exemplified in Table 1 (e.g., seeing contextual shifts, recognizing new patterns, finding creative insights). This view stresses that the interaction component of HII needs to be emphasized. The human should not be regarded as simply a passive recipient of information display, however creative that information display might be. The human needs to be able to manipulate and interact with the information. The ability to manipulate information and view it in different contexts is key to the elimination of cognitive biases and to the achievement of novel insights (e.g., finding the novel intelligence in massive data). The goal is a neo-symbiotic interaction between the human and the *information*.

Thus, requirements should be defined so that a neo-symbiosis can be achieved between humans and their technology. Questions to guide the requirements definition process for neo-symbiotic systems designed to facilitate HII include:

- *How can such systems be designed to mitigate or eliminate cognitive biases?* Detecting/recognizing possible bias is one part of the challenge; an equally critical R&D goal is to define mitigation strategies. What types of interventions will be effective, and how should interventions be managed? We suggest that a mixed-initiative solution will be required that maintains the supervisory control of the human.

- *How can such systems be designed to leverage the unique processing skills of humans?* A prerequisite here is to identify the unique processing skills of humans. Technologies and approaches for developing idiosyncratic user models would be most useful. Moreover, expert users can identify and contribute their own unique skills: Consider an image interpretation system in which an expert with knowledge of a certain area could correct and elaborate upon outputs of image interpretation algorithms.

- *How can such systems be designed to facilitate collaboration?* One aim is to realize the assertion made by Licklider and Taylor (1968) that people will be able to communicate more effectively through a machine than face to face.

- *How can such systems promote a more pleasurable experience?* The goal here is to address some of the objectives outlined by Hancock et al. (2005).

- *How can such systems help someone to leverage personal potential or overcome a personal deficit (e.g., through augmenta-*

tive/assistive technology)? A major area of interest for neurally-based symbiotic studies is the use of implant technology in which a connection is made between technology and the human brain or nervous system. Important medical applications include restoring lost functionality in individuals due to neurological trauma or a debilitating disease, or for ameliorating symptoms of physical impairment such as blindness or deafness. Other applications that do not address medical needs but instead aim to enhance or augment mental or physical attributes provide a rich area of research in the growing area of augmented cognition. Warwick and Gasson (2005) review the field of research and describes his research and experiences as a researcher and experimental subject who is the first human to have a computer chip inserted into his body that enabled bidirectional information flow and demonstration of control of a remote robot hand using the subjects' own neural signals (Gasson, Hutt, Goodhew, Kyberd & Warwick, 2002; Warwick & Gasson, 2005). Warwick and Gasson (2005) observe:

By linking the mental functioning of a human and a machine network, a hybrid identify is created. When the human nervous system is connected directly with technology, this not only affects the nature of an individual's ... identity, ... but also it raises serious questions as to that individual's autonomy.

It should be appreciated, however, that assistive technology need not necessarily entail implants or any involvement with neurology. Indeed a great deal has already been accomplished via adaptive software and input and output devices (Griffith, 1990; Griffith, Gardner-Bonneau, Edwards, Elkind & Williges, 1989).

- *What are implications and requirements for computer architectures to achieve neo-symbiosis?* A central point underlying neo-symbiosis is that humans need to be included in the computer architecture or system design. It is anathema to the concept of neo-symbiosis that computers and humans be regarded in isolation. They need to be considered together with the objective of each exploiting the other's potential and compensating for the other's weaknesses. Ideally the interaction between the two will achieve a multiplicative effect, a true leveraging.

Metrics: Measuring Success

An important question is how to identify neo-symbiotic design and how to assess it. It is important to recognize instances of neo-symbiotic design that are already among us in the form of productivity enhancement tools or job aids. For example, spell checking in contemporary word processors compensate for memory and perceptual/motor shortcomings; thesauruses leverage communicative abilities. Various creativity tools, such as concept mapping, leverage creative potential. In the augmented cognition domain, various neurologically-based "cognitive state sensors" are emerging as indicators of cognitive load and as potential cognitive prosthetics for medical purposes. In each of these cases, particularly the most recent developments that aim to enhance cognitive functions and effectiveness, evaluation methods and metrics are needed to guide research and facilitate deployment of technologies. For more advanced development of neo-symbiotic designs that aim to enhance human information processing and decision making (e.g., intelligence analysis performance) or knowledge/skill acquisition (e.g., training applications), we recognize the need for more rigorous evaluation methods and metrics that reflect the impact of the technology on performance.

Of course, standard subjective measures can readily be expanded to include neo-symbiotic potential. Many subjective measures are interpreted in terms of usability. There are several sources of established guidelines for usability testing (e.g., Nielsen, 1993). Commonly used criteria include efficiency, ability to learn, and memorability. Usability measures the address of the experience of users; whether or not they found the tool useful, easy to learn, easy to use, and so forth. Often, users are asked to provide this sort of feedback using qualitative measures obtained through verbal ("out loud") protocols and/or post-hoc comments (via questionnaires, interviews, ratings). Likert scales, in which respondents indicate their degree of agreement or disagreement with particular statements using numerical ratings, can use question stems such as: "Using this application/system enhanced my performance"; or "Using this application/system compensated for my information processing shortcomings."

Subjective measures such as these are designed to assess the acceptance by users of the system. It is unfortunate that the term subjective is used in a pejorative sense and that subjective measures are all too often regarded as second rate measures. Whether or not a system is perceived favorably and judged to be useful are central questions in evaluating the system's value. Especially relevant to neo-symbiosis is the user's assessment of the extent to which his or her potential has been enhanced.

It is possible to use magnitude estimation to assess the subjective amount, or lack of, neo-symbiosis in an application/system. In magnitude estimation (Stevens, 1975), stimuli are evaluated with respect to a standard stimulus, or modulus. That standard stimulus is assigned a value, and other stimuli are evaluated proportionate to it. So if the modulus was assigned a value of 50, and the stimulus being rated was regarded as half of whatever the rating dimension was, it would be rated 25. Were it regarded as having twice the value on the rating dimensions, it would be rated

100. A given version of Microsoft Word™ could be assigned a value of 50. If someone regarded another word processor as being twice as neo-symbiotic as this version of Word, it would be rated 100. Were it regarded to be only half as neo-symbiotic, it would be rated 25. A desirable property of magnitude estimation methods is that they produce ratio scales. Magnitude estimation is a remarkably robust methodology. Its validity has been demonstrated with stimuli ranging from the loudness of tones to the seriousness of crimes. It uses an anchor to a standard that allows proportional assessments of where an issue, item, stimulus stands with respect to that standard. Thus, statements can be made that a product is 20% better than a related product, 40% worse, and so forth. These ratings are more meaningful and interpretable than many other subjective rating techniques.

Whenever feasible, subjective measures should be supplemented with objective measures. Greitzer (2005a) has argued for development of measures of effectiveness based on performance impact in addition to the continued use of traditional subjective usability measures. User satisfaction is a necessary, but not sufficient measure. Behavioral measures are needed to address more cognitive factors and the utility of tools or technologies: Does technology X improve the throughput of cognitive tasks of type Y? Does it yield more efficient or higher quality output for certain types of tasks? Quantitative measures that assess utility may include efficiency in completing the task (time, accuracy, completeness). These will be most useful in comparing the utility of alternative tools or assessing the utility of a given tool vs. baseline performance without the tool. For example, in information analysis tasks, it has been observed (Scholtz, Morse & Hewett, 2004) that analysts tend to spend more time in data collection and report generation than in analysis activity (hence a kind of "bathtub curve" as described by Wilkins (2002) in the context of product reliability); tools or technologies that help alleviate the processing load for the collection phase and allow more time for analysis, for example, would be valued for their positive impact on performance (Badalamente & Greitzer, 2005). Time-based measures such as total time on task and dwell times can provide insight on user preferences and efficiency/impact of technologies being assessed (Sanquist, Greitzer, Slavich, Littlefield, Littlefield & Cowley, 2004). Other performance measures must be derived from specific decomposition of cognitive tasks. Greitzer (2005a) described examples of such analysis, within the information analysis domain, based on a decomposition of chains of reasoning (following the work of Hughes and Schum (2003) and analysis of behavior chains based on work of Kantor (1980) that was originally applied to evaluation of library science applications. While subjective measures provide weak support for neo-symbiosis, behavioral or performance measures provide strong support for neo-symbiosis. Absent behavioral or performance measures, questions remain as to the justification for the subjective ratings. Further research is needed to understand the basis for the subjective ratings.

SUMMARY AND CONCLUSIONS

The convergence of developments in different fields provides the foundation for a quantum leap in HII. Advancements in computer technology, cognitive theory, and neuroscience provide the potential for significant advances. Moreover, there is a movement for a more encompassing view of the scope of the field of human factors and ergonomics. The objective has been raised from making technology usable to using technology to enhance human potential, which was the original goal set by Licklider in 1960. The fulfillment of this objective will require collaboration and interaction among the fields of cognitive science, neuroscience, and computer technology. Most of the work in human factors and ergonomics

has been empirical. Only occasionally has the field drawn upon theory. The field of HII has been primarily technology driven. Programs and systems are developed on the bases of intuitions and what is regarded as cool and challenging by the developer, rather than from considerations of the information processing shortcomings and potential of the users. Very often techniques are not even subject to empirical assessment. But a strategy of generating an idea and then evaluating it empirically will not prove successful in the long run. HII requirements need to be developed not only on the basis of what a given system is being designed to accomplish, but also on the basis of theory and data in cognitive science and neuroscience.

To sum up, we have argued that the field of HII is on the threshold of realizing a new vision of symbiosis — one that embraces the concept of mutually supportive systems, but with the human in a leadership position, and that exploits the advances in computational technology and the field of human factors/cognitive engineering to yield a level of human-machine collaboration and communication that was envisioned by Licklider, yet not attained. As we have described, the field of human factors/HII is not static, but rather must inexorably advance. With advances in computer technology, cognitive science, and neuroscience, human potential and fulfillment can be leveraged more, yielding a spiral of progress: As human potential is raised, then that new potential can be leveraged even further. We think this vision provides a useful framework for cognitive informatics.

REFERENCES

Anderson, J. A. (2005a). Cognitive computation: The Ersatz brain project. In *Proceedings of the IEEE 2005 International Conference on Cognitive Informatics* (pp. 2-3). IEEE Computer Society.

Anderson, J. A. (2005b). A brain-like computer for cognitive software applications: The Ersatz brain project. In *Proceedings of the IEEE 2005 International Conference on Cognitive Informatics* (pp. 27-36). IEEE Computer Society.

Badalamente, R. V., & Greitzer, F. L. (2005). Top ten needs for intelligence analysis tool development. In *Proceedings of the 2005 International Conference on Intelligence Analysis*, McLean, Virginia.

Croft, W. B. (1984). The role of context and adaptation in user interfaces. *International Journal of Man-Machine Studies, 21*, 283-292.

Dreyfus, H.L. (1992). *What computers still can't do*. MIT Press/Cambridge Press.

Dreyfus, H. L., & Dreyfus, S. E. (1986). *Mind over machine: The power of human intuition and expertise in the era of the computer*. New York: The Free Press.

Fitter, M. J., & Sime, M. E. (1980). Creating responsive computers: Responsibility and shared decision-making. In H. T. Smith & T. R. G. Green (Eds.), *Human interaction with computers*. London: Academic Press.

Fitts, P. M. (1951a). Engineering psychology and equipment design. In S. S. Stevens (Ed.), *Handbook of experimental psychology* (pp. 1287-1340). New York: Wiley.

Fitts, P. M. (Ed.) (1951b). *Human engineering for an effective air navigation and traffic control system*. Washington, DC: National Academy Press, National Academy of Sciences.

Gasson, M., Hutt, B., Goodhew, I., Kyberd, P., & Warwick, K. (2002, September). Bi-directional human machine interface via direct neural connection. In *Proceedings of the IEEE Workshop on Robot and Human Interactive Communication* (pp. 265-270), Berlin, Germany.

Gershon, N. (1995). Human information interaction. In *Proceedings of the WWW4 Conference*, Boston, MA.

Greitzer, F. L. (2005a). Toward the development of cognitive task difficulty metrics to support intelligence analysis research. In *Proceedings of the IEEE 2005 International Conference on Cognitive Informatics* (pp. 315-320). IEEE Computer Society.

Greitzer, F. L. (2005b). Extending the reach of augmented cognition to real-world decision making tasks. In *Proceedings of the HCI International 2005/Augmented Cognition Conference*, Las Vegas, NV.

Greitzer, F. L., Hershman, R. L., & Kaiwi, J. (1985). Intelligent interfaces for C^2 operability. In *Proceedings of the IEEE International Conference on Systems, Man, and Cybernetics*.

Griffith, D. (1990). Computer access for persons who are blind or visually impaired: Human factors issues. *Human Factors, 32*, 467-475.

Griffith, D. (2005a). Beyond usability: The new symbiosis. *Ergonomics in Design, 13*, 3.

Griffith, D. (2005b). Neo-symbiosis: A tool for diversity and enrichment. Retrieved August 6, 2006, from http://2005.cyberg.wits.ac.za.

Griffith, D., Gardner-Bonneau, D. J., Edwards, A. D. N., Elkind, J. I., & Williges, R. C. (1989). Human factors research with special populations will further advance the theory and practice of the human factors discipline. In *Proceedings of the Human Factors 33rd Annual Meeting* (pp. 565-566), Santa Monica, CA. Human Factors Society.

Hancock, P. A., Pepe, A. A., & Murphy, L. (2005). Hedonomics: The power of positive and pleasurable ergonomics. *Ergonomics in Design, 13*, 8-14.

Hoffman, R. R., Feltovich, P. J., Ford, K. M., Woods, D. D., Klein, G., & Feltovich, A. (2002). A rose by any other name... would probably be given an acronym. Retrieved August 6, 2006, from http://www.ihmc.us/research/projects/EssaysOnHCC/TheRose.pdf

Hollnagel, E., & Woods, D. D. (1983). Cognitive systems engineering: New wine in new bottles. *International Journal of Man-Machine Studies, 18,* 583-600. Reprinted (1999) in 30th Anniversary Issue of *International Journal of Human-Computer Studies, 51,* 339-356. Retrieved August 6, 2006, from http://www.idealibrary.com

Hughes, F. J., & Schum, D. A. (2003). *Preparing for the future of intelligence analysis: Discovery – Proof – Choice.* Unpublished manuscript. Joint Military Intelligence College.

Joy, B. (2000, April). Why the future doesn't need us. *Wired, 8.04.*

Kahneman, D. (2002, December 8). *Maps of bounded rationality: A perspective on intuitive judgment and choice.* Nobel Prize lecture.

Kahneman, D. (2003). A perspective on judgment and choice: Mapping bounded rationality. *American Psychologist, 58,* 697-720.

Kahneman, D., & Frederick, S. (2002). Representativeness revisited: Attribute substitution in intuitive judgment. In T. Gilovich, D. Griffin, & D. Kahneman (Eds.), *Heuristics and biases* (pp. 49-81). New York: Cambridge University Press.

Kantor, P. B. (1980). Availability analysis. *Journal of the American Society for Information Science, 27*(6), 311-319. Reprinted (1980) in *Key Papers in information science* (pp. 368-376). White Plains, NY: Knowledge Industry Publications, Inc.

Kurzweil, R. (1999). *The age of spiritual machines: When computers exceed human intelligence.* New York: Penguin Group

Licklider, J. C. R. (1960). Man-computer symbiosis. *IRE Transactions on Human Factors in Electronics, HFE,* 4-11.

Licklider, J. C. R., & Taylor, R. G. (1968, April). The computer as a communication device. *Science & Technology, 76,* 21-31.

Maslow, A. H. (1970). *Motivation and personality* (2nd ed). New York: Viking.

Miller, G. A. (1956). The magical number seven, plus or minus two: Some limits on our capacity to process information. *Psychological Review, 63,* 81-97.

Nielsen, J. (1993). *Usability engineering.* Cambridge, MA: Academic Press/AP Professional.

Norman, D. A. (2004). *Emotional design: Why we wove (or hate) everyday things.* New York: Basic Books.

Norman, D. A. (2005). Human-centered design considered harmful. *Interactions.* Retrieved August 6, 2006, from http://delivery.acm.org/10.1145/1080000/1070976/p14-norman.html?key1=1070976&key2=3820555211&coll=portal&dl=ACM&CFID=554857554&CFTOKEN=554857554

Norman, D. A., & Draper, S. W. (1986). *User-centered system design: New perspectives on human-computer interaction.* Mahwah, NJ: Lawrence Erlbaum.

Parasuraman, R. (2003). Neuroergonomics: Research and practice. *Theoretical Issues in Ergonomics Science, 4*(1-2), 5-20.

Pirolli, P., & Card, S. K. (1999). Information foraging. *Psychological Review, 106*(4), 643-675.

Sanquist, T. F., Greitzer, F. L., Slavich, A., Littlefield, R., Littlefield, J., & Cowley, P. (2004). Cognitive tasks in information analysis: Use of event dwell time to characterize component activities. In *Proceedings of the Human Factors* and *Ergonomics Society 48th Annual Meeting,* New Orleans, Louisiana.

Schmorrow, D. D., & Kruse, A. A. (2004). Augmented cognition. In W. S. Bainbridge (Ed.), *Berkshire encyclopedia of human computer interaction* (pp. 54-59). Great Barrington, MA: Berkshire Publishing Group.

Schmorrow, D., & McBride, D. (2005). Introduction to special issue on augmented cognition. *International Journal of Human-Computer Interaction, 17*(2).

Scholtz, J., Morse, E., & Hewett, T. (2004, March). In depth observational studies of professional intelligence analysts. Paper presented at *Human Performance, Situation Awareness, and Automation (HPSAA)*, Daytona Beach, FL. Retrieved August 6, 2006, from http://www.itl.nist.gov/iad/IADpapers/2004/scholtz-morse-hewett.pdf

Sloman, S. A. (1996). The empirical case for two systems of reasoning. *Psychological Bulletin, 119*, 3-22.

Sloman, S. A. (2002). Two systems of reasoning. In T. Gilovich, D. Griffin, & D. Kahneman (Eds.), *Heuristics and biases* (pp. 379-396). New York: Cambridge University Press.

Stanovich, K. E. (1999). *Who is rational: Studies of individual differences in reasoning.* Mahway, NJ: Erlbaum.

Stanovich, K. E., & West, R. F. (2002). Individual differences in reasoning. Implications for the rationality debate. In T. Gilovich, D. Griffin, & D. Kahneman (Eds.), *Heuristics and biases.* New York: Cambridge University Press.

Stevens, S. S. (1975). *Psychophysics: Introduction to perceptual, neural, and social prospects* New York: Wiley.

Wang, Y. (2005a). On cognitive properties of human factors in engineering. In *Proceedings of the IEEE 2005 International Conference on Cognitive Informatics* (pp. 174-182). IEEE Computer Society.

Wang, Y. (2005b). On the cognitive properties of human perception. In *Proceedings of the IEEE 2005 International Conference on Cognitive Informatics* (pp. 203-210). IEEE Computer Society.

Warwick, K., & Gasson, M. (2005). Human-machine symbiosis overview. In *Proceedings of the HCI International 2005/Augmented Cognition Conference*, Las Vegas, NV.

Wilkins, D. J. (2002, November). The bathtub curve and product failure behavior. *Reliability HotWire, 21.* Retrieved August 6, 2006, from http://www.weibull.com/hotwire/issue21/hottopics21.htm

Zhang, J., & Norman, D. (1994). Representations in distributed cognitive tasks. *Cognitive Science, 18*(1), 87-122.

Zsombok, C. E. (1997). Naturalistic decision making: Where are we now? In C. Zsombok & G. Klein (Eds.), *Naturalistic decision making.* Mahwah, NJ: Erlbaum.

ENDNOTES

[1]   A research program at DARPA, Neurotechnology for Intelligence Analysts, seeks to identify robust brain signals that may be recorded in an operational environment and that are correlated with imagery data of potential interest to the analyst. Investigations of visual neuroscience mechanisms have indicated that the human brain is capable of responding to visually salient objects significantly faster than an individual's visuomotor response—i.e., essentially before the human indicates awareness. The program seeks to develop information processing triage methods to increase the speed and

accuracy of image analysis. http://www.
darpa.mil/dso/thrust/biosci/nia.htm

2   As Anderson (2005b) has observed, human
expertise in System 1 domains has been very
difficult to model in computers, and many
researchers (connectionists, behavior-based
roboticists) have used this to argue that
digital computer metaphor is flawed.

This work was previously published in the International Journal of Cognitive Informatics and Natural Intelligence, edited by Y. Wang, Volume 1, Issue 1, pp. 39-52, copyright 2007 by IGI Publishing, formerly known as Idea Group Publishing (an imprint of IGI Global).

Chapter XXIV
Politeness as a Social Computing Requirement

Brian Whitworth
Massey University, New Zealand

Tong Liu
Massey University, New Zealand

ABSTRACT

This chapter describes how social politeness is relevant to computer system design. As the Internet becomes more social, computers now mediate social interactions, act as social agents, and serve as information assistants. To succeed in these roles computers must learn a new skill—politeness. Yet selfish software is currently a widespread problem and politeness remains a software design "blind spot." Using an informational definition of politeness, as the giving of social choice, suggests four aspects: 1. respect, 2. openness, 3. helpfulness, and 4. remembering. Examples are given to suggest how polite computing could make human-computer interactions more pleasant and increase software usage. In contrast, if software rudeness makes the Internet an unpleasant place to be, usage may minimize. For the Internet to recognize its social potential, software must be not only useful and usable, but also polite.

INTRODUCTION

Social Computing

Computers today are no longer just tools that respond passively to directions or input. Computers are just as mechanical as cars, but while a car inertly reflects its driver's intentions, computers now ask questions, request information, suggest actions, and give advice. Perhaps this is why people often react to computers as they would to a person, even though they know it is not (Reeves & Nass, 1996). Miller notes that if I accidentally hit my thumb with a hammer, I blame myself not the hammer, yet people may blame an equally mechanical computer for errors they initiate (Miller, 2004). Software it seems, with its ability to make choices, has crossed the threshold from inert machine to interaction participant as the term human-computer interaction (HCI) implies. Nor are computers mediating a social interaction, like e-mail, simply passive, as the software, like a facilitator, affects the social interaction possibilities (Lessig, 1999). As computers evolve, people increasingly find them active collaborators and participators rather than passive appliances or media. In these new social roles, as agent, assistant, or facilitator, software has a new requirement—to be polite.

To treat machines as people seems foolish, like talking to an empty car, but words seemingly addressed to cars on the road are actually to their drivers. While the cars are indeed machines, their drivers are people. Likewise, while a computer is a machine, people "drive" the programs interacted with. Hence, people show significantly more relational behaviours when the other party in computer mediated communication is clearly human than when it is not (Shectman & Horowitz, 2003), and studies find that people do not treat computers as people outside the mediation context (Goldstein, Alsio, & Werdenhoff, 2002)—just as people do not usually talk to empty cars. Reacting to a software installation program as if to a person is not unreasonable if the program has a social source. Social questions like: "Do I trust you?" and "What is your attitude to me?" now apply. If computers have achieved the status of semi-intelligent agents, it is natural for people to treat them socially, and thus expect politeness.

A *social agent* is taken as an interacting entity that represents another social entity in an interaction, either person or group, for example, if an installation program represents a company (a social entity), the installation program is a social agent, if it interacts with the customer on behalf of the company. The interaction is social even if the social agent is a computer, and an install creates a social contract even though the software is not a social entity itself. In the special case where a software agent is working for the party it is interacting with, it is a software *assistant*, working both for the user and to the user. In such cases of human-computer interaction (HCI), social concepts like politeness apply.

If software can be social it should be designed accordingly. A company would not let a socially ignorant person represent it to important clients. Yet, often, today's software interrupts, overwrites, nags, changes, connects, downloads, and installs in ways that annoy and offend users (Cooper, 1999). Such behaviour is probably not illegal, but it is certainly impolite.

Selfish Software

The contrast to polite software is "selfish software." Like a selfish person who acts as if only he or she exists, so selfish software acts as if it were the only application on your computer. It typically runs itself at every opportunity, loading at start-up and running continuously in the background. It feels free to interrupt you any time, to demand what it wants, or announce what it is doing, for example, after installing new modem software, it then loaded itself on every start-up and regularly interrupted me to go online to check for updates to itself. It never found any, even after many days, so finally after yet another pointless "Searching for upgrades" message I (first author) decided to uninstall it. As in "The Apprentice" TV show, one reaction to assistants that do not do what you want is: "You're fired!"

Selfish software is why after 2-3 years Windows becomes "old." With computer use, the Windows taskbar soon fills with icons, each an application that finds itself important enough to load at start-up and run continuously. Such applications always load, even if you never use them, for example, I *never* use Windows messenger but it *always* loads itself onto my taskbar. When many applications do this, it slows down the computer considerably, and taskbar icon growth is just the tip of the iceberg of what is happening to the entire computer. Because selfish programs put files wherever they like, uninstalled applications are not removed cleanly, and over time Windows accretes an ever increasing "residue" of files and registry records left-over from previous installs. Giving selfish applications too much freedom degrades performance until eventually only reinstalling the entire operating system can recover system performance.

Polite Computing

Polite computing is about how software design can support HCI politeness. It is not about how people should be polite to people online, which various "online etiquette" guides cover. This chapter aims to define, specify, and illustrate an information vision of polite computing.

Politeness is distinct from both usefulness and usability requirements. Usefulness addresses a system's functionality, while usability concerns how people use that functionality. The first focuses on what the computer does, and the second on how the user gets the computer to do that. Polite computing, however, is not about what the computer does, nor how one can better get it to do it. It is about social relations rather than computer power or cognitive ease. It enables software that "plays well" in a social setting and encourages users to do the same. It addresses the requirements for social interaction, enabling better social collaboration, rather than better tool use. The contexts differ, so software could be easy to use yet rude, or polite but hard to use. While usability reduces training and documentation costs, only politeness lets a software agent work with a competent user without frustration. Both usability and politeness, however, fall under the rubric human-centred design.

BACKGROUND

The Oxford English Dictionary (http://dictionary. oed.com) defines politeness as:

… behaviour that is respectful or considerate to others

Considering and respecting others, a critical success factor in physical society, is equally relevant to online society. The predicted effect of polite computing is better human-computer interactions. While one may mistrust a polite door-to-door salesman as much as an impolite one, the polite one will get more "air time" because interacting with them is more pleasant. If politeness makes social interaction more pleasant, a polite society is a nicer place to be than an impolite one, and its people will be more willing to interact beneficially with others. Polite computing can contribute to computing by:

1. Increasing legitimate interactions.
2. Reducing anti-social attacks.
3. Increasing synergistic trade.
4. Increasing software use.

There is nothing to stop programmers faking politeness, just as nothing stops people in the physical world from doing so, but when people *behave* politely, cognitive dissonance theory finds they also tend to *feel* more polite (Festinger, 1957). Likewise, if programmers design for politeness, the overall effect will be positive, even though some may pretend.

Politeness Supports Legitimate Interactions

Legitimate interactions, defined as those that are both fair and in the common good, have been proposed as the complex social source of civilized prosperity (Whitworth & deMoor, 2003) and a core requirement for any prosperous and enduring community (Fukuyama, 1992). Conversely, societies where win-lose corruption and conflicts still reign are among the poorest in the world (Transparency-International, 2001). Legitimate interactions offer all parties a fair choice and are in the public good, while anti-social interactions, like theft or murder, give the "victim" little choice and harm society overall. In contrast, polite acts

Figure 1. The social choice dimension

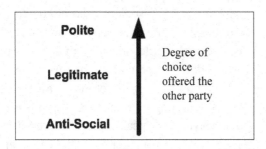

are *more than fair*. To do as the law requires is not politeness precisely because it is required, for example, one does not thank a driver who stops at a red light, yet one thanks the driver who stops to let you into a line of traffic. While laws specify what citizens *should* do, politeness is about what they *could* do. If politeness involves *offering more choices in an interaction than the law requires* then it begins where fixed laws end. If criminal acts fall below the law, then polite acts rise above it, and polite, legitimate, and anti-social acts can be ordered by the degree of choice offered to the other party or parties (Figure 1). In this view politeness increases social "health," just as criminality poisons it.

Politeness Reduces Anti-Social Attacks

Polite computing may have value, but should not it take a back seat to security issues? Is politeness relevant if we are under attack? Yet upgrading security every time an attack exploits another loophole, is a never-ending cycle. An alternative is to develop strategies to reduce motivation to attack (Rose, Khoo, & Straub, 1999). Politeness can help one common source of attacks—resentment or anger against a system where the powerful are perceived to predate the weak (Power, 2000). Often

hacking is vengeance against a person, a company, or the capitalist society in general (Forester & Morrison, 1994). Politeness contradicts the view that since everyone takes what they can, so can I. That some people are polite and give choice to others, may cause those neutral to society to copy, or those against society to become neutral. Politeness and security seem two sides of the same coin of social health. By analogy, a gardener defends his or her crops from weeds but does not wait for every weed to be killed before fertilizing. If politeness grows a better society, one should not wait to use it until every threat is purged. If security reduces anti-social acts, and politeness encourages social acts, they are complementary not mutually exclusive functions.

Politeness Increases Prosperity

Over thousands of years, as physical society became more "civilized," this has created enormous prosperity, so for the first time in history some economies now produce more food than their people can eat (as their obesity epidemics testify). The bloody history of humanity seems to represent a social evolution from *zero-sum* (win-lose) interactions, such as war, to *non-zero-sum* (win-win) interactions, such as trade (Wright, 2001). Scientific research illustrates this social synergy, as for researchers to freely give their hard earned knowledge to all seems at first foolish, but when a critical mass do this, people gain more than they could have by working alone. Synergy means that when many people give to each other, they gain more than is possible by selfish activity. The success of the open source software (OSS) movement illustrates this, as open source products like Linux now compete with commercial products like Windows. The mathematics of social synergy are that while individual gains increase linearly with group size, synergy gains increase geometrically, as they depend on the number of interactions not the number of group members. The Internet illustrates social synergy, as we each only "sow" a small part of it, but from it can "reap" the world's knowledge interactions.

Politeness Increases Software Use

A study of reactions to a computerized Chinese word-guessing game found that when the software apologized after a wrong answer by saying "We are sorry that the clues were not helpful to you" the game was rated more enjoyable than when the computer simply said "This is not correct" (Tzeng, 2004). Brusque and often incomprehensible error messages like the "*HTTP 404—File not Found*" response to an unavailable Web page can imply a user fault, while a message like: "*Sorry I could not find file xxxxx.*" does not. Accusatory error messages can rub users the wrong way, especially if it is a software error in the first place.

In general, politeness improves the social interactions of a society, which makes it a nicer place to be. The reader can judge for him or herself whether the world wide Web is currently a nice place to be or whether its "dark side" which includes spam, spyware, viruses, hackers, pop-up ads, nagware, identity theft, solicitations, pornography, spoofers, and worms (Power, 2000), means it could benefit from polite computing. If software were more polite, people might be more willing to use it and less willing to abuse it.

AN INFORMATION DEFINITION OF POLITENESS

Reinventing Politeness Online

To apply politeness to computer programming, it must be defined in information terms. If politeness is "considering others," then since different societies "consider" differently, what is polite in one culture can be rude in another. Given no universal "polite behaviour," there seems no basis to apply politeness to the logic of programming. Yet while different countries have different laws,

Figure 2. Social goal vs implementation

Goal	Implementation
Politeness	Etiquette
Legitimacy	Laws

the goal of fairness that underlies the law can be attributed to every society (Rawls, 2001). Likewise, different cultures could have different "etiquettes" but a common goal of politeness. Figure 2 distinguishes the goals of Figure 1 from their specific implementations. In this view, while each society may "implement" a different etiquette, politeness remains the common "design goal," just as legitimacy is the "spirit" behind laws that vary in detail between societies.

If politeness can take different forms in different societies, to ask which implementation applies online is to ask the wrong question. The right question is how to "reinvent" politeness in each specific online case, whether for chat, wiki, e-mail, or other groupware. Just as each different physical society develop local etiquettes and laws, so different applications may need a different politeness implementation based on a general design "pattern," specifying politeness in information terms (Alexander, 1964).

Informational Politeness

If the person considered knows what is "considerate" for them, politeness can be defined abstractly as *the giving of choice to another in a social interaction*. Doing this is then always considerate if the other knows what is good for them, though the latter assumption may not always be true, for example, a young baby. In a conversation, where the locus of channel control passes back and forth between parties, it is polite to give control to the other party, for example, it is impolite to interrupt someone, as that removes their choice to speak, and polite to let them finish talking, as they then choose when to stop.

An information definition of politeness is:

... any unrequired support for situating the locus of choice control of a social interaction with another party to it, given that control is desired, rightful and optional. (Whitworth, 2005)

Unrequired means the choice given is more than required by the law, as a required choice is not politeness. *Optional* means the polite party has the ability to choose, as politeness must be voluntary. *Desired by the receiver* means giving choice is only polite if the other wants it. "After you" is not polite when facing a difficult task. Politeness means giving desired choices, not forcing the locus of control, with its burden of action, upon others. Finally, *rightful* means that consideration of someone acting illegally is not polite, for example, to considerately hand a gun to a serial killer about to kill, is not polite.

Other Definitions

Some define politeness as "being nice" to the other party (Nass, 2004) and argue that when another says "I think I'm a good teacher; what do you think?" polite people respond "You're great," even if they do not think so. In this view, agreeing with another's self praise is considered one of the "most fundamental rules of politeness" (Nass, 2004). Yet while agreeableness may often accompany politeness, it does not define it if one can be both agreeably impolite and politely disagreeable. One can politely refuse, beg to differ, respectfully object, and humbly criticize, that is, disagree but still be polite. Conversely, one can give charity to others yet be impolite, that is, be kind but rude.

Being polite is different from being kind, for example, kind parents may not give an infant many choices, but politeness does not apply to young children who are considered to not yet know what they really want. Do software creators consider software users to be like little children, unable yet to exercise choice properly? While inexperienced users may happily let software do as it thinks is best, when children grow up they want more choice (as teenagers illustrate). The view that "software knows best" is hard to justify for the majority of today's computer-literate users. Perhaps once computer users were child-like, but today they want respect and choices from their software.

Impolite Computing

Impolite computing has a long history. Spam, for example, fills inboxes with messages users do not want (Whitworth & Whitworth, 2004) and is impolite because it takes choice away from e-mail receivers. Pop-up windows are impolite, as they "hijack" the user's cursor or point of focus and take away the user choice of what they want to look at. Users do not like this, so many browsers prevent pop-ups. Impolite computer programs can:

1. **Use your computer's services.** Software can use your hard drive to store information cookies or your long distance phone service for downloads.
2. **Change your computer settings.** Like browser home page, e-mail preferences or file associations.
3. **Spy on what you do online.** Spyware, stealthware, or software back doors that gather information from your computer without your knowledge or record your mouse clicks as you surf the Web and, even worse, exchange your private information with others.

For example, Microsoft's Windows XP Media Player, was reported to quietly record the DVDs it played and use the user's computer's connection to "phone home," that is, send data back to Microsoft (Editor, 2002). Such problems differ from security threats, where hackers or viruses break in to damage information. This problem concerns those invited into our information home, not those who break in, for example, "software bundling," where users choose to install one product but are forced to get many:

When we downloaded the beta version of Triton [AOL's latest instant messenger software], we also got AOL Explorer—an Internet Explorer shell that opens full screen, to AOL's AIM Today home page when you launch the IM client—as well as Plaxo Helper, an application that ties in with the Plaxo social-networking service. Triton also installed two programs that ran silently in the background even after we quit AIM and AOL Explorer. (Larkin, 2005)

Likewise, Yahoo's "typical" installation of their IM also downloads their Search Toolbar, anti-spyware and anti-pop-up software, desktop and system tray shortcuts, as well as Yahoo Extras, which inserts Yahoo links on your browser. It also alters the users' home page and auto-search functions to point to Yahoo by default. Even Yahoo employee, Jeremy Zawodny dislikes this:

I don't know which company started using this tactic, but it is becoming the standard procedure for lots of software out there. And it sucks. Leave my settings, preferences and desktop alone. (http://jeremy.zawodny.com/blog/archives/005121.html)

A similar scheme is to use security updates to install new products, for example:

Microsoft used the January 2007 security update to induce users to try Internet Explorer 7.0

whether they wanted to or not. But after discovering they had been involuntarily upgraded to the new browser, they next found that application incompatibility effectively cut them off from the Internet. (Pallatto, 2007)

Security cannot defend against people one invites in, especially if it is the security system taking advantage! However, in a connected and free society, social influence can be very powerful. In physical society the withering looks given to the impolite are not toothless, as what others think of you affects how they behave towards you. In old societies banishment was often considered worse than a death sentence. Likewise, what online users think of a company that creates a software agent can directly impact sales. A reputation for riding roughshod over computer user's rights is not good for business.

SPECIFYING SOFTWARE AGENT POLITENESS

The widespread problem of software that is rude, inconsiderate, or selfish is a general software design "blind spot" (Cooper, 1999). The specification of politeness in information terms is in its infancy, but previous work (Whitworth, 2005) suggests polite software should:

1. **Respect the other's rights.** Polite software respects the user, does not pre-empt user choices, and does not act on or copy information without its owner's permission.
2. **Openly declare itself.** Polite software does not sneak or change things in secret, but openly declares what it does, who it represents, and how they can be contacted.
3. **Help the other party.** Polite software helps users make informed choices, giving useful and understandable information when needed.

4. **Remember the interaction.** Polite software remembers past user choices in future interactions.

Respectful

Respect includes not taking another's rightful choices. If two parties jointly share a resource, one party's choices can deny the other's, for example, if I delete a shared file, you can no longer print it. Polite software should not preempt rightful user information choices regarding common HCI resources like the desktop, registry, hard drive, task bar, file associations, quick launch, and other user configurable settings. Pre-emptive acts, like changing a browser home page without asking, act unilaterally on a mutual resource and so are impolite.

Information choice cases are rarely simple, for example, a purchaser can use the software but not edit, copy, or distribute it. Such rights can be specified as privileges, in terms of specified information actors, methods, and objects (Table 1). To apply politeness in such cases requires a legitimacy baseline, for example, a software provider has no right to unilaterally upgrade a computer the user owns (though the Microsoft Windows Vista End User License Agreement (EULA) seems to imply this). Likewise, users have no right to unilaterally upgrade, as this edits the product source code. In such cases politeness applies, for example, the software suggests an update and the user agrees, or the user requests an update and the software agrees (for the provider). Similarly, while a company that creates a browser owns it, the same logic means users own data they create with the browser, for example, a cookie. Hence, software cookies require user permission, and users should be able to view, edit, or delete "their" cookies.

A respectful assistant does not interrupt unnecessarily, while selfish software, like a spoilt child, repeatedly does, for example, Windows Update advises me when it starts, as it progresses, and when it finishes its update. Its modal window interrupts what I am doing, seizes the cursor, and loses my current typing. Since each time Update only needs me to press OK, this is like being repeatedly interrupted to pat a small child on the head. The lesson of Mr. Clippy, that software serves the user not the other way around, seems still unlearned at Microsoft.

Table 1. Socio-technical actors, objects, and methods

Actors	Objects	Methods
People	*Persona* (represent people)	*Create/Delete/Undelete*
Groups	*Containers* (contain objects)	*Edit/Revert*
Agents	*Items* (convey meaning)	*Archive/Un-archive*
	- Comments (dependent meaning)	*View/Hide*
	- Mail (transmit meaning)	*Move/Undo*
	- Votes (choice meaning)	*Display/Reject*
		Join/Resign
		Include/Exclude

It is hard for selfish software to keep appropriately quiet, for example, Word can generate a table of contents from a document's headings. However, if one sends the first chapter of a book to someone, with the book's table of contents (to show its scope), every table of contents heading line without a page number loudly declares: "ERROR! BOOKMARK NOT DEFINED." This, of course, completely spoils the sample document impression, and even worse, this is not apparent until the document is received. Why could the software not just quietly put a blank instead of a page number? Why must it announce its needs so rudely? What counts is not what the software needs, but what the user needs.

Open

Part of a polite greeting in most cultures is to introduce oneself and state one's business. Holding out an open hand, to shake hands, shows that the hand has no weapon and that nothing is hidden. Conversely, to act secretly behind another's back, to sneak or to hide ones actions, for any reason, is impolite. Secrecy in an interaction is impolite because the other has no choice regarding things they do not know about. Hiding your identity reduces my choices, as hidden parties are untouchable and unaccountable for their actions. When polite people interact, they declare who they are and what they are doing.

If polite people do this, polite software should do the same. Users should see who is doing what on their computer. However, when Windows Task Manager shows cryptic process like CTSysVol. exe, attributed to the user, it could be system critical process or one left over from a long uninstalled product.

An operating system *Source Registry* could link all online technical processes to their social sources, giving contact and other details. "Source" could be a property of every desktop icon, context menu item, taskbar icon, hard drive file, or any other resource. A user could delete all resources allocated by a given source without concern that they were system critical. Windows messages could also state their source so users know who a message is from. Source data could be optional, making it backward compatible. Applications need not disclose themselves, but users will prefer sources that do. Letting users know the actions of their computer's inhabitants could help the marketplace create more polite software.

Helpful

A third politeness property is to help the user by offering understandable choices, as a user cannot properly choose from options they do not understood. Offering options that confuse is inconsiderate and impolite, for example, a course text Web site offers the choices:

- OneKey Course Compass
- Content Tour
- Companion Web site
- Help Downloading
- Instructor Resource Centre

It is unclear how the "Course Compass" differs from the "Companion Web site," and why both seem to exclude "Instructor Resources" and "Help Downloading." Clicking on these choices, as is typical for such sites, leads only to further confusing menu choices. The impolite assumption is that users enjoy clicking links to see where they go. Yet information overload is a serious problem for Web users, who have no time for hyperlink merry-go-rounds.

Yet to not offer choices at all, on the grounds that users cannot understand them, is also impolite. Installing software can be complex, but so is installing satellite TV technology. In both cases users expect to hear their choices in an understandable way. Complex installations are simplified by *choice dependency analysis* of how choices are linked, as Linux's installer does. Letting a user choose to install an application they want minus a critical system component is not a choice but a trap. Application-critical components are part of the higher choice to install or not, for example, a user's permission to install may imply access to hard drive, registry, and start menu, but not to desktop, system tray, favourites, or file associations.

Remember

Finally, it is not enough to give choices now but forget them later. If previous responses are forgotten, the user must redo them, which is inconsiderate. Hence, software that actually listens and remembers past user choices is a wonderful thing. Polite people remember previous encounters, yet each time I open Explorer it fills *its* preferred directory with files I do not want to see, then returns the cursor to me to select the directory *I* want to look at, which is *never* the one displayed. Each time, Explorer acts as if it were the first time I had used it, yet I am the only person it has ever known. Why can it not remember where I was last time and return me there? The answer is simply that it is impolite by design.

Such "amnesia" is a trademark of impolite software. Any document processing software could automatically open the user's last document and put the cursor where they left off, or at least give that option (Raskin, 2000). The user logic is simple: "If I close the file I am finished, but if not, put me back where I was last time." Yet most software cannot even remember what we were doing last time we met. Even within an application, like Outlook's e-mail, if one moves from inbox to outbox and back, it "forgets" the original inbox message and one must scroll back to it.

If a choice repeats, to ask the same question over and over, for the same reply, is to pester or nag like the "Are we there yet?" of children on a car trip. This forces the other party to again and again give the same choice reply, for example, uploading a batch of files creates a series of overwrite questions, and software that continually asks

"Overwrite Y/N?" forces the user to continuously reply "Yes." Hence, most copy software also offers the "Yes to All" *meta-choice* that remembers for the choice set. *Offering choices about choices* (meta-choices) reduces information overload, as users need only set repeated access permissions once, for example:

1. Always accept
2. Always reject
3. Let me choose

A general meta-choice console (GMCC) would give users a common place to see or set all meta-choices (Whitworth, 2005).

IMPLEMENTATION CASES

The Impolite Effect

In HCI interactions, impoliteness can cause a social failure every bit as damaging as a logic failure, for example, the first author's new 2006 computer came with McAfee Spamkiller, which when activated overwrote my Outlook Express mail server account name and password with its own values. When checking why I could no longer receive mail, I retyped in my mail server account details and fixed the problem. However, next time the system rebooted, McAfee rewrote over my mail account details again. The McAfee help person explained that Spamkiller was protecting me by taking control and routing all my e-mail through itself. To get my mail I had to go into McAfee and tell it my specific e-mail account details. That this did not work is less the issue than why this well known software:

a. Felt entitled to overwrite the e-mail account details a user had typed in
b. Could not copy my account details, which it wrote over, to create its own account

This same software also "took charge" whenever Outlook started, forcing me to wait as it did a slow foreground check for e-mail spam. Yet in 2 weeks of use, it never found any spam at all! I (first author) concluded it was selfish software, and uninstalled it.

Interaction Situations

Other human computer interactions where politeness applies include:

1. **Errors.** Polite error messages say *we* have an error rather than *you* have an error. While computers tend to take charge when things go well, when they go wrong, software seems to universally agree that the user is in fact "in charge." To ask what "we" (rather than you) want to do about an error implies the computer should also suggest solution options. Studies of users in human-computer tutorials show significant differences based on how politely the computer addresses the user, that is, users respond differently to "Click the Enter button" vs. "Lets click the Enter button" (Mayer, Johnson, Shaw, & Sandhu, 2006).

2. **Advice and Notifications.** To interrupt impolitely disturbs the user's train of thought. For complex work, like programming, even short interruptions can cause a mental "core dump," as the user drops one thing to attend to another. The real interruption effect is then not just the interruption time, but also the user recovery time (Jenkins, 2006), for example, if a user takes three minutes to refocus after an interruption, a 1 second interruption every 3 minutes can reduce productivity to zero. Mr. Clippy, Office '97's paper clip assistant, had this problem, since as one user noted: "It wouldn't go away when you wanted it to. It interrupted rudely and broke your train of thought." (Pratley, 2004). Searching the Internet for "Mr. Clippy" gives comments like *"Die, Clippy, Die!"* (Gauze, 2003), yet its Microsoft designer wonders: "If you think the Assistant idea was bad, why exactly?" (Pratley, 2004). To answer simply, he was impolite, and in XP, is replaced by polite smart tags.

3. **Action requests.** Asking permission is polite because it gives the other choice and does not pre-emptively act on a common resource, such as a zip extract product that puts the files it extracted as icons onto the desktop, without asking! Such software tends to be used only once.

4. **Information requests.** If software asks for and gets choices from a user, it should remember them. Polite people do not ask "What is your name?" every time they meet, yet software often has no interaction memory whatsoever, for example, when reviewing e-mail offline in Windows XP, actions like using Explorer trigger a "Do you want to connect?" request every few minutes. No matter how often one says "No!" it keeps asking, because the software has no interaction memory.

5. **Installations.** Installation programs are notorious for pre-emptive acts, for example, the Real-One Player adds desktop icons and browser links, installs itself in the system tray, and can commandeer all video and sound file associations. Customers resent such invasions, which while not illegal, are impolite. An installation program changing your PC settings is like furniture deliverers rearranging your house because they happen to be in it. Software upgrades continue the tradition, for example, Internet Explorer upgrades that make MSN your browser home page without asking. Polite software does not do this.

Online Learning

Online learning software, like WebCT or Blackboard, illustrates how politeness issues vary with channel type. While channel *richness* (rich vs. lean) was once thought the main property of computer-mediated communication (Daft & Lengel, 1986), channel properties like *linkage* (one-to-one, one-to-few or one-to-many) and *interactivity* (one-way or two-way) now also seem relevant (Whitworth, Gallupe, & McQueen, 2001). For example, *instructor-student* online communications, like e-mail, text messaging, chat, podcasts, cell phone, or video-computer interaction are usually *one-to-one* and *two-way*. In contrast, *instructor-class* communications are *one-to-many* and *one-way*. The rich-lean dimension is orthogonal to this distinction, for example, an instructor can post lean text assignments, graphical lecture slides, or rich video-lessons. E-mail still plays a major role in online learning, though it remains largely plain text, because it is interactive. Online learning system's e-mail and chat functions unnecessarily duplicate existing e-mail services, like Hotmail. Having a separate e-mail for each class taken or taught requires students or instructors to check each class e-mail, in addition to their normal e-mail. For online learning systems to create normal e-mail lists would be much more user considerate, as then students would only have to check their normal e-mail.

In 1:1 two-way communications, like e-mail, "the conversation channel" is the shared resource. Yet while physical society recognizes the joint ownership of communication channels and offers everyone the right not to interact (e.g., to remain silent, to not receive junk mail, to not answer the phone, etc.), the core e-mail system gives all senders the right to put any message into any receiver's inbox. This unfairly gives all rights to the sender and none to the receiver and enables the ongoing spam epidemic that plagues us all.

A more fundamental problem with e-mail in online learning is that one-to-one teacher-student interactions do not scale well (Berners-Lee, 2000). While one can as easily post lessons to a large class as to a small one, handling e-mails for classes over 50 can be difficult. The legitimacy baseline is that students have paid for class tuition, not one-to-one on-demand tuition. Experienced instructors often restrict the use of e-mail to personal requirements, like arranging meetings. They discourage its use for course content, for example, *"Sorry I could not make the last class, what did I miss?"* is a real student e-mail that I discouraged. Politeness in an interaction works two-ways, so training students to be e-mail polite is a valid learning goal, for example, polite e-mails are:

1. **Signed.** Give your name clearly—e-mails from nicknames like "fly-with-wind" are often unanswered.
2. **Understandable.** Give course/class number in the e-mail title so the instructor knows the context.
3. **Personal.** Use personal e-mail for personal issues, not issues that affect the entire class, for example, an online instructor may paste a "When is the exam?" e-mail into an online discussion board and answer it there, so other students can see the answer.

Class to instructor interactions, like an online assignment submission box, illustrate many-to-one one-way communication. For multi-choice quizzes, the computer can also grade the submissions and give student feedback. This is scalable as the computer can handle any class size, and can remember previous tests, telling the student if he/she is improving or not. However, while online exams do not need politeness, as students must take them, voluntarily online learning is a different matter. The distinction is:

a. **Formal testing quizzes.** Usually begin and end at a fixed time, shuffle questions and options to prevent cheating, and give little content feedback. Being mandatory, politeness applies only minimally.

b. **Informal learning quizzes.** Offer choices like pausing to restart later, optional tips, answer feedback, and choice of difficulty level. Being voluntary, politeness can help involve the student in the learning process.

If learning means changing ones own processing, a case can be made that all learning is voluntary. If so, polite interaction may help engage students in voluntarily online learning. The difference between a forced online quiz and an online learning experience may be politeness and respect. Online quizzes can support face-

to-face lessons, for example, if students answer online questions on a textbook chapter the week before lecture. This questioning encourages them to actively find information from the textbook, and prepares them for the weekly face-to-face class. Unlike a testing quiz, which is given *after* the class, and is graded by percentage correct, a "learning participation" quiz occurs *before* the taught class, and any reasonable participation (e.g., 30+%) gets full points. However, the quiz must be done in the week stated, and there are no "resits" for weekly participations. The quiz answers are not released until the week finishes, and students can do or redo the quiz any time in the given week. In practice, those who do poorly in testing quizzes also tend to omit the learning quizzes. However, the good students find them an excellent way to learn.

Figure 3. Getting quiz feedback in WebCT

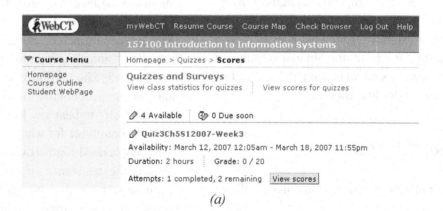

(a)

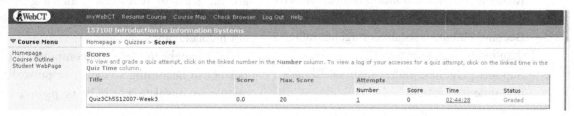

(b)

Most online learning systems seem designed to give information to teachers rather than students, who get learning feedback only with difficulty, for example, Figure 3a shows a "View Scores" button, which when clicked gives Figure 3b, that shows a score. Few students then realize that clicking the underlined "1" gives feedback on the right answers. While online teachers can "see" everything, like when and for how long students are online, students struggle to see what could help them learn in online software.

Class-to-class FAQ boards, where students answer each other's questions, are many-to-many, two-way interactions that scale well to all class sizes. Respecting and using class member knowledge is not only popular with students but for fast changing subjects, like Web-programming, almost essential. If young people learn mainly from their peers, involving their peers in online learning seems sensible, and polite computing could enable this.

Polite computing suggests voluntary choice is a new online learning dimension. Its application however, requires a complete redesign of current teacher focused systems like WebCT. The online classroom must move from what is essentially a software supported dictatorship to a system that invites voluntary student participation, based on a balance of rights and choices.

FUTURE TRENDS

Polite computing suggests computers will increasingly:

1. Remember interaction data rather than object data.
2. Become human assistants or agents rather than independent actors.
3. Support politeness rather than selfishness in online interaction.

Remember the Interaction

It is astounding that major software manufacturers like Microsoft gather endless data on users, but seem oblivious to data on how their software *interacts with the user.* Like Peter Sellers in the film "Being There," such software "likes to watch," but cannot relate to people. To spy on users at every opportunity is not a user relationship, For example, Mr. Clippy watched *your* document actions but could not see *his* interactions with you, and so was oblivious to the rejection and scorn he evoked. Most software today is in the same category, and modern airport toilets seem more aware of their users than the average personal computer. Hopefully tomorrow's software will make HCI memory its business, as its primary role will be to work for people, not for itself.

Computers as Assistants or Agents

There are several reasons why people should control computers, not the reverse. *Firstly*, while computers manage vast amounts of data with ease, they handle context changes poorly, and outside their fixed parameters can seem very stupid. So-called "smart" computing (Kurzweil, 1999) usually needs a human "minder." *Secondly*, computers are not accountable for what they do, as they have no "self" to bear any loss. If society makes people accountable for what computers do, as it does, people need control over computer choices. *Thirdly*, the resistance of people to computer domination is predictable. Software designers should not underestimate the importance of user choice. In human history, freedom and choice are the stuff of revolutions, and a grass-roots Internet movement against impolite software is not inconceivable.

Fortunately, the future of computers probably lies not in becoming so clever or powerful that people are obsolete, nor in being passive human tools, but in contributing to a human-computer combination that performs better than either people or computers alone. The runaway IT successes of the last decade (cell-phones, Internet, e-mail, chat, bulletin boards, etc.) all support people rather than supplant them. As computers develop this co-participant role, politeness will be a critical success factor. These arguments suggest that if the role of computers is to assist, they should learn to be polite.

Online Politeness Will Grow

Today, many users feel at war with their software: removing things they did not want added, resetting changes they did not want changed, closing windows they did not want opened, and blocking e-mails they did not want to receive, and so forth. User weapons in this unnecessary war include third party blockers, cleaners, and filters of various sorts, whose main aim is to put users back in charge of their computer estate. Such applications are the most frequent accesses at Internet download sites. Like all wars, if software declares war on user choice, everyone will lose in the long run. If the Internet is a battlefield, no-one will want to go there. Some compare the Internet to the U.S. Wild West, and others talk of the "hunter-gatherers of the information age" (Meyrowitz, 1985). Yet the Stone Age and the U.S. Wild West evolved into civil society, and so perhaps it is time to introduce civility to the Internet. What took physical society thousands of years may occur online in only a few years for example, Wikipedia began with few rules and one leader, but now to combat "trolls" who trash data, has many rules (including copyright) and many roles, like "Steward," "Bureaucrat," and "Sysop" (Whitworth, Aldo de Moor, & Liu, 2006). Yet the real force behind Wikipedia is the majority's enjoyment of working together considerately, not its ability to deal with the anti-social minority.

Many successful online traders find politeness profitable. EBay's customer reputation feedback gives users optional access to valued information relevant to their purchase choice, which by the previous definition is polite. Amazon gives customers information on the books similar buyers buy, not by pop-up ads but as a view option below. Rather than a demand to buy, it is a polite reminder of same-time purchases that could save the customer postage. Politeness is not about selling but improving the customer relationship that leads to sales. By giving customers choice, polite companies win business because *customers given choices come back*. Perhaps one reason the Google search engine swept all before it was that its simple white interface, without annoying flashing or pop-up ads, made it pleasant to interact with. Google ads sit quietly at screen right, as options not demands. Yet while many online companies know that politeness pays, for others the lesson is still being learned, and for still others, hit-and-run rudeness is an online way of life.

FUTURE RESEARCH

The users of modern software increasingly choose whether to use it or not, for example, President Bush's 2001 decision not to use e-mail because he did not trust its privacy. The ability of software to hold users hostage to its power may be declining. Where customers choose their software, a simple prediction is made: *Polite software will be used more and deleted or disabled less than impolite software.*

An experimental test of polite computing *value* requires a comparison of polite versus impolite applications on measures like willingness to use, attitude to the software, willingness to purchase, and user satisfaction. Politeness here is defined to apply not just to language, conversations, or people, but also to human-computer interactions.

Research can show if computer users really value politeness in HCI interactions like application installations, user help, online learning, e-mail, messaging, and bulletin boards, to mention a few. This politeness is not just the words used, but also the software actions taken. The relative value of the proposed politeness sub-aspects (respect, openness, helpfulness, and remembering) can also be compared. Correlational studies could compare rated application politeness with market success. Longitudinal studies could determine if successful applications become more polite over time. Ethnographic studies could explore how users perceive polite and impolite software.

The *scope* of online politeness also bears investigation. The definition implies that young or inexperienced users will tolerate impolite agents like Mr. Clippy more than experienced users. Also, it has been proposed that for interactions mandated by law, or other coerced acts, politeness will apply less. Other individual differences including gender, age, and culture, may also mediate the user reaction to impolite software. Cultural differences in polite computing raise highly complex issues of roles and social structures and may affect the boundary between what is required and what is polite.

CONCLUSION

Polite software asks before it allocates computer resources, openly declares itself and its acts, does not unnecessarily interrupt or draw attention to itself, offers understandable choices, and remembers past interactions. Conversely, impolite software acts without asking, does things secretly, interrupts unnecessarily, offers confusing choices, and has no recall of its past interactions with you.

If polite software attracts users, impolite software can drive them away. This implies a new type of IS error—*social error*. A program syntax error fails to support the needs of the computer technology. A software usability error fails to support the psychological needs of the computer user. However, a social error means the software fails to support the equally critical needs of human social interaction. While users misunderstand systems designed with poor usability, they understand impolite software all too well, and that is why they walk away from the interaction. Whether a system fails because the computer cannot run it, the user cannot run it, or the user *will not* run it, makes no difference. The end effect is still that the *application does not run*. A software social error gives the same outcome as a software crash or user failure. Indeed, social errors may be even worse, as it is in the nature of people to actively seek retribution against those who wrong others in social interactions.

A future is envisaged where software politeness is a critical requirement for socio-technical system success, especially where user willingness to participate counts. Polite computing could be taught in system design classes, along with other system requirements. A "politeness seal" could credit applications that give rather than take user choice. If physical society in general sees the value of politeness, online society should follow that lead. As software becomes not only useful and usable but also polite, the Internet may at last recognize its social potential.

ACKNOWLEDGMENT

Many thanks to Guy Kloss, Massey University, for his very useful comments and insights.

REFERENCES

Alexander, C. (1964). *Notes on the synthesis of form*. Cambridge, Ma: Harvard University Press.

Berners-Lee, T. (2000). *Weaving the Web: The original design and ultimate destiny of the world wide Web*. New York: Harper-Collins.

Cooper, A. (1999). *The inmates are running the asylum—Why high tech products drive us crazy and how to restore the sanity*. USA.

Daft, R. L., & Lengel, R. H. (1986). Organizational information requirements, media richness and structural design. *Management Science, 32*(5, May), 554-571.

Festinger, L. (1957). *A theory of cognitive dissonance*. Stanford University Press.

Forester, T., & Morrison, P. (1994). *Computer ethics*. London: MIT Press.

Gauze, C. F. (2003). *I see you're writing an article*. INK19. Retrieved on http://www.ink19.com/issues/march2003/webReviews/iSeeYoureWritingAn.html

Goldstein, M., Alsio, G., & Werdenhoff, J. (2002). The media equation does not always apply: People are not polite to small computers. *Personal and Ubiquitous Computing 6*, 87-96.

Jenkins, S. (2006). Concerning interruptions. *Computer, November*, 114-116.

Kurzweil, R. (1999). *The age of spiritual machines*. Toronto: Penguin Books.

Larkin, E. (2005). *PC World, December*, 28.

Lessig, L. (1999). *Code and other laws of cyberspace*. New York: Basic Books.

Mayer, R. E., Johnson, W. L., Shaw, E., & Sandhu, S. (2006). Constructing computer-based tutors that are socially sensitive: Politeness in educational software. *International Journal of Human Computer Studies, 64*(1), 36-42.

Meyrowitz, J. (1985). *No sense of place: The impact of electronic media on social behavior*. New York: Oxford University Press.

Miller, C. A. (2004). Human-computer etiquette: Managing expectations with intentional agents. *Communications of the ACM, 47*(4), 31-34.

Nass, C. (2004). Etiquette equality: Exhibitions and expectations of computer politeness. *Communications of the ACM, 47*(4), 35-37.

Pallatto, J. (2007, January 22). *Monthly Microsoft patch hides tricky IE 7 download*. Retrieved on http://www.eweek.com/article2/0,1895,2086423,00.asp

PCMagazine. (2001). *20th anniversary of the PC survey results*. Retrieved on http://www.pcmag.com/article2/0,1759,57454,00.asp .

Power, R. (2000). *Tangled Web: Tales of digital crime from the shadows of cyberspace*. Indianapolis: QUE Corporation.

Pratley, C. (2004). *Chris_Pratley's OneNote WebLog*. Retrieved http://weblogs.asp.net/chris_pratley/archive/2004/05/05/126888.aspx

Raskin, J. (2000). *The humane interface*. Boston: Addison-Wesley.

Rawls, J. (2001). *Justice as fairness*. Cambridge, MA: Harvard University Press.

Reeves, B., & Nass, C. (1996). *The media equation: How people treat computers, television, and new media like real people and places*. New York: Cambridge University Press/ICSLI.

Rose, G., Khoo, H., & Straub, D. (1999). Current technological impediments to business-to-consumer electronic commerce. *Communications of the AIS, I*(5).

Shectman, N., & Horowitz, L. M. (2003). *Media inequality in conversation: How people behave differently when interacting with computers and people*. Paper presented at the CHI (Computer Human Interaction) 2003, Ft Lauderdale, Florida.

Technology threats to privacy. (2002, February 24). *New York Times*, Section 4, p. 12.

Transparency-International. (2001). *Corruption perceptions*. Retrieved on www.transparency.org

Tzeng, J. (2004). Toward a more civilized design: studying the effects of computers that apologize. *International Journal of Human-Computer Studies, 61*(3), 319-345.

Whitworth, B. (2005). Polite computing. *Behaviour & Information Technology, September 5*, 353 – 363. Retrieved on http://brianwhitworth.com/polite05.pdf

Whitworth, B. (2006). Spam as a symptom of electronic communication technologies that ignore social requirements. In C. Ghaoui (Ed.), *Encyclopaedia of human computer interaction* (pp. 559-566). London: Idea Group Reference.

Whitworth, B., Aldo de Moor, & Liu, T. (2006, Nov 2-3). *Towards a theory of online social rights.*

Paper presented at the International Workshop on Community Informatics (COMINF'06), Montpellier, France.

Whitworth, B., & deMoor, A. (2003). Legitimate by design: Towards trusted virtual community environments. *Behaviour & Information Technology, 22*(1), 31-51.

Whitworth, B., Gallupe, B., & McQueen, R. (2001). Generating agreement in computer-mediated groups. *Small Group Research, 32*(5), 621-661.

Whitworth, B., & Whitworth, E. (2004). Reducing spam by closing the social-technical gap. *Computer, October,* 38-45. Retrieved on http://brianwhitworth.com/papers.html

Wright, R. (2001). *Nonzero: The logic of human destiny.* New York: Vintage Books.

Chapter XXV
Vive la Différence:
The Cross–Culture Differences Within Us

David Gefen
Drexel University, USA

Nitza Geri
The Open University of Israel, Israel

Narasimha Paravastu
Central State University, USA

ABSTRACT

In the ITC cross-cultural literature, we often talk about the differences among peoples and how their respective culture and history may affect their adoption and preference usage patterns of ITC. However, do we really need to look that far to find such cross-cultural differences? Considering language is one of the major defining attributes of culture, this article takes a sociolinguistic approach to argue that there is also a cross-cultural aspect to ITC adoption within the same culture. Sociolinguists have claimed for years that, to a large extent, the communication between men and women, even within the supposedly same culture, has such characteristics because men and women communicate with different underlying social objectives and so their communication patterns are very different. This article examines this sociolinguistic perspective in the context of online courses. A key finding is that although the stage is set to smother cultural and gender differences if participants wish to do so through ITC, gender based cultural patterns still emerge. These differences were actually strong enough to allow us to significantly identify the gender of the student, despite the gender neutral context of the course discussions. Implications for ITC, in general, in view of this Vive la Différence, are discussed.

INTRODUCTION

One of the major manifestations of culture is language and the way it affects communications: who we prefer to talk to and the sum of the underlying objectives of the communication. Communication is not a mere exchange of words. It is a social process and, as such, it is imbued with a social meaning of inclusion, exclusion, and social hierarchy. These cultural aspects are a prime aspect of cross-cultural research, including in the context of ICT information technology and communications, adoption, and usage patterns. But one need not look that far to find cross-cultural differences. They are here among us all of the time—that, at least, is the basic premise of sociolinguistics.

Sociolinguistics deals, among other things, with the way culture affects and determines communication. Most important in the context of this study is that culture is not only a manifestation of language and national heritage. Culture is also a matter of gender. Men and women communicate differently, and do so with different underlying social objectives. This is part of our evolutionary past (Brizendine, 2006), which also affects online collaboration (Kock & Hantula, 2005). Gender is so much a part of communication that in many languages, there are distinct rules in the language about how men and women should conjure the sentences they speak and their expected speech patterns. It is much more than superimposed linguistic gender segregation though. It is, at least in the view of sociolinguists, a matter of a cultural difference between men and women.

In general terms, men, according to sociolinguistics, communicate more with the objective of creating and preserving their social status, while women communicate more with the objective of creating rapport and social inclusion. Not surprisingly, the result of this is that communication across genders is often an exercise in cultural miscommunication (Brizendine, 2006; Tannen, 1994; Tannen, 1995). Indeed, when men communicate with each other, it is often on a basis of exchanging information, or as Tannen calls it "report talk," while women do so to exchange emotions, or as Tannen calls it "rapport talk" (Tannen, 1994). The consequence of this is often communication that are gender segregated (Hannah & Murachver, 1999; Yates, 2001).[1] Looking at this distinction in the context of virtual communities and supporting it, Gefen and Ridings (2005) commented that when men joined virtual communities composed of mostly male members, they did so with the declared objective of sharing information, while when they joined mixed gender virtual communities, it was more for emotional support. In contrast, women who joined mixed virtual communities did so for information exchange, but when they looked for emotional support, they too joined mostly female ones. Indeed, even in what should be gender and emotion neutral settings, women perceive more social presence in e-mail (Gefen & Straub, 1997) and e-commerce websites (Gefen, 2003).

The objective of this study is to examine whether the expected gender-related cultural differences in oral communication, predicted by sociolinguists regarding oral communications, hold true also in the explicitly created gender-neutral ITC environment of online courses, where the nature of the controlled course conversations make social dominance and rapport rather irrelevant. If these gender communication patterns hold true also in this scenario, then how much more so that such cross-cultural differences should hold true in other ITC induced environments. This is a crucial question because if true, then cross-cultural research in ITC should look not only across the border, but also within.

The data support the basic *Vive la Différence* proposition of the study even in the stoic context of online course discussions. Male students did prefer to respond to other male students and female ones to females, and men did show a more domineering attitude in their postings. Cross-cultural studies in ITC should consider gender as another dimension of culture.

Theory

The tendency of society toward being masculine or feminine is a central aspect of the cultural dimensions of peoples (Hofstede, 1980; Hofstede, Neuijen, Ohayv, & Sanders, 1990). However, is gender also an aspect within a culture? According to sociolinguistics, it is (Yates, 2001). In fact, the popular press sometimes even takes it a step further claiming, perhaps jokingly, that this gender difference might even take on celestial proportions (Gray, 1992). If this is so, then gender-related social behavior should come through even in the stoically enforced context of online courses, thus demonstrating the need to include gender as an aspect of culture even within a given national and linguistic culture, as also biology implies (Brizendine, 2006).

One of the major manifestations of culture is in language and communication. Communication carries with it not only information, but often also a very strong social message—a social message which is interpreted and sometimes also misinterpreted, within the cultural context of the speaker and listeners. Even the very way words are pronounced carries a cultural burden with it, making people identify or not with the speaker, based on the national or local culture implied in the accent (Deaux, 1984; Deschamps, 1982). Speaking in the accepted dialect can in fact make all the difference between whether people agree or disagree with a speaker, based almost purely on the manifestation of the presumed culture of the speaker (Abrams & Hogg, 1987). This additionally crucial social level of communication is a function not only of national and local culture but, according to sociolinguists (Tannen, 1994; Yates, 2001) and hormones (Brizendine, 2006),

also of gender. Men and women may communicate in what, on a superficial level, may seem as the same language, but the social message behind the words and this message is interpreted quite differently by the average man and the average woman. This is because men and women, on average, imbue and insert different social nuances into the message and do so even in languages, such as English, where there are no linguistically gender enforced styles. These gender related nuances can be so manifest as to result in the equivalent of cross-culture miscommunication (Tannen, 1994). Picking up on this idea, Gefen and Straub (1997) showed that women, across cultures, sense more social presence in work-related e-mails and that increased sense of social presence affect their perceptions of the usefulness and ease of use of the ITC and ultimately its usage. Expanding on this theme, Venkatesh and Morris (2000) showed that women are more affected by social norms in their adoption of ITC.

A salient example of this underlying social message in communication brought by Tannen (1994) is asking for directions. On the face of it, asking for direction is no more than just asking a stranger a question in what may seem a neutral environment. It could be regarded as information exchange and no more. However, this is not the case. Asking for directions also carries a social meaning. That is why men will often drive around for hours rather than ask for directions, while women will think nothing of it and do so without hesitation when they think they are lost. The reason for this, sociolinguists say, is that in asking for directions, men are subconsciously implying at least to themselves (certainly women are often surprised to hear this) that the other guy knows more than they do. The person being asked for directions certainly may know more, after all that is why they are being asked for directions, but it is admitting this that bothers men and makes them drive around for hours. Admitting someone else knows more than I do, to men, carries with it a social inferiority message of the other guy is better than I am in something. Men, unless aware of the stupidity of this underlying message, are loath to admit this supposedly social inferior standing. The same communication with women, however, carries no such subconscious implication. If anything, to women this creates a chance to engage with others, rapport, which they more willingly do than men (Tannen, 1994).[2]

This example, adapted from Tannen (1994), highlights the cultural social difference in communication between men and women. Beyond the meaning conveyed in the words themselves, men tend to communicate with the objective of exchanging information and in doing so establish their social pecking order. This is why men tend to try to control the conversation by talking more than others and employing various methods to silence or demote those who disagree with them. Generally, men, unless aware of the need to do otherwise, also tend to center the conversation more on themselves (Anderson & Leaper, 1998; Coates, 1986). Again, this is a manifestation of using conversation as a way of establishing the social pecking order. Tannen (1994) classes this communicational behavior *report* talk. In contrast, women tend more than men do to be inclusive in their conversational styles. This is because women are more centered on creating rapport, rather than self promotion (Holmes, 1992; Johnson, 1993; Kilbourne & Weeks, 1997; Lakoff, 1975; Mulac, Erlandson, Farrar, & Hallett, 1998; Tannen, 1994; Tannen, 1995). Tannen (1994) classes this communicational behavior *rapport* talk.

Supporting this report versus rapport distinction, previous research has claimed a greater tendency by men, at least in oral conversations, to try to dominate (Herring, 1993; Holmes, 1992) and control the discussion (Edelsky, 1993), to be more competitive (Kilbourne & Weeks, 1997) and more assertive by interrupting others (Anderson & Leaper, 1998; West & Zimmerman, 1983; Zimmerman & West, 1975), and generally be more forceful (Weatherall, 1998) and less

complementary (Coates, 1986; Yates, 2001). These gender-based differences in the cultural message imbued into the conversation are evident across cultures (Costa, Terracciano, & McCrae, 2001; Hofstede, 1980) and seem to also carry over to listserves (Herring, 1996b; Stewart, Shields, & Sen, 2001) and to e-mail in general (Boneva, Kraut, & Frohlich, 2001; Parks & Floyd, 1995). A direct consequence of these gender-based differences and preferences is that men and women tend to congregate into same-gender conversations (Tannen, 1994). Men talk more to other men than to women; women talk more to other women than to men. Interestingly, this happens also online in virtual communities where people have a much broader choice of communities to join and where they can hide their gender and identities or even masquerade as anything they wish to be known as (Gefen & Ridings, 2005).

The ITC in charge of discussions in online courses provides a unique opportunity to examine these cross-gender differences because it is possible to create what are arguably gender-neutral settings. Also, if, in these induced gender-neutral ITC settings, cross-gender differences exist, then these differences are probably not a matter of setting alone, but are a matter of the ingrained nature or nurture considerations extensively discussed in the cross-culture literature (Hofstede, 1980; Hofstede, et al., 1990) and should thus be controlled in the context of cross-cultural ITC research.

Whether cross-gender differences, such as gender congregation, apply also in online courses is actually an open question because parallels cannot be drawn with the closest equivalent, virtual communities, where these do apply (Gefen & Ridings, 2005). Virtual communities are not regulated by a moderator and people are free to come and go as they wish, without being graded on it. Moreover, in typical online courses, students do not interact with other students except in controlled threaded discussion settings where the teacher posts a question and the class then discusses it.

This discussion is usually graded. The discussion is asynchronous, so it is impossible to dominate air time or control the discussion and who talks when as in oral discussions. Inserting socially loaded comments and body language cues is also impossible. It is as close as possible to a gender neutral setting. Moreover, in contrast to virtual communities where people join for many reasons, including the stereotypical feminine rapport and the stereotypical masculine information exchange, the reason people join online class discussions is usually a matter of being forced to by the grading policy—a matter antitypical of both masculine and feminine stereotypical and sociolinguistic behavior. While gender-based communication patterns do occur in the regular classroom (Tannen, 1991), and some evidence does exist that men use the online environment more to access information and women more to converse (Herring, 1996a; Yates, 2001), how these apply to a supposedly gender-neutral setting, such as an online class, remains an open question. Should these gender-related communication behaviors carry over to these neutral settings, then it could be argued that they are another aspects of culture-induced behaviors.

HYPOTHESES

Accordingly, applying the underlying proposition that gender differences are not induced by the settings alone but rather are a matter of culture, then even in the relatively gender neutral ITC setting of online course discussions, some typical gender communication patterns should be evident. While the basic cross-gender difference of rapport versus report might be somewhat mute in these settings, other aspects, such as gender congregation, should still be evident. The rapport versus report distinction should be rather mute because online class discussions are deliberately not conductive for the feminine rapport type communication and are explicitly managed to

discourage the male dominating status building communication styles. Moreover, the technical settings in these ITC, such as the asynchronous nature of online course discussions, do not permit the students to control who speaks, when, what they say, and for how long—again making aspects of stereotypical male alleged domination conversation styles immaterial (Tannen, 1995; West & Zimmerman, 1983).

And yet, other aspects of typical gender behavior should come through if the proposition holds. Primary among these is gender congregation during discussions. Men's preference to respond to other men more than to women and vice versa could still come through even in these settings because there is nothing in the technical aspects of the ITC or in the way these conversations can typically be managed to exclude this possibility. There are no technical ITC aspects or plausible conduct rules that can make a student address comments, or not be able to address comments, by any other specific given student. Practically speaking, this should translate to a gender preference with men preferring to refer to other men and women to other women.

- **H1:** The number of references to postings by students of the same gender is higher than the number of references to posting of students from the opposite gender.

Although we do not expect students to resort strongly to their alleged stereotypical report versus rapport conversational styles in these ITC in general, some weaker aspects of these styles should still come through in conversational aspects, which are not forced by the ITC or typical course conduct regulations. One aspect in which these aspects should come through is in the extent of support given to positions presented by other students. Conventional political correctness in online courses may not be overly encouraging of blunt disrespect and challenging others, but there is a nuance students can play in whether they choose to be explicitly supportive of the postings of others or not. Extrapolating from the literature about typical gender conversational styles, and hence assuming these styles are culture induced and should therefore carry over also to gender neutral ITC settings: men should be less supportive of the positions of other students. Generally, men are supposed to be more assertive, competitive, and dominating (Anderson & Leaper, 1998; Edelsky, 1993; Herring, 1993; Holmes, 1992; Kilbourne & Weeks, 1997; Weatherall, 1998; West & Zimmerman, 1983; Zimmerman & West, 1975), and less complementary (Coates, 1986; Yates, 2001) than women. All these mount up to ways of shoring up one's own social standing, a motive strong among men but rather absent among women (Tannen, 1994). This behavior should especially come through strongly when male students refer to other male students because, extrapolating from sociolinguistics, they should be competing with each other. When male students refer to postings by female students the competition should be one way, only by the male student.

- **H2:** Men referring to postings by other men will be less supportive than women are.

With female students, on the other hand, inclusion should be a more dominant feature of the conversation, as it is in other settings (Tannen, 1994). A central strategy in creating inclusion is showing support and encouragement toward the other person. If this carries over to gender neutral ITC, then it could be expected that women will be more supportive of other women because of their tendency to be inclusive among other women.

- **H3:** Women referring to postings by other women will be more supportive than men are.

Method and Data

The data for this study were extracted from online course discussions in 14 online courses. There was an average of eight online course discussions in each online course. Every one of these online discussions was analyzed. For each student in each online course discussion, we recorded how many postings there were, how many related to a previous posting by other students in this discussion, how many of these references to previous posting were to postings by male students, how many of these were supportive, how many were to postings by female students and how many of these were supportive. A posting was counted as supportive if the student posting it explicitly stated agreement or support with a previous posting in this discussion. We then removed those records that related to students who did not refer to postings by other students in this specific online discussion. These records were removed from the analyses because evidently these students were not taking an active part in the specific conversation but only posting to fulfill the course requirements. This left us with 599 records, dealing with 83 students who each participated on average in 7.2 online course discussions. Among these 599 records, 381 were of men who took an active part in the online course conversation and referred to postings by other students in the specific conversation and 218 were by women. The data were classified by two raters. On the overlapping sample of 100 posting, which was classified by both raters, there was absolute agreement.

Supporting the stereotype of men trying to control the conversation (Edelsky, 1993), men did significantly ($T=2.751, p=.006$) post more (mean = 3.00, standard deviation= 2.096) than women (mean = 2.55, standard deviation= 1.542) and did significantly ($T=3.959$, $p<.001$) post longer messages (mean number of words = 346.30, standard deviation= 205.903) than women (mean = 286.99, standard deviation= 154.767).

Data Analysis

To examine hypotheses H1 through H3, we compared the means of men and women with a set of T tests. Men in a given online course discussion did not significantly (T=1.067, p=.286) refer more to others (mean=.69, standard deviation=1.255) than women did (mean=.58, standard deviation=1.032). However, men did significantly (T=2.525, p=.012) refer more to other men (mean=.45, standard deviation=.913) than women did (mean=.28, standard deviation=.605), although women did not significantly (T=.692, p=.489) refer more to other women (mean=.28, standard deviation=.620) than men did (mean=.24, standard deviation=.602). These results give partial support to H1. Gender congregation does occur, but primarily among men.

Surprisingly however, men in a given online course discussion were significantly (T=2.082, p=.038) more supportive of other men (mean=.14, standard deviation=.445) than women were (mean=.07, standard deviation=.254). This contradicts the expected direction in H2. Also, men did not significantly (T=1.544, p=.123) refer in a supportive manner to other students in general (mean=.20, standard deviation=.540) more than women did (mean=.13, standard deviation=.414). In fact, women were not significantly (T=.148, p=.882) more supportive of even only other women (mean=.06, standard deviation=.264) than men were (mean=.06, standard deviation=.289). This does not support H3. The hypothesized differences in the supportive behavior of students in online course discussions were not supported. Apparently, the courses were sufficiently gender neutral to make this otherwise typical behavior mostly insignificant.

We then examined if the gender of the student could be identified in a linear regression by the characteristics of postings the student made in the online course discussion. If this is so, it would lend more support to the claim that gender and communication style, also in these gender neutral settings, are related. In the linear regression, the gender of the student making the posting was the dependent variable. The length of the posting in words, whether this posting was supportive, and whether it was addressed to a student of the same or opposite gender, were the independent variables. In all, the explained variance was low at .02. The only significant determinant of student gender was the length in words of the postings the student made in this online discussion (β=.149, p<.001). However, when only the more active students were examined, the results became more convincing. When the analysis was limited to only those students who posted at least 3 postings in the conversation, there were 268 such records, the degree of explained variance became .15. The significant determinants were the length in words (β=.175, p=.004), the number of postings referring to previous postings by women (β=-.173, p=.006), and the number of postings referring to previous postings by men (β=.123, p=.048). In other words, among more students who participated more actively in the online course conversation, students who referred more to previous postings by men and less to previous postings by women were mostly significantly more likely to be men.

Discussion

Language is a central pillar of culture and subcultures within the dominant culture. It is a central pillar even within what may otherwise be considered the same national or historical culture. It is enough to read the famous words of George Bernard Shaw in *Pygmalion*, "An Englishman has only to open his mouth, in order to have another Englishman despise him," to realize how even dialects create a cross-cultural event. This is a conclusion supported by research (Abrams & Hogg, 1987). Along those lines of brilliant eloquence, this study presents another aspect of cross-cultural communication, the *Vive la Différence*, according to which gender too is a central cultural difference.

As sociolinguistics claim, men and women apply language, and communication in general, to such a differing social objectives that cross-gender communications can be sometimes best seen as nothing less than cross-cultural miscommunications among people with differing cultural backgrounds (Tannen, 1994). Examining a derivative of this sociolinguistic viewpoint, this study hypothesized that even in the gender neutral ITC environment of online course discussions with their asynchronous and topic focused orientation, cross-gender communication would show some aspects of a cross-cultural communication. These hypotheses were partially supported, but, the pattern in the data was strong enough to significantly allow the correct identification of the gender of the student participating in the online course discussion.

That gender should come through significantly in this otherwise deliberately gender and culture independent ITC setting lends support to the claim that there is a need to include gender as another significant aspect of culture, even within the same national culture environment. One should pay special heed to this conclusion because, to some extent, there is a voluntary gender segregation occurring in these discussions. This is something quite amazing when one stops to think about it, because it is occurring despite the gender neutral environment, which supports neither the typical male report type communication nor the typical female rapport type communication.

Before discussing these implications in detail, a word should be said about the limitations of the study. The data in this study came from a convenience sample. This is okay because the objective of the study was to show support to the need to include gender as an aspect of culture. Generalization was not the objective. Generalization requires replication in other and more varied ITC settings, including, but not limited to, other online courses and ITC supported business interactions. To this, one should add that no two courses are the same. Having said this though, the data of this exploratory study do warrant further investigation. Some gender behavior patterns did come through and did allow a significant identification

of student gender.

So what do the data tell us? Gender, as sociolinguists and eminent playwrights tell us, is also about culture. Cross-gender communications have cross-culture aspects to them. While it is still unknown whether these gender differences are ingrained or learned, they did come through even when the settings, such as the one of this study, should have made them mute. When considering how culture affects ITC adoption and usage patterns, and it does (Gefen & Straub, 1997; Rose & Straub, 1998; Straub, 1994), this aspect should be considered too. Although more research is needed, sociolinguistics is one possible theory base to support this inclusion. On a practical level, these conclusions imply some interesting tentative implications. If men and women communicate with different objectives and so understand messages differently, then awareness and practical steps to address these misunderstandings should be taken both in online conversations and in other instances of ITC.

Explaining the gender effect, by focusing on the culture of language, may also explain some previous research results. People are generally more accepting of answers given by a computer generated cartoon when the topic of the answer provided through this cartoon corresponds to its gender stereotypes: male cartoons about sports and female cartoons about fashion (Lee, 2003). If gender preference is so much part of our everyday behavior that people show a tendency to congregat by gender even in gender neutral discussions, then this carryover of oral discussion gender behavior might explain why this happens. The results also provide additional explanations why women sense more social presence in business e-mail than men do (Gefen & Straub, 1997). Again the carryover of the respective gender aspects of communication to an ITC environment, which is supposed to be gender neutral, might explain this.

Looking at the results in a broader manner, the results of the study, if generalized, tentatively suggest that just as culture should be a major aspect of ITC research, so should gender. ITC research, and especially human computer interaction research, is about many things, but one of its central topics of research is about how people use ITC to communicate with other people, be it through e-mail, e-commerce, or virtual communities. A key aspect in such communication, determining its meaning and success, is the use of language. Since language cannot be understood properly when analyzed devoid of its social underpinnings, these socially overlaid meanings should be part of any research on how ITC is used and how it supports communication among people. Ignoring these central social components, how they contribute to the meaning and value of ITC based communication, and especially how misunderstandings may arise when communicating across genders as they are across cultures, is tantamount to ignoring a central tenet of the ITC interaction process itself.

Including gender into human computer interaction research, however, requires a solid theoretical base. This lack of a strong theory base may explain why gender has not come up often before as a central aspect of this research. It is not enough to say there is a significant T statistic. There must also be a theory base, which can explain why there is this significance and so tie it into other research and a broader understanding. There might be undeniable physiological reasons which affect gender differences in ITC behavior, as some research suggests (Cutmore, Hine, Maberly, Langford, & Hawgood, 2000), but there are also cultural reasons, such as those presented in this study. These cultural psychological reasons are central in determining behavior. Sociolinguistics could be one theory base on which such understanding could be achieved. Looking at things through this theory could make our understanding richer and broader, and, more importantly, avoid a joint misclassification of men and women into one group, which ignores the different social meanings men and women attach to communication.

Unfortunately, while culture is recognized as a key issue in ITC adoption and usage patterns, most such research has chosen to ignore this aspect of gender. This may be because of political correctness constraints, but it is taking the unnecessary risk of being scientifically wrong. Smothering this cultural aspect not only hides significant relationships and blotches construct validity, but it also skews our understanding of the world. We know men and women have different managerial styles (Beasley, 2005; Boon, 2003) and handle domination and conflicts differently (Chan, Monroe, Ng, & Tan, 2006). We all know men and women think and communicate differently, whether saying so is or is not politically correct. It is about time ITC research also paid homage to gender. Ignoring gender may be a mistake, if gender differences come through even in the controlled settings of this study, how much more so that they should be evident in less controlled settings.

REFERENCES

Abrams, D., & Hogg, M. A. (1987). Language attitudes, frames of reference, and social identity: A scottish dimension. *Journal of Language and Social Psychology, 6*, 201-213.

Anderson, K. J., & Leaper, C. (1998). Meta-analyses of gender effects on conversational interruption: Who, what, when, where, and how. *Sex Roles, 39*, 225-252.

Beasley, A. L. (2005). The style split. *Journal of Accountancy, 200*, 91-92.

Boneva, B., Kraut, R., & Frohlich, D. (2001). Using e-mail for personal relationships: The difference gender makes. *American Behavioral Scientist, 45*, 530-549.

Boon, M. V. D. (2003). Women in international management: An international perspective on women's ways of leadership. *Women in Management Review, 18*, 132-146.

Brizendine, L. (2006). *The Female Brain*. USA: Morgan Road Books.

Chan, C. C. A., Monroe, G., Ng, J., & Tan, R. (2006). Conflict management styles of male and female junior accountants. *International Journal of Management, 23*, 289-295.

Coates, J. (1986). *Women, men and languages: Studies in language and linguistics*. London, UK: Longman.

Costa, P. T. J., Terracciano, A., & McCrae, R. R. (2001). Gender differences in personality traits across cultures: Robust and surprising findings. *Journal of Personality and Social Psychology, 81*, 322-331.

Cutmore, T. R. H., Hine, T. J., Maberly, K. J., Langford, N. M., & Hawgood, G. (2000). Cognitive and gender factors influencing navigation in a virtual environment. *International Journal of Human-Computer Studies, 53*, 223-249.

Deaux, K. (1984). From individual differences to social categories. Analysis of a decade's research on gender. *American Psychologist, 39*, 105-116.

Deschamps, J. (1982). Social identity and relations of power between groups. In H. Tajfel (Ed.), *Social Identity and Intergroup Relations* (pp.85-98). Cambridge, UK: Cambridge University Press.

Edelsky, C. (1993). Who's got the floor? In D. Tannen (Ed.), *Gender and Conversational Interaction* (pp. 189-227). New York: Oxford University Press.

Gefen, D. (2003). Tutorial assessing unidimensionality through LISREL: An explanation and example. *Communications of the Association for Information Systems, 12*, 1-26.

Gefen, D., & Ridings, C. (2005). If you spoke as she does, sir, instead of the way you do: A sociolinguistics perspective of gender differences in virtual communities. *The DATA BASE for Advances in Information Systems, 36*, 78-92.

Gefen, D., & Straub, D. W. (1997). Gender differences in perception and adoption of e-mail: An extension to the technology acceptance model. *MIS Quarterly, 21*, 389-400.

Gray, J. (1992). *Men are from Mars, women are from Venus*. New York: HarperCollins.

Hannah, A., & Murachver, T. (1999). Gender and conversational style as predictors of conversational behavior. *Journal of Language and Social Psychology, 18*, 153-174.

Herring, S. C. (1993). *Gender and democracy in computer mediated communication*. Retrieved from http://www.cios.org/www/ejc/v3n293.htm

Herring, S. C. (1996a). Posting in a different voice: Gender and ethics in computer-mediated communication. In C. Ess (Ed.), *Philosophical Perspectives on Computer-Mediated Communication* (pp. 115-145). Albany: State University of New York Press.

Herring, S. C. (1996b). Two variants of an electronic message schema. In S. C. Herring (Ed.), *Computer-Mediated Communication Linguistic, Social and Cross-cultural Perspectives* (pp. 81-106). Amsterdam/ Philadelphia: John Benjamins Publishing Company.

Hofstede, G. (1980). *Culture's consequences: International differences in work related values*. London, UK: Sage.

Hofstede, G., Neuijen, B., Ohayv, D. D., & Sanders, G. (1990). Measuring organizational cultures: A qualitative and quantitative study across twenty cases. *Administrative Science Quarterly, 35*, 286-316.

Holmes, J. (1992). Women's talk in public contexts. *Discourse and Society, 3*, 131-150.

Johnson, B. (1993). Community and contest: Midwestern men and women creating their worlds in conversational storytelling. In D. Tannen (Ed.),

Gender and Conversational Interaction (pp. 62-80). New York: Oxford University Press.

Kilbourne, W., & Weeks, S. (1997). A socio-economic perspective on gender bias in technology. *Journal of Socio-Economics, 26,* 243-260.

Kock, N., & Hantula, D. A. (2005). Do we have e-collaboration genes? *International Journal of e-Collaboration, 1,* i-ix.

Lakoff, R. T. (1975). *Language and woman's place.* New York: Harper & Row.

Lee, E.-J. (2003). Effects of "gender" of the computer on informational social influence: The moderating role of task type. *International Journal of Human-Computer Studies, 58,* 347–362.

Mulac, A., Erlandson, K. T., Farrar, W. J., & Hallett, J. S. (1998). Uh-huh. What's that all about? Differing interpretations of conversational backchannels and questions as source of miscommunication across gender boundaries. *Communication Research, 25,* 641-668.

Parks, M. R., & Floyd, K. (1995). *Making friends in cyberspace.* Retrieved from http://www.ascusc.org/jcmc/vol1/issue4/parks.html

Rose, G., & Straub, D. W. (1998). Predicting general IT use: Applying TAM to the Arabic world. *Journal of Global Information Management, 6,* 39-46.

Stewart, C. M., Shields, S. F., & Sen, N. (2001). Diversity in on-line discussions: A study of cultural and gender differences in listervs. In C. Ess and F. Sudweeks (Ed.), *Culture, Technology, Communication: Towards an Intercultural Global Village* (pp. 161-186). Albany, NJ: State University of New York Press.

Straub, D. W. (1994). The effect of culture on IT diffusion: E-mail and FAX in Japan and the U.S. *Information Systems Research, 5,* 23-47.

Tannen, D. (1991). Teachers' classroom strategies should recognize that men and women use language differently. *The Chronicle of Higher Education, June 19,* B1-B3.

Tannen, D. (1994). *You just don't understand women and men in conversation.* New York: Ballantine Books.

Tannen, D. (1995). The power of talk: Who gets heard and why. *Harvard Business Review, 73,* 138-148.

Venkatesh, V., & Morris, M. G. (2000). Why don't men ever stop to ask for directions? Gender, social influence, and their role in technology acceptance and usage behavior. *MIS Quarterly, 24,* 115-139.

Weatherall, A. (1998). Re-visioning gender and language research. *Women and Language, 21,* 1-9.

West, C., & Zimmerman, D. (1983). Small insults: A study of interruptions in cross-sex conversations between unacquainted persons. In B. Thorne, H. Kramarae, and N. Henley (Ed.), *Lauguage, Gender and Society* (pp. 103-118). Rowley: Newbury House.

Yates, S. J. (2001). Gender, language and CMC for education. *Learning and Instruction, 11,* 21-34.

Zimmerman, D., & West, C. (1975). Sex-roles, interruptions and silences in conversation. In B. Thorne, H. Kramarae, and N. Henley (Ed.), *Language and Sex: Difference and Dominance* (pp. 89-101). Rowley: Newbury House.

ENDNOTES

[1] These differences are also related to genetics and hormones (Brizendine, 2006).

[2] By the way, this is no joke. I tried it out on many of my students and almost unani-

mously all the men admitted to having been in this situation and driven around for hours, while almost all the women said they would ask for direction immediately.

This work was previously published in the International Journal of e-Collaboration, edited by N. Kock, Volume 3, Issue 3, pp. 1-15, copyright 2007 by IGI Publishing, formerly known as Idea Group Publishing (an imprint of IGI Global).

Chapter XXVI
Growing Up Wireless:
Being a Parent and Being a Child in the Age of Mobile Communication

Letizia Caronia
University of Bologna, Italy

ABSTRACT

This chapter illustrates the role of the mobile phone in the rise of new cultural models of parenting. According to a phenomenological theoretical approach to culture and everyday life, the author argues that the relationship between technologies, culture, and society should be conceived as a mutual construction. As cultural artefacts, mobile communication technologies both are domesticated by people into their cultural ways of living and create new ones. How are mobile phones domesticated by already existing cultural models of parenting? How does the introduction of the mobile phone affect family life and inter-generational relationships? How does mobile contact contribute in the construction of new cultural models of "being a parent" and "being a child"? Analysing new social phenomena such as "hyper-parenting" and the "dialogic use" of mobile phones, the author argues upon the role of mobile communication technologies in articulating the paradoxical nature of the contemporary cultural model of family education.

BEYOND THE USER-TECHNOLOGY DICHOTOMY: A PHENOMENOLOGICAL APPROACH TO EVERYDAY LIFE

"Some day we will build up a world telephone system making necessary to all peoples the use a common language, or common understanding of languages, which will join all the people of the earth into one brotherhood" (Dilts, 1941, p. 11, cited in de Sola Pool, 1977, p. 129)

Like an underground current, the same social discourse reappears each time a new technology enters the social world: the technology purportedly produces new unexpected behaviours and causes major changes in the way people live. Whether it is for the worse or for the better is not important. What matters more is the underlying unidirectional causal-deterministic model that putatively accounts for the influence of technologies in people's lives.

The deterministic approach to social phenomena and particularly to technological evolution has had a long and strong tradition that spans the 20th Century. Even if today no one would say "science discovers, industry applies, man conforms,"[1] the deterministic model persists in both scientific and commonsense approaches. At least within commonsense reasoning and theories, information and communication technologies are supposed to determine not only people's behaviours but also their attitudes, relationships, and even identities. Empowered technologies are perceived as overwhelming unskilled people as if they dominate their lives. Such a view of the role of technologies in people's everyday life has the hallmarks of all commonsense theories. It is self evident, taken for granted, and ready made. It shares commonsense's advantages: it provides easy to grasp explanations for a number of social events and allows people to cope with more dramatic circumstances. Like most practical reasoning, the one concerning information and communication technologies is a shortcut. It reduces the complexity of the phenomenon making it simpler and apparently more manageable.

Often echoed by media discourse and sometimes reinforced by references to simplified expert discourse, commonsense reasoning and layman theories constitute a shared cultural system through which we make sense of technologies in our daily life.

Although the deterministic approach to social phenomena has nurtured commonsense theories more than any other approach, it is not the only one. A major philosophical approach has been supporting concurrent views on social phenomena and providing a different paradigm for understanding technologies in everyday life: the phenomenological approach to social life.

Since Edmund Husserl's and Alfred Schutz's philosophical investigations, scholars in both Europe and the United States have emphasized the role of individuals in constructing culture, social organization, and their relation to the material features of everyday life contexts. Against any form of social and cultural determinism, ethnomethodology has demonstrated that people create their social and cultural world through their everyday actions and interactions (Garfinkel, 1967). Everyday practices of ordinary people are the effective tools that make supposedly passive users behave as active subjects. Defying and subverting any determinism of both dominant culture and the systems of production, social actors invent and create, moment by moment, the meaning and functions of things that circulate in their social space (De Certeau, 1984). Far from obeying implicit logics inscribed in goods, consumers develop their own tactics and follow paths in often unforeseen and unpredictable ways. The uses and gratification approach to information and communication technologies (Katz, Blumer, & Gurevitch, 1974) is consistent with this antideterministic paradigm. Proponents of this stream have shed light on the role of users' needs and goals in the adoption or rejection of a technology and its intended uses.

These approaches to social life and phenomena share a crucial theoretical assertion: the strength of human agency (Giddens, 1979, 1984) and subject intentionality in making the meaningful dimensions of the world people inhabit.[2]

Accordingly, everyday life is conceived as a never-ending cultural work through which social actors produce the meaning, structures, and social organization of the world they live in, as well as their own identities and those of the people they interact with. Everyday language and interaction are the primary tools of this culture construction. However, social structures as well as the material features of everyday life contexts are more than an inert background for culture construction.

Disregarding any radical subjectivistic drift, the phenomenological approach to culture and everyday life does not underestimate the constraints of the world of things nor does it claim for an omnipotent actor. Rather it conceives the process of culture creation as radically embedded in the cultural frames and the material resources available in the world people inhabit, which in turn makes this creation possible.

As renewed attention to the material aspects of social life indicates (Appadurai, 1986; De Certau, 1984; Gras, Jorges, & Scardigli, 1992; Latour, 1992; Semprini, 1999), the artifactual dimension of daily life is a crucial component that affects and is affected by everyday interactions, social organizations, and cultural frames of reference. Things, whether technological or not, participate in such a process of creating cultural models of living: as cultural artefacts, they are domesticated by users into pre-existing patterns of meaning and create new social scenarios and identities.

As people establish meaningful interactions with objects and artefacts, they make them exist in their social world, making sense of and domesticating them according to their frames of relevance and "moral economy" (Silverstone, Hirsch, & Morley, 1992). Literature on the social uses of media and the cultural ways of coping with a technological environment has shown how these uses, like other social practices, may be considered semiotic actions in the strict sense of the term; that is, ways of communicating and tools for constructing meanings and social realities.

The available technologies, the material features of the objects which support them and the daily routines they create or are integrated in, are all tools for the everyday production of culture and identities. Through media-related practices, individuals construct themselves in specific ways and produce the forms of their social participation (Caronia, 2002). Simply put, through our uses of media, through the way we act out these uses, we define (at least locally) the communities to which we belong and our identities.

We define but we are also defined. If face-to-face interaction and talk may still be considered the basic forms of socialization (Boden & Molotoch, 1994), the ways in which media uses become topics of everyday conversation are powerful tools to construct their meanings and the identities of those who use them. People's ways of using media, whatever real or imagined, enter everyday conversations as parts of the narratives through which people constantly construct who they are and who the people they talk about are (Ochs & Capps, 1996).[3]

If human beings construct the meaning of things and make sense of them according to their goals, the reverse is also true. Things are not neutral nor are they "pure" material objects waiting to be defined. Even though they do not determine people's life, things delineate the conditions of possibility for new behaviours and ways of life. Their features and engineering anticipate paths of action and project new possible identities for the users. By moving the image from the permanence of the analogical universe to the ephemeral digital world, the digital camera demands and proposes a radical nonrealistic ontology for photography. Even the social perception of the photographer's work and identity has changed. The digital camera has definitively legitimized photography as a manipulation of reality through iconic representation. Whereas the assumption of the nonreferential nature of documentary images has always been taken for granted by epistemologists and philosophers, the digital camera has integrated this representation of photography in the layman's culture. Allowing people to make, remake and unmake iconic representations of reality, the digital camera has produced a new everyday culture of photography.

Overcoming the "subject-object" duality, we need to rethink the relationship between humans and technologies in terms of reflexivity, that is, a mutual construction of meaning and reciprocal sense making.

This need is even more pronounced for information and communication technologies. Their progressive introduction into people's everyday life, the multiplication of possible new courses of action, and ways of communicating and getting information, expand the range of tools through which individuals construct culture and identities.

Faced with this changing and growing technological environment (Livingstone & Bovill, 2001), it then becomes relevant to investigate how the work of everyday culture construction may be affected by the new forms of technologically mediated actions, and vice versa.

The process of mutual construction among technologies, culture, and society may be analyzed at the macro level of patterns of diffusion and uses, as well at the micro level of ordinary everyday interactions. Drawing upon data from qualitative and ethnographic research on mobile communication devices in ordinary life,[4] this author of this chapter discusses the role of these technologies in the construction of family relationships and inner culture. Particularly, the chapter focuses on the following aspects: the creation of a cultural model of "parenting" (hyper-parenting), the dialogic use of mobile phones in connecting the different socio-cultural universes to which children belong (i.e., family and peer), and the role of mobile communication technologies in articulating the paradoxical nature of the contemporary cultural model of family education.

CONTEMPORARY STUDIES ON MOBILE PHONE DIFFUSION AND APPROPRIATION

In recent years, considerable research has examined the adoption and diffusion of mobile phone technology. It seems quite evident that, even though important differences exist across different countries (Kats & Aakhus, 2002), adolescents are a major well-established target for the adoption of this technology (Colombo, & Scifo, 2005; Kasesniemi & Rautianen, 2002; Ling, 1999; Lobet-Maris, 2003).

It is not surprising, then, that research has focused on young people's uses of the mobile phone, especially in European countries where the adoption rate among adolescents and young people had been quite high.[5] Investigating adolescents' uses of mobile phone, Ling and Yttry (2002) show how adolescents hypercoordinate their social life and construct social encounters moment-by-moment. Mobiles phones allow for "perpetual contact" (Katz & Aakhus, 2002), a form of social link that seems to fit perfectly with young people's peer culture and developmental tasks. Rather than voice calls, young people have made the Short Message System (SMS) their typical use of mobile phone (Cosenza, 2002; Grinter & Eldgridge, 2001; Grinter & Palen, 2002; Riviére, 2002) Along with the economic advantages, the diffusion of the SMS among teenagers may be explained by social and cultural factors (Taylor & Harper, 2003). The silent dimension of this distant communication is at the core of its domestication in young people's underground life both in the family and in school (Caron & Caronia, 2007). Allowing for silent and hidden communication, the mobile phone perfectly integrates a typical teenagers' cultural pattern: constructing their social world outside of their parents' control and the official rules governing life in school. Young people have also interpreted the technical constraints of SMS according to their specific peer culture. The limit of the numbers of available characters has been transformed into a resource for constructing a new language and new language games. Competence in this language defines the boundaries of a community of users, creates group membership and cohesion, and distances users from adults' culture (idem).

Studying teenagers' discourses on mobile phone, some scholars have noted that this technology is a detonator of social thinking: it provokes reflective thinking on the ethics, politeness, and aesthetic rules of everyday action and social life (Caronia & Caron, 2004). Reflecting upon social uses of the mobile phone, teenagers explore the identity-making processes involved in the presentation of oneself on a public scene. They interpret and make the uses of the mobile phone work as a social grammar through which people supposedly define themselves and those around them. In this sense, using a mobile phone in a teenage-appropriate way is not a matter of technical competence; it requires broader communicative skills that include cultural knowledge of when, where, why, and especially how to use this technology. Similarly, researchers have analyzed the normative aspect of mobile phone use among teenagers' groups. In particular, they focus on the implicit cultural rules governing the sharing of the technology (Caron & Caronia, 2007; Weilenman & Larsson, 2001). According to teenagers' cultural frames of reference, the ownership of a communication device is not an individual matter. Rather it is a radically social affair. Alliance and friendship, leadership and membership, require sharing individual property: mobile phones are loaned and borrowed among the members of the group and this performance entails a system of reciprocal obligations. This "gift exchange" (Mauss, 1954 {1924]) reinforces social links and ritually defines who belongs to the group.

These studies shed light on different aspects of what can be conceived as a single process: the domestication and integration of the mobile phone into youth-specific culture. The mobile phone seems to work as a developmental tool that meets the needs of the growing up process. Particularly, young people use it to attain a certain degree of autonomy with respect to family world, to mark their belonging to a community of peers, to create their specific social organization, and to develop the skills and share the knowledge needed to become competent members of their own community.

Less explored than the world of teens are the cultural and social micro-aspects involved in parents' uses of the mobile phone in communication with their children. Research on this issue mostly describes mobile phones' usefulness in mutual coordination of children and working parents and their perception of mobile phone as a security/safety/control device (Caronia & Caron, 2004; Ling & Yttri, 2002; Rakow & Navaro, 1993). These studies have investigated relevant dimensions of the process through which mobile phones affect and are affected by family culture. However, more detailed knowledge and a deeper understanding of the cultural and interpersonal aspects of such a process is required.

Our hypothesis is that this mobile communication device contributes to the creation of new cultural models of being a parent and being a child.

CULTURAL MODELS OF PARENTING: A THEORETICAL APPROACH

The cognitive approach to culture conceives cultural models as prototypical, language-based scripts of events, actions, and social actors. These shared definitions of situations supposedly work as frames of reference for inference-making and as guides for appropriate, mutually understandable, and accountable actions. Shared by individuals belonging to the same linguistic and cultural community, cultural models are models of reality as they define what counts as an occurrence of what type of event. They are also models for reality insofar as they are used as references to act in accordance with these shared definitions of social events. Cultural models thus constitute a background cultural knowledge providing resources to understand and to perform in culturally appropriate manners (D'Andrade, & Strauss, 1992; Holland & Quinn, 1987). Just as linguistic competence and grammatical knowledge make linguistic performance and language use possible, the shared set of cultural models of reality generates social actions. Conversely, people's actions, discourses, and behaviours are seen as merely reflecting or expressing their mental representations of the social world.

The cognitive approaches to social knowledge and praxis give primacy to knowledge over praxis, to culture over everyday actions and discourses. This top-down theoretical perspective has been strongly criticized and programmatically reversed by radical bottom-up views. Building upon philosophy of language and speech act theory (Austin, 1962; Searle, 1969), ethnomethodology (Garfinkel, 1967; Heritage 1984), social constructionism (Gergen, 1985), conversation analysis (Atkinson & Heritage, 1984), and discursive psychology (Edwards, 1997; Potter & Wetherell, 1987), conceive cultural models that organize everyday life in intersubjectively shared ways, as constructed moment by moment by the ways people participate in social events. Actions and discourses do not merely reflect an existing culture stored as information in people's minds. Rather, they are tools for constructing cultural definitions of reality. From a radical constructivist perspective, knowledge is thus a product of praxis.

In contrast, dialectical perspectives have emphasized the reductionism of both the knowledge oriented and action oriented approaches. Phenomenology (Giorgi, 1990), cultural psychology (Bruner, 1996), critical discursive psychology (Wetherell, Taylor, & Yeats, 2001), and contemporary linguistic anthropology (Duranti, 1997) propose a theoretical perspective that captures the reflexive relationship between culture and action. Individuals are historical beings belonging to an existing life-world. This background of taken-for-granted assumptions, beliefs, and traditions provides established, normalized ways of understanding the world and sets the limits and the opportunities for acting and thinking (Foucault, 1980). However, background cultural knowledge does not determine people's actions and behaviours. Through their everyday actions and discourses, individuals become crucial agents

of a creative process of culture making, remaking, and unmaking. In essence, "knowledge and praxis create each other" (Ochs, 1988, p. 15).

Praxis is also technologically mediated actions and communications. How does the use of mobile communication devices shape cultural models of "being a parent" and "being a child" and vice versa?

HYPER-PARENTING: A TECHNOLOGICALLY MEDIATED ACHIEVEMENT

As the mobile phone became a tool for parent-child communication, it has been shaped by a pre-established culture of parenting. Pagers and mobile phones have been interpreted by parents as means to exert control over and fulfil their responsibilities toward their children. They have thus been completely domesticated in the family's moral economy and transformed into tools for family socialization. By analyzing parents' and children discourses on their use of mobile phones, we can reconstruct the repertoire of official reasons family members invoke to make sense of the adoption of this technology.[6] Some patterns of meaning are recurrent, namely being in touch and responding to emergencies.

In the following example, Guy, a father in his mid-fifties, sees the mobile phone and pager as a kind of "umbilical cord," since they allow him greater contact with his children:

Guy: *But we also used it, now less, it used to be a lot like an umbilical cord with the kids. The kids could call us... Now it's less important... they're 19 and 20 now. They both have pagers. Bruno who didn't want one, we twisted his arm to get him to have one, so we could get in touch with him.*

Parents may also insist on their children calling them, as we can see in the following discussion between Louis (age 10) and his parents, Gerry and Madeleine (in their 40s) that lend him their cell phone to reach them:

Researcher: *Do you call your parents often?*

Louis: *Well, yes. Even when I'm going to school.*

Gerry: *Let's say you don't call, it's because we tell you to call...*

Researcher: *Why do you call them, for example?*

Louis: *Well! Sometimes when it's important or something that uh...*

Madeleine: *But he doesn't call us. We have to insist on him calling us.*

Gerry: *In fact, it's because we are starting to leave him at home alone a little. So we tell him, "before you go, you call."*

Children also can perceive the mobile communication device more as a kind of "electronic leash" that allows their parents to contact them at any time:

Barry (19 years old): *It is a pager heu.. (...) and then afterwards there, it happened, what we call.. it becomes a bit like an electronic leash for my mother...*

Researcher: *An electronic leash?*

Barry: *For my mother and then so... It lets her call me all the time and then uh... any time.*

Andrée (mother, age 50): *Well, it's true, I appreciate it.*

Barry: *Yeah, she finds it very useful.*

Andrée: *I can reach him everywhere because he has it and it's reliable, you always have it?*

Barry: *I alw... I almost have it all the time on me. Sometimes I forget but otherwise it is always on, always, always.*

The image of the cellular phone as a piece of emergency equipment is another recurrent pattern of meaning in parents' accounts of the reasons they introduced cell phones. Parents and children often construct narratives of hypothetical dangers and imagined scenarios in which having a mobile phone helps the owner resolve a problematic situation. The emergency discourse is actually one of the most recurrent themes in explanations of why the mobile phone came into informants' family and how they were supposed to use it:

Researcher: *You told me you'd have a cellular?*

Louis (son, age 10): *Yes.*

Madeleine (mother age 40): *When did we talk to you about having a cellular?*

Louis: *When we were in the car.*

Gerry (father, age 45): *That's right.*

Louis: *To call each other in emergencies.*

Gerry: *That is we will lend him one of our cell phones so that when he is on the mountain, if ever something happens, that he would get lost, like when he went to blue mountain and he got lost, well he would have his cellular and it is going to be programmed, because, you know, you can program the cell phone, so he will have to program the number.*

Louis: *At Green Mountain I had it.*

Gerry: *Had you lent it to him?*

Madeleine: *Yes I remember.*

As these examples show, the use and the functions of mobile phones are shaped by typical features of cultural model of parenting characteristic of contemporary western society. Exerting control over children, ensuring that they are safe, handling emergencies, managing time to create family moments, assuming responsibility toward children, supervising children's life out of the home, and mutual coordination to be in touch are all behaviours consistent with the cultural definition of being a parent. From this point of view, remote parenting (Caronia & Caron, 2004; Rakow & Navaro, 1993) seems to be nothing more than a new way to perform old functions and to act according to established models of fulfilling parental roles.

Our hypothesis is that mobile communication devices are not only an expression of an existing family culture and social organization, they are also ways to create them. By tracking their children's movements, finding out who they are spending time with, claiming to know that their children are safe, reminding their children when they have to be back or scolding them if they are late, parents realize the rights and duties involved in "being a parent."[7] By participating in these remote parenting interactions, children are socialized in the commitments and responsibilities of being members of the family. Mobile communication devices' practical uses are thus meaningful actions: they establish and confirm family boundaries, they state "who makes family with whom" and what behaviours belong to family members. They make the link between relatives permanent and work as teaching-learning strategies on the rights and duties governing family community life. Through the courses of action implicit in mobile phone use, parents do more than exert their role: they construct culture by legitimizing the definitions of what counts as "being a parent," "being a child," or "being a family" inscribed in their mobile phone mediated actions.

The following example from our ethnographic fieldwork on mobile use in the family sheds light on the cultural and social consequences hidden behind the most visible functions of remote parenting.

Scene: *It is Saturday afternoon in Bologna. Silvia, a divorced mother in her 40s, is talking on the land phone to her friend, participant researcher Laura. Mafalda, Silvia's oldest daughter, age 13, is in Milan at her father's house. Silvia's mobile phone rings:*

1. **Silvia to Laura:** *Wait, just a minute, it's "Serafini-Milano." (reading on the display)*
2. **Laura:** *Okay.*
3. **Silvia to Mafalda:** *Yes, sweetheart, I'm on the phone, talking with Laura.*
4. **Silvia:** *"Wear?" (English in original), W-E-A-R ? (spelling the word) It means to bear on the person.*
5. **Silvia:** *"Back?" (English in original), it means "at the rear" or "been returned," It depends. You have to consider the sentence.*
6. **Silvia:** *"Appear?" (English in the original), I don't know, wait, I'll ask Laura...*
7. **Silvia to Laura on the land phone:** *Laura, what does it mean, "appear?" A-P-P-E-A-R?*
8. **Laura:** *"To have an outward aspect."*
9. **Silvia to Mafalda:** *"To have an outward aspect." Laura said that it means to have an outward aspect.*
10. **Silvia:** *"Fail" (English in original), I don't know, I'll ask Laura.*
11. **Silvia to Laura:** *And "fail?" (English in original), F-A-I-L?*
12. **Laura:** *To deceive, fail, to not succeed in doing something.*

13. **Silvia to Mafalda:** *To not succeed, okay sweetheart? Is it correct? I love you.*

14. **Silvia to Laura:** *Hey, many thanks, many thanks from Mafalda, too. It's fantastic, I never do that, helping Mafalda with her homework in this way. She's in Milano and I'm in Bologna and you, you're at home, it's great!*

Remote parenting is more than an easy way to attain practical purposes or carry out typical functions related to the parental role. Through this mobile phone mediated interaction, Silvia is not only helping her daughter do her English homework. The sequence of her "mobile" actions is a meaning making devices.

Consider first the opening sequence of this multiparty telephone conversation. Silvia interrupts her conversation with Laura to give priority to her daughter's call (turn 1.). "It is Serafini-Milano": reading aloud the identity of the caller appeared on the display, she tells Laura whose needs come first. In this family culture "Serafini-Milano" is a shortcut for "daughters when they are at their father's house." Sharing this background local knowledge, Laura accepts Silvia's shift to her daughter's call (turn 2.). Acceptance is an action: through this action Laura legitimizes her being put in standby position. Then, Silvia does more than merely shift her attention to her daughter. After addressing Mafalda with some instances of intimate talk, she formulates this move with words (turn 3). Describing in words what one is doing is one of the linguistic moves though which participants negotiate the meaning of what is going on (Garfinkel & Sacks, 1970) and construct a shared definition of the event and its implications. This can be summarized as: "if children call, their mother is available and their needs come first."

The second part of the conversation is a typical mother-child scaffolding interaction: the mobile phone guarantees a direct, always open access to the caregiver and makes it possible to carry out this kind of joint action despite physical distance.

In the closing sequence, Silvia formulates what happened as a new, original way to perform as a parent (turns 13 and 14).

The actions performed in and through this technologically mediated conversation are culture building activities and socialization devices. By doing "being a parent" in certain ways, the mother locally constructs and proposes dimensions defining her cultural model of parenting: being always available, giving priority to children's needs over adults' needs, interrupting the ongoing course of action to open up a parallel one, using intimate talk to address one's own children, and giving children a scaffolding to overcome their difficulties.

At the same time, the mother's actions convey a cultural model of the child: a child is a demanding individual whose needs come first. He or she has the right to expect his or her parent to divert attention from an ongoing adult-adult interaction to take care of the children.

What about the other participants? By participating in such an interaction, Mafalda is learning more than the meaning of some foreign words: she is being socialised in the cultural models of "being a mother" and "being a child" that are at stake in this family. Accepting her role as a collateral participant, Laura legitimizes the definition, under construction, of "what is going on and why."

The participants officially involved in this interaction, are jointly constructing and ratifying, at least locally, a shared definition of "being a parent" and "being a child." That is, they are constructing a cultural model of parenting as a technologically mediated achievement.

If "reciprocal availability" can be considered a trait of an existing culture of parenting, how does mobile phone shape this trait?

Mobile communication devices are distinctive because they allow anytime and anywhere reciprocal availability. This is nothing more than a suggested way of acting, a "possible world" inscribed in the technology. It is through everyday and ordinary ways of using the mobile phone that this cultural model becomes a (technologically mediated) accomplishment.

A pre-existing cultural definition of being a parent has clearly shaped parents' and children's use of the mobile phone far beyond the management of urgency, safety, and control. In very reflexive ways, the use of this technology has created a new original way to be a parent. The possibility of remote parenting has been turned into hyper-parenting.

Through their everyday mobile interactions, parents and children have transformed physical distance into relational proximity; they have overcome the spatial and temporal constraints of face-to-face or traditional telephone interactions, and transformed almost every moment into an opportunity for coconstructing joint actions and care-giving. Family relationships seem to perfectly mirror the contemporary paradox of a wireless world producing hyperlinked people.

LINKING MACRO AND MICRO: SOCIO-CULTURAL CHANGES IN FAMILY EDUCATION

One of the most relevant contributions to the construction of the contemporary cultural model of parenting has been the historical change in the notion of parental authority. Since the end of the 17th Century, western societies have progressively moved from a political model of authority based on the concept of natural inequality and on the related notions of power and obedience to a definition of authority legitimized by a social consensus among equals. According to the political model, the pater familias' supreme authority over his children was analogous to that exerted by a sovereign over his subjects. Power and submission were the expected behaviours defining parents' and children's reciprocal and naturally unequal status. This notion of authority was profoundly questioned by Locke and Rousseau according to the principle of the natural equality of all human beings. Obedience to the authority does not stem from the presumed inferior status of some individuals. Rather, it derives from the social contract. Individuals have to obey the law because it expresses the will of all the people concerned.

Since Toqueville, and throughout the 19th Century, this model of authority has strongly affected western societies' macrohistory, politics, and laws. While in a slow often inconsistent way, it has also brought major changes to microhistory: it has affected the cultural models of all social relationships including those typical of the private family universe. The patria potesta no longer has a natural foundation, and negotiation is presumed to be at the core of family members' distribution of authority. The translation of this consensus-based model into actions and interaction is less obvious with respect to the parent-child relationship. Here, a "natural inequality" (now referred to as "asymmetry") is at stake: it defines the psycho-physical dependency of children on their caregivers. The gap in competences, skills, and knowledge is precisely what defines the reciprocal status of parents and children. Parents' authority—whatever that means—is a tool to overcome this gap, a necessary condition for children's development. Yet this necessity is no longer an argument for a power-based definition of parental authority.

At the end of the 20th Century, the inner logic defining parental authority was completely reversed. Until at least a century ago, parents had almost absolute power over their children, who were not considered to have rights. Now it is parents that have duties toward children. Most western societies have substituted the notion of patria potesta with those of parental cares and responsibilities, protection and supervision. The United Nations Convention on the Rights of the Child, introduced in 1989, emphasized that children have their own rights; adults' "authority" is clearly defined in terms of duties, obligations, and responsibilities that parents have over their children. The notion of power as the probability of obtaining obedience no longer defines the contemporary model of parenting.

How can this new image of a child as a subject that is no longer expected to obey be reconciled with the notion of parental authority and governance? How can authority be invoked without power? How does one cope with a child that is considered both a vulnerable and dependent individual and an autonomy-oriented person with rights?

Traditionally, parents had the right to exert power over children who had the obligation to obey. Aside from any other consideration, this model was inherently consistent. It offered a clear distribution of complementary rights and duties and traced a path for mutually coordinated actions.

The change in the definition of parental authority has broken the inner consistency of the traditional model. Now, children's rights and parents' duties often appear incompatible, and family education practices need to be conceived as ways to cope with the inherent paradoxes defining contemporary democratic education.

It may sound hazardous to relate these macro cultural, historical, and political changes to everyday life and social practices. Yet it is in the micro-order of ordinary life that cultural changes are both reflected and accomplished. The cultural changes in the status of children and in the notion of parental authority have directly and indirectly affected family education practices.

Aside from tragic exceptions, mainstream parents and children in contemporary western societies interact according to the social consensus framework. While recognizing the difficulties of creating such a consensus, sometimes shifting to or mythically evoking the simplicity of the authoritarian traditional model, contemporary parents have assumed the basic principles of democratic education.

Negotiation more than obedience, competence more than power, trust more than authority are the basic principles underlying parents' and children's reciprocal interactions. Mobile communication devices have been shaped by such a cultural framework. They have been appropriated as unexpected and efficient tools to negotiate parents' and children's often conflicting perspectives on children's developmental needs, and as ways to articulate their often incompatible rights and obligations.

In other words, mobile communication devices play a role in coping with the slightly paradoxical nature of the contemporary model of family education.

PARENTS' AND CHILDREN'S INCOMPATIBLE RIGHTS: MOBILE PHONES AS A NEGOTIATION TOOL

One of the domains where the paradoxical nature of parents' and children's reciprocal status emerges the most is children's gradual shift towards the peer universe.

As they grow up, children multiply their universes of references and have to negotiate their progressive belonging to multiple socio-cultural worlds. Family and peer community are different, often conflicting, demanding worlds.

It is mostly at this point in their developmental trajectory that pre-adolescents start demanding autonomy, freedom, and the right to make their own decisions, choices, and even mistakes. Moreover, it is then that they construct social links beyond their parents' filter. Not surprisingly, it is at this moment that parents officially enforce their responsibility, their obligation, or even their right to exert control and supervision. Less than 10 years ago, these conflicting perspectives were managed in two ways: talking with children about the where, when, what, and with whom of their extra-family life and negotiating the limits of time spent outside the home. These educational practices are rarely mutually exclusive. Depending on the family's pedagogical model and on children's behaviours and attitudes, the transition to the peer universe may be more dialogic-oriented or more control-oriented. In either case, borders are clearly identified and the transition becomes a field where parents' and children's differing perspectives often conflict.

As mobile phones became part of the family's technological equipment, they are interpreted as a means of coping with children's belonging to multiple socio-cultural worlds. They have opened a new arena to manage the transition from family universe to that of peers. Crossing the boundaries of these two worlds, mobile phones become tools to negotiate children's right to develop autonomy and parents' right to control a still dependent child.

Consider first the arrival of a mobile phone in children's life. Often, parents offer their children a mobile phone at some ritual milestone of their development. This gift-giving is a meaningful symbolic practice: parents recognize that their children have attained a stage of relative autonomy and allow them to privatize their social contacts. In contemporary societies, mobile phone gifts are rites of passage marking the (culturally perceived) beginning of adolescence. Like other goods provided by parents that symbolically mark the beginning of children's autonomy, the mobile phone marks also children's dependence on their parents for a wide set of needs and activities. Children's dependence on their parents for mobile phone use seems even more obvious when we look at management of the related costs. As some adolescents, age 15, explain[8]:

Researcher: *Generally, among your friends who have mobile phones, who pays?*

All: *Our parents!*

Mishan: *Well, I think it is half and half because teenagers want to have a little independence so they pay half. But they can't pay for the whole cost so their parents pay half.*

Since children or even adolescents do not have the means to cover the costs, parents pay the fees. As soon as they are able, adolescents want to express their independence and give themselves some freedom by taking responsibility for part of the cost. Yet when parents are paying all or most of the related costs, they acquire the right to set rules on mobile phone use. This economic leash defines the boundaries of children's autonomy. If the mobile phone is a bridge connecting children with the outside family universe, the bridge is built by parents who partially control access to this universe. Allowing for an economically controlled independency, mobile phones are used as cultural objects to mediate and gradually modulate children's construction of a life outside of family boundaries and constraints.

Besides the strategic use of costs, the role of the mobile phone as a mediating device emerges from the way it is used both by parents and children.

As a 15-year-old girl told us, parents often take advantage of the fact that their children have mobile phones to keep an eye on them, watch over them from a distance, and even control where they go:

Karine (age 15): *Well, it's because my parents, it's become like they really want to know where I am, so my parents always want to contact me, they're always afraid when I'm outside. When I'm out they can't contact me because there's no phone, when I'm at someone's it's okay but if I go somewhere and I don't call when I'm going, well they start freaking out, so… I need one.*

Anxiety when children go out is an emotional experience strictly related to parenting. Mobile phones allow parents to cope with such a common experience in a totally original way: they do not need to choose between either allowing children be out of supervision and enduring their own anxiety, or radically limiting children's social life to avoid painful apprehension. The mobile phone thus opens an alternative course of action:

Pénélope (age 15): *Often there are, well I know some where it's the parents who want to know where their kids are…*

Researcher: *Ah?*

Pénélope: *It's a form of security for them, like, you know, parents buy it for their kids to give them, to give the kids some freedom, but at the same time the parents can know where the kids are any time.*

For parents, the function at stake is not only to reduce their own apprehension. By tracking their children's movements and finding out with whom they are spending time, they fulfil the duties and rights related to their parental role while respecting the children's right to live an autonomous life. As we have seen in the extract above, adolescents seem to be quite aware of the dual nature of mobile phone contact. It is exactly this feature that allows them to use the technology in very strategic ways to negotiate their right to autonomy.

Adolescents usually accept that parents use cell phones to exert parental control. The duty to inform parents is generally well integrated in young people's specific culture: this ritual practice is commonly assumed to be a way to gain more permission:

Sophie (age 15): *It's safer, not just for us, but for our parents too… Sometimes there are families that are separated; in ours, we're all together, but even so my mother likes to be able to call me…*

Antoine (age 17): *In that sense, it's sure that it's another advantage, maybe to be able to get*

more permission to go out because you tell them something like "hey, you can call me any time, there won't be any problems."

Sophie: *"If there's anything, I'll call you, Mom, Dad…"*

Karine (age 15): *Because some people go out a lot, they have a really big social life and for their parents, it would help them a little.*

Researcher: *To be able to contact them?*

Karine: *To contact them, yeah, so the parents won't freak out, so they won't be there going "Aaaack!"*

As this discussion among adolescents shows, mobile phone has opened a totally new arena for negotiating children's belonging to both family and peer worlds. Allowing users to reach and be reachable all time, the phone creates a symbolic space where parents and children can take into account the rights of the counterpart. When provided with a mobile phone, children are willing to accept the parents' right to know where their children are, and they are willing to attend to and cope with their parents' anxiety (It's a form of security for them; It's safer not just for us, but for our parents too.). Conversely, helping them manage their own right to apprehension, mobile phones help parents cope with their children's right to go out and have a "really big social life:"

Layla (age 15): *Why did you get a mobile phone?*

Jean (age 15): *Well, one, to communicate, like to have more independence. You know, when your parents tell you, like in a mall, you have something, a means of communicating, to contact you. Like with your friends, let's say we say, "okay, let's meet like at the movie theatre."*

Layla (age 15): *Okay.*

Carl (age 15): *Me, it's about the same too. It's like the parent-child relationship. It's sure that you know if, if you're going to be late, you're on your way, so then you just have to call your parents on your mobile and then you tell them, "I'm coming, I'm about 15 minutes late, uh, I'm just in front of such-and-such a place, I'm coming." Then they say, "oh, okay, that's fine."*

Children consider autonomy, freedom, and peer life coordination the fundamental reasons for owning a mobile. However it is not surprising that they strategically focus on safety reasons when impressing on parents the need to get one. Grasping the unique opportunities they offer, adolescents use mobile phones as a means to act in ways that are consistent both with their needs and rights and with those of their parents.

Camera phones have amplified the repertoire of parents' and children's mediating tools. They provide parents and children with a more sophisticated strategy to negotiate their incompatible rights and to construct a bridge that connects the worlds of family and peers:

Layla (age 15): *Then you say, "yes, Mom, see my friends," then you take a picture with your phone. It's so your mom can see that you're really with your friends.*

Researcher: *Could you repeat what you just said?*

Layla: *It's because I say to myself, okay, let's say I call my mother, then my mother really wants to know if I'm somewhere or if I'm really with my friends, you take a picture, then you say, "yes, Mom, I'm with my friends, look."*

Researcher: *So you've got proof.*

Layla: *Yeah, I've got proof.*

Aside from their impressive role in creating a community of peer where instant pictures circulate and are shared by members, camera phones fit perfectly into parents' and children's typical interactions. It would be easy to invoke the image of Bentham's panoptikon and wonder if this kind of visual remote parenting is nothing more than a contemporary version of power and control dynamics. Rather, we propose a different interpretation that focuses on the strategic use of this otherwise controlling device: the dialogic use of mobile phones. By letting their parents enter their peer world, by giving them visual proof of what they probably have stated in words, adolescents establish a contract of trust with their parents. Gaining in trust implies gaining in freedom and autonomy. Adolescents have turned the constraints of remote parenting to their advantages as in peer culture gaining more freedom is an advantage. Less hidden then it once used to be, adolescents' underground life with respect to family can be strategically and at least partially shared with parents. The new sharable quality makes peer community experience a negotiable affair.

Sending photos via camera phone to parents may thus be seen as a paradox-resolving practice. In and through this process, parents and children articulate their symmetric and opposite rights, while creating much more room for negotiation and for consensus construction.

Mobile phones are also used to transgress this dialogic model. Transgressing family norms, pushing the boundaries of what has been consensually established as legitimate, and eventually breaking the terms of the trust contract, are all typical dimensions of adolescents' growing up process. Mobile phones can be strategically turned off (i.e., when children do not want to be reached by their parents) or simply ignored if the caller ID device signals that parents are calling:

Tania (age 15): *It's like, I don't really like that. You're with your friends and then your mother calls you.*

Researcher: *So, you'd rather not have one? It's your mother who insists?*

Tania: *Yeah, but it's really like, uh, to know where I am, if I'm going to be late or something.*

Researcher: *So how do you deal with it?*

Tania: *I turn it off.* [Laughs]

Researcher: *You take it but you turn it off...*

Tania: *Well, I turn it off, yeah, or else I say I was in the subway.*

The following is another example of the strategies used by adolescents to filter parental control calls. In this case an additional function of the technology enables Sandrine to transgress the rule:

Delphine (15 years old): *On top of that, I don't have call display, so I have no choice but to answer.*

Sandrine (15 years old): *I have call display, you know, when it's someone, let's say I'm somewhere and it's my parents and I don't want to talk to them, I don't want them to bug me, so I don't answer.*

Turning off the mobile phone and not answering if parents are calling are behaviours that have to be justified or accounted for: no signal and low battery are the arguments commonly used by children to justify their being unreachable. The need for explanations defines these behaviours as exceptional transgressions. Invariably, transgression reveals and confirms the rule at stake. In this case, the rule is dialogic use of the mobile phone, a pattern of interaction legitimizing both parents' right and duty to supervise their children and children's right to be autonomous.

PARENTS' AND CHILDREN'S DIALOGICAL USE OF MOBILE PHONES: CONCLUSIONS

Although they are incorporated in existing cultures of parenting and strongly dependent on each family moral economy, mobile communication devices nurture these worlds of meaning. Culture and praxis create each other. Everyday uses of mobile phone are no exception: they participate in the process whereby people constantly create and recreate their cultural ways of living their lives.

Entering the family's and teens' everyday life and allowing new forms of interaction (such as remote parenting), this device works as a culture making object. It plays a major role in the rise of new cultural models of "being a parent" and "being a child." Hyper-parenting is one such model.

Beside allowing coordination of children and working parents, besides facilitating single parents' multitasking or connecting divorced parents to their children living away from their home, mobile phones are used to create and constantly confirm social and affective links among parents and children. Building upon traits of a shared, pre-existing model of parenting and seizing the opportunities of mobile phone, parents in contemporary western societies go beyond its practical functions. They have transformed the "reaching children and being reachable" dimension into anytime and everywhere reciprocal availability. Wireless parents and children perform as hyper-linked members of a family. Beyond any practical purposes or topic of mobile conversations, it is the contexts of mobile phone use and the ways in which it is used that give their interactions meaning. Their mobile verbal exchanges are meaningful actions that define their social and affective ties as relevant and prior to almost any other course of action. Simply put, mobile phones have magnified and overstated a totally cultural and unnatural parental model: children come first. It may sound obvious, yet it is not.

Mobile phones uses confirm, naturalize, and literally objectivize what is nothing more than a socially constructed definition of "being a parent." These technologies participate in the silent and almost invisible process in and through which individuals create their cultural world as a quasi natural one.

The same process underlies the use of the mobile phone as a bridge connecting family and peer worlds. As we have seen, contemporary parents must contend with a definition of parental authority and children's rights that make family education almost paradoxical. Mobile phone use has been totally integrated in a dialogical model of exerting parenthood. Thanks to its engineering, it leaves room for negotiating the symmetric and opposite rights defining the status of contemporary children and parents.

The mobile phone has opened a symbolic space to manage the transition from family universe to that of peers and to cope with paradoxes of the developmental process such as the typical autonomy-dependency dimension. Parents and children use the technology to blur the boundaries of the different socio-cultural universes to which children belong, and to make a smooth supported transition from family culture to the peer world. In particular, the mobile phone is used by family members to negotiate the often conflicting perspectives of parents and children with respect to the developmental needs and to articulate an often incompatible system of reciprocal rights and duties.

In a social and historical context where parental governance is no longer legitimized by power and obedience, mobile communication devices are used as an educational tool consistent with a consensus-based notion of parental authority. Performing according to such a cultural and even normative model of being a parent is a way to constantly recreate it. Through a dialogic use of mobile phones, parents and children participate in the process of defining a contemporary model of family education as a democratic social practice.

REFERENCES

Appadurai, A. (Ed.). (1986). The social live of things. Cambridge, MA: Cambridge University Press.

Atkinson, J.M., & Heritage, J. (Eds.). (1984). *Structures of social action: Studies in conversational analysis.* Cambridge, MA: Cambridge University Press

Austin, J.L. (1962). *How to do things with words.* Oxford: Clarendon Press.

Boden, D., & Molotoch, H.L. (1994). The compulsion of proximity. In R. Friedland & D. Boden (Eds.), *Now/here. Space, time and modernity* (pp. 257-286). Berkeley, CA: University of California Press.

Bruner, J. (1996). *The culture of education.* Cambridge, MA: Harvard University Press.

Caron, A.H., & Caronia, L. (2001). Active users and active objects. The mutual construction of families and communication technologies. *Convergence. The Journal of Research into New Media Technologies, 7*(3), 39-61.

Caron, A.H., & Caronia, L. (2007). *Moving cultures. Mobile communication in everyday life.* Montreal, Canada: McGill-Queens University Press.

Caronia, L. (2002). La socializzazione ai media. Contesti, interazioni e pratiche educative, Milano: Guerini.

Caronia, L. (2005). Mobile culture: An ethnography of cellular phone use in teenagers' everyday life. *Convergence. The Journal of Research into New Media Technologies, 11*(5), 96-103.

Caronia, L., & Caron, A.H. (2004). Constructing a specific culture: Young people's use of the mobile phone as a social performance. *Convergence. The Journal of Research into New Media Technologies, 10*(2), 28-61.

Colombo, F., & Scifo, B. (2005). Social shaping of the new mobile devices. Representations and uses among Italian youth. In L. Haddon, E. Mante, B. Sapio, K-H. Kommonen, L. Fortunati & A. Kant (Eds.), *Everyday innovators, researching the role of users in shaping ICTs* (pp. 86-103). London: Springer.

Cosenza, G. (2002). I messaggi SMS. In C. Bazzanella (Ed.), *Sul dialogo*. Milano: Guerini.

D'Andrade, R., & Strauus, C. (Eds.). (1992). Human motives and cultural models. Cambridge, MA: Cambridge University Press.

De Certeau, M. (1984). *The practice of everyday life*. Berkeley, CA: University of California Press.

De Sola Pool, I. (Ed.). (1977). *The social impact of telephone*. Cambridge, MA: MIT University Press.

Dilts, M.M. (1941). *The telephone in a changing world*. New York: Longman's Green.

Doxa Junior. (2005). Indagine sui ragazzi tra i 5 e i 13 anni. Retrieved October 3, 2007, from http://www.doxa.it/italiano/nuoveindagini/junior_2005.pdf

Dunfield, A. (2004, November 12). Students like their cellphones. *Globe and Mail*. Retrieved October 3, 2007, from http://m1.cust.educ.ubc.ca:8200/news/studentslikecellphones

Duranti, A. (1997). *Linguistic anthropology*. Cambridge, MA: Cambridge University Press.

Edwards, D. (1997). *Discourse and cognition*. London: Sage.

Foucault, M. (1980). *Power/knowledge*. New York: Pantheon.

Garfinkel, H. (1967). *Studies in ethnomethodology*. Englewood Cliff, NJ: Prentice Hall.

Garfinkel, H., & Sacks, E. (1970). On formal structures of practical action. In J. McKinney & E. Tiryakian (Eds.), *Theoretical sociology: Perspectives and developments* (pp. 337-366). New York: Appleton.

Gergen, K.J. (1985). The social constructionist movement in modern psychology. *American Psychologist, 40*, 266-275.

Giddens, A. (1979). *Central problems in social theory: Actions, structures and contradiction in social analysis*. Berkeley, CA: University of California Press.

Giddens, A. (1984). *The constitution of society: Outline of the theory of structuration*. Cambridge: Polity Press.

Giorgi, A. (1990). Phenomenology, psychological science and common sense. In G.R. Semin & K.J. Gergen (Eds.), *Everyday understanding: Social and scientific implications* (pp. 64-82). London: Sage.

Gras, A., Jorges, B., & Scardigli, V. (Eds.). (1992). *Sociologie des techniques de la vie quotidienne*. Paris: L'Harmattan.

Grinter, R.E., & Eldridge, M.A. (2001). Y do tngrs luv 2 txt msg? In W. Prinz, M. Jarke, Y. Rogers, K. Schmidt & V. Wulf (Eds.), *Proceedings of the Seventh European Conference on Computer Supported Cooperative Work* (pp. 219-238). Dordrecht: Kluwer Academic Publishers.

Grinter R., & Palen, L. (2002). Instant messaging in teen life. In *Proceedings of the ACM Conference on Computer Supported Cooperative Work*. New Orleans, LA: ACM Press.

Heritage, J. (1984). *Garfinkel and ethnomethodology*. Cambridge: Polity.

Holland, D., & Quinn, N. (Eds.). (1987). *Cultural models in language and thought*. Cambridge, MA: Cambridge University Press.

Kasesniemi, E., & Rautiainen, P. (2002). Mobile culture of children and teenagers in Finland. In J.E. Katz & M.A. Aakhus (Eds.), *Perpetual contact. Mobile communication, private talk, public performance* (pp. 170-192). Cambridge, MA: Cambridge University Press.

Katz, J.E., & Aakhus, M.A. (Eds.). (2002). *Perpetual contact: Mobile communication, private talk, public performance*. Cambridge, MA: Cambridge University Press.

Katz, E., Blumler, J., & Gurevitch, M. (1974). *The use of mass communication*. Beverly Hills, CA: Sage.

Latour, B. (1992). *Aramis, ou l'amour de techniques*. Paris: la Découverte.

Ling, R. (1999). C'est bien d'être joignable: l'usage du téléphone cellulaire et mobile chez les jeunes norvegiens. *Réseaux, 92-93 ,* 261-291.

Ling, R. (2006). The role of mediated ritual communication. *Telenor*. Retrieved October 3, 2007, from httpp://intermedia.uib.no/public_files/_2006_06_mediated_ritual_communication.ppt

Ling, R., & Yttri, B. (2002). Hyper-coordination via mobile phones in Norway. In J.E. Katz & M.A. Aakhus (Eds.), *Perpetual contact. Mobile communication, private talk, public performance* (pp. 139-169). Cambridge, MA: Cambridge University Press.

Livingstone, S., & Bovill, M. (Eds.). (2001). *Children and their changing media environment. A European comparative study*. London: Lawrence Erlbaum.

Lobet-Maris, C. (2003). Mobile phone tribes. Youth and social identity. In L. Fortunati, J.

Katz & R. Riccini (Eds.), *Mediating the human body: Technology, communication and fashion* (pp. 87-92). Mahwah, NJ: Lawrence Erlbaum Associates.

Mauss, M. (1954 {1924]). *The gift; forms and functions of exchange in archaic societies*. Glencoe, IL: Free Press.

Ochs, E. (1988). *Culture and language development: Language acquisition and language socialization in a Samoan village*. Cambridge: Cambridge University Press.

Ochs, E., & Capps, L. (1996). Narrating the self. *Annual Review of Anthropology, 25,* 19-43.

Potter, J., & Wetherell, M. (1987). *Discourse and social psychology. Beyond attitudes and behaviour*. London: Sage.

Rakow, L., & Navaro, P. (1993). Remote mothering and the parallel shift: Women meet the cellular phone. *Critical Studies in Mass Communication, 10*(2),144-157.

Rivière, C. (2002). La pratique du mini-message. Une double stratégie d'extériorisation et de retrait de l'intimité dans les interactions quotidiennes. *Réseaux, 20*(112-113), 139-168.

Searle, J. (1969). *Speech acts*. Cambridge: Cambridge University Press.

Semprini, A. (Ed.). (1999). Il senso delle cose. I significati sociali e culturali degli oggetti quotidiani. Milano: Franco Angeli.

Silverstone, R., Hirsch, E., & Morley, D. (1992). Information and communication technologies and the moral economy of the household. In R. Silverstone & E. Hirsch (Eds.), *Consuming technologies. Media and information in domestic spaces* (pp.15-31). London: Routledge.

Taylor, A.S., & Harper, R. (2003). The gift of the gab? A design oriented sociology of young people's use of mobiles. *Computer Supported Cooperative Work, 12*(3), 267-296.

Weilenmann, A., & Larsson, C. (2001). Local use and sharing of mobile phones. In B. Brown, N. Green & R. Harper (Eds.), *Wireless world: Social and interactional aspects of the mobile age* (pp.99-115). Godalming and Hiedleburg: Springer Verlag.

Wetherell, M., Taylor, S., & Yates, S.J. (2001). *Discourse theory and practce. A reader.* London: Sage.

Withers, K. (2006). *Mobile have key role for young.* Institute of Public Policy Research. Retrieved October 3, 2007, from http://news.bbc.co.uk/go/pr/fr/-/2/hi/technology/6070378.stm

ENDNOTES

[1] This is the famous slogan of Chicago World's Fair in 1933.

[2] The notion of intentionality as the human competence in making sense of reality and in creating the crucial dimensions of people's *life-world* was introduced by Brentano and Husserl at the beginning of the 20th Century. It is perhaps one the more heuristic notions of XX century philosophy.

[3] Aside from any theoretical consideration, the relevance of talk-in-interaction in meaning making and culture construction has strong methodological consequences. Notably, it legitimizes the analysis of discourse as a social practice per se (Wetherell, et al., 2001). According to this framework, we conceive and analyze the uses of mobile communication devices as well as the discourses on such devices, as ways to make sense of them.

[4] This chapter draws on data from a 7-year multiple research project on the appropriation of communication and information technologies in families' and adolescents' worlds (Caron & Caronia, 2001, 2007; Caronia, 2005; Caronia & Caron, 2004). We used different yet complementary methodological and recording devices: family interviews and participant observation, log books on everyday practices, focus groups with adolescents, ethnographic case studies among natural groups of adolescents, analysis of naturally occurring mobile conversations and SMS exchanges. These studies have been conducted jointly with André H. Caron (Department of Communication, University of Montreal, Montreal), with financial support from CITÉ (Center for Interdisciplinary Research on Emerging Technologies, University of Montreal). I wish to thank my colleague André H. Caron for the support and the suggestions he gave me. Most of the ideas and interpretation proposed in this chapter have emerged from the joint analysis of data.

[5] In some countries the diffusion and appropriation of mobile phone by young people is an important social phenomenon. In Europe, 23% of children ages 8 to 10 have a mobile phone. In Italy, one in three children between ages 5 and 12 has and uses a personal mobile phone. At age 9, 28% own a mobile phone. Among 14 and 18-year-olds, the percentage of mobile use and ownership is around 100% (Doxa Junior, 2005). In Norway, nearly 80% of children ages 9 to 12 have and use a mobile phone. The percentage rises at 13 (around 96%) to reach 100% at 16 (Ling, 2006). In Britain, 49% of children ages 8-11 and 82% of 12-15 year-olds own a mobile phone (Withers, 2006). The phenomenon is less apparent in Canada but is still growing. According to Statistics Canada, 17.5% of children in primary school have a cell phone and 42.8% of high school students have one (Dunfield, 2004).

[6] The following verbatim come from family interviews made during a larger ethnographic research on the integration of new communication technologies in family

everyday life (Caron & Caronia, 2001).

[7] From an empirical point of view, we have strong evidences of remote parenting as a new way to perform the parental role. Whether it is considered as a way to dissimulate adults' escape from their responsibility or as a way to manage the contemporary parents' multitask life, strictly depends on the actors' points of view and cultural models of "what counts as good parenting." I advance the hypothesis that the common sense shared cultural model of "good parenting" is strictly anchored on notions as "face-to-face interaction" and "physical contact." On the basis of such a cultural model, remote parenting may be considered as not consistent with the ideal-typical behaviour of a "good parent." This is the point: are not these new communication technologies participating in the change of the cultural models we live by?

[8] All the following transcripts come from conversational focus groups with adolescents on their uses of mobile phones (Caron &Caronia, 2004).

Chapter XXVII
Digital Imaging Trek:
A Practical Model for Managing the Demand of the Digitally Enabled Traveller

Stephen C. Andrade
Johnson & Wales University, USA

Hilary Mason
Johnson & Wales University, USA

ABSTRACT

This chapter introduces the concept and activities of the digitally enabled tourist and the impact such as tourist has on the travel and tourism industry. It summarizes the existing and emerging technical environments that encourage the use of hand held digital recording devices and personal Internet communications. Additionally, it looks at ways tourists publish and exhibit digital visual and written artifacts of their travel experience. The chapter introduces general types of digital communication infrastructure to be considered by the industry to create an experience to support this type of tourism. The authors hope that further understanding of the digitally enabled tourist will inform travel professionals to better facilitate commerce and practice in the industry.

INTRODUCTION

Technology has had a great influence on the tourism and travel industry. In recent years digital communication platforms and technologies have evolved and become accessible to a wide mainstream audience of tourists and travelers. Organizations engaging in travel and tourism commerce need to understand this wave of innovative behavior among their customers. From cell phones to high speed wireless Internet connection to the variety of creative ways customers have applied digital technologies—the travel and tourism industry is being widely affected by these emerging trends in information and communications technologies (ICT). Is the digitally enabled traveler the wave of the future? How will companies and services shift business models to optimize the experience of people with digital devices? Are there commercial opportunities embedded in these? What does a traveler need to know to keep current with changing technologies? It is critical that services providers and travelers alike stay informed, because one thing is certain, technological innovation and change will be a constant companion for the travel and tourism industry.

This chapter provides insight into technology trends that will be helpful to the practitioner, student, educator and the tourist-travelers themselves. Being prepared to meet the new demands of customers will provide rewarding experiences for parties on all sides of the tourism equation.

BACKGROUND

Since the wide spread use of the telephone in the 1920s, information and communications technologies (ICT) have had a great influence on the industry of tourism. In the 1990s, the wide spread use of powerful desktop computers, enterprise wide systems, and the World Wide Web (WWW) continued to transform the way business was conducted in all facets of the travel and tourism. While ICTs have had a dramatic impact on the mechanics of tourism business practices, the virtual explosion of new inexpensive digital communication technologies is transforming the experience of tourism from the traveler's point of view.

The new generation of hand held mobile technologies, the expansion of wireless (WiFi) networks and the surge in digitally hosted social interchange services present new opportunities for engaging all sectors of the tourism industry. This new generation of technologies also presents new challenges to the industry to structure services with the digital service users in mind.

New services that provide online collaborative and social interaction through the World Wide Web now shape and influence vast communities of millions of online customers. Traveler-centered mobile technologies are increasingly used for many activities embedded in the tourist and traveler experience. This chapter will explore the model of the digital imaging trek and the digitally enabled traveler as a way to structure experiences to satisfy the demand of the technically savvy traveler in a world of advancing mobile technologies and online services. It also will provide basic technical background about the devices and infrastructure that drives these technological innovations.

Understanding the use of advanced hand held devices from the traveler's point of view is becoming more critical to tourism industry providers. Both new and veteran professionals in the tourism industry need to think about how these technologies influence the customers' choices, activities and ultimately their economic decisions about tourism. Customers have eagerly adopted the cheap and easy to use digital technologies. Tourism professionals need to understand the role mobile digital technologies play in the expanding global tourism field. For customers, mobile digital technologies are helping to shape the experience of tourism from initial research of a destination, through the reservation process to the final visual record of the experience.

Mobile digital technologies include a wide array of products that are inexpensive and easy to use. When mobile digital technologies are used to shape a tourist's experience they become powerful digital communication tools reaching out to an infinite audience of like-minded users on the World Wide Web. New products in cellular telephony, visual still imaging, motion and sound recording, wireless digital connections to the World Wide Web and the services on the World Wide Web, all converge to offer a digital environment unlike any before it. The combinations of these technologies are dynamic, unique and ever expanding. These digital technologies are in a constant state of enhancement—services become faster, devices become more powerful

Figure 1. Moore's Law

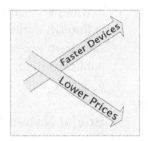

Moore's Law predicts: Computer chip devices get faster as prices come down over time.

and feature-rich, and prices come down. This evolution of technology is known as "Moore's Law" (see Figure 1). Just what is Moore's Law and why is it important?

Moore's Law is the observation made in 1965 by Gordon Moore, co-founder of Intel. In it he states that the number of transistors per square inch on integrated circuits had doubled every year since the integrated circuit was invented. Moore predicted that this trend would continue for the foreseeable future. In subsequent years, the pace slowed down a bit, but data density has doubled approximately every 18 months, and this is the current definition of Moore's Law, which Moore himself has blessed. Most experts, including Moore himself, expect Moore's Law to hold for at least another two decades. (http://www. webopedia.com)

Consider what it means to double the capacity of digital technologies every 12-18 months. Few if any physical systems or resources in the world of tourism have this capacity and potential. Moore's Law not only means faster and better technology, it also enables dynamic changes in the way people use technology. In fact, it is difficult to predict exactly how consumers will respond to innovative devices and new digital gadgets. Tourism profes-

sionals need to understand this dynamic process and prepare for the digitally enabled traveler.

Who is the Digitally Enabled Traveler?

The digitally enabled traveler is a new breed of traveler equipped with devices, connectivity, skill and motivation to create and access real-time, online, rich media knowledge bases of travel and tourism experience.

The digitally enabled traveler is motivated by the same principles as the conventional tourist. People involved in tourism are visiting locations for leisure, recreation, sight seeing, vacation and other activities. The global travel industry hosts not only tourists, but professional travelers on professional missions as well. People travel for business, cultural, scientific, educational, governmental and other kinds of activities in the world of global tourism. Most forecasts for travel of all types indicate a steady rise of 4% a year over the next decade. Even a causal observation in any busy transportation hub, such as an airport or train station will reveal how critical mobile technologies and wireless connections are to both the recreational and professional traveler alike.

People who travel with digital devices are highly motivated to stay connected to business and social networks. Minimally, most travelers today require basic voice and Internet connectivity service to maintain contact with families and tourism providers. Travelers want to stay in touch with the sources of lodging, travel bookings, reservations and other critical contacts during their trip. Some travelers thrive on constant digital connection to not only monitor progress in plans, but also stay in touch with their virtual communities.

Beyond the basic business function and family contact, travelers are using a wide array of digital devices to capture, record, edit, and exhibit the experience of tourism and travel. The days of a single film camera used in a casual manner to take pictures of highlights are over. As the tourism industry embraces near-endless global locations for travel destinations, travelers are highly motivated to capture and share their experience with digital recording and connection devices. Why? In spite of all the technical gadgetry, it is still human nature to want to discover and share a new experience. This mode of communication has been going on for generations, only now, it is played out on a global digital stage.

Digital still and video cameras along with powerful laptops and hand held devices have opened new territory for the digitally enabled traveler. These new digital technologies also offer new service-business opportunities for the tourism industry.

Today's digitally enabled traveler is highly motivated to stay in-touch with a virtual community of people through services on the Internet. With millions of people subscribing to World Wide Web sites that host virtual communities the trend of communicating in digital interactive space has been set. Social networking through digital services is widely accepted as common practice. This segment of the technology service industry is rapidly growing as the each successive generation matures into an economic demographic that can afford the expense of travel and tourism.

Millions of people are now involved in what is called "social networking." As counter intuitive as it may seem, the way to establish human bonds is through digital technologies. Numerous Web sites have been established as sources for self-published digital image galleries, digital video galleries, audio files, user profiles, and blogs.

Social Networking: The Latest Trend

Social networking systems are an emerging technology that is beginning to have a significant influence on how people communicate. Social networking systems are Web sites that offer a collaborative or shared virtual experience, generally around a particular theme or human interest. Visitors to the site can connect with each other through shared attributes, such as interests, activities, or geographic location.

Some social networking sites, such as Facebook (http://www.facebook.com), are designed simply to facilitate the process of making social connections. Other sites, such as Delicious (http://del.icio.us), offer a core application, such as allowing users to share Web site bookmarks. An essential quality of a social networking site is that it must allow users to share information via a network of nodes (users) and connections (users with similarities). Users also can easily identify other users with similar interests.

Most social network sites utilize the community to develop an ontology via tagging. Tagging is a simple method of allowing users to attach key words to a piece of data. Users searching for those keywords can then locate a wide variety of matching media. This works on the assumption that humans will generally choose similar terms to describe similar items. Most of the time, the assumptions works well, and people network with other people's experiences.

Tags are often represented in a "tag cloud" (see Figure 2). Larger text indicates a more popular tag. Other visualizations include history, topics, and information origin. This visual model of

Figure 2. Sample tag cloud

popularity makes these sites friendly to even the most non-technical visitors.

Social networking sites are beginning to have a large impact in business. Consider the common professional activity of attending industry-specific conferences. Attendees meet for seminars, meals, and networking. Several attendees may take photos of this event. They can upload their photos to a photo networking site such as Flickr (http://www.flickr.com), and tag them with the name of the conference. Anyone searching for the conference would be able to find a complete photographic record of the event.

Social networking has even made an impact in tourism. "Where Are You Now?" (http://www.wayn.com) is a site that connects travelers, for logging trips and comparing destinations, finding travel buddies, and making friends with like-minded people. WAYN even helps with off-line networking by allowing users to send SMS (short text messages) to each other's cell phones.

Social networking presents an innovative solution to the problem of information overload. By organizing information collaboratively, useful content filters toward the people who would most like it, while useless content is dropped

altogether. Finally, it is a core technology with implications that will touch all disciplines in the years to come.

A blog, or "Web log" for short, is a collection of posts around a theme or topic collected on a Web site. At the time of this writing, blog search firm Technorati (http://www.technorati.com/) was tracking 25.4 million blogs with 1.9 billion links.

A blog is a collection of time-stamped journal entries on any possible topic. Blogs cover every subject from politics to education to technology to one particular person's social life. Some blogs are only of interest to a few people while others have thousands of readers daily.

The Pew Internet Survey estimates that about 11%, or 50 million people, read blogs. (http://www.pewInternet.org/PPF/r/113/report_display.asp). Eighty percent of people contacted by the Business Blog Consulting Web site, a site focused on the growing use of blogs in business, believe that blogs are not a fad. Traditional media outlets (such as the BBC) have begun to add blogs to their media offerings.

The digitally enabled traveler is motivated to share experience in an immediate, visual and highly subjective manner. For a digitally enabled traveler, the personal reaction to a destination like a museum, a historic site, or a travel adventure is typically recorded as a highly personalized written blog. The digitally enabled traveler will supplement the blog with a gallery of digital images. The gallery will then be linked to a short video, compressed for Web hosting, of the activity at the site. With a reasonably fast wireless Internet connection or access to a local Internet café, this material can be posted within minutes of the experience, or in some cases, in near real time. Digitally enabled travelers with the proper digital gear and Internet connection can produce a personalized digital stream of video, images and words. Often defined as "rich" media, the mix of all these files—sound, still, motion, text—are a critical and creative connection to a virtual world for the digitally enabled traveler. For the digitally enabled traveler, contact with the social network on the Web is critical. This technical and artistic practice is easy to achieve and among the

members of the digital generation, a routine and necessary activity.

Table 1 offers a way to understand the devices, practices, skills, and motivations of a digitally enabled traveler.

Professionals in travel and tourism should understand that the focus of these technologies is the individual consumer, not necessarily the business enterprise.

Digital Imaging Trek: A Model for the Tourism Industry

The digitally enabled traveler is equipped with an endless array of digital products designed to capture and record the tourism experience. Through these devices travelers are highly motivated to stay connected to virtual communities online. Patrons of tourism will use their technology skills to create visual and rich media collateral—high quality digital media artifacts. There are countless Web-based outlets to connect the traveler's experience

Table 1. Understanding the devices, practices, skills, and motivations of the digitally enabled traveler

Device	Connectivity	Skill	Motivation
Cellular phone with low resolution camera function	Commercial wireless network, satellite connection in remote areas Multifunction chips available for international functionality Limited WWW access if available	Easy to use, entry level skill	• Basic voice communications; real time voice conversations with social and business network; voice mail. • Basic e-mail if function available • Basic organizational information: names, addresses, telephone, fax • Basic low resolution images, very limited storage • Limited to real time voice based research and basic business functions such as reservations, bookings, and so on • Limited keyboarding if necessary

Table 1. continued

Hand held multifunction PDA- personal digital assistant	Commercial wireless network, satellite connection in remote areas Multifunction chips available for international functionality Limited WWW access if available	Entry to moderate level, requires some experience	• Voice function if feature available on device • E-mail • Moderate organization of rich information itinerary, dates, addresses, images, URLs, and so on • Low resolution imaging if available, limited storage • Wireless connectivity to basic navigating on WWW • Basic keyboarding for research and booking business functions such as reservations, bookings, and so on
Battery power laptop with wireless connectivity	Commercial or free wireless, Internet café, locally provided high speed network connection Satellite connection in remote areas Wireless chip functional in international standards Access to rich sources of information on WWW	Moderate to advanced, able to detect wireless signal; may re-quire some basic problem solving Powerful image editing software applications	• Voice over IP if function available • E-mail, online social networking, post digital images and video • Advanced organization of rich information on device's data sources • Edits and stores high resolution still images and digital video with sound • Likely to use laptop for extensive research and business functions such as reservations, bookings, and so on • Uses laptop as critical extension of travel experience; connectivity to online, social network a priority
Digital still camera	Direct connect to laptop or other device with Firewire. Interconnect to Web through computer device	Easy to expert level skill	• Record images • Record technical file type and related information • Field edit • Organize image files • May be critical to business comm-unications • Critical to social network and social communications

Table 1. continued

Digital video camera	Direct connect to laptop or other devices with Firewire	Easy to expert level skill	• Record motion and sound • Record technical file type and related information • Field edit: shoot to edit • May be critical to business comm-unications • Critical to social network and social communications
Computing tablet	Direct connect to laptop or other devices with Firewire Essentially same connectivity as laptop, yet these devices are relatively new to the marketplace and not widely adopted by travelers	Moderate to advanced, able to detect wireless signal; may re-quire some basic problem-solving Application base still developing	• Typically less functional than laptop • Consumers are urged to match intended use to tablet functionality

and collateral to an eager virtual community and social interaction network. As digitally enabled tourism becomes an expectation among patrons and customers, tourism professionals need to understand and shape usage models.

The model of the digital imaging trek proposes information and technical architectures to capture travel experience, create a virtual record of tourism, and meet the demands of the digitally enabled traveler.

From early times of travel, the notion of a "trek" has long been regarded as a journey of self-exploration for the traveler. Many tourists and travelers today are seeking a heightened experience as part of their tourism through digital communication technologies. Putting practice in to models, especially the practice of the digital imaging trek, is a way to understand the processes and practices of the digitally enabled traveler (See Figure 3). Using all the digital tools available, a digital trekker will produce files from a wide range of sources and self-publish material in two methods; saved as CD-based files (or some other permanent memory such as DVD or portable USB Flash Memory) or published on the World Wide Web.

A typical day on digital imaging trek starts with a destination selection. Digitally enabled travelers will turn to the Internet to locate and decide upon a location. Whether it is a museum,

Figure 3. The general digital imaging trek model embraces technology communication devices and self publishing

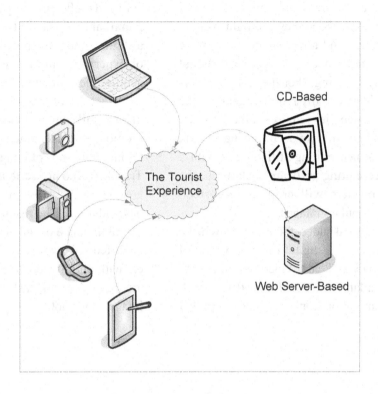

a regional historic location or a cultural performance, the digitally enabled traveler will seek all types of information from Web site based services to make plans. When made available on a Web based system, transportation schedules, phone numbers, hours of operations, special information about exhibits, costs, and other related information about the region, are always instantly available to the traveler. Web based systems allow the digitally enabled traveler to acquire information regardless of time and in a preferred language.

in digital imaging trek model, the traveler is focused on acquisition of digital still and video images that record the daily experience of the trip. In any environment—built or natural—the visitor will always encounter new scenes that are novel, exciting, and educational and from the perspective of the traveler, representative of the tourism experience. With cheap recording memory in the form of Flash Memory, a digitally enabled traveler has near infinite storage space to capture images. Digitally enabled travelers also can edit on the fly. The advantage of digital imaging over traditional film imaging is in the use of storage and field editing. If an image is not worth keeping, it can be immediately erased. Images worth keeping are filed and stored until needed later.

As the day progresses on the digital imaging trek, travelers will want to spend time reviewing images, editing images, and corresponding to the social network with e-mail, uploads and blogs. Editing and organizing images are tasks that most travelers will conduct when time is available. Typically image editing is done on a portable laptop computer. Many people prefer to travel with laptop computers as they are light weight, highly functional, and a repository of software tools and information necessary to conduct digital imaging while traveling. (For the business traveler, a laptop is practically required gear for the trip.) Editing image files requires some time and concentration and will like occur during a break in activities. When editing still images with a popular image editing software such as Adobe Photoshop, travelers will crop, color-correct, merge and manipulate images.

Similarly, digital video footage also will be edited. Travelers on a digital imaging trek will likely download and edit video footage with commonly available video editing software such as Adobe Premiere or Apple's iMovie and Final Cut Pro. Still image editing software and video editing software is widely available. With basic skill and proficiency, digital travelers can achieve remarkably high quality results. For travelers on a digital imaging trek, it is the primary focus of experience and a rewarding achievement to acquire these images.

The ease of use of digital imaging equipment—still cameras, video cameras and laptops, promotes the phenomena of "hyper-imaging"— taking thousands of images to sort through later. Travelers who are serious about digital imaging are continuously shooting images throughout the day and night. The result of hyper-imaging is an overabundance of images and footage that must be sorted and organized. Powerful laptop computers with optimized internal and external storage are prefect for this task. Sorting and organizing images and footage is typically done to suit the

Figure 4. Students and faculty from Johnson & Wales University on a digital imaging trek to Paris; wireless digital connection to the Internet is abundant in urban environments; checking e-mail and editing images in a street side café is now a common tourist experience

desires of the traveler on a digital imaging trek. Images are categorized by group or class and notated with keywords for access at a later time. Various gallery and filing software makes the task of organizing relatively easy.

A Short Primer on Digital Photography

Unlike film cameras, which store images on film, digital cameras capture images via electric sensors and store those images on reusable solid-state memory.

The first digital cameras targeted toward consumers were released in the early 1990s. Since then the digital camera revolution has taken off, and there are hundreds of models available. Competition has remained fierce and manufacturers are producing digital cameras with limitless capacity.

Just 15 years after the introduction of the first consumer digital cameras, current models are take pictures that are as high or higher quality than film cameras. Digital cameras take some getting used to, but tourists and travelers who taking digital imaging seriously will find numerous camera choices in the marketplace.

Digital cameras fall into three general categories: consumer, prosumer, and professional. Consumer cameras generally have a single, non-removable lens that mimics a standard 35mm film lens. However, manufacturers now produce consumer level models with nearly every feature of a traditional Single-Lens Reflex or SLR camera.

The term prosumer is a blend of "professional" and "consumer" and refers to consumers who demand more than the standard technology available while being unable to afford professional equipment. In the digital camera market,

Figure 5. Digital cameras are popular among travelers and tourists; they are portable, easy to use, and affordable

the prosumer devices are Single-Lens Reflex, or SLR, models, and are falling below the $1000 price point. Prosumers tend to be technologically savvy and more tolerant of quirks and bugs in new products.

Many professional photographers are moving entirely to digital photography, enticed by the low cost of shots, ease of printing, high resolutions, and ability to edit photos easily with software such as Adobe Photoshop. Professional cameras generally accept the same standard lenses as film cameras and store photos in RAW format, which allows for greater flexibility in editing. The RAW format can be thought of as a digital negative.

The editing and sorting activity is often a precursor activity to the act of e-mail, blogging and posting images on a Web site to interact with digitally connected social network. Travelers with a laptop and access to the Internet will use the online connection to communicate frequently and for sustained periods of time—sometimes hours at a time. If connectivity is available from a wireless service, the traveler with a laptop will connect, log in to services, and communicate on a frequent basis throughout the day. If the Internet connection is more concentrated, in an Internet café with computers for instance, the traveler will dedicate a portion of the day to connect and communicate online. It is not unusual to see Internet cafés through Europe and Asia, but the model is less attractive in the U.S. Internet connection services should allow the traveler to connect and spend as much time as necessary to conduct the typical activities as blogging, image posting, e-mail, checking itinerary, and so on. As the day winds down on the digital imaging trek, the digitally enabled traveler has acquired a new database of images, published and shared

Figure 6. Digital imaging trek file types, platforms, and purpose

File Type	Hardware Platform	Software Platform	Purpose
Text file	Laptop, desktop, or handheld device with keyboard. Privately owned, or available through Internet cafe	Word processor-editor software	Written log of experience. Creating and sending attachments on e-mail. Creating and posting blog on Web services
Still image	Digital still camera Cell phone with still camera function Multifunction still and video camera	Embedded software in camera platform. Image editing with additional software on laptop or other device	Create a visual record of still images of travel experience. Sort and publish on Web server to share with social network. Send as attachments in e-mail.
Motion images	Digital video camera Cell phone with motion camera function Multifunction still and video camera	Embedded software in camera platform. Editing with additional software on laptop or other device	Create a visual record of motion images and sound. Edit and publishing on Web site to share with social network. Send attachments.
Hyperlink	Web based hosting services – social networks	Embedded feature on Web site	Allows author to 'link' from one type of information to another. Series of links create trails for others to follow.

select image-files, and communicated stories of their experience with their social network online through e-mail and blogs.

Taking pictures on a vacation is not new to the world of tourism, but digital equipment has changed the business and behavior equation. Given the proper technical infrastructure, images can be acquired and posted—essentially published—to a world-wide audience in a matter of minutes.

Digital photos are easy to share. Most photos are already stored on a computer or memory card, and it is a simple matter to upload them to the Internet, either through a private gallery (such as the digitaltrek.org site), or a social photography Web site such as Flickr (www.flickr.com).

Most thriving urban centers and developed destination resort complexes have a mature ICT infrastructure to support instant access to the Internet. Even smaller rural locations now boast access to the greater world of the Internet. The goal of a traveler on a digital imaging trek is to capture and publish images that reflect travel experience in new places and foreign cultures.

Tourism and Information Architecture

It is critical that both traveler and tourism enterprise alike prepare for the use of digital technologies through "architecture." Travelers and organizations need to plan and think ahead of how to respond and conduct activities through the travel and tourism experience. While some things are left to chance or serendipity the deployment of digital infrastructure requires some thought. That plan is called "architecture."

Architecture for information services is similar to that of architecture for buildings—it is the deliberate planning, modeling, and delivery of ICT services. Architecture requires adopting a model of approach and solution, both in systems architecture and information architecture. How does a highly connected, fast speed digital environment that serves the digitally enabled traveler sprout up? It is not a singular act by any tourism organization, but a system wide policy approach of local and national partners in business and governmental bodies. In most cases, experts from companies that provide ICT services will consult on the array of services available in the technology marketplace.

Much of the communications infrastructure that has developed in the past decade is a confluence of commercial profit-driven interest, digital user culture, and regional policy and laws. The combined effect of the built ICT environment serves residents and visitors alike. Localities with new digital infrastructure enjoy digital connection to a broader world. Travelers to areas that are served with high speed digital services also reach out and use the infrastructure for all their related travel communication activities. This ever growing presence of widely accessible digital communication services represents different challenges to different cultures. While most Western cultural sensibilities accept the openness of access to the World Wide Web, other cultures are more circumspect and reserved, wishing to control the vast onslaught of information pouring out of the Web.

Cost has always been considered the primary barrier for entry in the world of ICT. The receding cost barrier—as Moore's Law predicts—has lowered the cost barrier, particularly with technology products and services. Tourist properties such as hotels and resorts now can achieve Internet access as easily as telephone access. In many instances, travel infrastructure such as airports, train stations, and the aircraft and trains themselves, provide Internet and advanced telephone access. Countries and regions are now adopting ICT's and installing a fiber-optic telecommunications system with wide spread wireless digital access points, which has distinct advantages over older, legacy "wire based" telecommunications infrastructures—particularly for the traveler.

In some ways, the new fiber and wireless based connectivity infrastructure offers advantages for the digitally enabled traveler.

Of course, this entire ICT infrastructure model represents enormous business opportunity for the properties in which they exist. Hotels, resorts, travel destinations, travel hubs, restaurants, coffee houses, business outlets can differentiate themselves from competitors by providing ICT for a fee to the traveler. Travelers in turn, view access to ICT as a cost associated with travel and plan to spend money to acquire it. It is common for travelers to purchase short term access to ICT services at these sites on terms ranging from a few hours to several days.

When collaboration on planning and development of digital infrastructure occurs, the stage is set to promote services to the digitally enabled traveler. A highly developed infrastructure and usage model promotes rapid creation and publishing of rich media collateral by the digitally enabled traveler. All parts of the technology infrastructure work in unison to support the activities of the traveler.

Digital communication technologies of many platforms have become accessible to even the most inexperienced traveler. Mobile technologies of all types and sizes and wireless network signal have brought the Internet to the most distant of locations. This convergence of technical infrastructure and tourism presents opportunities and challenges to the tourism industry.

Yet even as the cyber-record of digital travel experience explodes, there are many issues the profession must consider. The more available common digital technologies become, the more travelers and tourism enterprises grapple with the complexity (and confusion) of choices including but not limited to privacy, intellectual property, systems integration, systems management, training, best practice, and so on.

Digitally Enabled Travel: Knowledge Targets for the Novice

As the digitally enabled traveler becomes more of an influence in the world of travel and tourism, young professionals seeking degree based education and career opportunities in the field need to be familiar with basic technology. Whether looking at a college level curriculum or training opportunities for adults wishing to gain new skills, look for some of the topics covered here.

College level curriculum in hospitality, travel, and tourism programs should include an introductory level course in this area of digital technology. The topics taught in such a course do not necessarily have to be technical but young professionals entering the business should know the basics and be prepared to research and understand technology. A sample of college level curriculum might include topics such as the following.

Foundations in Technology

Many professionals and educators mistakenly think that learners know all there is to know about basic computer operations, productivity software and Internet access, Web searching and surfing. While these topics are often part of many school systems, not everyone has mastered basic skill and techniques in all these areas. Interacting with computer interfaces and mastering the sophistication of some productivity tools such as word processing, spreadsheets, databases and browsers requires instruction, time and practice. Many colleges, universities, technical institutions and similar educational organizations offer courses in computer technology. The popular press is filled with instructional books complete with CD based video for those who are adept at self instruction. Many conferences, training seminars, and "Webinars" (seminars of text, sound, and motion hosted on the Web), offer similar instruction. Regardless of the model one uses to get trained, using digital technologies requires constant "tune ups" to one's

Figure 7. The architecture for wireless network and infrastructure model for digitally enabled traveler

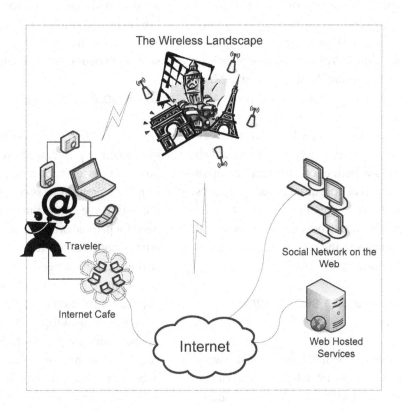

skill set. Find the type of education that works for you and take advantage of it.

Basic Information and Systems Architecture

Information and systems architecture introduces models to help solve problems in the field of technology. As with providing digital services for travels to use to communicate with social networks, technology applications start as a way to provide a solution to a problem.

While it is convenient to say technology will solve a problem or make some situation more efficient or less cumbersome, the idea has to be communicated in a visual model. Professionals

in the world of information technology communicate regularly with visual models that reflect the structure or architecture of a system. Devices and the networks that connect them are shown so all can understand and agree on system solutions. Understanding basic architecture in work flow, information flow, and management, networking, service devices, client side devices, and so on will be very valuable for new professionals in the world of hospitality, travel, and tourism.

Basic Web Design and Interface

Many professionals in the field of hospitality, travel, and tourism will likely be asked to participate in design teams to design and build Web sites that will host information for customers or be used internally as sources of information for the business enterprise. Conceptualizing and building a Web site is a skill that requires practice and experience although of software tools such as Microsoft FrontPage and Adobe (formerly Macromedia) Dreamweaver make it easy to try this activity. With a little training in software features of such applications, college level courses can quickly teach students the essentials in basic Web site design. This is both a technical and creative challenge, but most people quickly see the results of a little effort. For people just wishing to start with a simple Web site to host information about a trip or a destination, these tools are cheap, accessible, and relatively easy to learn.

Basic Digital Imaging and Image Manipulation

There are an abundance of off-the-shelf software tools in the marketplace that will introduce college student (or anyone with the motivation to learn) skills in digital imaging and image manipulation. While many people have digital cameras a course on digital photography will introduce a wide range of topics from composition to technical specifications. Understanding the wide range of options in today's digital cameras can be helpful for young professionals who need to deal with a customer base that is armed with the latest camera gadgetry. Learning the process involved in capturing an image and uploading an image to a devices that can store the image in important. More knowledge in these areas will help improve customer empathy and ultimately customer satisfaction.

Editing images in software like Adobe Photoshop has a double benefit to a college curriculum. Students with added technical skills such as digital photo editing are in more demand. Many businesses need such skills to help with developing creative collateral to promote the commercial activity of the business. Understanding the creative process from image acquisition to image editing also will help the professional in dealing with agencies that provide that service. For instance, image editing is a time consuming activity, and in negotiating advertising contracts, such knowledge will be helpful.

Desktop Publishing

Desktop publishing is a content area that will provide a young professional with the knowledge of how to put assets such as text and images together in print collateral to serve the business. Even in the digital age, many businesses still have a great need for printed products to advertise, inform and attract potential customers. Tourism properties still have a great need for pamphlets, brochures and signage to keep customers informed about policies, regulations, events, calendars, and so on. A course in desktop publishing will give practitioners an opportunity to learn a skill that will help promote and organize business. In desktop publishing, students can learn how to conceive and construct various types of print pieces using software such as Microsoft Publishing or Adobe Indesign.

Editorial, Content Creation and Content Management

While learning technical tools is vital, helping young professionals identify and manage the message is critical to the success of travel and tourism businesses. Courses that emphasize the basics of how to construct the message in both text and visual design are important for a basic college curriculum.

Systems and Technology Primer for the Digitally Enabled Traveler

As digital communications platforms and technologies have become adopted by a wide mainstream audience two factors have been critical to widespread use—practicality and ubiquity. Along with the explosion of digital gadgets, contemporary travelers now have high expectations of availability of connectivity and complimentary technologies.

If the tourism industry is to appropriately harness and cater to this new and demanding audience, the industry must build a model of digitally enabled travel that supports both traditional goals of tourism and the new goals of digital media acquisition. Understanding the pieces of the technology puzzle can serve as a starting point.

Several recent world events have highlighted the role mobile technology plays on the world stage. The first images of the London tube bombing in 2005 came from the cell phone cameras of survivors. These images were published by the BBC and forwarded around the world within minutes of the attack. Similarly dramatic images, particularly digital video, were quickly spread after the 2005 tsunami disaster in the Indian Ocean. Whether it is a global or local scale, digital imaging devices are ever present and serve as eyes to the world. Building a world class digital environment brings with it many more challenges, not just in the technical realm, but in the human realm as well.

A Word on Privacy and Security in the Digital Age

Privacy, security of information, copyright, information ownership, censored, and uncensored material are all issues that become concerns of the industry when technology is introduced. It is a grey area because decorum and respect relies as much on personal behavior as it does on personal technology. Travelers with powerful digital recording tools must understand the local cultural norms, as well as the global broadcast power of the World Wide Web.

Privacy is an important and sensitive issue. Visitors to a Web site may be reluctant to share information—such as their e-mail address—because they fear that their personal information will be sold and they will be subjected to unsolicited advertisements. Spam, the endless barrage of meaningless e-mail advertising, has become an onerous burden to all citizens using online tools. It is best avoided by constricting the use of e-mail addresses.

Information that may be personal or sensitive, such as vacation photos or a travel journal, should be posted with care. In many cultures people do not wish to have their images posted for the world to see. Privacy for individuals is a sensitive matter. Even in public tourism venues, digital photographers are challenged when taking images and asked to refrain. Religious and private properties often post requests to refrain from photography and video recordings.

Institutional Web sites should consider developing a privacy policy, or a legal statement that reflects what the institution may and may not do with information provided by users. The World Wide Web Consortium (the standards body for the Web) has developed the Platform for Privacy Preferences (P3P) (http://www.w3.org/P3P/), a standardized language which provides Web site administrators with a simple and automated way to quickly generate a customized policy for their site. Individual digital travelers, eager to capture a unique image, must apply their own standards. The golden rule though is "do unto others" as you would have done to yourself. Consider the impact of each image that is posted.

Travelers must be aware of their physical safety and security at all times. Broadcasting information on the Web can add to this worry. For example, travelers, especially solo-travelers, are advised against posting a personal and complete itinerary until their trip is complete. No only does it tell the world where you will be, but it also tells the world where you are not. Home safety as well as trip safety is the paramount concern.

With reasonable precautions, a Web site can *increase* safety. It allows a large number of people to check in on the well-being of travelers. While theft and other dangers cannot be eliminated, careful use of a Web site, instant messaging, and e-mail can reassure those back home. The personal technology of a digital enabled traveler is an attractive target for thieves. Common sense should guide the novice and experienced traveler in protecting personal possessions.

Table 2. Core components of an information technology system

Technology	Location	Skill-level	Description
Computer Client	Computing cluster such as an Internet café, business service office, hotel lobby, etc. One or more for use by customers	Basic to advanced software such as e-mail, word processing, file management; basic computer knowledge	The computer client serves as the starting point for the customer. Recreational and business travelers alike will budget time and funds to access basic computing services such as e-mail, word processing, file uploading.
Laptop Computers	Anywhere, travelers port and manage	Basic to advanced software such as e-mail, word processing, file management; basic computer knowledge	A laptop computer is a computer client and the traveler's link to the Internet and workstation for writing blogs or editing digital photos.
Card Readers	Anywhere	Basic computer knowledge required.	Digital cameras accept different memory cards depending on brand. A generic card reader will allow any computer to read any card from any camera, with no additional software.
Portable Storage	Anywhere	Basic computer knowledge required.	Backups are a major issue for travelers concerned about potential data loss (from theft or equipment failure). A portable hard drive (or a device that can burn CD's) provides a cheap and easy backup solution on the road. Small and easily packed.
Network-wired	Anywhere	Intermediate to advanced computer knowledge required to build and support. Entry level user knowledge to access and use.	Wired Internet connections are generally located in institutions (such as hotels, business services, universities), and may incur a cost for access.

Table 2. continued

Network-wireless	Anywhere	Intermediate to advanced computer knowledge required to build and support. Entry level user knowledge to access and use.	Wireless Internet connections can be found in built environments, particularly popular in urban settings with restaurants, parks, museums, hotels, and cafes.
Mass Storage	Any secure building location, typically attached to host devices such as advanced workstations or mainframes.	Intermediate computer knowledge required to configure, install and support.	A mass storage device, is a very large, commercial grade hard drive. It supports data and functions core to large businesses. While computer users may see the results of such devices in a routine Web search, these devices work in the background of daily user activities.
Servers	At a hosting company; typically a technology company which provides a secure physical location, as well as technical knowledge to support services. Locations are typically built specifically to house the servers.	Advanced technical skills in Web hosting and server based data services.	The server will host all of the content for a Web site and code for Web applications such as a gallery or blog. Often a class of computers known as workstations; function solely as servers. A hosting service provider will maintain and support all server hardware and software. Computer users access these devices through client computers to update Web sites, post images in galleries and blog.

Web Hosting: What Travel and Tourism Professionals Need to Know

All Internet applications such as a Web site or a search engine run on a server. The server is a computer workstation in a class of computing machines that is specially constructed to manage the constant demand of service to clients on the network. Servers require special software and in most cases, comparably advanced knowledge and skill to configure and maintain. While it is possible to run a server in-house, it involves purchasing a machine, installing and supporting an operating system and applications, and maintaining an "always-on" Internet connection. Managing a server requires routine management as well as prompt response emergencies, 24 hours a day, 7 days a week. For most travel and tourism providers, becoming a technology company is a distraction from the core business. It is generally advisable that any business requiring a host on a server be outsourced to a Web host business provider.

A Web host is a company that provides space on their Web servers, use of their programs, and a certain amount of bandwidth use for a monthly cost. Often referred to as a "solutions provider" or a "Web hosting service" the hosting company will handle all computer hardware and software issues such as installations, configurations, back-ups, updates, and any unforeseen maintenance. Of course, solution providers contract these services for a fee, but competition works in this marketplace

as it does in any other, and a shopper is wise to research and compare costs and services among a range of businesses.

There are many Web hosting companies and there are many attributes to consider when researching them. Choosing a hosting company is a long-term commitment. Transferring a site from one hosting service to another generally involves several days of unreliability and possible downtime. Carefully consider all of the factors onlined in Table 3 before making a decision.

All of these considerations are important indicators of a successful Web hosting experience. Remember, anyone can run a server, including a college student living in an apartment with a space for a computer on a network. Make sure that you are dealing with a professional company that has a reputation for handling routine business as well as crises. Like the travel and tourism industry, professional protocol in handling technical matters

Table 3. Qualities for evaluating a hosting company

Factor	Description
Reputation	Every company must market itself on its reputation for service to customers. Ask for reference of other businesses that have used the services. Search for comments on the Web about the company and its performance. Are there any instances of how the company performed in a crisis, such as a virus attack or power failure? Have you toured the facilities or conducted due diligence on the company?
Reliability	Does the company publish statistics on technical performance? What level of support and customer service contact is there? Will you be able to contact people in off hours? What kind of technology do they support? Is there a specific platform or hardware and software and do you recognize the vendor? Ask about back-up, power supply, physical security, data security, and so forth. Do they publish their reliability data? Conduct an Internet search through popular search engines to find information about them.
Technology	Is the hardware and software platform up to date and current? Can you speak to vendors who supply the company with technology. Do they publish any related information about platforms?
People	Making a business agreement is as much about people as it is price structure. Have you met the principals of the company? Are you generally familiar with their organization and business structure? Do you have confidence in the people you have met? Is there generally superior business communication to your proposals?

as well as high grades on customer service are key to sound business practice in the technology marketplace.

As with every business, hosting is about people as much as technology. Find a company with knowledgeable employees who are happy to deal with their clients. You should find support personnel who are professional, courteous and eager to answer questions at your knowledge level, no matter how basic or advanced.

Every good host publishes their uptime (the amount of time the service has run without interruptions) and customer testimonials. Don't necessarily trust the quotes on the company's Web site; do an Internet search with any popular search engine (Yahoo, Google, etc.), and find out for yourself.

Once you have identified a few companies that you feel comfortable dealing with, consider the technical requirements of your project. The first decision is about the type of hosting that the project requires. The options are:

- **Dedicated hosting** means that you are leasing an entire computer, which gives you access to the entire hard drive and allows you to make certain configuration requests that are not possible on a shared machine. By leasing a server (rather than purchasing it and placing it in your office), you outsource the need for physical setup, administration and backup services. You also avoid the upfront cost of a powerful machine, and take advantage of your hosting company's ability to quickly purchase and maintain the machine with professional qualified vendors.

- **Shared hosting**, sometimes called managed hosting, means that you are leasing part of a server, which you will share with other customers. This kind of plan generally involves very low monthly fees (as low as $10/month) and provides complete technical support. Unless you are hosting multiple blogs or Web sites, a shared hosting plan is probably sufficient.

Travel and tourism organizations could have a range of needs to contract an outside hosting provider. Setting up a Web page to inform customers of features and offerings of a property or package, or architecting more advanced online services for customers may be among the ideas you will have. The next step in this process of selecting a hosting provider is to explore what you want to do with your hosting provider. The type of service you offer will determine the software applications that the hosting provider will need to run on the server. Additionally, your requirements will guide the features that you'll select for the server. Each software package will list the special requirements on their Web site, but some general guidelines are:

- **Static Web page:** Simple Web pages that hyperlink information that is relatively static. Information does not change too often. Static Web pages require little to no special software or technical support.

- **Downloadable images:** No special requirements, similar to static Web page

- **Image gallery with uploading:** Image galleries containing collections of image (often hundreds and thousands) require server-side programs. Server side programs mean that special software has been loaded and manipulated to provide an easy user interface and experience. A database will be required to track and maintain a medium to large size collection of gallery images.

- **Blogs:** Blogs, or written text entries also require special server-side software to accepted entries, organize them and display them, blog software, like image galleries is generally database-driven.

Several hosts offer blog-friendly plans that require minimal configuration and no technical

Table 4. Criteria for evaluating Web hosting services

Feature	What to Look For
Technical Support	At the very least, 24-hour e-mail technical support. Also consider telephone support (generally, the company promises to address your problem and call you back within 24 hours).
Domain	Most hosting plans include one domain registration (for example, www.yournamehere.com) for free. Make sure that the price for a second is reasonable (not more than $20/year).
Disk space allocation	Disk space, the space on the hard drive that is allocated to you, should be adequate for your application. Storing Web pages or blogs requires a small amount of space, while storing photographs requires multiple gigabytes. Look for at least 10GB of space. Also, research in advance what it will cost to expand your allocated space. Understand the incremental hikes in cost for more disk space.
Server-side program access	The applications that you wish to run will guide your need for server-side program access. In general, look for PHP, which is a coding language that manages how customers see and interact with your services.
E-mail addresses	Your plan should offer the ability to create your own me@mydomain.com e-mail addresses. Web-based e-mail access is a nice feature for frequent travelers, and is offered at no additional cost by many hosts.
Bandwidth	Bandwidth refers to the total amount of data transfer between your server and visitors to your Web site. More bandwidth is good. Understand that bandwidth to the end user is limited by their personal connection and rate of speed.
Statistics	It's always helpful to know exactly how many visitors your site has. Hosting companies typically provide this information with some graphics and analysis.
Databases	If you wish to run a dynamic application such as a blog, you'll need access to a database.
Operating System	Your operating system choice should be guided by your application requirements. Most hosting plans are based on either Linux (which tends to be cheaper), or Windows.

skills. Lists of these can be found at http://word-press.org/hosting/ and http://www.sixapart.com/movabletype/hosting.

Identify your minimum technical requirements. In general, look for the criteria listed in Table 4.

More Technical Tools of the Digitally Enabled Traveler

Digitally enabled travelers will quickly embrace new and experimental technologies. For them, it is a challenge to figure out ways to adopt a technology and make it work in the daily flow of travel.

For instance, instant messaging, or "IM," is a technology for rapid-fire asynchronous messaging across a network. Instant messages can be thought of "instant e-mail," and are generally used to communicate to a select social network, but often composed on the computer screen while doing something else. Digitally enabled travelers multitask on the computer—that is, they conduct more than one activity at the same time—with ease.

IM was first popularized in the mid-1990s by ICQ, a product introduced by Mirabilis Ltd in 1996. Mirabilis Ltd was later acquired by America Online, which ran a competing product called "AOL Instant Messenger," or AIM. By acquiring

ICQ, AOL became the largest operator of instant messaging networks in the world.

Other competitors include Microsoft, which offers an instant messaging feature as part of the Microsoft Network (MSN), and Yahoo!, which offers the feature as part of their community-building options. All of these services are free to use, though some may display advertisements.

Unfortunately, all of these services are based on proprietary protocols and do not interoperate. Therefore, a digital traveler must choose the service that most of the people that they wish to communicate with use. If this is not practical, digital travelers can invest in a product such as Trillian, from Cerulean Studios (http://www.ceruleanstudios.com/), which is an IM program that supports all major networks.

Instant messaging is favored by digital travelers, because it allows instant communication with anyone on the network, no matter where their physically located. If a device (such as a computer or cellular telephone) has Internet access, it can connect to an IM network. This is an extremely low-cost method for travelers to communicate with their social network of friends, family, and colleagues around the world.

More recently, voice over Internet protocol (VoIP) has become an important buzzword in the latest digital tools becoming available to digital travelers. VoIP is a technology for transmitting traditional "telephone calls" over the Internet. Imagine using a laptop as a phone and conducting routine two-way audible conversations. Such calls are indistinguishable from normal Internet data and promise to make international conversational calls extremely cheap. Imagine no more phone calling cards and the end to frustrated travelers trying to decipher local and international calling codes.

While still in the early stages, VoIP is available to any digital traveler with a laptop, speakers, and a microphone. Services such as Google Talk or Skype (http://www.skype.com/) are up and running and can be used to converse with telephone quality audio for free. Skype also offers "Skype Out," which permits computers to connect with telephone numbers anywhere in the world for extremely reasonable rates.

Needless to say, it is important for travel and tourism organizations to be familiar with trends such as VoIP for two reasons. The early adopters of such technology—the digitally enabled traveler—are the bell weather for change in the industry. It won't take long for entrepreneurial technology providers to create a competitive business model for VoIP and shift the commerce to a new marketplace.

CONVERGENCE AND FUTURE TRENDS

Given the rapid evolution of digital communication tools, both hardware and software based, it is not hard to imagine that many of these products will continue to transform.

The technology industry is creating faster, lighter, devices that better integrate with each other. This trend of "convergence" is one to watch for. It wasn't long ago that a cell phone was simply a way to have voice conversations with other parties. Today, other features have converged on the platform of a cell phone. Is a cell phone a camera, a video recorder, a video viewer, organizer and personal digital library? The answer is "yes"—it is all those things and more.

A digital camera is no longer a camera; it is an image processing workstation. Images can be acquired, edited, filed, and stored. Images are dynamic files that merge and morph into other applications and devices through infrared proximity connections.

The ubiquitous iPod from Apple computer started off not too long ago as a just another platform for listening to music. Today an entire lucrative industry revolves around providing rich media content for viewing on a tiny screen. Need an exercise multimedia instruction package for keeping fit during travel, it can be purchased and downloaded to your iPod.

CONCLUSION

Digital gear to enhance the travel and tourism industry is a constantly evolving marketplace. The future is part evolution and part revolution, from wildly popular devices to culturally challenging information flow. Regardless of the intricacy, allure or popularity of digital devices, the seasoned digitally enabled traveler will always find ways of incorporating new devices and new services to enhance experience and communicate to a social network in digital space. Travel and tourism providers must influence the role of the digital imaging trek by understanding the role they themselves play in this ever changing landscape.

Who is the provider, the host, the arbitrator of this new world of digital travel? By seeing and understanding the big digital picture, tourism and travel providers will retain perspective and offer quality services to patrons worldwide.

NOTE

- All images are provided with permission to reproduce by the authors.
- Illustrations are public domain license free illustrations from Microsoft Visio.
- Figures representing models are provide with permission to reproduce by the authors.
- Illustrations in models are public domain license free illustrations from Microsoft Visio.

Chapter XXVIII
The U.S. Video Game Industry:
Analyzing Representation of Gender and Race

Janet C. Dunlop
Oklahoma State University, USA

ABSTRACT

Today's media are vast in both form and influence; however, few cultural studies scholars address the video gaming industry's role in domestic maintenance and global imposition of U.S. hegemonic ideologies. In this study, video games are analyzed by cover art, content, and origin of production. Whether it is earning more "powers" in games such as Star Wars, or earning points to purchase more powerful artillery in Grand Theft Auto, capitalist ideology is reinforced in a subtle, entertaining fashion. This study shows that oppressive hegemonic representations of gender and race are not only present, but permeate the majority of top-selling video games. Finally, the study traces the origins of best-selling games, to reveal a virtual U.S. monopoly in the content of this formative medium.

INTRODUCTION

Recently, the Chinese government banned 50 U.S. video games, top sellers worldwide, claiming that they are a negative influence on Chinese youth. This was seen by many as an attempt to maintain hegemonic codes in China (China Daily News Online, Sept. 28, 2005). However, throughout discussions of the role of media in establishing and perpetuating hegemonic codes in society, (Cortes, 2000; Fiske, 1992, 1994,; Gross, 2001; Hall, 2000; Hooks, 1990), few scholars address the video gaming industry's role in domestic maintenance and global imposition of U.S. hegemonic ideologies.

By and large, the most popular video games in the U.S. are also the best-selling games worldwide (Appendix B). The U.S. monopoly on the gaming software industry, as it applies to sociological effects on children, is paramount. This discussion is not to claim that all video games are bad. In contrast, games, such as *Star Wars: Knights of the Old Republic*, invite players to question ethical issues such as responsibility for one's actions. *Freedom Fighters* inverts the ideologies surrounding the U.S.-Iraq war, allowing players to question the difference between a terrorist and a freedom fighter. It points to the possibility that the labels lie only in what one believes is right and just. In *Tak and the Power of Ju Ju*, young players enjoy the role of an unlikely hero, a small, awkward tribesman who rescues the Pupununu people from the evil sorcerer, Tlalock. This game illustrates that heroism can be found in the most unlikely persons. This said, in the majority of these best-sellers, ideologies of capitalism, white male-dominance, and violence is blatant. Gamers gain prestige by earning points, which enable them to "buy" better equipment in the game. For example, in *ATV OffRoad Fury*, ATV riders can "purchase" better engines, better riders, and better equipment each time they win a race. This purchasing of gadgets is of unquestioned value, thus, capitalist ideologies are imbedded deep within the premise of the game. In this way, production or performance is constant and only consumption can be varied. Whether it is earning more "powers" in games such as *The Elder Scrolls II: Morrowind*, or earning points to purchase artillery in *Grand Theft Auto*, capitalist ideology is reinforced in subtle, engaging fashion. This study shows that the U.S. hegemonic codes of capitalism, gender, and race are not only present, but prevalent in the majority of video games. In addition, it indicates that the reason behind the monopoly of video game ideology is due to the U.S.'s domination of the gaming software industry production and sales.

THEORETICAL FRAMEWORK

In the same way that under-representation or negative stereotypical images have the ability to affect children's attitudes, values, and roles of themselves and others in society, the implications of racial diversity and stereotypes in video games have yet to be researched. A fair examination of the quality of any message that children receive also requires a close look at how people of color are depicted in video games. These images influence perceptions of societal roles, not only for youth of color, but also for white youth—boys and girls alike. In order to present a clear picture of the message that youth of all colors are receiving in video games, a racial analysis must be part of video game analysis.

Post-structuralist Jaques Lacan theorizes that in the pre-Oedipal stage, before babies develop language, they inhabit an imaginary speechless world between mother, child, and world. The acquisition of language results in the loss of the imaginary world identity with the mother, and thus, the child enters a (masculine) world that is structured by language (Crotty, 1998). Applying Lacanian symbolic theory, the individual forms identity of self and identity of others through the images one views. As the individual views images that resemble or do not resemble the self, she or he develops a perception of one's position in society (Crotty, 1998). Assuming this is true, the presence of symbolic annihilation in the video gaming industry for females and minorities is alarming. It is logical to apply Gross's (2001) ideas of symbolic annihilation to the video gaming industry where those who are at the bottom of the various power hierarchies will be kept in their places in part through relative invisibility (p.409). By focusing on the negligible representation of women and minorities, the following analysis of current popular video game selections suggests that representational issues may be at the core of the influence of gender and ethnicity on the adoption and use of gaming technology. Furthermore, it suggests that the global hegemonic effects of the U.S. monopoly of the gaming industry are an area for further research.

This article is intended to expand the work of cultural theorists Stuart Hall (2000), Bell Hooks (1991), Larry Gross (2001), and Herman Gray

(2001), who critically question the connection between popular culture and the representation of social groups. Although video game sales are a multi-billion dollar global industry, cultural scholars are markedly mute about the effects of video games. Leonard (2004) claims, "There is a marked failure to recognize video games as sophisticated vehicles inhabiting and disseminating ideologies of hegemony," (p. 3). Video games are part of a capitalist economy—but at what cost to the social development of youth? What about ethics? In this discussion, a sample of twenty top-selling video games is analyzed to determine messages about capitalism, race, and gender. While quantification of female and minority characters in a large sample of video games is equally important in achieving an analysis of representations in video games, this study is intended to elucidate and to understand the ideological terrain of popular video games. It is through this phenomenological observation of the games, the characters, the imbedded rules, and value systems, and through "thick description" that social meanings emerge (Geertz, 1983). This task is fundamentally important in reflecting on current video games and theories of identity development in youth.

THEORETICAL PERSPECTIVE

The effect of gaming on social development of youth is the issue that moved me to examine gender and racial representation in video games. While playing *Splash Down*, a jet-ski racing game with my six-year old son, he told me that he never wanted to be the girl riders (the game allows players to choose racers from a field of two men and two women) because, "they are slow and not as tough as the boys." Although his comment was inaccurate, the women racers in the game, maybe not as fast as the men, are more agile, and thus equally successful. It did cause me to take a step back and look at this game and others with a critical researcher's eye.

Up to this point, I had never noticed the scarcity of playable female characters in my son's games. This recognition led to a critical examination of not only the games we play, but those that many other gamers play. In order to examine games in this way, it is necessary to place groups who are most often marginalized, women and minorities, at the center of the researcher's gaze; this focus suggests a critical theory perspective.

Critical theory rejects any semblance of objectivity and instead examines an issue in hopes of creating social change. Rooted in Marxism and updated in the U.S. by the radical societal struggles of the 1960's, critical theory "provides a framework—both philosophy and methods—for approaching research and evaluation as a fundamentally and explicitly political, and as change-oriented forms of engagement (Patton, 2002, p.131). Harvey (1990) describes this as the process of creating an alternative body of knowledge that is internalized through ideas, but also externalized through our conscious manipulation of objects. Harvey (1990) concludes that

Knowledge changes not simply as a result of reflection but as a result of activity too. Knowledge changes as a result of praxis. Similarly, what we know informs praxis. Knowledge is dynamic, not because we uncover more grains of sand for the bucket, but because of a process of fundamental reconceptualisation, which is only possible as a result of direct engagement with the processes and structures which generate knowledge. (p. 23)

Also present in critical social research is the argument that race is a social construction rather than a biological category, which denies that "racism is just skin-deep" (Harvey, 1990, p. 157). Race is not an empirical social category; it is an ideological construct, signifying a socially constructed set of characteristics that define race (Cohen, 1988). The critical social perspective denies the notion that racism originates from biological differentiation but instead, sees racism as an "ideological code that seizes, opportunistically, on various ideological signifiers that work most effectively at any point in time to naturalize difference and legitimize domination," (Harvey, 1990, p.157). It is this active, political process, in which ideologies about knowledge and social identity are defined, that informs inquiry into the rapidly changing and adapting world of media. The question is how video game consumers perceive negative representation of race and gender. Horkheimer and Adorno (2001) have stated,

All amusement suffers from this incurable malady. Pleasure hardens into boredom because, if it is to remain pleasure, it must not demand any effort and therefore moves rigorously in the worn grooves of association. No independent thinking must be expected from the audience: the product prescribes every reaction: not by its natural structure (which collapses under reflection), but by signals. Any logical connection calling for mental effort is painstakingly avoided. (P. 82)

The images in video games are comfortable for young U.S. consumers, for they are both familiar and entertaining in their simplicity. Worrisome, however, is whether comfort leads to complicity in the messages some video games send.

VIDEO GAME STUDIES

Wilder, Mackie, and Cooper (1985) note issues of gender roles in video games. For example, there are few playable female characters and most female characters are seen in submissive, hyper-sexualized or victim roles. Gee (2003) recognizes the seductive power of the gaming format and the value of this format as a teaching tool. However, it was Provenzo's (1991) study of video game cover art that addressed games as "cultural texts that provide insight to ideas and values we hold as a culture" (p.99). Video games are participants in what Foucault (1980) describes as:

Dominant ways of knowing the world—making it meaningful—produced by those in power to make their ways of knowing circulate discursively around the world, generate 'regimes of truth' which come to assume an authority over the ways in which we think and act. (p. 230)

A perfect example of Foucault's (1980) notion of "regimes of truth" as expressions of hegemonic authority is in the thematic makeup of the most popular video games. In the same way Giroux argues that the U.S. cinema depicts a representation of "reality" as inner-city black-on-black youth violence, popular video games utilize gender and ethnic stereotypes in order to provide a familiar message for an over-entertained culture.

Video Game Violence Studies

Unlike the effects of racial and gender representation in video games on the identity development of youth, the psychological effects of video game violence has been well researched and well documented. Recent studies have shown the correlation between playing violent video games and decreased sensitivity to violent behavior, less trust, increased fearfulness, and decreased apathy (Griffiths, 1999). A number of recent studies have shown a relationship between playing violent video games and subsequent aggression (Anderson & Dill, 2000; Bartholow, Delamere & Waterloo, 2005; Schneider, Lang, Shin, & Bradley, 2004; Sestir, & Davis, 2005). Sakamoto (2005) reviewed Japanese literature to find maladaptive behavior in children who play violent video games. The findings in these studies establishes that video games do, in fact, affect the way some gamers think and act; therefore, it is imperative that studies likewise examine the effects of gender and racial representation. It is logical to presuppose that ethnic and gender roles in video games would likewise have an effect on gamers' thoughts and behaviors. However, there is a gap in the research, which correlates ethnic and gender roles in games to players' perceptions and subsequent behavior. Likewise, there are few qualitative analyses of racial and gender representation in games from a critical perspective (Dietz, 1998; Heintz-Knowles & Henderson, 2001).

Gender Roles

Study of gender roles in video gaming is essential because of the impact these games have on the formation of gender role expectations for both males and females. Although it can be argued that children who do not play video games are not influenced by the roles the games portray, this is not true. Every boy and girl exposed to video games takes in images and definitions of gender. In the same way any group forms ideas and behavioral expectations, through interaction with other boys and girls, these images and definitions become shared social experiences. Therefore, even children who do not play video games are indirectly affected by the images of gender that they portray (Dietz, 1998).

As Alloway and Gilbert (1997) suggest, such practices as surfing the Internet and reading video screens directly sustain and reinforce dominant discourses of hegemonic masculinity, by teaching skills that are potentially very powerful and useful in the communication technologies of the future. The vast selection of video games that attract male players, while alienating female players, may play a role in sustaining the glass ceiling of male hegemony in the lucrative, high-tech work force (Alloway & Gilbert, 1997; Heintz-Knowles & Henderson, 2001). Provenzo's (1991) research shows that through cover art, product description, and thematic images, current video game trends do exactly this.

From a critical theorist perspective, it seems that the video game industry may play into the power structure that sustains socioeconomic he-

gemony in two ways. First, video games are an important introduction to the world of computer technology. Becoming familiar with, comfortable with, and enjoying video games and computers may help girls develop an interest in careers in technology—a field in which women are significantly under-represented. According to U.S. Department of Labor figures, the percentage of women in the Information Technology (IT) industry declined by 18% in the last eight years, with females now representing only one quarter of IT workers. A recent study indicated that there is a correlation of computer and video games usage to gender differences in spatial ability—a desirable skill in IT professions (Terlecki & Newcombe, 2005). Although the number of female gamers is growing, they tend not to show interest in shooter games (games in which the player earns points by shooting targets or enemies) and fantasy games such as *Morrowind, Halo,* or *Eternal Darkness* (Hayes, 2006). In most fantasy games, playable characters are non-human and live in fantasy worlds in which these characters battle otherworld creatures in hopes of achieving domination. Girls and women more often choose casual games such as *Tetris*, relationship-centered games such as *The Sims*, or storied games, those in which playable characters are involved in a narrative and indirect competition (Angelo, 2004). According to Heintz-Knowles and Henderson (2001), there are powerful implications resulting from this trend. The scarcity of girl-friendly video games may send the wrong message to girls: using computers and video games are activities for boys and are not acceptable for girls. In addition, playing video games helps improve computer literacy by enhancing players' abilities to understand images in a three-dimensional space and to track multiple images simultaneously (p.22).

Marketing of games also plays a part and, perhaps, perpetuates the cycle of discrepancy between the numbers of boy and girl players. Tough competition in the video game industry means that only the topselling games survive. In order to reduce the chance of failure, producers and marketers of video games choose formulas that have proven successful in the past and attract predominately male players. Because "male games" are the majority produced, they are the most lucrative and the cycle continues. If, as Heintz-Knowles and Henderson (2001) propose, the lack of girl-friendly video games results in under-representation of women in technology professions (a highly lucrative and highly esteemed career path), then gender representation in video games is an important issue in gender equality.

These issues elucidate the bigger picture of how the video game industry, among other media, perpetuates hegemony by manufacturing stereotypical and, perhaps, sociologically damaging sexist and racist images of females and minorities. Moreover, the possible effects of misogynistic images and racist ideologies on any country currently struggling with women's rights or civil rights could be disastrous. Many of these images are so ingrained in dominant U.S. cultural expectations of women, ethic minorities, and their roles in society that they are perceived as normal. Thus, Gramsci's (2001) notions of social order being won and reproduced by ideological dominance emerge. Gramsci (2001) explains, in the most simplistic terms, that hegemony is the concept of a dominant way of seeing the world. It is different from ideology in that it depends on the expression of the interests of the ruling class and also on its acceptance of "commonsense" by those subordinated by it (Williams, 1983). One feature of hegemony is that in order for the powerful to maintain position, the weak must participate and agree. This is carried out in a delicate balance, whereby the dominant ideology includes bits of opposing views to appease the "mass society" (Horkheimer & Adorno, 2001). Hebdige (2001) describes Gramsci's notion of a "moving equilibrium," through which dominant ideology is, "winning and shaping consent so that the power of the dominant classes appears both

legitimate and natural," (p.204-205). In this way, subordinate groups are limited within an ideology that does not seem imposed, but instead, natural (Hebdidge, 2001).

Video Games and Gender Identity

Applying the framework of symbolic interactionism, it is known that individuals make meaning of their environment by using images and meanings that the members of that society share (Crotty, 1998). Individuals, therefore, assume roles according to society's norms or expectations. However, while there are societal norms surrounding each role, individuals also develop rules or identities that define what a particular role means to them. These meanings are often individualized and emotive in that our emotional and attitudinal responses are based on each individual's exposure to symbolic images (Angeles, 1992). Given that these societal roles are one facet used to define self, they also become a classification system by which we define the world, and ultimately, a basis for action (Mead, 1964). As Dietz (1998) states,

...they [individuals] are able to manipulate the way they "play" a specific role. Children, too manipulate and learn roles through childhood play. Play during childhood becomes an important component of socialization. (p. 426)

Mead (1964) suggests that individuals use the definitions of both themselves and others to interpret the action that surrounds them. Therefore, boys and girls depend upon images and societal expectations about both masculinity and femininity to interpret interaction and to form expectations of themselves and others. Thereby, it is known that a child's gender role expectations are affected by the messages and images of the various socialization agents to which she or he is exposed.

Mead (1964) describes how children "play" at something, pretending to be a mother, a father, a fireman, or a nurse, and in doing so, they develop gender identity through occurrences that they witness. Dietz (1998) argues that, in this process of defining gender, children will not only base gender identities upon interactions with others, but also on gender symbols (such as popular toys including Barbie dolls and G.I. Joe). Thus, feminine and masculine symbols, with which children interact, play an important role in the development of individualized gender expectations. Wilder, Mackie, and Cooper (1985) note that although video games have been seen as predominantly a masculine domain, as in other forms of technology, females have begun to play these games more. Therefore, the video game images of male and female characters inevitably affect the development of gender roles in boys and girls.

Scholars agree that the world of video games allows for subtle expression of consensual reality held by a culture (Espejo, 2003; Heintz-Knowles & Henderson, 2001; Poole, 2000; Provenzo, 1991). Video games provide insight into ideas and values we hold as a culture. Moreover, as Provenzo (1991) states,

[They]... represent cultural "texts" that can be read and interpreted on a number of different levels. In the case of women, the way in which they are portrayed, the roles they assume in game scenarios, and the extent to which they are included as part of the action of the games provide important insights into the role and status assigned to women in our culture. (p. 99)

By examining games from a gender perspective, we can see the games as socializing agents that teach both girls and boys about their roles in our society (Dietz, 1998; Espejo, 2003; Provenzo, 1991; Wilder, Mackie & Cooper, 1985). Of particular importance are the lessons that these "texts" are teaching girls and boys about body image, sexuality, dominance and submission (Provenzo, 1991; Heitz-Knowles & Henderson, 2001). Cahill (1994) argues that children rarely

challenge the authority of examples of gender roles in media. While women do appear in video games, their roles most frequently are as victims or sex objects (Dietz, 1998; Heintz-Knowles & Henderson, 2001; Provenzo, 1991).

One particular concern, when examining video games as gender socialization agents, is the hyper-sexualized image of women, or what Poole (2000) describes as "a ...deformed female character with massively enhanced breasts, eyes, and legs," (p.141). Even the characters regarded as most life-like, such as Lara Croft of Tomb Raider, who is touted by Poole (2000) as "a beautiful abstraction" boast scantily clad firm bodies with impossibly small waists and digitally enhanced breasts. Poole (2000) further states that this is all part of the allure:

... designers of the next generation of Tomb Raider games on Playstation 2 will surely be careful never to let Lara become too individuated. If she were to look photo realistic, too much like an actual woman, what seductiveness she possesses would thereby be destroyed. (p. 152-3)

This plays into society's love for the illusion of the "perfectly" built woman (Dietz, 1998; Poole, 2000). Examples are seen in digitally altered fashion model photos, prime time television stars, and in Barbie dolls. Poole (2000) explains this illusion further in the example of Lara Croft:

But surely she'll never be thoroughly realistic. For Lara Croft is an abstraction, an animated conglomeration of sexual and attitudinal signs (breasts, hot-pants, shades, thigh holsters) whose very blankness encourages the (male or female) player's psychological projection and is exactly why she has enjoyed such remarkable success as a cultural icon. (p. 153)

The video game female image is a warped mutation, seemingly formed from the battle between women's liberation and women's oppression. Female characters, such as Lara Croft, send a clear message to male and female players that it is okay for a woman to be tough and stand up for herself, as long as she looks sexy doing it. As Jhally (1999) explains, in media, masculinity is a performance in hyper-masculinity, and femininity is a performance in hyper-femininity.

METHODOLOGY

This study examined twenty top-selling games in the U.S created for Playstation 2 and Xbox. A sample of top-selling games from June 2002 was obtained from the industry's leader in sales rankings, gamemarketwatch.com (Appendix A), at the recommendation of an owner of four video game stores in my state (S.A. Bailey, personal communication, February 19, March 6, & April 17, 2004). The sample is intentionally nonrandom, for it was determined that a purposive sample of the most popular games would best resemble what young gamers are actually playing. Initially, Provenzo's (1991) format for analysis was used, in which he first analyzed the games selected in terms of the content of their cover, noting that these images provide visual text describing male and female status roles in American society. Secondly, utilizing Deitz's (1998) a priori codes, two coders played the games using the following categories: no female characters, female characters as hyper-sexualized objects or trophies (based on physical appearance, such as revealing clothing or unrealistic breast enhancement, or women awarded as prizes to male victors), females as the victim (women are kidnapped or assaulted), and females as the hero (action character who could possibly win the game). In addition, two more codes—games with no characters (such as automobile racing games) and characters presented as animals with no human characteristics—were added to the coding sheet.

Next, coders determined the race of each playable character according to the product descrip-

tion, which identified race, or by determining skin color or clothing (such as Native American headdress or Middle Eastern djellebas). Using a coding sheet with these categories, each game was evaluated. In addition, detailed descriptions of the roles of female and minority characters were obtained. Finally, using symbolic interactionism, a list of the most lucrative gaming software companies according to global sales revenue was obtained (Appendix B), to determine the origin of the company headquarters and founding date, thus forming a link between the common set of capitalist themes in the games, the origin of those themes, and the "understanding which has emerged to give meaning to people's interactions" with these texts (Patton, 2002, p.133).

FINDINGS

Cover Art

Games were analyzed using a tally system that identified males and females by their dress and physique, which was categorized as body image. In addition, male and female characters were categorized according to whether or not they were initiating action in the visual frame—for example, striking out with a weapon or as part of a military charge. Those initiating action were identified as dominant males or dominant females. Submissive characters, male or female, were identified as either being dependent upon or under the control of another figure. A final category included only graphic art or included a monster, animal, mythological or non-human figure, such as an automobile.

The results were that nine of the 20 included dominant males; none included dominant females, and half included graphic art with a non-human subject. *Medal of Honor: Frontline*, depicted only male soldiers in the cover, misrepresenting the growing number of female soldiers in service. More concerning perhaps is *WWE Wrestlemania*, which shows three massively muscular males on the cover; however, in playing the game, there are female characters that mark the division between wrestling periods by circling the wrestling ring in bikinis. In addition, female wrestlers are depicted with hyper-sexualized bodies. One buxom blond in a victory celebration over her opponent, tears off her blouse to reveal her lacy bra and swings her blouse over her head. The remaining games' cover art either depicted male characters or non-human subjects, such as automobiles (*Gran Turismo 3, Test Drive, ATV Off Road Fury*).

Only two games included a female on the cover, *Sonic Advance's* Amy, a female cutesy animal in a submissive pose, chin tucked down and smiling in demure fashion. *Grand Theft Auto 3* depicted one female character, Misty, a dancer at Sex Club Seven, a nude female dancing club, in the top right corner with her chin tucked down and gazing from heavily made up eyes. This illustrates the possibility that manufacturers choose advertising images that might attract young male players, while inadvertently alienating female players.

Product Description and Premise

Heintz-Knowles and Henderson (2001) showed findings in which a key factor in attracting female video game players was the game's premise. Those games that contained a story line were much more attractive and engaging to female players than sport or shooter games. Using the manufacturer's product description posted on Amazon.com, game premises were categorized. The following a priori categories based loosely on Provenzo's (1991) study were used:

1. A quest, including a female victim and male hero;
2. A quest, including a male victim and male hero;
3. A quest with a male victim and female hero;
4. A quest with male villain as protagonist;
5. A sport or shooter game without a story line;
6. Non human protagonists and antagonists.

Of the 20 game premises examined, a clear majority had male heroes and female victims or male victims and male heroes, while none had female heroes. Two games had themes involving the protagonist as a criminal (*Grand Theft Auto* and *Midnight Club*), and a great majority were racing, combat, or shooter games (*Medal of Honor Frontline, Grand Theft Auto, Gran Turismo 3, Dragonball Z, The Elder Scrolls III: Morrowind, Halo, Eternal Darkness, Yu Gi Oh Forbidden, Midnight Club: Street, Star Wars Episode 2, ATV Off Road Fury*). This data mirrors Dietz's (1998) findings that many of the current games are, in fact, combat, racing, and shooter games. In those with a story line, "…females are severely under-represented; they are generally cast in either insignificant props or stereotyped roles. Even when the female characters break out of the role of the helpless victim, their powers and strengths can be overshadowed by their hyper-sexualized bodies and attire" (p.30). Just as Dietz (1998), Heintz-Knowles and Henderson (2001), and Provenzo (1991) concluded in similar studies, these findings show that females are, in fact, under-represented and hyper-sexualized, perpetuating hegemonic ideas about gender roles for young players.

Body Image

In addition to game premise and cover art, the body images portrayed were analyzed. These were categorized as normal male, normal female (arms, legs, waists, and chests proportionate to those found in an average person) or as mesomorphic male (extremely muscular with arms, legs, waists, and chests disproportionate to those found in an average person) or hyper-sexualized female (disproportionate breast versus waist ratio). Of the male characters represented in the games, a significant majority was mesomorphic. Likewise, of the female characters, a clear majority was hyper-sexualized, and much fewer had normal body types, supporting an initial impression that the most purchased video games perpetuate amplified, unrealistic, and potentially damaging ideas about body image for young players.

Game Content

In this sample, games that had a story line revealed an overwhelmingly male gaze. For example, in playing *Grand Theft Auto 3*, two out of three female characters are employed at Sex Club Seven—a nude female dance club. The sign in front of the building reads, "Sex Club Seven—Where gentlemen go pop! 24 Hour a Day Fun for the Whole Family." In addition, Luigi, a male "gangster" owner touts, "You wanna have fun; you come to Luigi's. Luigi's girls are the best in town. Clean. Spic and span!" *Midnight Club: Street*, is a watered-down version of this game, with players racing through urban streets of New York and London. The game intro states that illegal street racing is the "new underground sport" for "speed freaks, car nuts, and *boy* racers." [Italics added]

Playable Characters and Race

Provenzo (1991), Dietz (1998), and Heintz-Knowles and Henderson (2001) assert that visibility is power in video gaming, and inclusion or exclusion of playable (characters that can be controlled in contrast to bystanders or props) characters, based on race or gender, sends important messages about power structure in our society. Using this premise as a guide, the playable characters in the games were analyzed. Every game in which race was identifiable included white characters, while only a few included playable black characters (*WWE Wrestlemania*, *Star Wars Episode II*) , and there was only a small number

of Hispanic, Asian, Native American, Middle Eastern, East Indian, or Islanders combined, but none of these were playable characters. Also significant is the point that all of the black characters are represented as either athletes or criminals in games such as *WWE Wrestlemania*, *Grand Theft Auto*, or *Midnight Club: Street*, perpetuating deep-seeded and damaging stereotypes. Gray (2001) describes this as production of blackness (and other minorities as well) through the "white eye," in which dominant media representations are *assimilationist* (invisibility) or *pluralist* (separate but equal) (p.450). It is logical to apply Gray's notions of assimilationist representations of blacks on television in the 1950's and throughout the 1960's as those that "…attempted to make blacks acceptable to whites by containing them or rendering them, if not culturally white, invisible." In addition, there is the "…threat of civilization being over-run or undermined by the recurrence of savagery…lurking below the surface" (Hall, p. 277). A recent trend in the U.S. video gaming industry is sport games such as *NFL Madden Football*, where African American athletes dominate the playable characters. Since 1989, 19 million units of *John Madden Football* have sold. However, Adam Clayton Powell III, son of Adam Clayton Powell Jr., the first African American Congressman, referred to this representation as "high-tech black face" in which "participants [are allowed] to try on the other, the taboo, the dangerous, the forbidden, and the otherwise unacceptable" (Leonard, 2005, p. 1). The minstrel show, or minstrelsy, was an indigenous form of American entertainment consisting of stereotypical comic skits, variety acts, dancing, and music, usually performed by white people in black face. Historian Eric Lott (1993) describes this trying on the other as a way to "facilitate safely an exchange of energies between otherwise rigidly bounded and policed cultures (p.18). While some may argue that players of color participate in the same ritual of "trying on the other," the difference is in the range of roles for white characters as compared to characters of color.

The under-representation and misrepresentation of people of color is a cultural text that may influence young players' perceptions about self and other, regardless of their own ethnic background. Perhaps, most destructive for any oppressed group is invisibility, for, as Jhally (1999) states in *Tough Guise*, "… in media, visibility is power." It seems that this is just one example of many of how media plays a role in perpetuating the socialization structures that promote hegemony in a society. Assuming the power of this medium to influence young players' views about themselves and those around them, it seems imperative to point out the origin of top-selling games. As illustrated in the introduction, video games are a global phenomenon, and thereby a global socialization agent.

DISCUSSION

The most lucrative gaming software (Appendix B) reveals that, while the leading gaming hardware companies, Sony and Playstation, suggest global influences, the software companies that produce the top-selling games are predominately U.S. companies. In the gaming industry, 95% of video games lose money and stop production, while only the top 5% are lucrative (Wikipedia, "Video Games," 2005). This results in an elite group of predominately U.S. software companies designing the games that send messages about gender, race, economics, and competition to a global audience. In addition, as discussed earlier, the most lucrative games become the "norm" in video games.

This study illustrates that the portrayal of women and minorities in top-selling U.S. video games is predominantly stereotypical, often hyper-sexualized, or worse yet, non-existent. While some sports games, such as *ATV Off Road Fury*, make an attempt to include female riders as playable characters, others such as *Gran-Turismo 3*:

A SPEC, *Medal of Honor Frontline*, *Test Drive*, *Wrestlemania*, and *Stuntman* ignore women altogether as participants. Games such as *WWE Wrestlemania*, *Grand Theft Auto*, and *Midnight Club: Street* depict women as mindless subordinate sex objects, while seemingly harmless games such as *Star Wars* and *Spiderman* place females in subordinate roles that are either props or much less important than men. These depictions of women are detrimental to girls and boys in that both may internalize these gender roles, playing a prominent role in the socialization of boys especially, who play these games more frequently.

Non-whites are very rarely represented, if at all. Some of the sporting games, such as *WWE Wrestlemania*, do include black and Hispanic male characters, but this is the only game in the top 20 list that includes non-whites in a positive representation. Lack of representation for both women and non-whites is perhaps the most damaging aspect of video game representation, for this amounts to symbolic annihilation, whereas those who are at the bottom of the various power hierarchies will be kept in their places, in part by their relative invisibility (Gross, 2001, p. 414). In sum, gamers are immersed in a white-washed, patriarchal view of the world.

CONCLUSION

Applying Mead's (1964) framework, showing that gender roles in both boys and girls are formed, in part, by visual examples they are exposed to during play, the purpose of this study was to analyze video games for their presentation of both gender and ethnicity. Most scholars agree that gender roles and ideas about ethnicity may be negatively impacted by visual and textual messages that some of these games illustrate (Provenzo, 1991; Dietz, 1998; Heintz-Knowles & Henderson, 2001; Poole, 2000). This study illustrates that the portrayal of women and people of color continues to be overwhelmingly stereotypical when they are represented at all. In addition, a vast majority of the games include violence in some form, ranging from violent and sometimes sexually explicit attacks on women, followed by subsequent violence by the heroes, to animated characters carrying automatic weapons and annihilating victims. These visual and thematic texts create a false reality that violence and victimization are normal components of society and that this is often amusing and fun.

In addition, thematic texts are built upon the ideologies of capitalism and consumption, thus presenting these ideas in a format that is a catalyst to the "process of normalization," or the process of hegemony (Marx & Engels, 2001). Further more, as Dietz (1998) states, in that video games are much more interactive than other media forms such as television or magazines, researchers should be cautious in minimalizing the effects of exposure to video games "based upon generalizations from research of other media forms" (p.440). Finally, because research has focused only upon the short-term effects of video game exposure, it is unclear what long-term effects and what effects from long-term exposure will occur. This discussion suggests that there is a need for more research to assess the effect of racial and gender representation in video games. Therefore, given the current trend of imbedded U.S. hegemonic ideologies of capitalism, and gender and racial misrepresentation or annihilation, it is important that continuing research be conducted to interpret what, if any, short-term and long-term effects emerge from this global socialization agent.

REFERENCES

Alloway, N. & Gilbert, P. (1997). Boys and literacy: Lessons from Australia. *Gender & Education, 9*(1), 49-62.

Angeles, P. (1992). *The Harper Collins dictionary of philosophy.* (2nd ed.). New York: Harper Collins.

Angelo, J. (2004, May 14). *New study reveals that women over 40 who play online games spend far more time playing than male or teenage gamers.* Retrieved June 3, 2006, from http://media.aoltimewarner.com/media/cb_press_view.cfm?release_num=55253774

Bartholow, B., & Sestir, M. (2005). Correlates and consequences of exposure to video game violence: Hostile personality, empathy, and aggressive behavior. *Personality and Social Psycholgy Bulletin, 11,* 1573-1586. Retrieved June 27, 2006, from PubMed database.

Cohen, P. (1988). The perversions of inheritance: Studies in the making of multi-racist Britain. In P. Cohen & Bains (Eds.), *Multi-racist Britain.* London: Pluto Press.

Cortes, C. E. (2000). *The children are watching: How the media teach about diversity.* New York: Teachers College Press.

Crotty, M. (1998). *The foundations of social research.* Thousand Oaks, California: Sage.

Delamere, F. M. (2005). 'It's just really fun to play!' A constructionist perpective on violence and gender representations in violent video games. *Dissertation Abstracts International, 65*(10-A), 3986.

Dietz, T. (1998). An examination of violence and gender role portrayals in video games: Implications for gender socialization and aggressive behavior. *Sex Roles, 38*(516), p.425-442.

Espejo, R. (Ed.). (2003). *Video games.* San Diego: Greenhaven Press.

Fiske, J. (1992). British cultural studies and television. In R. C. Allen (Ed.), *Channels of discourse, reassembled: Television and contemporary criticism* (pp.284-326). (2nd ed.) Chapel Hill: University of North Carolina Press.

Fiske, J. (1994). Moments of television: Neither the

text nor the audience. In E. Seiter, H. Brochers, G. Kreutzner, & E. M. Warth (Eds.), *Remote control: Television audiences and cultural power* (pp. 56-78). New York: Routledge.

Foucault, M. (1980). *Power/knowledge: Selected interviews and other writings, 1972-1977.* New York: Pantheon.

Gee, J. (2003). *What video games have to teach us about learning and literacy.* New York: Palgrave/St. Martin's.

Geertz, C. (1983). Thick description: Toward an interpretive theory of culture. In R. M. Emerson (Ed.), *Contemporary field research: A collection of readings.* Prospect Heights, Illinois: Waveland Press.

Gramsci, A. (2001). The concept of ideology. In M.D. Durham & D. M. Kellner (Eds.), *Media and cultural studies* (pp.43-48). Malden, MA: Blackwell.

Gray, H. (2001). The politics of representation in network television. In M. Durham & D. Kellner (Eds.), *Media and cultural studies: Keyworks* (pp.439-461). Malden, MA: Blackwell.

Griffiths, M. (1999). Violent video games and aggression: Review of the literature. *Journal of Aggression and Violent Behavior, 4*(2), 203-212. Retrieved June 2, 2006, from Ebsco host database.

Gross, L. (2001). Out of the mainstream: Sexual minorities and mass media. In M. D. Durham & D. M. Kellner (Eds.), *Media and cultural studies* (pp.405-423). Malden, MA: Blackwell.

Grossman, D. Lt. Col., & DeGaetano, G. (1999). *Stop teaching our kids to kill: A call to action against TV, movie & video game violence.* New York: Random House.

Hall, S. (2000). Racist ideologies and the media. In P. Marris & S. Thornham (Eds.), *Media studies: A reader* (2nd ed.; pp.271-282). New York: New York University Press.

Harvey, L. (1990). *Critical social research.* London: Unwin Hyman.

Hayes, E. (2006). Women, video gaming and learning: Beyond stereotypes. *Tech Trends, 49*(5), 23-28.

Hebdige, D. (2001). From culture to hegemony; subculture; the unnatural break. In M. Durham & D. Kellner (Eds.), *Media and cultural studies: Keyworks* (pp.198-216). Malden, Massachusetts: Blackwell.

Herz, J. C. (1997). *Joystick nation: How video games ate our quarters, won our hearts, and rewired our minds.* New York: Little, Brown and Company.

Heintz-Knowles, K., & Henderson, J. (2001). *Fair play? Violence, gender and race in video games.* Oakland, CA: Children NOW. Retrieved February 18, 2004, from ERIC database.

Hooks, B. (1990). *Yearning: Race, gender and cultural politics.* Toronto: Between the Lines.

Horkheimer, M., & Adorno, T. (2001). The culture industry. In M. D. Durham & D. M. Kellner (Eds.), *Media and cultural studies* (pp.71-101). Malden, MA: Blackwell.

Jhally, S. (Director). (1999) *Tough guise: Violence, media & the crisis in masculinity* [Motion Picture]. United States: Media Education Foundation

Lee, H. (1990). *Critical social research.* London: Unwin Hyman.

Leonard, D. (2004). Unsettling the military entertainment complex: Video games and a pedagogy of peace. *Studies in Media & Information Literacy Education, 4*(4), 17-32. Retrieved May 27, 2006, from www.utpjournals.com

Leonard, D. (2005). High tech blackface—Race, sports video games and becoming the other. *Intelligent Agent, 4*(4), Retrieved June 18, 2006, from http://www.intelligentagent.com/archive/Vol4_No4_gaming_leonard.htm

Lott, E. (1993). *Love & theft: Blackface minstrelsy and the American working class*. New York: Oxford University Press.

Marx, K., & Engels, F. (1976). Ruling class and the ruling ideas. In M. D. Durham & D. M. Kellner (Eds.), *Media and cultural studies* (pp. 39-47). Malden, MA: Blackwell.

Mead, G. (1934, 1964). *Mind, self and society*. Chicago: University of Chicago Press.

Newkirk, T. (2002). *Misreading masculinity: Boys, literacy and popular culture*. Portsmouth, New Hampshire: Heinemann.

Patton, M. (2002). *Qualitative research and evaluation methods* (3rd ed.). Thousand Oaks, CA: Sage.

Poole, S. (2000). *Trigger happy: Video games and the entertainment revolution*. New York: Arcade Publishing.

Provenzo, E. F. Jr. (1991). *Video kids: Making sense out of Nintendo*. Cambridge, MA: Harvard University Press.

Sakamoto, A. (2005). Video games and the psychological development of Japanese children. In D. W. Schwalb, J. Nakazawa, & B. J. Schwalb (Eds.), *Applied developmental psychology: Theory, practice and reform from Japan* (pp. 3-21). Greenwich, CT: Information Age Publishing. Retrieved May 27, 2005, from Ebsco host database.

Schneider, E., Lang, A., Shin, M., & Bradley, S. (2004). Death with a story: How story impacts emotional, motivational and physiological responses to first-person shooter video games. *Human Communication Research, 30*(3), 361-375. Retrieved May 27, 2006, from Ebsco host database.

Terlecki, M., & Newcombe, N. (2005). How important is the digital divide? The relationship of computer videogame usage to gender differences in mental rotation ability. *Sex Roles, 53*(5-6), 433-441. Retrieved June 3, 2006, from Ebsco host database.

Wilder, G., Mackie, D., & Cooper, J. (1985). Gender and computers: Two surveys of computer-related attitudes. *Sex roles, 13*(13), 215-228. Retrieved February 18, 2004, from ERIC database.

Williams, R. (2001). Base and superstructure in Marxist cultural theory. In M. Durham & D. Kellner (Eds.), *Media and cultural studies: Keyworks* (pp. 152-165). Malden, Massachusetts: Blackwell.

APPENDIX A

Top 20 Best Selling Video Games
Gamemarketwatch.com Internet magazine—June 2002

<u>Game Title</u>	<u>Gaming Software Company</u>
1. Medal of Honor Frontline	Electronic Arts
2. Grand Theft Auto 3	Rockstar Games
3. Gran Turismo 3: A-SPEC	Sony
4. Dragonball Z: Goku	Infogames
5. Spiderman: The Movie (PS2)	Activision
6. The Elder Scrolls III: Morrowind	Bethesda Softworls
7. WWE Wrestlemania X8	THQ
8. Test Drive	Infogames
9. Super Mario Advance 4	GBA
10. Halo	Microsoft
11. Eternal Darkness	Nintendo
12. Yu Gi Oh Forbidden	Konami
13. Midnight Club: Street	Rockstar Games
14. Star Wars Episode 2	THQ
15. Stuntman	Infogames
16. ATV Off Road Fury	Sony
17. Super Smash Brothers Melee	Nintendo
18. Sonic Advance	Sega
19. Yu Gi Oh Dark Duel	Konami
20. Spiderman: The Movie (Xbox)	Activision

APPENDIX B

Video Game Software Industry Leaders
Wikipedia Online Encyclopedia—Retrieved November, 2005

Company name	Headquarters	Founded
Gimple Software	U.S.—Pennsylvania	1984
Digi Design	U.S.—California	1985
Powersoft	U.S.—California	1985
Borland	U.S.—California, Georgia	1985
RAD Game Tools	U.S.—Washington	1988
Nu Mega	U.S.— Michigan	1973
Kinetix	U.S.—California	1983
Electric Arts	U.S.—California	1982
Equilibrium	U.S.—California	1989
Sonic Foundry	U.S.—Wisconsin, Pennsylvania	1991
Syntrillium Software	U.S.—California	1982
Cakewalk	U.S.—Massachusetts	1987
Creative Labs	Singapore	1981
Addison Wesley	U.S.—California	1996

This work was previously published in the International Journal of Technology and Human Interaction, edited by B. C. Stahl, Volume 3, Issue 2, pp. 96-109, copyright 2007 by IGI Publishing, formerly known as Idea Group Publishing (an imprint of IGI Global).

Index